Charlotte Frances Champion Crespigny nee Dana
(1820-1904)

Rafe de Crespigny

and

Anne Young

CHARLOTTE FRANCES CHAMPION CRESPIGNY NEE DANA
(1820-1904)

AND HER FAMILY IN AUSTRALIA

BY

RAFE DE CRESPIGNY
AND
ANNE YOUNG

BALLARAT, VICTORIA
AND
LILLI PILLI, NEW SOUTH WALES
AUSTRALIA

2020

© Copyright Richard Rafe Champion de Crespigny
and Christine Anne Young 2020

ISBN: 978-0-6481917-3-5 [hardback]
978-0-6481917-5-9 [paperback]
978-0-6481917-4-2 [e-book]

 A catalogue record for this book is available from the National Library of Australia

THE TAPESTRY DOG

During the last years of his life William Pulteney Dana (1778-1861), father of Charlotte Frances, lived in Shrewsbury with his daughter Anna Penelope (1814-1890), Charlotte Frances' elder sister who had married William Henry Wood. Anna Penelope inherited most of the family heirlooms and pictures, but as she and her husband had no children she left many of them to Charlotte Frances' family in Australia. Miniatures and photographs in that collection have provided several of the illustrations for this book.

One item listed is "the little dog lying on a red cushion which she worked." In context, "she" refers to Charlotte Frances, who embroidered the picture as a girl, presumably in her teens during the 1830s.

The picture was left to Charlotte Frances second daughter Viola (1855-1929), and after her death it was transferred to Viola's younger sister Rose Beggs (1858-1937). In Rose's will, made on 6 March 1931, number 8 of her bequests was:

I give to Geoff son of my nephew Constantine the tapestry-picture.

Constantine was Constantine Trent Champion de Crespigny (1882-1952); Geoff was Richard Geoffrey Champion de Crespigny (1907-1966). The picture is now held by Geoff's son Rafe.

The tapestry, still in very good condition, is some 185 years old. The frame was probably made in the 1890s, when Anna Penelope's bequest came to Australia.

Charlotte Frances Champion Crespigny nee Dana
Taken in Australia, the daguerreotype is probably dated about 1860, when she was turning forty.
The piece is now in the possession of the family.

INTRODUCTION

A great emigration necessarily implies unhappiness of some kind or other in the country that is deserted. For few persons will leave their families, connections, friends, and native land, to seek a settlement in untried foreign climes, without some strong subsisting causes of uneasiness where they are, or the hope of some great advantages in the place to which they are going.

Thomas Robert Malthus, An Essay on the Principle of Population *(1798)*

Charlotte Frances Dana and her second husband Philip Robert Champion Crespigny came to Melbourne in 1852. Through their son Philip, who took the full surname of Champion de Crespigny, they were the founders of the Australian branch of the family.

In *Champions from Normandy*, published in 2017, Rafe de Crespigny discussed the history of the family, later known by the surname Champion de Crespigny, from the earliest records in France to their forced emigration as Huguenots in the seventeenth century and then the establishment in England during the eighteenth century. The present volume considers the experiences of the first generation in Australia. It is centred upon the life of Charlotte Frances, for she and her brother were central to the decision to emigrate, and she lived to see her first great-grandchildren in the new country and the new century.

Born in 1820, Charlotte died in 1904, and that period of eighty-four years was a time of enormous and dramatic change. She was first a subject of King George IV, former Prince Regent, and she lived through the reigns of William IV and Queen Victoria into the first years of Edward VII. Her voyage to Australia in 1851-52 lasted four months; fifty years later a steamship passage took only six weeks, less than half that time. When she arrived in Victoria, travel was by horse and cart, often no faster than seven miles a day; she would later take a train from the goldfields town of Beaufort and reach Melbourne in a matter of hours; while at the time of her death the Wright brothers in the United States were making their first powered flights at Kitty Hawk.

So it was a time of progress, but it was also an age of uncertainty. Health and medicine were both erratic, and diseases which are now quite easily treated were dangerous and could be fatal. Infant or child mortality was very high – to such a degree that many children were baptised with the name of an older sibling who had gone before them: Charlotte had two brothers christened Francis Richard Benjamin, three called Douglas and two more named William. And even those who grew to maturity could be crippled or killed by accident or sickness: one brother died in his thirties and another at the age of forty; two young nephews died of scarlet fever and one of tetanus; and Charlotte's son Constantine Trent Champion Crespigny and her sister-in-law Sophia nee Walsh both died of tuberculosis.

Such dangers applied still more to women of the time. Childbirth always carried a risk and stillbirth was by no means uncommon, while the absence of any practical means of contraception meant that pregnancy was often frequent: Charlotte had seven children, but she had twelve full and half-siblings, both her father and her mother had twelve brothers and sisters, and her mother's father had sired ten more on another wife. Similarly, in her first marriage she experienced three pregnancies in three years, with one daughter who would live to maturity, a son who died in his very first year, and a third child which was still-born. With the vagaries of midwifery and the chances of infection, many women were weakened or simply worn out by such frequent fertility.

Apart from these physical matters, social and financial life could likewise be a question of fortune, good or ill. Charlotte's family could fairly be described as gentlefolk: her grandmother was the daughter of a Scottish baron; her grandfather came from a notable background in the American colonies; one of her uncles was a general in the British army and owned a landed estate; two of her aunts married wealthy men; and in 1839 Charlotte herself was married to a prosperous solicitor in Gloucestershire.

Such apparent security, however, could change very quickly. Soon after Charlotte's wedding her father's printing business failed and he was sent to prison for debt. Stripped of all property, he spent the last years of his life with a small pension in the home of his daughter and son-in-law.

Bankruptcy and indebtedness were indeed a constant threat: if a bank failed, its notes were worthless – and much of the currency in circulation was issued by private banks; the system of limited liability was not in common use, so the failure of a business could bring ruin to its owner; and a batch of unpaid bills could bring a cascade of misfortune.

The position was even more precarious for women. Until quite recent times, a married woman was identified with her husband, with no separate legal or financial existence, while unmarried women had limited opportunities for a meaningful career which might enable them to support themselves. Married, unmarried or widowed, most women were obliged to rely upon their families. When Charlotte Frances' husband Philip Robert was taken ill, he was entitled to a pension, but after his death there was no further official or government support; and her unmarried daughters Ada and Viola were equally dependent upon the goodwill of their more prosperous kinfolk.

One question may always be raised of any Australian whose family arrived within the last 250 years: "Why did they come?" For convicts, it was compulsory; very often, notably in the years of gold rush, it was the hope of sudden fortune. For Charlotte's brother Henry Edmund Dana, educated as a gentleman but with few opportunities at home, it was the hope of better prospects than could be expected in England – and for Charlotte and her second husband Philip Robert Champion Crespigny it was a means to escape the social and financial embarrassment of a dramatic and well-publicised divorce.

Regardless of such an erratic beginning, however, that second marriage was affectionate and companionable, and even after Philip Robert's sad slow death Charlotte was able to enjoy the support of her daughters and the successes of her son Philip and her grandchildren. In a letter of 1858, her father-in-law wrote in praise of her patience and courage, and of her determination to make the best of everything. The approval was well deserved, and her descendants can be grateful for the chances of fortune which brought her and her husband to their new country.

Richard Rafe Champion de Crespigny
and Christine Anne Young nee Champion de Crespigny
December 2020

CHRONOLOGY
1817-1904

Notes: Events which closely concern Charlotte Frances nee Dana are presented in Roman type.

Events concerning Charlotte Frances Dana's family, but with which she is not immediately concerned, are presented in *Italic* type. General historical events are presented in purple.

The abbreviations ChC and CdeC reflect variants in the family surname, whether Champion Crespigny or Champion de Crespigny. See pages 77-78.

1817	October: *birth of Philip Robert Champion Crespigny in Boulogne, France*
1820	22 February: birth of Charlotte Frances Dana at Albrighton, Shropshire
	April: baptism of Charlotte Frances
1835	June: John Batman, sailing with a party from Launceston in Van Diemen's Land [Tasmania] establishes a settlement at the present site of Melbourne
1836	October: Sir Richard Bourke, Governor of New South Wales, appoints Captain William Lonsdale as Chief Agent of Government, Police Magistrate and Commandant for the Port Phillip Region
1839	May: Charlotte Frances Dana marries John James of Newnham on Severn, Gloucestershire
	September: *Charlotte Frances' brother Henry Edmund Pulteney Dana arrives in Van Diemen's Land [Tasmania]*
	Charles Joseph La Trobe is appointed Superintendent of the Port Phillip District of the Colony of New South Wales
1840	July: birth of Charlotte Constance, daughter of John James and Charlotte Frances nee Dana
	August: Charlotte Frances' father William Pulteney Dana imprisoned for debt
1841	July: birth of John Henry, son of John James and Charlotte Frances nee Dana
1842	January: *Henry Edmund Pulteney Dana is appointed to command of the Native Police Corps of the Port Phillip Bay Settlement*
	March: death of the infant John Henry James
	July: Charlotte Frances James nee Dana suffers a stillbirth
1844	October: *William Augustus Pulteney Dana, younger brother of Henry and of Charlotte Frances, arrives in Melbourne*
1845	June: *William Dana is appointed an officer of the Native Police Corps*
c. 1845	Charlotte Frances James nee Dana meets Philip Robert Champion Crespigny [hereafter ChC]
1846	May: death of Charlotte Frances' mother Charlotte Elizabeth Dana nee Bayly
1847	August: Charlotte Frances commits adultery with Philip Robert ChC and becomes pregnant
	November: Charlotte Frances elopes with Philip Robert and the couple flee to St Malo in France
1848	May: Charlotte Frances gives birth to Ada, her first daughter by Philip Robert ChC
1849	February: divorce of Charlotte Frances by John James is approved by the ecclesiastical Court of Arches
	March/May: bill of divorce approved by Parliament
	July: Charlotte Frances nee Dana marries Philip Robert ChC at the British Embassy in Paris
1850	January: birth of Philip, first son of Charlotte Frances and Philip Robert ChC, at St Malo
1851	January: *William Walsh shoots William Dana, claiming he has committed adultery with his sister Sophia nee Walsh, the wife of Henry Dana*
	May: birth of Constantine Trent, second son of Charlotte Frances and Philip Robert ChC, at St Malo
	July: the Port Phillip Bay Settlement, formerly under the jurisdiction of New South Wales, becomes the separate Colony of Victoria, with Charles La Trobe as Lieutenant-Governor
	August: beginning of the gold rush in Victoria
	December: Charlotte Frances, Philip Robert and their children Ada and Philip sail from Southampton for Australia; *the infant Constantine Trent remains in the England in the care of his grandfather Charles Fox ChC, his grandmother Julia, and his aunt Eliza Constantia*

CHRONOLOGY

1852	April: Charlotte Francis and Philip Robert ChC arrive in Melbourne with their children Ada and Philip
	November: Philip Robert ChC is appointed an Assistant Commissioner for Crown Lands at the Goldfields
	death of Henry Dana; his will appoints William Dana and Philip Robert ChC as guardians of his children
1853	Philip Robert ChC stationed in the Castlemaine region; *Daisy Hill, south of Maryborough, is established as the Municipality of Amherst*
1854	December: *the Eureka Stockade insurgency at Ballarat*
1855	*government enquiries and amendments to the mining licence system*
	Philip Robert is appointed a Warden of the Goldfields and transferred to Amherst; he takes up residence at Daisy Hill Farm
	November: birth of Viola Julia Constantia, fourth child and second daughter of Charlotte Frances and Philip Robert ChC, at Daisy Hill
1856	November: *William Dana marries Sophia nee Walsh, widow of his brother Henry*
1858	November: birth of Helen Rosalie [Rose], fifth child and third daughter of Charlotte Frances and Philip Robert ChC, at Daisy Hill
1859	January: *Charlotte Constance James, daughter of Charlotte Frances by her first marriage, marries Francis Gamble Blood at Clifton, Gloucestershire*
	February: Philip Robert appointed Police Magistrate at Amherst
	July: Philip Robert elected Chairman of the Amherst Hospital Board, a position he holds for ten years
1860	April: *death of Sophia nee Walsh, widow of Henry Dana and wife of William Dana*
1861	October: visit of Governor Sir Henry Barkly to Amherst, he is received by Magistrate Philip Robert ChC
1862	January: *Back Creek is named Talbot and becomes a rival centre to Amherst*
1864	August: Philip, son of Philip Robert and Charlotte Frances [hereafter Philip CdeC]: the bushranger affair
1866	February: *Cecile Sophia, daughter of Henry Dana, marries James Colles, postmaster at Talbot*
	April: Philip CdeC: the incident at church
	June: Philip CdeC joins the Bank of Victoria
	October: *death of William Dana at Geelong*
1868	May: *death of Augustus, youngest son of Henry Dana*
1869	February: Philip Robert ChC is transferred to be Police Magistrate at Bairnsdale; he is accompanied by Ada while Charlotte Frances moves to Hawthorn in Melbourne with Viola and Rose
	April: Philip Robert is transferred back to Amherst-Talbot
	July: *Constantine Trent Champion ChC, second son of Charlotte Frances and Philip Robert, becomes an Ensign in the 69th Foot and is stationed in Canada*
	October: sale of Daisy Hill Farm
	November: *Charlotte Constance Blood nee James, daughter of Charlotte Frances by her first marriage, gives birth to a son, John Neptune Blood (1869-1942), grandson of Charlotte Frances*
1870	June: Philip Robert is transferred to Bright; Charlotte Frances and the family remain at Melbourne, but move to St Kilda
	Charlotte Constance Blood nee James obtains an uncontested divorce from her husband Francis Gamble Blood on grounds of his adultery
1871	February-September: Philip CdeC in the New Hebrides with his cousin George Dana
	March-April: Philip Robert is transferred from Bright to the Bendigo district
	May: Philip Robert is appointed to a long-term appointment as Police Magistrate at Ararat
	Constantine Trent ChC, having returned to England, is promoted a Lieutenant in the 41st Foot, stationed at Cardiff in Wales
	October: *Constantine Trent resigns his commission and retires from the army*
1872	December: *death of George Dana, son of Henry Dana, in the New Hebrides*

x

CHRONOLOGY

1875	March: *death of Charles Fox Champion Crespigny at Cheltenham, England*
	Philip CdeC and Frank Beggs are involved in a road accident at Beaufort
	November: Constantine Trent ChC arrives in Australia
1876	February: Charlotte Frances and Philip Robert's daughter Rose marries Frank Beggs at Ararat
	September/October: Philip Robert is afflicted by paralysis, probably from a stroke
	December: Philip Robert resigns his magistracy on account of ill health; the family moves to St Kilda in Melbourne
	[*about this time*] Philip CdeC is appointed head of an agency of the Bank of Victoria at Epsom near Bendigo
1877	June: Constantine Trent ChC is appointed Truant Officer in St Kilda
	October: Philip CdeC marries Annie Frances Chauncy
1879	March: Constantine Trent involved in an altercation while walking with his father Philip Robert at St Kilda beach
	June: birth of Philip, son of Philip CdeC and Annie Frances nee Chauncy, at Epsom
1880	Rose and her husband Frank Beggs take up residence at Eurambeen East
	August: Constantine Trent ChC and his brother Philip visit Sydney
1881	February: Constantine Trent ChC leaves Australia to return to England
1882	March: birth of Constantine Trent CdeC, second son of Philip CdeC and Annie Frances nee Chauncy, at Queenscliff[1]
1883	January: *Constantine Trent ChC dies in England after several months' illness*
	February: death of Annie Frances nee Chauncy, wife of Philip CdeC
1886	Philip CdeC transferred to be manager of the Elmore branch of the Bank of Victoria, near Bendigo
1887	Philip CdeC is appointed manager of the South Melbourne branch of the Bank of Victoria
1888/1889	Philip CdeC is appointed Assistant Inspector of the Bank of Victoria
1889	September: death of Philip Robert Champion Crespigny
1891	November: Philip CdeC marries Sophia Montgomery Grattan Beggs (1870-1936)
1892	May: banking crisis in Victoria; the Bank of Victoria briefly closes its doors, then enters a scheme of reconstruction
	September: birth of Francis George Travers CdeC, first son of Philip CdeC and Sophia nee Beggs
	December: Philip CdeC is appointed Assistant Inspector of the Bank of Victoria
1896-1903	the Federation Drought affects all Victorian agriculture
1897	April: birth of Hugh Vivian CdeC, second son of Philip and Sophia CdeC
1898-1904	the Eurambeen Letters
1900	September: Philip Champion de Crespigny, son of Philip CdeC and grandson of Charlotte Frances, marries Barbara Wilhelmina "Birdie" Walstab
1903	women have the right to vote in elections for the Australian parliament
	August: birth of Charlotte Frances' first great-grandchild, Annie Frances, daughter of Philip and Birdie nee Walstab; baptised 25 March 1904 in St Mary's, Caulfield
1904	July: birth of Charlotte Frances' second great-grandchild, Lorna Blanche, daughter of Philip and Birdie nee Walstab
	9 November: death of Charlotte Frances Champion Crespigny nee Dana

---

[1] As in the Notes above, the abbreviations ChC and CdeC reflect variants in the family surname: the elder Constantine Trent, second son of Philip Robert ChC and Charlotte Frances, was almost always known as Champion Crespigny; his nephew and younger namesake, however, son of Philip CdeC and Annie Frances Chauncy and grandson of Charlotte Frances, used the full form of Champion de Crespigny. See further at pages 77-78 below.

Contents

Introduction	vii
Chronology	ix

Chapter One
Prologue: The family background of Charlotte Frances nee Dana

The Dana family in America	1
Edmund Dana in England and Scotland	3
The children of Edmund Dana and Helen nee Kinnaird	14
William Pulteney Dana, father of Charlotte Frances	31

Chapter Two
The Road to Divorce

The Bible and the census	43
Breakdown	53
Divorce	59
France to Australia	67
A note on the Crespigny surname	77

Chapter Three
Victoria in the Gold Rush

The Dana brothers and the native police	79
Family in Victoria	95
Commissioner, Magistrate and Warden of the Goldfields	105
Letters from home	113

Chapter Four
Amherst and Talbot 1855-1871

Settlements at Daisy Hill	121
Public and private life	128
Farewell to Talbot	142
In search of Daisy Hill Farm: a note	145
Tragic cousins: George and Augustus, the sons of Henry Dana	149

Chapter Five
Ararat to St Kilda 1871-1889

Bairnsdale, Bendigo and Bright, with a brief return to Talbot	157
Magistrate at Ararat	163
Constantine Trent in Australia 1875-1881	173
Rose Crespigny and Frank Beggs	182
Philip Crespigny and Annie Frances Chauncy	191

Chapter Six
Eurambeen 1889-1904

The second marriage of Philip Champion Crespigny	207
The letters of Constantine Trent Champion Crespigny 1889-1896	207
Banks and the land: the crisis of the 1890s	216
The Eurambeen Letters 1898-1904	218

CONTENTS

CHAPTER SEVEN
    Epilogue: The immediate descendants of Charlotte Frances
          Champion Crespigny nee Dana

Philip Champion de Crespigny 1850-1927	253
Philip Champion de Crespigny 1879-1918	256
Constantine Trent Champion de Crespigny 1882-1952	259
Francis George Travers Champion de Crespigny 1892-1968	261
Hugh Vivian Champion de Crespigny 1897-1969	262
Royalieu Dana [Roy] Champion de Crespigny 1905-1985	263
Claude Montgomery Champion de Crespigny 1908-1991	264
Rose (1858-1937) and Frank Beggs (1850-1921)	265
Postscript: Ada, Viola and Rose	266
John Neptune Blood 1869-1942	267
BIBLIOGRAPHY	269
INDEX	275

ILLUSTRATIONS

The Tapestry Dog	Frontispiece 1
Charlotte Frances Champion Crespigny nee Dana *c.*1860	Frontispiece 2
Arms of the Barons Kinnaird and Johnstone baronets and those adopted by Edmund Dana	3
The Reverend Edmund Dana (1739-1823)	4
Barbara Lady Kinnaird nee Johnstone *and* William Johnstone Pulteney	5
Castle Gate House, Shrewsbury	11
Shrewsbury Castle	12
The Dana 1788	12
The New Gaol at Shrewsbury 1795	12
The main entrance of Shrewsbury Prison [present day]	12
The Dana and the eastern wall of the prison [present day]	12
The Church of Saint Andrew, Wroxeter	13
Lieutenant Pulteney Johnstone Poole Sherburne	19
New Amsterdam, Berbice, in the 1830s	20
Saint Chad's Church, Shrewsbury	23
The gravestone of Anne Frisby Fitzhugh nee Dana (1803-1850)	35
The Reverend Arthur Grueber DD	36
The Church of Saint Peter, Worfield	40
The Frontispiece of Charlotte Frances Dana's Bible	42
The shield on the christening box of Charlotte Frances Dana	43
The Bible of Charlotte Frances Dana	44
Extract from the 1841 Census sheet for Newnham in Gloucestershire	46
Extract from *Pigot's Directory of Gloucestershire* 1842	47
Anna Penelope Wood (1814-1890) with her father William Pulteney Dana (1776-1861)	51
Extract from the records of the British Embassy at Paris, 1849	68

Passport issued by the British Consulate at St Malo for Philip C Crespigny to travel to Paris 1849	69
Two extracts from the Registry of Christenings at the British Protestant Chapel in St Servan	70
A *goélette* [schooner] from Paimpol, Brittany	72
Model ship *Ariel* at sea at Grange, South Australia *c.*1950	73
Model ship *Ariel* at Lilli Pilli, NSW in 2020	73
Harefield House, Middlesex, as an Australian military hospital during the First World War	75
Census return for Harefield House in Middlesex 1851	76
Ford Madox Brown, *The Last of England* 1855	77
Bookplate of Constantine Trent ChdeC (1882-1952)	78
Black troopers escorting a prisoner from Ballarat to Melbourne 1851	83
The headquarters of the Native Police Corps at Narre Warren 1855	85
Aboriginal troopers, Melbourne police, with English corporal 1850	85
Aboriginal Police Force 1850: uniform of the black troopers	86
Commissioner's Tent at Ballaarat 1852, with native police in uniform	87
Henry Edmund Pulteney Dana *and* William Augustus Pulteney Dana	89
En route to the diggings 1851	91
The city of Melbourne, Australia, 1854	96
The Government Gold Escort 1852	97
William Augustus Pulteney Dana (1825-1866)	99
Heaton Champion de Crespigny *and* his wife Caroline nee Bathurst	101
Miner's Licence of the Colony of Victoria 1853 issued by Commissioner P C Crespigny	103
Licensing Diggers, Castlemaine Camp 1852	104
The Commissioner's Camp, Castlemaine (Mount Alexander) 1852	104
Golden Point at Forest Creek, Castlemaine 1858	109
The *Great Britain* steam-ship 1852	114
Charles [James] Fox Champion Crespigny (1785-1875)	117
Constantine Trent Champion Crespigny *c.*1862	119
The Road from Forest Creek to Bendigo 1852	120
Vom publick Haus zu Ballarat [View from the Pub at Ballarat] 1854	120
A spring cart and haulage drays	122
Eagle Hawk Gully, Bendigo 1852	124
Triumphal or Welcoming Arch	126
Amherst Town Hall	127
The Seventh Annual Amherst Hospital Fete at Talbot, Victoria	134
The Anglican Church of Saint Michael and All Angels, Talbot	135
Ada Champion Crespigny *c.*1855	136
Viola Champion Crespigny *c.*1865	136
Rosalie Helen ["Rose"] Champion Crespigny *c.*1870	137
The Odd Fellows Hall Talbot 1866	141
Crespigny's Hill from Pollocks Road, Amherst	147

CONTENTS

Crespigny Street, Talbot, looking west	147
HMVS Nelson at Williamstown 1898	150
Passenger list for *Gem*, arriving Port of Melbourne 4 October 1871	153
Port Resolution, Tanna, New Hebrides	154
Bright, Victoria, 1871	160
The gold-diggings at Ararat 1871	162
Ararat Court House	162
Beaufort Court House	168
Ararat Lunatic Asylum 1880	169
Ship *Sobraon* 1868	180
The tomb of Charles Fox Champion Crespigny (1785-1875) and of Constantine Trent Champion Crespigny (1851-1883) at Saint Peter's, Leckingham in Gloucestershire	182
Frank and Rose Beggs	190
St Marnock's homestead 2019	190
Annie Frances nee Chauncy 1877	192
Gravestone of Annie Frances Champion Crespigny nee Chauncy at Queenscliff	197
Queenscliff *c.*1882, with the Bank of Victoria building	198
The Melbourne and Hobson's Bay United Railway Company train of the Brighton line at South Yarra station *c.*1874	199
Philip Robert Champion Crespigny 1879	200
Brighton Beach, Victoria, in the early 1880s	202
Bushy Creek homestead	204
Eurambeen East homestead 2019	208
Philip CdeC 1894 with his second wife Sophia Montgomery nee Beggs and his sons Constantine Trent and Francis George Travers	212
A cave on Mount Cole	214
Mount Cole from Challicum 1852/53	215
Eurambeen Station homestead *c.*1900	218
Charlotte Frances Champion Crespigny nee Dana *c.*1895	218
The Canary Book	220
Lake Beaufort: the reservoir	224
Canaries	226
The Bank of Victoria building at Beaufort *c.*1900	233
Portrait of Dorothy Champion Crespigny by George Romney 1790	240
The Hall at Burton Latimer 1905	240
The Queen Victoria Memorial Pavilion at Beaufort	247
Gravestone of Philip Robert and Charlotte Frances Champion Crespigny	250
Philip Champion de Crespigny (1850-1927)	251
The Bank of Victoria building at 257 Collins Street, Melbourne, 1918	253
Philip Champion de Crespigny's house "Vierville" at Black Street, Brighton	254
Philip Champion de Crespigny (1879-1918)	255

The Australian Light Horse in Egypt	256
with Trooper Philip Champion de Crespigny	
Billjim at Sea	257
Constantine Trent Champion de Crespigny (1882-1952)	259
Francis George Travers Champion de Crespigny (1892-1968) 1917	261
Francis George Travers CdeC *with* **Beatrice Noel CdeC nee Court**	261
Hugh Vivian Champion de Crespigny (1897-1969)	262
The Wedding of Royalieu Dana with Nancy Temple Smith	263
Claude Montgomery Champion de Crespigny (1908-1991)	264
with his wife **Edith P [Patricia>"Pat"] nee Cary-Barnard**	
Francis "Frank" Beggs (1850-1921) at St Marnock's 1908	265
with Richard Geoffrey CdeC (1907-1966)	

SCANS OF LETTERS

Letter 3: started by Constantine Trent ChC [age 8]	119
continued by Charles Fox ChC 1859	
Letter 8: Philip Robert ChC to Charlotte Frances 1871	165
Letter 11: Eliza Constantia ChC to Rose ChC 1881	181
Letters 14 and 15: Annie Frances Crespigny nee Chauncy	194
to Rose Beggs nee Crespigny 1879	
Letter 17: Philip CdeC to his mother Charlotte Frances 1883	198
Letter 18: Constantine Trent CdeC to his aunt Ada 1889	209
Letter 22: Constantine Trent CdeC to his father Philip 1894	213

MAPS

Southeast Shropshire	8
Central Shrewsbury	10
The Bengal Presidency of British India	16
New York State and the Genesee Lands	32
Ireland	37
Shropshire, Worcestershire, Herefordshire, Gloucestershire	41
and southeast Wales	
Shrewsbury	49
Southern Engand and northeastern France	65
St Malo, Brittany, and its neighbourhood	71
Victoria, or Port Phillip District, 1851	81
The goldfields of Victoria	102
Amherst [former Daisy Hill] and Talbot [Back Creek]	110
The official survey of the township of Amherst 1855	112
The survey of Amherst 1864	146
and the possible extent of Daisy Hill Farm	
The region of Amherst and Talbot	148
with the suggested boundaries of Daisy Hill farm	
The New Hebrides 1884	151
Bright and Bairnsdale in eastern Victoria	158

Contents

Maryborough to Ballarat	159
Philip Robert Champion Crespigny's magistracies in the Western District	164
Southeast Melbourne, with indication of places associated with the Crespigny and Dana families 1870-1900	177
Eurambeen and Eurambeen East at the present day	185
Albury, Wodonga, Wagga Wagga, Gundagai, and Tumut	188
Brighton 1887	202
Part of the Western District of Victoria indicating the Eurambeen properties and Bushy Creek	208

Tables

Table 1:	A summary of the descent and kinship of Charlotte Frances Dana	xix
Table 2:	The Fitzhugh-Dana connection in nineteenth-century America	34
Table 3:	The Beggs family in Australia during the nineteenth century	203
Table 4:	The children and grandchildren of Charlotte Frances Dana	252
Table 5:	The great-grandchildren of Charlotte Frances Dana	268

Chart

Estimated population of Victoria at 31 December from 1851 to 1861	91

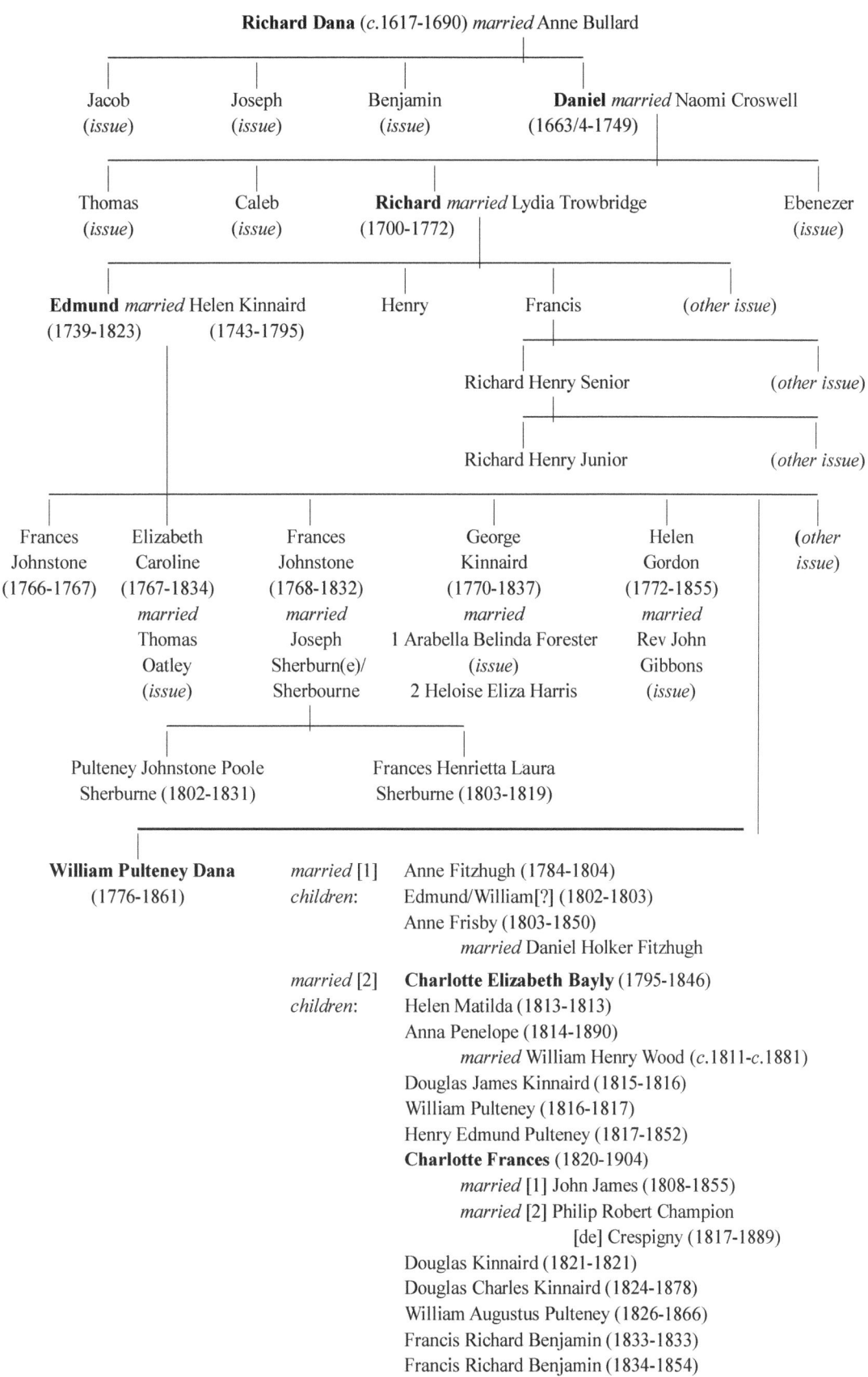

TABLE 1

A SUMMARY OF THE DESCENT AND KINSHIP OF CHARLOTTE FRANCES DANA

CHAPTER ONE

PROLOGUE: THE FAMILY BACKGROUND OF CHARLOTTE FRANCES NEE DANA

The Dana family in America
Edmund Dana in England and Scotland
The children of Edmund Dana and Helen nee Kinnaird
William Pulteney Dana, father of Charlotte Frances

The Dana family in America
There are several different accounts for the origins of the surname Dana, varying from the prosaic to the farfetched and romantic. Among the latter, one links the family to the Biblical prophet Daniel or to Dan, one of the lost tribes of Israel, while another refers to the mythical princess Danae, who was imprisoned in a tower by her father but was seduced by the Greek god Zeus, manifested as a shower of gold, and gave birth to the hero Perseus. A little more practically, but comparably unlikely, there is the suggestion of an Italian origin in Piedmont, with a putative link to the royal house of Savoy, future kings of Italy, and a family tradition of a French connection. There are more prosaic and England-based explanations, including the obvious one that it referred to a Dane or – in contrast – that it is an Anglo-Saxon name, taken from the word *dann*, meaning "valley," an early site of settlement. We may also note that a common pronunciation of the surname – *danner* – rhymes with the occupation of a tanner who treats hides to make leather.

In her Introduction to *The Dana Family in America*, Elizabeth Ellery Dana discounts all the more distant claims, and cites evidence of the surname in differing forms in Lancashire and Cheshire – particularly in Manchester during the sixteenth and seventeenth centuries. She observes in particular that Richard Dana, founder of the family in America, held official positions in Massachusetts which were unlikely to have been allowed to a foreigner, while a certain Richard Dana, whose family came from Kendal in the Lake District of Westmorland but who was baptised at Manchester on 31 October 1617, is not recorded again in England. Though recognising the evidence is no more than negative and circumstantial, she argues that:

> Many facts connected with his associations in Cambridge indicate that the man who was born in Manchester and disappeared from that town is identical with Richard Dana who lived in Cambridge from 1642 to 1690…[1]

The Introduction is followed by a series of extracts from documents of the sixteenth and seventeenth centuries, compiled in the late nineteenth and early twentieth centuries by Benjamin Dana and Joseph Gardner Bartlett. They list citations of people with the surname Dana or similar, including Danna, Danah, Danor, Danam and Danum, together with mentions in Kendal of Dawney, Dawnye, Daunay, Daynay and Dawnie; this last collection, affected by regional accents, is suggested as the original of the Dana surname, probably through a branch of the Dawney family of Yorkshire moving east into the Lake District.[2] Since spelling in the seventeenth century could be erratic – witness, for example, the different forms of William

---

[1] Dana Family in America, 9-10.
[2] Dana Family in America, 11-32 at 30.

CHAPTER ONE: PROLOGUE

Shakespeare's surname – while several documents are authorised by a "mark" rather than by a signature – indicating the person was illiterate – the variations are not surprising. And in modern times, as above, there is disagreement on pronunciation.

In her account of Richard Dana, Elizabeth Ellery Dana notes that he was the only person of that surname to come to America for the next two hundred years, and that he is the sole ancestor of the main American family.[3] There is no evidence of any later connection between Richard and his descendants in the American colonies – later the United States – and any kinfolk that he left behind in England.

It appears that **Richard** Dana came to Massachusetts in the early 1640s, for in a court document of October 1647 he affirmed that he had been working as a labourer some years earlier, and it was probably in 1647 that the General Court of the Massachusetts Bay Colony granted him land on the southern bank of the Charles River. A hundred acres in extent, it was in a good and convenient position, and Richard Dana continued to acquire property. He held several significant local offices: Constable; Viewer of Fences; Surveyor of Highways; and member of the Grand Jury of the Court of Assistants, advising the British Governor; and he was an early donor to Harvard College. He died of a fall in 1690.

Richard left four sons, twins Jacob and Joseph, Benjamin and Daniel, the youngest. **Daniel** (1664-1749) had a successful life and held local office,[4] but his third son **Richard** (1700-1772), first of the family to attend Harvard, became a magistrate and judge at Boston and was a leading figure in the agitation against the British imperial government which led to the American Revolution.[5]

In 1737 this second **Richard** Dana married Lydia Trowbridge (1711-1776), who bore him nine children; their eldest son, Edmund, is discussed below. One other son died in infancy, and another, Henry (1741-1761), died unmarried at the age of twenty. Four daughters also died as children, but Lydia Dana (1755-1808) married John Hastings, who served as a captain in the American army during the Revolutionary War.

Richard and Lydia nee Trowbridge's third son **Francis** (1743-1811), moreover, had a career at the national level. A leading lawyer and a close associate of George Washington, he was a member of the Continental Congresses of 1777, signed the Articles of Confederation in 1778, and was sent as Ambassador to Russia in 1780; the future President John Adams served there as his secretary. Again a member of Congress in 1784 and a leader of the Federalist Party, he later joined the Supreme Court of Massachusetts, and was Chief Justice from 1791 to 1806.[6] His son and grandson, Richard Henry Senior and Junior, were both lawyers; Richard Henry Senior (1787-1879) being also a well-known poet and literary critic, while Richard Henry Junior (1815-1882) was the author of *Two Years Before the Mast* and also compiled a substantial and detailed *Journal*.[7]

---

[3] Dana Family in America, 35.
[4] Item 570 of *Dana Family in America*, beginning at page 464, is an account of Daniel Dana; succeeding items deal with his descendants. See also *Anne's Family History* 2018/04/04.
[5] Dana Family in America, item 573 beginning at page 473.
[6] Item 582 of *Dana Family in America*, beginning at page 486, is an account of Francis Dana. Items 600 and 628, beginning at 504 and 526 respectively, deal with Richard Henry Senior and Richard Henry Junior.
[7] As will appear below, the *Journal* is an important source for the history of the Danas in England in the eighteenth and nineteenth centuries.

Edmund Dana in England and Scotland

Edmund Dana, eldest son of Richard, elder brother of Francis and later the grandfather of Charlotte Frances nee Dana, had a very different career.[8] Born at Charlestown, immediately north of Boston city across the mouth of the Charles River, on 15 November 1739, he entered Harvard in 1756 and graduated in 1759.[9] He was briefly apprenticed to a local doctor, but soon afterwards travelled to England and never returned to America.

Twenty years old, Edmund may have been formally in pursuit of medical qualifications, but it is not certain how serious he was about the project, and it is more likely that his primary concern was to travel and enjoy himself at his father's expense.[10] By 1764, however, he was at Edinburgh, where the university was known for its teaching in medicine and science, and he there met the Honourable Helen Kinnaird, daughter of Charles (1723-1767) the sixth Baron Kinnaird of Inchture and his wife Barbara nee Johnstone. The couple were married on 9 July 1765 at the church of Saint Cuthbert in the centre of Edinburgh.

Arms of the Barons Kinnaird and Johnstone baronets, and those adopted by Edmund Dana
[*Kinnaird and Johnstone from* Debrett *1904, Dana reconstructed by Rafe de Crespigny*]
The left-hand [dexter] *half of the Kinnaird shield is that of the family itself; the right-hand part comes from a later marriage. As members of the peerage, the Kinnaird family is entitled to supporters.*
The Kinnaird motto may be translated as He conquers who endures, *Johnstone's as* Never unready, *and Dana as* Safe by being cautious

The barony of the Kinnaird family was part of the peerage of Scotland, so the holder of the title was not automatically a member of the British House of Lords: a limited number of seats were available for peers of Scotland, and they had to be elected by their fellows. At the same time, however, Helen's mother Barbara was the daughter of the baronet Sir James Johnstone of Westerhall in Dumfries. Though the Danas were a respected colonial family, it was a considerable coup for a young American to marry the daughter of such a well-born and well-connected house; he was, however, considered to be very good-looking.[11]

---

[8] An account of Edmund Dana is item 581 of *Dana Family in America*, beginning at page 484.

[9] There is uncertainty about Edmund Dana's degree. Pattinson, *Shrewsbury Local History*, as immediately below, suggests that it was a Bachelor of Arts [BA], but *The Clergy Database*, as in note 20 below, states that he was ordained on the basis of a Master of Arts [MA] from Harvard.

The University of Cambridge in England has a system whereby a person who has graduated as a Bachelor can later pay a fee and receive the Master's degree: cambridgestudents.cam.ac.uk/your-course/graduation-and-what-next/cambridge-ma. The present-day graduate program at Harvard awards the Master's degree [abbreviated AM] only on the basis of academic work, but it is possible that the system in the eighteenth century was comparable to that of Cambridge in England.

[10] For example, Pattinson, *Shrewsbury Local History*, which has a brisk biography.

[11] His miniature portrait supports this. In 1785, when Edmund was in his middle forties, Abigail Adams, wife of the President of the United States, described him as "remarkably handsome:" note 33 at 13 below.

CHAPTER ONE: PROLOGUE

The Reverend Edmund Dana (1739-1823)
A miniature in the possession of the family

At the time of her marriage the Honourable Helen was still in her teens.[12] Unlike the situation in England, however, a woman in Scotland could marry at the age of twelve and did not need

---

In "A Search for the Arms of the Dana family," an essay published by *Anne's Family History* at 2014/05/24, Rafe de Crespigny has shown how the arms of a sixteenth-century London merchant William Dane were taken over by the Dana family of America. The earliest known use of the insignia was on the frame of a portrait of Richard Dana painted by John Singleton Copley about 1770 [Heckscher, *American Rococo*, 141-142], while Richard's son Francis had a bookplate engraved in the same style.

It is suggested that the adoption was made by Edmund Dana when he was in London during the 1760s. There is no evidence that any member of the family had been in England since the first Richard Dana departed for America about 1640, so Edmund was the first to have opportunity for the necessary research, and there was incentive for him to acquire some heraldry to match the family of his new wife. It would be natural for Edmund to advise his father and his brother of this initiative.

[12] There is some uncertainty about the age of the Honourable Helen. Her parents married in 1748 and she was their eldest child, so some have assumed that she was born in 1749.

England, Select Births and Christenings, 1538-1975, however, records the baptism of Helena, daughter of Charles Kinnaird at Kirk Andrews Upon Esk in Cumberland, just on the English side of the border with Scotland, on 17 March 1746. It is possible that Charles Kinnaird was the future baron, and he and Barbara nee Johnstone had anticipated their marriage. If so, Helen would have been nineteen when she married.

her father's permission to do so,[13] and Helen's parents were somewhat distracted, for Charles Lord Kinnaird was in the process of divorcing his wife on account of her "illnature." After firm negotiations, Barbara was left a pension of £130 a year, furniture valued at £100, and no access to her children.[14] Said to have been living in very depressed circumstances, she died in October, four months after her daughter's wedding. Charles followed her two years later.

Barbara Lady Kinnaird nee Johnstone
mother of the Honourable Helen Dana nee Kinnaird
portrait by Allan Ramsey 1748

William Johnstone Pulteney
brother of Barbara Lady Kinnaird
portrait by Thomas Gainsborough c. 1772

Though Rothschild describes the marriage as "unsuitable," there is no evidence that Helen's family had concerns.[15] The Dana family was not insignificant, and the mutual affection of the

---

On 27 November 1745 Charles Kinnaird was imprisoned at Edinburgh 'for holding treasonable correspondence with the Highlanders at Carlisle" – that is, with the forces supporting Prince Charles Stewart, "Bonny Prince Charlie" or the "Young Pretender," in his attempt earlier that year to overthrow the Hanoverian regime. He was released in December, but the incident may have been sufficient to delay a wedding until quieter times. [Walter Scot, a servant of Barbara's father Sir James Johnstone, was arrested with him, which indicates quite a close connection between the two families.] Source: "Extract of a Letter from Edinburgh" dated 28 November and published in the *Derby Mercury* of 29 November and the *Stamford Mercury* of 12 December; also Rothschild, *Life of Empires*, 16-17 with 318 note 28 quoting the *St James Evening Post*, London, of 3 and 24 December.

[13] In England, Lord Hardwicke's Marriage Act of 1753 (26 Geo.II. c.33) required that the ceremony had to be performed in a church, preceded by a call for banns or the obtaining of a marriage licence, while the marriage of a minor needed parental consent or at least acquiescence. The Act, however, had no effect in Scotland, and the village of Gretna Green, north of Carlisle and just across the border of the two kingdoms, became a popular destination for couples eloping from England.

[14] Rothschild, *Life of Empires*, 30-31.

[15] Rothschild, *Life of Empires*, 65, but *cf.* note 19 below.

Possibly through the connection of Edmund's marriage to Helen, the Dana family of Massachusetts and the Johnstones of Scotland corresponded with one another. George Johnstone, for example, supported the interests of the American colonists against the British East India Company [*e.g. Life of Empires*, 74-76] and on 8 June 1778 – in the middle of the Revolutionary War – he was writing from Philadelphia, Penn-

couple appears to have been genuine and long-lasting. Edmund himself, however, was well aware and appreciative of his good fortune. In a letter to his father Richard a month after the wedding he noted that one of Helen's uncles, George Johnstone, was Governor of West Florida and another, John, ruled a province in India.[16]

John Johnstone became extremely wealthy from his imperial service, but all family fortune was overshadowed by that of his brother William (1729-1805), who married Frances Pulteney in 1760. Frances' father Daniel was a cousin of William Pulteney, a leading politician who had been created Earl of Bath. He died in 1764, his only son William had died in 1763 and his younger brother General Harry Pulteney died in 1767. Daniel Pulteney, his sons and two elder daughters had also died by this time, and the vast estate was transferred to Frances and thus to her husband, who became known as the wealthiest commoner in England.[17] William changed his surname to Pulteney, and maintained it when he inherited the Johnstone baronetcy at the death of his elder brother James in 1794.[18]

The first three children of Edmund and Helen were born in London: Frances Johnstone in May 1766, who died one year later; Elizabeth Caroline in June 1767; and a second Frances Johnstone, in September 1768. Papers of the Kinnaird and Johnstone families demonstrate that they were willing to provide support,[19] and the couple's first two children were baptised in Saint Paul's Cathedral and the third child – the second Frances Johnstone – in the church of Saint Anne in Soho.

On 18 December 1768, at a ceremony in the Chapel Royal of Whitehall, Edmund was ordained as a deacon of the Church of England, and two months later he was made a priest.[20] The route of approval and acceptance was convoluted: authority for both appointments was given by Robert Lambe the Bishop of Peterborough on the basis of a Letter Dimissory from

---

sylvania, to Edmund's brother Francis [above at 2], now a member of the Continental Congress which headed the revolutionary government: the letter is quoted in one written to William Johnstone by a certain William Alexander on 8 October that year: call number mssPU 1-2087 in the William Pulteney papers held at The Huntington Library of San Marino, California.

[16] Rothschild, *Life of Empires*, 65 and note 28 at 357.

Florida had been ceded to Britain by Spain in the settlement at the end of the Seven Years War (1756-1763) and George Johnstone (1730-1787) was the first British Governor of West Florida from 1763-1767: *Life of Empires*, 20 and 35-45.

George's younger brother John (1734-1795) was a senior official of the British East India Company, with residence in Burdwan district of Bengal: *Life of Empires*, 21-22 and 46-58; there is a map at 16 below.

[17] Until the passage of the Married Women's Property Acts of 1870 and 1882, everything a woman owned – even her personal possessions – was controlled by her husband with very few restrictions: *e.g.* Poole, *What Jane Austen Ate*, 162-167.

[18] A biography of Sir William [Johnstone] Pulteney is at *History of Parliament online* 1754-1790 member/pulteney-william; see also Rothschild, *Life of Empires*, passim.

A biography of William Pulteney, Earl of Bath, is at *History of Parliament online* volume/1715-1754/member/pulteney-william.

[19] A letter of 6 September 1768 from John Johnstone to his brother William Johnstone/Pulteney [see below], discusses the support which might be jointly provided to Edmund Dana by the brothers, including George Johnstone: call number mssPU 1-2087 in the William Pulteney papers at The Huntington Library.

In a letter of 29 March 1775 Helen's brother George, who had succeeded their father and was now the seventh Baron Kinnaird, wrote to thank his uncle William Johnstone for providing assistance which he was currently unable to manage: call number mssPU 1-2087 in the William Pulteney papers at The Huntington Library. This may well relate to the additional living at Aston Botterill which William Pulteney arranged at this time: below at 8-9.

[20] Details of Edmund Dana's career in the Church of England are provided by *The Clergy Database* at jsp/persons/10426.

John Greene the Bishop of the neighbouring diocese of Lincoln. A Letter Dimissory is issued by one Anglican bishop to another, asking him to carry out the ordination on his behalf; the candidate is required to present the document to demonstrate his entitlement. Edmund may have received some training in his future duties, but the formal qualification was his MA from Harvard.[21]

Though both ceremonies of ordination were held at Whitehall, Edmund held office as deacon under the auspices of the Bishop of Lincoln, and he had a nominal appointment as Chaplain to his father-in-law Lord Kinnaird. More effectively, once he had been made a priest he received immediate and substantive appointment as Vicar of Brigstock with the chapel of Stanion. Both Brigstock and Stanion are in Northamptonshire, northeast and north of Kettering, but the parishes were in the diocese of Peterborough. In the Church of England, both vicars and rectors – as below – were responsible for individual parishes; the traditional difference was based upon the allocation of tithes, but the Rector was formally higher in rank and his position was usually more profitable. Edmund's actual salary was not very high, but in a letter to his father Richard soon after his appointment he explained his new situation and his decision to abandon his medical studies:

> My living has been magnified beyond measure, but I have great privileges in it wh[ich] no other person ever had upon acc[oun]t of its being upon an Estate of Mr Pulteney. I really understood before I took the gown that whatever deficiencys it labor[e]d under Mr Pulteney w[oul]d make good.[22]

In effect, therefore, Edmund had accepted the assurances of his new in-laws, and notably of his wife's uncle William Johnstone Pulteney, that a career in the church would be assured and well paid. Though the parish of Brigstock was controlled by the Crown through the Bishop of Peterborough, Edmund's letter indicates that the land was owned by William Pulteney and that his basic salary was supplemented. Given Pulteney's wealth and position, it would not have been difficult for him to persuade the bishop to find a place for his niece's husband, and a few years later he was able to act directly in the interest of his new client.

In November 1769, shortly after his appointment to Brigstock, Edmund Dana was admitted as a Sizar of Christ's College at the University of Cambridge. His entry in *Alumni Cantabrigienses*, however, suggests that although he may have intended to take the BD [Bachelor of Divinity] degree he did not in fact do so. Brigstock is forty-five miles/seventy kilometres from Cambridge, so it is not surprising if Edmund Dana found it impracticable to maintain his studies while ministering to his parish. Admission to the university, however, would have helped confirm his American qualifications.[23]

---

[21] *The Clergy Database* identifies the qualification for Edmund Dana's ordination as a deacon as *lit*, "The common abbreviation for 'literate' or '*literatus*'. Its use indicates that a clergyman did not possess a degree, but that he was judged by the bishop to possess sufficient learning to qualify for ordination."

[22] Rothschild, *Life of Empires*, 435 note 100.
  At 191 and 414 note 143, Rothschild also notes correspondence in September 1768 between William Pulteney and his younger brother John Johnstone (1734-1795), discussing support for the couple.

[23] *Alumni Cantabrigienses* adds a short account of Edmund Dana's background and clerical career, including his ordination and parish appointments, adding that he was also Chaplain to Lord Kinnaird.
  The significance of the term Sizar in this context is uncertain. Traditionally, a sizar received financial assistance from his college, sometimes acting as a servant to regular students. Sizars were generally more successful in gaining a degree than the average gentlemen undergraduates, so the appointment could be regarded as a form of scholarship. Since Edmund Dana was a mature man with a confirmed position, one

Chapter One: Prologue

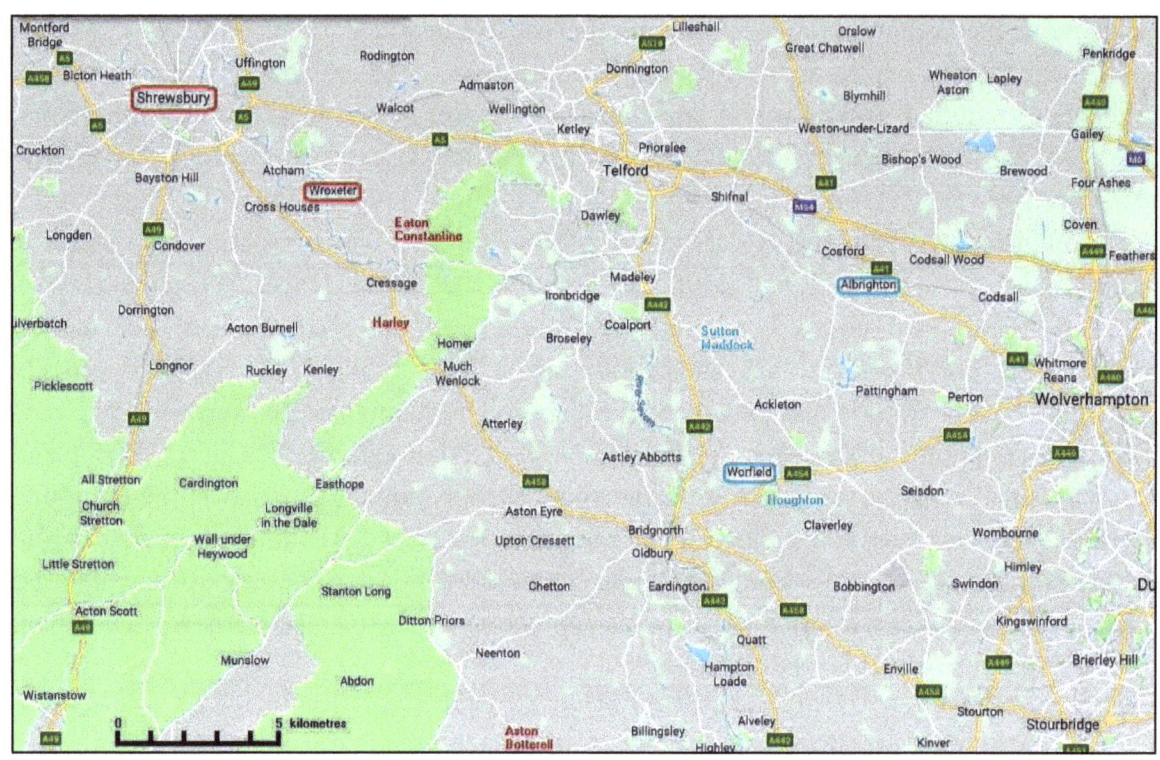

Southeast Shropshire; based on Google Maps
Sites marked in red relate to Edmund Dana; those in blue concern William Pulteney Dana

In November 1772 the Reverend Edmund Dana took up new duties as Vicar of the parish of Wroxeter in Shropshire, in the diocese of Coventry and Lichfield. Wroxeter is a village some five miles – less than ten kilometres – east of Shrewsbury. William Pulteney first entered Parliament in 1768 as member for Cromartyshire in Scotland, but he had substantial interests in Shropshire and had also contested the seat of Shrewsbury. He won a seat there at the election of 1774, and held it until his death in 1805.[24] Among his several estates in the region, William Pulteney was lord of the manor of Wroxeter and patron of several livings: that is, he had authority to name the priest who would head the parish as rector or vicar. The previous long-serving incumbent at Wroxeter, Robert Cartwright, had died, so the vacancy was free for him to nominate his nephew by marriage.[25]

Edmund Dana and his family now settled in the region of Shrewsbury, and William Pulteney continued his support. In 1775 the living of Aston Botterill became vacant through the death of the former Rector Nehemiah Tonks, and Edmund Dana was appointed to succeed

---

may assume the title was a compliment rather than indication of inferior status.

Alumni Cantabrigienses states that Edmund Dana took up residence at Christ's ten years later, in December 1780. By that time he was Vicar of Wroxeter and Rector of Aston Botterill, both far to the west, so it is unlikely he was able to stay for long. He never took a degree.

[24] One of William Pulteney's rivals in 1768, and his colleague from 1774, was Robert Clive, a major figure in the British conquest of India; his residence was a short distance north of Shrewsbury.

[25] Patronage of a living, also known as an advowson, was often held by the diocesan bishop, but many were in the hands of laymen. Formally, a lay patron presented the name to the bishop for approval, but there was strong legal presumption that the bishop would follow the advice.

It should be noted that patronage gave the right only to nominate the incumbent, not to require his subsequent dismissal. The patron could exercise his authority again only when a living became vacant through the death or departure of the incumbent.

An account of the parish of Wroxeter, with extracts from parish records, is at melocki.org.uk.

him. That parish was in a different diocese, Hereford, and was thirty miles/fifty kilometres southeast from Shrewsbury and Wroxeter, but there was a curate John Purcell: a curate served as an assistant and was authorised to care for the parish when the rector or vicar was absent. Purcell had been a student at Christ Church, Oxford, and held a Bachelor's degree, and at this time he was also the curate of another parish and full vicar of a third, all in the diocese of Hereford. There were some restrictions, but such pluralism of appointments was common: it improved the income of the titular priest, and the parishioners did receive some pastoral care.

In 1781 Edmund Dana was given two further appointments as Rector: to Harley and to Eaton Constantine.[26] Both parishes were in the diocese of Coventry and Lichfield and both lay southeast of Shrewsbury, Eaton Constantine just two miles from Wroxeter and Harley the same distance further on. The livings were formally in the gift of a certain John Newport, but he was evidently under age and William Pulteney was his official guardian.

Edmund's wife Helen continued to bear children: nine girls and four boys for a total of thirteen in the space of twenty-one years, of which three died in infancy. Their names and places of birth or baptism are listed below.[27]

Frances Johnstone (1766-1767)* [London]
Elizabeth Caroline (1767-1834) [London]
Frances Johnstone (1768-1832) [London]
George Kinnaird (1770-1837) [Brigstock]
Helen Gordon (1772-1855) [Brigstock]
Harriet (1774-1803) [Wroxeter]
William Pulteney (1776-1861) [Wroxeter]
Henry Bertie (1778-1798) [Wroxeter]
Barbara (1779-1779)* [Wroxeter]
Matilda (1780-1837) [Wroxeter]
Henrietta Laura (1782-1814) [Wroxeter]
Charles Patrick (1784-1816) [Wroxeter]
Maria (1787-1787)* [Wroxeter]

Such a number of children and of infant deaths was not unusual, but it was surely exhausting for the woman giving birth. Aged forty-five, Helen died at Shrewsbury on 17 April 1795 and was buried at Wroxeter on 22 April. She and Edmund had been married just three months less than thirty years; he did not marry again.

In a tradition which would be followed in the next generation, several children were given names from the Johnstone and Kinnaird families, together with Pulteney – naturally enough – and Gordon, from the family of Helen's paternal grandmother, also named Helen, daughter of the second Earl of Aboyne. Among the more regular Christian names, Frances Pulteney was the heiress wife of William Johnstone Pulteney; Elizabeth Johnstone (1728-1813) was a sister of Barbara Kinnaird;[28] and the name Caroline honours that of Barbara's husband Charles, Lord Kinnaird. A convenient courtesy, the system recognised the connection to Helen's noble relatives, and probably indicated hope for future favour.

---

[26] An account of the parish of Harley, with extracts from the parish records, is at melocki.org.uk.
[27] The names of female children are in *italics*. An asterisk * indicates death in infancy.
[28] Rothschild, *Life of Empires*, 307.

Chapter One: Prologue

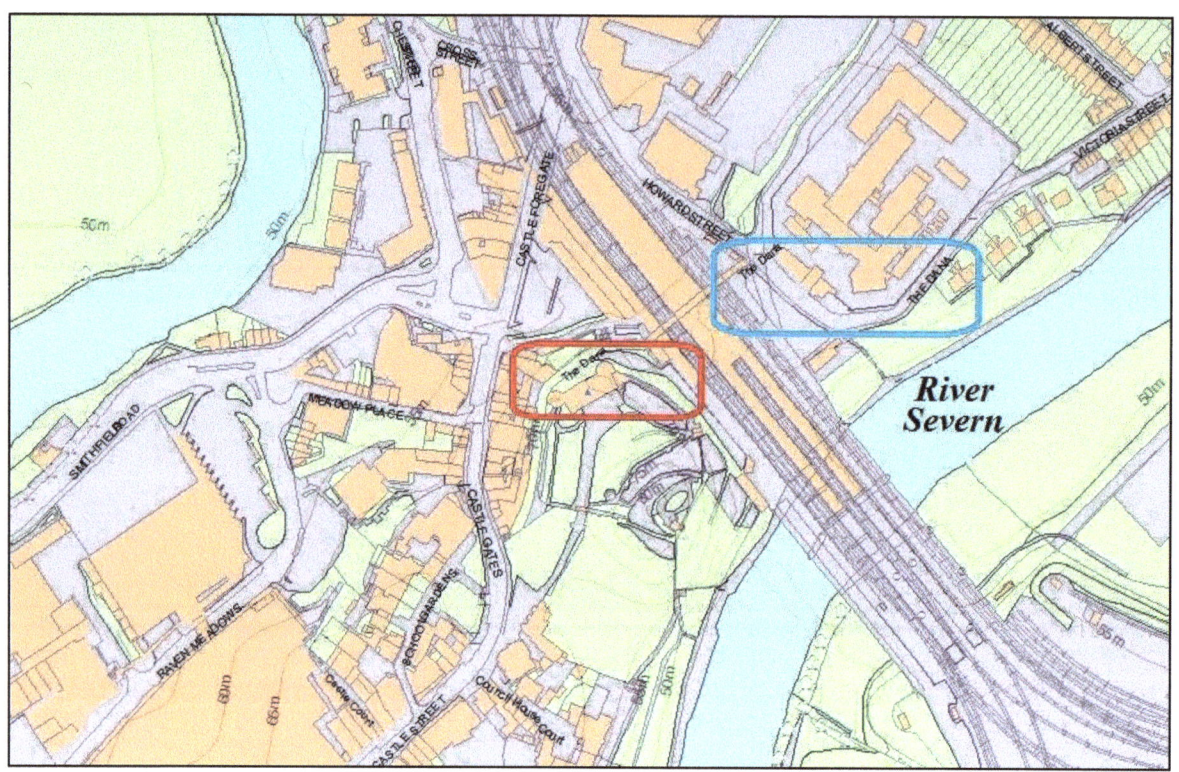

Central Shrewsbury, from the British Ordnance Survey
The red square identifies Shrewsbury Castle, and the eastern end of The Dana which then leads across the modern railway towards Shrewsbury Prison.
The blue square identifies The Dana passing the main entrance of Shrewsbury Prison, then turning northeast to continue above the bank of the Severn.

Though Edmund Dana had no previous contact with Shropshire, the patronage of William Pulteney gave status to the newcomer, while Wroxeter is a notable parish: a short distance east of Shrewsbury, it occupies the site of the former Roman town of Uriconium. Some time after his arrival, Edmund Dana became a local magistrate.

An early patron of the great engineer Thomas Telford, William Pulteney arranged for him to work on the refurbishment of Shrewsbury Castle during the 1780s, and a few years later had him appointed Surveyor of Public Works for the county, where he planned and constructed roads, bridges and canals. Edmund Dana was a member of the trust concerned with roads and streets, so the two men knew one another, and when Telford was commissioned to construct a new prison in the city, close to the castle, Dana had him construct a passage from the castle, across the line of the present-day railway, to the entrance of the prison and then along the River Severn. The route became known as The Dana, and custom applied the name also to the prison itself.[29]

Some sources claim that Edmund Dana lived in Castle Gate House by the entrance to the castle, and he may have done so at some period. From the time he arrived, however, all his children were born and baptised at Wroxeter, and his wife Helen died and was buried there.

---

[29] Pattinson, *Shrewsbury Local History*, observes that local pronunciation of the surname is *danner* rather than *darner*.

Castle Gate House, Shrewsbury
Photograph by Anne Young 2019

In 1856 Edmund Dana's great-nephew Richard Henry Dana Junior, grandson of Edmund's brother Francis, visited England and spent three days at Shrewsbury. On the first day he met his cousin Anna Penelope, Edmund's grand-daughter,[30] and her husband William Henry Wood escorted him on a tour of the city. He saw the castle, which had been the residence of William Pulteney, and the Dana Terrace, "principal walk of the castle, and named from the Rev Edmund Dana, who planned it." He was also shown an old house with black timber cross-beams, where the future King Henry VII was said to have spent the night on his way to defeat Richard III at Bosworth in 1485. There was, however, no mention of Edmund Dana living in Castle Gate House or anywhere else in the city and, since Anna Penelope had been nine years old and living near Shrewsbury when her grandfather Edmund died in 1823, we may assume that she would have remembered if he had done so.

Richard Henry Dana's entry for the next day, Sunday 10 August, records how he accompanied Mr and Mrs Wood to the evening service at Wroxeter. In romantic style, he tells how:

> Wroxeter is a fair specimen of the old English parish Church, parsonage and village. . . . . The church stands in the midst of the graves of the villagers, and the vicarage opens into the Church Yard. In this vicarage, lived and died, Edmund Dana, my grandfather's only brother. Here he officiated from 1766 to 1823 – a period of fifty seven years.[31] Here he brought his beautiful noble bride, a peer's daughter, in the bloom of her charm, and here he laid her, under the stone of the chancel, at middle life, the mother of twelve children, loved and honoured by all.[32] Here he lies by her side, and here most of his children are buried. . . . . Here grew up, here played, here walked and studied, and loved, and married,

---

[30] Richard Henry Dana's visit to Shrewsbury is described in his *Journal* at 784-787 He has Mrs Wood's first given name as Anne, but when probate was granted of her will after her death on 27 February 1890 the name was written Anna. Richard Henry may have misheard, or the editor misread his handwriting.

[31] Edmund Dana was ordained in 1766, but did not arrive at Wroxeter until 1772, so he was there only fifty-one years. Richard Henry Dana was presumably given the mistaken information by Anna Penelope Wood nee Dana: by 1856, 1766 and 1772 were far in the past and she no doubt confused the ordination with the appointment.

[32] In fact, Edmund and Helen had thirteen children, not twelve. Anna Penelope had probably forgotten – or never knew of – the birth and death of the first child of the marriage, the infant Frances Johnstone (1766-1767), whose name was later taken by the third daughter (1768-1832).

Chapter One: Prologue

Shrewsbury Castle
Photograph by Anne Young 2019

The Dana 1788
Watercolour by Michael 'Angelo' Rooker
from Shrewsbury Museums Service

The New Gaol at Shrewsbury 1795
Watercolour by John Ingleby

The main entrance of Shrewsbury Prison
Photograph by user Nabokov at Wikipedia 2009

The Dana and the eastern wall of the prison
Street view by Google Maps 2020

The Church of Saint Andrew, Wroxeter
Photograph by Anne Young 2019

those beautiful daughters, whom Mrs President Adams says were the most elegant women he saw in England, and whom George III called the roses of his court.[33]

He goes on to describe the church itself, with the tombs of Edmund Dana, his wife Helen, and several of their children, placed before the chancel.

Since 1781 Edmund Dana had been the incumbent of four parishes: Wroxeter, where he was vicar; together with Aston Botterill, Eaton Constantine and Harley, in each of which he was the rector. In January 1805, however, he relinquished his appointment at Harley. The process, known as "cession," is described by *The Clergy Database* as a means to control the excesses of pluralism, but in this case it was rather a matter of nepotism, for Edmund Dana's successor at Harley was his son-in-law John Gibbons, who had married his daughter Helen Gordon three years before.[34] Sir William Pulteney, who had inherited the Johnstone baronetcy after

---

[33] *Journal*, 785-786. Note 26 quotes a letter written in 1785 by Abigail Adams, wife of the second President of the United States:

> The finest English woman I have seen is the eldest daughter of Mr [Edmund] Dana, brother to our Mr [Francis] Dana; he resides in the country, but was in London with two of his daughters when I first came here. [She and her husband came from Boston, Massachusetts, and thus knew the Dana family.]

and

> I would not have it forgotten that her father is an American, and, as he was remarkably handsome, no doubt she owes a large share of her beauty to him.

This eldest daughter would have been Elizabeth Caroline (1767-1844). Eighteen years old in 1785, she married Thomas Oatley two years later: below at 14. Mrs Adams describes seeing her at Ranelagh, a pleasure park near Chelsea in London, and she later met her and her younger sister Frances Johnstone when they called upon her. She does not mention their attendance at court, however, and no evidence is provided for the comment attributed to King George.

[34] Below at 26.

CHAPTER ONE: PROLOGUE

the death of his elder brother in 1794 but kept the surname Pulteney, again served as the patron for the new appointment.

Soon after the transfer of Harley, and of rather more consequence for Edmund Dana and his children, Sir William Pulteney died. His first wife, the heiress Frances, had died in 1782, and in January 1804 Sir William made a second marriage to Margaret nee Stirling, daughter of a Scottish baronet. There were rumours that he was hoping for an heir of his own body, but he was now in his middle seventies and he died on 30 May of the following year. Surprisingly for a man of such extensive property and a qualified lawyer, he left no will, and the whole of his estate devolved to his only child Henrietta Laura, daughter of his first marriage, who held title as Countess of Bath; his widow received a small annuity. The situation became confused, but in June 1805 the Bradford estates in Shropshire, valued at £30,000 *per annum*, were transferred to William Harry Vane, Earl of Darlington, a kinsman by marriage to Henrietta Laura's father the late Earl of Bath.[35] There was certainly no direct benefit for the Dana family and – as we explore below – there may have been serious damage.[36]

Edmund Dana nonetheless maintained his local position and influence until his death on 7 May 1823. We have noted that Richard Henry Dana saw the tombs of Edmund, his wife Helen and several of their children when he visited Wroxeter in 1856, and he also remarked that the local bridge, a Roman column in the churchyard and several trees were named in his memory, while

> the old people of the parish still call him the "old gentleman", and look upon the present rector, who has been here twenty years, as the "new vicar", and complain of his innovations.[37]

The will of the Reverend Edmund Dana was proved at London on 22 May 1823. His estate – including some actual or potential holdings in America – was divided between his three children Elizabeth Caroline Oatley, Helen Gordon Gibbons and William Pulteney Dana and their heirs. His other surviving children, Frances Johnstone Sherburne, George Kinnaird Dana and Matilda Armstrong, were doing well enough not to require assistance, and the situation of his grandchildren by his youngest son the late Charles Patrick Dana was evidently too distant and too uncertain to be considered at that time.[38]

The children of Edmund Dana and Helen nee Kinnaird

Note: This section is concerned with the thirteen sons and daughters of Edmund Dana and his wife Helen, except for their seventh child and second son William Pulteney Dana. As the father of Charlotte Frances nee Dana he has a separate entry below.

Born in 1767, **Elizabeth Caroline** was the second daughter and the eldest to survive infancy.[39] In 1787 she married Thomas Oatley, whose family held a number of farms in Shropshire and Staffordshire. Their formal residence was at Bishton Hall near Little

---

[35] *The Public Ledger and Daily Advertiser*, 6 June 1805, page 2; *Bath Chronicle and Weekly Gazette*, 4 July 1805, page 4.
[36] Below at 31 and 35.
[37] Dana, *Journal*, 786.
[38] A copy of his will and its probate is at The National Archives; Kew, England; Prerogative Court of Canterbury and Related Probate Jurisdictions: Will Registers; Class: PROB 11; Piece: 1670.
  On Charles Patrick Dana and his children, see below at 28-31.
[39] An account of Elizabeth Caroline Dana is item 581ii of *Dana Family in America* at 485.

Haywood, some five miles or eight kilometres east of Stafford, but Thomas died in 1834 and when Elizabeth Caroline died ten years later she was buried at Albrighton in Shropshire, ten miles – fifteen kilometres – northwest of Wolverhampton.[40] She bore ten children; one of her sons became a clergyman, another was an officer in the army, and her daughters likewise married at that level of society.[41]

As we have seen, Edmund and Helen named two daughters **Frances Johnstone**: their first-born had died in infancy in 1767 and their third daughter was named for her – this was a common custom in an age of high child mortality. The second Frances Johnstone was born on 3 September 1768 and baptised on 6 October at the church of Saint Anne in Soho, London. Her baptismal name appears only as Frances; the Johnstone was added later or assumed as part of the surname.[42]

On 14 November 1793 Frances Johnstone Dana married Joseph Sherburne at Boston, Massachusetts. The local *Columbian Centinel* describes her as the daughter of the Reverend Edmond Dana DD [Doctor of Divinity], of Shrewsbury, England, and adds that she was a niece of the Chief Justice Francis Dana.[43]

The *Centinel* refers to Joseph Sherburne as "late from India." Baptised at Falmouth in Cornwall on 26 June 1751, he was the son of Joseph Sherburne (*c*.1725-1763) and Statira nee Fawkener. The 1782 *Index* of the East India Company in Bengal lists him as a Senior Merchant who had arrived in 1767, when he would have been sixteen years old.[44] He served in the Accountant's office, then became a Writer, a Factor and a Junior Merchant, and had also been a Deputy Superintendent of Police.[45] In 1787 he was appointed Collector of Birbhum, north of Calcutta. A Collector was the chief administrative officer of a district, with – as his title indicates – special responsibility for the gathering of tax revenue.

---

[40] Awkwardly, there are two villages called Albrighton in the county of Shropshire. One is a few miles north of Shrewsbury; the other, as here, lies northwest of Wolverhampton in Staffordshire. All references to Albrighton in the following text relate to the latter place, not to the village north of Shrewsbury.

[41] Item 581 of *Dana Family in America* at page 485.

[42] Accounts of the two Frances Johnstone Danas are items 581i and 581iii of *Dana Family in America* at 485.

[43] Issue of 20 November; transcribed by *US, Newspaper Extractions from the Northeast*, 1704-1930, 755. Apart from this, there is no evidence that Edmund Dana ever gained the degree of Doctor of Divinity.

One of the leading merchants of Boston at this time was Joseph Sherburne (1710-1799), whose portrait by John Singleton Copley was painted about 1770 and is now in the Metropolitan Museum of Art in New York. Frances Johnstone Dana's husband, however, however, was not this man, for the dates do not match, and though Joseph Sherburne of Boston had a son named Joseph, he died young: threefamilytrees.blogspot.com/2018/06/a-great-aunt-who-had-portrait-painted. Nor was there any connection between the two Sherburne families: had there been, we may fairly assume that the *Columbian Centinel* would have noted it in the same fashion as it identified the relationship of Frances Johnstone with Chief Justice Francis Dana.

The sources have variant spellings of the surname, whether Sherburn, Sherburne or Sherbourne. Allowing for hand-writing, it appears that Frances Johnstone used the spelling Sherborne in the Bible which she left to her god-daughter Charlotte Frances Dana, while the note of donation from Mrs McIvoe[?] in 1814 seems to have the form Sherbourne [Chapter Two at 43-44]; her Frances Johnstone's will, however, has the form Sherburne. Unless there is specific need to discuss the spelling, we use the form Sherburne.

[44] Listed in UK, Registers of Employees of the East India Company and the India Office, 1746-1939.

[45] In 1785 Joseph Sherburne had presented a memorial complaining of unfair treatment: To the Honorable the Court of Directors for the Affairs of the Honorable United Company of Merchants of England trading to the East Indies. Printed in Calcutta, the pamphlet presents a survey of his service to the Company and protests his failure to receive promotion. The British Museum copy has been digitised by Google Books.

The region had problems with banditry and border raiding and Joseph Sherburne established a very firm government, so that

> the two frontier principalities had passed from the condition of military fiefs into that of a regular British district, administered by a collector and covenanted assistants, defended by the Company's troops, studded with fortified factories, intersected by a new military road, and possessing daily communication with the seat of government in Calcutta.

Despite this record of success, however, in November 1788, after only eighteen months in office, he was recalled on suspicion of corruption.[46]

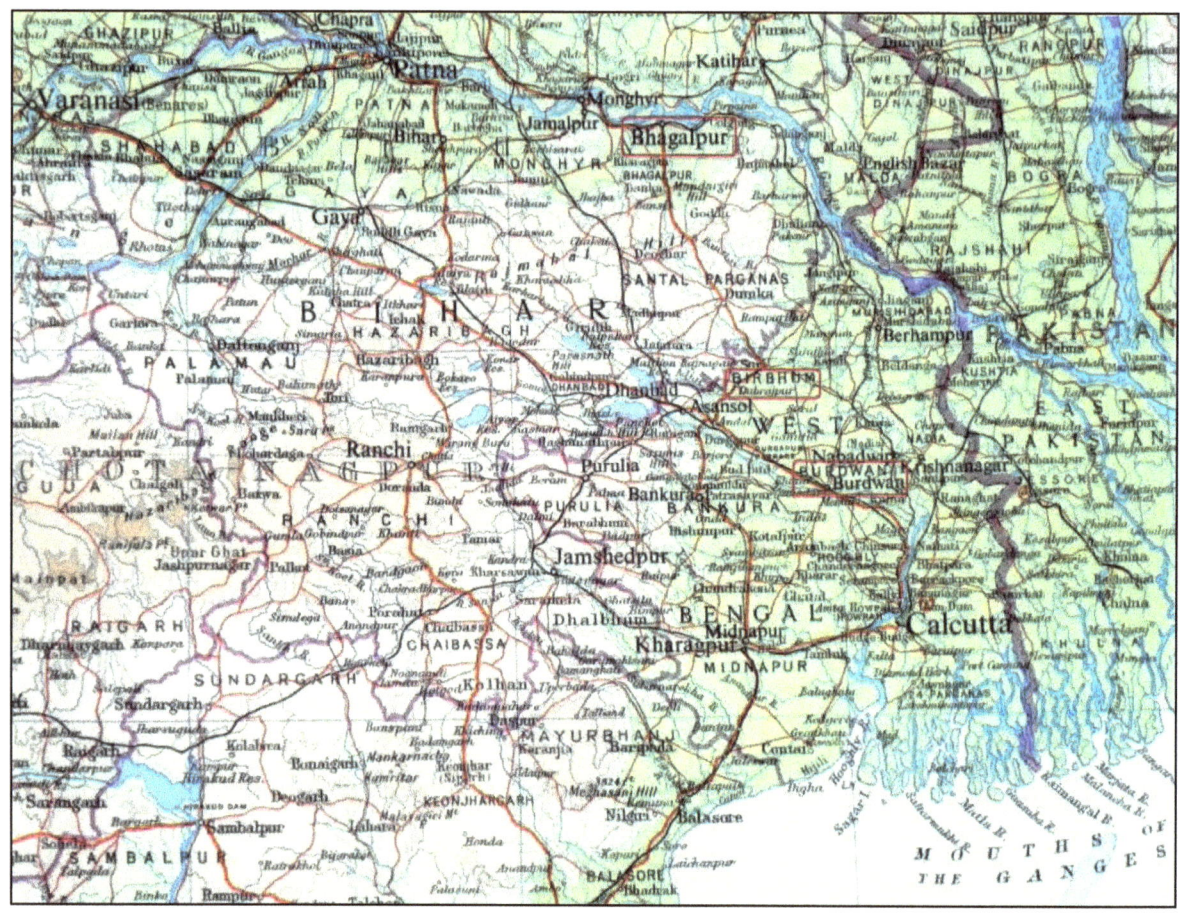

The region of the Bengal Presidency of British India
based on Times Atlas II
*Bhagalpur [formerly Boglepore or Boglipore] on the Ganges is identified in red,
as are Birbhum and Burdwan, north of Calcutta [on Burdwan, see note 16 above]*

It appears the suspicion was unfounded, for Joseph Sherburne was again employed by the East India Company, and he was presumably in Boston on business when he met Frances Johnstone Dana as she was visiting her American family.

It is not known when Joseph returned to India with Frances Johnstone, but in June of 1802 he was appointed Collector of the district of Boglepore in Bengal.[47] Boglepore or Boglipore, now known as Bhagalpur, is a city on the Ganges River in Bihar state of present-day India, some four hundred kilometres from Calcutta. Soon after their arrival, Frances gave

---

[46] Hunter, Annals of Rural Bengal I, 16-17.
[47] Listed in The Asiatic Annual Register 1802.

birth to a son, who was baptised Pulteney Johnstone Poole at Boglepore on 16 December. Ten months later, on 3 October 1803, a daughter was baptised Frances Henrietta Laura – her second and third names were those of William Pulteney's daughter the Countess of Bath.[48]

Joseph Sherburne died, however, on 15 July 1805. He left no will, so there was delay in settling his affairs, but on 13 December the administration at Calcutta granted probate to his widow for the substantial amount of 17,280 Rupees.[49] Much of the estate, however, was in real estate, and Frances Johnstone Sherburne was obliged to wait some time to sell and settle her property.[50]

In addition to these financial concerns, moreover, the will of Frances' brother Charles Patrick Dana, signed at Calcutta on 27 September 1814, appointed her as his Executrix, together with two friends in the service of the East India Company. Since Charles Patrick died two years later in July 1816, Frances was then responsible not only for his estate but also for his three orphaned children, all aged less than ten years old.[51]

In all these circumstances, it appears that Frances Johnstone Sherburne remained for several years in India. Other arrangements, however, were made for her own two children.

In its "Calcutta Gazette" section dated 12 December 1811, the *Madras Courier* of 31 December recorded that the Honorable East India Company ship *Metcalfe* had sailed in a convoy for Europe on the second of that month. The list of passengers included twenty-four children, boys and girls, and one of them was Frances Henrietta Laura Sherburne, now eight years old.[52]

During the nineteenth century it was customary to send young British children "home" for the sake of their health; the Indian climate was considered – with some reason – to be dangerous. One example of this practice was Rudyard Kipling, who was sent to England at the age of five and was boarded out at Southsea near Portsmouth during the 1870s. Though he occasionally visited relatives, he was largely in the care of strangers, and he did not see his parents for seven years. It is clear that the practice was already established in the early part of the century, for all other ships of the convoy had similar lists of children. Unaccompanied by their parents, they presumably had a general guardian on board and they were received on arrival either by relatives or, as in the case of Kipling, by some agency which would care for them.[53]

---

[48] The account of Frances Johnstone Sherburne nee Dana in Item 581iii of *Dana Family in America* at 485 mentions her marriage and her son Pulteney, but omits her daughter and has her residence only as London.

[49] *The Public Ledger and Daily Advertiser* of London recorded his death on page 3 of 10 February 1806, seven months after the event.

Probate of his estate is recorded by *Administration Archive* reference L-AG-34-29-2 Page/folio 57 Administrations – Bengal.

[50] The *Calcutta Gazette* of 21 August 1806 at page 8 has a public notice advising that the Adminstratix of the estate of the Joseph Sherburne is selling housing and premises in the district of Chouringhee in Calcutta. On 22 April 1813 the front page of the same journal calls a meeting of creditors of the estate to be held on 4 May.

[51] On Charles Patrick Dana, his will and his three children, see below at 28-31.

[52] *Madras Courier*, volume 27, number 1369 in The British Newspaper Archive. The children are listed in a separate section; adult passengers included married women, civil servants, army officers, and some French prisoners of war.

[53] Kipling was seriously ill-treated and abused by his hosts, and wrote of it in the short story "Baa Baa, Black Sheep" and later in his autobiography. One assumes, however, that other cases were less unfortunate.

Chapter One: Prologue

Records are incomplete, so it is not known when Frances Henrietta's brother was sent to England, but on 20 April 1813 Pulteney Johnstone Poole Sherburne, Gentleman, became an Ensign in the South Hampshire Regiment of Militia. Militia were a home guard or reserve force, and Ensign was the lowest commissioned rank of an infantry regiment, equivalent to a Second Lieutenant at the present day. Pulteney Sherburne had not yet reached his eleventh birthday, but the appointment was approved by the Lord Lieutenant of the county of Norfolk. It appears that Pulteney Sherburne had been sent to England in the care of his relatives, and his family were using connections to gain him seniority for a military career; his uncle George Kinnaird Dana, now a colonel, may have had some influence, but the sponsorship from the Lord Lieutenant of a distant county implies that the broad reach of the Johnstone family may also have been involved.[54]

Two years later, on 27 July 1815 Volunteer Pulteney Johnstone Poole Sherburne was commissioned as an Ensign (without purchase) in the First Regiment of Foot.[55] Also known as the Royal Scots, the First Regiment of Foot was one of the most senior in the British Army. At that time it comprised four battalions: two were in Canada, engaged in the War of 1812 against the United States; one was in France, having fought at the battle of Waterloo on 18 June; and the 2nd was stationed in India. Pulteney Sherburne was barely thirteen, and the *Gazette* entry for 1818 three years later, as below, states that he was on half-pay. He was not yet engaged in active service.

Commissions were normally acquired by purchase, a system designed to ensure that the army would be controlled by men of property, who were unlikely to support political or social disruption. It was possible, however, for a man to serve as a Volunteer or "gentleman ranker," and after a period as an ordinary soldier he could seek a commission without payment. It appears that, regardless of his notional service with the South Hampshire Militia, Pulteney Sherburne was following this pattern.

Three years later, on 6 March 1818 Ensign Pulteney Poole Sherburne was transferred from the First Regiment to the same rank with the Seventieth Regiment of Foot. He was now sixteen, old enough to undertake formal duties. The *Gazette* states that he had been at half-pay with the First Regiment, so although the 2nd Battalion was engaged in the Third Maratha War during 1817 and 1818 he had not taken part. Elsewhere, both the wars against Napoleon and against the United States had ended, and Pulteney Sherburne's new regiment was on garrison duty in Canada.

Four years later, on 26 April 1822 Ensign Pulteney J Poole Sherburne of the Seventieth Foot was transferred to be a Lieutenant in the First Regiment of Foot, again without purchase; his commission was soon afterwards amended to have had effect from 18 October 1820: he gained seniority, but he was not entitled to back pay.[56] The 1st Battalion of the First Regiment had lately been in Canada but was currently in Ireland; the 2nd Battalion was still in India

---

[54] British Army Officer Promotions 1800-1815, issue number 16722 Page 791. On George Kinnaird Dana, see below at 21-24.

[55] *London Gazette* Issue 17048 of 5 August 1815 at 1589.

[56] *London Gazette* Issue 17812 of 27 April 1822 at 694 and Issue 17816 of 11 May at 786.

  In email correspondence, Bruce Bassett-Powell of Uniformology.com remarks that, "The dramatic drawdown of regimental personnel after the Napoleonic Wars left many career officers without a regiment of their choice, so officers were transferred with or without purchase to any regiment they could find."

and engaged in the First Burma War of 1824-1826. Six months later, in October 1822, Lieutenant Pulteney J Poole Sherburne of the First Regiment moved once again, this time by exchange to the Fifty-Eighth Foot; both he and his opposite number were on half pay.[57]

Miniature portrait of Lieutenant Pulteney Johnstone Poole Sherburne
Bequeathed by his mother Frances Johnstone Sherburne to her niece and god-daughter
Charlotte Frances Dana and still in the possession of the family; see Chapter Six at 232.
Both the Seventieth Regiment and the Fifty-Eighth had uniforms with black facings and gold lace evenly spaced, so it is not possible to decide he is wearing. Similarly, the portrait could have been made in Canada – in which case it probably shows him in the uniform of the Seventieth – or during his period of leave in England in 1830, when he was in the Fifty-Eighth. It is most unlikely that anyone in Berbice had the necessary skill.

The Fifty-Eighth Foot, a single-battalion regiment, was at that time stationed in the West Indies, and Pulteney Sherburne was appointed Barrack-Master of the garrison at Berbice in what is now Guyana, on the north-eastern coast of South America. Taking its name from the major river of the region, Berbice had first been colonised by the Dutch, but the territory had been seized by Britain during the Napoleonic wars and it was formally transferred by treaty in 1814-15. In 1831 Berbice was absorbed into the larger colony of British Guiana.

The garrison was based at Canje Point, one mile from the colonial capital New Amsterdam. Responsible for administration and maintenance, barrack masters were subject to the Board of Ordinance, and were detached from their nominal regiment: the Fifty-Eighth Foot moved to Ceylon in 1828, but Pulteney Sherburne remained at Berbice. He did have a spell of home leave, for he signed his will at Burton in Wiltshire on 7 August 1830.

---

[57] *London Gazette* Issue 17872 of 23 November 1822 at 1915. As with the absence of back pay in the previous transfer, we must assume that the half pay appointment also reflects the reduction described in note 56 immediately above. See also note 58 immediately following.

Chapter One: Prologue

New Amsterdam, Berbice, in the 1830s
From Sketch Map of British Guiana *by Robert Hermann Schomburgk (1804–65) published London 1840; retrieved from World Digital Library: https://www.wdl.org/en/item/11335/*

The climate of Berbice is tropical, with heavy rainfall all the year round, the country is low-lying, with marshes, swamps and woodlands, rife with malaria and other diseases. In 1831, the garrison of some two thousand black troops and a thousand white lost 113 men to sickness. Pulteney Sherburne was one of them: he died on 28 June 1831 at the age of twenty-eight, and his will was proven in London on 12 September of that year.[58]

Pulteney Sherburne's sister Frances Henrietta Laura had died several years before, in November 1819 at the age of sixteen. It is not known where the children had lived when they were in England – one assumes that Pulteney Sherburne had been in Hampshire when he was enrolled in the militia in 1813, but he had been in Canada from 1818 and Frances Henrietta's death was recorded at Leyton in Essex, now part of the London Borough of Waltham.

A shipping record of March 1819 lists the departure of a Mrs Sherburne from Calcutta on the East India Company ship *Phoenix*.[59] Another Mrs Sherburne in India was recorded some fifteen years earlier, but it is very possible that this entry relates to Frances Johnstone – she may have arrived in time to see her daughter before she died.

Once in England, the inheritance from her husband Joseph was sufficient to maintain his widow in comfortable circumstances, for in 1826 Mrs Frances Johnstone Sherburne was living in London at Hans Place in St Luke, Chelsea, an attractive area with most respectable neighbours including colonels in the army and naval captains, churchmen and the Countess Grosvenor.[60] She would no doubt have seen her son Pulteney when he visited and made his will in August 1830, but his death in the following year left her childless.

Frances Johnstone Sherburne nee Dana died on 11 April 1832, a few months after her son, at the age of sixty-three. She was buried with her daughter at the church of St Mary the Virgin at Leyton in Essex.[61] Signed at Chelsea on 19 October 1831, soon after her son's death,

---

[58] The Monthly Military Obituary, published on page 3 of the *Morning Post* of 1 September 1831 recorded the death of Sherburne of the 56 Foot, Barrack Master at Berbice, with the annotation "h.p.," indicating that he was on half pay.
   There is an account of Pulteney Sherburne's military career, with details of Berbice and the British establishment there, at *Anne's Family History* 2020/07/18.
   A copy of his will and its probate is at The National Archives; Kew, England; Prerogative Court of Canterbury and Related Probate Jurisdictions: Will Registers; Class: PROB 11; Piece: 1790.

[59] Departures from Bengal Almanac, Bengal Directory, Calcutta Annual Register, Calcutta Directory and Calcutta Calendar 1819, transcribed by Families of British India (FIBIS).

[60] *London, England, Land Tax Records, 1692-1932*: Kensington and Chelsea; St Luke, Chelsea 1826, 10-11.

[61] Though her will, as below, asked that she be buried in the church at Wroxeter, the burial details are confirmed by the Essex Record Office at Chelmsford.

her will left generous bequests to her servants and a great quantity of jewellery and other items to friends and kinsfolk, with the residual estate divided between her nephew Charles Edmund Dana, whom she had cared for in India after the death of his father Charles Patrick, and her brother William Pulteney Dana.[62]

Twelve years earlier, when her niece Charlotte Frances, daughter of her brother William Pulteney Dana, was baptised at Albrighton in Shropshire on 16 April 1820 Frances Johnstone Sherburne had accepted responsibility as her godmother. Twelve years later she bequeathed her a miniature of her son Pulteney Johnstone Poole together with several items of jewellery, including a gold watch and chain, rings, ear-rings, brooches and bracelets, a tippet of sable fur and a large Bible. This last item, a handsome book with gold edging, was later used by Charlotte Frances to record her first marriage and children.[63]

George Kinnaird Dana was born on 12 September 1770 at Brigstock in Northamptonshire, where his father Edmund had lately been appointed Vicar, and he was baptised there on 25 October by the Reverend Richard Jones, Vicar of the neighbouring parish of Weekley; Weekley lies some ten miles/fifteen kilometres southwest of Brigstock, just north of Kettering. He was named for his maternal great-grandfather George Kinnaird (1691-1734), father of Charles, Baron Kinnaird.[64]

In the list of Commissions signed by His Majesty King George III for the Army in Ireland and dated 23 May 1786 George Kinnaird Dana was entered as an Ensign in the Thirteenth Regiment of Foot,[65] He was not quite sixteen years old.

First formed in 1685, from 1739 to 1766 the Thirteenth Regiment had been commanded by General Harry Pulteney, brother of the first Earl of Bath and immediate predecessor to William Johnstone in control of the family estates.[66] Until the middle of the eighteenth century regiments of the British army were identified by the names of their colonels, so the unit was known for several years as Pulteney's Regiment, but it was number thirteen in a order of precedence within the army, and when it was ordered in 1751 that regiments should be styled by their numbers; Pulteney's Regiment became the Thirteenth. Some years later, in 1782, a county designation was attached to each regular regiment of foot, so the Thirteenth Foot acquired a supplementary name as 1st Somersetshire. The system was intended to encourage local enlistment, but it was not particularly successful and regiments continued to recruit their men without regard for their nominal territory. We do not know whether George Dana was influenced in his choice by the old Pulteney connection or by the fact that Somerset is close to Shropshire; it may have been no more than chance and opportunity.

As the *Gazette* entry indicates, at the time George Dana joined in 1786 the Thirteenth Foot was stationed in Ireland, and it was still there when he was promoted Lieutenant at the

---

[62] A copy of her will and its probate is at The National Archives; Kew, England; Prerogative Court of Canterbury and Related Probate Jurisdictions: Will Registers; Class: PROB 11; Piece: 1801.
   Frances Johnstone Sherburne left substantial bequests to her servants, and a great quantity of jewellery and other items to different legatees. It is uncertain how much was left over to be shared by William Pulteney and Charles Edmund; on the latter, see further below at 30-31.
[63] Chapter Two at 43-45.
[64] An account of George Kinnaird Dana is in Item 596 of *Dana Family in America* at 499.
[65] *London Gazette* Issue 12768 of 11 July 1786 at 317; his surname is miswritten as Danx.
[66] Above at 6.

CHAPTER ONE: PROLOGUE

end of 1789.[67] In 1790, however, it was transferred to the West Indies, and when war broke out with revolutionary France it was briefly engaged in the rebel French colony of Saint-Domingue, now Haiti. Returning home in 1797, in 1801 the regiment was sent to Egypt to help deal with the French forces isolated there after the British naval victory at the Battle of the Nile in 1798. The success of the campaign was marked by adding a badge with a sphinx and the motto *Egypt* to the regimental colours.

Leaving Egypt in 1802, the Thirteenth Regiment was stationed first at Malta and then at Gibraltar. George Dana had evidently distinguished himself in the Egyptian campaign, for he had already been promoted Major and on 11 May 1802 he was awarded brevet appointment as a Lieutenant-Colonel in the Army.[68] Brevet rank placed an officer above his formal position in his regiment, and George Dana had expanded his horizons.[69]

In 1805 the Thirteenth Foot returned to England, and on 22 November 1806 Brevet Lieutenant-Colonel George Kinnaird Dana was appointed to substantive rank as Lieutenant-Colonel in the 6th Garrison Battalion; he was later advanced to full Colonel.[70]

Garrison Battalions, as their name implies, were reserve troops, primarily concerned to maintain defence and good order in potentially troublesome territory, and they were recruited from aging veterans or other troops considered unfit for front-line combat. The 6th Battalion was raised at Dublin from limited-service personnel of three regiments of foot, and it was stationed at Nenagh in Tipperary, some hundred miles to the southeast.[71] When Napoleon surrendered to the allies in April 1814, it was assumed that the days of large-scale conflict

---

[67] *London Gazette*, Issue 13174 of 13 February 1790 at 89.

[68] *London Gazette*, Issue 15478 of 8 May 1802 at 467-468.

[69] Adapted from Wikipedia, citing Holmes, *Redcoat*, 166–179:

The brevet conferred rank in the British Army overall, but importantly, not in the regiment. Advancement in the regiment could take place generally only by purchase (until 1871) or by seniority, ... and when there was a suitable vacancy (caused by the death, retirement or promotion of a more senior officer). For an officer on duty with his regiment, only regimental rank counted; if the regiment formed part of a larger formation then brevet rank could be used to determine command of temporary units formed for special purposes. In particular brigadier did not become a permanent rank until 1947, so command of brigades was determined by seniority, including by the date of promotion to any brevet rank. Thus it was possible for a regimental major to hold a brevet lieutenant-colonelcy with seniority over the commission of his own commanding officer as lieutenant-colonel and be given command of a brigade (potentially including his own regiment). Similarly, while the officer served in a staff position or as an aide-de-camp, then he could use his brevet rank. Appointment to a brevet also counted towards the requirement to have served for a sufficient time in a lower rank to be eligible for promotion (by purchase) to a more senior one.

[70] *London Gazette*, Issue 15977 of 22 November at 1523.

In June of the following year George had his younger brother William Pulteney Dana appointed Paymaster to the battalion: *London Gazette*, Issue 16040 at 837. See further at 35-36 below.

[71] An unfortunately fatal field day near Nenagh was reported by *Saunders's News-Letter* of 25 June 1811.

had ended – the Waterloo campaign of 1815 was an unexpected but comparatively short-lived resurgence of fighting. On 7 June 1814 George Dana was promoted Major-General,[72] and on 5 December the Garrison Battalion was disbanded.

From 1793 to 1802, therefore, George Dana had ten years of active service, but from the age of thirty-two he was in static positions, first in the Mediterranean, then in England and finally in Ireland. Now forty-five years old, he returned to England and purchased the estate of Winterbourne in Gloucestershire, just north of Bristol. He was formally made Lieutenant-General in 1830, but never held command at that rank.[73]

Saint Chad's Church, Shrewsbury
Photograph by Steve Aze at English Wikipedia

On 11 June 1795 George Kinnaird Dana had married Arabella Belinda Forester. Born in 1769, she was the daughter of Lieutenant-Colonel Cecil Forester of Ross Hall near Shrewsbury; her elder brother Cecil Weld later became the first Baron Forester. The wedding was celebrated at Saint Chad's Church, newly-built on an old foundation above the town.[74]

Two daughters were born to the marriage: Helen Kinnaird Dana on 25 March 1796; and Emma, who was baptised on 8 January 1797 and buried on 6 February. Emma may have been premature, but in any case there were no more children.

---

[72] *London Gazette*, Issue 16906 of 7 June 1814 at 1181.

[73] *London Gazette*, Issue 18709 of 23 July 1830 at 1534.

[74] Both Cecil Forester and his son sat as members of Parliament for the borough of Wenlock: historyofparliamentonline.org/volume/1754-1790/member/forester-cecil-1721-74 and volume/1790-1820/member/forester-%28afterwards-weld-forester%29-cecil-1767-1828. The wedding is recorded by *Pallot's Marriage Index* for England. Item 596 at page 499 of *Dana Family in America* is confused, for it appears to identify Lieutenant-General George Kinnaird Dana with the first Lord Forester, who was in fact his brother-in-law.

The entry records his daughter Helen Kinnaird, her marriage to George Oatley and their daughter Arabella Forester Oatley. There is no mention of the infant Emma nor, perhaps not surprisingly, of George Dana's second marriage and daughter, as below.

CHAPTER ONE: PROLOGUE

Arabella Belinda Dana nee Forester died in September 1836. Four months later, on 1 February of the following year, at the fashionable Saint George's Church in Hanover Square, London, George Kinnaird Dana took Heloise Eliza Harris as his second wife. He was a widower of sixty-six; she was a spinster, born at Marylebone in London about 1805 and aged in her early thirties.[75] The couple had very likely known one another for several years.

George Kinnaird Dana died on 28 June 1837. His will dated 6 June, three weeks earlier, left all his property to his beloved wife Heloise Eliza Dana. The only other bequest was to his sister Elizabeth Caroline Oatley, and that was no more than a mourning ring. His daughter Helen Kinnaird had married her cousin, Elizabeth Caroline's son George Edmund Oatley, a graduate of Oxford and a minister of the Church of England. He had died and she was now a widow, but her father gave her no mention.[76]

In the census of 1851, Helen Oatley was recorded with her daughter Isabella [miswritten for Arabella] and one servant at 88 Regent Street in Westminster; the house was shared with another, larger family. She died in 1854 at the age of fifty-seven and was buried in All Souls Cemetery at Kensal Green.[77]

The death notices of the *Argus* newspaper of Melbourne, Victoria, for 25 July 1854 included the following entry:

> On the 24th *inst*, at Lower Notting Hill, London, Helen Kinnaird, widow of the Rev George Edmund Oatley, only child of the late Lieutenant-General George Kinnaird Dana and niece of the late Lord Forester.[78]

The notice must have been copied directly from one which had been published in England, for Helen Kinnaird Oatley nee Dana had died in London on 24 March – not 24 July as the term *inst* would indicate – and was buried on 31 March. The news took four months to arrive by ship, but kinsmen in the antipodes were anxious to record their distinguished connection.[79]

Arabella Oatley, a spinster of 96 Denmark Road in Kilburn, Middlesex, died on 11 January 1894, leaving effects of £542.10s.1d; administration of her estate was granted five years later, on 29 March 1899 to a cousin, Mary Oatley.[80]

George Kinnaird Dana had left a considerable property: mansion, outbuildings and extensive grounds at Winterbourne, further parcels of land nearby and at neighbouring Frampton Cotterell, together with furniture, carriages, horses and cattle, money and securities. Soon after his death Heloise Eliza made application for a pension as a general's widow, but her request was refused.[81] There may have been debts, including mortgages on the properties, but

---

[75] Piece 012: D 1-164 in *British Army and Navy Birth, Marriage and Death Records, 1730-1960*, WO 42: Officers Birth Certificates, Wills and Personal Papers at 147.

[76] George Oatley received his MA degree from Oxford in 1820 and became Stipendiary Curate at Wroxeter, where his grandfather Edmund Dana was still the Vicar. After Edmund's death in 1823, George Oatley became a Curate at Little Wenlock, southeast of Shrewsbury and close to Harley. He died in 1831 at the age of thirty-five.

[77] London, England, Church of England Deaths and Burials, 1813-2003 for Kensington and Chelsea All Souls, Kensal Green at 334.

[78] Trove 4795540.

[79] Not surprisingly, they had no interest in Helen's half-sister Harriet nee Dana, Mrs Smith of Bristol: below.

[80] England & Wales, National Probate Calendar (Index of Wills and Administrations), 1858-1995, 1899 page 25.

[81] Piece 012: D 1-164 in *British Army and Navy Birth, Marriage and Death Records, 1730-1960*, WO 42: Officers Birth Certificates, Wills and Personal Papers at 146.

in any case the inheritance disappeared very quickly: Winterbourne was sold in August 1838,[82] and on Saturday 27 June 1840

> the Court for the Relief of Insolvent Debtors announced that orders had been issued for the vesting with the Provisional Assignee, at their own Petitions, the Estates and Effects of the following persons...

the last name on the list is that of Eloise Eliza Dana, widow, late of No 3, Old-park, Bristol, now in the Gaol of Bristol.[83]

Heloise Eliza was later released from prison, and in 1844 she married for the second time. Her new husband Russell Hipkins, who had also been married before, was a carver and gilder, master of a business employing two men. The couple lived at Saint Pancras in London, but Russell died in 1861. In the census of that year Heloise was listed as an Independent Lady, but by 1871 she was on Parish Relief. On 6 February 1874 Heloise Hipkins, now described as a servant, died in the Saint Pancras workhouse.[84]

Besides his apparently estranged daughter Helen Kinnaird Oatley, George Dana had a second child: on Saturday 17 February 1844 the *Reading Mercury* Notices of Births, Marriages and Deaths announced that the son of Mr James Smith, bootmaker of that city, who was also named James Smith and was himself a bootmaker in Bristol, had there married Harriet, daughter of General Dana, on 31 January.[85]

Harriet Dana was first recorded in the census of 1841, when she was living – possibly as a servant – in the household of Mr Gauntlett, a tea dealer of Bath; she is described as twenty-five years old. Census ages were generally rounded, but that indicates she was born about 1816, and the birth-place is given as Ireland. In 1851 she was living with her husband and two children near Bristol: she is now described as thirty years old, born at Nenagh in Ireland. Ten years later, in 1861, she was forty-eight, married but living apart from her husband; her occupation is given as a school mistress.

In the censuses of 1871 and 1881 Harriet Smith is still said to be married but is living alone. Aged sixty and then seventy, she is described as a school mistress and later as an "annuitant" –receiving a pension which was presumably based upon her previous earnings. Her birth year may now be calculated as 1811, and while the 1881 census has no account, the place of birth given in 1871 was again Nenagh in Ireland.

Whether born in 1811, 1813 or 1816, it is improbable that Harriet was the daughter of George Dana's wife Arabella Belinda, who would have been in her forties, and impossible that she was a child of Heloise Eliza, who was barely ten at that time: she must have been the result of an affair with a local woman when the Garrison Battalion was in Ireland. There is no information on her mother, nor on how Harriet came to be acknowledged and received in England, but it does appear that she was given a fair education, sufficient for her to earn her living later as a school-teacher.

---

[82] The notice of sale was published on the front page of *The Bath Chronicle and Weekly Gazette*, issue 3794 for Thursday 30 August.
[83] *London Gazette*, Issue 19870 of 30 June 1840 at 1562-1563.
[84] London, England, Church of England Deaths and Burials, 1813-2003 at 71.
[85] From British Library Newspapers.

CHAPTER ONE: PROLOGUE

Harriet's estranged husband James Smith is recorded by the census of 1861 as a lodger living alone in Bristol, but cannot be reliably traced further. Two children of the marriage – a son and a daughter – were baptised at Bristol on 21 October 1849: Harriet Elizabeth, born in 1847 and living with her mother in 1861, died soon after the census, aged just fourteen; the son, James Kinnaird, born in 1845, married Elizabeth Sarah Durban in 1866 and had two sons and one daughter. There were further descendants, but the lineage becomes increasingly hard to identify.

Helen Gordon, fifth child and fourth daughter of the Reverend Edmund Dana and Helen nee Kinnaird, was born at Brigstock on 26 February 1772.[86] Her father transferred to Wroxeter in November and she was not baptised until 26 March of the following year. The family returned to Brigstock for the ceremony, which was again carried out by their neighbour the Reverend Richard Jones of Weekley. Continuing the family custom, Helen's second name commemorated her maternal great-grandmother Helen Kinnaird nee Gordon (1689-1731), mother of her grandfather Charles, Baron Kinnaird.

In 1800, in a ceremony at Saint Chad's in Shrewsbury, Helen Dana married John Gibbons, a graduate of Clare College, Cambridge, and in 1805 her father Edmund ceded the parish of Harley so that his son-in-law could become the Rector there.[87] In 1856 Richard Henry Dana said they were living in Harley,[88] but the census of 1851 had recorded them at Cheltenham, and though John Gibbons is still described as a clergyman, he was now eighty-eight years old and had evidently retired.[89] Helen Gibbons nee Dana died at London in 1855 at the age of eighty-three, but her husband survived her by another three years. When probate was granted for his will it was stated that he had died at Harley in December 1858.[90]

The couple had three children, William Henry Kinnaird Gibbons (1802-1873); Helen Kinnaird Gibbons, who died in 1820 while still in her teens; and Harriette Anne Matilda Gibbons (1807-1885) who married Thomas Plowden Presland of Cosford Grange near Shifnal in Shropshire. Both she and her brother were prosperous, but neither left children.

Harriet Dana was born in 1774 and christened at Wroxeter on 26 September. She married John Mare Wood at Saint Mary's Church in Shrewsbury on 25 November 1800, but died on 27 February 1803, after a long and painful illness.[91] Aged thirty-one, John Wood did not marry again but went to Oxford and graduated BA in 1807 and MA in 1811.[92] Even before

---

[86] *Dana Family in America,* Item 581v at pages 485-486, has her date of birth as 26 February 1773. The census of 31 March 1851 lists her [as Mrs Gibbons] as being seventy-nine years old and living at Cheltenham, and the record of her burial at Marylebone on 22 August 1855 says that she was eighty-three when she died: *London, England, Church of England Deaths and Burials, 1813-2003 for Kensington and Chelsea All Souls, Kensal Green* at 506. It therefore appears that she was born in 1772, presumably on 26 February.

[87] Above at 13.

[88] *Journal,* 418.

[89] 1851 England Census for Cheltenham in Gloucestershire, district 1bb, page 738.

[90] England & Wales, National Probate Calendar (Index of Wills and Administrations), 1859 Wills Gabb-Gynne at 50

[91] *Dana Family in America,* Item 581vi at page 486 lists her as Harriot, but has an account of her marriage and her husband.

Her death was reported by the *Morning Chronicle* of 5 March 1803 on page 4. She was staying at the time in the house of Sir William Pulteney at Weymouth.

[92] *Alumni Oxoniensis* 2:iv at 1599.

this, however, he had been appointed Vicar of Stottesdon in Shropshire, in the diocese of Hereford under the patronage of Sir William Pulteney in 1805. He was found insolvent in 1829 and again in 1834; he died later that year.

William Pulteney Dana (1776-1861), father of Charlotte Frances Dana, is discussed below.

Henry Bertie Dana was born at Wroxeter on 6 January 1778 and baptised on 26 January. He died at Shrewsbury on 6 June 1798 at the age of twenty and was buried at Wroxeter.[93]

Barbara Dana was born at Wroxeter on 18 April 1779 and baptised there on 25 May. She died on 13 December of that year and was buried at Wroxeter three days later.[94]

Matilda Dana was born at Wroxeter on 13 June 1780 and baptised on 14 July.[95] In 1801 she married William Armstrong (1755-1837), who rose to high rank in the British Army.[96]

William Armstrong was almost forty years old when he was commissioned as an Ensign in 1794 and then as Lieutenant in a Londonderry company. When the French General Hoche led an attempted invasion in 1796, William Armstrong gained recognition as a military engineer planning defence works, and he later commented with influence on fortifications in England. Appointed to the staff of the Commander-in-Chief in Ireland in 1808, he became a Colonel in 1813 and was promoted Major-General in 1819.[97]

William and Matilda had no children. They spent some years in Londonderry [also known as Derry], but later moved to Paris, where they were described as being well-established in society, with friends among leading citizens and literary figures, members of the nobility and even King Louis Philippe. Matilda died there on 22 June 1837 at the age of fifty-seven, and William followed her on 10 October, aged eighty-two.[98]

Henrietta Laura Dana was born at Wroxeter on 13 August 1782 and baptised on 26 November.[99] Her name was chosen in courtesy to Henrietta Laura, Countess of Bath, the daughter of Sir William Pulteney.

On 14 July 1813, at a ceremony in Saint Mary's Cathedral at Limerick in Ireland, Henrietta Laura Dana married Andrew Aiken of Newry. She died in September of the following year, soon after giving birth to a daughter. The child was baptised Henrietta Laura.

Though Andrew Aiken came from a landed family, he was bankrupted in 1817 and all his property, including leases on houses and tenements in Newry, land he was due to receive by inheritance from his father John Aiken and money from an annuity, was distributed among his creditors.[100] It appears that his daughter Henrietta Laura Aiken never married, for *The Dana Family in America* records her still living under her maiden surname in 1886.

---

[93] *Dana Family in America*, Item 581viii at page 486.
[94] *Dana Family in America*, Item 581ix at page 486.
[95] *Dana Family in America*, Item 581x at page 486 mentions her birth, her death and her marriage.
[96] *London Gazette*, Issue 17505 of 12 August 1819 at 1442.
[97] There is a detailed account of William Armstrong's career in Philippart, *Royal Military Calendar* IV, 25-29 item 602.
    Lieutenant-General George Kinnaird Dana, as above, has an entry in Philippart at III, 344, item 508, but it is no more than a single paragraph with a summary of his promotions.
[98] Births, Deaths, Marriages and Obituaries in the *Belfast News-Letter* of Tuesday 31 October 1837.
[99] *Dana Family in America*, Item 581xi at page 486, records her marriage and her daughter.
[100] *Dublin Evening Post* of 25 October 1817.

CHAPTER ONE: PROLOGUE

Born at Wroxeter on 24 June 1784 and baptised on 23 July, **Charles Patrick Dana** entered Shrewsbury School in 1799 at the age of fifteen.[101] In 1802 he was commissioned as an Ensign in the Twenty-Third Regiment of the Bengal Native Infantry in the service of the East India Company, and was promoted Lieutenant in the following year. In 1816, however, Charles Patrick Dana, now a Captain in the Twenty-Third Regiment, died at sea on the East India Company ship *Sir Stephen Lushington* as it was sailing to England.[102]

It is not known when or whether Charles Patrick Dana was married, but he had at least three children, for they are named in his will of September 1814: Frances Harriet, Charles Edmund and Henrietta Matilda.[103] Frances Harriette Fitzpatrick Dana was baptised at Calcutta on 20 May 1814; she had been born, however, on 4 April 1807.[104] Charles Edmund Dana was born on 11 February 1809 but was baptised at Calcutta on 2 July 1815.[105] Henrietta Matilda was baptised only in 1818: her date of birth is not mentioned, but she received a private christening from the chaplain of the garrison on 6 February;[106] she was obviously born before her father made his will. No godparents are listed in any of these records, but it is probable

---

[101] *Dana Family in America,* Item 598 at page 503, has a summary of Charles Patrick and his children.

[102] *Asiatic Journal and Monthly Miscellany* III (April 1817), 407 [Asiatic Intelligence, Calcutta]. The ship was named for Sir Stephen Lushington, Baronet, Chairman of the East India Company. According to the record of *Departures from The Bengal and Calcutta Directories 1816*, transcribed by Families of British India (FIBIS), Lieutenant Dana sailed from Calcutta on the *Sir Stephen Lushington* in January of that year, while the *Asiatic Journal* dates his death to 9 July and gives his rank as Captain. There is no detail of Charles Patrick Dana's death, nor is the date entirely certain.

Both the *Bath Chronicle* "Births, Deaths, Marriages and Obituaries" of 6 February 1817 at page 4, and *The Gentleman's Magazine,* 87.1 for March 1817 at 283, record the death of Charles P Dana, youngest son of Rev Mr Dana, of Shrewsbury, on his passage from the East Indies to England; one has evidently copied from the other, and both accounts were published well after the event.

Charles Patrick Dana was a member of a tontine – a contributory scheme common at that time by which members put in money and the last person to survive collected the whole amount. It appears that he had been entered into this form of lottery as a child, but *Irish Tontines Annuitants 1766-1789* in the National Archives of Ireland, reference NDO 2/32 at page 107, lists his death "before 10th October 1816."

One of Charles Patrick Dana's executors, Lewis Wiggens, applied for probate on 21 September 1816. [Lewis was a cousin from the Kinnaird side of the family; the surname was generally spelt as Wiggins.] The documents refer to him as the "late" Charles Patrick Dana but do not give the date of his death.

Until the 1830s, ships from India to Britain sailed around the Cape of Good Hope of South Africa, so a passage took four to six months and an exchange of correspondence might take a year or more: Headrick, "A Double-Edged Sword," 54. We do not know when the *Sir Stephen Lushington* arrived in England, but ships meeting at sea would commonly exchange information, so the news of Charles Patrick's death may have been passed earlier to an India-bound vessel.

[103] *British India Office Wills & Probate* Wills Bengal 1780-1938; Archive reference L-AG-34-29-28, pages 405-408.

The copy of the will has the second name of the elder daughter as Harriet, and she was christened Harriett, but she was later known as Harriette: the full form appears in the census list of 1861 as below, and in the probate of her will.

[104] *Christenings at Calcutta Fort William in Bengal AD 1814*. She is identified only as the daughter of Lieut Charles Patrick Dana; other entries give the mother's name, but not in this case.

The third given name is transcribed as Fitspatrick, but the original is best interpreted as Fitzpatrick. Fitzpatrick might indicate "child of Patrick" and was presumably a reference to the child's father, but Frances Harriette did not use the name in later life.

[105] Christenings at Calcutta Fort William in Bengal AD 1815, named only as Edmund.

As in note 104 immediately above, while other entries identify the mother, this one mentions only the father, Lieut Charles Patrick Dana of the 23rd Regiment of Native Infantry. Furthermore, other entries describe the child as *D* [daughter] or *S* [son], but Edmund is marked *NS* [natural son].

[106] *Garrison Fort William, Register of Baptisms 1818*, page 627, named only as Matilda. As with her brother and sister, her father is named but there is no mention of her mother.

that the infant's aunt Frances Johnstone Sherburne, sister of her father, took responsibility for her.[107]

Perhaps more notably, there is no evidence of a formal marriage, nor any reference to the children's mother in the will or other sources. It is possible that records have been lost and/or that the mother had died, and it could be that the children were the result of a series of casual liaisons, but it is far more likely that the children were the result of a long-term local marriage with an Indian woman. With very few British women available, such arrangements were common, but the legal rights of a native wife were limited and Anglo-Indian or "Eurasian" children could also be in difficulty without a true-born Briton to sponsor them.[108]

There is no further reference to Henrietta Matilda Dana, and we must assume that she died quite soon after her baptism. In June 1822, however, the ship *Ganges* departed Calcutta for England with two child passengers, Master and Miss Danna; it is most likely that they were Charles Edmund and Frances Harriette, now thirteen and fifteen respectively.[109] They can have stayed for only a few months, for on 21 May 1823 Miscellaneous Bond 3926 was issued by a British court to guarantee the passage from England to India for Charles and Frances Dana.[110] It was nonetheless common for children to be sent "home" for a time as a means to establish their status, and that appears to have been the purpose of the expedition.

That marginal status was under some threat during these years, for an increase in Christian missionary activity meant that children of mixed race – formerly quite regularly accepted – began to be looked upon with a degree of racial and cultural disapproval.[111] It was significant, however, that Charles Edmund and Frances Harriette were accompanied on their return voyage by Mrs Everina Hovenden and her daughter Sophia, and the Miscellaneous Bond indicates that they were travelling as a single party. The Reverend Walter Hovenden was Chaplain and Secretary to the Bengal Military Orphan Society which provided benefits for officers' children, legitimate and illegitimate. So Charles Edmund and Frances Harriette Dana had in some form come under the aegis of the society.

On 23 July 1827 Frances Harriette married John Asprey Wood, Second Lieutenant in the Twenty-Fifth Regiment of Bengal Native Infantry, in Saint Paul's Cathedral at Calcutta. She was just twenty years old and her husband was also under age, but the wedding was held by licence and a "Next Friend" R Stephenson and two witnesses were present for the occasion. Notably, moreover, the ceremony was conducted by the Reverend Hovington, with the permission of the cathedral's resident chaplain J D Henderson.[112]

---

[107] On this question, see 17 above and 30 below.
[108] The nature of such marriages and the situation of the wives and children are discussed by Hawes, *Poor Relations*, particularly at 9-11 and 14-20. A substantial article in Wikipedia on "Anglo-Indian" takes much of its information from that source.
[109] Madras Almanac [Departures] 1821-1824, 3 June 1823, transcribed by Families of British India (FIBIS).
[110] For a similar arrangement of bonds, see page 55-56 in Chapter Two.
[111] Hawes, *Poor Relations*, as cited in note 108 above.
[112] Parish register transcripts from the Presidency of Bengal 1713-1948, Archive reference N-1-18, Folio 75.
The Dana Family in America, Item 598ii at page 503, records her marriage and two children, but suggests that Stevenson may be the name of Charles Patrick Dana's wife and Frances Harriette's mother. That section in the register, however, is for "Parents or next Friends," and it is most likely that R Stevenson was in the latter category. Three other names in that column are those of men; the others have only initials but were probably also male.

CHAPTER ONE: PROLOGUE

The couple had two sons, Charles George, born in 1831, and James Stead, born in the following year; two daughters had been born earlier, but their names are not known and they died very young. John Asprey Wood died in India in 1833 and his widow Frances Harriette soon afterwards moved with her sons to England, living first in Surrey and later in St John's Hill, Shrewsbury.[113] Her younger son James Stead died in 1855, and Frances Harriette in 1861; Letters of Administration for probate were granted to her surviving son Charles George Wood, but the estate was less than £200.[114]

Charles George Wood became a surveyor. In 1874 he married Mary Anne Greenwood, but they had no children. He died at Blackheath, Kent, in 1892, leaving an estate of just £88.15s; his widow died in 1901.

In his *Journal* for 1851 Richard Henry Dana recorded an account of his English cousins from his kinsman John Hastings.[115] He makes reference at that time to Frances Harriette – Mrs Asprey Wood – and her sons, but it does not appear that he met any of them when he visited Shropshire himself five years later.[116]

Elizabeth Ellery Dana, however, had later contact with Charles George Wood, for *The Dana Family in America* records his marriage to Mary Anne Greenwood in 1872 and his death at London in 1892.[117]

Charles Edmund Dana, son of Charles Patrick and brother of Frances Harriette, was in England again just a few years after his return to India. He may have returned there about the time of his sister's marriage in 1827, when he would have been eighteen years old. He was close to his aunt Frances Johnstone Sherburne, for in her will of 19 October 1831 she named him as a residual legatee with her brother William Pulteney Dana.[118] His address at that time was South Crescent, Bedford Square, London, close to the British Museum in the heart of Bloomsbury, and he was a member of the staff of the London Oriental Institute. An advertisement in *The Atlas* of 1833 explained the services it offered:[119]

> **EDUCATION FOR INDIA**
> HAILEYBURY AND ADDISCOMBE STUDENTS may, during their vacation, prosecute the following branches, viz.– Hindustani, Bengali, Persion, Arabi, Classics, Mathematics, Civil and Military Drawing, &c, at the LONDON ORIENTAL INSTITUTE, 2, South Crescent, Bedford Square, the conductors of which studied the eastern languages with learned natives, and have prepared some hundreds of gentlemen for the East India Service.

---

[113] The census of 1841 records her and her two sons in Stoke next Guildford, Surrey; the census of 1861 has her at Saint Chad, the suburb of Shrewsbury, with her son Charles George.
  As sons of a deceased officer, the Bengal Military Orphan Society paid a pension for both boys, with a final grant when they turned seventeen: see their entries from Bengal Military Orphan Society 1820-1857, transcribed by Families of British India (FIBIS). Their mother would have received the pension money.

[114] England & Wales, National Probate Calendar (Index of Wills and Administrations), 1858-1966, 1861 at 148.

[115] *Journal*, 419. Richard Henry identifies his informant only as Mr Hastings, but it was probably John Walter Hastings (1819-1883). John Walter's father Edmund Trowbridge Hastings (1789-1861) was the son of Captain John Hastings (1754-1839) who had married Lydia nee Dana (1755-1808): above at 2. Their grandson John Walter Hastings, a year younger than Richard Henry Dana Junior, was his second cousin.
  See further below at 31 and 35, and Chapter Two at 51 and 53.

[116] *Journal*, 419 and 784-787, and above at 11-13.

[117] Item 598 at page 503; also England & Wales, National Probate Calendar (Index of Wills and Administrations), 1858-1966, 1893 at 201.

[118] See above at 20-21 with note 62.

[119] Issue of 22 December at page 15.

The East India College at Haileybury in Hertfordshire was established to prepare its pupils for the Indian civil service, and the Addiscombe Military Seminary performed the equivalent function for the army, comparable to the Royal Military Academy at Sandhurst. Knowledge of the relevant languages would be useful to those entering the Company's service, while private colleges such as this could also act as "crammers," helping their students pass the necessary examinations for entry. For a young man of mixed heritage such as Charles Edmund Dana, appointment at the Institute offered a good career.[120]

It appears, however, that Charles Edmund may have left the Institute, possibly after the death of his senior colleague Sandford Arnot. In 1836 he was living at Albrighton, home of his uncle William Pulteney Dana, but he died on 15 February of that year at the age of twenty-seven. His death was announced in the *Wolverhampton Chronicle and Staffordshire Advertiser*, which identified him as a grandson of the late Reverend Edmund Dana, and he was buried in the church at Wroxeter on 18 February.[121]

The thirteenth and last child of Edmund Dana and Helen nee Kinnaird was baptised **Maria**. Born at Wroxeter on 6 May 1787, she died just three weeks later, on 27 May.[122]

William Pulteney Dana, father of Charlotte Frances
William Pulteney Dana, seventh child and second son of Edmund Dana and Helen nee Kinnaird, was born at Wroxeter on 13 July 1776 and baptised there on 1 August.[123] He was named specifically for his mother's uncle and the family patron William Pulteney, and he may indeed have had great expectations from that connection.

We have noted that when Sir William Pulteney died in May of 1805 he left no will, and his vast property was thus inherited by his daughter Henrietta Laura, Countess of Bath, with a small pension to his widowed second wife.[124] In its issue of 18 June, the London *Public Register and Daily Advertiser* added a somewhat cryptic item:

> The circumstance of Sir William Pulteney having died without a will, is of very unfortunate consequence to a youth whom Sir William has educated as his son. This young man bears a high character; and the interposition of the friends of Sir William's heirs at law is anxiously expected, and we believe promised, in this young gentleman's favour.

The name of the young man is not mentioned, and the entry is no more than gossip – certainly the records are clear that no-one but Henrietta Laura obtained any great inheritance. In his *Journal* entry for 1851, however, following the report of his kinsman John Walter Hastings, Richard Henry Dana recorded a general expectation that William Pulteney Dana would inherit his uncle's American property.

---

[120] The head teacher of Hindustani at the Institute was Sandford Arnot [whowaswho-indology.info/331/arnot-sandford]. Following his death in 1834, Edmund Dana swore to the authenticity of a codicil to his will: he had known him for several years and recognised his handwriting.

[121] The *Chronicle and Advertiser* of 24 February reported that he died at Dogpole, a district of Shrewsbury, but has no indication of the cause. His residence in Albrighton is given by his burial record.

[122] *Dana Family in America,* Item 581xiii at page 486.

[123] The dates of William Pulteney Dana's birth and baptism are recorded by *Shropshire, England, Extracted Church of England Parish Records*.

  Dana Family in America, item 587 at pages 499-503, has a long entry for William Pulteney Dana, with a list of his descendants both from his first marriage in America and his second in Ireland.

[124] Above at 14.

CHAPTER ONE: PROLOGUE

It appears likely that William Pulteney Dana was the unfortunate protégé referred to by the *Public Register and Daily Advertiser*, and this is further supported by the history of the Pulteney Estates in upstate New York.

New York State and the Genesee Lands
The red line east of Rochester indicates the Preemption Line
place-names in red relate to the Pulteney Estates

At the time of the American Declaration of Independence in 1776 the territory in the further western part of present-day New York State was largely occupied by Indian tribes of the Iroquois confederacy, and in the conflict which followed they allied themselves to the British. Since one reason for the colonists' rebellion was their desire to expand westwards at the expense of the native tribes, the Iroquois' decision was sensible, but they suffered when their former protectors were defeated. By the end of the eighteenth century – encouraged by small payments and false treaties – the native tribes had largely been driven away.

The situation was confused by dispute between the colonies of New York and Massachusetts. Based upon seventeenth-century colonial charters, Massachusetts asserted a claim to the region of Buffalo, Rochester and the Genesee River.[125] As New York had since expanded north along the Hudson River, however, Massachusetts was separated from the territory concerned, and by the Treaty of Hartford in 1786 it was agreed that the region was now part of New York but that Massachusetts held a pre-emptive right of purchase for land formally

---

[125] On the original Massachusetts Bay Colony, with a notional claim to territory as far as the Pacific Ocean, see the entry in Wikipedia and its accompanying map. Following the success of the Revolution, a constitution was adopted in 1780 under the formal style of Commonwealth of Massachusetts. The distinctive title, however, has no practical or legal significance: Massachusetts is a state like any other of the United States.

held by the Iroquois. The border between the two holdings was marked – rather uncertainly – by the so-called Preemption Line. Two years later Massachusetts sold the right of purchase to private investors, and the territory was opened for white settlement.

The man chosen to manage the enterprise was Charles Williamson, a Scotsman and former army officer, who took up his post in 1792. Before any land could be sold, the region had to be developed with roads and places for settlement, and costs rose very quickly. Besides these necessities, moreover, Williamson had grand designs to develop a local centre at Bath – named for William Pulteney's base in England – but land sales were comparatively slow and over the eight years up to 1800 expenditure amounted to ten times the receipts.

At this point Sir William – as he now was – took over control, negotiating the dismissal of Williamson and installing his own agent with firm instructions to bring the finances into balance. It took ten years to do this, but the Pulteney Estates were maintained successfully thereafter, until the last land sale at the beginning of the twentieth century.[126]

Though Sir William rearranged the management, we must assume he was too occupied with affairs at home to visit the Estates in person. William Pulteney Dana, however, was there, for in 1800 he married Anne Fitzhugh at Geneseo on the Genesee River.

The Fitzhugh family had lately come to the Genesee from Maryland, bringing slaves with them to work on their property. They were kin to George Washington, and Anne's father Peregrine had served as his Aide-de-Camp and rose to the rank of Colonel in the American army.[127] Anne, born about 1784, was some sixteen years old at the time of her marriage while William Pulteney Dana was in his middle twenties.

It is not known where William Pulteney Dana had received his education. He is not listed among the students of Shrewsbury School, nor among the alumni of Oxford or Cambridge.[128] He must have arrived in America in the late 1790s, for he had surely been there some time in order to make the acquaintance of the Fitzhugh family and to obtain consent to marry their daughter. He had very likely been sent by William Pulteney to assess the situation and report back: a young man in his early twenties would have had neither the authority nor the experience to take action on his own.

William Pulteney Dana and Anne nee Fitzhugh had two children. The first was a son whose name is uncertain – whether Edmund or William or perhaps both; born in 1802 he died in the following year. The second child was a daughter, born at Geneva on Lake Seneca on 23 December 1803 and baptised Anne Frisby; the second name being her grandmother's maiden surname. Her mother Anne nee Fitzhugh died shortly afterwards, probably in 1804 from the effects of childbirth.

Soon after his wife's death William Dana departed for England, leaving his daughter in the care of her mother's Fitzhugh family. There is no reason to believe he ever saw her again.

---

[126] There is a favourable account of Charles Williamson in Green, *History, Reminiscences, Anecdotes and Legends* at 30-41, and another is provided by Charles Williamson, "Pulteney Estates in the Genesee Lands;" the latter author is presumably a descendant of the original manager.

[127] The Fitzhugh family is discussed by Green, *History, Reminiscences, Anecdotes and Legends*, 70-71. Having arrived with some thirty slaves, Peregrine Fitzhugh purchased a considerable tract of land, divided it into allotments, freed his slaves and distributed it among them; it became known as Nigger Hollow.

[128] William Pulteney Dana's brother Charles Patrick is the only person of that surname mentioned in the list for Shrewsbury School, while the surname Dana appears only twice in the records of Oxford and Cambridge: besides Edmund Dana's brief enrolment in 1769 [above at 7] a certain Obadiah Dana of Manchester graduated from Trinity College, Oxford, in 1678 and later became a monk.

CHAPTER ONE: PROLOGUE

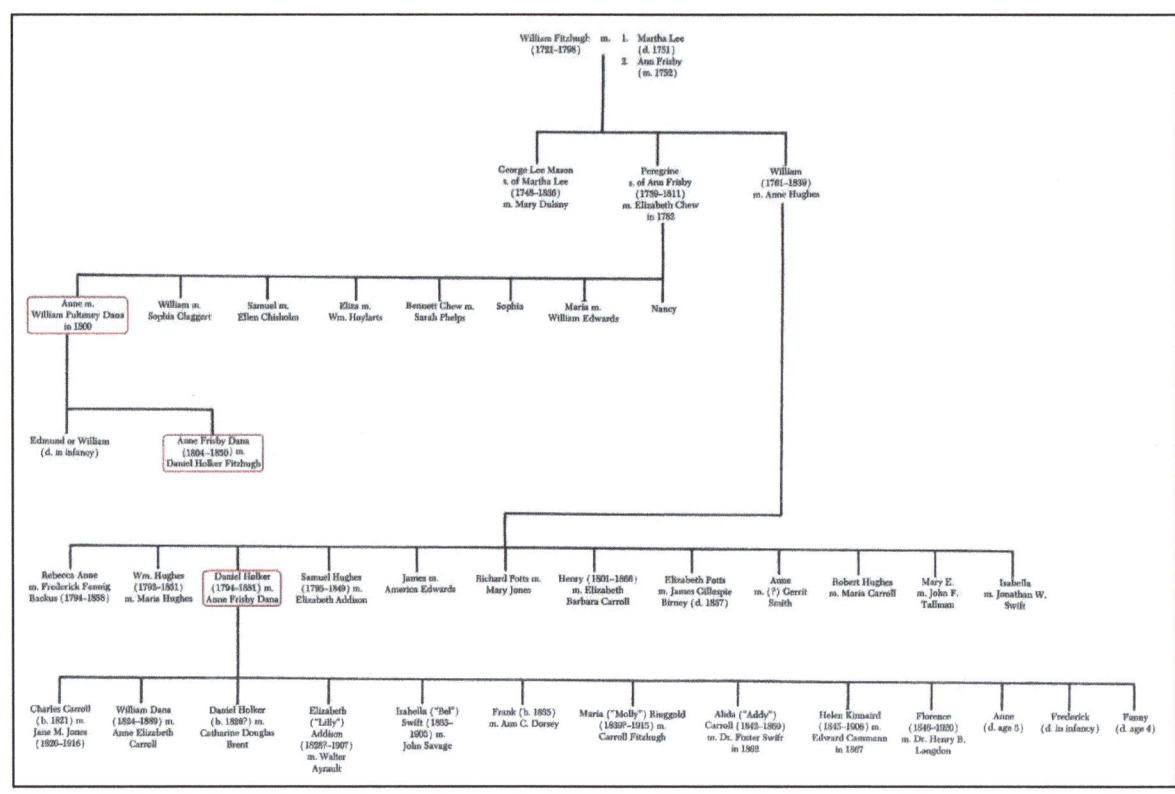

*Table 2: The Fitzhugh-Dana connection in nineteenth-century America
showing descendants of the marriage of William Pulteney Dana and Anne nee Fitzhugh
adapted from an appendix to* The Journal of Richard Henry Dana, Jr, *edited by Robert F Lucid*[129]

In April 1820 Anne Frisby Dana married her first cousin Daniel Holker Fitzhugh at Geneseo in Livingston County, New York State; he was twenty-six years old, she was sixteen. Their first child, Charles Carroll, was born nine months after the wedding, in January 1821, and they had twelve more children: three died as infants and the last, Florence, was born in 1846 when her mother was forty-three.[130] Anne herself died on 21 February 1850 aged forty-six. She was said to have contracted "ship fever" – a form of typhus – while attending a poor family newly arrived at Sonyea, just to the south of Geneseo.

Anne's husband Daniel Fitzhugh died in 1881 at the age of eighty-seven. His obituary in the *Dansville Advertiser* of 28 April describes an active life of local leadership, remarking that he was personally generous but a good businessman, with a constant care for the management of his landed property. Richard Henry Dana Junior met him in 1843 and described him as "an intelligent, gentlemanly man, possessing high character, as well as wealth and influence."[131]

---

[129] There is no information on the dates of birth of the three children of Daniel Holker Fitzhugh and Anne Frisby nee Dana who died young. Though they are placed at the right of the last line on the table, it is most unlikely they were actually born after Florence (1846-1890): their mother Anne would then have been in her mid-forties, extremely late for child-bearing.

[130] *Dana Family in America*, Item 597 at pages 499-502, has a list of the children and further descendants of Anne Frisby nee Dana.

[131] geni.com/people/Daniel-Fitzhugh/6000000004047277257; the middle name, however, is miswritten as Hughes rather than Holker. The *Dansville Advertiser* refers to him as Dr Daniel H Fitzhugh but gives no account of the qualification he had for the title. In his account of their first meeting in 1843 Richard Henry Dana refers to him simply as Mr Fitzhugh: *Journal*, 148.

Some years later, in 1851, Richard Henry Dana visited the family at Geneseo [*Journal*, 308-311], and

The gravestone of Ann[e] Frisby Fitzhugh nee Dana (1803-1850)

Besides the death of his young wife, in 1804 William Pulteney Dana was also faced with the news that Sir William Pulteney had married for a second time on 3 January. His father Edmund Dana had benefitted greatly from the Pulteney patronage, and William Pulteney Dana was very likely a protégé and potential heir to some of his great holdings. Such expectations, however, were now in danger, and it is likely that William Pulteney Dana returned to England at this time in the hope of confirming his position and obtaining some part of what he may have been promised – as indicated by the *Public Register and Daily Advertiser*.

Writing in his *Journal* on the report of the English family by his cousin John Hastings, Richard Henry Dana would later claim that William Pulteney Dana lost his hopes of inheritance because he had quarrelled with Sir William,[132] and it may well be that the tensions of the time brought such a result. His aging patron, possibly hoping for a male heir of his own body, is unlikely to have welcomed the importunities of his namesake and former favourite. In any event, the absence of a will was fatal to any hope of an identified inheritance, and despite the good wishes of the *Public Register and Daily Advertiser* it is clear that Sir William's daughter Henrietta Louise had limited interest in providing further support to the Dana family. William Pulteney Dana may have received a small payment or annuity, but it was not noteworthy and there was nothing more to be expected.

In general, apart from the absence of any substantial inheritance from Sir William and the fact that he had left his daughter in America, there is no good information on William Pulteney Dana's activities at this time. It is doubtful he ever returned to America, and certainly not for any length of time, for it was announced in the *London Gazette* of 20 June 1807 that on 10 June William Pulteney Dana Esquire had been appointed Paymaster to the 6th Garrison Battalion. The identification as "Esquire" indicated that he was a private citizen who had held no previous commission, but the position carried the rank of a Captain, and even after the battalion had been disbanded William Pulteney Dana was entitled to a half-pay pension for the rest of his life.

As we have seen, William Pulteney's brother George Kinnaird Dana had been named

---

in 1854 Daniel Fitzhugh and his daughter Isabella stayed overnight with the family at Cambridge – he is referred to at that time as Dr Fitzhugh [*Journal*, 619].

[132] Below at 51 and note 16.

Lieutenant-Colonel of the 6th Garrison Battalion when it was formed in November 1806, and he later became the full Colonel. Appointment of a paymaster was evidently in his gift, and he used it to benefit his brother, six years the younger.[133] The battalion was stationed at Nenagh in Tipperary until its disbandment in 1814 after the first surrender of Napoleon. So William Pulteney Dana was seven years in Ireland, and he met there and married Charlotte Elizabeth Bayly, daughter of the Reverend Henry O'Neale Bayly (1756-1826), Vicar of Nenagh for the Church of Ireland.[134]

Miniature portrait of the Reverend Arthur Grueber DD
Headmaster of The Royal School, Armagh, 1754-1786
The item is in the possession of the family

Nenagh was a major town of Tipperary, and the Bayly family was well established in the county. John, father of the Reverend Henry Bayly and grandfather of Charlotte Elizabeth, had been High Sheriff in 1759; Henry Bayly himself was a graduate of Trinity College, Dublin, and Charlotte's mother Anna Penelope was a daughter of the Reverend Arthur Grueber DD (1716-1788), distinguished and long-serving headmaster of The Royal School, Armagh, in northern Ireland. Both families were respectably wealthy.[135]

The first child of William Pulteney Dana and Charlotte Elizabeth nee Bayly was Helen Matilda, who was born on 24 February 1813. She was baptised in Saint Munchin's Church, Limerick, on 2 April, presumably because of family connections; she died, however, on 3 December of that same year. A second daughter, named Anna Penelope for her grandmother, was born at Dublin on 11 March 1814.

---

[133] Above at 22 with note 70.

[134] The Church of Ireland had been established by King Henry VIII when he broke from Rome in the 1530s. Though a member of the Anglican communion, it was formally separate from the Church of England, with doctrines more influenced by Calvinism. Almost all the communicants were members of the English-speaking minority: the Scots who came to northern Ireland in the seventeenth century were mostly Presbyterian, while the Irish-speaking majority remained Roman Catholic

[135] There is a detailed account of the Bayly family [also as Baily] and their relatives at monchique.com/Ochanoff/ohanov/ochanoff/2649.htm. Charlotte Elizabeth was one of thirteen children born to Anna Penelope Bayly nee Grueber and her husband the Reverend Henry.

The Grueber family were of Huguenot descent: the Reverend Arthur's father Nicholas and grandfather Daniel had come as refugees to England in 1685. They developed gunpowder factories there, and Nicholas later moved to Ireland and established another at Dublin. See *Anne's Family History* 2020/12/09.

Ireland
Showing sites of interest to William Pulteney Dana and Charlotte Elizabeth Dana nee Bayly

CHAPTER ONE: PROLOGUE

As the Garrison Battalion was disbanded in December 1814, William Pulteney and Charlotte Elizabeth Dana moved to England, and their third child, Douglas James Kinnaird, was born in Shropshire on 20 March 1815. Baptised at Wroxeter by his grandfather the Reverend Edmund on 19 April, he died just one year later and was buried in the same church on 10 April 1816. A fourth child and second son, named for his father William Pulteney, was born in September 1816 but died in March of the following year. So Charlotte Elizabeth had four pregnancies in four years but only one child, Anna Penelope, survived infancy.

The run of misfortune was interrupted by the fifth child and second son, for Henry Edmund Pulteney Dana, born on 28 December 1817 and named for his two grandfathers, would live to adulthood. On 22 February 1820, just over two years later – a longer gap than in previous years – another sister was born, and on 16 April she was baptised Charlotte Frances: the first name for her mother and the second for her aunt and godmother Frances Johnstone Sherburne.

More children followed. Douglas Kinnaird Dana was born and died on 17 November 1821, but Helen Kinnaird Dana, born on 28 March 1823; Douglas Charles Kinnaird Dana, born on 25 December 1824; and William Augustus Pulteney Dana, born on 2 August 1826 – all lived to full age. Finally came two boys christened Francis Richard Benjamin: the first was born and died in 1833; the second, his namesake, was born in 1834 and died at the age of twenty in 1854.[136]

According to the Genealogy of *The Dana Family in America*, the first two children of William Pulteney and Charlotte Elizabeth Dana were born in Dublin but all the others were born at Sutton House in Albrighton, in the east of Shropshire near Wolverhampton.[137] At some point, however, the family moved ten miles south to Roughton Hall by Worfield.[138] Both Sutton House and Roughton Hall were held on leasehold, not with full ownership.

There is no good way to assess William Pulteney Dana's financial resources. He certainly had half-pay from his military appointment as Captain in the Garrison Battalion, though that cannot have been a great deal; and he may have received something from his late patron Sir William Pulteney or from a settlement with Sir William's daughter Henrietta Laura the Countess of Bath. He had property in Cambridge, Massachusetts, which may have come from his father the Reverend Edmund, eldest son of Richard Dana, or possibly from Sir William

---

[136] There is some confusion whether there were in fact two boys named Francis Richard Benjamin Dana. The first of that name, however, was baptised at Albrighton on 15 June 1833, and the second underwent the same ceremony on 22 April 1834; the elder brother must have died.

The census of 1851 records Francis Richard Benjamin Dana at the age of seventeen: employed as a railway clerk, he was living in Shrewsbury with his sister Anna Penelope and her husband William Henry Wood; the other member of the family was William Pulteney Dana, now aged seventy-six. See above at 11-13, where the *Journal* of Richard Henry Dana records his visit to Shrewsbury in 1856; by that time Francis Richard Benjamin was dead.

[137] Sutton House, also known as The Old Hall, was demolished and replaced in 1861: archiseek.com/2013/st-cuthberts-albrighton. Its replacement suffered the same fate a hundred years later.

The house at this time was an eighteenth-century brick building, with three stories and a hipped tile roof; there was a walled garden: shropshirehistory.org.uk/collections/getrecord/CCS_MSA 16315.

[138] Randall, *Worfield and its Townships*, has an account of Roughton Hall at 104-105. It was an ancient house but not a particularly large one.

Pulteney. And at some time he had a printing business, probably based on Shifnal or Bridgnorth; this would later be a source of serious trouble.[139]

It does appear that he was able to maintain his growing family in style suitable to that of a local gentry, and they moved in that society. They were, after all, well connected: there was the aristocratic lineage of the Kinnairds and the Johnstones, the long record of the Reverend Edmund Dana at Wroxeter and in Shrewsbury, and – albeit in Ireland – the respected position of the Bayly family of Charlotte Elizabeth. In his own generation, William Pulteney Dana's elder brother George Kinnaird was a Lieutenant-General; his sister Elizabeth Caroline had married into a good farming family; Frances Johnstone was the widow of an officer in the East India Company; Helen Gordon was married to a vicar; and Matilda's husband, William Armstrong, was a Major-General.

Little is known of the children's upbringing or education. The girls were probably taught at home or by the local clergyman, and it appears that Charlotte Frances learnt to play the piano[140] – the others may have done so too. We are told that William Augustus Pulteney Dana, born in 1826, attended Bridgnorth Grammar School, presumably in the early 1840s, and Henry Edmund, nine years older, may have done so before him.[141] Bridgnorth is close to Worfield and Thomas Rowley the headmaster had raised the school to a very high standard. On the other hand, while Henry was certainly recognised as a gentleman,[142] there is no record of any military service or training. One may suspect that while the social status of the family was satisfactory, the potential for advancement and future prosperity were limited.[143]

On 14 May 1839, in the parish church of Saint Peter at Worfield, William Pulteney Dana's daughter Charlotte Frances married the solicitor John James of Gloucestershire. She was just nineteen, he was twelve years older, a respectable gentleman, established in his profession with a handsome fortune; it was surely regarded as an excellent marriage. The ceremony was carried out by the curate Cornelius Farnworth Broadbent, and witnesses included the father and mother of the bride, her elder sister Anna Penelope, and a brother, three sisters and two male cousins of the bridegroom.[144] Though John James' father, also named John James, and his wife Anne were no doubt present at the wedding, they are not listed among the witnesses.

The newly-wed couple then journeyed to Mr James' residence at Newnham-on-Severn, ten miles south of the city of Gloucester and eighty miles from Charlotte Frances' former home in Shropshire.

---

[139] On the fate of the printing business, and on the property in Cambridge, Massachusetts, see Chapter Two at 48-50.

[140] See Chapter Four at 140.

[141] Entry for Henry Dana in *ADB* 1, 278 by Marilynn L Norman, though the name is miswritten as Bridgeworth High School. It is now known as the Bridgnorth Endowed School.

[142] See the comments of the Colonial Treasurer of Van Diemen's Land in Chapter Three at 80.

[143] Fels, *Good Men and True*, 44-47 and notes 10 to 12 at 266-267, discusses the background of Henry Edmund Pulteney Dana. She is somewhat dismissive of his family, whose position was better established than her interpretation allows, but she observes that there is no mention of him at the Royal Military College at Sandhurst, nor among the cadets of the East India Company, where his uncle Charles Patrick Dana and his uncle by marriage Joseph Sherburne had both served.

As she points out, however, when Henry Edmund first arrived in Van Diemen's Land – later Tasmania – in 1839 he had recommendations to the Governor, Sir John Franklin, so the family had some contacts.

[144] Certified Copy of the Entry of Marriage for the Registration District of Bridgnorth, number 18 of 1839, General Registration Office, London: MB 311433 of 7 August 1984.

CHAPTER ONE: PROLOGUE

Though the alliance was clearly approved by both families, and the age difference was not remarkable, one may wonder how the nineteen-year-old bride had met her future husband: their homes were some distance apart and there seems no necessary reason for them to have crossed paths. Aged in his thirties and well established in a good legal practice, however, John James may well have turned his thoughts to matrimony, and Charlotte Frances would have "come out" into adult society at the age of eighteen. They may have met at some social gathering in a spa town such as Cheltenham, which lay between their places of residence, while it is also possible that the families had business contacts.

For a solicitor such as John James, Charlotte Frances Dana would have appeared a suitable wife. Her family seemed well established, with a connection to nobility and to high-ranking military officers and interests in India and America. On their side, Charlotte Frances' parents may have welcomed the connection to a prosperous professional, and would surely have encouraged the marriage.

For the society of the time, there was nothing unusual about the situation, but it was a considerable change for Charlotte Frances. One may doubt that she had any long or close acquaintance with her new husband, while her life was now very different, with formal responsibility for a substantial household and with social and marital duties in a new, strange environment, far from her family and her former home.

The Church of Saint Peter, Worfield
Photograph by J Taylor 2005

Shropshire, Worcestershire, Herefordshire, Gloucestershire and southeast Wales
based on Google Maps
Albrighton and Newnham-on-Severn are indicated in red

The Frontispiece of Charlotte Frances Dana's Bible

CHAPTER TWO

THE ROAD TO DIVORCE

The Bible and the census
Breakdown
Divorce
France to Australia
A note on the Crespigny surname

The Bible and the census
When Charlotte Frances Dana was baptised on 16 April 1820, her aunt and godmother Frances Johnstone Sherburne gave her a small camphorwood box with a silver plaque on the lid, engraved with the arms of the Sherburne and Dana families and the motto "In God Alone I Trust." It was an elegant and suitable gift for a christening, though the insignia was not quite correct: the Dana arms had been appropriated by Edmund Dana without good authority; and the Sherburne family of Lancashire, whose arms are combined with them on the shield, is unlikely to have had any close relationship with that of Joseph Sherburne of Cornwall who had married Frances Johnstone nee Dana.[1]

The shield design on the christening box of Charlotte Frances Dana
On the left [dexter]: *Sherburne: quarterly, 1st and 4th:* vert [*green*], *an eagle displayed argent* [*silver*];
2nd and 3rd: argent, a lion rampant vert.
On the right [sinister]: *Dana: or* [*gold*], *a chevron engrailed between three hinds gules* [*red*].
The box was lately in the possession of Mrs Nancy Movius, great-grand-daughter of Charlotte Frances.
It is now held by her grand-daughter Katherine de Crespigny O'Donovan nee Movius.

Frances Johnstone Sherburne's will, proven after her death in 1837, gave a number of items of jewellery to her god-daughter, together with a Bible. Twelve inches by fifteen at the cover, and four inches thick, this substantial volume was printed in London in the early nineteenth century. It was probably covered originally in leather, but has since been rebound in red.

A set of inscriptions on the opening sheet provide a history. The first reads:
The gift of Helen Reid McIvor[?][2]
To her beloved and most respected Friend
Mrs Frances Johnstone Sherbourne
   June 28th 1814 –

---

[1] On the box and its shield, and the arms of Dana and Sherbourne, see Rafe de Crespigny, "A Search for the Arms of the Dana family," an essay published in *Anne's Family History* 2014/05/24.
[2] The writing of the surname is not clear: it could be McIvor or McIvoe. There is no independent or external evidence to determine which is correct.

CHAPTER TWO

The second inscription reads:
> *The Gift of Mrs Frances Johnstone Sherborne*
> *to her Niece and God daughter Charlotte Frances Dana*
> *by her will –*

The Bible of Charlotte Frances Dana

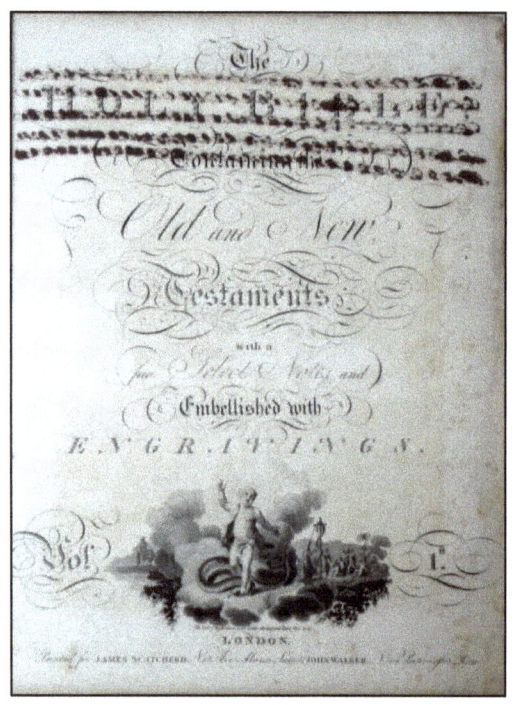

Title page, with lines of obliteration from the obverse

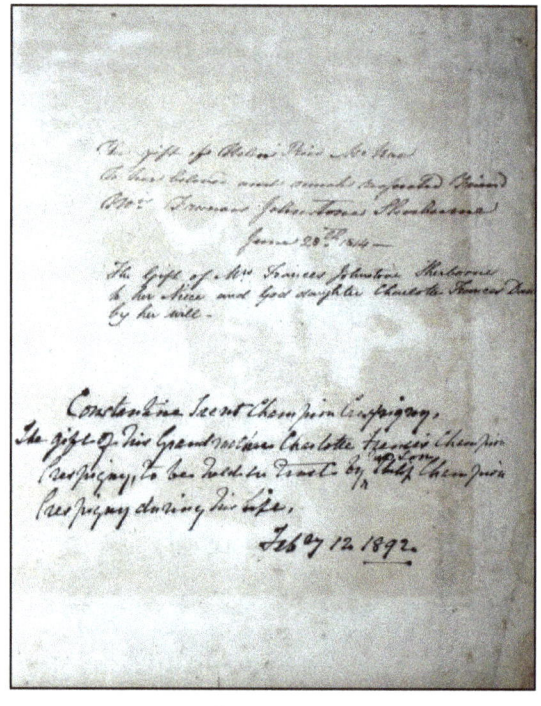

Dedication page

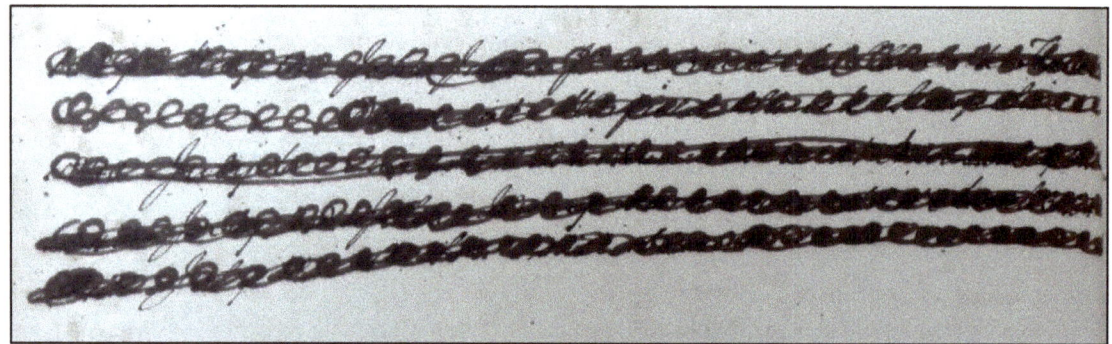

The obliterated text on the reverse of the title page and facing the dedication page

The third inscription reads:

> *Constantine Trent Champion Crespigny,*
> *The gift of his Grandmother Charlotte Frances Champion Crespigny,*
> *to be held in trust by her son Philip Champion Crespigny during his life,*
> *Feb'ry 12 1892*

Some writing is difficult to interpret: the surname of the first donor may be McIvoe rather than McIvor, or perhaps another variant; while the surname of Frances Johnstone appears to be written Sherbourne in the first inscription but Sherborne in the second. We follow the spelling "Sherburne" except, as here, where there is direct quotation of an original text. [We may also note that the inscription of 1892 has the family name as Champion Crespigny; not, as in current usage, Champion de Crespigny – that matter is considered below.][3]

Rather more significant, however, is the set of inscriptions on the reverse of the title page, which were later almost obliterated by heavy dark-brown lines of scribbling – so heavy that the markings can be seen through the top of the title page.

Although it has thus been covered over, however, with the aid of strong light and a magnifying glass it is possible to discern much of the information contained in the first inscription. It appears to have been written by the same hand as that which wrote the second inscription and also – though it was composed some fifty years later – the third inscription, which was signed by Charlotte Frances herself.

The wording may be construed as follows:

> *1839 May 14 John James Jr married Charlotte Frances Dana*
> *at Worfield Church, Salop [Shropshire]*[4]
> *1840 July 6 Charlotte [?].....born at home [?]*
> *1841 July 20 [?or 14 ?] John Henry [?] born......died March 3 1842*
> *1842 July 2 a Son stillborn*

The information is confirmed by official records. The British General Register Office holds volumes of lists of births and death for different local offices, arranged in collections of three months at a time, and the birth of Charlotte Constance James was registered at Westbury-on-Severn in the July-September quarter of 1840. In the following year, 1841, the birth of John Henry James was registered at the same office during the July-September quarter, and the death of John Henry James was recorded there in the January-March quarter of 1842. In addition, the parish records of Newnham Saint Peter give the date of his burial as 7 March. Since a stillborn child had legally never lived, no record was required – but the mother knew.

The census of 1841, the first full assessment of the population, collected information on every household throughout the British isles. Censuses had been carried out since 1801, but the Population Act of 1840 ordered that the count should apply to every household on a single day, created enumeration districts small enough to deal with this requirement, and set penalties for any failure to comply. Taken on Sunday 6 June, the survey included names, ages, sex, occupation, and the county of birth or whether it was overseas.

---

[3] On Sherburne/Sherburn/Sherbourne, see note 43 to Chapter One. On Champion Crespigny/Champion de Crespigny, see 77-78 below.

[4] As in Chapter One at 39, the father of Charlotte Frances' husband was also named John James. Though he is not listed as a witness to the marriage in 1839, he was in active legal practice with his son, who is accordingly identified as John James Junior.

CHAPTER TWO

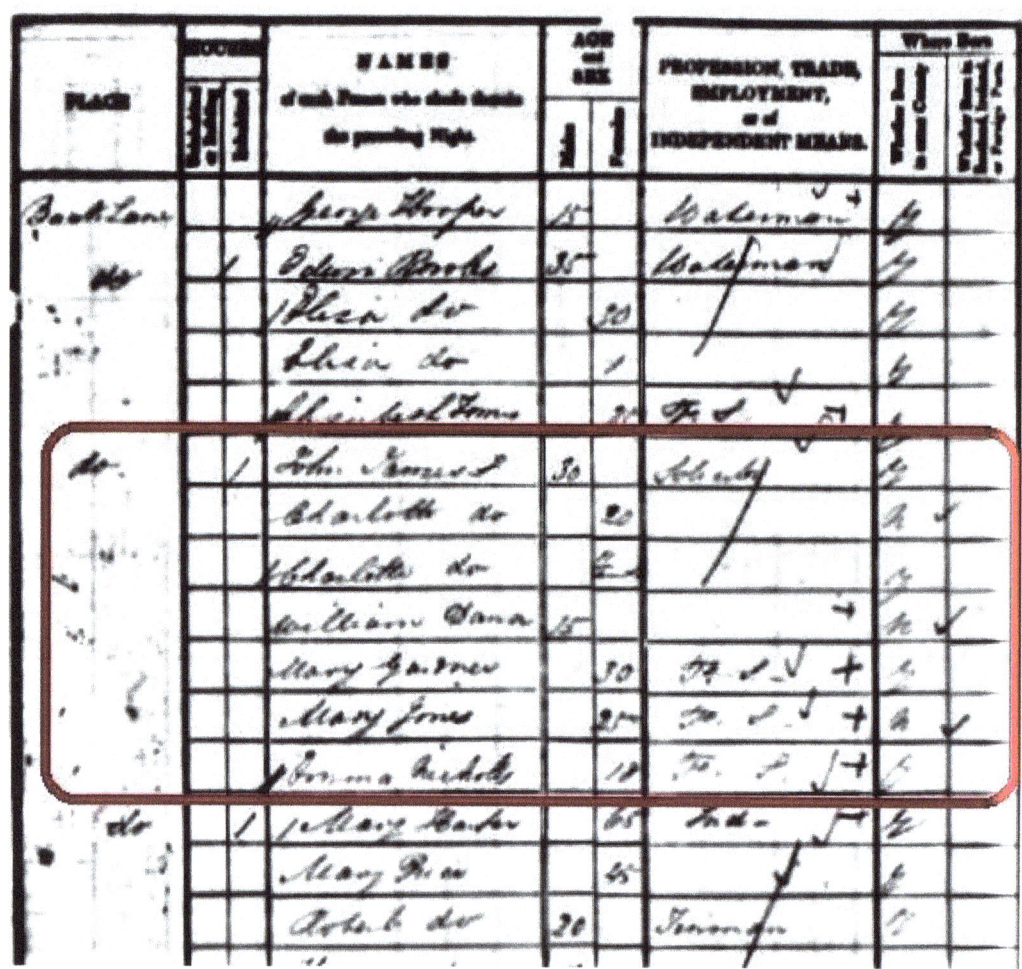

Extract from page 11 of the 1841 Census sheet for Newnham in Gloucestershire, district 8
The entry for John James Jr, Solicitor, and his household is identified in red.
Mary Jones, Mary Gardner and Emma Nicholls have their occupations identified as FS: Female Servant.

On this basis, therefore, we have an account of Charlotte Frances and her husband living at Newnham-on-Severn two years after their marriage. Their house was in Back Lane – which cannot now be identified – and the occupants were listed as:

John James Jr[5]   Head of Household   profession Solicitor
    male aged 30   born in Gloucestershire? Yes
Charlotte *ditto*   *no occupation given*
    female aged 20   born in Gloucestershire? No
Charlotte *ditto*   *no occupation given*
    female 11 months   born in Gloucestershire? Yes
William Dana   *no occupation given*
    male aged 15[6]   born in Gloucestershire? No
Mary Gardner   employment Female Servant
    female aged 30   born in Gloucestershire? Yes
Mary Jones   employment Female Servant
    female aged 25   born in Gloucestershire? No
Emma Nicholls   employment Female Servant
    female aged 18   born in Gloucestershire? Yes

---

[5]   The transcription of the census return has the surname miswritten as Janzer: the handwriting in fact has John James Jr, as in note 4 immediately above, but it is easy to misread.
[6]   This must be Charlotte Frances's young brother William Augustus Pulteney Dana, born in 1826.

In similar fashion, John James Senior, Attorney-at-Law, is also recorded living at Newnham, though the name of the street is illegible. He and his wife Anne are both described as sixty years old, and three of their children were living with them: Mary Phoebe, Charles and Frances; all are described as twenty years old and Charles is identified as an Attorney-at-Law.[7] The household had one manservant and three female servants, one of whom was Mary Nicholls, likely the mother or a sister of Emma working for John James Junior.

Besides the census information, the firm John James and Son, Attorneys and Solicitors, was recorded in 1837 by *Robson's Commercial Dictionary of Newnham*, and in 1842 *Pigot's Directory of Gloucestershire* listed the firm as attorneys and clerks to turnpike trusts, no doubt a profitable set of contracts.

NEWNHAM

Is a small and ancient market town, in the hundred of Westbury, and division of the Forest of Dean; 116 miles w. n. w. from London, 12 s. w. from Gloucester (the nearest railway station), and 6 s. from Mitchell-Dean; situated on an eminence rising from the western bank of the Severn, which is here nearly a mile in width at high water. In the reign of Edward I this town was governed by a mayor and burgesses; but at present the government is vested in two constables, appointed at the court leet of the lord of the manor (the Rev. Edward Jones), held annually at the 'Bear Inn.' Newnham once sent two members to parliament, but for many years has ceased to be so privileged; and its general consequence has been more upon the decline than the increase. The inhabitants of the town derive some advantage from its proximity to extensive coal and iron mines; and the railroad and Berkeley canal facilitate the conveyance of their produce. The navigation of the river at this part is difficult, and the shoals, even at high water, dangerous. The tide rises here in one solid wave, which rushes up the river, at the rate of five miles an hour, with impetuous fury and a resistless surge, and is termed 'the boar.' A quay for vessels of one hundred and fifty tons burden is on the verge of the river, and a few small vessels are built and launched from the yards on its banks.

The parish church of St. Peter stands on a cliff, sixty feet high, rising from the banks of the Severn; it is built with some curiously sculptured stone, conjectured to have been preserved from the ruins of a more ancient edifice, which stood at a place called Nab's-end. The living is a perpetual curacy, in the gift of the corporation of Gloucester. The Independents have a place of worship; and there are some charities by which the poor are benefited, and a bank for savings. The market day is Friday, but it presents scarcely any appearance of business different from other days in the week. The fairs are entitled to be held June 11th and October 18th; the privilege is, however, of trifling (if any) advantage to trade. Population, in 1831, 1,074, and, in 1841, 1,105.

POST OFFICE, James Powell, *Post Master*.—Letters from LONDON, &c. arrive (by mail cart from GLOUCESTER) every morning at half-past five, and are despatched thereto every evening at six.—Letters from SOUTH WALES (through CHEPSTOW) arrive every evening at six, and are despatched thereto every morning at half-past five.—Letters from BIRMINGHAM, LIVERPOOL, MANCHESTER, and the North, arrive (from GLOUCESTER) every morning at a quarter before eight, & are despatched to that town every afternoon at half-past five.

NOBILITY, GENTRY AND CLERGY.
Bathurst Rt. Hon. Chas. Lydney park
Boevey Crawley Sir Ths. Flaxley abbey
Combs Rev. Benjamin, Newnham
Hepburn Mrs. Mary, Little Dean
Jones Rev. Edward, Hay hill
Knowles Miss Hannah, Newnham
Malpas Rev. Jos. Hy. Awre vicarage
Morris Mrs. Mary, Newnham
Nash Miss Amelia, Newnham
Noel Hon. William M. Clanna falls
Palmer Mrs. Catherine, Newnham
Parsons Rev. James, Little Dean
Philips Miss Elizabeth, Newnham
Protheroe Edward, esq. Newnham
Pyrke Joseph, esq. Dean hall
Sayer Rev. John, Slown Arlingham
Thomson Mr. Thos. Sidney, Newnham
Torey Mr. Thomas, Newnham
Wait John, esq. New house

ACADEMIES AND SCHOOLS.
Bisp Daniel (brdg. & day) Broad oak
Coombs Rev. Benj. (boarding & day)
Moore Mary (day)
Playsted John (day)

PROFESSIONAL PERSONS.
Bird Henry, surgeon
Bullock Thomas, attorney
Hunt William & Henry, surgeon
James John & Son, attorneys and clerks to turnpike trusts
Lucas John, attorney
Mason Roynon, attorney and clerk to the magistrates

BANKS.
GLOUCESTERSHIRE BANKING COMPANY (branch)—(draw on Jones, Loyd and Co. London)—Simon R. Strode, manager
SAVINGS' BANK (open on Mondays) Simon R. Strode, actuary

FIRE, &c. OFFICE AGENTS.
NORWICH EQUITABLE (fire) Joseph Philpots
PHŒNIX (fire) Simon R. Strode
UNIVERSAL (life) Roynon Mason

INNS & PUBLIC HOUSES.
Anchor, John Jones
Bear Hotel (posting and passage house) John Miles Robertson
George, James Wallis [Dean
George Inn, William Wood, Little

Extract from Pigot's Directory of Gloucestershire 1842

---

[7] Charles (1817-1851) was now twenty-three. The first-mentioned sister would be Mary Phoebe (1813-1899), who should have been recorded as twenty-five rather than twenty. Charles' younger sister Frances had been born in 1819; she died in 1886.

Another sister, Amelia Charlotte (1815-1898), was already married to the attorney John Stanley and living at Bitton, east of Bristol. In 1844 Mary Phoebe also married a lawyer, Henry Sydney Wasbrough; in 1851 she was living with him and their son at Clifton, a suburb of Bristol.

John James Senior died in 1849, and the census of 1861 records his widow Anne, seventy-nine years old, as the head of a household which included her forty-nine-year-old son Edward James. She died two years later and he died in 1875 at the age of sixty-four: the record of his death and probate of his will gives his full name as Edward Lloyd James; it is likely that Lloyd was the maiden surname of his mother Anne.

CHAPTER TWO

In contrast to the James family, Charlotte Frances' father William Pulteney Dana had suffered serious reverses, for in August 1840, the year after his daughter's wedding to John James, he was in prison for debt.[8] The *London Gazette* announced that on Saturday 15 August the Court for Relief of Insolvent Debtors had ordered that the Estates and Effects of the following persons – on their own petitions – should be vested with the Provisional Assignee: among those named was

> William Pulteney Dana, late of Saint John's hill, Shrewsbury, Salop [*i.e.* Shropshire], Captain, on half pay, in the British Service. – In the Gaol of Shrewsbury.[9]

Embarrassingly, as we have seen, the prison at Shrewsbury was commonly known as the Dana, after the terrace built by William Pulteney's father the Reverend Edmund.[10]

Imprisonment for debt had been a feature of English law for centuries, and conditions could be harsh, with the additional problem that a person in prison would naturally find it difficult to arrange repayment, and was likely to be placed in even greater difficulty by the costs incurred in the prison itself, whether regular living expenses or the fees and bribes charged by the gaolers.

In some response to this, the Insolvent Debtors (England) Act of 1813 established Courts for Relief of Insolvent Debtors and provided that after fourteen days in prison debtors could make an agreement for the fair distribution of their assets, both present and future, with their creditors. The process was supervised by a Provisional Assignee appointed by the court, and if no creditors objected the debtor might then be released. In 1825 the Bankrupts (England) Act allowed debtors to take the initiative, rather than waiting for creditors to act, so William Dana and his fellow-unfortunates were able to present petitions to begin the proceedings.

William Pulteney Dana was accordingly released from prison, and when his case was heard by the Court at Shrewsbury on 5 December he is said to have been living again at Saint John's Hill, but now lodging with a Mr Smith. In that report he is described as

> Printer, previously of Roughton-hall, near Bridgenorth, and formerly of Albrighton, near Shiffnall, Shropshire, Captain on Half-pay, in the British Service, during the whole of the time, and out of business.[11]

On 5 March 1841 the *Gazette* announced that the case had been adjourned. In that notice, William Pulteney Dana is again recorded as lodging with Mr Smith in Saint John's Hill. He is described as a painter – surely miswritten – and his former addresses are again cited as Roughton Hall near Bridgenorth, preceded by Shifnal. He is now identified as Paymaster on half-pay of the 6th Garrison Battalion in the British Army, and it is again stated that he was out of business during the whole of the time.[12]

From the references to his previous addresses it is likely that the printing business had been carried out in one or both of the small towns Shifnal and Bridgnorth. Roughton is just a

---

[8] Much of the discussion which follows on this topic is informed by *Anne's Family History* 2017/04/13.

[9] Issue 19885 published 18 August 1840, pp 1921-1922. By an unfortunate coincidence, William Pulteney Dana's sister-in-law Heloise Eliza, widow of his elder brother the late Lieutenant-General George Kinnaird Dana, was in prison at Bristol for the same cause at this same time: Chapter One at 25.

[10] Chapter One at 10.

[11] *London Gazette* Issue 19913 of 13 November 1840 at 2558.
Here and below, the *Gazette* uses the name Bridgenorth; the present-day spelling is Bridgnorth.

[12] *London Gazette* Issue 19958 of 5 March 1841 at 627-628.
In the notice of 15 August Shifnal was spelt with two *l*s; here it has one – the present-day form. Albrighton is not specifically mentioned.

couple of miles from Bridgnorth, and though Shifnal is further from Albrighton it may have appeared to be a centre large enough to provide a market. The phrase "out of business" was a guarantee that the enterprise was not trading while insolvent – as in the present day, penalties for that could be severe.

The adjournment of 5 March 1841 marked a pause in the proceedings, and the matter was not raised again for another two years.

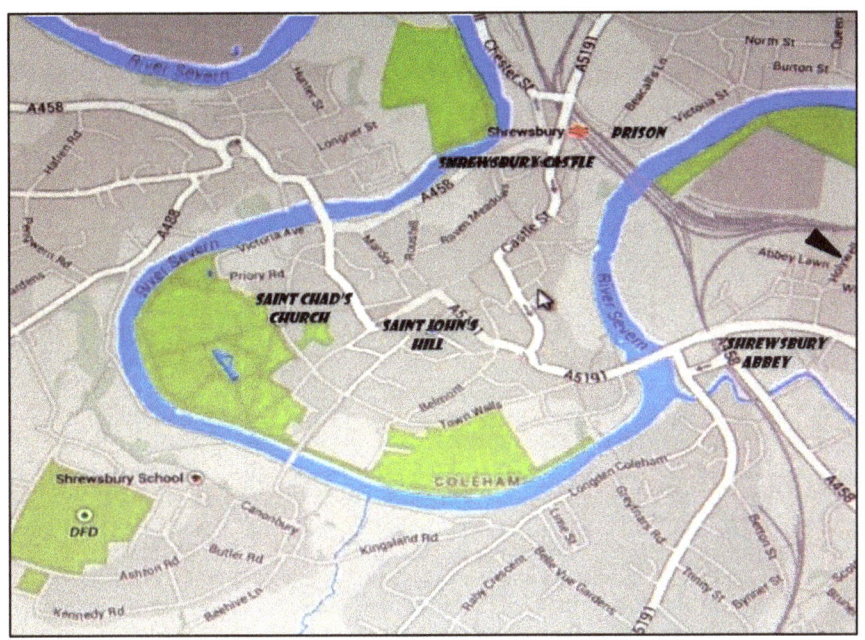

Central Shrewsbury
The Dana terrace ran from the castle, past the front of the prison, to join Victoria Street above the Severn
Holywell Terrace in the parish of Holy Cross and Saint Giles is indicated by the arrow on the right

By the time of the census held on 6 June 1841 William Pulteney Dana had left his lodgings in Saint John's Hill and was living with his family at Holywell Terrace in the parish of Holy Cross and St Giles, close to the site of Shrewsbury Abbey and a short distance across the Severn from the castle and the prison. He is now described as sixty years old – he was a month short of his sixty-fifth birthday – and his wife Charlotte as forty. Their daughters Anna Penelope and Helen Kinnaird – here called Ellen – were with them, and their youngest son Francis Richard Benjamin.[13] William Pulteney Dana described his occupation or profession as "Army," and despite his losses he was apparently able to sustain the household – including

---

[13] Several of the ages given by the census are more or less wrong. Charlotte Elizabeth was forty-five or forty-six and should have been described as in round terms as forty-five; Anna Penelope, born in March 1814, was twenty-seven but is described as twenty; Helen was eighteen but her age is rounded down to fifteen – acceptable but misleading – and Francis Richard Benjamin was seven years old, not eight: on this last, see Chapter One at 38 with note 136.

The eldest son, Henry Edmund Pulteney Dana, was already in Australia [below at 74 and Chapter Three at 79] while his younger brother William Augustus Pulteney Dana was staying with his sister Charlotte Frances and her husband John James [above at 46]. Douglas Charles Kinnaird Dana, however, currently sixteen, does not appear in this census.

In 1843 Helen Kinnaird Dana married Stephen Allaway, an ironmaster of the Forest of Dean in Gloucestershire who became a magistrate and deputy lieutenant of the county. They had four children and she died a wealthy widow in 1882. It does not appear she had any further contact with her father's family.

Douglas Charles Kinnaird Dana became a policeman. In 1844 he married Margaret Mortimer Boyce. They had five children, but later separated. He died in 1878 at King's Norton in Worcestershire, now part of Birmingham; she died in 1899.

CHAPTER TWO

three female servants – on his half-pay and perhaps some money from America as below; this last, however, was still vulnerable to his creditors. His situation is certainly reduced from the days of Sutton House and Roughton Hall just a few years earlier, but the debts remained and the process was continuing.

On 3 March 1843, a notice in the *London Gazette* announced the final stage of the affair: a meeting of creditors at Bridgnorth and the selling and dispersal of William Pulteney Dana's property in Massachusetts.

> In the Court for Relief of Insolvent Debtors.
> In the Matter of William Pulteney Dana.
>
> NOTICE is hereby given, that a meeting of the creditors of the estate and effects of the said insolvent will be held, on Monday the 20th day of March instant, at the Crown Inn, in the town of Bridgnorth, in the county of Salop, at eleven o'clock in the forenoon of the same day precisely, to assent to or dissent from the assignees of the said insolvent's estate and effects selling and disposing, by public auction or otherwise, and at such time and place as the majority of the creditors may determine, of all the right, title, interest, and estate whatsoever of the said insolvent of, in, and to all and singular the lands, tenements, and hereditaments of and belonging to him the said insolvent, situate in the town of Cambridge, in the county of Middlesex, and Commonwealth of Massachusetts, in North America, consisting of a certain tract or piece of land, formerly called the Oysterbank, but now called Pine-grove, containing, by estimation, including the streets, squares, and passage-ways, about fifteen acres, and also of a messuage or dwelling-house and buildings, standing and being thereon, or on some part thereof; and also to assent to or dissent from the said assignees bringing and prosecuting any action or actions at law, or suit or suits in equity, or taking any other proceedings whatsoever against the said insolvent, or his said estate and effects, in any court or courts of the Commonwealth or State of Massachusetts aforesaid, or in any other court or courts whatsoever and wheresoever, in order to attach the said messuage or dwelling-house, buildings, lands, hereditaments, and premises, and have the same sold; or for the creditors of the said insolvent setting off their respective debts in order to satisfying the same; and on other special affairs.

With this distribution, it appears that all assets had been realised and distributed. There may have been something left over from the sale, but it is more probable that everything was taken to satisfy the debts in whole or in part, and that William Pulteney Dana had now no more than the half-pay from his old appointment in the army. In the census of 1851, taken for the night of Sunday 30 March, he is again recorded as living at Holywell Terrace, now aged seventy-six and Captain and Paymaster in the Army.

Extract from page 22 of the 1851 Census for Holywell Terrace in the parish of Holy Cross and Saint Giles, Shrewsbury

In this household, however, the head is now his son-in-law. William Henry Wood, described as an Assistant Clerk at the County Court, was married to William Pulteney Dana's daughter Anna Penelope. Anna Penelope's mother Charlotte Elizabeth Dana nee Bayly had died in 1846, but Anna Penelope's young brother Francis Richard Benjamin Dana, seventeen years old, is also living there, employed as a Railway Clerk. A certain Bertha Mitford Reynolds, aged eighteen, is identified as a visitor, and there were two female servants: a cook and housemaid, the latter just sixteen years old.

Anna Penelope Wood (1814-1890) with her father William Pulteney Dana (1776-1861)

It is not an impressive establishment, and Richard Henry Dana records in his *Journal* the report of his cousin John Hastings that

> ... Anne, married to Mr Wm Henry Wood, lives in Holywell Terrace, Shrewsbury. Mr Hastings says she is of the salt of the earth ..... Her father and brother live with her, & she does everything in the world for them. ..... Mr Wood is an excellent man, in some office in the Court of Chancery, with a small salary, but has no property or expectations, as his father has become insolvent.[14]

As to William Pulteney Dana, Hasting's report is quite damning:

> Mr Wm Pulteney Dana is living in Shrewsbury, old, rather infirm, irritable, tyrannical, & poor. Indeed, he is a melancholy spectacle. The grandson of a peer, with the best of prospects in life, his indolence, pride and want of principle have reduced him to such a low condition. He has been through insolvency, & lives on a small pension from his office in the army, which is, I believe, that of a half-pay captain.[15]

On the following page he concludes the entry:

> Hastings seems much affected by the state of the family. He says they are treated with respect & looked up to as connected to the aristocracy, & have a good deal of pride of character, but they have met with many reverses. The influence of their uncle, Sir Wm Pulteney, would have put them all forward into the first stations, & did do much for them, but Mr Wm P Dana quarreled with his uncle, and cut himself from his chances of fortune and preferment. It is generally supposed that Sir Wm P intended to leave him his American property.[16]

---

[14] *Journal*, 418.
[15] *Journal*, 417-418.
[16] *Journal*, 419; see also Chapter One at 35.

Chapter Two

Though it is based upon a second-hand report from a distant land, this latter assessment appears fair, and in some contrast to the first. As discussed, we do not know the cause or nature of any quarrel between Sir William Pulteney and his namesake nephew, but it cannot be said that Sir William cut him from his will, for he did not leave one. Otherwise, it is not surprising that William Pulteney Dana, now in his seventies and approaching the end of his life, may have felt infirm, impoverished and irritable – and was sometimes demanding. He had reason for family pride, but there is no specific evidence of indolence or lack of principle. For one reason or another he had encountered many disappointments: the failure of the Pulteney inheritance; the early death of his first wife Anne nee Fitzhugh and the loss of their daughter; and the embarrassment of debt, imprisonment and insolvency. Many members of his family had done well or married well, but William Pulteney Dana had failed to fulfil his great expectations, and he ended his days as a widower, lodging in the house of a son-in-law – himself in no strong position.

At the census count on Sunday 7 April 1861 William Pulteney Dana, now eighty-four, was still at Holywell Terrace with his daughter and son-in-law. He died three months later, on 29 June, and was buried at Wroxeter on 5 July. Probate to his will was granted to his daughter Anna Penelope on 31 July; the value of his estate was less than £50.

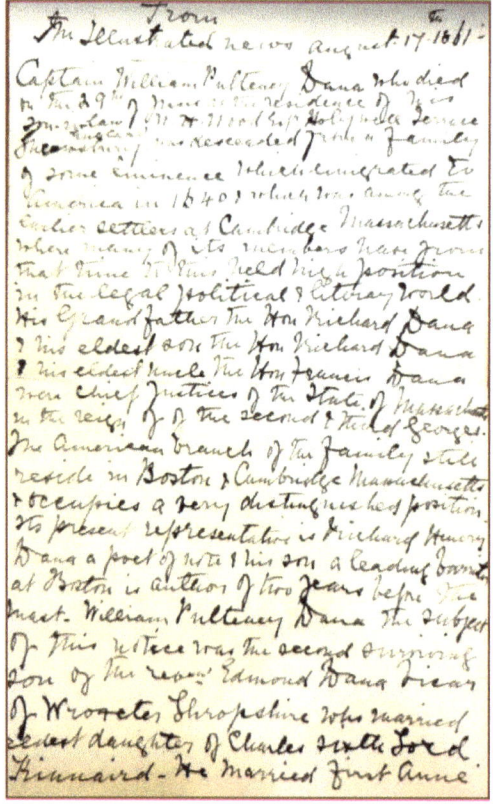 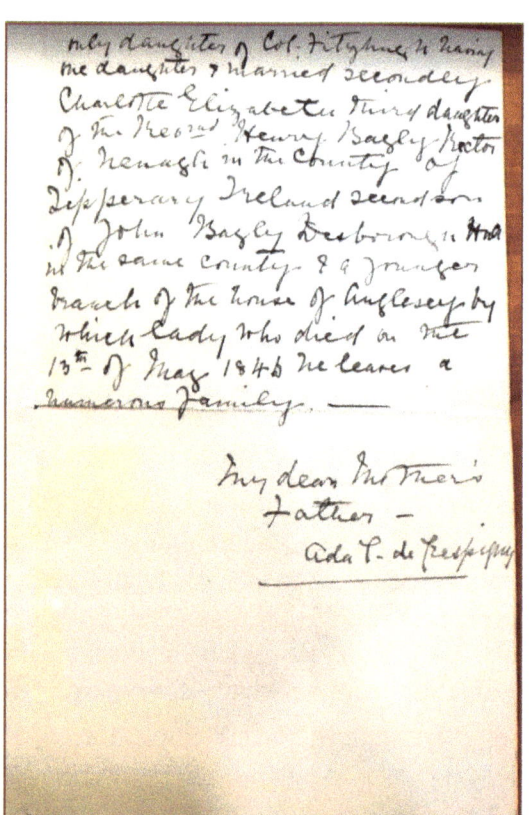

A quasi-obituary of William Pulteney Dana, with chief emphasis on his family connenctions, was published by The Illustrated London News *on 17 August 1861;*
His grand-daughter Ada CdeC made a copy.

The copy was probably done several years later, for in 1861 Ada was only thirteen, and this handwriting appears more mature. Furthermore, she uses the CdeC form of the family surname, and that was adopted in Australia only towards the end of the nineteenth century: see page 78 below.

Humiliating though it was, insolvency and imprisonment for debt were not uncommon. We have seen that the father of William Henry Wood had also been made insolvent, and the father of the novelist Charles Dickens was among the more celebrated sufferers. When William Pulteney Dana's case was first mentioned in the *London Gazette* of 18 August 1840 there were almost fifty others in the same circumstances, and when he was brought before the court at Shrewsbury on 13 November twelve others were also dealt with. Similar if not greater numbers appear in other issues of the *Gazette* – and it was published every fortnight. Several were private persons, but the majority appear to have been engaged in trade, for until the passage of the Joint Stock Companies Act in 1844, followed by the Limited Liability Act of 1855, investment in any business was potentially dangerous, while small enterprises could not be separated from their owners: the failure of one could bring ruin to its proprietor – and all were vulnerable to bad debts.

For Charlotte Frances James nee Dana, however, lately married to a prosperous lawyer with a secure position and income, her father's misfortunes were surely an embarrassment. At the time of their wedding in May 1839 her family were living at Roughton Hall, but fifteen months later, just at the time Charlotte Frances' first child was born, her father was in prison for debt and proceedings were under way to strip him and his family of all assets save his pension from the army. This is hardly the aristocratic connection the James family can have expected, and it likely caused tension in the newly-established household.

One year later, in July 1841, Charlotte Frances gave birth to the couple's son John Henry, but the boy died nine months later, in March 1842. Charlotte Frances was already pregnant for a third time, again with a son, but he was stillborn in July of that same year.

This sad combination of events might make any woman depressed, and very likely had an effect upon Charlotte Frances and her marriage. In the three years since their wedding in 1839, she had been with child three times, but after the stillbirth of 1842 there is no record of any further children or even a pregnancy. For people of that time, before modern methods of contraception, pregnancy was a normal and common condition for a healthy married women, and family records, as above and elsewhere, indicate that children could be expected every one or two years.[17] Charlotte Frances and her husband had been well capable of conceiving a child, but they had no more and the marriage does not now appear happy.

Breakdown

In his account of his cousin John Walter Hastings' report on the Dana family in England in 1851, Richard Henry Dana wrote in his *Journal* that:

> The second sister, Charlotte, who is said to have been very beautiful, married Mr James, a solicitor, a man of respectability & handsome fortune, living in Gloucestershire. But she has brought ruin upon herself & disgrace upon her name by eloping with a young man named De Cressiguy, son of a gentleman of large fortune, & leaving her husband & one daughter, a girl of 8 or 9 years. By some means or other, I know not what, the guilty pair are married in France, & live in great poverty & obscurity near Paris, Mr De C's father having reduced him to the smallest possible allowance. The poor woman is completely heart-broken, & is said to be too good to live under the sense of guilt. They expect, at any time, to hear of her death. This has been a dreadful blow to her family.[18]

---

[17] Edmund Dana and his wife the Honorable Helen Kinnaird, for example, had thirteen children in twenty-one years, and William Pulteney Dana had two children in two years by his first wife Anne nee Fitzhugh and ten children in twenty years by his second wife Charlotte Elizabeth nee Bayly; miscarriages or still-births, of course, were not normally recorded.

[18] *Journal*, 418. The surname De Cressiguy is either miswritten or mis-transcribed for de Crespigny. The

CHAPTER TWO

The account is close, but not quite accurate, and the forecast would prove mistaken.

Philip Robert Crespigny was born at Boulogne-sur-Mer in France on 4 October 1817, and baptised there in the British Chapel on 22 August 1825. Despite the birthplace and the surname, he was English by nationality of Huguenot descent. Members of the family had come to London at the time of the Revocation of the Edict of Nantes by Louis XIV in 1684, and Philip Robert's great-grandfather and grandfather, both named Philip (Philip I: 1704-1765; Philip II: 1738-1803), were lawyers at the Court of Arches, dealing with matters of marriage and divorce, wills and probate, and the law of the sea. It was a specialist jurisdiction – subsumed into general British law in the mid-nineteenth century – and a very profitable one, and both men made good marriages. Philip II was a Member of Parliament and had extensive holdings of land; his brother Claude (1734-1818), great-uncle of Philip Robert, was Receiver of the Droits of the Admiralty for more than thirty years and was made a baronet by the Prince Regent, future King George IV.[19]

Philip Robert's father, Charles [James] Fox Champion Crespigny (1785-1875), named after the leading politician of the time, a friend of his father,[20] was the second son of Philip II by his fourth wife, Dorothy nee Scott. He had two elder half-brothers by his father's first wife and one each by the second and third wives, both of whom died in infancy. He had an elder full brother, George (1783-1813), and an elder sister Eliza (1784-1831); a younger sister, Dorothy, was born and died in 1800.

Philip II died in January 1803 and in March of the following year his widow Dorothy nee Scott married Sir John Keane, a baronet and member of the parliament of Ireland. In April 1804 George took a commission in the army: engaged in the Netherlands and in the Peninsula War in Spain, he rose to the rank of Major, but was killed at San Sebastian in 1813. In September 1804 Eliza eloped to Gretna Green and married Richard Hussey Vivian; he served with the Duke of Wellington in Spain and at Waterloo, became a lieutenant-general, a knight of the Bath and of the Order of Saint Michael and Saint George, and was made first Baron Vivian in 1841.

Charles Fox Crespigny had matriculated to Cambridge University in 1803 at the age of eighteen. He was a member of Trinity College, and though there is no account of his taking a degree, records in that field are not complete. In 1804, aged nineteen, he became a Cornet –

---

surname is confusing and its use is also confused: at this time it appeared variously as Crespigny, Champion Crespigny, Champion de Crespigny and de Crespigny. There is discussion below at 77-78, and an account of the history of the family from earliest times to the beginning of the nineteenth century is given by RdeC, *Champions from Normandy*. Philip Robert normally used only the surname Crespigny, sometimes with the initial *C* for Champion, but very seldom with the prefix *de*.

In similar fashion, Philip Robert normally used only the first of his two given names. Since the name Philip is common in the family, however, he is regularly identified in the present work as Philip Robert.

[19] RdeC, *Champions from Normandy*, 162-167.

[20] It is uncertain whether the full given names were Charles Fox or Charles James Fox; there is said to have been some confusion at the baptism: *Champions from Normandy* at 173. He normally signed as Charles Fox, but on one occasion he used the initials CJC: Chapter Three at 117.

Somewhat unexpectedly, the death certificate of his son Philip Robert, issued in Australia in 1889, gives the name of his father as Charles James Fox Crespigny: Chapter Five at 201. A photocopy of the certificate is in Grayden, *Chronicle*, 31, and the Victorian Registry of Births, Deaths and Marriages for 1889, reference number 10924, likewise has the given names of Philip Robert's father as "Jas Fox Chas."

Anne's Family History 2018/01/26 has an entry for Charles Fox Crespigny, including a fragment of a hagiographical memoir by his grandson Charles Stanley Champion Crespigny (1848-1907).

second lieutenant – in the First (Royal) Dragoon Guards, a senior regiment of cavalry, and in 1808 he was promoted Lieutenant, without purchase. The regiment was at that time stationed in England, and Charles Fox Crespigny sold his commission and left the service in 1811.[21]

There were reasons for this. His father Philip had left substantial properties, with his two sons by Dorothy nee Scott, George and Charles Fox, as residual legatees; Dorothy, Philip's brother Claude the later baronet, and a personal friend Stafford Squire Baxter were named as Executors and presumably guardians until the two heirs came of age.[22] By 1809, however, when the First Dragoon Guards sailed for Spain, Charles Fox Crespigny's elder brother George was already with the army there and Charles Fox, now in his middle twenties, could fairly be expected to attend to their estates. There was no immediate family to look to otherwise: his mother Dorothy had a young child by a new marriage, his elder half-brother Thomas had died in 1799, and Thomas' younger full brother Philip (1765-1851), a lawyer at the Court of Arches, had travelled to France during the Treaty of Amiens, which paused the hostilities between Britain and Napoleonic France in 1802; but was interned there when war broke out again in May 1803.

The estates were widely spread: the will of Philip II identifies land-holdings in East Anglia – Norfolk, Suffolk and Cambridgeshire – in London and Bath, and at Llangasty Talyllyn in Breconshire in Wales.[23] In 1812 Charles Fox Crespigny was High Sheriff of Breconshire:[24] the office no longer gave significant authority and was rather a courtesy title granted for a year to a leading landholder, but it did indicate that he had been resident in the county, at least in 1811.

Charles Fox Crespigny was also a Justice of the Peace in Suffolk,[25] however, and the borough of Aldeburgh, which was entitled to send two members to the Parliament at Westminster was directly under his control.[26]. He was certainly in the county during the second half of 1812, for he fathered a child there: Emily Crespigny Hindes was baptised at the church of St Mary-le-Tower at Ipswich in Suffolk on 20 April 1813. Her mother was also named Emily, and though the name of the child's father was not formally recorded the second baptismal name is significant.[27]

On 14 July 1830, moreover, Charles Fox Crespigny of Aldeburgh in Suffolk stood surety for a court-issued bond on behalf of Mrs Eliza Blundell and Miss Emily Hindes, sailing as passengers to Bengal. The so-called "fishing fleet" of Englishwomen hoping to marry a promising young man in British India was a well-known phenomenon of the nineteenth

---

[21] His appointments appeared in the *London Gazette*, issues 15726 of 7-11 August 1804 at 953 and 15882 of 18-21 January 1806 at 77. His resignation and sale of commission were noted by Stephen Champion de Crespigny.

[22] See RdeC, *Champions from Normandy*, 175.

[23] RdeC, *Champions from Normandy*, 175, citing the will of Philip Crespigny, proven on 7 March 1803.

[24] *London Gazette* Issue 16565 of 21 January 1812 at 142, and Issue 16580 of 3 March 1812 at 425.

[25] According to the UK National Archives, the Essex Record Office holds a collection of correspondence from and to Charles Fox Crespigny, JP.

[26] Charles Fox Crespigny had inherited the patronage of the borough from his father Philip II. At the election of 1813 the two successful candidates each paid £6000 for his sponsorship. In 1818 he sold his interest for £39,000: RdeC, *Champions from Normandy*, 173.

[27] In the census of 1861 there was an Emily Hindes, aged sixty-six, listed as living alone in Aldeburgh High Street and maintained by "Annuity Property." Born about 1795, she would have been of age to bear a child in 1812. It is very likely that she was the mother of Charles Fox Crespigny's daughter and that he had supported her thereafter. She died in 1870.

CHAPTER TWO

century Raj, and it appears that Charles Fox Crespigny had arranged for seventeen-year-old Emily to enter that marriage market. Eliza Blundell had married George Snow Blundell, an officer in the army of the East India Company, just one month before, and Charles Fox Crespigny was paying her fare in exchange for her assistance as a guardian and chaperone.[28]

The initiative was remarkably successful, for on 1 December 1832 Emily Hindes married Major George Petre Wymer at Neemuch, east of Udaipur, south of Gwalior and now in the northwest of the state of Madya Pradesh; the ceremony was witnessed by George Snow Blundell, Captain in the Fifty-First Regiment of Native Infantry.

Born in Norfolk in 1788, and twenty-five years older than his wife, George Wymer was a fine soldier who rose to be a general and a knight of the Bath. There were five children of the marriage, four born in India; the first two, a daughter and a son named George Crespigny, both died there in infancy.[29] Returning to England about 1850, the family lived on the Isle of Wight and in London, where Sir George died in 1868, with obituaries in the *Gentleman's Magazine*, the *Morning Post*, the *Illustrated London News* and elsewhere. His widow, known as Dame Emily, died in 1891.[30]

On 20 March 1813, just about the time that his illegitimate daughter Emily Hindes was born, Charles Fox Crespigny married Eliza Julia Trent (1797-1855). Twelve years his junior, she was the daughter of John Trent (1770-1796) and his first cousin Elizabeth nee Phipps (1774-1836). The Trent and Phipps families both held plantations and slaves in the West Indies, but John Trent had come to England and purchased Dillington House in Somerset.[31] He died in August 1796, six months before the birth of his daughter Julia and her twin brother Francis Onslow. Elizabeth married again and had one more daughter, but her second husband Arthur Branthwayte, from a landed family in Norfolk who became a captain in the Dragoon Guards, was lost at sea in December 1808. She evidently had family money and did not marry again.

When Julia Trent married Charles Fox Crespigny, the ceremony was held at fashionable Saint George's Church in Hanover Square, London; the bride was still a minor, and her widowed but remarried mother Eliza Branthwayte gave her permission. Witnesses were the bride's brother John Constantine Trent and the bridegroom's half-brother Philip, who had escaped from his French internment in the previous year.[32]

---

[28] The bond was issued in the names of Chas F Crespigny and Philip C Toker of Doctors' Commons. Philip Toker was Charles Fox Crespigny's nephew, daughter of his half-sister Clarissa who had married Edward Toker, also a lawyer of the Court of Arches based on Doctors' Commons.
Anne's Family History 2019/11/27: "A Passage to India" describes the system in further detail and has more information on the fortunes of Emily Hindes as below.

[29] The grave of George Crespigny Wymer at Simla is described, overgrown with grasses, ferns and lichen, by in an essay "Out of Society" by Rudyard Kipling, first published in the *Civil and Military Gazette* of 14 August 1886.

[30] The website ghgraham.org/georgepetrewymer1788.html has an account of George and Emily Wymer and their children, with extracts from censuses, obituaries and the probate of wills.
Somewhat strangely, after her husband's death Emily describes herself in the census returns as being born in France. Given that she was baptised at Ipswich, this is most unlikely. She was possibly seeking to explain her unusual middle name, or simply reflecting the real experience of her step-siblings as below.

[31] Phipps, *Life of Colonel Pownoll Phipps*, has an account of the families. www.seavingtonwebmuseum.org.uk has a history of Dillington House at Ilminster in Somerset by Ewen J H Cameron [1998 revised 2008], including the brief tenure by the Trent family.

[32] Internment in France under Napoleon, while no doubt frustrating, was comparatively comfortable. Most exiles were held at Verdun in the northeast, which is said to have been a centre of lively society. Philip

Charles Fox and Julia Crespigny first lived at Aldeburgh, and their first child, Charles John, was born there on 20 June 1814 and baptised on 16 August. In 1815 the family moved across the Channel to France. Napoleon had surrendered to his allied enemies in April 1814 and was exiled to Elba, an island in the Mediterranean off the Italian coast, and – as in the period after the Treaty of Amiens in 1802 – many British gentry were glad to take the opportunity to visit the continent, while it may also have seemed sensible discretion to avoid the second household of Emily Hindes and her daughter.

There is no way to tell quite when Charles Fox Crespigny and his family made the move, but we know that his and Julia's second child, George Blicke, was born at Antwerp on 31 October 1815.[33] Since it is unlikely Julia would have travelled overseas at an advanced stage of pregnancy, they probably came to Europe in the spring or early summer. The situation soon became uncertain, however, for Napoleon returned to power in France in March and embarked on the northern campaign that led eventually to his defeat at Waterloo on 18 June.

It is possible the family had been in Paris and found it necessary to flee to the north, and there is a claim that Charles Fox Crespigny was present at the celebrated ball held in Brussels on the eve of Waterloo: his brother-in-law Sir Richard Hussey Vivian had an invitation, and Charles may have attended as a guest.

Following the birth of George Blicke the family lived for several years at Boulogne-sur-Mer, just across the Channel from Dover, and further children were born there: Philip Robert on 4 October 1817; Eliza Julia on 3 May 1819; and Eliza Constantia Frances in July 1825. Eliza Constantia Frances was baptised at the British Chapel of Boulogne on 31 July 1825, and her two brothers George Blicke and Philip Robert on 22 August. The brothers may have been christened earlier, but the ceremony under British auspices served to register their births for purposes of citizenship. Charles Fox and Julia Crespigny had no more children.

It is not known when Charles Fox and Julia returned to England, though it was probably in the second half of the 1820s, soon after the birth of Eliza Constantia Frances. By that time the boys would have been ten years old or more, and though there are no records of their schooling both George Blicke and Philip Robert gained university entrance, so we may assume they had acquired at least a secondary education in England. It is not known where the family lived, and it is possible they did not return to East Anglia: properties in London

---

Crespigny was later transferred to the neighbourhood of Paris, and he married the wealthy heiress Emilia Wade in 1809. His escape was likely assisted by bribery. See also *Anne's Family History* 2013/09/01, citing notes by Stephen CdeC.

The earlier experience of the Phipps family provides a striking contrast. In 1788 Elizabeth Phipps' father Constantine had moved to Caen in Normandy, where his wife's family were living, as he believed it would be cheaper than England and that the children would receive a better education. Though the Revolution broke out in the following year, the region was at first largely unaffected.

In 1792 the Phipps' cousin John Trent came to visit and became engaged to Elizabeth. Believing the wedding should be held in England, the parents went there with four of their children, leaving eight behind under the care of Penelope, age seventeen. When war was declared three months later, however, the children were caught in France and the parents could not return to them. Dependent for six years on the kindness of neighbouring French families, they were unable to get away until 1798, a year after their father had died in England. See Phipps, *Life of Colonel Pownoll Phipps*, 17-42, with *Anne's Family History* 2017/04/04 and 2018/04/18.

[33] Sources vary on the spelling of George's second given name, but there appears to be a slight preponderance for the final *e*, so we give it throughout as Blicke.

CHAPTER TWO

and in Bath were available, and when George Blicke entered Cambridge in October 1832 his address was given as Talyllyn House in Breconshire.

Though Charles Fox Crespigny had been to Cambridge and his younger sons George Blicke and Philip Robert went there too, the elder brother Charles John did not attend university. Later in life he described himself in census reports as a "Landed Proprietor;" it appears that he lived off the income from his father's estates and may have taken a part in running them.

George Blicke Crespigny was admitted to Trinity Hall just before his seventeenth birthday.[34] The Hall was known for legal studies, and in the following year, 1833, George Blicke was also enrolled at Lincoln's Inn in London, a stepping stone for admission to the English bar. It is not known whether he completed his degree, but there is no record of his matriculation at the university itself, and in January 1836 he joined the Twentieth Regiment of Foot as an Ensign – second lieutenant. He was promoted Lieutenant in July 1839 and Captain in June 1842, all three commissions being obtained by purchase.[35] He later became Lieutenant-Colonel and Paymaster at the School of Musketry. Married with children, he died at Folkestone in 1893.[36]

Philip Robert Crespigny was admitted as a Fellow-Commoner of Downing College at Cambridge in November 1838. He was then twenty-one years old, comparatively late for an undergraduate, and one must assume that, like his eldest brother, he had limited enthusiasm for higher education.

Students at this time were ranked by prestige, cost and privilege. Noblemen held the highest position, while Commoners, also known as Pensioners, paid for their own tuition, board and lodging. Fellow-Commoners, between the two, paid higher fees but enjoyed more privileges, including the right to dine at high table with the full Fellows of the college. More to the point, as the compilers Venn remark in their Introduction to *Alumni Cantabrigienses*,

youths of social and political importance.....generally entered as fellow-commoners, and, as they did not contemplate proceeding to a degree, they often neglected to matriculate.[37]

For many gentlemen, attendance at Cambridge or Oxford was a rite of passage rather than a search for qualification, and Philip Robert Crespigny may never have seriously sought a degree or received one: as with his brother George, there is no university record of his matriculation or graduation. In the early 1840s there are references to his attendance at social functions in Cheltenham – notably balls and galas in full or fancy dress – and at least from his mid-twenties he appears – like his brother Charles John – to have been to some degree involved with the family properties.

According to a later statement by John James, husband of Charlotte Frances nee Dana, Philip Robert first made the acquaintance of his family when he was arranging the conveyancing of farm bought by Charles Fox Crespigny; Philip Robert was acting as his father's agent. A brief

---

[34] *Alumni Cantabrienses* Part II, Volume 2 at 175 lists all members of the family who attended the university in this period, including the descendants of Philip II and those of his brother Claude the first baronet.

[35] *London Gazette* Issue 19351 of 29 January at 169; Issue 19752 of 19 July at 1437; Issue 20111 of 17 June 1842 at 1654.

[36] An obituary of Colonel George Blicke Crespigny appeared in the *Folkestone Express, Sandgate, Shorncliffe & Hythe Advertiser* on 8 July 1895.

[37] Part I, Volume 1 at v.

notice in the *London Daily News* of Monday 19 February 1849, reporting cases heard by the Court of Arches on the previous Saturday, reads:

> JAMES v JAMES. – DIVORCE
>
> This was a suit promoted by Mr James, a solicitor, residing in Gloucestershire, against his wife for a divorce, by reason of adultery. It appeared that Mr James, in his professional capacity, had the disposal of an estate, which was purchased by a Mr Crespigny, and which led to an introduction of his son, Mr Philip Champion Crespigny, to Mr James's family, with whom Mrs James afterwards eloped.
>
> The court thought the facts were fully established beyond all doubt, and pronounced for the divorce.

The circumstances appeared straightforward and the case was easily approved at this stage, while John James' statement serves to explain how his wife met Philip Robert Crespigny. Still more to the point, we are told elsewhere that Philip Robert soon afterwards went to live at the property, a small farm close to Newnham the home of the James family.[38]

We do not know when the farm was purchased, but it was probably in the mid-1840s, when Philip Robert Crespigny was in his late twenties and Charlotte Frances James nee Dana was about twenty-five. She was, we have suggested, very vulnerable. She had borne a daughter and a son, but the boy died in 1842 after just nine months, and a third child was stillborn three months later. At the very same time Charlotte Frances' father William Pulteney Dana had suffered the humiliation of imprisonment for debt and insolvency, and was being stripped of his possessions to satisfy his creditors. Her husband John James, twelve years the elder, was perhaps not sympathetic and it is likely the couple had become estranged. In 1846, moreover, Charlotte Frances' mother, Charlotte Elizabeth nee Bayly, died at Shrewsbury on 13 May and was buried at the family church in Wroxeter six days later. Her daughter may have felt very isolated.

One source suggests that the affair had been encouraged by John James' own suspicions, as the lack of her husband's trust encouraged Charlotte Frances to fulfil his fears.[39] In any event, by the middle of 1847 Charlotte Frances and Philip Robert had embarked on an affair, for it appears that Charlotte Frances became pregnant by him in August of that year. Their first daughter would be born on 15 May 1848 – but several questions had to be dealt with, the road to divorce was a long one, and their daughter Ada would be born out of wedlock.

Divorce[40]

The decision of the Court of Arches in February 1849 marked only the first stage of divorce proceedings at that time.

---

[38] The *Hereford Times* for Saturday 25 March 1849 has a report of the case in the House of Lords on page 6. It includes this information which is omitted by the account in the London *Times* [below].

[39] An article entitled "Opprobriums of Law" with this interpretation appeared in *The Hull Packet and East Riding Times* of Friday 30 March 1849 as the divorce case was proceeding before the House of Lords.

Yorkshire is a long way from London and even further from Gloucestershire, but rumour and suspicion may have been widespread, and the article refers to the case as "probably one of a large class."

[40] An account of the divorce proceedings, with quotations from relevant sources, is given by *Anne's Family History* at 2013/04/01.

Stone, *Road to Divorce*, 183-369, has a detailed account of divorce law at this time, the first half of the nineteenth century.

CHAPTER TWO

Based on Doctors' Commons, south of Saint Paul's Cathedral in the City of London, the Court of Arches exercised jurisdiction on behalf of the Archbishop of Canterbury over marriage, divorce, wills and their probate. Cases were based on the tradition of Roman law, as opposed to the Common Law which applied in regular English courts and, by a quirk of circumstance, the Court of Arches dealt also with maritime affairs, for these usually involved international disputes and Roman Law was standard in the rest of Europe. Philip Robert Crespigny's grandfather and great-grandfather, both named Philip, had been active practitioners at the Court of Arches, and his great-uncle Sir Claude the first baronet had, as we have seen, been Receiver of the Droits of Admiralty.[41]

The ecclesiastical judgement by the Court of Arches formally ended the marriage and allowed the former partners to separate; it did not, however, authorise either of them to remarry. That required a private Act of Parliament, which was both difficult and expensive to obtain.

As first step in the procedure, the aggrieved husband was expected to sue his wife's lover for "criminal conversation." Despite the term "criminal," such cases were civil actions, heard before the King's or Queen's Bench in a Common Law jurisdiction, and if the defendant was found guilty he could be required to pay heavy damages, sufficient to harm any estate and often enough to drive the guilty party into insolvency and imprisonment for debt.

Assuming the action for "*crim con*" was successful, the husband could then petition the House of Lords for a full divorce. By the time of James *v* James, the essential requirements for a successful petition had been largely established:

> The first was plausible, if often only circumstantial, evidence of the wife's adultery, testified to by two or more witnesses. The second was evidence of good marital relations prior to the adultery. The Lords tried to make sure that there was no sign of extreme prior negligence, neglect, separation of beds, or formal separation. The third was the absence of any act of adultery or cruelty by the husband which could have driven the wife to adultery. [In addition...] the House of Lords also insisted on proof of a successful outcome to an ecclesiastical court suit for separation and a common law action for *crim con*, or a plausible explanation why none was possible.
>
> The last requirement was that there should be no evidence of joint collusion between husband and wife in organizing the divorce proceedings, either by arranging for the former *crim con* action or ecclesiastical suit to go undefended, or by not enforcing payment of damages.[42]

In practice, of course, as two successive Lord Chancellors recognised at this time, collusion was almost impossible to prove, and "the passage of a divorce bill was virtually automatic if it had been preceded by a successful separation suit and *crim con* action."[43] In most cases, the first draft of the bill granted the innocent husband the right to marry but denied it to the guilty wife; this proviso, however, was regularly removed from the final act.

Leaving aside the action for *crim con* and the potential damages – which, as we shall see, proved not to be relevant to James *v* James – the costs of an action in the Court of Arches plus those of a private Act of Parliament could be extremely high. Figures vary, but in 1850 an unopposed suit in the Court of Arches, followed by the parliamentary bill of divorce, is said

---

[41] RdeC, *Champions from Normandy*, 147 and, on Sir Claude and the Droits of Admiralty, 163-164.
[42] Stone, *Road to Divorce*, 323-324.
[43] Stone, *Road to Divorce*, 324.

to have amounted to almost £5000, equivalent to some half a million Australian dollars at the present day, and that excludes the costs of witnesses and other incidental expenditure. As Stone remarks, access to such a procedure was the privilege of the wealthy landed, business or professional classes, and at this period there were no more than two or three cases in any one year.[44]

Each petition for a parliamentary divorce had first to be approved by the House of Lords, and the second reading was the important one. The first reading entailed little more than placing the matter on an agenda, but the second took the form of a full trial, with witnesses subject to cross-examination. The third reading was again rather a matter of form, and though the Lords' decision was subject to review by a Select Committee on Divorce Bills of the House of Commons it was generally accepted. Returned once more to the Lords, very occasionally with amendments, it could then receive the royal assent and become law.[45]

Just three weeks after the Court of Arches had approved an ecclesiastical divorce, the second reading of the private bill for "James's Divorce" was heard by the House of Lords on 20 March 1849. It was reported by the *Times* on page 7 of its issue of the following day.

In accordance with tradition, the Lord Chancellor, most senior legal officer of the kingdom, was the presiding officer at the meeting; in 1849 the office was held by the Right Honourable Charles Pepys, Baron Cottenham and a member of the Privy Council. Eight peers are listed as present, including the Duke of Wellington, hero of Waterloo and a former Prime Minister; Lord Stanley, a future Prime Minister;[46] Lords Brougham and Campbell, a past and a future Lord Chancellor; and Lord Ellenborough a former Governor-General of India. The list finishes "&c," implying there were others in attendance, but this is in any case a most impressive gathering to deal with a single item of private concern, and one may understand why the action was expensive. With paragraphing adjusted for clarity, the full report of the *Times* reads as follows:[47]

HOUSE OF LORDS, Tuesday, March 20.
_____

At the conclusion of the appeals this afternoon,
Their Lordships ordered the counsel and parties to be called in.

JAMES'S DIVORCE.

Mr Serjeant WRANGHAM[48] stated that he appeared at their Lordships' bar on behalf of Mr John James, the promoter of this bill. Mr James was a gentleman in very extensive practice as a solicitor at Newnham, in the county of Glocester, and on the 14th May, 1839, had been united to the object of his dearest affections, Miss Charlotte Frances Dana. The ceremony was solemnized at the parish church of Warfield, in the county of Salop [Shropshire], and from that moment until the event which had led to the present proceedings the parties had lived on the most affectionate terms. Mr James was one of the most indulgent of husbands, and had afforded his

---

[44] Stone, *Road to Divorce*, 356 and Table 10.1 at 325.
[45] Stone, *Road to Divorce*, 323.
[46] Edward George Geoffrey Smith-Stanley, later the fourteenth Earl of Derby but at that time known simply as Lord Stanley, was Prime Minister in 1852 and held that office in two subsequent terms.
[47] *Anne's Family History* at 2013/04/01 has copies of several newspaper items, including the account of proceedings in the House of Lords published by the *Times*. The *Morning Post* has a similar report.

CHAPTER TWO

wife every luxury that his circumstances would admit of. On the part of Mrs James it would seem that down to the moment of her departure she had continued to lead her husband to suppose that her feelings towards him had in no way diminished. She appeared by all outward signs to be still the same loving and affectionate wife.

Towards the latter part of 1847, in consequence of the delicate state of her health, Mr James had brought his wife up to London to consult some of the leading physicians, and the result was, that he was induced to take a cottage near Ventnor, on the Isle of Wight.[49] Thither he accompanied his wife, taking only their daughter and one servant with them, intending that one of the other servants should follow them.

After they had been there some time, Mr James received a letter from Mr Wintle, his partner at Newnham, wherein that gentleman stated, that the servant who was about to join them at Ventnor had been spreading some reports which were unfavourable to the character of Mrs James, and urging that Mr James would go home and prevent the servant from going to Ventnor.

Mr James told his wife what had occurred, and at the same time assured her that he totally disbelieved the calumny. It was, however, arranged that he should return home and prevent the servant in question going to Ventnor and dismiss her from his service. The parting on this occasion of Mr and Mrs James, their Lordships would hear from one of the witnesses whom he should call, was not simply exceedingly affectionate, but was extremely affecting. Mr James left his wife with the confidence that he had quitted her in the pride of her innocence and love.

But it would be proved to their Lordships that on the very night of his departure Mrs James had eloped with a gentleman, who turned out eventually to be Mr Philip Champion Crespigny, who, for some time prior to Mr and Mrs James leaving Newnham, had resided at a small farm near that place, which had been purchased by his father.

On the departure of Mr James the lady manifested very great distress, and at night, when her servant went to her bedroom as usual to assist her in undressing, she declined her aid, and, after a little time, she dismissed her to her own room. On the following morning, when the servant came downstairs, finding the door of her mistress's room open, she went in, when, to her surprise and alarm, she discovered not only that the lady had not occupied her bed, but that she had eloped, for she was nowhere to be found.

In her room, however, Mrs James had left two letters, of which the following were copies. The first was addressed to her husband, and the second to her servant, and was dated –

Friday Night, Nov 12, 1847

I know not, my beloved husband, how to write to you. My head is confused with all I would say to you; I have been in vain endeavouring

---

[48] Digby Caley Wrangham (1805-1863) was a leading barrister of the day. Serjeant-at-Law (SL) was a senior appointment, comparable to and now superseded by the title of Queen's Counsel (QC) or [in some states and territories of Australia] Senior Counsel (SC).

[49] A shorter version of the case in *The Era* weekly newspaper of 25 March at page 13 identifies the lodging as Madeira Cottage. A substantial brick house of two stories, Madeira Cottage still stands at the at the junction of High Street with Bannock Road [formerly Slay Lane] in Whitwell, a village to the northwest and slightly inland of Ventnor.

to calm my worn and harassed mind. Oh! May the Almighty support you and give you strength to bear this.

But one only thought has darkened my brain since you left me, and, dreadful as it is, it is the only atonement I can make. I cannot live, John, and feel myself a blight upon you and on our sweet and innocent child – death is preferable to disgrace – and yet I have so little merited it.

Eternally you have been so good, so kind, and so affectionate. Oh! Still think as kindly of me when I am no more. The slight wrongs I have done let these bitter tears wash from out your heart, and may God pardon my slanderers, as I do. Oh, live to protect and guard our child. She will be a comfort and a blessing to you, and your own good heart will bring you peace.

I am alone;– no one near to stay me. What can I do? – no one near to stay me. What can I do? – wretched, miserable outcast, beggar, bankrupt of all I ever possessed – my fair name. Oh, my head is gone – would that my heart were broken quite! Oh God! Have mercy upon me and pardon and pity me

Bless you, John! God bless you, ever and ever – both in this world and the next!

CHARLOTTE

The next letter was to the servant, and ran thus:–

Do not be frightened, Estcourt, at my going away. I know you will be kind and good to my darling child. Let her believe I am gone home – though it is to my long and last one. I leave you money (£5), which will pay all till your master comes again. I ask you to be kind and good to the child, and do not let her feel for her poor mother.

Friday night.

Their Lordships would observe that by these two letters Mrs James would appear rather to have contemplated the commission of suicide than the adoption of any other or more criminal act.

It had been arranged before Mr James left Ventnor that a relation by marriage should stop with Mrs James, a Mrs Bamford, and when she arrived on the following morning the servant placed the two letters in her hand, and having opened and read a portion of that which had been intended for Mr James, that lady communicated to the unhappy husband what had taken place.

Inquiries were instantly set on foot, and, after considerable difficulty, the parties were traced to Southampton, then to Havre, then to Rouen, then to Paris, and ultimately to a place near St Malo, where a copy of the present bill, together with a copy of their Lordships' order for its second reading, were eventually served upon and fully explained to Mrs James.

That lady, on that occasion, said that nothing wrong had taken place between Mr Crespigny and herself until subsequently to her leaving Ventnor, and she also raised an objection to the last clause in the bill, which went to prohibit her ultimate marriage with that gentleman.[50]

---

[50] This clause was indeed omitted in the final form of the act. The process of inclusion and then removal was standard practice: above at 60.

CHAPTER TWO

> It would be proved also that at each place to which the parties had been traced they had passed and lived as man and wife, occupying the same rooms and the same bed, and that they had gone by the names of Mr and Mrs Rae and Mr and Mrs D'Estair, under which title they were at present living at St Malo.
>
> Having proved these facts, he humbly submitted that their Lordships could have no difficulty in reading the bill a second time.
>
> A number of witnesses were then called, whose testimony went to corroborate in every particular the statement of the learned serjeant; and
>
> > Mr C G Jones, of Gray's-inn-square, the solicitor for the husband, stated, that he produced a copy of the registry of the marriage between Mr and Mrs James, whom he had constantly visited. They had lived on the most affectionate terms, and had had two children, one of whom only had lived. Since Mrs James had gone off another child had been born.[51]
> >
> > He heard of the elopement about the 17th of November, and had at once set out on his enquiries. He first went to Folkestone and Dover; but at neither place could he learn anything of the fugitives. He then, accompanied by one of Mr James's brothers,[52] had gone to other places, and at length, on the 25th of the same month, they obtained a clue at Southampton, which ultimately led to their discovery.
> >
> > He also stated that he had used every effort to induce Mr Crespigny to put in an appearance to an action for *crim con*, but without effect. Indeed, whenever he had had reason to think that gentleman might be in England, he had issued a writ. He had sued out at least seven or eight writs, but in no one instance had an appearance been entered.
>
> The evidence having been brought to a close,
> The Lord Chancellor was understood to move the second reading of the bill, which being agreed to,
> The bill was read a second time accordingly.

At first sight, this is a model petition for divorce, fulfilling all the requirements listed above: evidence of adultery, including the birth of a child which is not the husband's; good – indeed excellent – marital relations right up to the time of elopement; generous and most affectionate conduct by the husband, even acknowledged by Charlotte Frances' parting letter; and though there had been no action for *crim con*, firm evidence that every effort had been made to take one.

On the other hand, considering that the matter was heard by some of the most senior, experienced and competent men of the time, it is extraordinary that no-one asked questions about some of the stranger aspects of the case as presented:

- What was wrong with Charlotte Frances that required her to seek medical advice in London, and why was it regarded as best for her health to retire to a cottage on the Isle of Wight – where she does not appear to have ever been before – rather than returning home to be cared for by a competent local doctor?

---

[51] This is a reference to Ada, first daughter of Charlotte Frances by Philip Robert Crespigny; she had been born on 15 May 1848, ten months before the date of this hearing.

[52] As in note 7 above, John James Junior had two brothers, Edward Lloyd (1811-1875) and Charles (1817-1851). It is uncertain which took part in the search.

- Other than a general assumption of female hysteria, how is her conduct of Friday 12 November to be explained? First she is demonstrating obvious and touching affection for her husband as he departs; then she writes a note which indeed sounds like a preliminary to suicide;[53] and then she elopes at night with Philip Robert Crespigny.
- Finally we may observe that Charlotte Frances' absence was first discovered by a servant on 13 November and advised to Mrs Bamford on the following day. It is reasonable that some time elapsed before John James could be informed and then that he could arrange for his friend and colleague Mr Jones of London to begin a search on 17 November. But why did that search commence at Dover and neighbouring Folkestone rather than at Southampton, which is far closer to the Isle of Wight – indeed just across the Solent? And why did not John James return immediately to Ventnor, rather than leaving it to his brother one week later? The first trace was found on 25 November, almost two weeks after the elopement – perhaps they did not want to catch the fleeing couple?

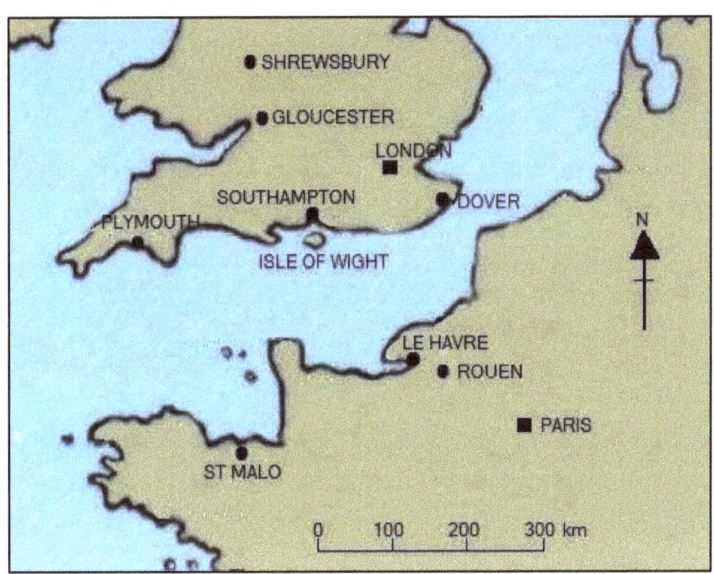

One circumstance which was mentioned and was surely significant, but which was not explored, was the birth of Ada on 15 May 1848. Despite her assertion that "nothing wrong had taken place between Mr Crespigny and herself until subsequently to her leaving Ventnor [in mid-November]" Charlotte Frances would have been three months pregnant when she saw the doctors in London just a few days before that time, and one must assume they were capable of recognising her condition. Whatever he may have believed before, John James should then have been fully aware of the situation – and he does not appear to have been under any illusion that the child was his own.

From that time on at the very least, therefore, and quite likely for several weeks beforehand, John James, Charlotte Frances and Philip Robert Crespigny were engaged together in arranging the elopement and the divorce. John James would not have wanted to continue with an adulterous wife and someone else's child, and everything that happened on the Isle of Wight and afterwards must have been done in collusion.[54] It is impossible to tell whether the

---

[53] It is presumably some account of this letter, at second or third hand or yet further removed, which caused Richard Henry Dana to write of her likely death or even suicide: above at 53.

[54] One further question is raised by the very presence of the family Bible in Australia: how did it get there? It is most unlikely that Charlotte Frances took it with her on the journey with John James to London, then to the Isle of Wight, and then on the elopement to France. A substantial volume, it must surely have aroused suspicion if she had taken it when she left home, and it would have been something of a nuisance on a

witnesses were suborned or were simply deceived by the married couple acting a charade, but we may suspect the number of people aware of the truth would have been kept to a minimum: bribery is one thing, blackmail an unwanted complication.

Perhaps the weakest point was Charlotte Frances' farewell letter. She may have intended to confirm the good conduct of her spouse and their mutual affection, but the exaggerated and melodramatic style fits badly with the events that followed. One feels she should have been given better guidance, though it must be acknowledged that the requirements for a successful petition of divorce – that the husband must have behaved well and there be mutual affection, but adultery must be proved – are somewhat contradictory.

Other petitions at this time were rejected on grounds of collusion, but in this event all went well. Charlotte Frances and Philip Robert made their way to France; no case was brought for criminal conversation; and the bill of divorce allowed both husband and wife to remarry. It probably received final approval in April or May of 1849, and at the beginning of the volume for the Twelfth and Thirteenth Year of the Reign of Her Majesty Queen Victoria, published by Eyre and Spottiswoode in London in 1849 as *A Table of All the STATUTES passed in the SECOND Session of the FIFTEENTH Parliament of the United Kingdom of Great Britain and Ireland, 12o and 13o VICT*, there is a list of "Private Acts, not printed." Item 28 on page xxii identifies

> An Act to dissolve the Marriage of John James with his now Wife, and to enable him to marry again; and for other Purposes.

In 1853 John James married Arabella Veronica Dighton, who bore him a daughter in that same year; she was baptised Vera Maria. After John James died two years later, his widow married Stanley Napier Raikes at Bombay in 1858 but had no further children. Vera Maria James married William Alves Raikes – a kinsman of her stepfather – and bore him three sons; she died in 1942.[55]

The last time Charlotte Frances nee Dana saw her daughter Charlotte Constance James would have been in late October or early November of 1847, when she left their home in Newnham to travel to London – and then to Ventnor and to France. Charlotte Constance had just passed her seventh birthday, but despite all the emotional words and kind wishes in her mother's letters on the Isle of Wight, it does not appear that Charlotte Frances made any attempt to contact her again – nor even to enquire about her. There may have been some correspondence, now lost, but there is no record of it. It was a principle of English law throughout the nineteenth century that a guilty wife lost all rights of custody and even contact with the children of the former marriage:

> A wife convicted, or merely accused, of adultery could be virtually certain that she would never again be permitted to set eyes on her children.[56]

It was a hard system, and one may doubt John James would have sought to make it easier. It is equally hard to contemplate the effect upon their daughter Charlotte Constance.

---

    midnight flit from Ventor. One must assume it was collected later – but that raises more questions about contact between the formally alienated families.

[55] *Anne's Family History* at 2019/07/19 has a detailed account of Charlotte Constance Blood nee James as below. The entry also provides information about Arabella Veronica nee Dighton, her daughter Vera Maria and their marriages.

[56] Stone, *Road to Divorce*, 171.

When John James died in 1855, he left substantial property, including houses and land. A marriage settlement and life interest went to his second wife Arabella Veronica, but there were generous bequests and trusts for his "beloved daughter" Charlotte Constance and her half-sister Vera Maria.

Four years later at the age of eighteen, in January 1859 Constance James married Francis Gamble Blood, an army officer of wealthy family; she was then eighteen years old. The couple had no children for ten years until their son John Neptune Blood was born in November 1869. In June of the very next year, however, Charlotte Constance Blood was granted a divorce from her husband on grounds of his adultery; he did not contest the case.[57]

Francis Gamble Blood died in 1881, leaving Charlotte Constance "his widow" as beneficiary and administrator of his estate, some £13,000. She did not marry again and died in 1935 at the age of ninety-five. She had made no will, but her son John Neptune Blood was granted administration of the estate, almost £20,000. A graduate of Oxford and a barrister, he died unmarried in 1942.[58] It is most improbable that the two families of Charlotte Frances nee Dana made any attempt at connection.

France to Australia

On 18 July 1849, a few weeks after Parliament had approved her divorce from John James, Philip Robert Crespigny married Charlotte Frances nee Dana at the British Embassy in Paris. The event was announced in several English newspapers, including the *London Standard*, *Berrow's Worcester Journal* and the *Bristol Times and Mirror*; the last would have circulated in Newnham-on-Severn, Charlotte Frances' former home with John James.

MARRIAGES
July 18, at the British Embassy, Paris, by the Rev Archdeacon Keating, Philip Champion Crespigny, Esq, youngest son of Charles Fox Champion Crespigny, Esq, to Charlotte Frances, second daughter of Captain William Pulteney Dana.[59]

It had not been an easy time, however, and the situation was not yet by any means secure.

According to the evidence of John James' solicitor Mr Jones, given to the House of Lords on 20 March 1849, in November of 1847 Charlotte Frances and Philip Robert had been followed from Southampton to Le Havre, then to Paris, and they were eventually found near St Malo in Brittany.[60] We are not told why they had taken such a roundabout route – it may have been necessary to register in Paris before taking residence in France – but they evidently settled in that area, for their first child was born there on 15 May 1848.

Still seeking to pass incognito, Philip Robert and Charlotte Frances gave their surname as D'Estrée. Mr Jones would tell the House of Lords that the eloping couple had been calling themselves Rae and D'Estair, and D'Estrée is presumably a development of this last – or he

---

[57] The case of Blood v Blood was reported by the *Hampshire Telegraph and Sussex Chronicle* of 22 June 1870, being issue 3949: retrieved from *Gale nineteenth century British Library newspapers* through the National Library of Australia.

[58] An obituary from the *Gloucester Citizen* is copied in Chapter Seven at 267.

[59] Charlotte Frances was actually the fourth daughter of William Pulteney Dana: besides her elder sister Anna Penelope (1814-1890), there was the short-lived Helen Matilda (1813-1813), both born to his second wife Charlotte Elizabeth nee Bayly [Chapter One at 36]; and there was also his daughter Anne Frisby Dana (1803-1849), child of his first marriage to Anne Fitzhugh [Chapter One at 33]. For the purposes of the announcement, however, it was reasonable to identify Charlotte Frances as his second daughter.

[60] Above at 63.

CHAPTER TWO

may have been slightly mistaken. It is possible their true identity was not discovered until after Ada had been born and christened, and only then was Charlotte Frances served with the writ of divorce. The formal proceedings could not commence until that time.

Two pages from the records of the British Embassy at Paris, 1849
The wedding of Philip Robert Crespigny and Charlotte Frances nee Dana is identified on 18 July

Despite the embarrassment and the very considerable costs, however, there were advantages to divorce. Ada, of course, was not acknowledged by John James, and she felt the stigma of illegitimacy all her life,[61] while by the time the parliamentary divorce was approved Charlotte Frances was already pregnant with her second child by Philip Robert. Philip was born on 4 January 1850, six months after his parents' wedding, and was christened on 14 January by the Reverend John Penleaye in the British Chapel at St Servan.

This time the surname appears as Crespigny, while both father and son have the given names Philip Champion, with Champion serving as a second personal name.[62] The Reverend Penleaye and other members of the local British community surely noticed the difference.

---

[61] Her great-nephew Francis Philip (Frank) Champion de Crespigny (1918-2010) remembered her: "Mad as a snake; never got over it."

[62] Apart from the supernumerary Champion, the boy had no given name but Philip. His father, however, had been baptised Philip Robert at Boulogne-sur-Mer in 1822. To save confusion, this work regularly refers to him as Philip Robert.

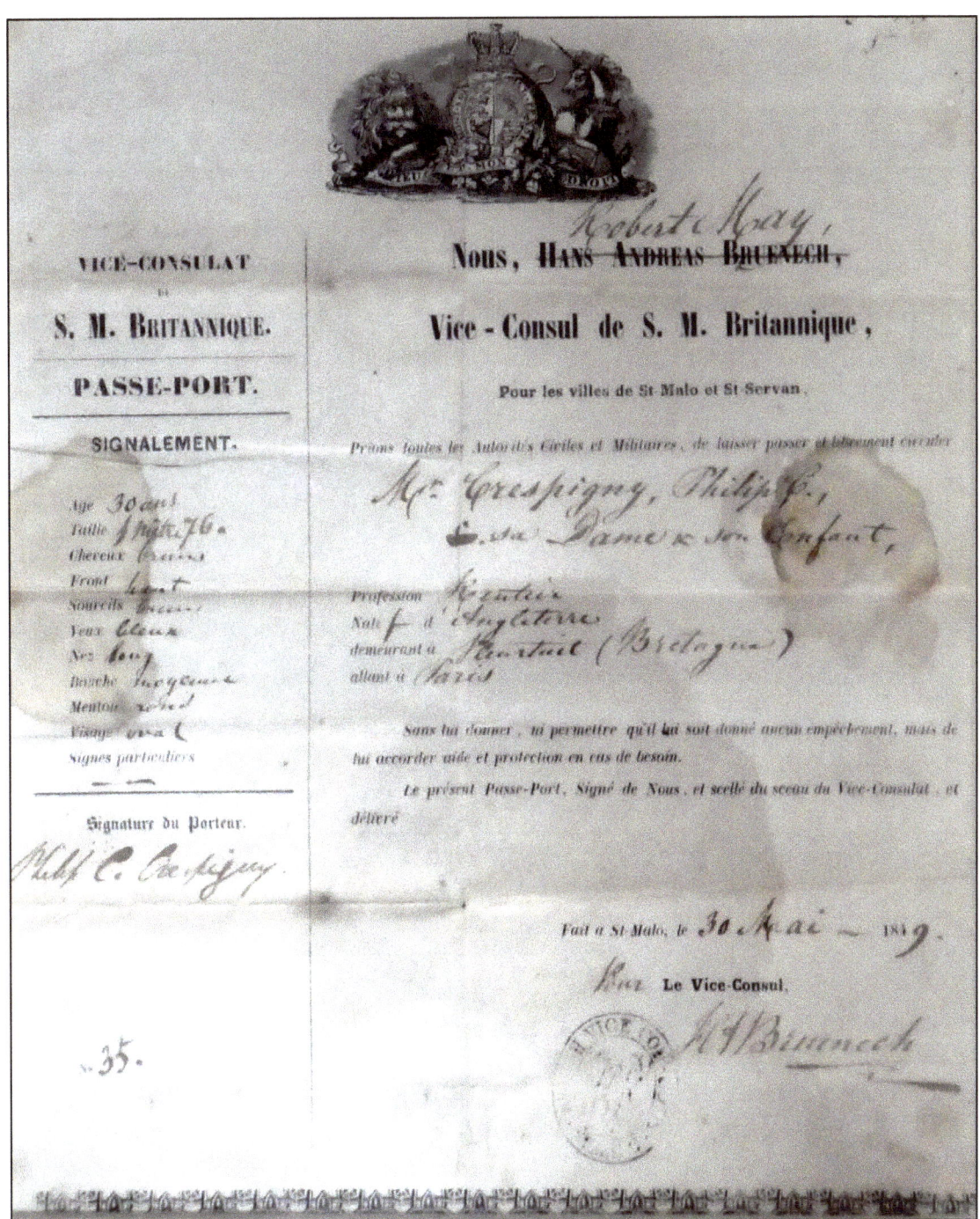

*Passport issued on 30 May 1849 by the British Consulate at St Malo
for Philip C Crespigny [Philip Robert Champion Crespigny] to travel to Paris
with his wife/lady companion [sa Dame] and a male child [son Enfant: this last, of course, was incorrect]*

The document was signed on behalf of the Vice-Consul; the reverse was stamped by the office of the mayor of St Malo on 30 May, by the British Embassy at Paris on 19 July, and by the prefecture of police at Paris on 20 July.

Passports at that time did not have photographs, but they did describe the bearer. The column on the left hand side headed Signalement [*Description/Particulars*], *identifies Philip Robert as:*

Age: 30 years	Height: 1 metre 76 cm	Hair: brown
Forehead: high	Eyebrows brown	Eyes: blue
Nose: long	Mouth: medium	Chin: round
Face: oval	Distinguishing marks [Signes particuliers]: none	

It was standard practice to record a man's beard or moustache [e.g. Russell, Special Correspondent, *315, describing the papers of a French soldier killed at Sedan in the Franco-Prussian War], so Philip Robert was probably clean-shaven at this time. Compare, however, his photograph of 1879 in Chapter Five at 200.*

CHAPTER TWO

Two extracts from the Registry of Christenings at the British Protestant Chapel in St Servan
showing [above]: the baptism of Isadora Ada Charlotte surnamed D'Estrée on 4 July 1849
and [below, identified in blue]: those of her brothers Philip Champion Crespigny on 14 January 1850
and Constantine Trent Pulteney Crespigny [usually as Constantine Pulteney Trent] on 28 May 1851
Source: Grayden, Chronicle, documents at 31

In the records of baptism the family address is given simply as St Malo, but on the passport issued for Philip Robert, Charlotte Frances and their infant daughter to travel to Paris for their wedding in 1849 it appears as Pleurtuit, a village on the east of the River Rance opposite St Malo and south of Dinard.[63] They had evidently purchased or leased a house there and they remained for two years, from 1849 to 1851. Their third child and second son was born on 5 May 1851 and christened Constantine Trent Pulteney at St Servan on 28 May.[64] Several kinsmen of Philip Robert's mother, Julia nee Trent, had borne the personal name Constantine, while Pulteney was a tribute to Charlotte Frances' family.

By this time, however, it had become apparent that the family could not remain indefinitely in France. Since the divorce case was concluded, it was formally possible for Philip Robert and Charlotte Frances to return to England as husband and wife, but there were surely problems.

---

[63] The writing of the name on the passport is difficult to read, and appears more like Fleurtuil. There is, however, no such place anywhere near St Malo, and we must assume it is Pleurtuit.

[64] The order of his given names, however, appears more commonly as Constantine Pulteney Trent, and he is often identified as Constantine Trent without the Pulteney.

Constantine Pulteney Trent's great-nephew, second son of his brother Philip, was named in his memory as Constantine Trent. He was known privately as Con, but after he was knighted in 1941 he was formally identified as Sir Trent.

St Malo, Brittany, and its neighbourhood
detail from Michelin France *2003 sheet 35*
St Servan-sur-Mer, south of St Malo, and Pleurtuit, south of Dinard, are identified in blue

Despite the energy with which John James' solicitor Mr Jones claimed to have pursued Philip Robert for an action of criminal conversation – with its implication of heavy damages – it had been something of a formality for the divorce, and is unlikely the attempt would have been renewed now the proceedings were over. There was increasing rejection of the idea that a woman was her husband's property, and it was now believed that demanding money for her misconduct was unacceptable.[65] If there ever had been a threat, it existed no longer.

Two major difficulties were, firstly, the possible embarrassment and potential ostracism of returning to society after a well-publicised and widely discussed divorce; and second, somewhat related, the difficulty of finding meaningful employment for Philip Robert. Discussing the case in March 1851 – albeit at second- or third-hand – Richard Henry Dana expressed firm disapproval and, in a sense of *Schadenfreude*, described the couple as living in poverty near Paris, with some expectation that Charlotte Frances might kill herself for

---

[65] See, for example, Stone, *Road to Divorce*, 297.

shame.⁶⁶ He was of course mistaken: they were successfully married, living near St Malo, with Charlotte Frances expecting her third child.

It is impossible to say what prospects there may have been in England. Evidence is vague and contradictory, but indications are that members of the aristocracy and landed classes were more tolerant, while those of professional and business background could be stricter. Where Charlotte Frances might have found herself on this spectrum is difficult to say: divorced from a lawyer, but married to a family with at least some connection to the gentry. She may not have wished to find out.

Richard Henry Dana also claimed that Charles Fox had reduced his son's allowance, and there are indeed indications that he was less wealthy than before.⁶⁷. Philip Robert describes himself as "gentleman" or "esquire" on the children's baptismal certificates, and his passport of 1849 has his profession or occupation as *Rentier*: of independent means. Nothing is known about the size of the house the family was living in, nor the number of servants, but though expenses in Brittany need not have been high there is no mention of employment.

Philip Robert had probably some command of the French language, for he had been born at Boulogne and spent some years there as a child, but he had no obviously marketable skills. It is likely that he passed some time at Saint Malo building the model yacht *Ariel*, probably with the aid of a local boat-builder or a fisherman out of season. Some five feet/1.5 metres from keel to mast-head and from bowsprit to stern, the ship is mentioned in a letter by Charlotte Frances in Australia,⁶⁸ it came later to her daughter Rose Beggs, then to Rose's

A goélette [*schooner*] *from Paimpol, a hundred kilometres west of St Malo in Brittany*
from a nineteenth-century postcard

---

⁶⁶ *Journal*, 418, quoted at 53 above.
⁶⁷ Chapter Five at 173-174.
⁶⁸ Letter 49 from Charlotte Frances to her daughter Ada, 24 November 1903: Chapter Six at 246.

Model ship Ariel *at sea at Grange, South Australia* c.1950

Model ship Ariel *at Lilli Pilli, NSW, 2020*

great-nephew Richard Geoffrey CdeC (1907-1966), and is now with Geoff's son Rafe. The style is that of a Breton schooner – and this period of enforced idleness appears to be the only occasion Philip Robert would have had opportunity for such a project.

Earning money in England was likely to be difficult. Though he had been, however briefly, at Cambridge University, Philip Robert had no formal qualifications. He was not a lawyer, and if he had acquired any experience in dealing with his father's landed estates it was probably no more than incidental. And while he might not be ostracised in the manner that Charlotte Frances might have feared, his reputation as a co-respondent in a scandalous divorce was not a factor in his favour. Why would anyone employ him?

At this point in a difficult set of circumstances, Charlotte Frances' brothers appear to have offered a solution – though not an easy one.

We have seen that the marriage of Philip Robert Crespigny to Charlotte Frances nee Dana had been reported in several newspapers in England soon after the ceremony in Paris on 18 July 1849. Five months later, on 15 December, a short item in almost exactly the same words was published by the *Melbourne Daily News*.[69]

By this time, two of Charlotte Frances' brothers, Henry Edmund Pulteney Dana (1817-1852) and William Augustus Pulteney Dana (1826-1866) were both in Australia, Henry in charge of a force of native police and William one of his officers.[70] Their story is considered in the next chapter, but it appears that despite the distance they were in good contact with their sister and were aware of her situation. As Commandant of Native Police, Henry Dana had a substantial position in the new-found settlement and was on good and trusted terms with Charles La Trobe, the Superintendent of Port Phillip District who would become Lieutenant-Governor of Victoria in 1851.[71] It is probable that Henry suggested Charlotte and her family come to Australia, and offered some assurance that he could find her husband a position in the government service.

The invitation would have arrived early in 1851, but there was one immediate difficulty: Charlotte Frances was pregnant at the time and Constantine Trent was born on 5 May. While some migrants to Australia were accompanied by their small children, and there could be a number of births during a three-month sea passage, it was not an ideal plan.

The alternative was little better, but no doubt seemed so at the time. With great generosity, Charles Fox Crespigny and his wife Eliza Julia undertook to care for their new-born grandson and to bring him up in England.

Domestic arrangements were already complicated, for the census of 30 March 1851 recorded Charles Fox and Eliza Julia Crespigny at Harefield House in Middlesex. Some

---

[69] Trove 226324213.

[70] The use of the name Pulteney in this later generation of the Dana family is slightly confused. Both Henry Edmund and William Augustus had the third given name of Pulteney. Both made use of all three, but the use is not constant and the spelling often omits the first *e*. Given that their father's effective connection to the Pulteney family had ended in 1804 – as in Chapter One at 35 – it is a little strange that the name was still in use. See also Fels, *Good Men and True*, 265 note 4.

[71] The first permanent white settlement in what is now Victoria was at Portland Bay in the southwest in 1834, but John Batman established a settlement at present-day Melbourne in 1835 and Captain William Lonsdale was appointed police magistrate and superintendent of the Port Phillip District in the following year; he was succeeded by Charles La Trobe [also as Latrobe] in 1839. The District was a subordinate territory of New South Wales, based upon Sydney, until its establishment as the independent colony of Victoria under the British crown in July 1851. In 1901 Victoria became a state of the Commonwealth of Australia.

twenty miles northeast of London, the property was formally owned by Charles Fox's elder half-brother Philip, now eighty-five years old. Philip, as we have seen, had been interned in France during the Napoleonic wars after the ending of the Treaty of Amiens in 1803. He had there married the wealthy heiress Emilia Wade and subsequently escaped to return to England.[72] The couple had no children, and Emma died in 1832. In 1848, at the age of eighty-one, Philip had been assessed as a "lunatic" and placed in the care of his half-brother and sister-in-law; he was probably suffering from senile dementia.[73] Also in the household at Harefield were Charles Fox and Eliza Julia's younger daughter Eliza Constantia Frances (1825-1898), their eldest son Charles John (1814-1880) and his son, their grandson, Charles Stanley (1848-1907). Born in June, Charles Stanley was just three years older than his cousin Constantine Trent. There were nine female servants and three male "doormen."

During the First World War Harefield House served as an Australian military hospital.
It is now a specialist heart and lung centre within the British National Health Service

In 1847 Charles John Crespigny had married Emma Margaret Smith, daughter of a civil servant in the East India Company, but she died two months after the birth of their son Charles Stanley, and he returned to live with his parents. He would make a second marriage in 1854, to Margaretta Amyatt Brown, but she died in the following year, one week after giving birth to a son who lived just one day. He married for a third time in 1859, but had no children by his new wife, Frances nee Plunkett.[74] The census of 1861 recorded Charles John and Frances living at Cheltenham in Gloucestershire with his son Charles Stanley and a single servant. For several years in the 1850s, however, Charles Stanley had also stayed in the

---

[72] See above at 56 and note 32.
[73] An account of the Commission of Lunacy, which had been initiated by Charles Fox, was published by the *Cheltenham Examiner* of 13 December. The hearing took place in the drawing room of Harefield House, Philip himself was examined, other witnesses were called, and the jury returned a unanimous verdict.
[74] After Charles' death, Frances married John Russell Reynolds (1828-1896), a distinguished physician and neurologist with appointment to Queen Victoria; he was made a baronet in 1895. See also Clayton, *Martin-Leake*, 8.

CHAPTER TWO

care of his grandparents, and letters to Australia refer to his companionship with Constantine Trent. Charles Fox's wife Eliza Julia died in 1856, but her unmarried daughter Eliza Constantia Frances played a considerable role in caring for the two boys.

Census return of 1851 for Harefield House in Middlesex
While Philip Champion Crespigny is named as the Householder, he is identified as a "lunatic" and his brother Charles Fox ChC is identified as the head of the household; both are described as Landed Proprietors. Charles Fox's son Charles John is marked as the Guardian of the Householder [Philip].
Charles Fox ChC's wife Eliza Julia, their daughter Eliza Constantia [Frances] and their grandson Charles [Stanley] are also listed. The census was taken on 30 March – Constantine Trent ChC had not yet been born.

In the spring of 1851, therefore, Philip Robert and Charlotte Frances Crespigny brought their children Ada, Philip and Constantine Trent from France to England. Late in November they left Constantine Trent, now six months old, with his grandparents and his aunt, and on 4 December the rest of the family – husband and wife, two children, and one servant – sailed from Plymouth in Devon on the ship *Cambodia*. Among just over three hundred passengers, they were the only party in cabin class, the highest grade of accommodation.[75]

Constantine Trent would not see his parents or his brother and sister again for twenty-four years.[76]

---

[75] Victoria, Australia, Assisted and Unassisted Passenger Lists, 1839-1923; United Kingdom Immigrants 1850-1854, 191-203 at 203. See also Chapter Three at 95-96 and note 64 to Chapter Five.

[76] This was the second time Charlotte Frances had left a child behind: the first was her daughter Charlotte Constance James, abandoned when she eloped with Philip Robert four years earlier. Almost half a century before, Charlotte Frances' father William Pulteney Dana had also left a daughter in America: Chapter One at 33.

Based upon the fact that Philip Robert and Charlotte Frances were in France in 1848 when a rebellion deposed King Louis Philippe, an enthusiastic family legend claims that they were close personal friends of the monarch and were obliged to escape on the first available ship – to Australia. This is nonsense: Charlotte Frances was fully occupied at that time with having her first baby – out of wedlock – by Philip Robert, and they would not travel to Australia for another three years.

FORD MADOX BROWN (1821-1893): THE LAST OF ENGLAND; OIL ON PANEL 1855
NOW IN THE COLLECTION OF THE BIRMINGHAM MUSEUM AND ART GALLERY

A note on the Crespigny surname

There was some confusion about the surname Crespigny and its variants at this time. The family was originally French, based in Normandy, and until the early seventeenth century the surname was Champion. In 1617, however, Richard Champion married Marguerite nee Richard, and through her acquired the small estate of Crespigny – Crépigny in present-day orthography. As Champion was a common surname, members of the family frequently called themselves Champion de Crespigny or even de Crespigny as a means of distinction.

The Richard family, previous owners of Crespigny, were Huguenots – French Protestants – and Richard Champion and his descendants adopted that creed. At the end of the century, however, as Louis XIV sought to force Huguenots back to Roman Catholicism the Champion de Crespigny family – with many others – took refuge in England from his persecution.

Chapter Two

For most of the eighteenth century the family regularly used the surname Crespigny for both official and private purposes, with Champion appearing rather as a secondary name. Champion de Crespigny was used in some formal documents such as wills, however, and two houses were given the name Champion Lodge. When Claude Crespigny (1834-1818) was granted a baronetcy in 1805, however, he adopted the full surname Champion de Crespigny and his descendants followed; often reducing it in practice to de Crespigny.

Sir Claude's younger brother Philip Crespigny (1738-1803), however, father of Charles Fox and grandfather of Philip Robert, did not make the change, and he and his descendants continued to style themselves Crespigny, with Champion as a secondary name, sometimes expressed only by the initial C; examples may be found in the passport and other documents relating to Philip Robert in France in the late 1840s.

For much of the nineteenth century, therefore, though members of the two lineages were related as cousins, they used different versions of the surname and slightly different coats of arms. It was not until the latter part of that century that the non-baronet branch of the family took Champion de Crespigny as the full and formal surname, and it was not adopted in Australia until the 1890s, at the instigation of Philip Robert and Charlotte Frances' son Philip.

Bookplate of Constantine Trent ChdeC (1882-1952)
grandson of Philip Robert Champion Crespigny and Charlotte Frances nee Dana,
showing the basic coat of arms commonly used by the Australian family.
A formal blazon would be: Quarterly: 1 and 4 (Champion de Crespigny), *argent [white], a lion salient sable, armed and langued gules [a black lion leaping, with red claws and tongue], in dexter base, a fer de moulin pierced of the second [in the lower left corner, a formalised cross with a central hole]; a crescent for cadency. The lion salient may also appear as* rampant *[clawing, with one foot off the ground.*
2 and 3 (Vierville), azure, three bars argent *[blue, with three white bars].*
The CdeC family had married with the Vierville family in the seventeenth century, and attached their arms. The small crescent of cadency, indicating a second son and his descendants as a junior branch, was adopted by Philip Champion Crespigny (1738-1803), younger brother of the first baronet Sir Claude (1734-1818) and father of Charles Fox Champion Crespigny.
Sir Claude adopted the full surname Champion de Crespigny, and his descendants in the baronet lineage followed. Descendants of Philip and Charles Fox kept the shorter surname until the late nineteenth century.
As the male line of the baronetcy ended in 1952, the crescent of cadency became unnecessary.
Further discussion of the surname, the history and the arms is in RdeC, Champions from Normandy

CHAPTER THREE

VICTORIA IN THE GOLD RUSH

The Dana brothers and the native police
Family in Victoria
Commissioner, Magistrate and Warden of the Goldfields
Letters from home

The Dana brothers and the native police
Born in 1817, Henry Edmund Pulteney Dana was the fourth child of William Pulteney Dana and his second wife Charlotte Elizabeth nee Bayly.[1] An older sister and an older brother had died in infancy, however, so Henry was the eldest surviving son; Anna Penelope, born in 1814, was his elder sister. Charlotte Frances came next in 1820.

There is little information about Henry Dana before his arrival at Launceston in Van Diemen's Land – now Tasmania – on 3 September 1839.[2] There are various theories about his education and prior experience, but it does not appear that he had any formal qualifications or training. He did, however, have the manners of a gentleman and letters of introduction to the Governor, Sir John Franklin.[3]

No specific reason is known why Henry Dana decided to come to Australia. Passages took three months, so he would have embarked in early June or the end of May, at least a year before his father's imprisonment for insolvency. There may have been forewarnings, and perhaps an increasing shortage of money, but it is likely the young man was finding limited opportunity in England. As Fels remarks, though he may have people to recommend him, he had no obvious sponsor in the civil or military hierarchy. The most useful would have been his uncle, Lieutenant-General George Dana, but he was long retired and had died in 1837.[4]

---

[1] On many occasions in this work it has seemed sensible to use the full personal names of individuals – as, for example, referring to Charlotte Frances nee Dana to distinguish her from her mother Charlotte Eliza nee Bayly and from her daughter Charlotte Constance James. For the two brothers Dana considered here and below, however, use of the full names would be clumsy and unnecessary. We refer to them simply as Henry and William.

On the other hand, as remarked in note 70 to Chapter Two, both Henry Edmund Pulteney Dana and his younger brother William Augustus Pulteney Dana regularly used all three of their personal names – though with variant spellings of Pulteney – and all three initials.

A number of official documents have Henry's second name Edmund as Edward. The two forms are often interchanged, but Henry was surely named after his grandfather the Reverend Edmund Dana, and that is the style he used on personal forms such as his marriage certificate and the birth certificates of his children.

[2] Van Diemen's Land had been named after Antony van Diemen, the Governor of the Netherlands East India Company who sent Abel Tasman to circumnavigate Australia in 1642. In 1803 the British colony of New South Wales established a small military outpost near present-day Hobart, and the island was made a separate colony in 1825.

For the first part of the nineteenth century Van Diemen's Land was the major penal settlement in Australia, but transportation of convicts ended in 1853 and the name was changed to Tasmania in 1857.

[3] The Shipping List published by the *Launceston Advertiser* of Thursday 5 September recorded the arrival of the barque *Arab*, 291 tons, on 3 September; the passenger list included Mr Henry Edmund Dana: Trove 84752591. All passengers appear to have travelled in the same class.

Fels, *Good Men and True*, 44-47, has an account of Henry Dana's background and his initial reception. He had very likely attended Bridgnorth Grammar School: Chapter Two at 39.

[4] On George Kinnaird Dana (1770-1837), see Chapter One at 21-24.

CHAPTER THREE

At that time a steady pressure from economic conditions was encouraging emigration from Britain, and though the greater number crossed the Atlantic to Canada or the United States the Australian colonies were a recognised destination. In the early 1830s, as the South Australian Company was seeking settlers for its venture at present-day Adelaide, one of its major expenses was publicity:

> Leaflets were scattered among the people broadcast, and not only hundreds but thousands of desirable immigrants had their minds directed towards the object of getting away from the curse of over-competition and into a land where their energies might have freer scope. Advertisements were inserted in the leading newspapers, and a good deal of literature on the subject of colonisation was kept in stock.[5]

So information and encouragement were widespread, and the propects for many young men appeared greater than at home.

Despite his letters of recommendation, Henry Dana did not obtain government appointment in Hobart. A memorandum from the Colonial Treasurer to the Colonial Secretary gave some reasons – in kindly fashion:[6]

> I had an interview with His Excellency this afternoon and explained to him my reasons for not recommending the appointment of Mr Dana.....
>
> Though I have not the slightest objection to make against Mr Dana personally, and on the contrary cheerfully admit the advantages of having a young man attached to my office who is evidently a thorough gentleman, still he will be for a considerable time of little use as an assistant to me, never having been a clerk before and therefore having no knowledge of accounts or book-keeping...

One may suspect that this was in any case not the sort of work that Henry Dana had in mind, and that both he and the Colonial Treasurer were fortunate their relationship went no further.

Unsuccessful in that possibility, Henry Dana looked to the Australian mainland. At the beginning of 1840 he worked in partnership with Robert Savage on the sheep run Nangeela near Portland Bay, but the seasons were bad, the venture did not do well and the property was sold at a sheriff's sale eighteen months later. A sheriff's sale is the public auction of a property which has been foreclosed because the mortgage payments have not been kept up – Nangeela fetched £230, no more than the cost of a bullock dray and the team to draw it.[7]

In *Letters from Victorian Pioneers*, the more successful squatter John Robertson of Wando Vale described the young men who took properties at this time:

> Few of them knew anything of mechanics, and they were totally unable to make comfort for themselves or their servants..... The three eventful years, which will long be remembered in this colony, of 1841-2-3, swept off most of these young gentlemen with their herds and all.[8]

Now styling himself as Captain Dana,[9] Henry returned to Van Diemen's Land and sought appointment in charge of the Customs office at Launceston, again without success. Soon

---

[5] Sutherland, *The South Australian Company*, 40.
[6] Job applications and comments, CSO [Colonial Secretary's Office] 5/212/5285, in the Archives Office of Tasmania; quoted by Fels, *Good Men and True*, 47.
[7] Fels, *Good Men and True*, 47 and 266 notes 14 and 15, citing also John G Robertson of Wando Vale near Casterton in western Victoria in *Letters from Victorian Pioneers*, 25.
[8] Robertson as above.
[9] Fels, *Good Men and True*, 47, remarks that the original licence for Nangeela identifies Henry Dana with the title Captain: "though there is no hint of military rank in the Van Diemen's Land correspondence; the military title is a Bass Strait acquisition."

afterwards, however, claiming some experience in dealing with the aborigines, presumably in the Portland Bay area, he managed to persuade George Robinson, Protector of Aborigines in the Port Phillip District, to propose him as an officer of the Native Police, and he supported Robinson's recommendation with his own importunities to Charles La Trobe, Superintendent of the District. In January 1842 he was given charge of the Corps. The salary was not high – £100 a year – but this was the maximum La Trobe was entitled to authorise without reference to Sydney.[10] Henry Dana was no doubt glad to have it and there was room for development.

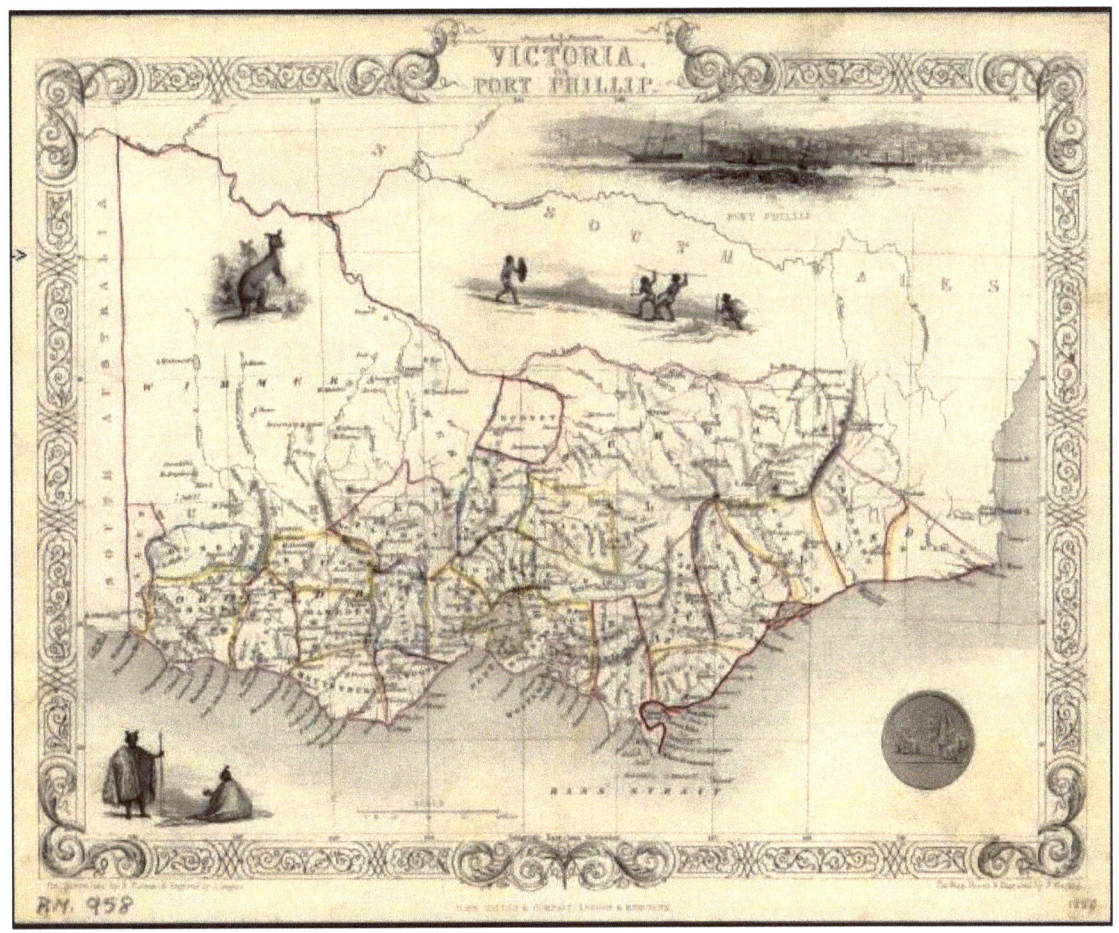

Victoria, or Port Phillip District, 1851
Map drawn & engraved by John Rapkin; illustrations by A. Warren and engraved by J Rogers;
John Tallis & Company, London and New York 1851; copy from the National Library of Australia

In an entry headed "Native Police," the *Port Phillip Gazette* of 2 March approved the new establishment:

> Mr Dana, lately holding the commission of Lieutenant in Her Majesty's army, has received instructions, through the local government, to organise a corps of native police. The system entirely meets our approbation; it will certainly prove a good way of employing native adults, and may become advantageous to the colonists....
>
> Mr Dana has been allowed to select out of the Yarra Yarra tribe, now nearly extinct, twelve men most suited to the undertaking. Some are remarkably intelligent – many have long been in communication with Europeans – and all can talk so much English, as to render it unnecessary for the officer to acquire the native tongue before joining the force.

---

[10] At *Good Men and True*, 48, Fels remarks that there was no formal letter of appointment, but only verbal instructions. The *Port Phillip Gazette*, as immediately below, has the salary as £120, but Fels' statement of the limit to La Trobe's discretion is presumably correct.

CHAPTER THREE

> Mr Dana has been appointed on a salary of £120 a year, with the prospect of being confirmed in the post with a higher salary, should he succeed in the task committed to his care and sagacity.[11]

On 15 April, perhaps with a touch of irony, the Hobart *Courier* announced that

> The friends of that enterprising settler H P Dana, Esq, will be much gratified at hearing of his being appointed to the command of the Melbourne Native Mounted Police.[12]

The idea of using a native police force to support the colonial government had been attempted before. In 1837 Captain William Lonsdale, first Superintendent of the Port Phillip District,[13] had been faced with the need to establish control and good order in the newly-established settlement. While neither the white settlers nor the local aborigines were a cause of serious trouble, there was concern about runaway convicts and the threat of bushrangers, and Lonsdale had only some thirty men of his own infantry regiment and a few civil police under his command. Warning the colonial administration in Sydney that his force was too small for effective action, he asked for a detachment of mounted police. After some discussion Governor Sir Richard Bourke authorised him to recruit and make use of "the Aboriginal natives."

In many respects, a native police force offered an excellent solution to several of the problems which faced the fledgling government of the District. It introduced a number of natives to the discipline and the benefits of European society, encouraging their future assimilation; it created a means for communication between settlers and local tribes; and – perhaps best of all – it was inexpensive: black troopers were far less costly than white ones.

It was nonetheless an extraordinary venture, for the men to be recruited were full-blood aborigines who had only recently encountered white men and their ways. Mounted on horses and supplied with guns, they were not only expected to assist in dealing with other natives but were also authorised to supervise and if necessary to arrest British settlers and convicts. Lonsdale and others believed the program would "civilise" the men and, by degrees, wean them from "their native habits and prejudices." In practice, the men of the Native Police Corps negotiated between two worlds. Provided with rations and uniforms and encouraged in *esprit de corps*, they acquired essential English and carried themselves well in settler society, while despite tribal tensions they enhanced their position in their own communities.[14]

This circumstance, however, while it made the native troopers exceptional, meant that they could not be readily settled within the regular discipline of a Western-style police or military force. Men might be recruited for service, and they regularly behaved in orderly fashion and effectively, but they were always volunteers and they held no abstract allegiance to any white-man's regime. Their loyalty was personal, and British officers had to earn their respect and gain their trust. Their commander needed a special combination of qualities: a

---

[11] Trove 225012744; paragraphing adjusted for clarity.
It may be observed that Henry Dana is identified here only as a Lieutenant, not as a Captain, while the regiment in which he may have served is – not surprisingly – unnamed.

[12] Trove 2954501.

[13] The Port Phillip District was named in honour of Captain Arthur Phillip, first Governor of New South Wales. Whereas the given name Philip is spelt with one *l*, his surname had two.

[14] Fels, *Good Men and True*, 15-22, has a sensitive discussion of the mixed and often contradictory motives of the different parties to the program.

strong personality; a total lack of prejudice about colour or caste; a great sense of concern for those under his charge; and a high tolerance for their individual needs.

Black Troopers Escorting a Prisoner from Ballarat to Melbourne 1851
from William Strutt, Victoria the Golden: Scenes, sketches and jottings from nature, 1850-1862
Collection of the Victorian Parliamentary Library

For there was a further factor in the nature of the native policemen: as members of tribes they had social and ritual responsibilities outside the bonds of government service. There were occasions for hunting, for meetings and for ceremonies which could require attendance at several times of the year, notably in the summer months from December to March, and absence with or without leave was ingrained in the conditions of service. Any officer who could not recognise that reality was doomed to fail.

The first recruitment for a native police force took place in the second half of 1837, and the first commander was Christiaan de Villiers.[15] Born to a good family background in South Africa in 1808, he came to Port Phillip from Launceston in July of 1836 and, according to Lonsdale when he recommended his appointment, he had lived among natives and had gained their respect and affection.

The new Corps attracted fifteen men, and headquarters were set at Narre Warren, in good country thirty-five kilometres southeast of Melbourne, where buildings for accommodation and stores were constructed, together with a parade ground.[16] Unfortunately, however, the enterprise lasted just ten weeks, for there were complaints from the head of a local mission, the Reverend George Langhorne, who saw de Villiers as a rival to his own authority and whose vision for the native people did not include such independent action.

Under this pressure, with only limited support from Lonsdale, de Villiers resigned in indignation. After several months' confusion, the Corps was re-formed once more under his command, now based at Melbourne, and it operated effectively both locally and on patrol to

---

[15] An account of de Villiers and his enterprises is given by Fels, *Good Men and True*, 12-41.
[16] The place was initially known as Nerre Nerre Warren, but we follow the modern usage.

CHAPTER THREE

the Goulburn River. As Langhorne continued to interfere, however, de Villiers resigned again, and though Langhorne sought to take over the men simply walked away. This second troop was disbanded in January 1839 after no more than fifteen weeks. De Villiers retired into private life, kept an inn, and played no further part.

Attempts were made over the next few years to use natives as police under Protectors of the Aborigines, but that system was designed to bring native people into settled reservations; the men were clumsily managed, the program was unsuccessful, and the experiment was left in abeyance.[17]

From the time of his appointment in 1839 Superintendent La Trobe had been under pressure from outlying settlers, from public opinion in Melbourne and from colonial headquarters at Sydney, to provide an effective police force for country districts where there was a general need for security against both the native tribes and European runaways and robbers. Regular police were suitable for local disturbances, but they were not widely effective and, as always, they were considered expensive and extravagant. In 1841 La Trobe resolved to revive the native police after the system which had applied under de Villiers, and he was persuaded that Henry Dana was a suitable leader.

La Trobe would later recall how "circumstances encouraged me to make the trial [of reviving the scheme], and Mr Henry P Dana was, on his own urgent and repeated applications, with but moderate encouragement in many respects, authorized to undertake the task."[18] Though the two men would become close friends, they do not appear to have had any previous contact, and one must assume it was Henry Dana's enthusiasm that got him the job – while there may not have been many applicants for such a strange position.

In January 1842 Henry Dana was accompanied to Narre Warren by Assistant Protector William Thomas. This had been the headquarters site of the first venture, but it had later been developed as a settlement station for the natives, with huts for their white supervisors, a paddock for grazing and some planting of wheat and potatoes. The people were unwilling to settle permanently, however, and equally reluctant to earn their rations by daily work in the fields, so the new program was received with a good deal of interest. As recruitment took place over the first weeks, rations, clothing and blankets were distributed, and on 23 February 1841 there was an inaugural ceremony. Dressed in new uniforms, the troopers were addressed in English and in translations of their own languages, and were then formally sworn in, each making his mark. Almost every man was the leader of a tribal group and the total of this initial contingent was twenty-two. In later years the figure would reach forty or fifty.

The effect of the first ceremony was confirmed by a formal parade each Sunday, followed by prayers or a church service. Discipline was loose, for it is difficult to punish men who can walk away at any time, and the chief sanction for bad behaviour was a few days solitary confinement, a serious matter for men who relied heavily on kinfolk and community. The common offences were absence without leave – though leave was regularly granted for good cause – and drunkenness.

---

[17] Fels, *Good Men and True*, 32-41, discusses this policy.
[18] In January 1853, following Henry Dana's death, La Trobe wrote to Sir John Pakington, former Secretary of State for War and the Colonies, praising his achievement. The full text of his letter is printed as an appendix to *Letters from Victorian Pioneers* at 266-269; this passage is at 267. See further below at 95.

The Headquarters of the Native Police Corps at Narre Warren
Sketch by Eugene von Guérard, 21 February 1855
Collection of the State Library of New South Wales

Aboriginal troopers, Melbourne police, with English corporal, 1850
from William Strutt, Victoria the Golden

Chapter Three

The heart of the Corps was the troopers' personal and mutual loyalty to the officers and their fellows, to the prestige of the uniform, the horses, the swords and the guns, and to the sense of pride gained by playing a recognised role in the settler community, with authority among their tribal fellows for such an achievement.

Above all, as commander of the enterprise Henry Dana established a personal connection to his men and to their families. He was careful of their health and cared for them when they were sick, while his regulations insisted that the [white] non-commissioned officers should treat their troopers "with the greatest forbearance and humanity;" any complaints of ill-treatment were to be reported promptly to the commander.[19] More generally, Henry Dana had a strong personality, enhanced by a natural arrogance, a sense of style and a taste for display. The Port Phillip District had many officers and men in uniform, but Dana was willing to match the best. His officers were splendid in blue and gold, red and white, with black Wellington boots, "so gorgeous as to belong nowadays in comic opera."[20] Non-commissioned officers – white sergeants or corporals and some native corporals – could be even more distinctive, with the addition of a long carbine, pistols and a sword. The troopers wore fine quality cloth, with uniforms of blue or green, depending upon the season, enhanced with red.

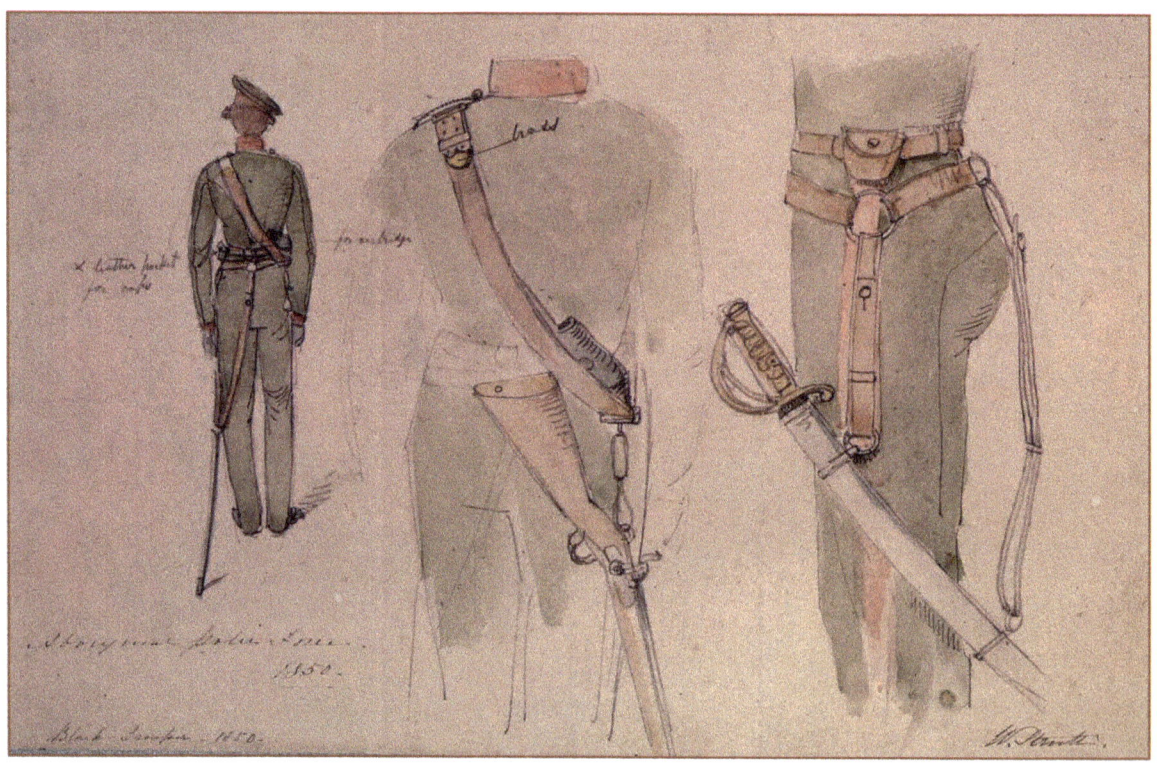

Aboriginal Police Force 1850: Black Troopers, pencil and watercolour by William Strutt
From Victoria the Golden
One of Strutt's earliest commissions, this sheet of sketches shows the winter uniforms of the Native Police Corps, green with a red stripe on the trousers, red collar and cuffs, a cap with a matching band, leather belts and a sash with brass buckles. Each man was armed with a sword and a bayonet, and carried a short carbine and a leather cartridge box.

The native police had the same responsibilities towards the settler community and the tribes of the region as their white counterparts, and Superintendent La Trobe decided how they

---

[19] The Rules and Regulations of the Corps of 1842 are in Appendix A of Fels, *Good Men and True*, 228-232.
[20] Fels, *Good Men and True*, 84-85.

would be deployed. The basic procedure was that of the traditional policeman on the beat. The Corps was divided into three divisions and each season, while one remained at headquarters the others "perambulated" one of the three territories into which Port Phillip District was divided: Portland Bay – now the Western District – Lower Murray or Gippsland. They made frequent patrols, establishing a forceful presence for the law and, as Dana put it in his Rules and Regulations of 1842, and confirmed in correspondence with La Trobe,

> They are at all times to be in readiness when called upon by any Magistrate to accompany him forthwith to assist in the capture of any bushranger or runaways he may require intelligence of, or to act under his orders in quelling any riot or disturbance.[21]

Commissioner's Tent, Ballaarat *by Thomas Ham (1852)*
with native police in blue summer uniform
National Library of Australia Rex Nan Kivell Collection

Though they could on occasion deal with disputes or problems with native tribes, such matters were only a small part of their responsibilities. Similarly, though aborigines' abilities in tracking is celebrated in legend, and Dana's men naturally paid attention to traces left by fugitives or those who were lost, they were not primarily concerned with such skills.[22] They were members of a regular police force, and a successful one.

Recent articles reflecting modern sensitivities, including the current entry in Wikipedia, give particular attention to the role of the Native Police Corps as killers of aborigines, and there is no question that such deaths occurred when the police were in pursuit of those who

---

[21] Fels, *Good Men and True*, 231, also 114.
[22] Marilynn Norman's entry on Henry Dana in the *Australian Dictionary of Biography* makes this comment as a criticism, but we believe she misses the point. Troopers of the Native Police Corps were not simple auxiliaries using native skills. They were working as equals with white men in white men's fashion, but were willing and able to use their tracking ability to assist them in that purpose.

had attacked settlers and taken sheep or cattle. Despite hostile interpretations, however, it does not appear these were massacres for the sake of it, nor that the native police of Victoria were bloodthirsty. On the contrary, Superintendent La Trobe received regular reports and approved the conduct of Dana and his men, and in his letter of 1853 he emphasised that the Corps

> at once formed a link between the native and the European, and gave many opportunities for the establishment of friendly relations. ...[It] gave confidence to the settler, removed the pretexts under which he would feel justified in taking redress into his own hands, and left no excuse for the vindictive reprisals which have been a blot upon the early years of the settlement.[23]

The displacement of aborigines by the settlers was inevitable, but the men of the native police were neither vicious nor traitors to their people.[24]

One aspect of native police work was escort and guard duty, and through this means Henry Dana and Superintendent Charles La Trobe became close companions and friends. La Trobe was concerned to learn as much as possible about the territory for which he was responsible, and over the years of his appointment he made many journeys into the surrounding country, some to visit established settlements and outstations, others to explore the unknown.[25] In March 1845, for example, he travelled 1,400 kilometres in fifteen days though southern Gippsland, accompanied by Frederick Powlett, local Commissioner for Lands, and Henry Dana with a troop of his police. In the winter of 1847 there were three trips to the southwest, with a fourth to Gippsland in November. And in 1849 La Trobe and Dana became dangerously lost in the difficult country north of Cape Otway.

These were not large expeditions, and the difficulties of travel through dense bush and across uncharted rivers meant that those engaged got to know one another well, both in dealing with the problems of the day and in camp at night. So Henry Dana would have been well acquainted with La Trobe, and was in many respects closer than most of his regular officers. It is clear from the later encomium that La Trobe was aware of his faults, but he also recognised his abilities and his dedication to the Corps.[26]

Henry Dana's brother William Augustus Pulteney Dana, eight years the younger, arrived in Melbourne on the *Reward* on 30 October 1844 and joined the Native Police Corps on 1 June 1845. In doing so he took the place of Sergeant Peter Bennett, who had been a competent officer but was accused of cowardice and dismissed. Details are vague and conflicting, and there is room for suspicion, but La Trobe approved Henry Dana's recommendations.[27]

---

[23] See *Letters from Victorian Pioneers* at 267 [note 18 above], quoted by Fels, *Good Men and True*, 107 [1983 edition].

[24] Finnane, "Law and Regulation, 407-408, has a summary discussion of the relationship between the native police forces of different colonies and the indigenous people. While remarking on the brutal reputation of the native police in Queensland, he observes that the Native Police Corps in the Port Phillip District had "aims [which] were more benign than the later history of such forces suggests."

[25] References to these expeditions, based upon La Trobe's notes made at the time, are given by Hiscock, "La Trobe and his Horses."

[26] Below at 95 and above at note 18.

[27] The dismissal of Bennett and the appointment of William Dana are discussed by Fels, *Good Men and True*, 152 with note 56 at 275. See also the Madden case immediately below.

William had already become known as one of the young gentlemen about town, the "swell portion of creation," as the journalist Edmund Finn put it.[28] Powerfully built and arrogant like his brother, he was also a troublemaker. On 5 June, almost immediately after his appointment to the police, he horsewhipped Gildon Manton, brother-in-law of Henry's wife Sophia, for what he claimed to have been loose talk about private family matters. Charged with assault on 7 June, William was fined £5 and bound over to keep the peace.[29]

Henry Edmund Pulteney Dana   *William Augustus Pulteney Dana*
Daguerreotypes in the possession of the CdeC family

Just one week later, on 14 June, the District Court heard a confusing case concerning Patrick Madden, formerly a household servant of Henry Dana. It was claimed that he had absconded on 10 May, but in answering the charge Madden alleged he had been threatened with a pistol by William Dana and assaulted by Henry. Evidence was contradictory, with allegations of some unspecified "unpleasantness" within the Dana household, but Madden was sentenced to lose his wages. Former Sergeant Bennett of the Native Police Corps gave evidence unhelpful to the brothers, and it emerges from the context that he had been employed with the Corps at the time of the incident but no longer held that position. Again, there is room for suspicion. Though the case of Madden *v* Dana was due to be tried before a jury in November, it was withdrawn before it came to court – there is no explanation or further information.[30]

Despite this record of actual, threatened or alleged violence, at the end of the year William was promoted to be third officer of the Native Police Corps.[31]

---

[28] Writing as "Garryowen," Edmund Finn was a leading reporter for the *Port Phillip Herald*, and his *The Chronicles of Early Melbourne* is a major source for the history of the colony. Strongly critical of the Dana brothers, he referred quite frequently in a pejorative sense to their "black" or "sable" troopers.

[29] The case was reported in the *Port Phillip Herald* of 11 June [Trove 224810552 (page 3)], and is mentioned also by Garryowen, *Chronicles*, 966, though Gildon Manton's personal name is miswritten Gideon by both sources. Gildon Manton's wife Julia Ann nee Walsh was the sister of Henry Dana's wife Sophia.

[30] The Madden case was reported in the *Port Phillip Patriot and Melbourne Advertiser* of 17 June 1845 and was the centre of an indignant article "The 'Dana's, and their Doings" in the same paper on 24 June: Trove 226346507 and 226346723. The cancellation of the jury trial was mentioned in the *Cornwall Chronicle* of Launceston, Tasmania in its issue of 29 November: Trove 66267923.

[31] The date of William Dana's entry into the police force and of his appointment as third officer are given on

CHAPTER THREE

The *Returns of the Colony of New South Wales*, prepared at Sydney each year, included an appendix on *Establishments at Port Phillip*, with a list of civil officers, their dates of appointment and promotion, and their salaries. In 1846 Henry Dana, Commandant of the Native Police, received £250 a year, William Walsh his second officer £100 and William Dana as third officer £60. Two sergeants received £40 and £30, a corporal £20, and native troopers 11 shillings and 3 pence.[32] The salary of the commander of the [white] Mounted Police was only £110, while his sergeants received £42 and corporals £32. Elsewhere, the Collector of Customs at Melbourne had a salary of £500, Police Magistrates and the Chief Protector of Aborigines £300, and Assistant Protectors £250, the same as Henry Dana's. Since his starting salary five years earlier had been just £100, he had done well.

In May of 1846, less than six months after his promotion, William Dana was again in trouble. Attending a theatre with some friends, he was smoking a cigar when the manager told him to stop. William refused and, apparently drunk, not only fought the attendants who attempted to remove him but also issued a challenge to every other man in the dress circle. The police arrived before this could be taken up, and William was arrested. He appeared in court a few days later and was fined 40 shillings, not for smoking but for resisting arrest.[33]

In general, however, and despite criticism from hostile journalists like Garryowen, the Native Police Corps and their commanders were effective, successful and popular. There are several accounts of Henry Dana's ability to end threatening situations involving both whites and blacks with a display of force but without bloodshed, and one remarkable compliment may be found in the *Returns of the Colony of New South Wales* (*Establishments at Port Phillip*) for 1849, where the salaries of officers in the Native Police were still higher than those of the regular Mounted Police, but a note at the foot of the relevant page observes that

> The Legislative Council having refused to vote any sums for the maintenance of the Mounted Police at Port Phillip for the year 1850, the above Establishment ceased accordingly on 31 December 1849.[34]

At the beginning of 1850, therefore, the Native Police took over the greater part of the functions of the former Mounted Police, as well as their barracks at Richmond with stables and horses. In his mid-year report to La Trobe, now Lieutenant-Governor of the newly-independent colony of Victoria, Henry Dana claimed that the Corps had never been in better condition, and by the end of the year there were plans for further expansion, with additional troopers and more outstations.[35] The situation, however, would change very quickly.

---

page 460 of *Returns of the Colony of New South Wales* (*Establishments at Port Phillip*) for 1846. In *Good Men and True* at 233, however, Fels has William already identified as third officer in December 1845.

[32] *Returns of the Colony of New South Wales* 1846, pages 352-353. *The Port Phillip Patriot Almanac and Directory for 1847*, published by that newspaper in Melbourne, has the same figures for the salaries of the senior officers, but mentions only four native troopers at 3 pence *per diem*. As discussed above, attendance was erratic, particularly in the summer months, and most troopers appear to have worked for little more than the uniforms and rations – probably shared with their families.

[33] Garryowen, *Chronicles*, 476. Reports of the case appeared in the *Port Phillip Gazette and Settler's Journal* issues of 20 and 27 May: Trove 225064280 and 225065247.

[34] *Returns* 1849, page 460.

[35] Fels, *Good men and True*, 201. The colony of Victoria became independent of New South Wales on 1 July 1851, and Charles La Trobe, hitherto Superintendent of the Port Phillip District, was named Lieutenant-Governor. Henry Dana's report for the first half of the year was dated 29 August.

Gold had been found in Australia before the 1850s, but not in forms suitable to individual enterprise. The California rush of 1848, however, had shown that alluvial gold could be extracted by mining and panning without major equipment, and when gold was discovered in Australia, first at Bathurst in New South Wales and then at Ballarat in Victoria – the richest alluvial field yet discovered – the effect was dramatic. The find at Ballarat was made in August of 1851, and by the end of that year it was claimed that half the men of the colony had gone to the diggings.[36]

En route to the diggings 1851
from William Strutt, Victoria the Golden
William Strutt (1825-1915) was in Victoria from 1850 to 1862 and went himself to look for gold at Ballarat

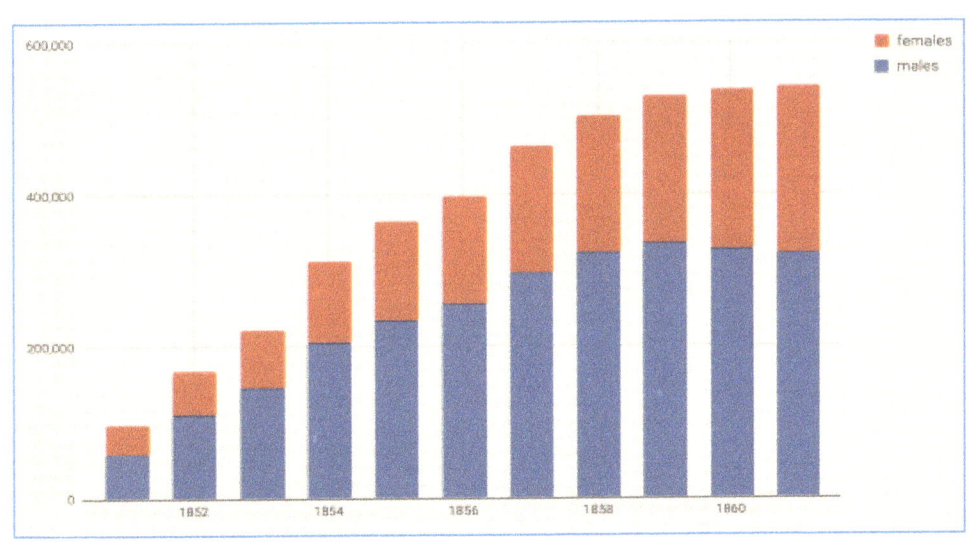

Estimated population of Victoria at 31 December from 1851 to 1861[37]

---

[36] There are many sources for the history of gold in Victoria, notably Blainey, *Rush that Never Ended*, and there is a useful entry in *Australians: a historical dictionary*.

[37] From Searle, *The Golden Age*, reproduced at http://education.sovereignhill.com.au/media/.

Chapter Three

At the same time, moreover, the population had vastly increased. In 1851 the non-indigenous inhabitants of Victoria numbered 77,000; in the following year 90,000 new settlers came to Melbourne; and by 1857, just six years later, there was a total of 411,000.[38] The population of Melbourne alone rose fourfold from 29,000 in 1851 to 123,000 in 1854. The strain on the administration, exacerbated by the effect of so many men leaving their regular employment – government or private – can barely be contemplated. When Henry Dana described the gold rush of 1851 as an "extraordinary revolution of the times," it was very fair comment.[39]

The effect on the Native Police Corps was twofold. Firstly, the men who departed for the fields included many soldiers and police, and the administration was compelled to rely increasingly upon Dana's men for work which they had not done before and for which they had little liking. One of the new requirements was for guard duty at Pentridge Gaol, where white prisoners were held for work on the roads. This was an essentially static responsibility with regular shifts, quite different to ranging on horseback – and aboriginal culture did not take well to the restriction of liberty, their own or anyone else's.

Another new and unwelcome duty lay in the goldfields themselves: the collection of licence fees from the miners. Given the problems and costs of controlling a community in such a sudden state of turmoil, it was not unreasonable for La Trobe and his administration to seek some source of revenue, but miners objected strongly to what they considered an unfair imposition, while the police themselves were obliged to pay more attention to collecting the fees than to dealing with crime. Dana's men bore much of the opprobrium and hostility. Black men on horses, armed with swords and guns and arresting men for failing to pay an unpopular levy, were an invitation to trouble. All parties suffered for it, while the *Argus* referred to the native troopers as a "Satanic Battalion of Black Guards."[40]

Secondly, moreover, many of the European officers, sergeants and corporals themselves left for the goldfields, and they were followed by a number of the men who had been under their command. In one case, an entire patrol happened upon a reef of gold and both the white men and the black agreed to quit the service. Reporting the resignations and departures to La Trobe on 26 November, Henry Dana observed, "The men leaving at this particular time will be of much inconvenience to the service as I shall have much difficulty in replacing them." Indeed, as Fels remarks, "It could be said that the Corps died here" – at the end of 1851.[41]

As Fels further observes, however, the damage to the Native Police Corps came not only from the effects of the gold rush but also from problems among its most senior commanders, including Henry Dana.

---

[38] Richard Broome, *Arriving*, 76: "So great was the influx that fifty-six percent of those Europeans living in Victoria in December 1852 had arrived in that year, while eighty-six percent of those in the colony in December 1854 had come in the previous three years."

[39] Report to the Colonial Secretary of Victoria early in 1852, quoted by Fels, *Good Men and True*, 202.

[40] Issue of 1 October 1851: Trove 4780769; Fels, *Good Men and True*, 215.

The *Argus* was regularly critical of Dana and his troopers. In the issue of 29 September the Geelong correspondent had criticised Henry for issuing miner's licences on a Sunday: Trove 4780714. As Fels remarks at 214, this was actually to benefit the miners themselves, while Dana made a point of regular Sunday service to encourage his troops: above at 84. The Geelong correspondent went on to claim that

... nothing short of the appointment of a more fitting man in his place there, will give satisfaction.

The licence fees and the general discontent which they caused are discussed in more detail below at 105.

[41] *Good Men and True*, 219. Dana's report was dated 26 November.

Whether one regards his policy as justifiable reliance upon men he could trust or simply as nepotism, Henry Dana had surrounded himself with relatives. In 1845 he arranged the appointment of his brother William as the replacement for Sergeant Bennett whom he had dismissed on dubious grounds,[42] and even before this he had chosen his brother-in-law William Walsh as his second in command.

William Hamilton Walsh had arrived at Port Phillip in January 1842. His father, also William Hamilton Walsh, former officer in a British infantry regiment and later a magistrate, had died in Ireland the year before, and his mother and eight of her children – three sons and five daughters[43] – migrated to Australia. Eighteen years old at the time, William was the eldest of the siblings. On 8 February 1844 his sister Sophia Cole Hamilton Walsh married Henry Edmund Dana in Saint James' Anglican Church, Melbourne,[44] and on 1 January 1845 W H Walsh became second officer of the Native Police Corps. Like the later appointment of William Dana as third officer, this required official approval, and it was duly given.

On the evening of 13 January 1851, William Walsh shot William Dana on the parade ground of the Corps headquarters in Narre Warren.[45] The injury was severe: the shot was fired from only a few feet away and the ball hit William Dana on the right, just below the ribs, and passed through his body. At first he was thought to be in danger of death, and as he recovered he was granted sick-leave on half pay and permission to return for a time to England.

A trial was held in March, and William Walsh was sentenced to seven years prison with hard labour. There are differing accounts of the incident, but no good reason was found for his action, and the best explanation at the time was that he had been drunk or temporarily insane; the *Argus*, however, suggested that Walsh had objected to an undue familiarity by William Dana towards his wife Isabella, whom he had married just the year before.[46]

Later that year, however, a petition for clemency was presented to La Trobe by Walsh, his wife and his mother, and they gave a different story: that William Dana had been having an affair with William Walsh's sister Sophia, wife of his brother Henry Dana, and William Walsh had objected. The petition was rejected, but in June of 1852 William Walsh was considered to be in danger for his health and was granted remission and release. He died in January of the following year at Port Fairy near Portland, aged twenty-nine.

Considering all circumstances, William Walsh may have been correct in his allegations. Born in 1827, Sophia nee Walsh was ten years younger than her husband Henry Dana but only one year younger than his brother William. She and Henry had five children together, but it is quite possible that, regardless of the relationship, a man of her own age may have

---

[42] Above at 88.

[43] Mary Ann nee Bissett (*c*.1793-1869) married William Hamilton Walsh (1784-1841) at Quebec, Canada, in 1815. They were together twenty-five years and she bore him a total of eighteen children.

[44] Saint James' Church was on the corner of Collins and William streets. It is one of three buildings in Melbourne which have survived from before the gold rush - though it was demolished in 1913-1914 and reconstructed on a new site at Flagstaff Gardens.

On the birth of the couple's first son, William Harry Pulteney Dana, see 98 and note 64 below.

[45] The incident and its aftermath, with conflicting explanations, are discussed by Fels, *Good Men and True*, 202-206, and by Blake, *Captain Dana and the Native Police*, 43-45.

There were contemporary reports in the *Port Phillip Gazette,* the *Melbourne Daily News* and the *Argus*: *e.g.* Trove 224813549, 226521051 and 4775665, and an account appears in Garryowen, *Chronicles*, 390.

[46] William Walsh had married Isabella nee Smith in the Scot's Church, Melbourne, on 13 February 1850. Blake, *Captain Dana and the Native Police*, follows this interpretation.

CHAPTER THREE

appeared attractive. How far the connection developed is uncertain, but later events indicate there was suspicion within the family.[47]

Such obvious hostility among their officers must have affected the morale of their native followers, and the European officers who replaced William Walsh and William Dana proved quite unsatisfactory. The gold rush would always have caused problems, but the loss of senior leadership – and William Walsh in particular had been popular and successful – meant that great pressure was placed upon Henry Dana just as the structure of his command was melting away.

Through all of 1852, as the numbers of native police diminished, the only means to maintain the functions of the Corps was to enrol and train Europeans to serve on mounted patrols and to guard the transport of gold. Already in May Governor La Trobe had come to the conclusion that "the Native Police has served its time and that it is vain to attempt to maintain it longer." And the process was reflected in official correspondence, for by gradual stages Henry Dana was described and addressed not as Commandant of the Native Police but as Commandant of the Mounted Patrol.[48]

On 24 November of that year, however, Henry Dana died in his rooms at the Melbourne Club. He had caught a chill while in chase of bushrangers on the Mornington Peninsula, and the cause of death was given as an inflammation of the lungs. He was thirty-four years old.[49]

Henry Dana was buried at Saint Stephen's Church in Richmond,[50] and the *Argus* of 26 November reported on the funeral:

> The remains of the late H E P Dana, Esq, JP, were yesterday borne to their last resting place. The funeral procession left the Melbourne Club shortly after 12 o'clock. The body was placed in a hearse, the mourners following after on horse-back and on foot comprising the relations and friends of the deceased gentleman, amongst whom were many heads of departments in the Government. The horse of the deceased, led by a trooper, followed the remains of his master, and was immediately succeeded by a body of the mounted patrol, of whom Captain Dana had been the commandant. About thirty of the cadets and the gold police and a company of the 11th Regiment concluded the mournful parade.[51]

And in an article of reminiscences published some forty-five years later, the policeman-historian John Sadlier recalled the day:

> On 25 November 1852, I happened to be standing in Elizabeth-street, Melbourne, when I saw a semi-military funeral pass towards the old cemetery in William-street. Most of

---

[47] Below at 97-98.

[48] Fels, *Good Men and True*, 200-201.

[49] The Melbourne Club had been established in 1838, but the present building at 36 Collins Street dates from 1859. The club-house was then at number 257 Collins Street, considerably further down and on the opposite side, between Elizabeth and Swanston streets. The site was later occupied by the Bank of Victoria, since demolished, and is now Emirates House: McNicoll, *Number 36*, 31 and 60-61; also *Anne's Family History* 2014/10/30 and below in Chapter Seven at 254.
Henry Dana's death is mentioned by McNicoll at 49.

[50] The article by Sadlier, below, says the funeral procession was travelling to the old cemetery on William Street, west of Elizabeth Street. The burial certificate, however, copied in Grayden's *Chronicle*, says that the ceremony was performed by the Reverend James A Clowe at Saint Stephen's Church in Richmond, which is east of the city. Sadlier was writing many years later and probably recalled some details wrongly.

[51] Quoted by Selby, *History of Melbourne*, 102-103. [The date is miswritten as 20 November: the funeral was held on 25 November and a report was published in the newspapers on the following day].

those who followed were officers and men in uniform and on horseback, and what most struck the new chum, as I then was, was the large number of black troopers – about forty, I should suppose – that brought up the rear. There was one who seemed to be chief mourner – a tall young man, fair, and wearing a long flaxen beard. His handsome face looked worn, as if from recent sickness. This mourner was William Augustus Pulteney Dana, and the coffin contained the body of his elder brother, Henry Edmund Pulteney Dana, commandant of the corps of native (aboriginal) troopers ...[52]

On 22 January 1853, two months after Henry Dana's death, Lieutenant-Governor La Trobe wrote to Sir John Pakington with an account of his achievements and a request for some official support for his family:[53]

I have no hesitation in saying that the entire credit [for the success of the Native Police Corps] is due to Mr Dana, for no one who did not bring to the work his tact, energy, firmness, and moral and physical powers of endurance, could have succeeded. The service was a most peculiar one in every point of view, entailing much self-denial and many sacrifices but it suited his natural temper and talents, and even ministered to his foibles. He may have had his failings, but that he spent himself freely in the service with singleness of purpose, and that the hardships and exposure which it inevitably entailed undermined his constitution and brought him to a premature grave, there can be no question.

Family in Victoria

We have observed that a notice of the marriage of Charlotte Frances nee Dana to Philip Robert Crespigny had been published in the *Melbourne Daily News* on 15 December 1849, so Charlotte Frances was in contact with her brothers there and had no doubt told them of her situation.[54] Since Henry Dana had by that time established a position for himself and for William, and had influence in the local administration, we may assume he suggested that she and her new family might join them in Australia and that he expected to be able to arrange some position for his new brother-in-law.

There is no account of the contents or the dates of the correspondence which took place, but the decision must have been taken about the middle of 1851, and the family left France and then England at the end of that year. Their ship *Cambodia* was new, built at Sunderland near Newcastle-upon-Tyne in 1850. Nine hundred tons, she was certified A1 at Lloyds and sheathed with metal for speed. She was nonetheless 116 days at sea, almost four months, as winds were either light or contrary, and even after she reached the entrance to Port Phillip Bay there was a day's wait on account of a shortage of pilots to guide her through the heads.[55]

---

[52] This is the beginning of "The Brothers Dana," an article published under the heading "Oldtime Memories" in *The Australasian* newspaper of 26 March 1898: Trove 138664222. The passage is quoted by Fels, *Good Men and True*, 136. The article includes an account of the background and experience of the brothers but, as Fels remarks at 46 and 265 note 10, there is no evidence for Sadlier's remarks on that line.

[53] See also above at 84 with note 18. This passage is in *Letters from Victorian Pioneers* at 268-269. Sadly, however, Henry Dana's widow and children received very little support: below at 98 and 149-151.

[54] Chapter Two at 74.

[55] Recording the arrival at Geelong on 1 April, the *Argus* of 31 March remarked on the delay. The voyage had commenced at London, but sailing time was calculated from the stop-over at Plymouth: Trove 4784104.

The *Isabella Watson*, which had sailed from Plymouth on 3 December, one day before the *Cambodia*, arrived a few days later but hit a reef off Point Nepean; nine passengers were drowned. *The Cornwall Chronicle* of Launceston, Tasmania, Saturday 10 April 1852, recording the events of the previous Sunday 4 April, remarks that for a time it was believed the wreck was the *Cambodia*: Trove 65579271.

CHAPTER THREE

Cambodia eventually arrived at Point Henry, the landing place for larger vessels at Geelong, on 31 March 1852, and a day or so later Philip Robert and Charlotte Frances Crespigny came to Melbourne with their children Ada and Philip. There were more than three hundred other immigrants on board, but the Crespigny family were the only cabin passengers. Cabin class provided the highest quality accommodation and the family were accompanied by a servant, probably a woman; her name, however, was not recorded and there is no account how long she stayed with them or what she did afterwards.[56]

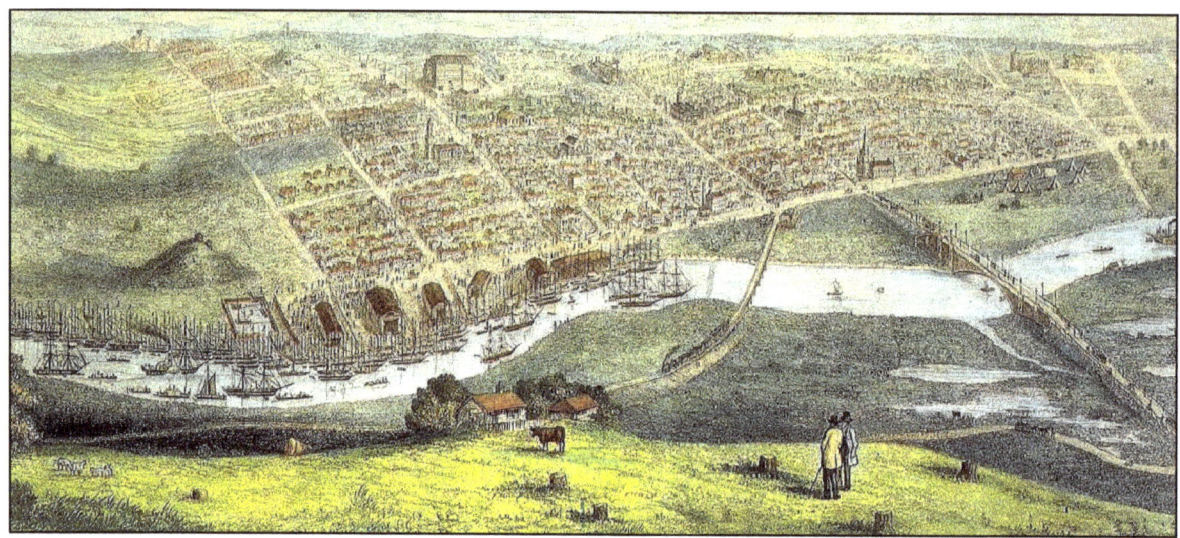

The city of Melbourne, Australia, 1854
drawn by Nathaniel Whittock from official surveys and from sketches taken in 1854
by G. Teale Esqr. of Melbourne; published by Lloyd Brothers & Co, May 9, 1855

There was evidently enough money in first instance, but the situation must have been awkward. The main contact, of course, was Charlotte Frances' brother Henry, but although he was the same age as Philip Robert they had probably never met. Henry had left England in 1839, just when Charlotte Frances was marrying her first husband John James, and Philip Robert had no connection at that time. In any case, by the time they arrived Henry had troubles of his own, domestically and professionally.

For his part, though William Dana had been staying with his sister in 1841, when she was married to John James,[57] and been on sick-leave in England since the incident with William Walsh in January 1851, it is uncertain whether he had any opportunity to see his sister and her new husband while they were preparing to leave France and travel to Australia. He did return to Victoria in the middle of 1853, and Henry then arranged his appointment as officer in charge of a division of the mounted patrol supervising gold escorts on the last section of the route from Bendigo to Melbourne.[58]

Given the confusion of Dana family affairs at this time, it is not entirely surprising that some time passed before a position could be arranged for Philip Robert. On 18 November 1852,

---

[56] Passengers are listed by *Inward Overseas Passenger Lists (British Ports)*, Public Record Office Victoria Microfiche VPRS 7666, copy of VRPS 947.
    Anne's Family History 2013/04/01 discusses the arrival, and there is an account of the ship and the voyage in Chuk, *The Somerset Years*, 157-160.
[57] Chapter Two at 46.
[58] Fels, *Good Men and True*, 220 and note 67 at 282.

however, several months after his arrival, he was appointed an Assistant Commissioner of Crown Lands for the Gold Fields. In a sign of the difficulties faced by the government as it sought to deal with the effects of the massive gold rush, the announcement was not published by the official *Gazette* until 14 October 1853, eleven months later.

When gold was discovered at Bathurst in February 1851, the colonial government of New South Wales followed British law, asserting the right of the Crown to all gold that was found and insisted that anyone who sought to mine it must hold a licence to do so.[59] Commissioners and Assistant Commissioners were appointed to administer each new field, to adjudicate disputes and, most important, to collect payments for the licences. Victoria became an independent colony in July of the following year, but when gold was found at Clunes in that same month and then at Ballarat in August Lieutenant-Governor La Trobe adopted the same policy: commissioners were appointed and the first licences were issued in September.[60]

The salary of a Commissioner was £300 a year, equal to that of a Magistrate, and Philip Robert Crespigny as an Assistant Commissioner received £250, the same as his brother-in-law Henry Dana, Superintendent of Police.[61]

The Government Gold Escort 1852
from William Strutt, Victoria the Golden

Six days after the announcement of Philip Robert's appointment, however, Henry Dana died and there were serious family matters to attend to.

Whatever dealings Henry Dana's wife Sophia may have had with her brother-in-law William or anyone else, she and her husband were thoroughly estranged. When Henry Dana was taken ill in mid-November he was lodging at the Melbourne Club, not at the family home, and his will of 21 November, composed three days before his death, contains no mention of her, neither as a beneficiary – though she did have some property of her own – nor as an executor. His estate was shared among his children, while his brother William and his brother-in-law Philip Champion Crespigny were named as sole guardians. Executors were Philip Crespigny, Frederick Armand Powlett, Commissioner for Lands, and Evelyn Pitfield Shirley Sturt, Magistrate at Melbourne.[62]

---

[59] For example, Blainey, *Rush that Never Ended*, 20-22.

[60] The nature of the commissioners' work is discussed in more detail below at 105-110. We have already observed the problems which the licensing system caused for the Native Police Corps: 92 above

[61] Figures vary, with the website education.sovereignhill.com.au stating that a Commissioner's salary was £500, and another source suggesting £700. We follow Withers, *The History of Ballarat*. Some of the difference may be due to varying levels of rank and responsibility and, as in note 30 to Chapter Four, part may be an amount allowed for official expenses.

[62] Frederick Powlett had been with Henry Dana on at least one of La Trobe's expeditions into the Victorian country: above at 88. Evelyn Sturt was a younger brother of Charles Sturt the celebrated explorer. Sturt Street and Dana Street are now two major thoroughfares in Ballarat.

CHAPTER THREE

Besides this written rejection, it is said that Henry's brother William and his sister Charlotte Frances Crespigny refused to allow Sophia to visit him, even on his deathbed,[63] and one cannot believe they would have acted in such a way against his will.

The rejection was maintained until late in 1854, two years after Henry Dana's death, when his brother William found Sophia and the children living at Launceston in poverty and distress. He arranged to get them food and credit, and criticised the executors of the will for their plight – though since he shared the children's guardianship with Philip Robert he surely had some responsibility himself. Neither he nor Philip Robert, however, had been in a position to keep track of them, for Philip Robert was at the goldfields and William was first at McIvor – now Heathcote – and later Inspector then Superintendent at Kilmore, sixty kilometres north of Melbourne, while Sophia and the children had moved to Tasmania.[64]

In December of that year, soon after he had found Sophia and her children at Launceston, William remarked in a letter to the family friend Trevor Winter that

> I do not intend to defend her conduct as regards her one peculiar failing, far from it, but it does not justify the means by which the remedy is to be applied.[65]

There is no way to tell, however, whether the failing of Sophia concerned her handling of money or to some sexual misconduct. In any event, William married her two years later, on 21 November 1856, in a Wesleyan [Methodist] chapel at Launceston. They had one son, William Harry Pulteney Dana, who was born at Melbourne in October 1858 but died there in January 1859, three months later.[66] In that same year Sophia contracted phthisis – tuberculosis – and she died after a fifteen-month illness in April 1860, also at Melbourne.

William became Superintendent of Police at Hamilton in the Portland Bay District, and transferred to Geelong in 1863. In August 1866 he married for a second time, to Antoinette Camilla Besserot nee Weber; born at Prague in Bohemia – now the Czech Republic – the daughter of a professor of mathematics, she was herself a widow. Two months later, however, on Friday 5 October William Dana died of apoplexy – a stroke. There were no children of the brief marriage, but in the following year the Victorian parliament voted a grant of £1000 to the widow of the late Captain Dana.[67]

---

[63] Fels, *Good Men and True*, 204 with note 12 on 281 citing a letter of 10 July 1853 from Trevor Winter to his elder brother Samuel Pratt Winter. Samuel Pratt Winter was an old friend of Henry Dana, and his younger brother Trevor took over from William Dana after his departure for England in 1851. Trevor, however, was dismissed after a few months for drunkenness, so his evidence may not be entirely reliable.

[64] The Melbourne *Argus* of 20 May 1854 reported the death of Henry and Sophia's eldest son, William Harry Pulteney Dana, at Franklyn/Franklin Village, just south of Launceston: Trove 4807910. It appears Sophia was living there, and she probably continued to do so until her marriage to William in 1856.

The notice says that the boy was eleven years old when he died, so he would have been born in 1843. Henry Dana and Sophia Walsh, however, had married on 8 February 1844, and William Harry Pulteney Dana's baptism was registered in 1845. Henry and Sophia's daughter Cecile was born 3 October 1845 so their oldest son was probably born at the end of 1844, and was nine years old when he died.

The cause of death was given as scarlatina – scarlet fever – the same disease that would kill his brother Augustus in 1868: Chapter Four at 149-150.

[65] Fels, *Good Men and True*, 204.

[66] Sophia had two sons named William Harry Pulteney Dana [the use of the more casual form Harry rather than Henry seems deliberate]. The first, born to her first husband Henry Dana, died in 1854, as in note 64 above. The second, here, was the short-lived child of her second husband, Henry's brother William. It was not uncommon to name a child after a deceased sibling, but this is perhaps more unusual.

[67] Melbourne *Argus*, 2 August 1867: Trove 5774021. On 21 November of the following year Mrs Dana sailed for London on the *Norfolk*: *Argus* of 23 November; Trove 5833031.

In his article on the Dana brothers in the *Australasian* of 1898, Sadlier compared William Dana to Captain Desborough, a leading figure in the novel *Geoffrey Hamlyn* by Henry Kingsley, popular in the day:

> Captain Desborough has been mentioned before in these pages. He was an officer in the army, at the present time holding the situation of Inspector of Police in this district. He was a very famous hunter-down of bushrangers, and was heartily popular with every one he was thrown against, except the aforesaid bushrangers.[68]

William Augustus Pulteney Dana (1825-1866)
Superintendent of Police at Geelong c.1865
A miniature in the possession of the CdeC family

Several newspapers of the time recorded William Dana's death,[69] and when his funeral was held on Sunday 7 October it was attended by senior officers of the police and the local administration, while the lengthy procession from Christ Church to the cemetery was watched by several thousand people. The burial was accompanied by *quasi*-military honours, with a firing party from members of the police force.

Chief mourner was Philip Robert Crespigny, Police Magistrate at Talbot, south of Maryborough and some 150 kilometres from Geelong. The *Talbot Leader* states that he learned of his brother-in-law's illness on the Friday morning and took the midday coach to Geelong, but arrived after William's death. He was joined by William's two nephews, sons of his brother Henry: George Jamieson Kinnaird Dana, seventeen years old and already

---

[68] Extract from Chapter 35 of *Geoffrey Hamlyn*.
    Like his brother Henry, William is frequently referred to as Captain Dana, but while Henry appears to have promoted himself [above at 80 with note 9], William's rank was associated with his appointments as Superintendent at Kilmore, Hamilton and Geelong.
    The *Talbot Leader*, cited below, says that William held his commission as head of the Native Police Corps, but there is no record that he held that office; it is surely a conflation with Henry.

[69] *Anne's Family History* at 2016/07/05 reproduces several articles, including an account of the funeral from the *Geelong Advertiser* of 8 October 1866.
    There is also a detailed article in the *Talbot Leader* of Tuesday 9 October, which was interested because of the connection to Philip Robert, the local magistrate, and because the local postmaster James Colles was married to Cecile Sophia, daughter of Henry Dana and niece of William: Chapter Four at 140. The *Leader* has not yet been digitised by the Trove program of the National Library of Australia, but Grayden, *Chronicle*, has a photocopy from a microfilm of the issue.

CHAPTER THREE

employed as a clerk at the Bank of Victoria; and Augustus Pulteney Dana, aged fifteen, a pupil at Mr Morrison's College.[70]

William Dana, as we have seen, left no children of his own. Henry Dana and Sophia nee Walsh had five, though one daughter, Charlotte Elizabeth Kinnaird, had been born in 1848 but died very soon afterwards,[71] and their eldest son, William Harry Pulteney Dana, had died at Launceston of scarlet fever in April 1854.[72] The three who survived were Cecile Sophia, born in 1845, with George and Augustus as above, born in 1849 and 1851. Though Henry Dana's will had entrusted the children's guardianship to his brother William and his brother-in-law Philip Robert Crespigny, it appears that immediate responsibility had been transferred to his friend Evelyn Sturt. Further accounts of the daughter and the two sons are given in the following chapters.[73]

Somewhat disconcertingly for Philip Robert Champion Crespigny, soon after his arrival in Victoria he had also to deal with the fact that his second cousin Heaton Champion de Crespigny, grandson of Sir Claude the first baronet and son of Sir William the second baronet, was also in the colony – and Heaton was as black as a family sheep could be.

As a young man, Heaton had served in the British navy against Napoleonic France, but in 1815 he became a student at Trinity Hall, Cambridge. On 19 December 1819 he was ordained by Henry Bathurst, Anglican Bishop of Norwich, as a clergyman of the Church of England, and in April he was appointed to the parish of Neatishead in Norfolk and later also to Stoke Doyle in Northamptonshire. He had not yet graduated, but the favourable treatment was explained when he married the bishop's daughter Caroline in June 1820; it is said that she had at some time been a mistress of the celebrated poet George Gordon Byron.[74]

Four sons were born to the couple in the following years, and income from two livings should have assured them a comfortable life, but by 1828 there were financial and other difficulties and Bishop Bathurst was writing to his son Henry that

> [Heaton] is certainly possessed of considerable natural quickness and very gentlemanly manners; if to these he added a well regulated mind and better temper…

Soon afterwards Heaton was harassing his father-in-law for financial aid, and in that same year he was first involved in a duel with a putative enemy of his father Sir William,[75] then attempted to blackmail his cousin the Earl of Plymouth.[76] He took refuge in Paris from the

---

[70] Born in Scotland and a graduate of the University of Aberdeen, George Morrison (1830-1898) was a distinguished teacher who became the founding Principal of Geelong College, a joint venture of the Anglican and Presbyterian churches. The College is still one of the leading private schools of Victoria.

[71] This child was born and died at Western Port, a large bay immediately east of the Mornington peninsula and some eighty kilometres south of Melbourne. There are no further details nor any explanation why the birth took place there; it may have been on grounds of – hoped-for – health.

[72] See note 64 at 98 above.

[73] On Cecile Sophia nee Dana, see Chapter Four at 140. On her brothers Augustus Pulteney Dana and George Jamieson Kinnaird Dana, see Chapter Four at 149-156.

[74] *Anne's Family History* has sites concerning Heaton CdeC, with an account of his marriage at 2016/04/15. The possibility of a liaison with Lord Byron is raised in Caroline's Wikipedia entry [note 77 below].

[75] The complex details of the affair are discussed by *Anne's Family History* 2014/04/19.

[76] Heaton's mother, Lady Sarah nee Windsor (1763-1825), was a daughter of Other Lewis Windsor (1731-1771), fourth Earl of Plymouth. The title passed to his brother Other Hickman Windsor (1751-1799), the fifth earl. His son, Other Archer Windsor (1789-1833), sixth earl, was Heaton's first cousin and the one who suffered his machinations.

complications of these affairs, but in December 1828 he was charged on account of the blackmail. When bail was granted he was taken by his friends to a lunatic asylum, and a few weeks later Lord Plymouth consented to end the proceedings provided Heaton left England.

Heaton Champion de Crespigny and his wife Caroline nee Bathurst
(1796-1858) (1798–1862)
Attributed to Philip August Gaugain (1791–1865), the portraits are now at Kelmarsh Hall, Northamptonshire

Resigning from his parish at Neatishead, Heaton duly travelled with Caroline to Germany and to Switzerland, where their first child Eyre Nicholas had been born in 1821. They returned quite soon, however, for their fourth child Claude Augustus was born at Norwich in 1830. In 1833 Heaton was still in England, for he was declared insolvent in January of that year; in October he resigned his position at Stoke Doyle.

In 1837 Caroline nee Bathurst bore their fifth child, named Augustus Charles, but her father died about that time, leaving her money of her own, and she left Heaton and her newborn son to live permanently at Heidelberg, where she gained reputation as a poet and a translator.[77] At the time of the census of 1841 Heaton CdeC was living at Pirton in Oxfordshire with his son Augustus Charles, now aged six, and a servant Jane Lovegrove. Though still described as a clergyman, he was not the vicar of the parish, for that office was held by the Reverend Thomas Durrell. Late in 1842 Jane Lovegrove, twenty years old, gave birth at Sandgate in Kent to a son named William Augustus DeCrespigny Lovegrove.[78]

Ten years later, in 1852, Heaton and his son Augustus Charles came to Australia as part of the great immigration for gold. Heaton was now in his late fifties, but Augustus Charles was seventeen and no doubt fit to work in the diggings while Heaton held a clerical position. On 7 June 1853 the *Victoria Government Gazette* announced Heaton's appointment as Clerk of Petty Sessions at Amherst (formerly known as Daisy Hill).[79] One month later, however, on 12 August, a new appointment was made to Amherst and Heaton was transferred north to Kerang, on the River Murray between Swan Hill and Echuca.

---

[77] See, for example, her entry in Wikipedia as "Caroline [Champion] de Crespigny."
    Eyre Nicholas (1821-1895) became a doctor and was known as a botanist. Claude Augustus (1830-1884), was an officer in the Royal Navy and served under Sir James Brooke, Rajah of Sarawak, where he discovered oil. The couple's third son, Albert Henry (1824-1873), was an officer in the Austrian army.
[78] *Anne's Family History* 2018/02/22.
[79] The gold rush town of Amherst, south of Maryborough, had been known as Daisy Hill, but the name was changed about this time. See further below at 111-112, with a map.

Chapter Three

Heaton was almost twenty years older than his cousin Philip Robert, and it is not known whether the two men had met, but the scandals of 1828 were well publicised in newspapers of the day. It is likewise unrecorded whether they met in Victoria, though that was a smaller community, and Philip Robert could have assisted Heaton in his application for appointment. The salary of a Clerk of Petty Sessions was only £100, however, Heaton was a well-educated man, the gold rush had left the government very short of staff, and discovery of gold at Daisy Hill had brought sufficient numbers to the area to need some form of legal attention. The Clerk, however, was a secretary and record-keeper, with no jurisdiction or special authority, and any cases, normally criminal matters, were heard by a visiting magistrate. Philip Robert, moreover, based on Castlemaine, may not have been delighted to have his embarrassing relative in office so close by; the swift move from Daisy Hill to distant Kerang was very possibly made at his instigation.

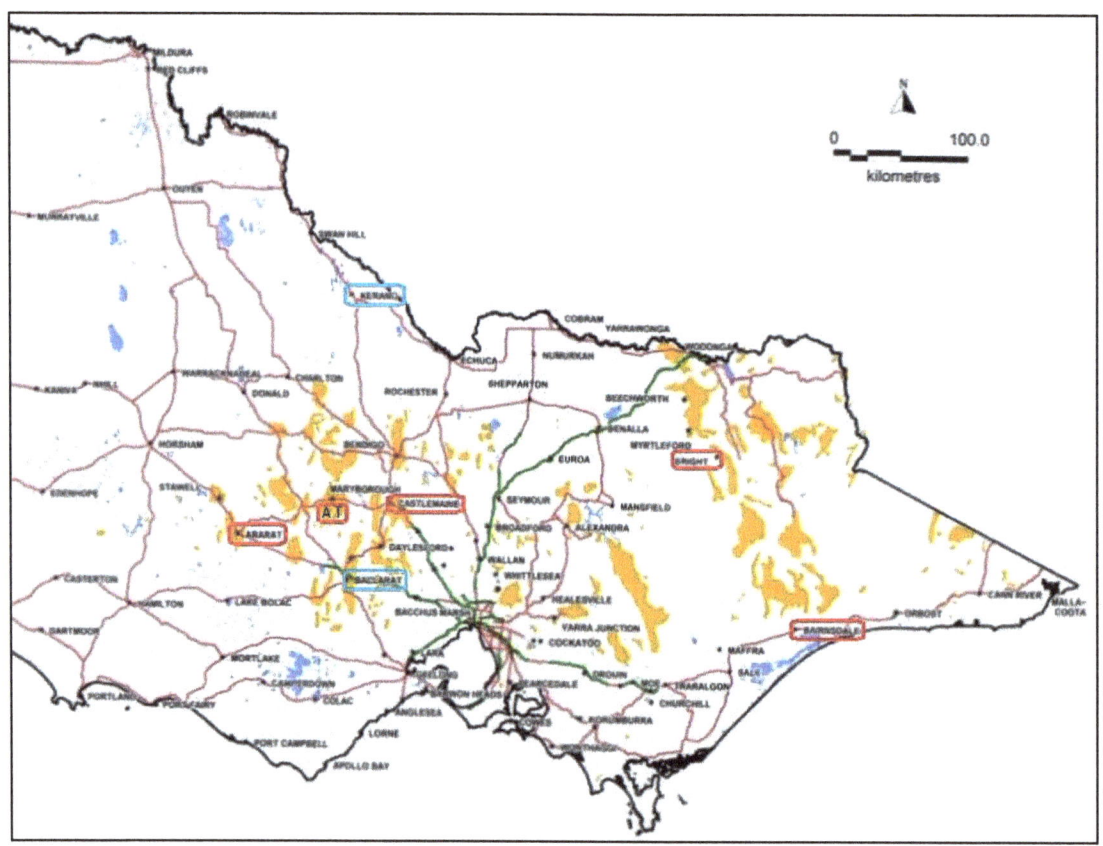

The goldfields of Victoria
Sites associated with Philip Robert Crespigny are indicated with red
A=Amherst [originally known as Daisy Hill]; T=Talbot [formerly Back Creek], south of Maryborough
Sites associated with Heaton de Crespigny are indicated in blue

Kerang, however, was not a place for gold, and Heaton and his son soon moved to Ballarat, where Heaton died from the effects of a stroke on 15 November 1858. His death certificate again recorded his occupation as a clergyman; his will was later proven in England for a property less than £1000, and he is there described as a clergyman and gold miner.

Augustus Charles, now twenty-two and described as a clerk, was the informant for his father's death certificate and had an obituary published in a local newspaper:[80]

---

[80] *Ballarat Star*, Friday 19 November 1858: Trove 66051259.

> DIED
> On the 15th instant, at the Nightingale Hotel, Township of Ballarat West, of serous [*sic*] apoplexy, aged 62 years, the Rev Heaton Champion de Crespigny, MA, Incumbent of the livings of Neatishead, in the county of Norfolk, and Stoke Doyle, in the county of Northamptonshire, of Trinity Hall, Cambridge; fourth son of the late Sir William Champion de Crespigny, Bart, MP, and Lady Sarah, fourth daughter of Windsor fourth Earl of Plymouth, and son-in-law of Bathurst, late Bishop of Norwich, and uncle to the present Sir Claude Champion de Crespigny.[81]

Augustus Charles CdeC returned to England, where in 1881 he was Secretary of the Chandos Club in London and a Fellow of the Royal Geographical Society. He later moved to Texas in the United States, and died at Houston in 1905.

A Miner's Licence of the Colony of Victoria
Issued 5 July 1853 by Commissioner P C Crespigny for the Loddon District, which included Mount Alexander
From the collection of the State Library of Victoria
Philip Robert's signature is rather more scrawled than it was on his passport from St Malo to Paris in 1849: Chapter Two at 69. He no doubt issued several such licences each day and wrote in some haste each time.

---

[81] Heaton's elder brother, Captain Augustus James CdeC, had died in 1825. His son Sir Claude William (1818-1865), became the third baronet when he succeeded his grandfather Sir William in 1829.

Chapter Three

Licensing Diggers, Castlemaine Camp. 1852
Watercolour by S T Gill from the collection of the State Library of Victoria
Note that the miners are obliged to gather in an enclosure. The mounted police here are white, not native.
This scene may be compared with those presented on page 87 above and immediately below.

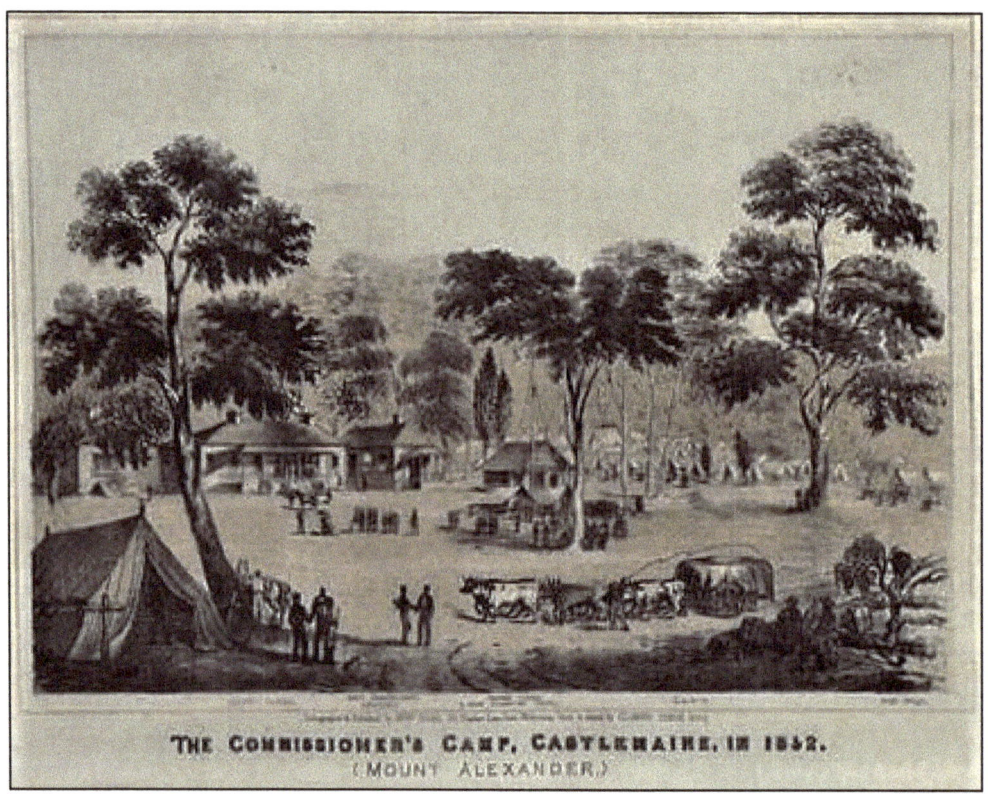

The Commissioner's Camp, Castlemaine (Mount Alexander), in 1852
Lithograph by Edward Gilks (1822–1886); collection of the National Gallery of Australia
Though the scene purports to be essentially the same as that in the picture by S T Gill above, there are notable differences.

Commissioner, Magistrate and Warden of the Goldfields

Philip Robert Crespigny's appointment as an Assistant Commissioner of Crown Lands for the Goldfields in November 1852 marked the beginning of a career which would continue almost twenty-five years. The work was legal and administrative, but the title of the office, the circumstances and the duties changed considerably over the course of time, and the first years were particularly difficult.[82]

Philip Robert's first posting was to the Tarrangower Field by Maldon, fifteen kilometres northeast of Castlemaine,[83] and like his colleagues, he was involved with the enforcement of miner's licences and the inspection and enforcement of claims.

Apart from the natural difficulties of jurisdiction and judgement in a territory as confused and conflicted as the lands of the gold rush, the requirement for a miner's licence was a major problem. The fee was set at 30 shillings a month. This was a considerable amount: there were 20 shillings to the pound, so the annual fee was £18 – the same as the full-year salary of a white mounted policeman. Furthermore, the licence was required whether or not any gold was obtained; it was a licence to hunt, not to find.

Certainly the revenue from the licences went some way towards covering the costs of administering and servicing the numbers of miners and new settlers who spread across the country in search of mineral wealth. There was also, however, some hope that the cost might dissuade would-be fortune hunters from abandoning their regular paid work for the chance of striking it rich.[84] In that respect, it was a high impost and widely resented.

The system was maintained in New South Wales, somewhat more leniently, but it was a source of increasing discontent in Victoria, culminating in the Eureka incident at the end of 1854. Though the rebel miners and their stockade were swiftly overrun by professional troops, the loss of life – more than twenty miners and six soldiers – was widely criticised and there was a general agreement that the protests had been justified.[85]

A Gold Fields' Commission of Enquiry was established in response to the affair, and in July 1855 the Victorian government abolished the licence system and replaced it with miners' rights, which were less expensive and included the right to vote, while further funds were realised by a tax on exports of gold. Commissioners were replaced by Wardens with similar powers, notably to deal with disputes about alleged encroachment of one man's claim into another's, while elective courts were established in gold mining districts to set regulations and to provide a route for appeal from a Warden's decision. By further legislation two years later, the elective courts were replaced by Courts of Mines held by a judge of County Court level, with broad jurisdiction over all disputes but with possibility for appeal to the Supreme Court

---

[82] The following discussion of the administrative system relies heavily upon Hamilton, "Adjudication on the Gold Fields in New South Wales and Victoria in the 19th Century." A more general but most helpful account is given by Blainey, *Rush that Never Ended*, chapters 2 to 4 at 13-58.

[83] The field was named from nearby Mount Tarrangower, and the settlement of Maldon which developed there was declared a town in 1856. It is now in the Shire of Mount Alexander.

[84] On that problem, see 80 above.

[85] The story of Eureka Stockade is well discussed elsewhere and it is unnecessary to give a detailed account. Concerned members of the family, however, may be assured that there is no record of any Dana or CdeC directly involved. Philip Robert and Charlotte Frances Crespigny were probably at Castlemaine, William Dana was at McIvor/Heathcote, and Heaton CdeC should have been at Kerang – though it is possible that he had already made his way to Ballarat.

CHAPTER THREE

of the colony. In addition, whereas Commissioners' and Wardens' decisions had frequently been informal and were often undocumented, records were now required for all cases.

As policy changed after the Eureka incident, however, the Commission of Enquiry held sessions also at Castlemaine, and Assistant Commissioner Philip Champion Crespigny was summoned to give evidence in response to some individual complaints:[86]

Survey Office, Castlemaine.
THURSDAY, 4TH JANUARY, 1855.
PRESENT: Mr Westgarth, in the Chair; Mr Fawkner, Mr Hodgson, Mr O'Shanassy, Mr Strachan, Mr Wright.

Francis Brady examined.

5028   Have you a complaint you wish to bring before the Commission?
– Yes.

5029   Have you a written note of your case?
– No, nothing but a memorandum. Some four months ago my mate and I were at work in Golden Gully, Forest Creek, having no licenses, and on one day, not a general hunting day, Mr Crespigny came round the back way, and called two policemen and took us both into custody, and at the same time took no other digger, and he fined us each £5; that was paid, one of them to Mr Crespigny and the other into the police station.

5030   There were two of you?
– Yes. Some short time afterwards a general rush took place; in the meantime I took out a license, and he came down to me, and I asked him why he had imposed a penalty of £5 for the first offence, having been three years on the diggings and taking out licenses regularly, but not having one then, not having been lucky then; and he said the instructions from the Government were to impose the full penalty, but I know that on that day, he being out hunting, he only imposed a penalty of £1 on other parties, and on applying at the Police Office to know whether that amount of fine has been paid in, I find it has not been.

5031   Is that all your complaint?
– That is all.

5032   Can you state what day this was?
– I cannot.

Philip Champion Crespigny, Esq, examined

5033   Do you remember fining this man?
– Yes, perfectly.

5034   Have you any record of the disposition of the fine?
– Yes, I have.

5035   He states you never paid it into the Police Court?
– I remitted it through the Gold Office to Melbourne, as I do all my fines.[87]

5036   As a fine?
– Yes.

5037   Not as a license collection?
– Not as a license collection.

---

[86]   www.parliament.vic.gov.au/papers/govpub/ VPARL1854-55NoA76p181-365.pdf at 269-270. For easier reading, paragraphing has been altered from the original.

[87]   There was a central Goldfields Office at Melbourne, but this is obviously the local one at Castlemaine.

5038   Have you any attested return of your having remitted it?
– I have asked Mr Naylor to bring up the book from the Gold Office, in which that remittance is described, and I expect him here every minute.

5039   Can you give any explanation why you fined this man £5 and other diggers only £1?
– Yes, the place where Brady was fined is close to the police station at Forest Creek. I had been in the habit of meeting the police from Castlemaine when going out in search of unlicensed miners, and I had always hitherto found on my arrival there that the people working in that gully were in the habit of leaving there when I came, knowing what I was coming for, consequently a great number of these miners were in the habit of mining without a license; such being the case, I passed by one day when I was not expected to go out after unlicensed miners, and I purposely looked out for any people I saw mining there.

I saw Brady and his mate. I immediately went up to them, and hailed the police at the station, and gave them into custody. I think Brady was standing outside the ground; his mate jumped into the hole and hid himself in the hole. I told the policeman there was a man gone down the hole, and he halloed out to him, but he did not answer, and I said, "Policeman, you had better go down," and on my saying that the man came up, and I then thought it was a very proper case to inflict the full penalty.

I do not know whether I am authorised in shewing you a circular letter which I have received, but I have been instructed by my superiors to take vigorous measures to enforce the license fee, as there was a short-coming in the revenue, and I think I can prove that the revenue was very much improved by it, and that at last there were very few men without licenses in my district.

5040   Which is your district?
– Golden Point.

5041   What was the date of the circular to which you refer?
– May 17th. I have one letter here on the same subject.

5042   *By Mr Hambrook*: I understand you to say, that you had received orders from your superior officers to enforce the license fee, and that you had done so, and that you had observed a great increase in the revenue as the consequence of it?
– Yes.

5043   Will you look to that statement of the quarter's revenue (*handing a newspaper to the witness*), and see what is said about it?
– I do not see that that has anything to do with this case.

There were no further questions. Philip Robert is clearly confident and competent, but one can appreciate the ill will associated with the licencing system.

The problems of a short-staffed government remained, however, and in June 1855 Philip Robert had to deal with a dispute at Mount Alexander, richest field in the colony, just north of Castlemaine, this time with no police support.[88] As the *Mount Alexander Mail* reported:[89]

---

[88]   On Mount Alexander see, for example, Blainey, *Rush that Never Ended*, 33:
Ballarat could not compete with Mount Alexander, and it is doubtful if any goldfield could have equalled Mount Alexander within six feet of the surface.

[89]   Issue of Friday 29 June 1855: Trove 202633503. Paragraphing has been amended from the original.

CHAPTER THREE

A MINING DISPUTE

On Wednesday, a circumstance occurred at the newly discovered Quartz Hill, Golden Point, which exemplifies, in very forcible manner, the operation of the new regulations as applied to quartz mining.

It seems a party of five individuals, who had for some time been prospecting the surrounding country, discovered, a few days since, a quartz vein of more than ordinary richness. In accordance with the clause of the Act regulating the leases of quartz clams, the party applied for a lease, paying down the deposit of twenty-five per cent on 63*l* [£63], for a claim sixty-three yards in length. The Commissioner acting as Warden handed a receipt for the money, and the party went on their way rejoicing and took possession of their claim.

Shortly afterwards the place became rushed, and several miners commenced their operations on the claim belonging to the original party. The lesser applied for redress to the Warden who granted the claim, and that functionary appeared on the ground, on Wednesday, as the champion of the law to administer justice between the disputants.

Mr Crespigny, the aforesaid champion, said he had not demanded the required fee of 2*l* [£2] before adjudicating in the matter, because he knew there would be some difficulty in obtaining it. He came to the spot to endeavour to reconcile the conflicting interests of the diggers, and he would confer with both parties and see if some arrangement could not be made.

The Commissioner then read from the Act, and said that the original party were entitled to their claim, but unfortunately, from the defective state of the police force, he was unable to protect them in their rights, and they must submit to be rushed by the diggers unless the matter could be amicably settled. He should tender back the money which had been paid for the lease, and he would appeal to the good feeling of the diggers to deal liberally with those who had been the means of discovering the reef.

Several diggers here protested against the absurdity of allowing one party to possess themselves of a quartz vein to the exclusion of all future comers, and many asserted that the claim of sixty-three yards would occupy many years of working. On the other hand, the prospectors produced the Warden's receipt, and claimed their rights under the new Act.[90]

After a great deal of discussion, the original party seeing the hopelessness of insisting on their title to the claim they had paid for, consented to break up their party, and to accept separate claims of twelve square feet along the vein, with a wall of two feet between each claim. That is to say, the discoverers of the spot agreed to take the same sized claim as any five men who rushed the locality afterwards would be entitled to.

The deposit of twenty-five per cent was then handed back to those who had paid it, and the discoverers were allowed the choice of ground, the diggers all protesting that they would take care that the original party were protected in the possession of their claim.

The best of the joke, however, has yet to come. The party who had thus been thrust out of their legal rights, expressed some degree of satisfaction at the turn matters had taken, asserting that the promise of the diggers to see justice done to them was of infinitely more value that any protection Government could give. The dispute had saved them the payment of the royalty of one-twentieth portion of their gains, and the rent of 63*l* would also be saved to them, and would go towards purchasing a crushing machine.

---

[90] This was the Act for the Better Management of the Goldfields (Act 18 Vict.37) of 12 June 1855.

> This little circumstance forms the best comment on the new regulations that could possibly be made. Mr Crespigny, on leaving the ground, was loudly cheered by the assembled diggers.

News of the incident travelled, for the Melbourne *Argus* reprinted the account *verbatim*, then followed it with criticism of the government for its failure to provide adequate police support to enforce its new legislation.[91] As it remarks,

> It cannot be expected that every such discussion as that described above shall terminate as satisfactorily. Some disputant, in the excitement of debate, may become personal, and provoke a breach of the peace. Other elements, such as reference to country and creed, may be introduced, and serious affrays may take place in consequence, while Mr Crespigny looks blandly on, and excuses himself from interference on the plea of perfect helplessness! A pretty prospect for the Gold-fields!

Golden Point at Forest Creek, Castlemaine 1858
Photograph albumen silver attributed to Richard Daintree; from the collection of the State Library of Victoria
Philip Robert Crespigny had been Commissioner and Warden three years before.

Despite the unkind remark about Philip Robert, the *Argus* itself pays unwitting tribute to his skills of negotiation. It is clear that he lacked the resources to enforce the law as it had been made – and if he had attempted to do so the affair could have turned very violent. As it was, he managed to calm a potentially dangerous situation and found a form of agreement which left everyone satisfied. Given the potential for trouble, one may feel he deserved the cheers.

---

[91] The *Argus* column appeared on page 4 of the issue of 3 July; the comment was reprinted in turn by the *Mount Alexander Mail* in its issue of the following Friday, 6 July: Trove 4810990 and 202631114.

Chapter Three

It is apparent from the item in the *Mount Alexander Mail* that the terms Commissioner and Warden were interchangable at this time, at least in common parlance. From Philip Robert's point of view, despite new legislation, the position was little changed from the time of his first appointment. His decisions were always subject to review, and better documentation might be required, but the responsibility for good order remained. Now in his late thirties, Philip Robert appears to have maintained an appropriate air of authority, combined with a sensible flexibility and common sense. When it was learned in July that he would be transferred to the region of Maryborough, fifty kilometres west, several men of Golden Point sent a petition to the Governor, Sir Charles Hotham, asking that he be kept in position:

> Your memorialists beg leave to assure your Excellency that the integrity of conduct displayed by Mr Crespigny, and his strict discharge of every duty, combined with his gentlemanly bearing to all and every one, render that officer's removal from among them a subject of sincere regret.[92]

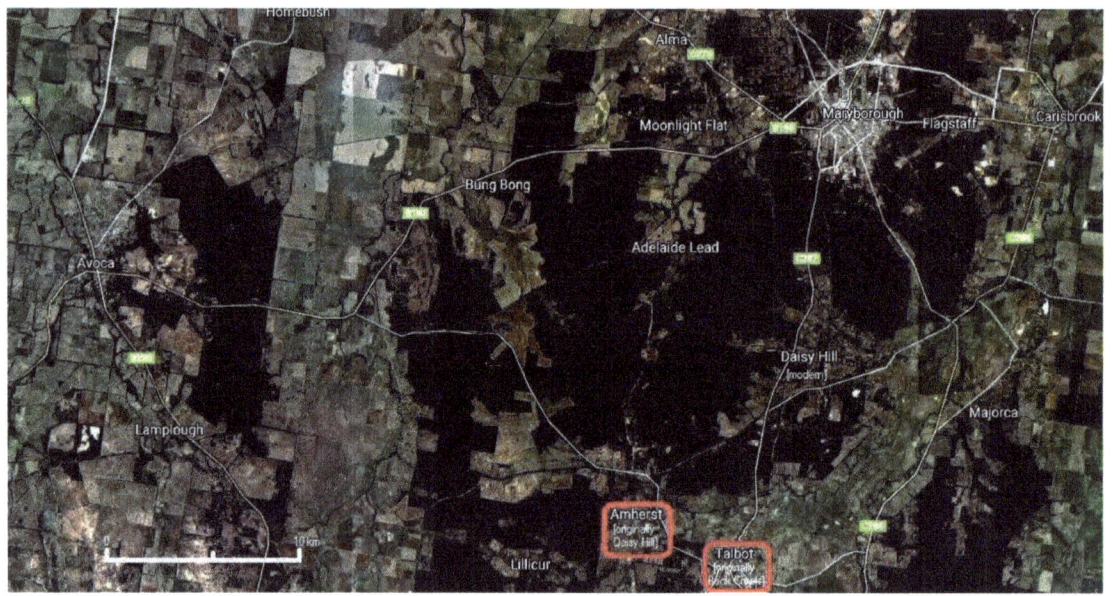

Amherst [former Daisy Hill] and Talbot [Back Creek] on modern Google Maps
Note the present-day site of Daisy Hill slightly to the north.

The petition was not successful, for on 25 November 1855 Charlotte Frances and Philip Robert's fourth child and second daughter, Viola Constantia Julia,[93] was born at Daisy Hill, twenty kilometres south of Maryborough.[94] A third daughter was born there three years later, on 15 October 1858. Christened Helen Rosalie, and known as Rose, she was the fifth and last child of Charlotte Frances by her second husband Philip Robert Crespigny.

There had been a claim of gold at Daisy Hill Creek as early as 1849, but no substantial finds were proven and the government managed to limit the publicity and discourage would-be prospectors. In 1852, however, there were further discoveries and some miners came across

---

[92] The Melbourne *Age* of 20 July 1855 at page 6 quotes the petition in a despatch from Daisy Hill – soon afterwards changed to Amherst as below. The issue of 10 July, from the *Age* correspondent at Forest Creek, had remarked on the local desire to have Mr Crespigny as Warden. See Trove 154894089 and 154894953.

[93] She was christened Viola Constantia Julia, though the second and third names sometimes appear in reverse order. She was generally known as Viola or Vi.

[94] Strictly speaking, the name of Daisy Hill had been changed to Amherst five years before, but the names were for some time used interchangeably in different documents.

from the Castlemaine area. A hotel, stores and a blacksmith's were constructed, officials were sent to sell licences, and a Police and Commissioner's Camp was established in October as a centre for administration. In 1853 the name of Daisy Hill was changed to Amherst,[95] and a Court of Petty Sessions was established, primarily for criminal cases, which were dealt with by a visiting magistrate.[96]

Success and numbers fluctuated, however, as gold was found at Avoca and other sites and men left to chase their fortune, and though several wives and companions of the miners stayed behind by December 1853 the population was significantly diminished and Amherst appeared little more than a supply and staging point for better fields in the region. The village was surveyed and officially established in 1855, however, and as more gold was discovered the miners returned in numbers estimated at ten thousand, together with some two thousand Chinese, who had their own quarrels. The area was over-crowded and lawless, with claim-jumping, robberies, bushrangers and the occasional murder, and very few police to control it. There was a notable riot at the Adelaide Lead, north of the town, in July, and at the end of the year, just at the time Philip Robert was transferred, gold was found near the cemetery midway between Amherst and Back Creek and five thousand diggers broke down fences to quarry on land which had been sold by the government and developed as private farms. The police who attempted to clear them away were themselves driven off, and Warden Crespigny was abused, pelted with mud and stoned. The reforms following the Eureka incident at Ballarat had given miners more status than before, but the confusion was so great that in August 1856 they and the store-keepers made a joint petition for a local court to be set up. This was not done immediately, but the Commissioner's Camp was moved closer to the centre of the new township.[97]

As elsewhere in Victoria, the first years of the gold rush saw official resources badly stretched, and supervision was very *ad hoc*. Though there are earlier references to various commissioners or assistant commissioners in the area of Daisy Hill/Amherst for short-term emergencies, the appointment of Philip Robert late in 1855 appears to have been the first to offer a degree of continuity. The situation began to improve from 1858, when Amherst was approved as the centre of a Municipal District. A local council took office at the beginning of January 1859, and government approvals were given for the construction of a court house, a warden's office and a gold house. Philip Robert's position was confirmed in February, when an entry in the *Gazette* announced his appointment as Police Magistrate.[98]

---

[95] The new name was probably chosen in honour of William Pitt, first Earl Amherst, who was a former Governor-General of India and sometime head of a mission to China.

Awkwardly, the name Daisy Hill now refers to a village further north towards Maryborough.

[96] As at 101 above, Philip Robert's cousin Heaton CdeC had been named the first Clerk of this Court, but was transferred shortly afterwards.

[97] Flett, *Maryborough, Victoria: goldfields history*, has an account of these places at this period: Chapter 7 deals with "The Early Days of Amherst-Talbot," and Philip Robert's difficulties at the cemetery are described at 66-67.

[98] *Victoria Government Gazette* 27 of Friday 25 February 1859 at 357, reporting a decision of 21 February. The construction of the court house and other works were noted in the first Half-Yearly Report of the Municipal Council of Amherst, *Gazette* 94 of Friday 17 June 1859 at 1286-1287. *Cf.* however, Chapter Four at 125 with note 18.

In the postscript to Letter 3 below at 118, Philip Robert's father Charles Fox ChC congratulates him on being "*en permanence*" at Amherst and remarks that the family in England had received the letters from

Chapter Three

Six years after his first appointment at an Assistant Commissioner in 1852, Philip Robert, Charlotte Frances and their family had at last gained tenure in a specific district, and marked an end to a comparatively peripatetic life. Wardens could be sent to deal with any new field, and although he had been some time in the area of Maryborough and had already spent three years at Amherst, the gazettal of 1859 meant that Philip Robert's could expect to remain in office for some years to come, and the family might establish a reasonably permanent home. This was surely a relief for his wife Charlotte Frances, and provided stability for their children: Ada, now eleven; Philip, nine; Viola, three; and Rose, just three months old.

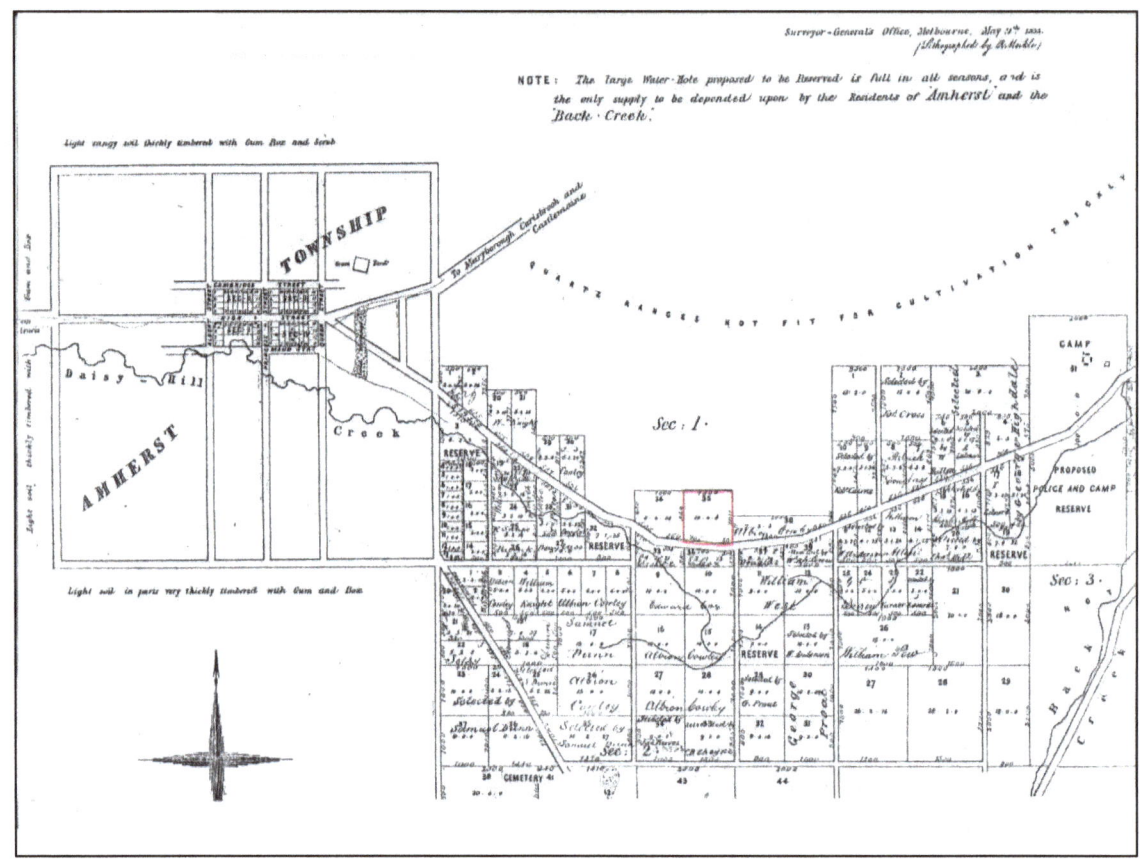

The official survey of the township of Amherst 1855
The ten-acre block which would be purchased by Philip Robert Crespigny in 1864 is identified with red
Photocopy from Grayden, Chronicle

While he was stationed at Maryborough, in May 1854 Philip Robert had purchased fifty-seven acres of land at Muckleford, a short distance to the southwest; the cost was £111 and 4 shillings. He still held the land in June 1856, for Philip C Crespigny was registered as voter number 1280 in the Maldon Division of North-western Province on the basis of that holding – women did not have the vote, so there is no reference to Charlotte Frances. The family had moved to Amherst-Talbot at the end of the previous year, however, and the land was sold in the following month, July, for the sum of £256: Philip Robert had doubled his money in little more than two years.[99] There appears to be no record of what property was held or where the

---

Australia up to 12 February. Philip Robert must have known about the appointment in advance and mentioned it in his correspondence. It is clear from that context that the change was not only a matter of position but also one of tenure.

[99] A copy of the certificate of purchase is in Grayden, *Chronicle*, together with a plan of the allotment. A second document, headed "Memorial," and being item 735 of Book 39, testifies to the sale and transfer of

family stayed in the first years at Amherst, but in 1864 Philip Robert acquired a ten-acre block some two kilometres to the east of Amherst and within a few years his holding had expanded to more than eighty acres. It was given the name of Daisy Hill Farm, and part of the land is still known as Crespigny's Hill.[100]

Letters from home

Some fifty letters to and from members of the Crespigny/CdeC family during the nineteenth century were in the possession of Philip Robert's grandson Constantine Trent CdeC (1882-1952). They had probably been collected by his aunt Ada (1848-1927), eldest daughter of Philip Robert and Charlotte Frances, and Constantine Trent made a few annotations – identified in the following texts as by CTCdeC.

After Constantine Trent's death in 1952, his second wife Mary Birks nee Jolley, Lady de Crespigny, had the letters typed by Ms W M Walsh and distributed copies among the family. We obtained a set through Constantine Trent's elder son Richard Geoffrey CdeC, our father and grandfather. The originals are now in the State Library of South Australia.

The great majority of the letters were written by or to Charlotte Frances during the later years of her life, but there are some earlier ones sent from England to Australia and within Australia. Transcriptions of the first four are given below; others appear in later chapters. Paragraphing is slightly adjusted for easier reading.

Letter 1
From: Eliza Julia Champion Crespigny nee Trent [wife of Charles Fox ChC]
To: Ada and Philip ChC

[from ENGLAND][101]
[undated, about 1854][102]

My dearest little Ada and Loup Loup![103]

A thousand thanks for your nice little letter which delighted me. Little Conny[104] could not read them but Charlie[105] learnt them by heart and repeated them to the little darling.

---

[100] the property and gives the price. On the move to Amherst-Talbot; see 98 above.
Chapter Four at 147.
[101] As in Chapter Two at 74-76, Charles Fox and Eliza Julia ChC had been living with Charles Fox's elder half-brother Philip at Harefield House in Middlesex when the census was taken on 30 March 1851. Philip died, however, in May of that year, and it is probable that the property was sold soon afterwards. The family was living now either at London or at Cheltenham – as in Letter 2 below.
[102] Eliza Julia nee Trent, mother of Philip Robert and grandmother of Ada and Philip, died on 17 July 1855, so this letter was written before that date.
[103] Philip Robert and Charlotte Frances' eldest son Philip, born in France, had the variant nicknames of Loup-loup, Loup and Loo [from the French *loup*="Wolf"]. He and Ada were brother and sister to Constantine [Conny] as below.
Ada was born in May 1848 and Philip in January 1850, so they were at this time about six and four. They had probably had help writing to their grandmother in England. Eliza Julia is a little unclear whether there were one or two letters.
[104] As in Chapter Two at 74-76, Constantine Pulteney Trent ChC had remained with his grandparents and family when his parents left for Australia. Born in May 1851, he turned three in 1854.
[105] Charlie is Charles Stanley ChC (1848-1907). Son of Charles John (1814-1880), eldest son of Charles Fox Crespigny and Eliza Julia nee Trent, he was first cousin to Constantine, and was living with him under the care of his grandparents: Chapter Two at 75-76. Born in June, he was just three years older than his cousin Constantine and was now turning six.

113

CHAPTER THREE

I hope Ada has received the little books I sent her by this time and that you have both had a ride in Papa's new carriage. Grandpapa will send you some seeds for your garden by the Great Britain Steam Ship and I hope you will have as much pleasure in growing your mustard and cress as Charlie has.[106]

Conny and Charlie are always talking of you and longing to have you both as playfellows. Do send me word what I can send you my little darlings to amuse you. I am very glad the boots fitted so well.

Goodbye to you both. Conny and Charlie send you many kisses and I am ever your Affte Gd Mama.

Gd Papa and Aunt [Constantia][107] send you many loves and kisses.

The Great Britain *steam-ship in 1852, refitted for the Australian trade*
Coloured lithograph by Samuel Walters

Letter 2
From: Charles Fox Champion Crespigny
To: Philip Robert ChC

CHELTENHAM
Gloucestershire
9th Jan'y 1858

My dear Phil,

As Constantia has written to you and told you all about us, it is almost needless for me to add a line, but she says even a line will be welcome and that I must not let the post go without my mite. I am sorry that your last letter left your dear Charlotte in weak, impaired health, yet the wonder is that in her delicate state to have gone through so much hard toil and constant cares and anxieties that she is as well as she is. She really has patience and courage to bear up against all the troubles she has had to struggle with and seems determined to make the best of everything in this rugged life. It is the true philosophy of life and she deserves to be well and happy.

---

[106] The *Great Britain* was designed by Isambard Brunel and constructed in 1843. Her main propulsion was by a steam engine but she had several masts and sails. She was originally designed for the trans-Atlantic trade, but her owners fell into financial trouble due to the length of time and the cost of her construction, and in 1852 she was sold and re-rigged for the Australia route, arriving for the first time at Melbourne in November 1852. Over the following thirty years she made repeated passages to Australia, averaging some sixty days – two months – for a one-way passage. [Compare the 116 days taken by the sailing ship *Cambodia* less than a year before, leaving England early in December 1851 but not arriving until the end of March 1852.]

[107] Eliza Constantia Frances Crespigny (1825-1898) was the youngest child and unmarried daughter of Charles Fox Crespigny and Eliza Julia nee Trent: Chapter Two at 75-76. She is the "Constantia" of the following Letter 2, and is referred to on several later occasions.

To do battle with the troubles and ills of life and to overcome them will give zest and delight. When youth and strength and health are called to the task it is most satisfactory and pleasant to reflect you are able to exert energy enough to compass the cares and business of each succeeding day. If I was fifty years younger I should, if I enjoyed health and strength as formerly, take delight in the sort of life you lead, especially in looking forward by my industry and carefulness to realize a property for the future wants of my family. Go on and prosper, you must succeed in the end – if not to be rich at least to ensure a competence, a property at least sufficient to support your family with common care and attention in easy circumstances. If you do that it is enough for all beyond in the imaginings of parade and vanity.[108]

I was vexed to find that you had been worried by the resentment of some fellows petitioning for your dismissal on account of your farm.[109] On the score of attention to your duties you fortunately are able to defy their fixing a plot to injure. I hope no consideration on that ground no on any other will ever induce you to resign or give up your Wardenship. I have no doubt you could not only prove that you have never neglected any duty but that you could defy them to show that any Warden has done it better, if as well. If idle fellows out of resentment for punishment bringing petitions and charges against the Wardens, are to be listened to, and the Wardens able to demonstrate that they have zealously and creditably performed their duties are not to have the support of the Government, it will be never possible for the Wardens to perform their duties with confidence and zeal.

Your plan of making your farm a secondary consideration and rigid attention to duties the first must ensure your safety from the aspersion and malignity of these fellows. The worst likely to happen to you if their charges made any impression on the Governor would I imagine be your removal on account of your farm to another district, but it would surely be better for you to give up the farm than your appointment and you should well weigh this and be prepared to decide in the event of the alternatives being ever forced upon you. Do not be influenced by the irritation of the moment but by the result of your unbiassed mature reflection of the plan most conducive to your future interests and to your family. I have no doubt your farm will pay yet I fear you overestimate the value. You must calculate sometimes on drought and failure of crop. There is never a drought to cut short the pay of your Wardenship.

Have you made the acquaintance of Sir H Barkly? Of course you made the attempt when you were in Melbourne.[110]

---

[108] Here and in other places, while Charles Fox Crespigny shows paternal affection and encouragement, he also makes it clear that he is not going to provide any money to the family in Australia.

[109] Following his transfer to Amherst-Talbot in 1856, Philip Robert had acquired land at Daisy Hill near Amherst; the property would eventually amount to eighty-three acres: Chapter Four at 136 and 145-149.

In January 1857, however, complaints were raised when he used his authority as Warden to force the abandonment of diggings in a potentially lucrative field at Amherst, as the land was designated for public use. There was considerable indignation, culminating at a public meeting in September where a petition was voted calling for his dismissal. Among other criticisms, it was claimed that he was a large land-owner and paid more attention to his private business than to his duties as a public officer.

Philip Robert may well have been concerned at all this, but in August of that year he was gazetted as a Magistrate, and the matter was eventually resolved in November 1858, when he permitted a party of miners to follow a lead across the main street of the town [!], provided they made good the damage.

See Trove 87996874 [*Bendigo Advertiser*, 22 January 1857], 7137047 [*Argus*, Melbourne, 14 August 1857], 253585695 [*Maryborough and Dunolly Advertiser*, 29 September 1857], and 64509653 [*Portland Guardian and Normanby General Advertiser*, 26 November 1858].

[110] Sir Henry Barkly was Governor of Victoria from December 1856 to September 1863. Despite any family connections in England, it is unlikely a provincial magistrate could be on easy terms with the governor.

CHAPTER THREE

I wrote some time since for a supply of seeds to send out to you, the same as last year. I have not yet received them. It was about this time in January last they were sent to you as Gibby wrote word he could not get at the seed sooner.[111]

Constantia has of course told you that she enjoys good health. She goes out very little, sometimes to an evening party – never to dinner, as we do not give any nor see anyone or very rarely – never a party. I find it better on score of expense and every other score to keep at home quietly.[112] On this plan I keep better health which at my age is a consideration for me but not so pleasant for Constantia, but that I cannot help. She is all contentment and satisfied. The care she takes in your dear Con and the delight she has in him is not to be described. It will be a great loss and pain to us to part with him when the time comes that he must go to school. He says positively that he will not go till he is eight and gets on so well with us that it will be time enough. I much wish to live long enough to see him grow up and started in the world but this is hardly to be expected.

When old enough and if we think it will be best to send him to the College here – 600 boys![113] but it is very good and terms very moderate, within sixty pounds a year – if a boy is at a boarding house, the last forty and twelve or fourteen to the college and about twelve per annum to hire the presentation or pay about one hundred in purchase of a presentation which is always saleable when you want it no longer. I have offered to pay for Charlie's if Charles will send him there and I think Charles has made up his mind to do so.[114] I much wish the two dear boys to be brought up together. They are exceedingly fond of each other. Conny is of course exceedingly fond of Constantia but he will say that he likes me but "except you know my Papa and Mama and my brothers and sisters, I like them best of all." He is often talking of you all and asking various questions about you. He has excellent qualities and gets on well in everything. He never will be idle a moment but must read or write or draw, but it would be needless to speak of him as I am sure Constantia has told you all about him. He is delighted now with Charles with us for his holidays.

Charles is on the lookout for a fair partner, has not yet fixed on the fortunate girl destined to make him happy. He says he likes them young! and he is getting old for the tender age of 17 or 18! Before the Ides of May he will probably decide. A wife is really necessary to his happiness and he will make a good husband.[115]

Unmarried and with no pursuit no hobby or occupation he finds it hard work to get through the day with pleasure or satisfaction.

As to Politick I know not what to say. "The Times" will do that better than I. The business of mutiny and cold-blooded murders in India has been most atrocious

---

Three years later, however, Philip Robert formally welcomed Sir Henry when he visited Back Creek/Talbot in 1861: Chapter Four at 126.

[111] This "Gibby" in England cannot be identified. There can be be no connection to the "Gib" or "Gibbie," of Eurambeen in Victoria forty years later: *cf.* Chapter Six at 210 and 239, with notes 12 and 123.

[112] Though Charles Fox ChC inherited considerable wealth, including much landed property, he had sold off a good deal and it appears that he now feels less prosperous. See further in Chapter Five at 174.

[113] Cheltenham College was founded in 1841, catering for both boarders and day pupils.

[114] "Charles" is Charles John ChC, eldest son of Charles James Fox. "Charlie'" is Charles Stanley ChC, son of Charles John; note 105 above

[115] As in Chapter Two at 75, Charles John ChC had been married twice: first to Emma Margaret nee Smith, who died in 1848 after the birth of their son Charles Stanley; second to Margaretta Amyatt nee Brown: they were married in 1854 and she died in 1855.

Following the Roman calendar, the Ides of May fall on the 15th day of that month. In the following year 1859, at the age of 45, Charles John married for the third time, to Frances nee Plunkett; born in 1835, she was then 24.

and disgusting.[116] I fear we shall not see the end of it for some time. Our people have on every occasion behaved nobly and won the admiration of all Europe. In the commercial we have had such panic and crash as never before known. This misery has affected the chief commerce of Europe but most the United States and England. It is thought the worst is over after misery far and wide and most severely felt – numbers of poor men thrown out of employment and on the parish thousands!

Perhaps it will not meet with much acceptance or interest with you what I am going to send you which is an explanation of an important Prophecy – never before made out – as clear and plausible. It will amuse if it does not convince you. I feel myself that I have been successful – if you at all take in my view it is matter of serious import to us all and will bid us set our houses in order, as I hope and believe yours is.[117]

I can only now add now, sincerely and affecly, with very best love to you all,

I am Yours

C J C[118]

I have not mentioned George.[119] He has been rather better for Watson's medicine but he will not take care of himself. He gives preference to quackery rather than to medical science and calls our preference to the last our prejudice. If he will go on in his own prejudice he must abide the consequences. I think Lizzie is on our side.[120] It is a sad pity while within reach of fair treatment of medical science that he should obstinately go on to destruction, careless of his health and eating and drinking all he is forbidden! However I hope now before too late he will turn over a new leaf. He promises another visit to Dr Watson shortly.[121]

I must give you Conny's last remark to Constantia just reported: He said: "Grand P was sent to school at 5 years old because he was not loved. Now I am so much loved you will not bear to part with me at 8. You will not know how to let me go to school." The fact is I was so hideous they could not bear the sight of me and till 5 I was left always with servants in the country.[122]

---

[116] The Indian Mutiny broke out in May 1857. The initial massacres in many places, and particularly that of Cawnpore in June were ferocious [note 125 below]. In due course the British restored the balance of atrocity and the Mutiny was largely ended by June 1858.

[117] This was presumably some millennial forecast; the document has not survived the letter it accompanied.

[118] Philip Robert's father is generally known as by the personal names Charles Fox, but there is uncertainty whether he had not been baptised as Charles James Fox, the full name of the great parliamentarian who was a close friend of his father Philip Crespigny. He normally signed as Charles Fox, but on this occasion – assuming the original manuscript has been correctly transcribed – he used the initials CJC. See Chapter Two at 54, and also RdeC, *Champions from Normandy* at 173.

[119] George Blicke ChC (1815-1893), second son of Charles James Fox, was a younger brother of Charles John and elder brother of Philip [Robert]: Chapter Two at 57.

[120] Elizabeth Jane nee Buchanan (1827-1897) married George Blicke ChC in 1851.

[121] George Blicke ChC was at this time 42. He died 35 years later, at the age of 77.

[122] At least in maturity, however, Charles Fox ChC appears to have been a good-looking man.

CHAPTER THREE

Letter 3
From: Constantine Pulteney Trent ChC [and his grandfather Charles Fox ChC][123]
To: Philip Robert ChC [his father]

[LONDON]
[April 9, 1859]

My dear Papa

I beg you will write to me next time. I am sorry Mama had rheumatism when you wrote. Charlie has got the measles. I have seen a panorama[124] of Delhi with the Massacre of Cawnpore![125] My Aunt did not go as she could not stand <u>that</u>, so I went with Payne.[126]

I am too busy <u>pasting</u> in my scrap-book to finish this myself. Charlie and I had no more pictures to paste, but Grdpapa went out and brought us home 4 dozen old "Punch's." I send my love to all and remain

Your affecte
Con

[*Subscript*] April 9th: What fearfully hot weather you have had! I am very glad you are *en permanence* at Amherst.[127] We have your letters up to Feby 12.

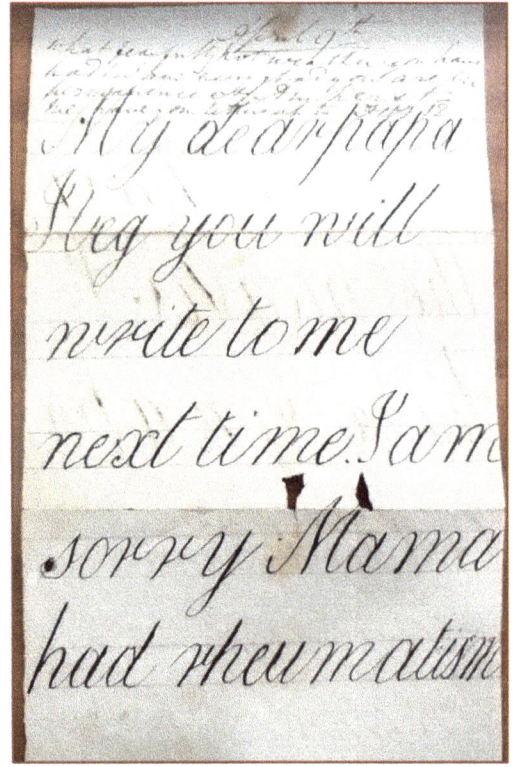 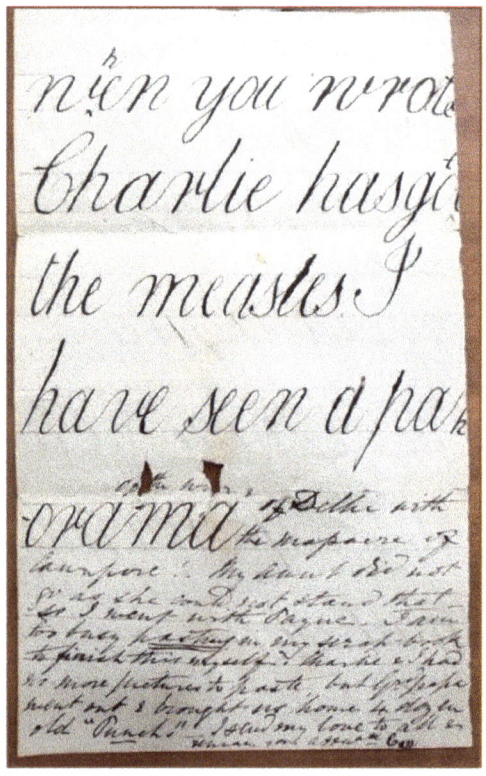

Letter 3: started by Constantine Trent ChC [age 8], continued by Charles Fox ChC

---

[123] Constantine Trent ChC, born in May 1851, was now just under eight years old.
[124] Note by transcriber Walsh: From here adult writing by Charles Fox ChC.
[125] The siege of Cawnpore [modern Kanpur] concluded on 24 June 1857 with the slaughter of the British defenders as they sought to leave under promise of safe conduct.
    Panoramas were common forms of exhibition at this time. The spectators entered a large room and the event was displayed on the surrounding walls, normally in two dimensions but aided by special lighting.
[126] Payne is not mentioned or identified elsewhere. She/he was presumably a servant.
[127] Philip Robert had been appointed Police Magistrate at Amherst in February 1859: above at 110-111.

Letter 4
From: Eliza Constantia Frances ChC [Aunt Constantia]
To: Ada Isadora Charlotte ChC [age 14]

CHELTENHAM
May 19th, 1862

My dearest Ada

I was delighted to receive your very nice note and to read such a cheering and pleasant account of you all and I am sure it must fill you with joy to see your dearest Papa's health so wonderfully improved. I hope both he and your dearest Mama continue well. It was also a great comfort to me to find you were all getting the better of that dreadful whooping cough. Your dear brother Con is not looking well just now and I shall be glad when we can go to the sea or somewhere for a change next month and when you receive this I hope we shall be <u>not here</u>. Perhaps we shall go to Malvern as that is much nearer than the sea-side and the mountain scenery is very beautiful.[128] Con would enjoy it I think even more than the sea.

A young friend of ours at [Cheltenham] College here has asked Con to take a long walk with him on Saturday and he is looking forward to it with great joy! The young Collegian is much older than Con who is rather proud of being patronised by him but I don't much like Con going out in the scorching sun and shall persuade them to put off their walk to the evening.[129]

I have nothing more to tell you, my dearest Ada, except to beg you to write to me as often as you can and to tell me <u>all about</u> each one of the family at Daisy Hill. With fondest love to all

Ever yr Affte Aunt E C F Crespigny

Constantine Trent Champion Crespigny
c.1862

---

[128] The Malvern Hills in Worcestershire are twenty miles/thirty kilometres northeast of Cheltenham in neighbouring Gloucestershire. The nearest seashore would be south of Bristol, some fifty miles to the southeast.
[129] Constantine Trent ChC is now eleven years old.

The Road from Forest Creek to Bendigo 1852
[*In Wintertime Impassable for Mud*]
Engraving by S T Gill
Philip Robert Crespigny was Commissioner and Warden at Forest Creek a few years later [Chapter Three at 106-107]. This picture shows the road which led north past Maryborough, but it is doubtful that any communications in this part of the world were a great deal better.

"Vom publick Haus zu Ballarat [View from the Pub at Ballarat]" 1854
Pencil sketch by Eugene von Guérard (1811–1901)
Collection of the Art Gallery of Ballarat
Von Guérard had come to Australia in 1852 in hope finding gold, but after some years with small success he returned to his profession as an artist. Ballarat was a typical tent city of the goldfields

Chapter Four

Amherst and Talbot
1855-1871

Settlements at Daisy Hill
Public and private life
Farewell to Talbot
In search of Daisy Hill Farm: a note
Tragic cousins: George and Augustus, the sons of Henry Dana

Settlements at Daisy Hill

For thirteen years, from the end of 1855 to the beginning of 1869, Philip Robert was local magistrate for the municipal borough of Amherst – formerly Daisy Hill – which included the neighbouring settlement of Back Creek – later named Talbot – five kilometres to the south-east.[1] Reflecting changes in official policy through the disruptions of the gold rush. he was given varied and additional titles and duties. From his first appointment as an Assistant Commissioner for Crown Lands in 1852, he was gazetted a Magistrate for the Colony of Victoria in 1853. He became a Warden of the Goldfields in the reformed system after the Eureka incident, was confirmed as Warden under the revised arrangements of January 1858, and was named Police Magistrate at Amherst in February 1859. At the same time, as the government sought to deal with Chinese immigrants and miners, he was made Chinese Proctor in 1858 and Chinese Protector one year later.

The last of these offices, whether Proctor or Protector, was not created with particularly benevolent intent, but as a means to control the numbers of Chinese nationals who came to the goldfields. In theory, the Protector served as guardian and magistrate for the alien community, but in practice his duties were primarily to tax its members and keep them under supervision. Legal proceedings were bedevilled by problems of translation, for very few Europeans had more than a smattering of any Chinese language or dialect, and disputes could become hopelessly confused when each party insisted that their opponent's rendering of the evidence was false or mistaken.[2]

Otherwise, in the English-speaking jurisdiction, Philip Robert and his colleagues had two separate responsibilities. As Police Magistrate he held heard civil and criminal cases; as Warden he adjudicated between rival claims and disputes relating to the mining of gold.

For his first appointment to Mount Alexander near Castlemaine, it appears that Philip Robert travelled alone and lived in a tent on the diggings.[3] Charlotte Frances and the children Ada and Philip presumably remained for a time in Melbourne, but joined him soon afterwards.

Travel was not easy. Men could go on horseback, but a woman with two small children was obliged to take a carriage of some form, and the same transport was required for any

---

[1] Back Creek took its original name from the watercourse which ran through it.
[2] The article by Bryans, "'A Tolerable Interpreter'," especially at 133-136, discusses the administration of Chinese miners and the problems of translation.
[3] In a court-case held on 1 June 1853 a certain Peter Robinson, tent-keeper, was charged with theft of a bottle of brandy, another of sherry, and one of porter [dark beer or stout] from the tent of P C Crespigny. He claimed, however, to have taken the items in error when clearing up after an evening party attended by two other gentlemen. He was found not guilty. Trove 4793362; *Anne's Family History* 2019/10/25.

CHAPTER FOUR

furniture, even the most basic such as beds, tables and chairs. The roads were no more than winding tracks and often impassable in bad weather or the wrong season.

There is no direct record or description by or about Charlotte Frances and her experiences,[4] but Philip Lamothe Snell Chauncy (1816-1880), who was a direct contemporary of Philip Robert and whose daughter Annie Frances would marry his son Philip, was also travelling at that time and has left a detailed account. Living in Melbourne, he was appointed Surveyor at McIvor – now Heathcote – in September 1853, and travelled there with his wife and three children, all under five and one of them six months old. As a government official, with an allowance for expenses, he purchased a horse, a "tilted spring cart" and tents,[5] and his party was accompanied by two drays from the Commissariat Department with their baggage.

A spring cart, with haulage drays in the background
From http://boobookbacktracks.blogspot.com

Here are some extracts from his description:[6]

> The journey to McIvor, seventy-two miles, occupied ten days, of which it rained on nine. On the 14th September the road lay between fences, and the cart and drays were sometimes bedded in the mud. We passed through a beautiful country, laid out in farms and partly cultivated. The village of Flemington is a long straggling place, about four miles

---

[4] Henderson, *Early Pioneer Families*, 237, says that the family "travelled by bullock dray through dense bush." This was indeed a regular form of transport at the time, but there is no specific authority for the statement.

[5] A spring cart, or sprung cart, was a lightweight two-wheeled horse-drawn carriage with road-springs.

[6] *Memoirs of Mrs Poole and Mrs Chauncy*, 43-46; paragraphing adjusted for clarity.
   The Memoirs of Mrs Chauncy, by her husband Philip Lamothe Snell Chauncy, District Surveyor, Ballarat; written for the instruction and comfort of their eight children, was first published in Ballarat in 1873. Susan Augusta nee Mitchell (1828-1867) married Philip Chauncy in 1848. "Gentility and a Gold Rush: the story of Susan Mitchell," an extensive review of the *Memoirs*, was published by the West Australian on 27 July 1929: Trove 32296763; *Anne's Family History* 2018/01/09.
   Susan Augusta [below as "Susie'] was Philip Chauncy's second wife. His first wife, Charlotte Humphreys Kemmis (1816-1847), had died without children. *Anne's Family History* 2013/08/25.
   Philip Chauncy's sister Theresa (1807-1876) was a noted artist [*Anne's Family History* 2018/04/18]. She first married John Walker and later George Herbert Poole. Philip first composed his *Memoirs of Mrs Poole* as a separate document; the two works were published together in 1976.

from Melbourne. The road was thronged with people, mostly on their way to the diggings.

On the third night we encamped at the Rocky Waterholes,[7] and towards morning a violent storm came on, sweeping over us and carrying away our tent, left us exposed to the rain. Having righted the tent, we turned in again, and rose at daylight. We soon finished breakfast, and were ready to start, when two men came up, and demanded rent for our having encamped on their land, although it was open, unenclosed ground. As I could not disprove their assertion, I was glad to get rid of them by paying their demand.

When twenty-six miles [forty-two kilometres] from Melbourne the axletree of our vehicle broke in two while it was raining. I had five hired men with me, and set them to work to put up a tent, under which I got my dear wife and children. We then emptied and turned over the spring-cart, and spliced the axle with saplings and cord…..

On the 17th we passed over the most difficult and dangerous part of the road we had yet travelled on. Susie and the children walked the greater part of the day, and at one time, while Betsy, the servant, was carrying little Philly [Philip Chauncy, age two and a half] through a bog, she got stuck fast in the stiff mire up to her knees, and was with difficulty dragged out. After a journey of nine miles, we encamped in a black forest, in the neighbourhood of many other travellers, and of some "coffee shops," where sly grog was always sold. Many bad characters were said to be lurking about there, and we had to take especial care of the horses…..

On the 18th we travelled over some better country, and leaving the Kilmore road on the right, stopped to dine about noon, having made four miles [6.5 kilometres], and ascertained at a cottage that we had passed Kilmore without seeing it.[8] The mud was so deep that I could with difficulty get into the town on horseback. I bought some bread … at a shilling a pound, and butter at five shillings a pound. Hay was £100 a ton delivered in Kilmore, and £60 at the stack. I gave thirty-five shillings a bushel for damaged oats, and was asked 18s for a burnt damper. There were about two thousand people in Kilmore, and trade seemed to be very brisk, but the streets were absolutely impassable for a cart with anything in it; I could scarcely flounder through on horseback.

Having returned to our camp, we had proceeded another mile when the heavy dray got hopelessly bogged, so we unloaded and encamped again…..

On the 20th my cart got stuck so firmly in the mud that the new English harness was broken in the endeavour to drag it out…..

Wednesday, 21st. – … Crossed some dangerous deep creeks, and got bogged again. We made fourteen miles today.

22nd. – Reached the Commissioner's camp at the McIvor diggings, where we were well received by Mr Walter Brackenbury, the Gold Commissioner, who ordered a comfortable tent to be at once prepared for us, and every attention to be given to our comfort. There were about three thousand diggers and storekeepers on the ground (some with their families, and all living in tents)… I had brought four tents with me, which were put up, and in a day or so everything was in order.

As Philip Chauncy observed, McIvor/Heathcote was a little more than seventy miles from Melbourne; it is now 110 kilometres on the Northern Highway. Castlemaine, where Philip Robert brought his family at about the same time, is 120 kilometres from Melbourne. So the distances were comparable, and the roads can have been no better.[9]

---

[7] The site known as Rocky Waterholes was close to Kalkallo, on the Hume Freeway some thirty kilometres north of Melbourne.

[8] Kilmore is sixty kilometres north of Melbourne.

[9] *Anne's Family History* 2014/07/22 has an account of Philip Chauncy and his family at Heathcote.

CHAPTER FOUR

There is also an account of Martha Clendinning, who travelled from Melbourne to Ballarat early in 1853.[10] She and her sister had a bullock dray for their baggage, but they themselves covered the 115 kilometres on foot; it took them a week. Once there, Ballarat too was a tent city, with canvas only gradually replaced by wooden huts, often roofed with bark, and sometimes both roofed and clad with corrugated iron, which was comparatively easy to transport for the area it could cover.[11] Larger and more substantial buildings would follow, but the first goldfields settlements were tent cities and shanty towns.[12]

Eagle Hawk Gully, Bendigo 1852
Water-colour by S T Gill 1872, from a drawing made at the time
State Library of Victoria

Martha's Clendinning's husband was a medical doctor, not a miner, and Martha ran a store with her sister, but even for such educated and enterprising people daily life was difficult. Government officers such as Philip Robert Crespigny and Philip Chauncy might receive assistance, but private individuals had to cope for themselves. In any case, the necessities were awkward and time-consuming to manage, and though some furniture was cobbled together on the spot, items such as bedsteads, bedding and mattresses, tables and chairs and cooking equipment were best brought in.

---

[10] The story of "Martha Clendenning: a woman's life on the Goldfields," is told by Louise Asher in *Double Time* at 52-60.

[11] Techniques and types of early construction are discussed by Connah, '*Of the Hut I Builded*,' particularly at 67-72. On general problems of transport by land, see Blainey, *Tyranny of Distance*, 142-143.

[12] In the census of 1861 the municipality of Amherst, with a population just over two thousand, had nineteen brick or stone dwellings, 158 made of wood or (corrugated) iron, 7 of slab, bark or mud [*i.e. pisé*/tamped earth], and 435 tents or dwellings roofed with canvas. On the census, see further below at 128. Many records list the numbers and types of dwellings; these figures are taken from Table XXXIII.

Cooking was generally outdoors on an open fire: tents were inflammable and a sheltered fireplace with a chimney took a deal of construction – so an umbrella was necessary when it rained, and flies were always a nuisance and a potential source of disease. Water had to be carried from a nearby stream – often muddied by gold-seekers or polluted by other activities further up. Sewerage was basically non-existent. Outhouses or similar shelters were built over holes in the ground, which could then be filled in again or were sometimes emptied for use as fertilizer, particularly in Chinese market gardens.

For women and children in particular, health – both public and individual – was always a matter of concern. With low levels of sanitation in the goldfields, disease – notably typhoid – was a danger, especially to young children, and few families escaped the death of a small child. "Little Philly," the son of Philip Chauncy who was carried through the mud by the servant girl Betsy on the way to McIvor, died there six months later at the age of three.[13] Even in England during her first marriage to John James, when conditions were better and help more available, Charlotte Frances lost a son and also suffered a still-birth.[14]

Childbirth was dangerous to any woman, with a one to two percent chance of a mother's death from each experience: not great odds in themselves, but cumulative over time. Besides natural pain and exhaustion, loss of blood or an awkward presentation could prove fatal, and there was high possibility of infection – puerperal fever – for several weeks afterwards.[15] The threat was present on every occasion, even in developed communities, but it was enhanced by the primitive arrangements of the new settlements in Australia. Midwives, no matter how experienced, were not necessarily competent, while many doctors were even more ignorant and were perhaps more likely to bring infection on their instruments and their hands.[16] In her marriage with Philip Robert, however, Charlotte Frances bore five children without serious after effects, and all lived to maturity. She was fortunate.

With the establishment of a new municipality in 1859, followed by the establishment of a court house, a warden's office and a gold house – albeit in rented accommodation in a public house – Amherst became a local centre for law and government. In that same year, however, a major discovery of gold at Back Creek was followed by the "Scandinavian Rush" which brought fifteen thousand miners, so that the population rose to rival that of Amherst and Philip Robert had more than enough to occupy his attention.[17] So great was the change that when funds were allocated for a permanent court house with other offices the new building was erected at Back Creek. Questions were asked in Parliament, but the Commissioner for Public Works James Goodall Francis explained that the decision had been made upon the recommendation of Mr Crespigny the resident Police Magistrate.[18]

---

[13] *Anne's Family History* 2013/09/27 discusses "Sick Children" in Australia, including three-year-old Philip Chauncy.
[14] Chapter Two at 45.
[15] Shorter, *History of Women's Bodies*, 98 and 241. His Chapter 5 discusses "Pain and Death in Childbirth" and Chapter 6 "Infection after Delivery."
[16] When a hospital was established at Amherst in the early 1860s [below at 132-134] there was no provision for a maternity ward. Children were born at home.
[17] See, for example, vhd.heritagecouncil.vic.gov.au/places/12192/download-report, a Database Report on the Scandinavian Lead by Heritage Council Victoria.
[18] Reports were carried by the *Age* of 1 and 8 February 1860: Trove 154879673 and 154879538; also in the *Argus* of 1 February and the *Geelong Advertiser* of 8 February: Trove 5695994 and 148788636.

CHAPTER FOUR

Triumphal or Welcoming Arch
Arches such as these were frequently set up when a notable visitor was received. This one was erected at Emerald Hill in the south of Melbourne for the Duke of Edinburgh, son of Queen Victoria, in 1867. Those prepared for Sir Henry Barkly at Amherst and Back Creek would have been in the same style but less elaborate.

The plain name of Back Creek was now considered unworthy of the newly-enlarged and prosperous settlement, and after a number of representations by the council the government agreed to a change of name. In October 1861 His Excellency the Governor Sir Henry Barkly toured the Maryborough region, and on 17 October he visited Amherst and Back Creek.[19]

The community made the most of the event, with ceremonial arches of welcome constructed at both Amherst and Back Creek. The one at Amherst Town Hall was particularly fine:

> The centre arch was wide and lofty, flanked on either side by a smaller archway. The apex of the centre arch was occupied by a crown and several flags, conspicuous amongst which was the British ensign which moved somewhat lazily to the slight breeze that came up in fits and starts during the morning. Immediately in front of the Town Hall, and forming a human lane for His Excellency to pass through into the Hall, were two lines of neatly dressed children, representing the various schools in Amherst.

As Sir Henry and Lady Barkly arrived by coach, they were formally welcomed by Philip Robert Crespigny, Warden of the District and the senior government official, then travelled on with a confused escort of horsemen, each seeking to ride close to the guests of honour. After a brief stop at Amherst to receive and respond to a loyal address, the vice-regal party galloped on to Back Creek for another set of loyal and welcoming deputations. No possible group appears to have been omitted, though there was a deal of complaint at the speed of the procession which prevented people from marching in company and meant that the National Anthem had to be replaced with a hasty cheer.

---

[19] A detailed account of the day, with extensive quotations from *The Northwestern Chronicle*, the local newspaper, in its issue of Sunday 19 October, is given by Kau, *The Governor's Visit to Back Creek/Talbot* at 5. The passage on the welcoming arch is at 10.

The day concluded at the Theatre Royal with "a banquet of a very superior kind, made in the most liberal manner," followed by more loyal addresses, from the Municipal Council, members of the Roads Board, miners, farmers, the Independent Order of Odd Fellows and the German community.[20] Each was received and responded to by Sir Henry with every sign of pleasure – and patience. He announced, moreover, that Back Creek would be renamed Talbot, and the local newspaper promptly changed its title from *North-Western Chronicle* to *Talbot Leader and North-Western Chronicle*, with its first issue under the new name appearing on 22 October. When the town was eventually gazetted with the name Talbot two months later, on 13 January 1862, the name was changed once more, to *Talbot Leader*. The Shire of Talbot would be proclaimed in 1865.[21]

The reference to a Theatre Royal at Back Creek/Talbot indicates the borough was substantial, with a fair supply of public buildings. A post office was opened at Amherst in 1856, as soon as the village had been surveyed, and an Anglican school was established later that year, followed by a Wesleyan [Methodist] church in 1857, a national school in 1858 and a Presbyterian school in 1860. A warden's office and gold repository had, as we have seen, been constructed soon after the gazettal of the municipality in 1859, and the Town Hall was built in that same year.

Amherst Town Hall
Constructed 1859-1860, demolished 1947
From the collection of the Talbot Arts and Historical Museum, reproduced in Kau, The Governor's Visit

---

[20] The Independent Order of Odd Fellows was founded as a friendly society for mutual benefit with international connections. The first branch in Victoria had been formed at Melbourne in 1846 and more were now spread all over the colony.

[21] The County of Talbot had been established in 1849, covering territory from north of Maryborough south to Mount Macedon, and from Castlemaine in the east to Avoca in the west. Up to this time, however, no settlement had been given that name.

Kau, *From Back Creek to Talbot*, 8, suggests that the county was named for a family of the Irish peerage, with a seat at Malahide near Dublin [*cf.* the Beggs family in Chapter Five at 183]. William Talbot (1784-1845), a cadet of that lineage, came to Van Diemen's Land in 1820 and became a successful woolgrower in northeast Tasmania. Kau argues that he and his nephews Samuel and Richard were members of Victorian society and acquaintances of Lieutenant-Governor La Trobe, so the name was chosen as a generic courtesy.

CHAPTER FOUR

At one time or another there are said to have been as many as forty thousand miners in the district, but figures may be seriously exaggerated. The official census of the Colony of Victoria, held on 7 April 1861, recorded the population of the municipality of Amherst as 2,080, of whom 1,314 were men and 766 were women. In December of the previous year, however, an official count of miners employed in the Amherst [Mining] District recorded 7,100, and this floating population swelled the local numbers of more settled residents.[22] Presumably conflating these figures, the *North-Western Chronicle* of 7 May 1861 claimed that the settled population was just over nine thousand.[23] In any event, besides the continued mining for gold, by 1865 *Bailliere's Victorian Gazetteer* was recording general stores, factories and tradesmen's enterprises, a mechanics' institute with a library, two breweries and almost twenty hotels.

Increasingly overshadowed by its neighbour, Amherst was replaced by Talbot as the centre of the borough in 1875, but through the 1880s gold became more difficult to find and extract, the mines closed and population began to decline. Talbot is now a small local centre, and Amherst, which was badly affected by bushfire in 1985, is little more than a ghost town – its major remaining site is the cemetery. In the time of Philip Robert and Charlotte Frances, however, both places were thriving.

Public and private life[24]

As indicated by his reception of Governor Sir Henry Barkly at the visit of October 1861, Warden and Police Magistrate Philip Robert Champion Crespigny was the senior government representative at Amherst-Talbot. The municipal borough had a mayor and councillors, and elections were held for the Legislative Council and the Legislative Assembly, upper and lower houses of the colonial parliament, but the Warden and Magistrate was responsible for checking the electoral lists for these last, and within the borough his rank was comparable to that of the mayor. Earlier in 1861, for example, he had received a deputation of leading citizens seeking his support in persuading the authorities at Melbourne to consolidate official buildings in Back Creek/Talbot, and the report of the discussion makes it clear that he was the natural person to make such representations on behalf of the local community.[25] In similar fashion, he appeared as one of several expert witnesses before the Gold Fields Royal Commission of Enquiry which was established by Sir Henry Barkly in 1862 and reported to Parliament in the following year with proposals for revisions of legislation.[26]

Apart from such practical duties of judgement and official advice, Philip Robert and his fellow-magistrates were "key agents of administration, the representatives at local level of the reach of government," and their status was enhanced by symbolism, with black judicial robes on the traditional British model, and substantial court houses constructed to enhance the local settlement and impress its citizens with the authority of the law.[27]

---

[22] The Victorian census returns has data for the municipality of Amherst in Table XVIII at 28. The figures for the numbers of miners were in official *Goldfields Statistics, 1860*, presented to Parliament and recorded by the *Argus* of 3 May 1861: Trove 5699858.
[23] Cited by Grayden, *Chronicle*.
[24] There is a discussion of Philip Robert's time at Amherst-Talbot in *Anne's Family History* at 2017/04/23.
[25] *North-Western Chronicle* for Thursday 14 March 1861, quoted by Grayden, *Chronicle*.
[26] www.parliament.vic.gov.au/papers/govpub/VPARL1862-63No10P151-200.pdf at 177-182.
[27] Finnane, "Law and Regulation," 397-398.

As Police Magistrate Philip Robert was responsible for a reasonably well-defined district extending some twenty to thirty kilometres about his two main courts at Amherst and Talbot. Below his jurisdiction, Courts of General or Petty Sessions under territorial magistrates of lower rank or Justices of the Peace had authority to deal with minor offences and disputes. Above, appeals against his decisions could be heard in the County Court, which was based at Maryborough but sometimes held local sessions.[28] In 1861 police resources for Amherst-Talbot comprised a sergeant, a senior constable, three mounted police, and eleven regular constables. No doubt reflecting a greater number of miners and more problems in consequence, Back Creek/Talbot had far the larger share of that force.[29]

According to the official *Statistics for the Colony of Victoria for the Year 1860*, Philip Robert received £750 a year,[30] a handsome sum and three times the £250 he had received at the time of his initial appointment as an Assistant Commissioner for Crown Lands in 1852.[31] Ten years after the commencement of the great gold rushes, administration was more settled, while government revenue had increased from some £1.5 million in 1851 to over £3 million in 1860.[32]

Philip Robert surely earned his money. In addition to his duties as Magistrate and Warden, he was appointed on occasion to supplementary positions as Receiver and Paymaster for the government, and also as Coroner. He was required to hold court at both Amherst and at Back Creek/Talbot, and a newspaper calculation for the second six months of 1862 found that he had attended at Amherst on 27 days and at Talbot on 101 days; allowing for weekends and a Christmas holiday, that is 128 days out of a possible 140.[33] During the same period two years later he was at Talbot Police Court on 97 days, hearing 260 cases and 82 applications for licences.[34] He was sometimes assisted by one or more Justices of the Peace, but frequently sat alone.

Late in 1860, however, there was a lengthy period of illness. In October of that year a friend, Reynall Johns, recorded visiting the family at Amherst; Philip Robert was crippled with sciatica and was said to have had an epileptic fit three months earlier.[35] The situation was serious enough that a petition was raised in November with more than a thousand signatures, asking that the government appoint a certain Mr Fyfe as replacement for "Mr Crespigny, who has been seriously ill and is not likely again to resume duty." When a

---

[28] Valuable sources of information on the structure of the judiciary, particularly the functions of magistrates, justices of the peace and their courts are *Australians 1838*, Weber, "Origins of the Victorian Magistracy," Lowndes, "Australian Magistracy," and the account of the Magistrates' Court of Victoria published by the Public Record Office Victoria.

[29] www.parliament.vic.gov.au/papers/govpub/VPARL1860-61NoA15.pdf at 3. Prepared in response to a question in parliament, the document gave an account of the strength and disposition of the Police Force.

[30] www.parliament.vic.gov.au/papers/govpub/VPARL1861-62No3Pi-68.pdf at 26.

When he was obliged to retire on ground of ill health in 1876 Philip Robert's salary is said to have been £650. The difference may be accounted for by assuming that the additional £100 was an allowance for expenses and not formally part of his stipend. See Chapter Five at 172 with note 44.

[31] Chapter Three at 97.

[32] 1851: www.parliament.vic.gov.au/papers/govpub/VPARL1853-54NoA31.pdf at 40;
1860: www.parliament. vic.gov.au/papers/govpub/VPARL1861-62NoA11P1-80.pdf at 3.

[33] Talbot Leader and North-Western Chronicle, 27 January 1863, Grayden, Chronicle.

[34] *Talbot Leader*, 17 March 1865; Grayden, *Chronicle*.

[35] Reynall Everleigh Johns, *Diary*, in the Australian Manuscripts Collection of the State Library of Victoria, indexed by Denis Strangman; discussed by Cooper, "Rediscovered Victorian."

CHAPTER FOUR

deputation of citizens, headed by two local members of parliament, presented it to the Chief Secretary of the colony, however, it was explained that Mr Fyfe was currently too junior for such a position. No mention was made of Philip Robert's incapacity, and it appears that he resumed his duties quite soon afterwards.[36] In 1866 he was again on leave for three months, though this was not necessarily due to ill health.

In June 1865, however, an indignant letter to the *Talbot Leader* from "Pro Bono Publico" complained that he was not sitting frequently enough or long enough:

> For instance, that gentlemen arrives at the Courthouse generally about eleven o'clock in the forenoon, manages to get comfortably esconced in the judicial armchair about half an hour subsequently, and no matter of what importance the case on which he is engaged may be, or how near its completion, adjourns for an hour at one o'clock, returns to his agricultural retirement and domestic bliss in the rural vicinity of Amherst, for the purpose of recruiting the exhausted judicial facilities, and probably is prepared in 30 or 40 minutes after the expiration of the "hour" to resume the judicial functions. At four o'clock our estimable dispenser of the law again adjourns, and his work (if so plebian an expression can with propriety be used with regard to Philip Champion Crespigny Esq, PM) is concluded.

This eloquent piece of satirical invective received a response three days later, when the editor of the *Talbot Leader* published a note to say that Mr Crespigny's recent absences from the local court had been caused by the need to him to hear cases at Avoca while the magistrate there was on leave. While this did not quite answer Pro Bono's complaint, it did show the spread of responsibilities.[37] In similar fashion, two years earlier, Philip Robert had been obliged to attend to a rush at Majorca, both as a magistrate and as Warden to deal with disputed claims,[38] and there were intermittent complaints of the shortage of magistrates in the region as a whole.[39]

The varied cases which he heard were reported in detail by the *Talbot Leader and North-Western Chronicle*, later renamed the *Talbot Leader*, and several are cited or quoted by Grayden's *Chronicle*. They included applications for licences to sell alcohol, and prosecutions for doing so without a licence; frequent charges of drunkenness, including furious driving while under the influence; housebreaking and horse-stealing; and assaults – some with a knives. Two of the more notable were:

The Rape Case: In May 1865 a young Irishwoman, Mary Wolfendale, accused James Cousen of having imprisoned her in a cellar and sexually assaulted her in November of the previous year. She was forcefully cross-examined by Mr H H Hoskins, acting for the defendant, and Magistrate Crespigny dismissed the case even before the defence was concluded. The *Talbot Leader* of 30 May expressed surprise at his decision.

Embezzlement: In September 1865 Mr Frederick Odell Monckton, long-time Clerk of the Court of Petty Sessions at Talbot, was accused of misappropriating £100 from the courthouse safe. He had left Talbot without leave, and Magistrate Crespigny promptly

---

[36] Melbourne *Age*, 17 November 1860: Trove 154883959.
[37] Pro Bono Publico's letter, written on 19 June, was published on 20 June. The *Talbot Leader's* response appeared on 23 June; both are quoted by Grayden, *Chronicle*.
[38] *Talbot Leader*, news items of 24 and 28 April 1863, cited by Grayden, *Chronicle*; and "The Warden's Boundaries," 9 June 1863; quoted by Grayden, *Chronicle*.
[39] *Talbot Leader and North-Western Chronicle*, "A Scarcity of Magistrates," 16 May 1862; quoted by Grayden, *Chronicle*.

arranged a warrant for his arrest, but an initial charge was abandoned on a technicality. On a second hearing, however, despite an energetic defence by Mr Hoskins, Monckton was committed for trial.

The case was heard at Maryborough General Sessions in February 1866, and Monckton was found guilty. An appeal to the Supreme Court, arguing that the evidence was insufficient to justify the verdict, was rejected in June.[40]

Mr Hoskins was a local solicitor, but he frequently appeared in court as an advocate, and he was well known for the enthusiasm with which he presented his arguments. In a case before Warden Crespigny on Friday 30 April 1869 one miner, represented by Mr Hoskins, accused another of encroachment on his claim. The *Talbot Leader* described the occasion:

> Mr Hoskins, and Mr Walsh of Ballarat, appeared to do battle for their respective clients, and fought with the utmost pugnacity. We need scarcely tell Talbot readers who expended the most powder, but we may inform the far off public that that it would take a good many Ballarat lawyers to put Mr Hoskins down; for he has a good library, his office is convenient to the court, and many of the audience will rush out with the utmost celerity and return at his bidding with convincing-looking files well knowing that this gratuitous service will be amply rewarded by hearing British and Colonial law cases cited with an amount of energy quite refreshing in these undemonstrative days.
>
> The fact is Mr Hoskins must fight, and is not particular where he hits; consequently on Friday he had a fling at his more learned brother's horsehair, as he designated the barrister's insignia [a wig], then a scrimmage with the clerk of the court because he lent a law book to the Warden when a ruling from the bench was demanded; and finally, twice threatened his Worship with a *mandamus* if he would not go on with the hearing of a case.[41]
>
> Mr Crespigny was so very courteous, and so slow to check amidst these boisterous proceedings, as to lay himself open to the charge of vacillation.

This was one of many such incidents. Mr Hoskins also served as Mayor of Talbot from 1865 to 1868.[42]

One more case, reported in the *Maryborough and Dunolly Advertiser* on Friday 4 September, deserves special mention, if only for the quality of the prose:[43]

> The case of the Police *v* Terrill and Watton, arising out of a demonstration which took place on Talbot Flat, on the night of the 23rd ult [23 August], was heard before P C Crespigny, Esq, PM, at the Talbot Police Court, on Monday last, and resulted in the acquittal of the prisoners. A brief review of the case may not be uninteresting to our readers.
>
> For some six months past a storekeeper named Whittle, who resides on Talbot Flat, was to all intents and purposes making love to the daughter of a highly respectable neighbouring gentleman, and gradually succeeded in ingratiating himself into the good graces of not only the daughter, but also the father and mother. Time wore on, his visits

---

[40] The later stages of the case were reported, for example, in the *Age* of 1 March 1866 [Trove 155046663], and in the *Argus* of 22 June [Trove 155044208].

[41] A writ of *mandamus*, made to a superior court, asks it to instruct the junior level to carry out a duty.
    Warden Crespigny was proposing to adjourn the case from Friday to the following Thursday. Since it is unlikely that an appeal to the Court at Maryborough would have been heard in less than a week, Hoskins' threat was somewhat empty.

[42] *E.g. Ballarat Star*, 27 April 1866: Trove 11286908. The *Talbot Leader* of 15 October 1867 also mentions Mr Hoskins as Mayor.

[43] Trove 253525475.

CHAPTER FOUR

were not "few and far between," and he frequently had the felicity of attending balls and quadrille parties in the company of the daughter, accompanied by her mother.

A gradual change is perceptible in the conduct of the gallant Whittle; rumour with her thousand tongues is busy, it ekes out that the daughter is supplanted in the affections of the enviable Whittle by the mother, and the rumour is verified by the fact of the redoubtable Whittle skedaddling with the mother.

When young folks or old fogies were guilty of such sins in the old country, they found a refuge in Gretna Green, or they wisely placed a long distance between themselves and those from whose care they had escaped; but Whittle and his paramour showed a more plucky spirit – climacteric influences may account for it. The main road, only, divides the present residence of the unnatural mother from her husband's roof, under which dwelleth her children.

Expressions of sympathy with the sorrowing husband and the motherless children were on every lip, and the indignation of the populace resolved itself into giving the guilty pair ocular and auricular demonstration of their abhorrence of the outrage upon morality committed by them. A crowd collected on the main road, an effigy of Whittle was carried before them, to be burned within sight of the original. Whittle presents himself; groans and hisses; and an occasional volley of stones, *à la Tipperary*, assail him; windows are smashed in; himself and his paramour seek refuge from a neighbouring magistrate in vain, and finally accept a night's lodging from Sergeant Boyle, in the new lock-up at the Camp.[44]

It was for carrying the effigy that Terrill and Watton were arrested. Mr Wells appeared for their defence, and the trial was listened to by a crowded Court.

When the effigy was produced in Court, at the request of Mr Wells, the effect upon the audience can be easier imagined than described. The Bench, the Bar, and the crowded Court were for some minutes convulsed with laughter. The decision of the bench was received with unrestrained applause by those who were present, and Mr Wells, at the termination of the case, handed over his fee for the defence of the prisoners to be given to the Amherst hospital.

The effigy is still in the custody of the police, and if it were possible to steal it, the original intention of hanging it would be carried out, and we are informed that the sum of five pounds has been offered for it, but wisely refused by those in whose safe keeping it is for the present.

In many respects, outside his legal duties, Philip Robert's most substantial public contribution was to the local hospital.[45]

In the first years of the gold rush at Daisy Hill/Amherst and Back Creek there had been no effective medical aid available for any of the several thousand miners working in the district. Accidents and illness had often to be dealt with on a very amateur basis, no establishment

---

[44] We must assume the "neighbouring magistrate" was Philip Robert Crespigny, for the main road passed his property as well as Mr Whittle's and that of the unfortunate husband, and there was no other magistrate in the district. This did not prevent him hearing the subsequent case.

Though the reference to Tipperary implies that it is an Irish custom, "rough music" or charivari was common in England and Europe as a show of disapproval against people who had offended the accepted norms of good behaviour; the name charivari is thought to be a corruption of vulgar Latin. The core of the demonstration was a rowdy gathering, often in procession, with a great deal of noise made by banging pots and pans. It could turn violent, so Mr Whittle and his companion were probably wise to seek protection.

The camp in which they found refuge would have been the Commissioner's Camp at Amherst [Chapter Three at 111]. Presumably now known as the Warden's Camp, it was the local police headquarters and had some facilities for holding prisoners.

[45] A history of the hospital is provided by Brewster, *Amherst District Hospital 1859 to 1933*.

provided long-term nursing, and the potential for mortality was high. Through local initiative a basic "timber ward" was set up in 1857. It is said to have provided care in ten beds, but there are few records and little is known. More to the point, while there was government support available, it was necessary to establish a formal Board of Management, overseen by trustees, in order to apply for funds and take responsibility for their expenditure.

On 21 July 1859, at a public meeting to elect such a Board, Philip Robert was chosen to be the first president, and he held that position for ten years until 1869.[46] The local Dr Dow was the first House Surgeon, and a Dr Radcliffe was House Physician.

The Amherst District Hospital was formally opened on 1 January 1860. Though it comprised at that time no more than the original timber ward and a newly-built cook-house, roofed in iron, the Board had asked for money to be included in the next Government Estimates, and over the following years there was an annual grant of some £1500. This was supplemented by subscriptions of £1 a year from local people, who were thus entitled to hospital treatment at need. Half that amount, ten shillings, bought the right to attend as out-patients, and local councils paid £5 to cover their employees. The region serviced covered the gold fields as far as Avoca and Lamplough, and the beds were almost always full. The vast majority of patients were miners and the most common problem was injury, frequently involving the loss of a limb or an eye.

A second wing was opened in February of 1862, and a central building at the end of the following year. This last had been delayed by the late approval of the government grant, but the initial cost was covered by a local appeal which raised £500. One feature of the fund-raising program was the Hospital Fete, first held in 1865, which developed into a major local celebration and even attracted the attention of the national press.

---

[46] Brewster, *Amherst District Hospital*, 63, has a list of office-holders based upon records held by the Talbot Museum. She has P Crespiney [*sic*] as president for seven years, from 1859 to 1866. The *Talbot Leader*, however, cited by Grayden, *Chronicle*, records the annual meeting held on Thursday 28 January 1869, when Mr P C Crespigny was nominated for a further term as president. He declined, however, as he would be leaving the district within a few days, but remarked that he had had the honour of being elected each year since the earliest date of the institution.

At 67, the *History* lists past officials, but no president is recorded after P C Crespigney in 1866 until Mr Stewart Symes in 1875. The *Talbot Leader* report, however, states that Mr Moritz Cohn, the Mayor, was elected to succeed Mr Crespigny; he probably held office for the next six years.

CHAPTER FOUR

*The Seventh Annual Amherst Hospital Fete, held at Talbot, Victoria,
1st November 1871*
From Illustrated Australian News for Home Readers, *Melbourne
Monday 4 December 1871, page 221*

On 24 February 1865 *Victoria Government Gazette* announced that the Governor and his Executive Council had declared The Amherst District Hospital to be a body politic and corporate under the terms of the Act for Hospitals and Charitable Institutions. Contracts for the construction of a third wing were invited in that same year, the work began a few months later, and the building was completed in 1867. The hospital was now one of three in the region, the other two being those of Ballarat and of Maryborough, both much larger centres. It was later extended further, and despite a steady decline of local population the hospital maintained its operation for almost seventy years until a final closure in 1933.

Such a large and swift increase in the function and facilities of the hospital during the years of Philip Robert's presidency – beginning with a single wooden ward and concluding with four substantial buildings – demanded a great deal of attention and energy. Besides questions of finance and accountability, and the arrangements for contracts and construction, there were problems of water supply, road access, fencing and general maintenance, all of which had to be dealt with, and there were occasional difficulties with doctors and the nursing staff. It was an impressive development for a very new venture, and Philip Robert showed remarkable administrative skill in a very different field.

At one time or another Magistrate Crespigny was also chairman or president of the Amherst Mechanics Institute – which housed the local library – and of the Anglican community.[47] A Church of England school had been opened at Amherst in 1856, and a there was a Wesleyan/

---

[47] In July 1863, for example, he was re-elected president of the Mechanics Institute, and in October he took the chair at a formal meeting held after the Church of England Tea Festival and Sacred Concert: *Talbot Leader* 21 July and 16 October, cited by Grayden, *Chronicle*. In the following year he was a member of the committee of an Anti-Transportation Meeting.

Methodist church, but it was some time before the local Anglicans had a proper building for worship or, indeed, a full clergyman to take services. In February 1861 a General Meeting of Members of the Church of England at Talbot reported that the diocese of Ballarat had not yet allocated a priest to the district, and they were compelled to rely upon a lay preacher from Lamplough, twenty-five kilometres away. A wooden building had been constructed to serve as a venue until something more permanent could be erected, but it was flattened by a storm – which also stripped many of the canvas houses in the town – just as it was about to be handed over. Until recently, with the kind permission of Police Magistrate P C Crespigny, Sunday morning services had been held in the court house, but it had now been found that evenings were more convenient, so the Presbyterian church was being rented at the cost of £1 a week.[48]

Like the hospital though on a smaller scale, such civic activities were supported by volunteers and fund-raising. The balance sheet presented at the Anglican General Meeting identified £25 received from church collections and £100 from the proceeds of the Bazaar, and in May 1862 Charlotte Frances, Mrs Crespigny, was presiding over tables at such a function.[49]

We may assume that a temporary building was eventually constructed, but work on the permanent church of Saint Michael and All Angels commenced only in 1870, and it was opened on Trinity Sunday 1871. Built of bluestone in Gothic Revival style, it is one of the finest and oldest surviving buildings in Talbot. Though Charlotte Frances and Philip Robert Crespigny may have seen the beginning of the work, however, they had left the district before it was completed.[50]

The Anglican Church of Saint Michael and All Angels, Talbot[51]

---

[48] *North-Western Chronicle*, 7 February 1861; Grayden, *Chronicle*.

[49] Talbot Leader and North-Western Chronicle, 27 May 1862; Grayden, Chronicle.

[50] Trinity Sunday in 1871 was 4 June; Philip Robert and his family had been at Ararat since May: Chapter Five at 161.

[51] In similar fashion, though there were many Irish people on the gold-fields, including at Amherst and Talbot, and they brought with them a strong Roman Catholic tradition, the community was less publicised. It appears to have followed the Anglican model with a temporary construction, but the foundation stone for the church of Saint Patrick was laid in 1869: "Solemn Functions in Talbot;" the Roman Catholic *Advocate* for 16 October 1865. The ceremony had been held on 26 September; the estimated cost of the building, also to be constructed of bluestone, was £3000. The building survives, but it was sold in 1977 and no longer serves as a church.

CHAPTER FOUR

As "Pro Bono" remarked in his letter to the *Talbot Leader*, Philip Robert and his family were living at this time on a property midway along the road between Amherst and Back Creek/Talbot. Given the name Daisy Hill Farm – from the previous name of the area and the creek which ran through it – it eventually comprised eighty-three acres – 33.5 hectares – with a substantial house.[52]

This was a working property, for the *Talbot Leader* of 15 February 1867 mentioned that a severe windstorm had demolished a stack of hay weighing several tons, spreading sheaves of grain in every direction. Given Philip Robert's responsibilities as a magistrate, there must have been hired help, but no matter what assistance there may have been on the farm and in the household, a great deal must have fallen upon Charlotte Frances, and through all their time at Amherst-Talbot she and Philip Robert were dealing with four children, three of them teenagers. Between 1859 and 1869 Ada grew from twelve years old to twenty-two, Philip from nine to nineteen, Viola from four to fourteen, and Rose from one to eleven. In England, Constantine Trent, eight to eighteen, passed through school and entered the British army.

Ada Champion Crespigny
c.1855

Viola Champion Crespigny
c.1865

Though he was obliged to travel widely in the district, Philip Robert was normally able to sleep at home, so there were few occasions to write letters within the family. One, however, addressed to Ada, was probably written when he was away in Melbourne about 1860:

Letter 5
Dearest little Mouse,
    A little bird has just told me that you have been a dear good little girl, and I shall therefore get the prettiest present for you I can. Tell Loup [Philip] that I shall not forget to buy him something too, and if the little bird tells me he has been very good, I will get whatever I think he will like best. I shall be back very soon after you get this letter, so mind be very good children and be very kind indeed to dear Mama. I will not forget

---

[52] An advertisement in the *Ballarat Star* at the time of the family's departure from Amherst-Talbot has a description of the property: 133 below. Philip Robert gave his address as Daisy Hill Farm, Talbot, when he wrote to the Melbourne *Argus* on 27 August 1864 supporting the account of his son Philip about his encounter with a bushranger. The letter was published by the newspaper in its issue of 2 September: Trove 5747472. The incident is discussed below.

something for Bab and Polly. Goodnight darling Mouse. I hope soon to give you all a great big kiss.

Your most affec
Father, P C C

Rosalie Helen Champion Crespigny ["Rose"]
c.*1870*

Ada was at this time about twelve years old, and the nickname "Mouse" may indicate that although she was the eldest she was quiet and shy. "Loup," in contrast, from the French for a wolf, refers to Philip, who turned ten in 1860 and appears always to have been energetic. "Bab" and "Polly" are presumably the two youngest children; Viola, turning five, and Rose, two – they would have been pet names, for no reason now known, and were probably not maintained for long. Philip, however, was known to the family as Loup or Loo for much of his life.

With such a nickname, it is not entirely surprising that Philip was involved in the most trouble. In August 1864 the *Talbot Leader* reported on the "Daring Attempt to Murder the Son of Mr P C Crespigny, Police Magistrate of this District." According to Philip, then fourteen years old, on Friday 12 August he saw a man lurking near the barn. He ran away when he was challenged, and though Philip pursued he could not find him. On the following night he was seen again, and both Philip and his father gave chase, but again without success. On Sunday Philip went for a walk, taking a gun with him, and saw the man some distance away. The fellow threatened to shoot if he did not put down the gun, and when Philip instead raised his weapon he did indeed fire, wounding Philip slightly on the shoulder. Philip fired back, hitting his opponent's thumb, so that he took refuge behind a tree and then fled. Police were called and made a search, but nothing was found. That evening the man was seen by Philip, and also by his eighteen-year-old cousin Cecile Sophia Dana who was staying with the family, but the fellow ran off again, and though there were renewed searches by the police there were no further sightings.

There were other reports of a mysterious and/or suspicious stranger in the district, but Philip's story does have curious elements. The *Dunolly Express* cast doubt, and was followed

CHAPTER FOUR

by the Melbourne *Argus*, and although Philip Robert wrote to confirm his son's account and offered a reward for information, the satirical magazine *Punch* of Melbourne published jokes and verses of doggerel on the subject. Amidst suggestions that the incident had been an exaggerated accident, the affair eventually blew over and was forgotten.[53]

Less dramatically, in October of the following year a saddle was stolen from the horse of Mr Crespigny, junior, but was then found hidden behind a hedge quite close to the site of the robbery.

A few months later, on 1 April 1866 – a most appropriate day – Philip was involved in a ridiculous incident in the church of Saint Michael at Talbot; that is the temporary structure which served the congregation before the permanent stone building was completed in 1871.

It appears that as the minister was giving his sermon, he noticed Philip looking at his watch – not once but twice. Interrupting his address, he made a point of calling the boy out for discourtesy. Admittedly, men's timepieces at that time were fob or pocket watches, not worn on the wrist, so even a surreptitious glance would have been comparatively noticeable. It is nonetheless extraordinary for the preacher to make such a fuss, and the situation got worse, culminating in a report published by the *Maryborough and Dunolly Advertiser*. That newspaper is not yet digitised, but the item was reprinted in the *Ballarat Star* of Wednesday 4 April 1866 under the heading "A Nice Youth:"[54]

> A scene in St Michael's Church, Talbot, is thus referred to by a correspondent of the *M and D Advertiser*:– "A noteworthy incident happened in St Michael's Church, on Sunday. The evening service was honoured by the presence of some of the members of our police magistrate's family, when the conduct of Mr Crespigny, junior, (a youth, I suppose of about nineteen or twenty years of age), was such as to draw forth a personal reproof from the minister, who told him (stopping in the middle of his sermon for that purpose) that his conduct 'was annoying to him and offensive to others.'
>
> "One would have thought that the reproof thus publicly given would have the salutary effect of taking down a peg or two a cub (for he can be no gentleman) whose sole idea consists of an overweening sense of his own and his family's importance, and whose conduct was insulting to a minister of God.
>
> "But, mark the sequel. No sooner had the congregation left the church, than this hero accosts the clergyman, and, demanding an apology, invites the rev gentleman 'outside.' On being told that his conduct was disgraceful and that he had better 'go away,' the insensate boy climaxed his folly by talking about 'satisfaction,' and saying he should 'be heard of to-morrow.'
>
> "Fortunately, his notoriety is already so unenviable that one of the church committee, who was present, deemed it his duty to accompany the clergyman beyond the gate, in case this candidate for the Yarra Bend [Lunatic Asylum] should attempt personal violence."[55]

Copies of the report appeared not only in the *Mount Alexander Mail* of neighbouring Castlemaine, but also in the *Age* and the *Leader* of Melbourne, and even as far away as the

---

[53] Issue of Tuesday 16 August; Grayden, *Chronicle*. An account of the incident and its further repercussions is given by *Anne's Family History* at 2017/01/17.
[54] Trove 155047396. Paragraphing is amended for clarity.
[55] Yarra Bend Asylum was a hospital for the insane. It was maintained under various names from 1848 to 1925.

Tumut and Adelong Times of New South Wales. One week later, however, the *Maryborough and Dunolly Advertiser* carried a riposte, which was printed in the *Ballarat Star* as follows:[56]

> A few days since a paragraph appeared in our columns, extracted from the *M and D Advertiser*, which attributed rather discreditable conduct to Mr Crespigny, jun, while at church at Talbot.
>
> It appears that the whole affair was greatly exaggerated. A correspondent writing to the above journal says:– "I certainly think that the onus of attempting to cast unmerited odium on Mr Crespigny, jun, rests with the preacher, who caught sight of the junior Crespigny's watch (would you believe it, Mr Editor, that the fact of this young gentleman having twice looked at his watch in the course of the sermon constituted the sum total of his offence).
>
> "The bad taste and manifest unfairness of your correspondent in dragging the official position of Mr Crespigny into this matter, is only exceeded by the rev gentleman.
>
> "Happily, Mr Crespigny and family are too much respected in the neighbourhood in which they reside to be injuriously affected by anything that can be said against them, especially when emanating from an individual who, assassin-like, stabs in the dark, sheltering himself behind an anonymous signature."

Perhaps fortunately for the broader reputation of the family and of Philip in particular, the same text and disclaimer was published in the *Mount Alexander Mail*, in the *Age* and in the *Leader*. The *Tumut and Adelong Times* failed to mention it, but that probably didn't matter.

Indeed, the mind boggles at the preacher's conduct. Philip Crespigny was not nineteen or twenty years old at this time – he was sixteen – and however he may have behaved it is extraordinary to interrupt a sermon in order to "reprove" a boy in the congregation. It is hard to believe that even a fob watch can have been so disruptive as the clergyman claimed.

From Philip's point of view, such public embarrassment would have been quite shocking, the more so as the watch in question was very likely a recent present, and whether or not he did indeed challenge the clergyman to a duel, it is not surprising if a young man of spirit responded in some way.

In any case, what can have possessed the minister to call out and abuse the son of one of the leading members of his congregation? Apart from Philip Robert's position as a magistrate, the family had been strong supporters of the local church: Philip Robert had lent his courtroom for their services and Charlotte Frances was involved in fundraising.[57] It was hardly a wise move, and one may wonder how the incident was eventually resolved, and whether the minister remained much longer in the parish.

No matter the circumstances, moreover, the initial report is vicious. There must have been several people who, for one reason or another, disliked or were envious of the magistrate and his family, but this is particularly hostile and abusive, and it is notable that it was published in the Maryborough paper, while the *Talbot Leader* appears to have made no reference to the affair. Perhaps that was a matter of local courtesy.[58]

More generally, it is interesting to observe how newspapers of the time, beside more practical matters of politics, commerce and shipping, and substantial items from overseas,

---

[56] Trove 112868619.
[57] Above at 135.
[58] Grayden, *Chronicle*, cites or quotes references to Philip Robert and his family from the local newspaper, but has no mention of the affair. It is unlikely he would have omitted it.

Chapter Four

filled their columns with such items of potentially libellous gossip and passed them so swiftly from one to another – almost as well as present-day Facebook.

At the time of the bushranger incident in 1864, one of the sightings reported by Philip had been in the company of his cousin, Cecile Sophia Dana, who was staying with the family at the time. She was the daughter of Charlotte Frances' elder brother Henry Edmund, who had died in 1852 but had appointed his brother-in-law Philip Robert as one of the guardians of his children together with his brother William.[59] It appears the families were in regular contact at this time and the Dana cousins came quite frequently to Talbot. Born in October 1845, Cecile Sophia was some three years older than Ada Crespigny and five years older than Philip; her brothers George Jamieson Kinnaird, born in 1849, and Augustus Pulteney, born in 1851, were slightly older and younger than Philip.

Two years later, however, when their uncle and stepfather William Pulteney Dana died at Geelong in October 1866, the Dana children were already separated. George was employed in the Bank of Victoria and Augustus was still at school,[60] while Cecile Sophia was at Talbot, married to the postmaster James Colles. The wedding had taken place at the church of Saint Mary in Hotham [North Melbourne] on 20 February of that year;[61] the bridegroom was just over forty, his bride not yet twenty.

James Colles had dealt with Philip Robert in the case of embezzlement by Mr Monckton the former Clerk of Petty Sessions,[62] and Sophia presumably made his acquaintance while she was staying with the family. The couple had seven children, all but one of whom reached maturity, and descendants are still living in Victoria.[63]

As Philip Robert turned fifty in 1867, he and Charlotte Frances could be content with their position. It was not England – whatever that country might have held for them – but they had achieved a respected position in their community and a fair degree of prosperity. With Philip Robert's salary and profits from the farm, they lived in a substantial house, whose furnishings included a piano, so Charlotte Frances could practice the skills she had been taught as a child, and her daughters could learn music in their turn.

In September 1867 the *Talbot Leader* recorded that a committee had been formed to develop a series of Entertainments to be held in the Talbot Odd Fellows Hall; the proceeds would be devoted to the relief of distressed persons residing in the district. Mrs Crespigny, her daughters the Misses Crespigny and Philip, Mr Crespigny junior, were all involved and took part.[64] The second concert included a duet on the pianoforte by Mrs Crespigny and Mrs Cohn, wife of the Mayor, and Miss Crespigny sang "Sweet spirit, hear my prayer."[65]

---

[59] Henry Dana's death and the arrangements for his children are described in Chapter Three at 97.

[60] Chapter Three at 99-100. There are further accounts of George and Augustus in a separate section, *Tragic cousins*, at 149-156 below.

[61] The marriage was announced in the Melbourne *Argus* of 23 February: Trove 5774086. From 1855 to 1887 the present-day suburb of North Melbourne was known as Hotham in honour of Sir Charles Hotham, Governor of Victoria from 1854 to 1856.

[62] Above at 130-131.

[63] On Sophia, see also Chapter Three at 100.

[64] *Talbot Leader* for 24 September, cited by Grayden, *Chronicle*. The further accounts below appeared also in the *Leader*, in each case on a Tuesday issue. The paper was published on Tuesdays and Fridays, we may assume that each of the concerts had been held on the previous Saturday.

[65] *Talbot Leader*, 15 October. "Sweet spirit, hear my prayer" is an aria from the opera *Lurline*, based on the legend of the Rhine maidens. With libretto by Edward Fitzball and music composed by William Vincent

The Odd Fellows Hall Talbot 1866
Wood engraving by Samuel Calvert; collection of the State Library of Victoria

In the third concert, the second part commenced with a recitation by Mr Horne and Mr Crespigny junior.[66] The fourth concert included a duet on the pianoforte by Miss Crespigny and Miss Dallimore, and Miss Crespigny sang the romantic ballad "Kathleen Mavourneen."[67] In the fifth concert, with Philip Robert Crespigny in the chair, Miss Crespigny played a solo piece on the pianoforte.

There is no firm indication which sister performed which item, but one suspects the Miss Crespigny who played the piano was not the one who sang, and it appears more likely that Ada, nineteen, would have been the pianist and Viola, now twelve, the singer. Rose, nine, was probably not a performer. Miss Dallimore may have been their music teacher.

In the winter of the following year, 1868, there was a similar program of Popular Readings, several of them chaired by Magistrate Crespigny. At a meeting of the organising committee reported by the *Talbot Leader* on 25 September, however, Mr Crespigny – this time not in the chair,

> drew attention to the fact that some pieces of a description scarcely contemplated by the originators of the popular readings movement had been presented on the occasion of the last entertainment, and moved that the attention of the sub-committee for drawing up the programmes be especially directed to the necessity of due care being observed in their compilation.

His motion was seconded and carried.[68] There is no further information on what the offending items may have been.

Wallace, it was first performed in London in 1860 and was extremely successful. Many of the pieces were published as parlour songs.
[66] *Talbot Leader*, 29 October.
[67] *Talbot Leader*, 12 November. Composed in 1837, the Irish song – "Kathleen my beloved" – was widely popular during the American Civil War in the early 1860s.
[68] Transcribed [possibly with slight errors] by Grayden, *Chronicle*.

CHAPTER FOUR

Farewell to Talbot

As early as 1867 there had been concern in Talbot that a gradual loss of population after the glory days of the gold rush was rendering the district vulnerable to retrenchment and to an eventual division and/or absorption into the larger centres of Maryborough and Avoca. Such rumours were discussed by the *Talbot Leader* in an editorial of 14 May, followed by an eloquent protest at the government's high-handed conduct by a correspondent from Avoca, who feared the same loss of status. That danger passed, but the situation remained uncertain.

At the beginning of 1869, however, the threat became real, for the government began a program of economies, which included a reduction in the number of magistrates throughout the colony and a consequent extension of the districts to which each one was allocated. An editorial in the *Talbot Leader* of 8 January protested angrily that:

> The task of retrenchment in which the Government is at present engaged is not being honourably carried out, and unless great modifications are speedily made to it a storm of opposition will gather through the country ....

and on 12 January a large group of citizens attended a public meeting in the Borough Hall of Talbot to protest official plans for "the removal by the Government of the general sessions, the police magistrate, the receiver & paymaster and the detective officer from this town." Among many arguments, it was affirmed that "No work was more arduous than that performed by Mr Crespigny during the rush, and from their mining prospects at present the warden's duties would be greatly increased, and the necessity for a warden to be stationed here, felt in as great degree as ever."[69]

The government nonetheless moved very quickly, though not in the manner that had been feared. Instead, orders were sent transferring Philip Robert to Bairnsdale in Gippsland, 450 kilometres away, while his position as Police Magistrate at Talbot was taken by Mr Charles Cholmeley Dowling, who had held the same office at Creswick, fifteen kilometres north of Ballarat and thirty to the south of Talbot.

In effect, the district controlled by the Talbot jurisdiction was now extended to the south to include Creswick, and Magistrate Dowling took over this larger territory. In order to make room for him, Magistrate Crespigny was transferred to Bairnsdale, which had also extended its territory to the north, and the unfortunate magistrate at Bairnsdale lost his position.

Not unreasonably, the people of Bairnsdale similarly objected to the loss of their officer Mr Alfred William Howitt. There was a large and indignant public meeting on 23 January, and a strongly-worded memorial was sent to the Minister of Justice.[70] There had been some hope of a change of mind, but on Thursday 4 February the *Ballarat Star* reported:[71]

> It appears that the people of Bairnsdale were too precipitate in congratulating themselves upon the Government having acceded to the prayer of their petition to allow Mr A W Howitt to retain his office of PM for that district. Tuesday's *Gipps Land Times* [sic] says:– We were informed upon reliable authority last evening that the Government will adhere to their original determination to remove Mr Howitt, and that his successor, Mr

---

69   *Talbot Leader*, 15 January, cited and quoted by Grayden, *Chronicle*.
70   *Gippsland Times*, Saturday 23 January: Trove 61342442. A parallel memorial from the residents of Omeo in the Victorian Alps, ninety kilometres north of Bairnsdale, was sent on 26 January; its text is reproduced in the *Gippsland Times* of Tuesday 2 February: Trove 61342470.
71   Trove 112883092.

Crespigny, with his daughter, is now actually on his journey to Bairnsdale to assume the administration of justice.

The matter was then clarified by the *Gippsland Times* of Tuesday 9 February:[72]

> The memorialists for the re-instatement of Mr Howitt have received a very courteous letter from the Law Department, regretting that circumstances so ordered it necessary to dispense with the services of that gentleman, and stating that, as Mr Howitt was junior of all police magistrates in the colony, the Minister of Justice had no alternative.
>
> It is to be regretted that this fact was not made known by the Government earlier, since a great deal of misapprehension and misrepresentation would have been obviated.

Despite such explanations, and a degree of public acceptance of the need for economy, Mr Howitt had surely been badly treated.

It may be observed that although the *Victoria Government Gazette* mentioned appointments to local offices, it did not announce changes of tenure. As examples:

- In *Gazette* No 1 for 1869, published on 5 January, page 1 contains a list of Justices who are appointed to be Police Magistrates of Victoria with effect from 29 December 1868. Philip Champion Crespigny is listed at Talbot and Alfred William Howitt is listed at Bairnsdale.
- The next relevant entry is in *Gazette* No 10 for 1869, published on 12 February, where page 282 announced the appointment of P C Crespigny, Police Magistrate at Bairnsdale, to be a Coroner; the original document is dated to 8 February.

There is no entry relating to the dismissal of Mr Howitt from his position at Bairnsdale, nor anything concerning Mr Crespigny's transfer there.

For his part, while Philip Robert had at least kept his office as a magistrate, he was entering a period of confusion and disruption which continued for more than two years, with transfers to no fewer than five districts, while he and his family suffered from frequent moves to distant territory, generally with very short notice. As an immediate example, the news of his transfer too Bairnsdale was broken early in January, the *Talbot Leader* published its indignant editorial on 8 January, and the public meeting of protest was held on 12 January. Within three weeks, however, Philip Robert was the "former magistrate" at Talbot: though he did not leave until 3 February, his successor Dowling presided for the first time at the Police Court and in the Warden's Court on Monday 1 February.

On Tuesday 2 February, the eve of his departure, Philip Robert was guest of honour at a fine farewell banquet, held in the Borough Hall and reported in detail and at length by the *Talbot Leader*. Sixty gentlemen – no ladies – were present, and the Talbot Brass Band added to the occasion. After grace had been said and loyal toasts drunk to the Queen, the royal family and the Governor, Moritz Cohn the Mayor proposed the toast to Mr Crespigny, remarking, *inter alia*, that

> He regretted to think that a man like Mr Crespigny, who during a period of fifteen years – the fourth of an ordinary man's life – had been located in their midst, had formed a home and had brought up a family, should now have to go to a new place and new people, and to undergo at his age the inconveniences and discomfort consequent on such a removal.

On the other hand,

---

[72] Trove 61342505.

CHAPTER FOUR

> he considered that it was a proof of the Government's appreciation of him that they had transferred him to a place where there was a greater amount of work for him to do than there had been in this locality lately.

The toast was drunk with enthusiasm, and the band played "For he's a jolly good fellow," accompanied in song by the assembled company.

In his reply of thanks, Philip Robert spoke of the kindness and support which he and his family had received from the community, and referred in particular to

> the occurrence of a bush fire near his house, when the residents of the neighbourhood had rushed to assist him in saving his property......
>
> He could testify to the attention and consideration he had received both in sickness and in health, and he could not depart without publicly expressing his deepest gratitude for the past and present kindness.

Mr Hoskins, Magistrate Crespigny's long-term colleague and frequent sparring-partner in court, then proposed a toast to Mr and Mrs Crespigny and their family, and

> He alluded to the arduous nature of Mr Crespigny's duties in this district for years after the rush, duties which he had often carried out under circumstances of great personal inconvenience, and regardless of wind and weather had four or five times a day travelled to Talbot and from thence to distant parts of his division for the purpose of deciding those dispute which in mining matters at that time were constantly demanding settlement.

The evening continued with further speeches – including a toast to the [absent] ladies – music and song, including "Auld Lang Syne;" "My dear old wife and I" sung by Mayor Cohn; and "England, empress of the sea" with all the company joining loudly in the chorus. The final pieces were "Saint Patrick's Day in the Morning" and the National Anthem;

> and thus concluded one of the most successful and enjoyable gatherings we remember to have been present at in Talbot.[73]

On the following day, as Philip Robert travelled to Bairnsdale with Ada, now almost twenty-one, to take up his new position, Charlotte Frances was obliged to stay behind to close up the house and to sell the farming equipment. Advertisements in the *Avoca Mail* and other local newspapers in early February announced that:

> THE Sale by Auction of Farming Implements, Drays, Waggons, Chaff-cutter &c., &c., the property of Philip C. CRESPIGNY, Esq, P M, who has been removed from the district, will take place without any reserve, at one o'clock p.m., on Wednesday, February 17th, at his residence, situate between Talbot and Amherst.
>
> For particulars, *vide* posters:
>
> W. M, WISE
> Auctioneer[74]

---

[73] *Talbot Leader*, Friday 5 February 1869; Grayden, *Chronicle*.
[74] Trove 252153208. The same advertisement no doubt appeared in other local papers, but these have not been digitised. It was not placed in any Ballarat publications, but farming equipment would be of limited interest to townspeople, and country papers covered the area adequately.

For the time being, the house and its furnishings remained, but it was a sad and difficult time for Charlotte Frances.

In search of Daisy Hill Farm: a note

We have seen that Philip Robert Crespigny had purchased fifty-seven acres of land at Muckleford, east of Castlemaine, when he was stationed there in 1854, and that he sold the property for a handsome profit when he was transferred to Amherst in 1856.[75] Thirteen years later in August 1869, during his shorter, second posting at Amherst, he offered a property of eighty-three acres for sale by auction; the text of the advertisement is below.[76] There is some uncertainty, however, where this farm was situated and the territory which it covered. This note considers the question.

TALBOT

SATURDAY 14th AUGUST

At Twelve o'clock noon

TO MINING SPECULATORS, CAPITALISTS FARMERS AND OTHERS

JAMES S STEWART is favoured with instructions from P C Crespigny, Esq, PM, (who is leaving that part of the district), to SELL BY PUBLIC AUCTION, at Wrigley's Hotel, Talbot, on Saturday, 14th August, at noon,

THE WHOLE OF MR CRESPIGNY'S

V E R Y   V A L U A B L E   F A R M

CONTAINING 83 ACRES,

Situated on the Main road, between Talbot and Amherst, in the centre of and within easy access of the best markets in the colony.

The land is very good, easily tilled, and is undoubtedly auriferous, gold having been found in the farm, and in the land surrounding it on three sides. In the paddocks immediately adjoining some very rich claims are at present at work, viz – The Colleen Bawn, Tara's Hall, Pocahontas, and others, the returns showing that nearly £30,000 worth of gold has been extracted from the adjoining land during the last few years. Plans of the land, drawn by Mr Mining Surveyor Smith, of Talbot, from actual survey, showing that the property appears to be the outlet of a vast extent of rich auriferous country, and that the various leads therefrom have been traced within a short distance, and in the direction of the property, can be seen at the office of Mr Mining Surveyor Smith, or of the Auctioneer, Talbot.

There is a large Dwelling-house, Stable, Barn, and the various necessary outhouses in connection with farming erected on the property; likewise a large orchard and garden.

Title perfect.

Terms at sale.

---

[75] Chapter Three at 112.
[76] *Ballarat Star* of Thursday 5 August 1869: Trove 112891274. The entry was repeated on Saturday 7 August and on the following Tuesday 10 August. It very likely appeared in other publications.

On Philip Robert's second appointment at Amherst-Talbot in 1869-1870, see Chapter Five at 157-159.

CHAPTER FOUR

On 26 November 1864 Philip Robert received title to a plot of 10 acres and 8 perches [10.0.8] – just under 4.5 hectares[77] – being allotment 35 of Section One in the Parish of Amherst in the County of Talbot; the amount paid was fifteen pounds, one shilling and sixpence. His holding was then registered under the Real Property Act, and on 21 July 1865 it was entered on Folio 26475 in Volume 133 of the Register Book. The document, which has been photo-copied by Grayden, *Chronicle*, includes a surveyor's description of the boundaries and also a small plan of the block and its neighbouring allotment 34.

Grayden also provides two relevant photocopies:

- The first, taken from the original government survey of the site of Amherst in 1855, is reproduced in Chapter Three at 112; the future holding of Philip Robert Crespigny is outlined in red.
- The second, shown below, and associated with documents relating to the purchase of 1864, shows part of the parish map of Amherst from that period; the name of the holder of block 35 is now given, slightly mistakenly, as C P Crespigny..

It may be observed that the survey has been extended to the north, and that there are now several larger blocks close to the original Crespigny one.

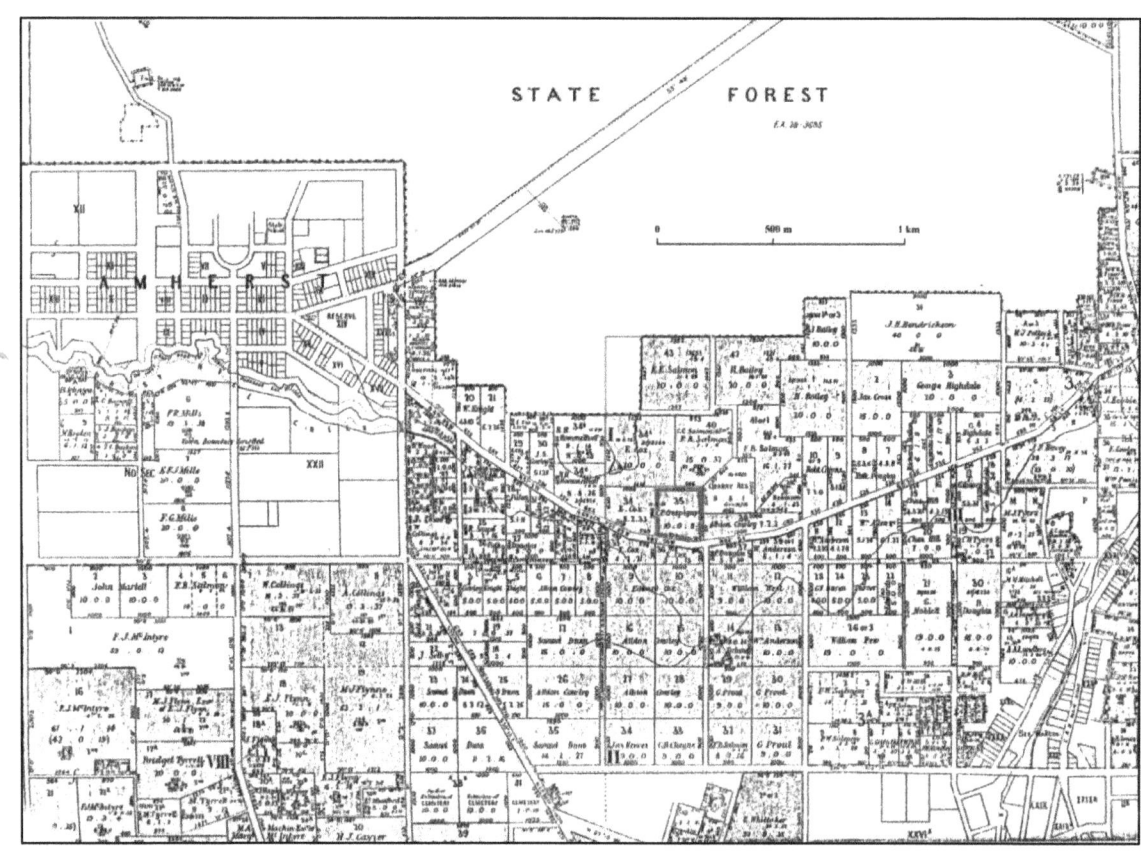

The survey of Amherst 1864, and the possible extent of Daisy Hill Farm
The original block held by Philip Robert Champion Crespigny is marked in red on black
and the putative expansion to 83 acres is outlined in red

In his letter to the *Talbot Leader* in June 1865 the correspondent Pro Bono referred to Philip Robert's farm as lying in the "rural vicinity of Amherst," and the advertisement of August

---

[77] In traditional English measurement, an acre comprised four roods and a rood contained forty perches. Philip Robert Crespigny's property was thus described as 10 acres, 0 roods, and 8 perches.

The Registrar-General's Guidelines used by the Land Registry of New South Wales equates one acre to 0.4047 hectares; a hectare being 10,000 square metres. Our calculations follow this formula.

1869 describes it as situated on the main road between Talbot and Amherst. At the present day, moreover, there is rising ground called Crespigny's Hill just where block 35 was, on what is now the junction of Pollocks Road with Salmon Road, two kilometres from the former site of Amherst township and three from Talbot.

Crespigny's Hill from Pollocks Road, Amherst

The most convenient route from the farm to Talbot would have been south along Salmon Road, then left into Crespigny Street – named for Philip Robert and identified on the second map.[78]

Crespigny Street, Talbot, looking west

Grayden's *Chronicle*, however, has no record of the purchase of any more than the ten acres obtained in 1864: so there remains a question of the additional land which went to make up the eighty-three acres advertised in the *Ballarat Star* in 1869. It is often impracticable to trace sales and purchases of land in this period, and we are fortunate that Grayden managed to find as much documentation as he did, first relating to the land at Muckleford and then to the acquisition of the original ten acres near Amherst.

If we consider the second map, however, and the blocks neighbouring number 35, there

---

[78] At the present day, the westward extension of Crespigny Street has been abandoned, so Talbot must be approached by way of Avoca Road. The old line, however, can still be identified on the modern map.

appears a possible solution. Immediately west of the Crespigny block, number 34 is described as 8.2.33 [*i.e.* eight acres, two roods and 33 perches] and is attributed to E Cox.[79] Immediately to the north of that block 34 is another labelled as block 34A, also attributed to E Cox but substantially larger at twenty acres [20.0.0]. North of the Crespigny block number 35, moreover, block number 40 is attributed variously to F B and G C Salmon, with area just over fifteen acres [15.0.37]. North again, and bordering on the twenty acres held by E Cox and the fifteen of the Salmons, block 43 of twenty acres is attributed to E E Salmon.

If we sum the area of these five contiguous blocks, the result is as follows:

Block number	attributed to	acreage [rounded]
35	Crespigny	10
34	Cox	8
34A	Cox	20
40	Salmon	15
43	Salmon	<u>20</u>
Total		**73**

This is ten acres short of the eighty-three which were advertised for sale in 1869, and the balance may have been made up from part of the twenty acres of block 47, attributed to H Bailey, or possibly from the unsurveyed land immediately to the west of block 43.

The region of Amherst and Talbot at the present day; from Google Maps
The suggested boundaries of Daisy Hill farm are outlined in red

---

[79] This is presumably the same landowner as the Edward Cox holding property south of the road.

Since there is no indication when the various blocks identified on the map of 1864 were actually taken up and/or occupied, the reconstruction cannot be certain. Nonetheless, an outline of the possible and approximate boundaries of the Crespigny property, known for a time as Daisy Hill Farm, is identified with orange on the modern map.

Tragic cousins: George and Augustus, the sons of Henry Dana[80]

Following the death of William Dana at Geelong in October of 1866 the Crespigny family at Talbot had limited contact with Charlotte Frances' surviving nephews George Jamieson Kinnaird Dana and Augustus Pulteney Dana, sons of her elder brother Henry. As above, the young men's sister Cecile Sophia had married the postmaster James Colles and was living close by, but her brothers were based at Melbourne and Geelong and it does not appear that they visited very often in later years.

Augustus, the youngest, had a sad life. Born in 1851, he was one year old when his father died, estranged from Augustus' mother Sophia nee Walsh. She then took Augustus, his two brothers and his sister from Melbourne to Launceston, where they lived in poverty and where his eldest brother William Harry died in 1854. The family was rescued by his uncle William, who married Sophia in 1856 – Augustus was five at that time.[81]

When Augustus was seven, his half-brother William Harry – son of his mother and stepfather, who had been given the same name as his dead elder brother – was born and died three months later. And very soon afterwards his mother Sophia contracted tuberculosis, suffering a harrowing fifteen months sickness before her death in 1860. Twice orphaned, Augustus was now ten in the care of his stepfather uncle.

The family was then at Hamilton in the Portland Bay District, and it cannot have been easy for William to manage his duties and care for three children of his late brother. When he was transferred to be Superintendent of Police at Geelong in 1863 Augustus and his brother George were sent to school at Mr Morrison's College, later Geelong College.

In 1866, when Augustus was fifteen, William married again but died just a few weeks later. George had now left school and was a clerk at the Bank of Victoria in Melbourne while their sister Cecile Sophia, five years older than Augustus, was married and living at Talbot. So the boy was alone at school, under the formal guardianship of his father's old friend Evelyn Sturt, Magistrate at Melbourne.

One year later in November 1867 Augustus, now sixteen years old, was declared uncontrollable – he had presumably been disruptive and badly behaved both at school and at home. Magistrate Sturt arranged his committal as a ward of the state, and paid ten shillings a week for his keep. Augustus absconded for a short time in January 1868 but was retaken and returned, and in February he was moved to the training ship *Nelson* with nominal rank as an ordinary seaman.[82] Three months later he contracted scarlatina [scarlet fever], and he died on

---

[80] *Anne's Family History* 2012/04/25 has a short entry on George and Augustus, and is a more detailed account of Augustus at 2017/04/26.
[81] Chapter Three at 98.
[82] Laid down in 1809, commissioned in 1814 and named after the hero of Trafalgar, *HMS Nelson* had been a traditional sailing ship of the line, with three decks and 120 guns. In the 1850s, however, she was converted to a two-deck steamship, still with auxiliary sail, armed with forty-six guns.

In 1867 *Nelson* was transferred to the Victorian government for use as a training vessel, and on 8 February 1868 *HMVS Nelson* arrived at Hobson's Bay, by the mouth of the Yarra on the northernmost point

CHAPTER FOUR

30 May after three days illness. Young people are particularly vulnerable to the disease, and before modern antibiotics the mortality rate could be as high as 25%.[83]

HMVS Nelson *at Williamstown in 1898; she was sold soon afterwards*

Augustus was buried in Williamstown cemetery. Though he was given a funeral in naval style – perhaps to encourage his former comrades to better conduct – his grave is unmarked. His death certificate, moreover, has the name of his father wrongly as George Dana, inspector of police, and his mother is "not known." This is barely six months after he had been placed in care by a leading magistrate, and it seems extraordinary that no-one checked the file and/or advised Mr Sturt and obtained better information.[84]

From this summary alone, it is not surprising if Augustus was "uncontrollable" at the age of sixteen. He had never known his father, he had suffered poverty and hardship with his mother, he had seen her death and that of a brother and a half-brother, and he had also lost his stepfather and uncle. There may have been contact with his sister and the Crespignys in Talbot, but they were a long way away and Cecile Sophia was married and had other interests. Brother George was at Melbourne, but he was two years older, he was working and playing football and may not have had much free time – and he was probably closer to his cousin Philip Crespigny, who had joined him as a clerk in the Bank of Victoria. It is obvious that Augustus was disturbed and confused, and he was surely lonely and lost.

Besides his work at the bank, **George** was an energetic and successful footballer in the developing code of Australian Rules.[85] In 1866, at the age of seventeen, he was a leading member of the South Yarra team, scoring the deciding goal in a semi-final against Royal Park. The final score in that match was two goals to nil[!] and South Yarra went on to defeat the Melbourne club for the premiership and the Challenge Cup.[86] In 1867 George joined

---

of Port Phillip Bay immediately south of the city of Melbourne.
[83] Augustus's elder brother William Harry Pulteney Dana had died on the same affliction in 1854: Chapter Three at 98.
[84] *Anne's Family History* has an account of Augustus Dana at 2017/04/26.
[85] *Anne's Family History* 2017/04/29 discusses George Dana as a football-player. The early development of the game is explained by Ian Turner, "The Emergence of Aussie Rules."
[86] *Bell's Life in Victoria and Sporting Chronicle* for the Saturdays 15 and 22 September 1866: Trove

Melbourne, and on 8 June he was playing against his former team-mates of South Yarra.[87] He is not mentioned in reports of the following seasons, however, for he had left the Bank of Victoria to travel and trade in the islands of the South Pacific.

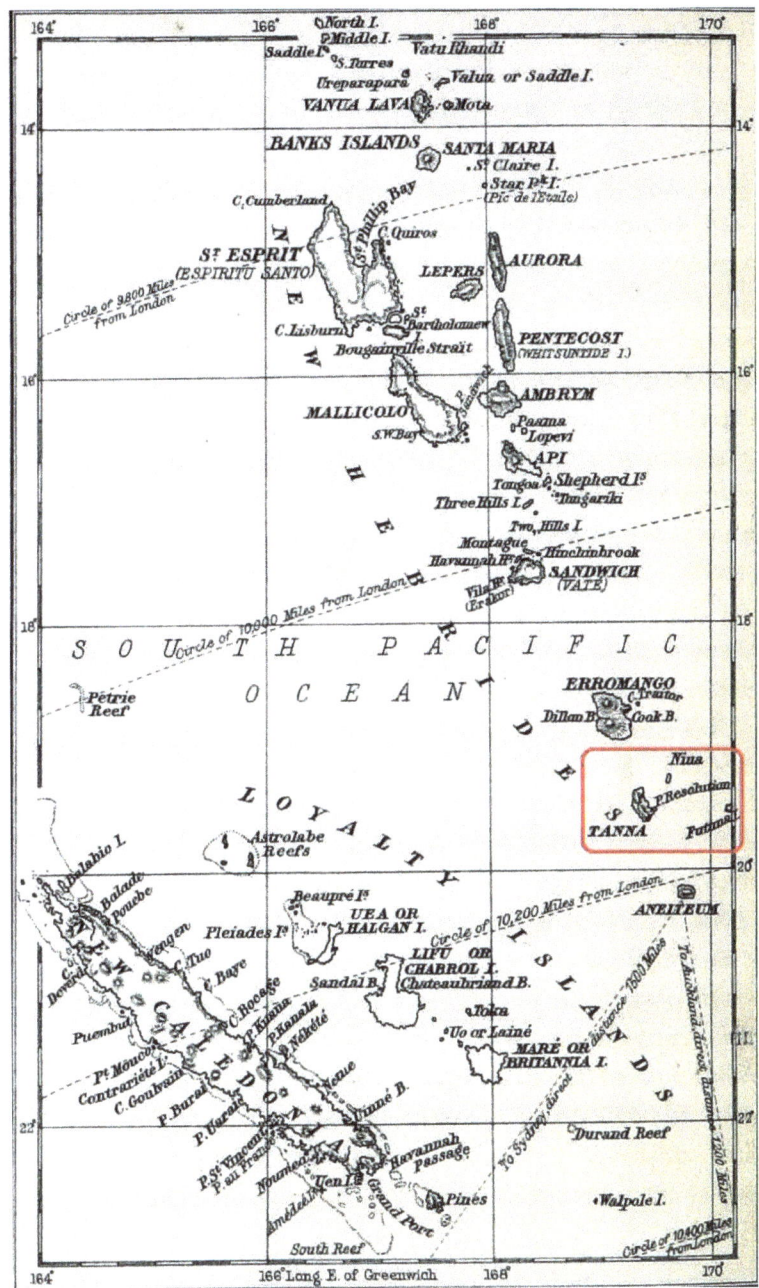

The New Hebrides, from a British map of 1884
The island of Tanna [also written as Tana], with Port Resolution, is indicated in red; Port Vila, now the capital of Vanuatu, is on the island of Éfaté, which appears on this map with the name Sandwich, or Vaté.

There was at this time a degree of interest in the possibilities of plantation production in the New Hebrides archipelago. Named by Captain Cook and now Vanuatu, the islands were largely controlled by rival native tribes, some encouraging white settlement while others objected or sought to steal from the newcomers. Though there was European influence it was uncertain territory: not until 1906 would Britain and France establish joint rule as a

---

199057292 and 199060355.
87 *Argus*, Saturday 8 June, page 5: Trove 5769138/513796.

condominium.[88] To some young men in Australia, however, the islands appeared to offer a land of opportunity, and George Kinnaird Dana was one of those young men.

It is not certain when George Dana arrived in the New Hebrides, for he may have spent time working or trading elsewhere in the Pacific. About 1868 or 1869, however, he was joined by two others, James Fraser Bell and William Alister Ross, and in partnership with James Bell he acquired a small schooner, the *Gem*, 52 tons, and took up land on the island of Tanna to establish a plantation for the production of cotton and/or of copra.[89] The father and the uncle of James Bell were dead, but both had been businessmen and his mother had married a doctor in Hobart, so there was probably some money available.

James Bell had also been a clerk, in the National Bank, and he was a little older than George Dana; his younger brother Henrie was the same age.[90] William Ross, whose father was also dead but who had family based at Geelong, was the nephew of an accountant, so again there was reason for them to be acquainted and to have some access to funds.[91] It may be observed that all these young men had lost their fathers and had no close ties in their home community.

On 23 January 1871 the *Gem* arrived at Port Melbourne from Levuka in Fiji by way of Tanna in the New Hebrides. Cabin passengers included James F Bell, age twenty-three and G K Dana, twenty-one.[92] Nine months later, on 4 October the *Gem* arrived again at Port Melbourne from Nouméa in New Caledonia, with cabin passengers Henry Bell, age twenty-two, George Dana, also twenty-two, and P C Crespigny, twenty-one.

These are inbound records; those outbound are not available, nor are the inbound records of the New Hebrides or New Caledonia. The Melbourne *Argus*, however, reporting the arrival at Hobson's Bay on 5 October, also gave the names of the passengers – slightly corrupted – and remarked that *Gem* had sailed from Nouméa on 16 September: so the passage had taken just under three weeks.[93] From other reports, it appears that *Gem* made quite frequent voyages from Melbourne to various Pacific islands as far as present-day Kiribati; there were several ships of that name, however, so this one is difficult to trace among newspaper texts which are often corrupted as they are digitised.

On the other hand, while it is not certain when George Dana first travelled into the South Pacific, these arrivals in 1871 are the only occasions that he returned. Since Philip is recorded

---

[88] The territory became independent in 1980 and is now the Republic of Vanuatu. The capital, Port Vila, is on the island of Éfaté. The island of Tanna/Tana, as below, lies some distance to the south of Éfaté.
  The archipelago of New Caledonia, also named by Cook, has been a French possession since 1853. The capital and largest town is Nouméa.

[89] Copra, also called cobra, is the dried meat or kernel of the coconut, from which coconut oil is extracted.
  At 52 tons, *Gem* was very small. Frederick Alexander Campbell, author of *A Year in the New Hebrides* as below, made the same voyage on "the little brigantine *Dayspring*," which was measured at 120 tons.

[90] The personal name of this young man and of his father is given variously as Henry, Henri and Henrie. Though the family came from Scotland, the last and more unusual form appears to be correct.

[91] A number of reports would be published on the fate of the young men. This account of their connection is taken from the *Ballarat Star* of 1 September 1871: Trove 197565565. An entry in the Melbourne *Weekly Times* of 2 September remarks that a brother of William Ross was a member of the staff of the *Geelong Advertiser*: Trove 220407389.

[92] The *Age* of 25 January: Trove 203014974.

[93] The *Argus* report of 7 October is at Trove 220407320.
  Shipping was reported by several different newspapers, and there are a number of entries for this arrival of the *Gem*. Not surprisingly, the names of passengers are variously transcribed.

as returning just once, in October of that year, it appears that he went with his cousin George on the outward passage in January or February, stayed for about eight months, then came back with him to Melbourne in October. He had been working at the Bank of Victoria since June 1866,[94] so he had been in direct contact with his cousin. It appears that he had either resigned from the bank or taken leave of absence to explore the possibilities of the islands.

List of passengers on the Gem, *arriving at the Port of Melbourne on 4 October 1871*

During his visit, however, things went very wrong, for on 28 July James Bell and William Ross were murdered by tribesmen on Tanna. The Australian newspapers published several reports of the incident, with commentary, and the Melbourne *Leader* and the *Geelong Advertiser* of 31 August carried a full account of an "inquest" held immediately afterwards, with statements from George Dana and several other witnesses, including natives whose reports were taken by translation.[95]

It appears that Bell and Ross had been on their way to a plantation owned by Henry Ross Lewin, and were being guided there by a native employee when they met a group of five tribesmen who offered to take over. These latter, however, then killed the two young men and stole their clothes and their revolvers. There was some suggestion that they been intending to

---

[94] Philip's obituary, published by the Melbourne *Argus* on 12 March 1927, mentions the year and month that he joined the bank: Trove 3843151.

[95] The *Leader* report is at Trove 196836553, and that of the *Geelong Advertiser* at Trove 148766652. Others appeared in the *Ballarat Star* of 1 September [Trove 197565565] and in a letter from the New Hebrides published by the Sydney *Evening News* on 25 September [Trove 129962412].
   There were also death notices:
   - in the *Mercury* of Hobart, where James Bell's mother, now Mrs Doughty, was living: Trove 8873161;
   - in the Melbourne *Argus*, where Bell's late father had been a merchant: Trove 5854797;
   - and in the Melbourne *Age* and *Geelong Advertiser* for William Ross: Trove 203009208 and 150417971.

eat the bodies but were disturbed and put to flight by a search party which had been called by a friendly native. The five murderers were described and named, but nothing more could be done – they belonged to a tribe that was known to be troublesome, and there was no military or police capacity to make arrests or undertake a punitive expedition.

James Bell had left his property to his brother Henrie, who now held a part-share with George Dana in the small schooner *Gem*. After the return to Melbourne in October, however, it appears that Henrie had had enough of the Pacific and resolved to find his fortune in other parts of the empire. In January 1880 he married Jessie Robina Kennedy at Calcutta; she died giving birth to a daughter later that year and the census of Scotland in 1881 recorded Henri Bell and his infant daughter Margaret living at Edinburgh with his widowed mother-in-law Margaret Kennedy. Henri Bell gave his occupation as "Tea Planter," but it does not appear that he ever returned to India, for Henry John Bell, aged forty-two, died at London in 1891.[96]

In similar fashion, the few months' experience of the islands had been enough to persuade Philip Crespigny not to return. Many years later he would describe to his grandson Philip George the uneasy feeling of being moored in the evening on a small ship just off-shore, with a strong sense of hostile eyes in the woods a short distance away.

He also regarded it as a mark of good fortune that the Bank of Victoria was prepared to take him back, for it was a general rule that a man who had left that service should not be employed again [97]

Port Resolution, Tanna
From Campbell, A Year in the New Hebrides
The term "Delt" at lower left is an abbreviation for deliniavit *= "drawn by," indicating that Campbell made the original sketch. The name of the engraver is at lower right, but is illegible in this format.*

---

[96] Despite the more regular spelling of the name, the age is correct and we may assume this is the same man. His daughter Margaret Jessie Robina Bell appears to have stayed with her grandmother in Edinburgh and married a man named Adams and later a man named Reid: the National Probate Calendar of England and Wales records that the widowed Margaret Robina Adams Reid or/nee Bell died at Edinburgh on 9 December 1957: www. ancestry.com.au/interactive/1904/32858_605905_2360-00166.

[97] Personal communication from Philip George (1906-2001).

George Kinnaird Dana, however, did go back to the New Hebrides, but though he sought to protect himself against future attacks with a loaded gun, his precautions were insufficient. A traveller in the region, Frederick Alexander Campbell, who published an account of his experiences in 1873, told of his death:[98]

> *Port Resolution, Tana*
> *December, 1872*
>
> There are two traders' establishments here, the occupants of them being engaged principally in the manufacture of cobra from cocoanuts and the collection of sulphur.[99] Until lately one of these establishments was in charge of a young man named Dana.
>
> He was one of that unfortunate expedition that left Melbourne some years ago to settle upon this island. Two of them – Messrs Ross and Bell – were killed by the natives; and now Dana, poor fellow, has met his death here too.
>
> Going out one Sunday alone, with his gun, it went off accidentally, inflicting a very bad wound in the leg. He was conveyed home by natives, and Mr Neilson [the local missionary] went down to attend to him. For some days he seemed to be on a fair way to recovery, but then, quite unexpectedly, he took lockjaw, and shortly afterwards died.[100]
>
> It is sad to see a young man like that dying alone, on a heathen island, far from his friends and relatives, with no-one to care for him except the kind-hearted missionary, near whose station the accident happened to occur.
>
> It is a lonely miserable life which many of these traders lead. They are continually shooting one another, or shooting themselves…

An announcement of George Dana's death was published in the Melbourne *Argus* just over three months later, on Tuesday 1 April 1873:

> **DANA**.– On the 20th December, 1872, at Port Resolution, Tanna, of an accidental gun-shot wound, George Kinnaird Dana, aged 23 years and seven months, the last surviving son of the late Captain H E P Dana.

There was a family legend that George and his friends, including Philip Crespigny, had engaged in "blackbirding," the recruitment or kidnapping of men from the islands to work as indentured labourers in plantations, particularly the cane fields of northern Queensland. This was indeed prevalent at the time, but there is no evidence that the young men from Melbourne were involved in it. In *A Year in the New Hebrides* Campbell has a lengthy passage describing the trade and expressing his strong disapproval. Had George Dana been involved, we may fairly assume Campbell would have said so.[101]

On the contrary, rather than kidnapping natives from the islands to work elsewhere, the young men from Melbourne were attempting to establish plantations on the island and recruited native people to assist them. They were welcomed by many, for they brought money and opportunity rather than taking men away, and it was said that James Bell in particular had been well-liked and popular. Not all the tribes agreed, however, and while there are claims of cannibalism amongst the local culture, there is even firmer evidence of

---

[98] *A Year in the New Hebrides*, Letter XII at 172-173. Paragraphing adapted.
[99] Mount Yasur, an active volcano on Tanna, is a source of sulphur.
[100] Tetanus is a disease caused by bacteria which can enter the body through the skin. It causes severe muscle spasms, and the symptoms frequently appear first in the jaw – hence the term "lock-jaw." It is prevalent in tropical countries, and though it can now be prevented by immunisation with vaccine, a person who is infected requires intensive treatment, often over several months, and even with modern medicine the fatality rate can be ten per cent.
[101] *Year in the New Hebrides*, Letter XVI at 204-212.

theft and violence. Much of the British empire was founded and maintained by lonely men in isolated outposts of Africa, India, and southeast Asia, whether as soldiers, rulers, traders or planters. The settlers in the New Hebrides were seeking to follow that pattern, but they were operating at the outer edges of effective control – and it was all just too far away.

CHAPTER FIVE

ARARAT TO ST KILDA
1871-1889

Bairnsdale, Bendigo and Bright, with a brief return to Talbot
Magistrate at Ararat
Sickness and retirement
Constantine Trent in Australia 1875-1881
Rose Crespigny and Frank Beggs
Philip Crespigny and Annie Frances Chauncy

Bairnsdale, Bendigo and Bright, with a brief return to Talbot:
In a letter to his ten-year-old daughter Helen Rosalie, written at Bairnsdale one month after his departure from Talbot, Philip Robert wrote:

Letter 6 2 March, 1869

My own darling little Rose,

I must apologise for not answering your dear little letter before. I am so very glad to hear that Vi and you have been such very good children and taken such care of your poor Mother in that dreadful <u>sale</u> and the other miseries since we left.[1]

Poor dear little love, how delighted I was to hear of the narrow escape you had! – from the falling tree I mean. Vi will soon be going to Inglewood and your poor Mother will have no one but you.[2] What care you will take of each other! How I long to be with you.

You would laugh if you could see poor Ada and I keeping house together.[3] When we first commenced I thought I could have it all my own way and make her tidy and so forth – but hitherto she says she will begin tomorrow! But tomorrow never comes. I much fear I shall be beaten in my attempts at making her tidy!

Now good-bye, my own darling, with love in which Ada joins me.

Your most affectionate Father
P C Crespigny

According to the *Gippsland Times*, which was published on that same day at Sale, seventy kilometres to the west of Bairnsdale, Philip Robert had been bitten by a horse just a few days before this letter was written.[4] Naturally enough, he did not mention this to his daughter.

The *Gippsland Times* also remarked that it expected his injury would prevent him from visiting Grant and Omeo. The goldmining township of Grant, now abandoned, lies a hundred kilometres northwest of Bairnsdale, just beyond Dargo; Omeo is 120 kilometres north of Bairnsdale, on what is now the Great Alpine Road. Both were in hilly and even mountainous country, so Philip Robert's duties entailed considerable travel.

Ten days after this letter was written, however, the *Talbot Leader* of 12 March 1869 reported:

---

[1] This must be a reference to the sale of equipment from Daisy Hill Farm: Chapter Four at 144.
[2] Born in 1855, Viola Julia Constantia was now thirteen years old. Inglewood is a small town some forty kilometres northwest of Bendigo. Viola was presumably going to stay with some friends there, but nothing more is known.
[3] Born in 1848, Ada was turning twenty-one.
[4] Cited by Grayden, *Chronicle*.

CHAPTER FIVE

> We hear that in consequence of the removal of Mr Dowling, PM, to Geelong, Mr Crespigny, our late Police Magistrate, will resume his duties in that capacity in Talbot and also act at Clunes and Creswick. The return of Mr Crespigny to this district from Bairnsdale to which he was lately transferred, may be expected in a week or so.[5]

Clunes lay twenty kilometres to the south, and Creswick, where Magistrate Dowling had been stationed before he took Philip Robert's office at Talbot, was another ten kilometres further towards Ballarat.

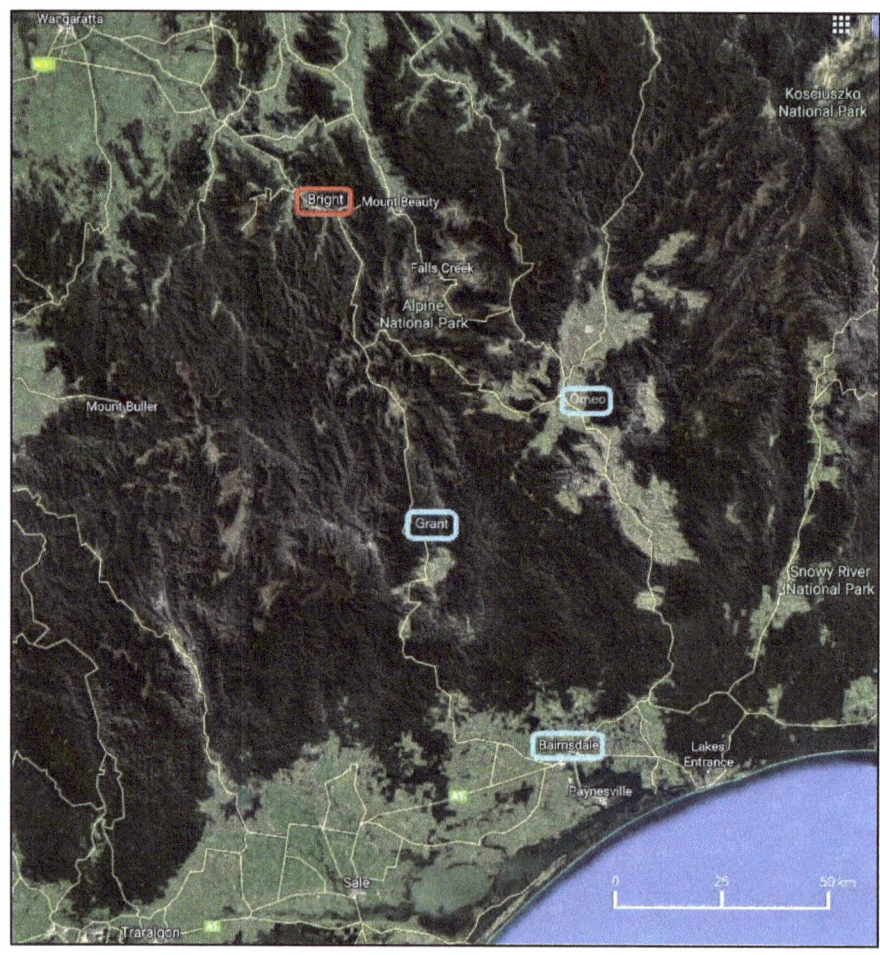

Bright and Bairnsdale in eastern Victoria
Showing the sites of Philip Robert Crespigny's magistracies 1869 and 1870-1871
Grant and Omeo were part of the Bairnsdale circuit

Three weeks later, Magistrate Crespigny attended his first hearing of the new arrangement in the Talbot Police and Warden's Court on Monday 5 April, and he now also held regular court at Clunes, at Creswick and at Learmonth, twenty kilometres east of Creswick.[6]

Philip Robert's tenure as magistrate and warden for the enlarged district of Talbot, Clunes and Creswick lasted just over a year. Issues of the *Talbot Leader* for that period have unfortunately been lost, as have those of the *Creswick and Clunes Advertiser*, while there are no more than passing references or quotations in the *Star* and *Courier* of Ballarat. Criminal

---

[5] Transcribed by Grayden, *Chronicle*.
By coincidence, the next issue of the *Leader*, on 16 March, reported that the Amherst District Hospital had just received the amount of £3 and 17 shillings, being the balance from the banquet which had farewelled Magistrate Crespigny in January.

[6] E.g. *Ballarat Courier*, 11 January: Trove 191562886.

158

and civil cases were heard regularly, and Magistrate Crespigny was a member of the local Lands Commission, but the only personal reference was in June 1870, when he suffered a fall from his horse and a neighbouring magistrate had to act in his office at Clunes.

Maryborough to Ballarat
Showing the sites where Philip Robert Crespigny held court 1869-1870

It was in that same month of June that Philip Robert was transferred once again, this time to Bright, in the hill country of the Victorian Alps southeast of Wangaratta. While not so far as Bairnsdale, it was nonetheless some four hundred kilometres from the region of Ballarat and more than three hundred from Melbourne. The *Talbot Leader* criticised the appointment, and the Melbourne *Age* quoted its comments, prefacing them with the remark that "Here is a grievance for the consideration of the Government:"[7]

"Last week," writes Tuesday's *Talbot Leader*, "Mr P C Crespigny and his family took their departure from this district, Mr Crespigny going to Bright, and his family remaining at Hawthorn. We believe that Bright is almost inaccessible, owing to the bad weather – at least it is to any but those who can endure the roughest kind of travelling.

"Mr Crespigny is one of the eldest servants in the Government employ, and we certainly think that he has not been treated with that consideration to which he is entitled in being removed to a district that will necessarily involve a long separation from his family.

"We have heard it intimated that he will not remain long at Bright, and we hope that the rumour is true, for there are plenty of magisterial appointments that could be given to

---

[7] Issue of Thursday 28 July: Trove 189330876/18286153.

CHAPTER FIVE

> Mr Crespigny, that would not involve the expense of keeping two establishments, and the separation of himself from his family.
>
> "In leaving this district, with which he has been connected for the last twelve years, Mr Crespigny and his family carry with them the good wishes of all."

Even before this, in August 1869 the property known as Daisy Hill Farm on the road between Amherst and Talbot had been advertised for sale, including the house and outbuildings, with an additional promise of possible mineral wealth. It must have been a difficult decision, but the rapid transfers from Talbot to Bairnsdale and back again were surely unsettling, and the general sale of equipment at the beginning of the year meant that the farm could no longer be worked by the family.[8] It is possible there had been some notice of the coming transfer, or it may simply have seemed more sensible to prepare in general terms for some such move and to realise the capital.

Bright, Victoria, in 1871
From the website Bright Pictorial Heritage 1850 to 2011, *compiled by Robert J Padula*

The item quoted from the *Talbot Leader* implies that Charlotte Frances and at least two of their daughters had settled in Melbourne before Philip Robert was sent to Bright. Son Philip had been at the Bank of Victoria in Melbourne since 1866, and is probable that the family considered Melbourne offered greater possibilities for the younger children: Viola was now fifteen years old and Rose was twelve. There would be more to interest them generally, while the educational, social and cultural opportunities were broader than Talbot could offer. The street address in Hawthorn is not recorded, and we do not know whether Ada had stayed with Philip Robert while he was in Talbot – as she had at Bairnsdale – nor whether she went with him also to Bright.

Philip Robert was indeed only a few months at Bright, but his comment in one case while he was there attracted some attention and appeared in several Victorian newspapers and further afield. The *Ballarat Courier* of Tuesday 7 February 1871 reported:

> A rather curious caution was given the other day to a prisoner on his discharge by the Bright bench. It may be remembered (says the *Ovens Spectator*) that a Chinaman named

---

[8] Chapter Four at 144.

Ah Sou, who had been in hospital, under remand for attempting to commit suicide, was on his recovery transmitted to the Bright bench. Mr Crespigny, PM, on discharging him, warned him that if he did not cut his throat more effectually next time he would be punished.[9]

By 18 March 1871, however, the *Ovens and Murray Advertiser* was noting that another magistrate was acting for Philip Robert while he was said to be on leave,[10] and the leave developed into another short-term posting, this time in the area of Bendigo. On 15 April the *Bendigo Advertiser* mentioned him holding court at Eaglehawk, a gold mining town just six kilometres to the west, and a few days later he held a Warden's Court to consider mining matters.[11] He was then at Huntly, twelve kilometres northeast of Bendigo,[12] and again at Eaglehawk, but on 10 May the *Ballarat Star* quoted a report from the *Beaufort Chronicle* that he had been appointed to be the next Police Magistrate at Ararat.[13] Two days later, on Friday 12 May, the *Ararat and Pleasant Creek Advertiser* noted that:

> Mr Crespigny, our new Police Magistrate, who is to succeed Mr Daly, has arrived and will commence his duties today.[14]

In contrast, and with some confusion, the *Ballarat Star* of Wednesday 17 May reported that:[15]

> Mr Crespigny the new Police Magistrate for the Ararat district (says the [*Beaufort*] *Chronicle*), arrived in Beaufort on Tuesday night on his way to Ararat, and sojourned at Scharp's hotel. Mr Crespigny has not determined which of the two towns he will make his residence.

Through all these various and shifting appointments, Charlotte Frances and the family stayed in Melbourne, though they were now at St Kilda rather than at Hawthorn. A notice in the *Victoria Police Gazette* of 13 June 1871 under the heading Property Lost notes:

> LOST by Mrs Charlotte Crespeigny [*sic*], on the 3rd instant, in St Kilda, a small gold chain about 12 inches long, smooth pattern, two seals and locket attached, one seal bloodstone engraved with a rose and scroll border, the second a cornelian with stag's head and holly-bush in the mouth, on the reverse side "Sevenbank;" the locket is heart-shaped containing different shades of hair.—8th June 1871

The *Gazette* has a separate section for items which have been stolen, so this was a genuine loss. Though the insignia cannot be related to the Kinnaird family – which had a different shield and crest – nor to any known other, the items were surely heirlooms and the locks of hair were family remembrances, so the loss was annoying and sad. There is no mention of anything being found and recovered.

---

[9] Trove 191645774. Similar items appeared in the *Ovens and Murray Advertiser*, published at Beechworth, in the *Argus* and *Advocate* of Melbourne, and in the *Mount Alexander Mail* of Castlemaine. Attributed to the *Ovens Spectator*, it was also published by the *Wallaroo Times and Mining Journal* of Port Wallaroo on Spenser Gulf, at the far side of Yorke Peninsula in South Australia.

Many Chinese names of this period are reported as beginning with *Ah*. This was a traditional and largely meaningless prefix for any personal name.

[10] Trove 196415867.

[11] Trove 87968940 and 87968999.

[12] Trove 87969222.

[13] Trove 197562563.

[14] 165 kilometres from Melbourne on the main western highway, Beaufort is forty-five kilometres east of Ararat and was part of Philip Robert's new district.

The *Ararat and Pleasant Creek Advertiser* is not digitised for this period. Extracts and quotations are given by Grayden, *Chronicle*.

[15] Trove 197562767.

CHAPTER FIVE

Eugene von Guérard, *The gold-diggings at Ararat* 1871
Collection of the National Gallery of Victoria

The Court House at Ararat
From Wikipedia Commons; photographer Mattinbgn 2011
Construction was completed 1866-77, so Philip Robert Champion Crespigny would have presided here.
The design has similarities to the court at Beaufort, constructed in 1864 [below at 168].

An Assessment of the Borough Rates of St Kilda made on 4 January 1872 identifies Philip Crespigny as the occupant of a wooden house in Lambeth Place.[16] Someone of a different name – illegible – is given as the owner, so the family was renting the property while Philip Robert himself was in Ararat, and probably also while he had been at Bright, Bendigo and Talbot.

When Philip Robert was transferred to Bright in June 1870, the *Talbot Leader* and the Melbourne *Age* remarked on the lack of consideration which the government had shown him, and the record of those years indeed displays an extraordinary degree of ill treatment, which one can only assume was occasioned by a combination of insensitivity and a gross lack of competent planning.

In sum, after ten years at Amherst-Talbot, in February 1869 Philip Robert was dispatched to Bairnsdale, displacing the previous incumbent, who was left without a position. Two months later he was back in Talbot, remaining there just over a year – with time to sell his house and farm. There followed nine months at Bright, from June 1870 to April 1871; a little more than one month in the area of Bendigo; and finally a transfer to Ararat, with some hope of a longer tenure.

Much of the turmoil was ascribed, with varying degrees of courtesy and sympathy, to a lack of funding and a resultant need for economies. Whatever the reasons, however, the difficulties of travel, of carrying out a responsible job in one different community after another, and the problems of finding suitable accommodation for himself and for his family through all these changes of circumstance, must have been a constant and exhausting source of strain. Philip Robert was now in his fifties, and he could certainly have been better treated.

On 8 January 1869, just as Philip Robert and his family were obliged to embark on their peregrinations, the *Talbot Leader* complained that "The task of retrenchment in which the Government is at present engaged is not being honourably carried out," and continued the article with references to "extraordinary vagaries," "the running of a muck at all the institutions of the up-country districts" and sheer folly – a kind of madness which no Government should be guilty of..."[17] The writer had a point.

Magistrate at Ararat

As Philip Robert Crespigny took up his new position as Police Magistrate at Ararat, he wrote to his wife Charlotte Frances on several different matters, but chiefly about the arrangements he was attempting to make for their accommodation in the district. One may observe the affection with which he writes to his spouse of twenty years.

> **Letter 7** [Monday] 10th July 1871
> My own dearest Love,
>   I got home all right on Sunday afternoon having only got another [break-]down of the spring of the coach about a mile beyond Burrumbeet![18] It is extraordinary it should have occurred going backwards and forwards to Melbourne! I was not

---

[16] *Rate Book* for the City of St Kilda 1872, at 241.
[17] Photocopied by Grayden, *Chronicle*.
[18] Some 135 kilometres from Melbourne on the main western highway, Burrumbeet is twenty-five kilometres west of Ballarat and seventy-five from Ararat.

CHAPTER FIVE

however detained long on the road – only about an hour. I forgot to leave you Paling's cheque for 3 pounds which I now enclose.[19]

I have been very busy all day writing letters and as I have no time to spare for this one must now conclude.

I have been looking at a house about 3 miles from this place as from all I hear Reid's house is not to be had – at least I think so. I will give you all particulars tomorrow.

In great haste
Ever thine, P C C

The region of Philip Robert Champion Crespigny's magistracies in the Western District
from Google Maps
Castlemaine and Maryborough are in the upper and central right; Talbot is identified with a T
Ararat and Stawell are on the left; EE marks the site of the Beggs family properties at Eurambeen near Beaufort
Glenthompson and Wickliffe are in the lower left; BC marks the site of Bushy Creek station
SM in the centre marks the site of St Marnock's station, later held by Frank and Rose Beggs nee Crespigny

Letter 8 was written on the following day; the search for accommodation was still inconclusive.

Ararat
11 July 1871

Dearest Love,

Mr Nicholas has not arrived yet and is not expected here for another week but I fear there is no chance of our getting Reed's house – that is to say <u>with</u> the paddock – without which it would be useless. However, as soon as Nicholas comes here if I find out that he does not want the house and paddock, I will make application for it forthwith to rent.

---

[19] It is not possible to discover anything more about Mr Paling, nor about Mr Reed mentioned in the next paragraph, whose house Philip Robert was eventually unable to buy. In cases like this, where people cannot be further identified, we do not add a footnote or cite them in the index.

Seeing how uncertain Reed's house was I went to look at another house about 3 miles from here on the Avoca Road.[20] It has forty or fifty acres of land attached to it and I think would suit us very well – the only thing is we should have to keep a <u>trap</u> and horse. It is uncertain whether this house is to be let and I shall only know in about 2 months' time. It is a wooden building rather <u>nice</u> looking, with a very nice garden in front.

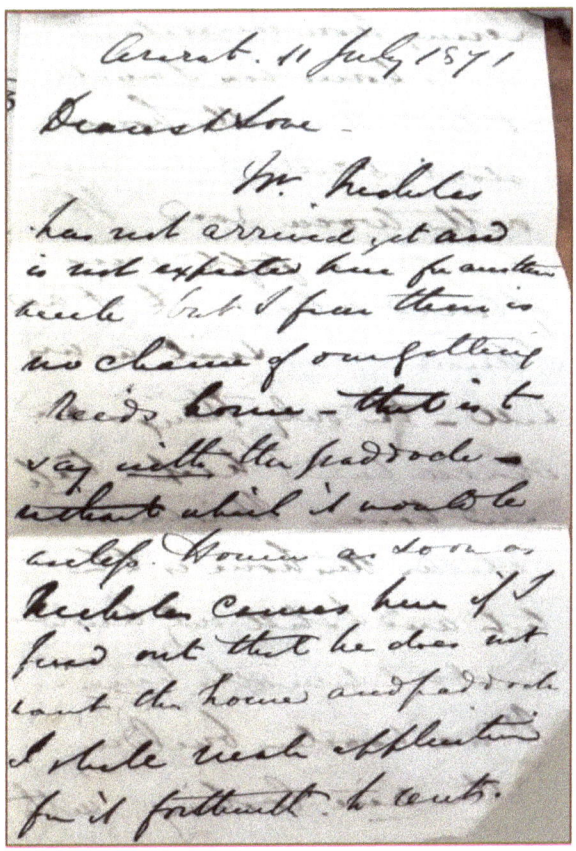

This will not prevent me looking after Reed's house if it is to be had. Reed is going to sell all the furniture including a <u>trap</u> which I suppose judging from the way ours sold at Daisy Hill is worth about 15 or 20 pounds. I have some idea of buying it as it would suit us very well but in doing so I shall consider well whether we can <u>afford</u> it so you need not be afraid of my getting into <u>further difficulties</u>![21]

The house that Cope lived in I have not yet seen but I intend to do so on Saturday or Sunday next. I start tomorrow afternoon for Beaufort and will not return until Thursday afternoon, but I much fear it will not suit as tho it is a remarkably pretty place it will require such a great repair that I doubt whether the purchase (sold about 5 Augt next) would be an outlay. I shall however see it. You may depend upon it I will do the very best I can to get us a house.

When I got here on Sunday I found a letter from Matthew reminding me of the fifteen pounds bill. It also said that the 6 months expires on the 10th inst, so I wrote to remind him of his error. I also sent him a bank draft for 15 pounds. I at the same time telegraphed to Webb to know whether he intended to <u>complete</u> the purchase on the 20th inst. I got a telegram from him the same day saying: "Yes, for aught I know to the contrary." I however have an impression that he won't have the money to pay.

---

[20] Avoca is about sixty-five kilometres by road northeast from Ararat.
[21] There is no information on what financial error Philip Robert had made before.

CHAPTER FIVE

We shall however see. I also wrote to Matthew to say I was perfectly ready to pay the fifty pounds which Webb deposited.[22]

I had [a horse, name illegible] taken out yesterday by the groom but he was so frightfully fidgetty that after going about 5 miles he was obliged to bring him back. I got on him today determined to walk him until I found he was quiet. I walked him about 5 miles and then took him a canter of 10 miles! so you need have no fear about him. He will be <u>as quiet as a lamb</u> tomorrow for my journey to Beaufort.

I was very glad to get your letter this morning! If you get a letter from the blacksmith at Creswick please forward it. You will find a pair of woollen socks in the dining room and I <u>think</u> I left a pair of gloves, yellow, the same I bought for my visit to the Govr.[23] Please send them by the <u>post</u>.

I shall certainly write home and not forget to send the <u>document</u> to Constantia for her £200.[24] I told Matthew that after Webb's telegram of which I sent him a copy that I was certain he intended to conclude the purchase! – but still between you and I, I am very doubtful whether he will really do so.

I have written you a very hurried letter but if anything else strikes me I will write to you again tomorrow before leaving for Beaufort. I trust the change of air is doing Fanny Were good.

With fondest love to all,
Ever thine, P C C

No time to read this over.
Errors excepted.

A few weeks later Philip Robert wrote to his daughter Rose, now thirteen years old:

Letter 9   25th August, 1871

My dearest Rose,

I have to thank you for your <u>naughty</u> letter of the 23rd inst.! I am delighted to hear that Ada and Vi enjoyed themselves at the Ball: and that they were not burnt in dressing or set the house on fire! and that Ada did not keep Vi and her Mother waiting! How did you get on with Mrs Henderson on the night of the Ball?

I hear from your Mother that you have made great progress in your music and singing! I am very anxious to hear you but I suppose I am doomed to wait for two or 3 months until I can get a house for you up here. I am delighted to hear that poor Thyrza is going to stay with you! I have looked in the *Argus* of yesterday but cannot find her name mentioned in the list of arrivals from Tasmania – but I suppose she will come today or tomorrow.

I fear your poor Mother has been greatly overworked lately! It is time for her to have a little rest! Surely Ada might assist her a little! I promised your Mother I would write to her today so must now say adieu, so with fondest love and kisses to you and

Believe me ever,
My darling child
Your most affectionate Father
P C Crespigny

---

[22] Webb may have been the intending buyer of Daisy Hill Farm. The matter is not mentioned in later letters.

[23] The Governor of Victoria at this time was Sir John Henry Thomas Manners-Sutton, Knight Commander of the Order of the Bath and Viscount Canterbury since 1869. There is no record when Philip Robert visited him; he probably attended a general reception.

[24] As was common at this time, "home" in this context refers to England. Eliza Constantia Frances Crespigny, Philip Robert's sister, had been the primary carer for his and Charlotte Frances' son Constantine Trent, who was now twenty years old and an officer in the British army; below at 173.

The letter is addressed to "Miss Rose Crespigny, St Kilda," so Charlotte Frances and all three daughters were still in Melbourne. [Philip, currently on leave from the Bank of Victoria, was with his cousin George Dana in the New Hebrides.][25]

For his part, Philip Robert was already on post. The *Ararat and Pleasant Creek Advertiser* reported on Friday 12 May 1871 that:

> Mr Crespigny, our new Police Magistrate, who is to succeed Mr Daly has arrived and will commence his duties today. Mr Daly will shortly take his departure for Wood's Point, the scene of his future labours.[26]

An article in the Melbourne *Herald*, published on 31 January 1872, identified the districts for which each magistrate was responsible and where they held their courts. Philip Robert, based on Ararat, sat also at Beaufort and Moyston while Mr Dowling, returned from Geelong to Talbot, sat again at Creswick, Clunes and Learmonth.[27]

Irritatingly, there is no record where Philip Robert and Charlotte Frances were living in Ararat. From the correspondence above, we may assume they found a property in the countryside nearby, but no newspapers or official documents offer anything more specific.

They had retained accommodation in Melbourne, however, for a lengthy account of the Mayor's Ball, published in the *Weekly Times* of 30 August 1873, lists Miss Crespigny – among an enormous crowd – in costume as "Winter."[28] There is no mention of a partner, nor are we told which Miss Crespigny: Ada was now twenty-four and Viola was almost eighteen; Rose, fifteen, was probably too young for such frivolities.

In the mean time, Philip Robert was carrying out his duties as a magistrate. Among many cases, in September 1871 he had to deal with an awkward charge of embezzlement against the Clerk of Petty Sessions at Beaufort,[29] and in 1872 there was disagreement among members of a Court of Petty Sessions.

In the latter case, it appears that an employee of a Mr Little was found to have been driving sheep afflicted by scab through the Wimmera District, which had been declared clean of the disease. Mr Little was charged under the provisions of the Scab Act, but the Justices of the Peace who heard the case were persuaded that the fault lay only with the drover, and that his employer was not responsible. Magistrate Crespigny, however, who was also a member of

---

[25] Chapter Four at 152-154.

[26] Wood's Point lies 180 kilometres east of Melbourne, in the Shire of Mansfield. Following the discovery of gold nearby the town grew rapidly in the 1860s, but the population declined through the 1870s and 1880s and is now very small.

The *Mount Ararat Advertiser* was first published in 1857, and was renamed the *Ararat and Pleasant Creek Advertiser* in 1861 – Pleasant Creek was the original name of the town of Stawell, thirty kilometres northwest of Ararat; the name was changed also in 1861, but the newspaper kept the earlier form until 1885, when it changed to be the *Ararat Advertiser*, a masthead retained to the present day.

Few issues of the newspaper have been digitised, and none from the years that Philip Robert Crespigny was magistrate at Ararat. Grayden, *Chronicle*, however, has several transcriptions of relevant items; this is one of them.

[27] Trove 245700546. Though the *Ararat and Pleasant Creek Advertiser*, as immediately above, dealt with both Ararat and Stawell, the two towns were under different jurisdictions. See further below at 171.

From a reference in the *Ararat and Pleasant Creek Advertiser* of 29 October 1875, it appears that Philip Robert also sat at Wickliffe, fifty kilometres south of Ararat: Grayden, *Chronicle* and below at 171.

The *Beaufort Chronicle*, local paper for that settlement, has not been digitised, but it was quoted by several neighbouring newspapers such as the *Star* and *Courier* of Ballarat and the *Geelong Advertiser*.

[28] Trove 223791178/23348755.

[29] Trove 150418195 and 197565930.

CHAPTER FIVE

the bench, dissented. The verdict was appealed, and on 10 September the Supreme Court found that the original decision had been mistaken. The matter was referred back to the lower court for correction.[30]

Beaufort Court House
Photograph by Anne Young 2019
Built of local brick in 1864, until 1982 the Court House was used by the Court of Petty Sessions, the County Court and the Court of Mines. It is now occupied by the Beaufort Historical Society.

In February 1875 the *Ballarat Star* reported the sad case of Bridget Franc, accused of assaulting her eleven-year-old daughter. A senior constable, two witnesses and the girl herself testified that her back and legs had been covered with bruises from the beating.

> The police-magistrate commented severely on the mother's inhuman conduct, and then sentenced her to a fortnight's imprisonment without the option of a fine.

At the same session an engine-driver was charged with the careless use of fire on a section of the Ararat railway. His defence argued that he could not be held responsible for any damage from sparks which escaped from the funnel of the engine. Magistrate Crespigny accepted that this objection was fatal to the case and dismissed it.[31]

The *Victoria Government Gazette* lists parallel appointments for Philip Robert as Coroner and as Official Visitor at the Ararat Lunatic Asylum, constructed some five years earlier in the middle 1860s. He was also a member of the local Land Board, where he sat regularly in the company of the District Surveyor, Philip Lamothe Snell Chauncy, whose daughter Annie Frances would marry his son Philip a few years later.[32]

---

[30] Sterling v Little, reported by the *Argus*, 11 September 1872: Trove 5838545.
    A skin infection caused by a mite, sheep scab is highly infectious and can be transferred by contact.
[31] The two cases are reported at Trove 208251481.
[32] For example, Trove 199330078; and below at 191.

Ararat Lunatic Asylum 1880

Of comparable importance for the future, there were several occasions that Philip Robert heard cases in company with George Beggs (1816-1879), a grazier who served as a Justice of the Peace.[33] George and his brother Francis (1812-1880) were in partnership at Eurambeen, ten kilometres to the west of Beaufort, and Francis's eldest son, also Francis but commonly known as Frank, was the same age as Philip the son of Philip Robert and Charlotte Frances. The two young men were friends, though on Wednesday 31 March 1875 the *Ballarat Star* reported that:

> A serious accident happened to Mr Crespigny, son of the police-magistrate at Ararat, when returning from Beaufort to Ararat in company with Mr F Beggs, jun, in a buggy from the Easter sports. He took too sharp a turn in going round Mr Prentice's corner of Havelock street, causing the near wheels to go into a deep drain, capsizing the buggy, and effectually putting a stop to any further progress in travelling. On extricating Mr Crespigny he was found insensible, and continued so for some two or three hours. Medical aid was called in at the Golden Age hotel, whither he was removed; and it was found that the injuries he had received had caused concussion of the brain. Mr Beggs fortunately escaped with a few slight bruises about the face and shoulders.[34]

A more up-to-date account was offered by the *Ararat and Pleasant Creek Advertiser* of the same day, with differences:

> Mr Crespigny, junr, met with a very severe accident on Monday evening, when driving from the ground where the Beaufort Athletic Sports were held to the Golden Age Hotel, in company with Mr Beggs and Mr A Campbell. The latter, who was steering, found it necessary to cross a deep rut to avoid a cart, and the shock was so great that not only Mr

---

[33] *E.g.* Trove 207641274 and 211002072.
[34] Trove 208252734.

CHAPTER FIVE

> Crespigny but Mr Beggs was thrown out. The latter had his lip badly cut, but Mr Crespigny struck his head violently on the ground, and lay insensible. He had to be removed to the hotel, where he continued without consciousness for eight hours. Mrs Crespigny who was sent for, drove down at once to attend to her son. We are happy to learn that the patient's consciousness is restored, and the case promises to progress favourably.[35]

Where the Ararat newspaper is vague, the *Ballarat Star* makes it clear that Frank Beggs was a passenger. The Ararat report, however, identifies the driver as a Mr Campbell, not Philip Crespigny; it also offers a slightly different reason for the accident and states that Philip had been unconscious for longer but adds that he was making a good recovery.

Three weeks later, a more serious example of an accident with a horse and cart gained the attention of Philip Robert in his capacity as Coroner. According to the *Advertiser* of Tuesday 20 April,

> A travelling tinsmith named M'Alpine was killed at Buangor Station on Thursday last. The unfortunate man was feeding his horse at the dinner hour, and after taking off the nosebag the winkers [*i.e.* blinkers] by some means fell from the horse's eyes causing him to bolt. In trying to pull the animal up the wheel of the dray passed over the deceased, causing internal injuries which resulted in death. The matter was duly reported to Mr Crespigny, who did not consider an inquest necessary under the circumstances of the case.[36]

Also in April 1875, an elected Member of the Legislative Assembly, Michael Byrne Carroll, was accused of forgery and fraud. It was alleged that he had persuaded Goldsborough and Company, wool-brokers – later combined to form Goldsborough Mort and now part of Elders Limited – to purchase wool that would be supplied by local farmers; Mr Carroll acted as go-between, handling the money and arranging documentation. It turned out, however, that the farmers received no money, and many denied having signed the receipts or the liens which had been placed upon their produce.

As Mr Crespigny and two justices of the peace committed the defendant for trial, the prosecutor Mr C A Smyth objected to the grant of bail, as the offences were serious and there were a number of other counts of forgery pending. When bail was nonetheless approved for the amount of £2000, with two sureties of £1000 each, Mr Smyth objected again:

> Mr Smyth was very sorry to have to object to this but he now held in his hand a certified rule for the sequestration of the estate of Mr Carroll under hand of the judges of the Supreme Court. Under these circumstances the personal bail of Mr Carroll was worthless, and he must object. If Mr Carroll felt aggrieved it was open to him to apply to the Supreme Court for an order for bail to be taken.
>
> He mentioned this because he wished to relieve the local Bench of responsibility The Bench had committed [the defendant for trial] and, under the circumstances he submitted they must refuse bail and the responsibility of accepting it would be left to the Supreme Court.

The Bench did now refuse bail and Mr Carroll was taken to the Ararat Gaol.[37]

---

[35] Transcribed by Grayden, *Chronicle*.

[36] Transcribed by Grayden, *Chronicle*; Buangor is midway between Ararat and Beaufort on the road to Ballarat and Melbourne; there was a railway station there which is now out of commission.

[37] Melbourne *Argus* of 16 April 1875: Trove 11515419.

Three months later the former parliamentarian was found guilty by a jury of the Supreme Court and was sentenced to fourteen years hard labour. The judge observed that the penalty was deserved because such conduct by a man in Mr Carroll's position could destroy all confidence in business. The prisoner "seemed rather astonished at the severity of the sentence."[38]

Sickness and retirement

In 1876 Philip Robert Champion Crespigny, now approaching sixty, had been Police Magistrate at Ararat for five years. We have considered some of his cases above, and mention a few from the second half of that year: on 27 June he acted as Coroner in the inquest on a fatal railway accident; on 26 September he sentenced a man to two months imprisonment for stealing clothing; and three days later he heard an appeal against the decision of a licensing magistrate and ordered the transfer of the right to sell alcohol at the Shire Hall Hotel from one applicant to another.

Besides these local matters, in September Philip Robert's jurisdiction was temporarily extended to Stawell, thirty kilometres to the northwest, because the magistrate there was on sick leave. It was a short-term solution to quite a minor problem, but it roused a flurry of indignation locally and led to questions in the Legislative Council, where it was argued that Stawell was a far more important centre, while the population of Ararat "mostly lived on government money."[39] The matter, however, soon became moot – at least so far as Philip Robert was concerned.

During twenty-five years in government employ, as Warden and later as Magistrate, Philip Robert had travelled widely in Victoria, often under harsh conditions – frequently shared with Charlotte Frances his wife. He had suffered some sickness, notably in 1860;[40] in 1866 he took three months leave, possibly on account of ill health; and he experienced disruption and difficulty during the several transfers from one centre to another over the two years from February 1869, when he departed Talbot, to May 1871, when he was finally posted to Ararat.[41] There were also the usual problems with horses: the occasional fall and the inevitable bite. In October 1875 the *Ararat and Pleasant Creek Advertiser* reported that he missed a court sitting at Wickliffe, fifty kilometres to the south, on account of a sudden illness: he had to send a telegram to explain his absence. Considering the nature and circumstances of the times, however, Philip Robert had had a healthy life.

It was probably quite surprising, therefore, when the *Advertiser* of Tuesday 4 October 1876 reported that

> Mr Crespigny, Police Magistrate for the district, is at present suffering from a severe illness, induced by changing from warm to cold bathing on Friday morning last. Medical aid was at once procured, and we are happy to say that Mr Crespigny is out of danger, although it is not likely he will be in a condition to resume his duties for a week or two. Drs Gordon and Mercer were the first to visit Mr Crespigny after the attack, and we understand that both were hopeful of the case. Mr Crespigny has been doing a good deal

---

[38] *Argus* of 26 July: Trove 11520916/242510.
[39] Trove 139770684, 590081 and 5903896.
[40] Chapter Four at 129.
[41] See above in Chapter Four at 142-144 and in Chapter Five at 157-163.

CHAPTER FIVE

of trying work throughout the district of late, which may to some extent account for the rather sudden and unexpected illness.[42]

Other local papers provided similarly optimistic reports, but the situation became steadily more serious. By 27 October, three weeks later, though Philip Robert was reported to be better a relieving magistrate had been appointed to act in his place, and on 24 November Mr Crespigny was granted three months leave of absence. Finally, yielding to the inevitable, it was announced in the *Victoria Government Gazette* of Friday 5 January 1877 that

---

RESIGNATION

The Governor, with the advice of the Executive Council, has accepted the resignation by
P C CRESPIGNY, ESQ,
of the offices of Police Magistrate, Warden, and Coroner.

JAMES McCULLOCH
For the Minister of Justice

Crown Law Offices,
Melbourne, 29th December 1876

When Philip Robert Champion Crespigny died in September 1889, the official certificate gave the cause of death as a general paralysis lasting thirteen years.[43] Rather than a change in bathing, it seems most probable that the initial cause was a stroke.

At the time of his resignation, the Victorian government granted Philip Robert a "Gratuity" of £487 and 10 shillings. Very sensibly, he repaid the money in full and took a pension at £260 a year; he would have qualified for the pension at the age of sixty, but because of his disability he was allowed to access it earlier. The income was considerably less than the £650 annual salary he had received on active duty as a magistrate,[44] but though the figure remained the same for the next thirteen years its purchasing power also stayed largely steady. The pension, however, ended with his death, and there was no provision for his widow Charlotte Frances.[45]

The family returned to St Kilda near Melbourne, where Charlotte Frances and the children had stayed when Philip Robert was first moving to Ararat. They first lived in Grey Street, but in 1882 they rented a wooden house with six rooms at 6 Robe Street, and stayed there until shortly before Philip Robert's death.[46]

---

[42] This and the following citations are taken from transcriptions in Grayden, *Chronicle*.

[43] A photocopy of the death certificate is provided by Grayden, *Chronicle*. See also below at 201.

[44] For examples, The Treasurer's Statement of the Receipts and Expenditure of the Consolidated Revenue and other Moneys, year ending 30th June 1879;accompanied by the Report of the Commissioners of Audit and by the Documents specified in the Forty-Eighth Section of the Audit Act, Victoria 1879, at 48 with footnote: www.parliament.vic.gov.au/papers/govpub/VPARL1879-80NoA12p1-50, and Statistical Register of the Colony of Victoria for the year 1880, compiled from official records in the office of the Government Statist; Part I. Blue Book, presented to both Houses of Parliament by His Excellency's Command, Victoria 1881, at 17 with footnote 5: www.parliament.vic.gov.au/papers/govpub/VPARL1881 No1.

Philip Robert is said to have received £750 a year in 1860, at the time of his first appointment to Amherst. As discussed in note 30 to Chapter Four, however, £100 of this amount may have been an allowance for expenses, and the salary itself was just £650. We may observe that – like the pension – salaries and other expenditure remained at the same level for many years,

[45] parliament.vic.gov.au/papers/govpub/VPARL1890NoA3p101-204 at 105.

[46] Sands and McDougall's *Melbourne Directory* for 1880 at 230 and for 1881 at 236 list Philip C Crespigny at Grey Street in St Kilda; there are no earlier records.

Sands and McDougall's *Melbourne Directory* for 1882 at 383 lists Philip C Crespigny at Robe-street, St

Constantine Trent in Australia 1875-1881[47]

In March 1875, eighteen months before Philip Robert was taken ill at Ararat, his father Charles Fox died at Cheltenham in England. He was buried at Saint Peter's Church, Leckingham, just outside the town, and the Australian family placed a notice in the *Argus* which was published on 13 May:

> **CRESPIGNY**. – On the 4th March, at 11 Royal-parade, Cheltenham, England, Charles Fox Champion Crespigny, aged 90.

The same announcement appeared in the *Australasian* on 22 May.[48]

The will of Charles Fox Champion-Crespigny was proved on 13 April. The executors were Eliza Constantia Frances his daughter and George Blicke Champion de Crespigny his son. Eliza Constantia still gave her address as 11 Royal Parade in Cheltenham, while George Blicke, Lieutenant-Colonel in the army, was living in Folkestone. The estate was described with "Effects under £5,000,"[49] though is not clear whether this included the house at Royal Parade. In the following year, however, though Eliza Constantia was still in Cheltenham she had moved to Priory Street, and appears to have been living in a considerably smaller house.[50]

Charles Fox Crespigny had inherited considerable wealth from his father Philip but managed to get rid of almost all of it. Two specific examples are recorded: in 1818 he sold the patronage of the parliamentary borough of Aldeburgh for £39,000 and in 1837 he sold properties in Wales for £60,000; so in just two sales he realised £100,000.[51]

The census of 1841 recorded Charles Fox Crespigny living at Cheltenham with his wife Julia nee Trent, his daughters Eliza Julia and Eliza Constantia Frances, his brother-in-law Francis Onslow Trent, three female servants and a manservant. Ten years later, as we have seen, he was at Harefield House in Middlesex, caring for his mentally-afflicted half-brother Philip,[52] but by 1861 he was back in Cheltenham, now in the house on Royal Parade. Seventy-five years old, he is described as a widower and "Esquire, Deputy Lieutenant of Suffolk;" his wife Julia nee Trent had died in 1855 and their elder daughter Julia Eliza in 1848. Eliza Constantia Frances, unmarried at the age of thirty-five, was effectively in charge; grandson Constantine Trent, now ten, is identified as a scholar; and there is a cook, a parlour-maid and a housemaid.[53] Ten years later the household is the same, with Constantine Trent an Ensign in the Sixty-Ninth Regiment, though servants no longer include a dedicated cook.[54]

Kilda, and this continues over following years. The 1886-1887 *Rate Book* for the Borough of St Kilda, West Ward, at entry number 3905 has Philip Crespigny, Gentleman, living at 6 Robe Street, with the owners of the property identified as Executors of Clendennan[?], a deceased estate. The *Victorian Post Office Directory* for 1888 likewise has Phillip [*sic*] C Crespigny at Robe Street, St Kilda.
On Philip Robert's residence at the time of his death, see 187 below.

47 Constantine Trent ChC is discussed by *Anne's Family History* 2013/04/07.
48 *Argus*: Trove 11516711 and 11516889 (a first version on 10 May had "Chiltern Road" for Cheltenham, and a corrected form was published three days later); *Australasian*: Trove 143014982.
49 England & Wales, National Probate Calendar (Index of Wills and Administrations), 1858-1995 for Charles Fox Crespigny 1875.
50 Letter 10 below at 176. See also Google Maps and street views.
51 On Aldeburgh, see Chapter Two at 55; RdeC, *Champions from Normandy*, 173.
On the Welsh properties, see for example Morgan v Holford, reported in the *Silurian, Cardiff, Merthyr, and Brecon Mercury, and South Wales General Advertiser* for 1 January 1853 at page 3.
52 Chapter Two at 75-76.
53 The form has Constantia's age as thirty, but she was born in 1825.
The other grandson Charles Stanley, now twelve years old and also identified as a scholar, had returned to the care of his father Charles John, eldest son of Charles Fox, who had a separate establishment in

CHAPTER FIVE

In his Letter 2 of January 1858, Charles Fox had already remarked to Philip Robert that he finds it "better on score of expense and every other score to keep at home quietly,"[55] and he does not appear to have been particularly wealthy at any period from the 1840s. The establishment at Cheltenham in 1841 is comparatively modest,[56] that of 1851 at Harefield House is to a considerable degree his half-brother Philip's, and the Cheltenham ménages of 1861 and 1871 are again quite small.

There is no way to judge how an inheritance amounting to hundreds of thousands of pounds can have been reduced to less than five thousand. Charles Fox Crespigny was generous: he took in two grandsons, attended to the upbringing and education of Constantine Trent and paid for his commissions into the army; he may have paid something towards the cost of Charlotte Frances' parliamentary divorce from her first husband; and his grandson Charles Stanley, who was brought up in his household with his cousin Constantine Trent, composed a most affectionate essay in his memory which remarked upon his lack of concern for money and his kindness to every beggar, deserving or not.[57]

None of this, however, can account for the disappearance of a fortune worth tens of millions in present-day currency. There is no evidence that Charles Fox was a gambler or a wastrel, and one must assume there had been some serious loss through a faulty investment or possibly the failure of a bank – until the establishment of the principles of limited liability in the mid-nineteenth century, all investments were risky.

It is in any case clear – as he had indicated to Philip Robert many years before[58] – that the Australian family had no expectations from Charles Fox's will. One thing that did happen, however, was that soon after his grandfather's death Philip Robert and Charlotte Frances' third child and second son, Constantine Trent Champion Crespigny, came out to Australia, meeting his parents and his elder siblings for the first time in more than twenty years – and the two youngest for the first time in their lives.

According to Hart's *Army List* for 1870, Constantine Trent Pulteney Champion-Crespigny had purchased a commission as an Ensign in the Sixty-Ninth (*The South Lincolnshire*) Regiment of Foot with effect from 14 July 1869 and was then with the regiment in Canada.[59] In May of 1870 there was a cross-border raid by Fenians – an Irish Republican organisation based in the United States – which was faced and defeated by British and local troops at the battle of Trout River. Constantine Trent presumably took part in this campaign, but it appears that he returned to England when the regiment was transferred to Bermuda later that year, for

---

[54] Cheltenham with his third wife Frances nee Plunkett: Chapter Two at 75 and note 115 to Chapter Three. One of the servants, Susan or Susanna Tolman, had stayed with the family during the intervening ten years; she is now the senior, but appears to have remained a housemaid.
[55] Chapter Three at 116.
[56] Charlotte Frances' first husband, the solicitor John James, had also three servants: Chapter Two at 46.
[57] Chapter Two at 75-76. *Anne's Family History* at 2018/01/26 has the text of Charles Stanley's encomium.
[58] Letter 2 in Chapter Three at 116, as cited in note 55 above.
  Charles Fox was said to have reduced Philip Robert's allowance about 1850: Chapter Two at 53. This may have been a matter of economy rather than of moral disapprobation. Charles Fox had an illegitimate child of his own and treated her and her mother generously: Chapter Two at 55-56. Far from disapproving, moreover, he would later write of Charlotte Frances in most kindly terms: Letter 2 in Chapter Three at 115.
[59] *The New Army List*, 1870, at 215.

we have seen above that at the time of the census taken in April 1871 he was staying at his grandfather's house in Cheltenham.[60]

The *London Gazette* of 9 May then records the appointment of Ensign Constantine Trent Pulteney Champion-Crespigny to be Lieutenant in the Sixty-Ninth Foot; the promotion was made by purchase, and took effect from 10 May. Six months later the *Gazette* announced his transfer to the Forty-First (Welch) Regiment of Foot, taking the place of his cousin Lieutenant Charles Stanley Champion Crespigny, who was retiring from the service.[61]

There is something a little suspicious about this series of appointments and transfers. Among the reforms introduced about this time by the Secretary of State for War Edward Cardwell, the Regulation of the Forces Act 1871 provided that regiments with only one battalion should combine into one of a number of districts identified for recruiting and administrative purposes. Under these arrangements, the Forty-First and the Sixty-Ninth were linked together with their depot at Cardiff, a hundred kilometres from Cheltenham. Part of the new arrangement, moreover, was that one battalion would be based at home while the other was overseas. So Constantine Trent had first obtained leave from his original regiment – now in Bermuda – and then transferred to its associate, stationed quite close to his grandfather's residence.

In the following year, however, the *London Gazette* of 18 October announced that
> *41st Foot.* Lieutenant Constantine Trent Pulteney Champion-Crespigny retires from the Service, receiving the value of his commission. Dated 19th October, 1872.[62]

In light of later events, the earlier transfers may have been occasioned by ill health, and his retirement was on the same grounds. In Letter 10 below, his aunt Eliza Constantia remarks, "'Twas a sad fate for him to lose his profession and to be an idle man at 25," which certainly indicates that he was reluctant to leave the army and may have been invalided out, while the description of his illness in Letter 11 suggests he may have suffered from tuberculosis.[63]

It is not known what Constantine Trent did immediately after he had left the army, but soon after the death of his grandfather Charles Fox in March 1875 he came to visit his family in Australia. On 17 August he left London on the iron-hulled clipper ship *Melbourne*, travelling cabin class,[64] and he arrived at Hobson's Bay, Port Melbourne, on 16 November. This was a maiden voyage, and the *Argus* of Wednesday 17 November not only reported the *Melbourne*'s arrival but added an article on the new vessel.[65] The passage, however, still took three months by sail, whereas the steamship *Great Britain* had been averaging two months since 1852.[66]

Though there is no information on Constantine Trent's activities in the eighteen months after his arrival in Victoria, we may assume he had some money of his own – at least from the sale of his commission and perhaps something from his grandfather's estate – and that he

---

[60] Above at 173.
[61] Issues 23735 at page 2223 and 23796 at page 4664.
[62] issue 23910 at page 4939.
[63] Below at 176 and 180. Henderson, *Early Pioneer Families*, 240, says that Constantine Trent sold his commission after he had been badly injured in an accident. This may be correct, based on information which is not now apparent, but we know of no authority.
[64] Cabin Class – also called Saloon Class – was the best of three possible levels of accommodation.
[65] Trove 7425119.
[66] Note 106 to Chapter Three.

CHAPTER FIVE

spent several months visiting his parents, his brother and his sisters. We are assured that he was made welcome, but it was surely a strange situation: twenty-five years old, meeting his immediate family for the first time in a totally strange country, and with all his previous experience made largely irrelevant by his illness. A letter from his aunt Eliza Constantia Frances in England, written to her newly-married niece Rose, Constantine Trent's youngest sister and now the wife of Francis/Frank Beggs – reflects the position:

Letter 10
                      Priory Street
                      CHELTENHAM
                      12th May, 1876

My dear Rose,

 I have not written to you since your marriage but I very often think of <u>you all</u> and especially of you and your dear Frank, and believe me, you are all very dear to me for yr loved parents' sake tho' so far away and <u>unknown</u>.[67] Con being amongst you seems to bring you all even <u>nearer to my heart</u> than ever, and <u>you</u>, the youngest of all my nieces, yet the first to marry, you of whom your dear Mother has so often written in deep sorrow and anxiety when you have been laid upon a bed of sickness,[68] – you can hardly imagine the tender interest I take in you, or how earnestly I wish and how fervently I pray that your married life may be blessed with true happiness, for dear Con assures me your husband is one of the best fellows he ever met and sure to make you happy! And the satisfaction and comfort yr parents feel in seeing their darling married to one they have so long known and esteemed must, I think, render yr happiness as perfect as it is possible to be in this world.

 Con had been enjoying himself immensely in your house when he last wrote to me. It was such a pleasure to him to see his little sister in her dignified matronly character! Poor Con! 'Twas a sad fate for him to lose his profession and to be an idle man at <u>25</u>. But the love of parents, brothers and sisters which you have <u>all</u> so freely and fondly bestowed upon your newly imported brother, has brightened his life, hitherto so sadly clouded, and if only his hopes of <u>employment</u> are realised, I trust his life may yet be a happy and useful one.

 I feel so grateful to <u>everyone</u> of those who have been so kind to Con and I know how kind and hospitable your father-in-law has been and how he has enjoyed himself at Eurambeen (I don't know if I spell the name right!). I suppose Con rides with you sometimes when you are together. Mount him on a good horse and he is at the summit of felicity! He has told me of the rides he has enjoyed. He must be dreadfully missed in your old home, particularly, I should think, by Vi, as she is nearest yr age. I hope she enjoyed the ball at Woolaston to which she was enabled to go by yr dear Frank's kindness.[69]

 Try and find time now and then to write to yr old Aunt, my dear Rose, and with much love to you both

                      Believe me always
                      Yr affte Aunt
                      E C F Ch. Crespigny

---

[67] On the marriage of Rose and Frank Beggs, see below at 182-183.
[68] There is no way to tell whether Rose had suffered serious illnesses as a child, or whether this is no more than a reflection of traditional maternal concern.
[69] There is now a Wollaston Bridge and Wollaston Road in the north of Warrnambool, which presumably took the name from a property nearby, owned by friends of the Beggs family.

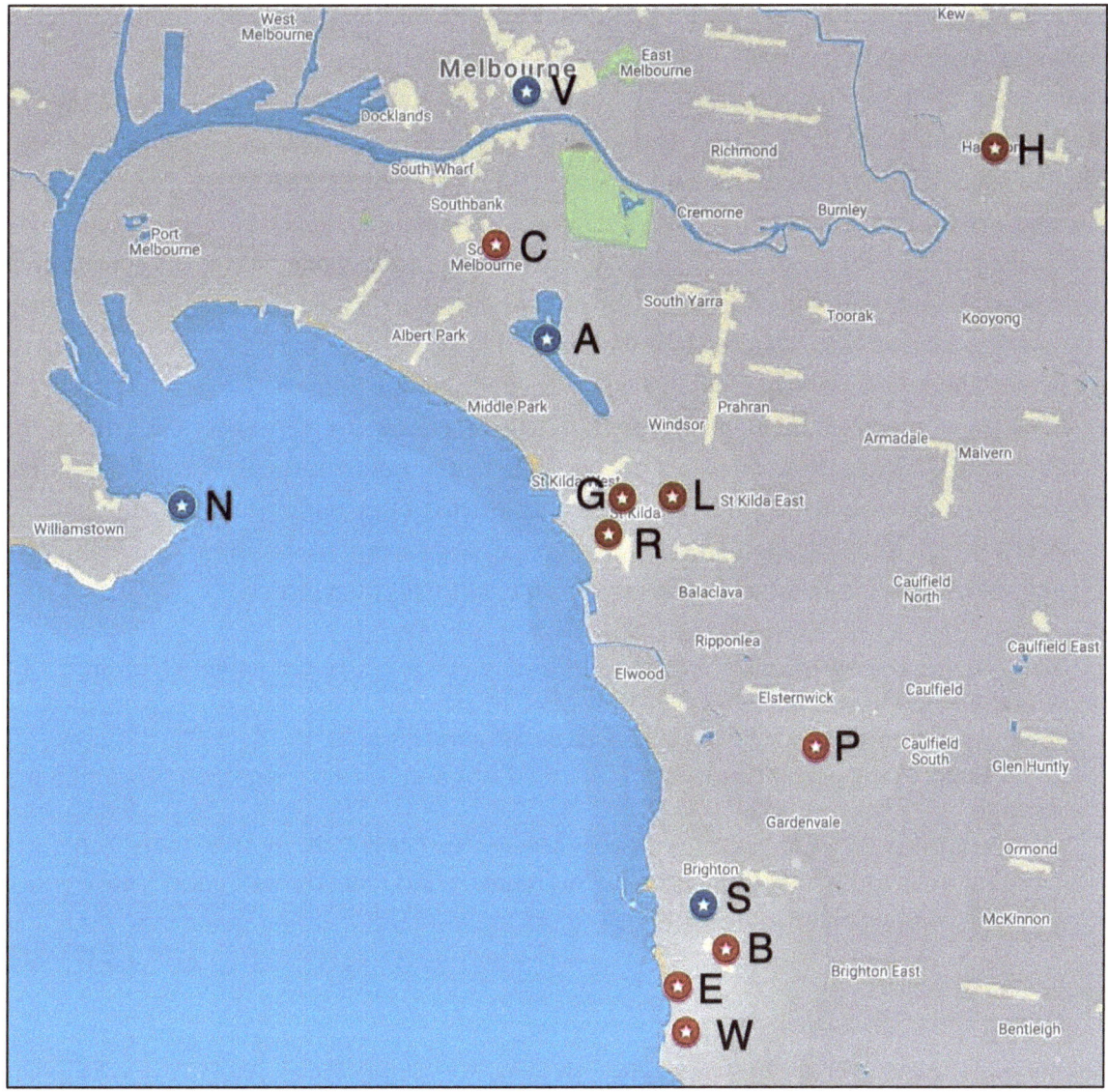

Southeast Melbourne from Google Maps
with indication of places associated with the Crespigny and Dana families 1870-1900

- **H**   Hawthorn: *Charlotte Frances and family 1870*
- **L**   Lambeth Place, St Kilda: *Charlotte Frances and family 1872*
- **G**   Grey Street, St Kilda: *Philip Robert, Charlotte Frances and family 1876-1881*
  and *Gurner Street, St Kilda: Constantine Trent ChC 1877-1881*
- **A**   *Albert Park*
- **R**   Robe Street, St Kilda: *Philip Robert, Charlotte Frances and family 1882-1888*
- **C**   Clarendon Street, South Melbourne: *Philip 1887-1888*
- **E**   Esplanade and St Kilda Street, Brighton: *Philip 1889-1892*
- **V**   Head office of the Bank of Victoria in Collins Street: *Philip from 1889*
- **W**   "Wyndcote" at Tennyson Street, Brighton: *Philip 1892 to 1894*
- **S**   *Brighton Grammar School*
- **P**   Gladstone Parade, Elsternwick: *Philip 1894-1908*
- **B**   Black Street, Brighton: *Philip 1908-1927*
- **N**   Mooring site of the training ship HMVS Nelson *at Williamstown:*
  Augustus Pulteney Dana 1868 [Chapter Four at 149-150]

CHAPTER FIVE

It was soon after this, in December 1876, that Philip Robert was obliged to retire from the position at Ararat and the family moved to Robe Street in St Kilda.

Constantine Trent took accommodation nearby in Gurner Street, and in June of 1877 he found employment as the Truant Officer for St Kilda and Prahran, ensuring that children attended school. The Victorian Education Act of 1872, first of its kind in the British empire, provided for secular, free schooling of all children between the ages of six and fifteen, with attendance required for no fewer than sixty days in any six months. The requirements were first enforced only by Boards of Advice for parents, but this method had limited success, and from 1876 truant officers were appointed, with authority to call parents to account for the absence of children from school and to instigate prosecutions in the most serious cases. The system and the principles upon which it was based were comparatively new, and Constantine Trent's military background – and his connections to the police through his father's former magistracy – may have helped him obtain the position and carry out its duties.[70]

A few weeks after his appointment Constantine Trent wrote to the *Argus* complaining of greyhounds in Albert Park attacking other dogs, including his own terrier.[71]

TO THE EDITOR OF THE ARGUS

Sir. – Seeing a letter in your impression of to-day headed "The Greyhound Nuisance," I would beg to tell you that a terrier of my own, of especial value, was severely mauled some three months hence, by a pack of these ferocious brutes.

Thanks to my prompt assistance, fractured ribs and a broken leg constituted all the damage.

Surely it is very hard that so pleasant a resort as Albert Park must be sacrificed every morning to the proprietors of these noxious animals. Hoping you will insert this in your valuable columns, I am, &c,

C T C Crespigny

Glanmire-house,
Gurner Street, St Kilda

The letter was published on 7 July, but since the attack is said to have taken place in March or early April, and Constantine Trent had already acquired a dog by that time, it appears that the family had taken up residence early in the year, soon after Philip Robert's forced resignation from Ararat.

Two years later, in March 1879, Constantine Trent was involved in an awkward incident when walking at South Beach with his father Philip Robert.[72] Seeing a man, Mathias Lyons, apparently ill-treating his wife, he went up and spoke to him. Lyons, predictably, told him to mind his own business, but Constantine Trent followed him to his house – and Lyons then took his walking stick from him and hit him over the head with it.

Constantine Trent summoned Lyons for assault, and the case was heard before the Mayor of St Kilda and three justices of the peace on Friday 14 March. Lyons claimed, however, that

---

[70] On the Education Act and its requirements for compulsory schooling, followed by the appointment of truant officers, see Long, *History of State Education in Victoria*, 65-66 and 83. Constantine Trent's appointments were announced in the *Argus* of 15 and 16 June: Trove 59257301 and 5925845. Newspapers of the time contained a good deal of discussion on questions of truancy.

[71] Trove 5928476.

[72] South Beach is the present St Kilda Beach, which is close to Robe and Gurner streets.

he had not been abusing his wife, but that they had been dealing with a child who wanted to be carried and he had tapped his wife on the shoulder in play. The bench dismissed the case.

The affair was reported by the local paper, *The Telegraph, St Kilda, Prahran and South Yarra Guardian*, to the disadvantage of Constantine Trent, who appears as an interfering, weak busybody.[73] There are, however, other aspects to the affair:

Firstly, though the origin of the dispute was Mr Lyons' treatment of his wife, Mrs Lyons made no appearance. This, of course, was inevitable: a wife could not be called to give evidence against her husband, and she might have suffered severely if she had done so.

Second, Mathias Lyons was the appointed herdsman of the municipality of St Kilda, so had connection to leading citizens; this despite a number of incidents over several years involving cows wandering or being attacked by his dogs, one – disputed – about the ill-treatment of a horse, and another for threats and abusive language. In all those cases, the St Kilda newspaper gives him sympathetic support.[74]

So Constantine Trent may have been in the right, but his quixotic enterprise would not have been welcomed by the woman he sought to assist, and locals were unlikely to appreciate it.

The newspaper also remarks that Constantine "was forcibly reminded that he was not the stronger" when Lyons took his stick from him and beat him with it. Indeed, it is not sure how physically strong Constantine Trent was: it appears that he had been invalided out of the army, he is known to have been seriously and fatally ill later, and the stick may well have been for support rather than for use as a weapon. This would make his conduct all the more courageous and Lyons all the more the bully he was claimed to be.

We may note that although Philip Robert was a witness of at least some of the incident, he could have played no part in the affair. He was seriously ill, and though his experience and standing as a former magistrate might have been helpful he was in no condition to intervene. It does appear, however, that he was physically still able to manage himself independently – not in a wheel chair or a bath chair – for otherwise Constantine Trent would not have left him in order to accost and then follow Mathias Lyons.

On Monday 9 August 1880 the Melbourne *Age* reported that the ship *Wotonga*, owned by the Australasian Steam Navigation Company, had departed from Hobson's Bay the main port of Melbourne on 7 August, heading for Sydney; the *Sydney Morning Herald* of 10 August reported her arrival on the previous day. The passenger list in the *Age* included the names of C T C Crespigny and P C Crespigny: the first is Constantine Trent; the second is his elder brother Philip Champion Crespigny, who may have been travelling on behalf of the bank or was perhaps on a short period of leave – Constantine Trent's father Philip Robert was surely too unwell to travel. The *Herald* has C P and P C Crespigny: Constantine Trent was evidently using the initials of his first name and his third, Pulteney. Melbourne newspapers do not list the passengers on all the ships arriving from other colonies, so we have no idea when Constantine Trent and Philip returned, or whether they did so together. Philip was married with a young son, however, so it is unlikely he would have wanted to stay away for long.

On 14 February of the following year 1881, however, the *Argus* reported that on 12 February the *Sobraon* of 2131 tons had cleared out from Hobson's Bay for London via Cape Town and

---

[73] Trove 114580222.
[74] For examples: Trove 109631338 and 109630872, 114578989 and 114578830, also 108982378.

CHAPTER FIVE

St Helena; Mr C P De Crespigny was one of several saloon [first class] passengers for London.[75]

A three-masted ship built in Scotland and named for a British victory against the Sikhs in India twenty years before, *Sobraon* had made her maiden voyage to Australia in 1866. With a composite hull of teak wood on an iron frame, and capable of carrying two acres of sail when fully rigged, she could make the passage in two and a half months, and she was popular with passengers as she had a water condenser, a large ice chamber and livestock for fresh milk and meat.

Ship Sobraon *in 1868: from the collection of the State Library of Queensland*

Sobraon arrived in England in May, and Constantine Trent returned to live with his aunt Eliza Constantia in Gloucestershire. He had been five and a half years in Australia. It may have been hoped that a different climate would improve his health, but it appears rather to have deteriorated, and he probably returned to England for medical treatment. His condition, however, became steadily worse, and two letters from Eliza Constantia to his sister Rose Beggs describe his illness and death.

Letter 11

29 Kingsholm Road
GLOUCESTER
4th Aug, 1881

My dear Rose,
    Con wishes me to tell you how glad he was to get your letters and how much he regrets his inability to answer them. He has been very weak and ill ever since his return. A few weeks ago there was some slight improvement. The intense heat we had seemed not only to benefit his lungs but to relieve his fever. Certainly he ceased during those extremely hot days to suffer from daily attacks of fever, tho' in some ways the intense

---

[75] Trove 5977412.

heat tried him severely. But with a sudden change in the weather and fall of temperature his fever returned with increased severity. One of the lungs got worse and had to be treated with repeated blisters. It is now better but the daily attacks of fever are <u>terrible</u>, lasting sometimes 8 hours during which he suffers acute headaches, shortness of breath, cough and nausea. He seems sometimes ready to die, so <u>very ill</u> is he.

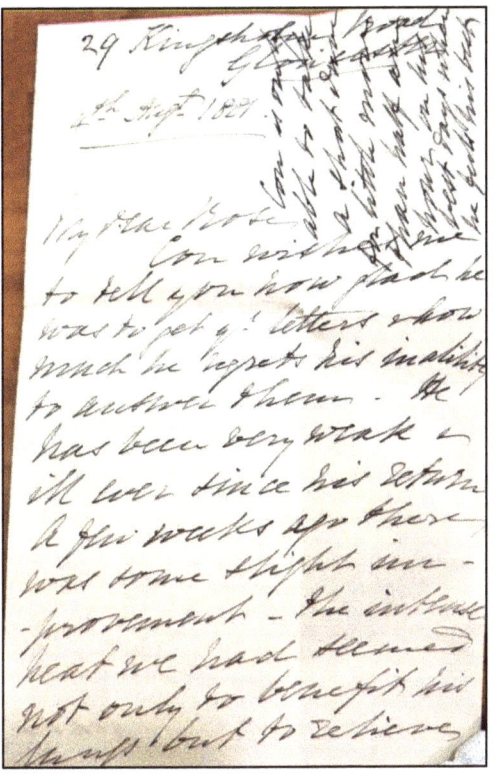

Under these circumstances I am sure you will see how difficult it is for him to write even a few lines to his Mother and I am always trying to impress upon him that he <u>ought not</u> to tax his strength by writing, and that if he <u>must</u> write, it should be <u>only</u> to his Mother and let <u>that</u> be considered enough for the family. I feel sure <u>you</u> will forgive him for deferring to write to you till he is better, altho' it is a <u>very</u> great pleasure to him to hear from you. I hope this will find you and your husband pretty well. I was sorry to hear that he had not been well.

With fond love from Con and much from me

Ever Yr affte Aunt
E C F Ch Crespigny

Con is only able to take a short drive for little more than half an hour on his best days when he feels his best.

Letter 12 Tuesday, 6th March [1883]

My dearest Rose,

Just one line to enclose 2nd half £5 notes. I hope you recvd first half all safe in last mail.[76]

My heart aches for yr poor Mother who would now, as I believe, be receiving my letter of 25 January, telling her how near death her darling was – tho' I scarcely knew that

---

[76] One means of sending money with some security by post was to cut banknotes in two. The notes were printed with a number in two places. With only one number, half a note was valueless, but when the two halves were put together they could be credited with a bank. It is uncertain what was to be done if one half was simply lost in the mail!

CHAPTER FIVE

> he must be taken from me the very next day. I miss him more and more and long to go to him.
>
> God bless you and your husband, dearest Rose.
>
> Your affte Aunt
> E C F Ch Crespigny

Constantine Trent Pulteney Champion [de] Crespigny had died on 26 January at the age of thirty-one. A notice placed by the family in the Melbourne *Argus* of Saturday 24 March says that his death took place at the residence of his aunt at Clevedon in Somersetshire.[77] Clevedon is at the mouth of the River Severn, twenty kilometres west of Bristol; it is probable that he had been brought there in the hope that the sea air might assist him.

Constantine Trent was buried with his grandfather Charles Fox in the graveyard of St Peter's Church, Leckingham.

The tomb of Charles Fox Champion Crespigny (1785-1875)
and his grandson Constantine Pulteney Trent Champion Crespigny (1851-1883)
at the churchyard of Saint Peter's Leckingham, near Cheltenham in Gloucestershire
Photograph by Anne Young 2019

Rose Crespigny and Frank Beggs
As indicated in Letter 10, Rose the youngest daughter of Charlotte Frances and Philip Robert had married in 1876. The wedding was announced with a misprinted notice in the *Argus* of 8 February, corrected by the issue of the following day:[78]

---

[77] Trove 8505991.
[78] Trove 7431514 followed by 7431650.

Marriages

BEGGS-CRESPIGNY. – On the 3rd inst, at Christ Church, Ararat, by the Rev Canon Homan, Francis Beggs, eldest son of Francis Beggs, Esq, of Eurambeen, to Helen Rosalie, third daughter of P C Crespigny, Esq, PM, Ararat.

The notice appeared also in the *Australasian* of 12 February but, somewhat surprisingly, not in the Ararat or Ballarat newspapers, nor did they publish an account of the event in any general notices or social notes.

We have seen that George Beggs, a Justice of the Peace, had heard a number of cases with Philip Robert, while George Beggs' nephew, eldest son of his brother Francis and best known as Frank, was a friend of Rose's brother Philip.[79] At the time of their wedding Rose was seventeen years old and Frank, born at Geelong soon after his parents had landed in Australia, was twenty-five.

Francis (1812-1880) and George Beggs (1816-1879) landed at Melbourne in March 1850, accompanied by their sister Sophia Montgomery (1813-1887) and Francis' wife Maria Lucinda nee White (1826-1914). Francis and George's brothers, Hugh Lyons Montgomery (1815-1885) and Charles Montgomery (1819-1897) came separately, but both married in Victoria, Charles in 1851 and Hugh in 1853. They arrived, therefore, at about the same time as Charlotte Frances, Philip Robert and their family, but circumstances were different.[80]

The four brothers and their sister were all children of Francis Beggs (1770-1839) by his second marriage, to Clamina Lyons nee Montgomery (1787-1821).[81] A prosperous linen merchant of Dublin, Francis Beggs also held landed properties, and all the children were born at Malahide, just south of Dublin, at a house called The Grange. The Lyons and Montgomery families of Francis' wife Clamina were members of the Anglo-Irish gentry and Clamina's mother Catherine was a daughter of Gustavus Hamilton, fourth Viscount Boyne. In the same fashion as the Kinnaird and Pulteney connection was remembered by the Danas, many of the Beggs family had Lyons or Montgomery among their given names.

When the elder Francis Beggs died in 1839, however, his children may have been less well off. For one thing, there were a large number of them: Francis' first wife Jane nee Montgomery had borne him four children, and Clamina had five sons and four daughters.[82] Some may have died in infancy or childhood, but at least nine of the siblings reached full age, so individual shares of the family property would not have been large.

Perhaps even more significantly, from 1845 to 1849 Ireland was afflicted by the Great Famine, caused by late blight, a fungus disease which attacked the potato, staple diet of the

---

[79] Above at 169-170.
[80] Alexander/Persse, *Tree, Rock and Gully*, has essays on the Beggs and related families. "The Beggs Family of Eurambeen" in that collection is an extract from the memoirs of Theodore Beggs (1859-1940), seventh child and second son of Francis and Maria Lucinda, and younger brother of Rose's husband Frank; it is cited as Theodore Beggs, "Memoir."

Theodore and his two younger brothers, Robert Gottlieb (1861-1939) and Hugh Norman (1863-1943), have a joint entry in the *Australian Dictionary of Biography*.

Other accounts of the family in Australia are in de Serville, *Pounds and Pedigrees*, 460, and Henderson, *Early Pioneer Families*, 249-257. A summary genealogy is at the end of this chapter.

[81] The *Probate Record and Marriage Licence Index 1270-1858* of Dublin, Ireland, records the grant of the marriage licence for Frances Beggs and Clemina Montgomery in 1808 – the spelling of the personal names is eccentric.
[82] Despite the common surname, Jane and Clamina were not closely related.

CHAPTER FIVE

poor. It is estimated that a million people died of starvation or from consequent diseases such as typhus, and with minimal assistance from the government at London even the greatest landholders suffered through the loss of rents from families unable to pay or through the demands on their resources for famine relief. Affected by the crisis, as many as two million emigrants are thought to have left Ireland, the great majority to the United States, but many to Australia and other British colonies.

It was against this background and under these circumstances that members of the Beggs family came to Australia. They were not penniless: Francis had a university education from Trinity College Dublin, and he and his new wife Maria Lucinda, his brother George and their sister Sophia Montgomery all travelled as cabin [first class] passengers.[83] They had money to purchase land and they had acquired some experience of farming, albeit in the very different conditions of Ireland.

On 8 August 1850 two sisters Jane and Catherine Meehan placed a rather touching advertisement in the *Melbourne Daily News*:[84]

> **NOTICE**
> **MESSRS** Francis Beggs, and George Beggs, and Miss Sophia Beggs, late of Feltrim Farm, County Dublin, who arrived in this Colony about 10 months since per the "Statesman," are requested to acquaint the undersigned who have just arrived from Adelaide with their place of abode.
> JANE MEEHAN
> CATHERINE MEEHAN
> August 5, 1850

Feltrim is a short distance southwest of Malahide, and the farm had evidently been part of the family estates. The *Statesman* had left London on 1 November, called at Plymouth in Devon – where the Beggs party probably got on board – and arrived at Port Adelaide on 12 February. She stayed there dealing with cargo until 9 March, when she left for Melbourne; the Meehans had presumably met the Beggs during their stay.[85] Catherine Meehan would marry Charles Montgomery Beggs in the following year.

In October of 1850, a few months after their arrival, a Mr Beggs of Geelong paid £7,750 for two properties on the Campaspe and Goulburn Rivers in central Victoria; this was probably one of the brothers, most likely acting in consortium or partnership.[86]

Francis and George initially took up separate properties: Francis was first at Gnarkeet near Lismore while George was for a time in partnership with his brother-in-law Humphrey Grattan, a friend from Ireland who had married his sister Sophia Montgomery. About 1855 George Beggs and Humphrey Grattan purchased Mount Cole station near Beaufort, but in 1857 Francis bought Grattan's share of the property while Humphrey and Sophia moved to Gowangardie east of Shepparton; Charles and his wife Catherine nee Meehan were fifty kilometres away, in the area of Violet Town.[87] Mount Cole station was renamed Eurambeen, and the partnership of G and F Beggs became known for fine merino sheep and wool.

---

[83] Trove 4767687. Theodore Beggs' "Memoir", however, says that they had to provide their own furniture, some of which was used later in houses at Eurambeen and at St Marnock's [below at 189].
[84] Trove 226518539.
[85] Trove 38443043 and 195939538.
[86] Trove 94914215
[87] There is now a Feltrim Road running northwest from Violet Town; it very likely took its name from a

At the same period, with financial assistance from his brother Francis, Hugh Beggs was acquiring his own property at Bushy Creek near Glenthompson, sixty kilometres south of Ararat and a hundred kilometres southwest of Beaufort. So Francis, George and Hugh were separated from their other brother and their sister by some two hundred and fifty kilometres, the distance between Beaufort-Ararat and Shepparton-Violet Town.

Eurambeen and Eurambeen East at the present day
from Google Maps: Beaufort and the Great Western Highway are at the upper right and centre
St Marnock's station, later owned by Frank and Rose Beggs [176 below] is shown at the lower left

One further – slightly more distant – member of the family had also come to Australia. William Montgomery, son of the elder Francis Beggs by his first wife Jane nee Montgomery and thus half-brother to the earlier arrivals, had a son named Thomas Alexander (1839-1920). On 9 October 1858 Thomas sailed cabin class from Liverpool on the *Greyhound* of the Black Ball line, reaching Hobson's Bay in the Port of Melbourne three months later on 8 January. Nineteen years old at that time, he spent some years gaining experience with his half-uncles at Eurambeen, but in 1865 he married his cousin Clamina Florinda Faris (1841-1895) and in the following year they took over Moglonemby Station near Violet Town.[88]

---

station established by Charles Montgomery Beggs and called after the family farm in Ireland.
[88] Clamina Montgomery Beggs (1811-1890), first child of the elder Francis Beggs and his second wife Clamina Lyons nee Montgomery, had married John Faris (1801-1869). Though they both lived and died in Ireland, four of their twelve children came to Australia, while Thomas (1844-1856) was lost overboard on the voyage.

CHAPTER FIVE

In 1878 Francis and George ended their partnership and divided the property, George taking Eurambeen East and Francis Eurambeen West – later known simply as Eurambeen. Each was about the same size: freehold of 8400 acres, or thirty-four square kilometres, with additional Crown Lands under long-term lease.[89]

Early in 1879, soon after this rearrangement, George Beggs died. He had married Charlotte Elizabeth White (1836-1921), younger sister of Maria Lucinda the wife of his elder brother Francis, in 1854. They had three daughters: Frances Georgina (1856-1932), Catherine (1859-1938) and Madeline (1860-1915), but their only son, George Warren (1870-1873), had died in infancy. After George's death his widow and daughters moved to Elsternwick in the south of Melbourne: it was not practicable for women to maintain such a property.[90]

Letter 10 from Eliza Constantia, writing in May 1876, refers to Constantine Trent visiting Rose a few weeks after she and Frank had married,[91] but it is not clear where the couple had made their home in the first years after the wedding. It does appear that Frank spent some time with his uncle Hugh Lyons Montgomery Beggs at Bushy Creek: after his father Francis died in 1880, Hugh chose him as executor of his will in his stead.[92]

In February 1873, however, Frank Beggs and a partner named William Norman had made a successful claim for a land lease near Tumut in New South Wales, and in January 1874 the *Government Gazette* announced that the fair annual value of their property, identified as Blowering East, had been assessed at £10.[93] In November of that year, moreover, Frank took up another claim of 960 acres, also in the south of Tumut. It was presumably a neighbouring property, and though Frank's was the formal name on the lease it was likely included in the partnership.[94]

Tumut is more than 650 kilometres from Ararat, but it is surely significant that the railway running north and northeast from Melbourne reached Wodonga on the River Murray in November of 1873. Victoria had been a great deal more enterprising than New South Wales in this regard: the first line to reach the Murray – at Echuca – had opened up the southern part of the neighbouring colony to transport south through Melbourne, Geelong and their ports. Railway construction from Sydney on the other hand, was hampered both by the Great Dividing Range and by a lack of government interest. The main south line did not reach Wagga until 1879 and it was linked to the Victorian network at Albury and Wodonga only in 1883. Until that time, communications north of the Murray relied partly on river boats

---

[89] Theodore Beggs, "Memoir," 11.
[90] The 1914 Electoral Roll for the Subdivision of Elsternwick in the Division of Henty records Charlotte Elizabeth and her three daughters at Gladstone Parade, Elsternwick. Each of them died at that address, and all were buried at Eurambeen.
[91] Above at 176.
[92] Hugh Lyons died in 1887, and a report of his probated will was published by the journal *Table Talk* of Melbourne on 28 October of that year: Trove 146710712/17657061.
[93] *Evening News*, Sydney, 5 February 1873 and 12 January 1874; Trove 107178243 and 107142721,
[94] *Evening News*, Sydney, 25 November 1874, and *Wagga Wagga Advertiser and Riverine Reporter*, 5 December; Trove 107137011 and 104117319.

The *Evening News* does not mention the site of Frank Beggs' acquisition, and the Wagga newspaper has it in the parish of Bayong in the district of Tumut. Bayong is very likely a miswriting for Bogong; at the present day the designated Bogong Peaks Wilderness is just to the east of the Blowering Dam, south of Tumut.

As may be seen below, Frank was often in his home territory in the Western District of Victoria, and his partner William Norman would have dealt with matters in his absence.

but more generally on the horse-coach network of Cobb and Co; many men, of course, travelled on horseback.[95]

Just as the connection to Echuca had offered opportunity across the Murray, the same potential could be seen as the railway approached Wodonga and the eastern Riverina from Albury north to Wagga. It was no doubt for this reason that the Beggs family took an interest, and that Frank chose to take up land at Tumut, a rich – albeit hilly – pastoral area which had been settled since the 1830s and 1840s.

Despite his interest in southern New South Wales, however, Frank returned frequently to Victoria. On 24 December 1874, three weeks after taking up the second parcel of land at Tumut, he was at court in Beaufort to accuse a certain William Meadows of driving sheep without giving notice – a form of trespass. The case was heard by Philip Robert Crespigny as Police Magistrate, with two Justices of the Peace, one of whom was George Beggs. Nobody raised any question of impropriety about an uncle hearing his nephew's case, and William Meadows was fined one shilling with five shillings costs.[96] In March of 1875 Frank attended the Beaufort Sports and suffered the carriage accident with Philip Crespigny, and in February 1876, of course, he married Philip's sister Rose in Ararat.[97]

In following years Frank is recorded again at Glenthompson: in March of 1877 he offered a reward for a black sheepdog named Slut, which had been lost or stolen from Bushy Creek; and in February 1878 he is listed among the competitors at the Dunkeld Athletic Sports Meeting, with a handicap of six yards in the hundred-yards sprint; Dunkeld is midway between Glenthompson and Hamilton, and Frank is now twenty-eight.[98]

Later that year, however, Frank and Rose moved to the property in Tumut, New South Wales. In October the partnership of Beggs and Norman purchased eight hundred sheep,[99] and Letter 14 below, written to Rose by Annie Frances, wife of her brother Philip, on 25 January 1879, mentions how Frank had sent Philip a copy of a Wagga newspaper: Wagga Wagga was the major town of that region. Two months later in Letter 15, Annie Frances commiserates on the lack of a railway line from Albury to Tumut.[100] As we have seen,

---

[95] There are many accounts of the development of communications at this period, but a few citations are:
Chronicle of Australia, 327 [Echuca 1864], 358 [Wodonga 1873], 394 [Albury-Wodonga 1883];
Blainey, *Tyranny of Distance*, 242 [on Echuca], 250-251 [Wodonga and Albury], 143-144 [Cobb and Co];
www.nswrail.net: railway expansion in New South Wales.

[96] *Ballarat Star*, 25 December; Trove 208250566.

[97] Above 169-170 and at 183.

[98] *Hamilton Spectator*, 22 March 1877 and 16 February 1878; Trove 226041511 and 226067930.

[99] *Wagga Wagga Advertiser*, 26 October 1878; Trove 101939860.

It was in that same month of February that Frank entered into a very loose arrangement with a certain Thomas Allen, who undertook to train a greyhound for him: Allen was to enter the dog into the Ararat Puppy Stakes; if it won, Allen would have half the prize money; if it lost, Frank would reimburse him for the entry fees. In the event, when the race was due to take place Frank was in Tumut and Allen could not raise the money for the entry, so the dog did not run.

Then, however, Allen sold the animal to someone else, without telling him that it actually belonged to Frank. When Frank returned and demanded his dog back, Allen counter-claimed for the costs of twelve months' feeding and training.

Both cases came to court at Wickliffe in February of the following year, and both were dismissed, while the magistrate made some comments on the unsatisfactory form of the original agreement. He did, however, order the dog be returned to Mr Beggs: *Hamilton Spectator*, 6 March 1879; Trove 226055655.

[100] Letter 14 at 194 below; Letter 15 at 195.

As Frank was engaged in a court case at Wickliffe in February, Rose was probably at Tumut by herself. Letters 15 and 16 mention a visit from Ada in March and May, and Frank may have escorted her there.

CHAPTER FIVE

however, Albury had as yet no railway connection anywhere to the north, and even when the main line was completed the branch from Gundagai through the hills to Tumut was not constructed until 1903; it was abandoned in 1984.

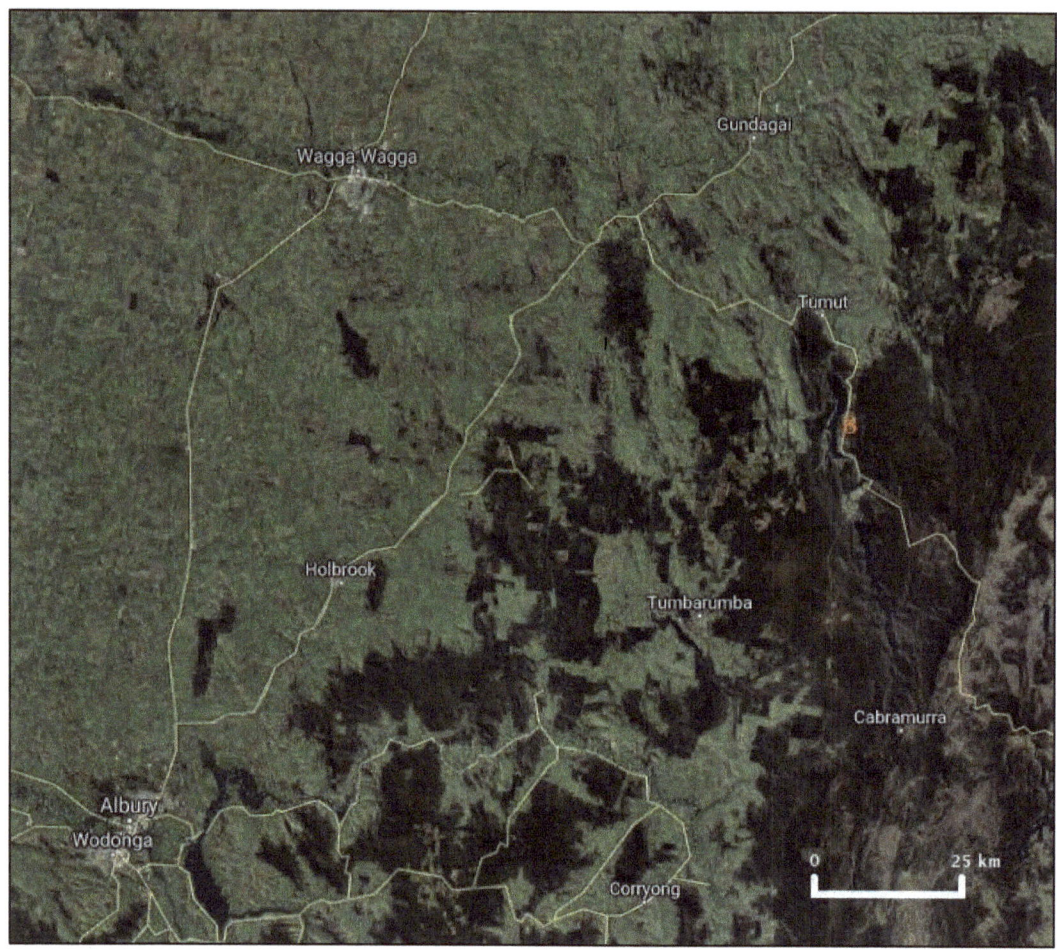

Albury, Wodonga, Wagga Wagga, Gundagai, and Tumut
from Google Maps
The area of Frank Beggs' properties at Blowering and Bogong south of Tumut is indicated with B

Though Frank thus held property in southern New South Wales from 1873, it is not possible to judge how long he and Rose actually lived there. Some sources suggest that Frank spent two years in the colony, but his involvement was obviously more extensive, though it was punctuated by lengthy periods at home in Victoria.[101]

Regardless of detailed timing, however, the Tumut venture ended in 1881.

Following the death of his brother and former partner George Beggs in January 1879, Frank's father Francis took a three-year lease of Eurambeen East. He died in December 1880, and twelve months later, as the lease was due to expire, the property was advertised again.[102]

---

[101] An obituary in the *Argus* of 29 August 1921 after Frank's death on 25 August says that "Except for two years in New South Wales and a brief period in Ireland, he resided in the Beaufort district all his life:" Trove 4665587. Theodore Beggs' "Memoir" describes how the family spent a few years in Ireland during the middle 1860s, when Frank would have been in his teens: Alexander/Persse, *Tree, Rock, and Gully* at 13. The two years in New South Wales, however, cannot be strictly correct.

Besides the obituary in the *Argus*, similar texts and tributes were published in other newspapers of the time. One which appeared in the *Pastoral Review* is in copied in Chapter Seven at 265-266.

[102] *Argus*, 8 December 1881; Trove 11526096.

> **EURAMBEEN EAST ESTATE**
> Near Beaufort
> To be **LET**, by **TENDER**
> TENDERS will be received on or before 3 p.m. of Thursday, 8th December next, for LEASING the above ESTATE, containing about 8397 acres, and known as the property of the late George Beggs. There is a commodious bluestone dwellinghouse of 11 rooms on the estate, and the estate is otherwise well improved.
> For terms and particulars apply to
> TAYLOR, BUCKLAND, and GATES, Geelong or Melbourne

Returning from New South Wales, Frank took over the lease, first in part and then in full, and he and Rose lived there for more than twenty-five years.[103] Frank became known as a breeder and judge of sheep, and the wool that his properties produced gained high prices. His brothers Theodore, Robert Gottlieb and Hugh Norman later formed a partnership which bought or leased several properties, but Frank preferred to operate on his own account and did not join them. All, however, remained on excellent terms.

Frank was a skilled horseman – as a young man he won prizes – and he had successes in local racing, notably with a horse named St Marnock's. Marnock was an Irish saint of the seventh century, and there is a Port-St-Marnock northeast of Dublin. Brown in colour, St Marnock's had many successes during the 1890s, including a tie in the Grand Stand Stakes at Ararat in February 1895. He also won show ribbons and was later a successful and sought-after sire.[104]

In 1908 Frank and Rose moved some twenty kilometres to the southwest, where they built a new homestead and established a garden which became celebrated. They called the property St Marnock's, and the grave of their champion horse had a place of honour by the entrance gate.[105]

Frank and Rose had no children. Frank died in 1921, and his nephew Theodore George, son of his brother Hugh Norman, purchased St Marnock's from his widow. The property was valued at almost £20,000, with sheep, cattle and horses worth £3,000, and a further £1,000 for equipment, furniture and some financial investments [106]

Rose went to live with her sisters Ada and Viola in Brighton, just south of Melbourne. Following their deaths in the late 1920s Rose moved to a new residence, still in Brighton, which she named "St Marnock's" in memory of the former holding. She died in April 1937.[107]

---

[103] Theodore Beggs, "Memoir," 11, says that he initially entered a five-year contract for only two thousand acres, but when that expired he took another lease for the whole of the station.
[104] *Ballarat Star* of 25 February: Trove 203152252; There is an account of St Marnock's career and his eponymous station in *Anne's Family History* at 2019/08/01. Sources differ whether there was a possessive apostrophe in the name, but the weight of usage is in its favour.
[105] Melbourne *Punch*, Thursday 13 August 1908, page 24: Trove 176018320.
[106] Frank's will was approved for probate on 11 November 1921, with his widow Rose as executor..
[107] See further in Chapter Seven at 266.

Chapter Five

Frank and Rose Beggs

St Marnock's homestead 2019
Photograph by Anne Young

Philip Crespigny and Annie Frances Chauncy

After his excursion to the New Hebrides in 1871, Philip Robert and Charlotte Frances' son Philip returned to work at the Bank of Victoria, where he held a number of clerical positions, first in Melbourne and then in a series of local offices. In the mid-1870s he was transferred to head the agency at Epsom, just north of Sandhurst/Bendigo and a sub-branch of the main office there.[108]

On Thursday 25 October 1877, eighteen months after his sister had married Frank Beggs, Philip married Annie Frances Chauncy.

Born at Heathcote in Victoria on 25 April 1857, Annie Frances was now twenty, seven years younger than her husband. Her father, Philip Lamothe Snell Chauncy, was District Surveyor for Ararat, and was a member of the local Land Board with Magistrate Philip Robert Crespigny;[109] he was also a Justice of the Peace and would have sometimes joined him on the bench. Annie Frances' mother Susan Augusta was a daughter of the Reverend William Mitchell (1803-1870), long-term missionary of the Church of England on the Swan River in Western Australia. Susan Augusta died in 1867, however, when Annie was ten.[110]

Annie Frances was a close friend of her future sister-in-law Viola Crespigny, six months her elder, and she wrote to her a few weeks before the wedding:

Letter 13[111]   26 Sept/77

My dearest Vi,

Thank you ever so much for all the trouble you have taken about the wretched old trimming, is it not annoying? The dress is all made except the braid and I can't get it anywhere.

Do you think the colour I enclose pretty for bridesmaids? I think it perfectly lovely only I am so frightened they'll call it green and it is not really but a moonlight colour. Does mauve suit you? Don't show this letter or the pattern to anyone and mind you don't lose it, as I want it. Your Mama would eat me perhaps if she thought it was green and I was going to have it. I think it was nasty of you to tell them all what I said the last time I wrote about the bridesmaids' dresses. I thought you never showed my letters to anyone. I never do yours.

Isn't the time drawing fearfully near? I tremble in my shoes when I think of it. I am going to have a very pale blue silk for the Cup, I think,[112] and a lovely light grey silk and cashmere for a travelling and going away dress and of course a lot of muslins and things for the summer. If you would tell me exactly what day you will be going up and you

---

[108] Epsom is now a suburb of Bendigo.
The name of Bendigo was taken from a local creek which was itself named for a local character called Abednego [from the biblical *Book of Daniel*]. The county was established as Bendigo, but for most of the nineteenth century the town itself was officially called Sandhurst. The name was changed to Bendigo as the result of a plebiscite in 1891: *e.g.* Trove 88961098.

[109] The *Ballarat Star* of 27 November 1874, for example, records a sitting of the Beaufort Land Board, where Mr Crespigny P M was sitting with Mr Chauncy the District Surveyor and Mr Manners MMB [Member of the (Ararat) Mining Board]: Trove 199330078.

[110] Susan Augusta nee Mitchell, second wife of Philip Chauncy, was the subject of his *Memoir of Mrs Chauncy*: note 6 to Chapter Four. Greenslade, *Mitchell Amen*, has a detailed biography of the Reverend William, and there is an entry in Wikipedia.

[111] The head of this letter is annotated "my mother" and "my aunt" by Constantine Trent CdeC (1882-1952). Annie Frances would have been with her father in Ararat, while Viola was at St Kilda with her family; Philip Robert had left office on account of ill health at the end of 1876.

[112] The Melbourne Cup race of 1887, held on Tuesday 6 November, was won by the bay colt Chester. The weather was wet: Cavanough and Davies, *Cup Day*, 44-46.

Chapter Five

don't mind I could tell Robertson and Moffat to send some things out to you and you could bring them to me, carriage is so expensive.[113] You can stay on your way a night, can't you?

Good-bye, my dear old lamb,
Annie Chauncy

Best love to dear Bruin,[114] your Mother, Ada and Con.

Annie Frances nee Chauncy
at the time of her wedding to Philip Champion Crespigny in 1877
Studio photograph in the possession of the family

---

[113] Robertson and Moffat on Bourke Street were leading drapers of Melbourne.

[114] Bruin is a nickname, but it is difficult to tell for whom. The other three mentioned are Charlotte Frances, her daughter Ada and her son Constantine Trent ChC (1851-1883), who was currently in Australia. It appears in context that Annie Frances is referring to Philip Robert her future father-in-law; this, however, is somewhat informal; Charlotte Frances is referred to as "your Mama" or "your Mother."

In Letter 15 below, Annie refers to "Bar," and this variant may be a reference to Constantine Trent ChC: 195-196 with note 132.

Formal reports of the wedding were carried by the *Ballarat Star* of 26 October and by the *Courier* on the following day, each with slightly different attention to detail.

The *Star*:[115]

> At St Paul's Church on Thursday, Miss Chauncy, eldest daughter of the local district surveyor, was married to Mr Philip Champion-Crespigny, jun, of Ararat.
>
> The ceremony was performed by the Rev R T Cummins, and the church was crowded, the spectators being for the most of the fair sex.

In fact Annie Frances was the second daughter of her parents and Philip was no longer at Ararat. The *Courier* of 27 October was rather more detailed and more accurate:[116]

> **MARRIAGES**
>
> CRESPIGNY–CHAUNCY. – On the 25th October, at St Paul's Church, by the Rev R T Cummins, Philip Champion Crespigny, manager of the Bank of Victoria at Epsom, and eldest son of P C Crespigny, Esq, late police magistrate at Ararat, to Annie Frances, second daughter of Philip Chauncy, J P, district surveyor at Ballarat.

The *Camperdown Chronicle*, however, published three days later – Camperdown is more than a hundred kilometres southwest of Ballarat – describes an awkward disturbance:[117]

> Miss Chauncey was married at St Paul's on the 25th inst to a Mr Crespigny, who hails from Ararat. The church was crammed, larrikins and larrikinesses being in great force, and very rowdy. The Rev R T Cummins, who tied the knot, at one time said that he would not go on with the service unless they behaved themselves. But they did not behave well, and the minister did go on to the bitter end.

Though details are slightly mistaken and vague, the disturbance does appear noteworthy. There is no indication what gave rise to it, whether it was directed at one or other of the bride or groom; or whether the cause was no more than young nuisances with nothing better to do. It seems sad for Annie Frances, however, for she had obviously been planning and looking forward to the day.

Three later letters from Annie Frances, written in 1879, are preserved; all were addressed to her sister-in-law Rose Beggs:

Letter 14   Epsom
                                                                    January 25th/79

Dearest Rose,

   I was so glad to get your long letter. It was so good of you writing so soon. We heard from your Mama today that Ada is to go up to you. How glad she must be! You will pity me when I tell you Connie had to go back last week. She was only with us a month. I do miss her so dreadfully now she has gone. I never missed anyone so much.[118] Of course I am not lonely as Loup is at home all day but it is so nice having a girl to speak to as well.[119] There are no girls in Sandhurst.

---

[115] Trove 199841514.

[116] Trove 211534603. Though he is described as a manager, Philip held formal title only as Agent; he was not yet the manager of a branch.

[117] Trove 64012654, discussed by *Anne's Family History* 2012/04/25.

[118] This is Annie's sister Constance (1859-1907). Born on 26 April, she was almost exactly two years younger than Annie, who was born 25 April 1857.

[119] Loup or – more commonly later – Loo is the family nickname for Philip, Annie's husband: Chapter Three at 113 with note 103 and Chapter Four at 136-137.

CHAPTER FIVE

Letters from Annie Frances Crespigny nee Chauncy to Rose Beggs nee Crespigny
Letter 14, page one; 25 January 1879   Letter 15, page one; 23 March 1879
[*The last paragraphs and the signature of letter 14 are cross-written at the top of the first page*]

The Wagga paper came this morning for Loup.[120] He sends Frank his best respects and says tell him he is very much obliged to him and sends him last Saturday's *Argus* and *Punch*.[121] Tell him also how deeply we regret to hear of his uncle's death.[122] Loup will write to him shortly.

Is Miney still in Melbourne? When is she going to Queensland? What a pretty name she has chosen for her baby.[123]

The Orrs gave a children's fancy-dress party last week in Ballarat. Amy, Fred, Clem and Totty Hale who is staying with them, all went and had great fun.[124] Amy went as "Nancy Lee" in a fishwife's dress of navy blue turned up and trimmed with red and white

---

[120] Wagga Wagga in New South Wales had two newspapers at this time, the *Advertiser* (formerly known as the *Wagga Wagga Advertiser and Riverine Reporter*) and the *Express*.

[121] Like the *Argus*, *Punch* was published in Melbourne.

[122] George Beggs, uncle of Frank, had died at Eurambeen East on 17 January.

[123] Clamina ["Miney" or "Minie"] nee Beggs (1858-1904) was the sixth child and fifth daughter of Frank's parents, Francis Beggs and Maria Lucinda nee White. She had married Walter Henry Davidson in 1877, and their first child, born in Toorak, Melbourne, on 14 November 1878, was named Ethel.

Walter was a partner with his brothers-in-law George and John Whittingham – married to his sisters – in Alice Downs station near Blackall in western Queensland. Because Clamina was only nineteen when she married, her parents made him promise not to take her with him immediately from Victoria to the outback. He returned for the baby's birth, however, and soon afterwards Clamina and the infant accompanied him back to the north. They were there seven years, but then returned to Victoria and purchased Coliban Park near Castlemaine.

Ethel nee Davidson (1878-1975) married the future General Sir Brudenell White (1876-1940) in 1905. Alexander/Persse, *Tree, Rock, and Gully*, 15-26, transcribes "Memories of my Childhood" by Ethel, Lady White, from her hand-written notebook. See also Derham, *The Silence Ruse*, 174.

Ethel Davidson appears frequently in the Eurambeen Letters below [*e.g.* 29, 30] and in Chapter Six.

[124] The Orr family cannot be readily identified, but Amy Blanche Chauncy (1861-1925), Frederick Philip

stripes, a fishwife's basket on her back and a high mob cap trimmed with blue and red ribbons.[125] Connie said she looked so pretty. Fred hired a Corsair's dress from a dramatic club in Ballarat and was gorgeous in the extreme. Clem went as Punch; he got a nose and chin from town.[126] He frightened the youngest little Orr to bed and was in a great rage at first because he could get no partners. Tot went as a *vivandiere* with a scarlet jacket and cap braided with gold etc and a little barrel slung on her shoulders.[127]

I hope you will write to me again soon. Give my love to Frank. Loup joins me, and best love to you.

Ever your most affec^{ate} Sister
Annie Crespigny

Letter 15
Epsom
23rd March/79

My dearest Rose,

I have been blaming myself very much for not answering your last letter sooner and thanking you for writing me such a long interesting one. We have had Tise and her baby staying with us for the last fortnight.[128] They returned to Melbourne yesterday. While they were here I did not try to write any letters as I never can write and talk at the same time and we had such a lot to things to talk about.

So Ada is with you at last. Give her my best love and thanks for her long interesting letter. Tell her I will answer it soon. What a time it takes to reach you. It makes you seem so terribly far off. Will they ever have a railway connecting Albury and Tumut?[129] I have been as far as Wodonga and Albury when Willie was living there serving out his articles. How pretty the country is in New South Wales. I do wish we lived there. Loup hates this colony [Victoria].[130]

I hope you really are coming down in October and will prepare to pay us a good long visit. I shall be so delighted to see you again. It will be two years then since we met. Mr Burford is going to live in lodgings on a farm somewhere in this direction. We are hoping it will be close to us so that we can often see him. It will be so nice for Loup to

---

Lamothe Chauncy (1863-1926) and Clement Henry Chaucy (1865-1902) were the younger sister and brothers of Annie Frances. On Totty/Tot Hale, see note 128 below.

[125] "Nancy Lee" was a popular song at this time, about a sailor celebrating the beauty and virtue of his wife.

[126] The traditional figure of Punch, as in Punch and Judy, was recognised by his hooked nose and large chin.

[127] *Vivandières* (the name is related to English "viands") were women attached to French or other European armies, selling provisions and sometimes other comforts. They commonly wore a costume related to the uniform of the regiment which they accompanied.

[128] Annie's sister Theresa Snell Chauncy (1849-1886) had married Samuel Aubrey Hale (1847-1922) in 1870. Their fifth child was Philip Chauncy Hale, born in 1876, and the sixth was Arthur Mitchell, born about 1880; the "baby" is probably Arthur Mitchell.

The couple's eldest daughter was named Amy Charlotte. Born in 1870, soon after her parents' marriage, she is probably the "Totty/Tot" Hale mentioned in Letter 14 above: she would have nine years old at the time of the fancy-dress party: note 124 above.

[129] See above at 187-188.

[130] Annie's brother William Snell Chauncy (1853-1903) became a lawyer in New South Wales. Her half-uncle, also named William Snell Chauncy (1820-1878), a surveyor like her father Philip, was District Surveyor of Belvoir/Wodonga in Victoria from 1856 to 1870 and was responsible for the Union Bridge across the Murray. [The name Belvoir was changed to Wodonga in 1869.] It is possible that this family connection was some basis for the younger William Snell Chauncy to take his articles in Albury.

Apart from the lack of agreeable companions at Epsom, referred to several times in these letters, no reasons are given for Philip's dislike of Victoria. He may have served at a branch of the Bank of Victoria in New South Wales, or travelled there privately, but his only known visit was the voyage to Sydney with his brother Constantine Trent in 1880, the year after this letter was written: above at 179.

CHAPTER FIVE

have someone he cares about to talk to occasionally.[131] There is not a man in S'hurst he likes much. I believe it is the only hope for poor little Bar, coming up country again and doctors say a farm life is so good for consumptive people.[132]

We expect Vi before long. .....[133]

Letter 16
Epsom
4th May 1879

My dearest Rose,

I enclose a few lines in Loup's to thank you for your last letter which came at Easter. I was so glad to get it and Ada's. Please give her my love and thanks. Loup of course has told you any news there is to tell, so however much I wished I could not send a long letter.

I miss Vi so dreadfully. I have been in the dumps ever since she left.[134] Loup borrowed a buggy yesterday and took me a drive into S'hurst, the first time I have been out for goodness knows how long and as I had to spend all the time shopping it was not very festive.

Mr and Mrs Kirby who were married yesterday week were to arrive in Sandhurst yesterday after only a week's honeymoon. Wasn't it short? They have such a nice well-furnished house and I do hope will be jolly people "the like of which" are badly wanted here.[135]

I hope you will write soon again. Your letters are such a treat. I always like hearing little things about your house etc. Give Ada and Frank my love and with a great deal for yourself.

Ever believe me
Your loving Sister, Annie

Tell Ada I will write to her soon.

Annie Frances and Philip had two children, both sons. The first was born on 18 June 1879 in the residence of the Bank of Victoria in Epsom and was baptised Philip, like his father with no second name. Two years later Philip was promoted to be manager at Queenscliff, south of Geelong on the Bellarine peninsula, and Annie Frances gave birth to their second son in the residence there on 5 March 1882.[136] He was named Constantine Trent, after his uncle.[137]

The elder Constantine Trent died in England in January 1883, and on 21 February, shortly before the news of his death had reached Victoria, Annie Frances died at the age of twenty-five. Her death was announced in the *Argus* of Friday 23 February and she was buried in the local cemetery.[138]

---

[131] Though this Mr Burford was evidently a good friend of Philip, nothing more is known of him.

[132] Though she lists "Con" in the postscript to Letter 13 above, certainly referring to Philip's younger brother Constantine Trent, this mention of consumption/tuberculosis makes it possible that "Bar" is an affectionate nickname for him. The letter was written just after the unsatisfactory court case against Mathias Lyons: above at 178-179.

[133] Transcriber Walsh notes here that "The last part of this letter seems to be missing."

[134] Annie was pregnant at this time. Her first child, Philip (1879-1918), was born six weeks later.

[135] The Melbourne *Argus* of 29 April reported that Edmund Wilmer Kirby, a solicitor of Sandhurst/Bendigo, had married Luisa Mary nee Turner at St Kilda on the 26th: Trove 5941174.

[136] *Anne's Family History* 2017/04/19 discusses Queenscliff in 1882. The name of the town was sometimes spelt with a final *e*.

[137] Constantine Trent Champion de Crespigny (1882-1952) became a noted physician and pathologist in South Australia. "Con" to family and friends, after he was knighted in 1941 he was formally known as Sir Trent.

[138] Trove 8498656.

The gravestone of Annie Frances Champion Crespigny nee Chauncy at Queenscliff
The original inscription was later amended to include references to her two sons:

> SACRED
> TO THE MEMORY OF
> ANNIE FRANCES
> *THE BELOVED WIFE OF*
> PHILIP CHAMPION CRESPIGNY
> WHO DIED 21ST FEBRUARY 1883
> AGED 25 YEARS
> BLESSED ARE THE PURE OF HEART, FOR THEY
> SHALL SEE GOD: ST MATTHEW
>
> ALSO IN MEMORY OF
> PHILIP
> OF THE 2ND AUSTRALIAN LIGHT HORSE
> *ELDER SON OF THE ABOVE*
> KILLED IN ACTION IN PALESTINE
> 14TH JULY 1918
> FIGHTING IN THE CAUSE OF
> HONOR, FREEDOM AND JUSTICE
> AGED 39 YEARS
>
> *AND OF*
> CONSTANTINE TRENT
> CHAMPION DE CRESPIGNY
> K.B, D.S.O, M.D., F.R.C.P.
> OF ADELAIDE, SOUTH AUSTRALIA
> *YOUNGEST SON OF THE ABOVE*
> 1882 - 1952

CHAPTER FIVE

Annie Frances' death certificate gives the cause as pelvic cellulitis, a bacterial infection which can now be treated with antibiotics; the condition had been apparent for three weeks before her death. It may have been the aftereffect of childbirth eleven months before, but had more probably developed from a third pregnancy which never came to term.

A postcard view of Queenscliff c.1882: Hesse Street from Baillieu's Tower with the Bank of Victoria building in the centre foreground

As a sad postscript, there survives a letter written by Philip to Charlotte Frances his mother welcoming her to Queenscliff.

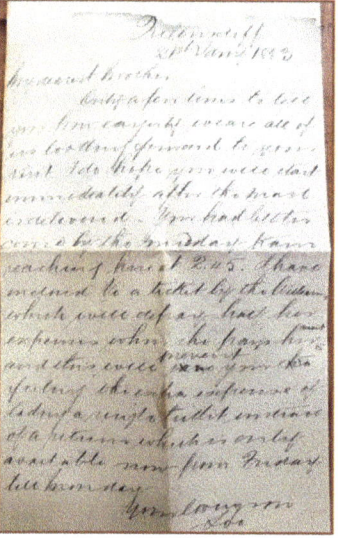

Letter 17 21st Jan'y 1883
My dearest Mother,
    Only a few lines to tell you how eagerly we are all of us looking forward to your visit. I do hope you will start immediately after the mail is delivered. You had better come by the mid-day train reaching here at 2.45. I have enclosed Vi a ticket by the Williams which will defray half her expenses when she pays her visit and this will prevent your feeling the extra expense of taking a single ticket instead of a return which is only available now from Friday till Monday.

Your loving son
Loo

Annie Frances became ill a few days later, and she died just one month after the letter was written.

The widower Philip was thus left with two small boys, one four years old and the other less than twelve months. As manager of a branch of the bank, however, he had accommodation provided, and his salary was sufficient to maintain a household of servants, including a nursemaid or governess for the children. There is no documentation, but it is very likely that one or other of his sisters Ada and Viola lived with the family to help with the children.

Late in 1886 Philip was transferred to the Elmore branch of the bank, northeast of Bendigo, but within a few months he was transferred again to the important branch at South Melbourne and by 1887 he was living there at Clarendon Street, in a large brick house of thirteen rooms owned by the Bank of Victoria.[139] He was still there in 1888, but at the end of that year or early in 1889 he moved to Brighton. In the *Rate Book* for the Town of Brighton of 1889, item 1780 of an assessment made on 20 March identified Phillip [*sic*] C Crespigny, Banker, living on Esplanade in the South Ward. The house of nine rooms, built of brick, was rented from a certain Daniel George, who also owned the place next door.

There were several reasons for the move, and a very basic one was that Philip had been promoted from the South Melbourne branch to the head office of the Bank of Victoria as Assistant Inspector of Branches. This was a senior position, ranking with the manager, the auditor and the accountant, and a considerable achievement for a man just forty years old.[140] While he no longer had access to the housing which the bank provided for the managers of its individual branches, he had the opportunity and resources to find accommodation at any place within reasonable range of the city.

199
Photograph held by the Public Record Office of Victoria

Brighton was a sensible choice. It was an attractive area, growing in popularity as the railway

---

[139] The 1887 *Rate Book* for the City of South Melbourne at 163 and the 1888 *Rate Book* at 171. The *Victorian Post Office Directory* of that year has Philip's entry immediately above that of his father in Robe Street, St Kilda: 178 above. The map at page 177 identifies this and other sites mentioned below onto a present-day map of south eastern Melbourne.

[140] A formal advertisement for the Bank of Victoria, published in the Melbourne *Leader* of 2 November 1889 lists the hierarchy at the head of the bank: Trove 198059625.

    Philip's obituary in the *Argus*, as in Chapter Seven at 253, states that he became Assistant Inspector in 1892. The evidence here, however, indicates the appointment was some three years earlier.

connection to central Melbourne now provided a good and inexpensive service.[141] Philip's parents Philip Robert and Charlotte Frances, and his two sisters Ada and Viola had been living at either St Kilda or Brighton for several years, and Brighton Grammar School was convenient for his two boys Philip and Constantine Trent, now ten and seven years old. Just at this time, moreover, his father had become increasingly frail.

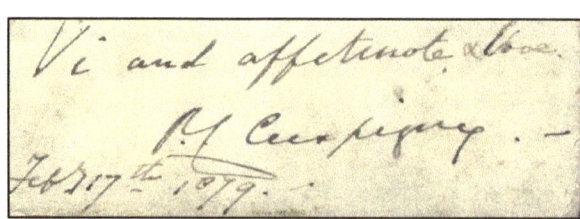

Philip Robert Champion Crespigny in 1879 at the age of sixty-one
The studio photograph by Foster and Martin of Melbourne is in the collection of his great-grandson John Chauncy CdeC (1908-1995). The inscription on the back to Philip Robert's daughter Viola is dated 17 February 1879, two years after the illness which compelled his retirement from office as magistrate at Ararat.
  The photograph which is commonly used – as in Henderson, Early Pioneer Families, 237 – and which is shown alongside, has been cropped from this larger picture. The walking stick and the position of the arms may indicate the effects of a stroke.

---

[141] Bate, History of Brighton, 194.

Though Philip Robert's paralysis had been sufficiently severe to compel his retirement as a magistrate in 1876,[142] he was not at first fully incapacitated, for in March of 1879 he had been able to walk along South Beach at St Kilda.[143] His condition steadily deteriorated, however, and ten years later it was terminal. He died on 13 September 1889. The death certificate gives the address as "Esplanade, St Kilda Street, Brighton Beach, Borough of Brighton, County of Brighton."[144]

It was a long, cruel ending to a forty-year marriage which had begun in such dramatic circumstances: clandestine adultery and a child born before wedlock; romantic elopement across the Channel followed by a scandalous divorce; then a new life to be made in a strange, harsh land while a new-born son was left behind. From all the evidence, however, it had been a successful and affectionate companionship – which must have made the slow but fatal process of Philip Robert's paralysis all the more affecting. At the time of his death, he and Charlotte Frances had seen two grandchildren, Philip's sons Philip and Constantine Trent; but they had also seen the deaths of their own son Constantine Trent and their young daughter-in-law Annie Frances.

Her husband's death left Charlotte Frances in a difficult financial position. He had, as we have seen, received a pension after his forced retirement, but that ended at his death, and the government made no further payments to his widow. Charlotte Frances did have some shares in various companies, but they cannot have been a major source of income,[145] and she was largely dependent upon such family support as could be provided. For the time being, she and her daughters Ada and Viola continued to live with Philip at the Esplanade, but – as in Chapter Six following – there was a strong connection to Rose and her husband Frank Beggs and his family at Eurambeen near Beaufort. Dating is uncertain, but it appears that Viola was staying with Frank and Rose at their property Eurambeen East from about 1891, and Charlotte Frances went to join that family in 1894. With occasional visits to Melbourne, she would live at Eurambeen for the last ten years of her life.[146]

---

[142] Above at 171-172.
[143] See the incident of Constantine Trent ChC and Mathias Lyons at 178-179 above.
[144] The death of Philip Robert Champion Crespigny in the District of Brighton was registered by Henry Addis, reference number 10924. A photocopy of the certificate is in Grayden, *Chronicle*, 31, but is too faint to be reproduced here.

The notice of Philip Robert's death in the *Weekly Times* of 21 September states that he died "at his late residence, Esplanade, Brighton:" Trove 220418232. The only entry for Crespigny in the Brighton *Rate Book* of 1889, however, is at 114-115 and relates to Philip C Crespigny, Banker. So Philip Robert was no longer the [nominal] head of a household; he and Charlotte Frances were living at their son's establishment.

The somewhat strange address given by the death certificate may best be explained by the fact that St Kilda Street, coming from the north, links with The Esplanade near the [now Royal] Brighton Yacht Club. The order of items in the *Rate Book* indicates that Philip Crespigny's house was on the Esplanade, just south of the connection with St Kilda Street.

[145] On Philip Robert's pension, see above at 172. For references to Charlotte Frances' share-holdings, see Chapter Six at 237 and 238.
[146] See Chapter Six at 211-213 with Letters 20 and 23.

Chapter Five

Brighton Beach, Victoria, in the early 1880s
Wood-engraving from Picturesque Atlas of Australasia,
after a drawing by Albert Henry Fullwood (1863-1930).

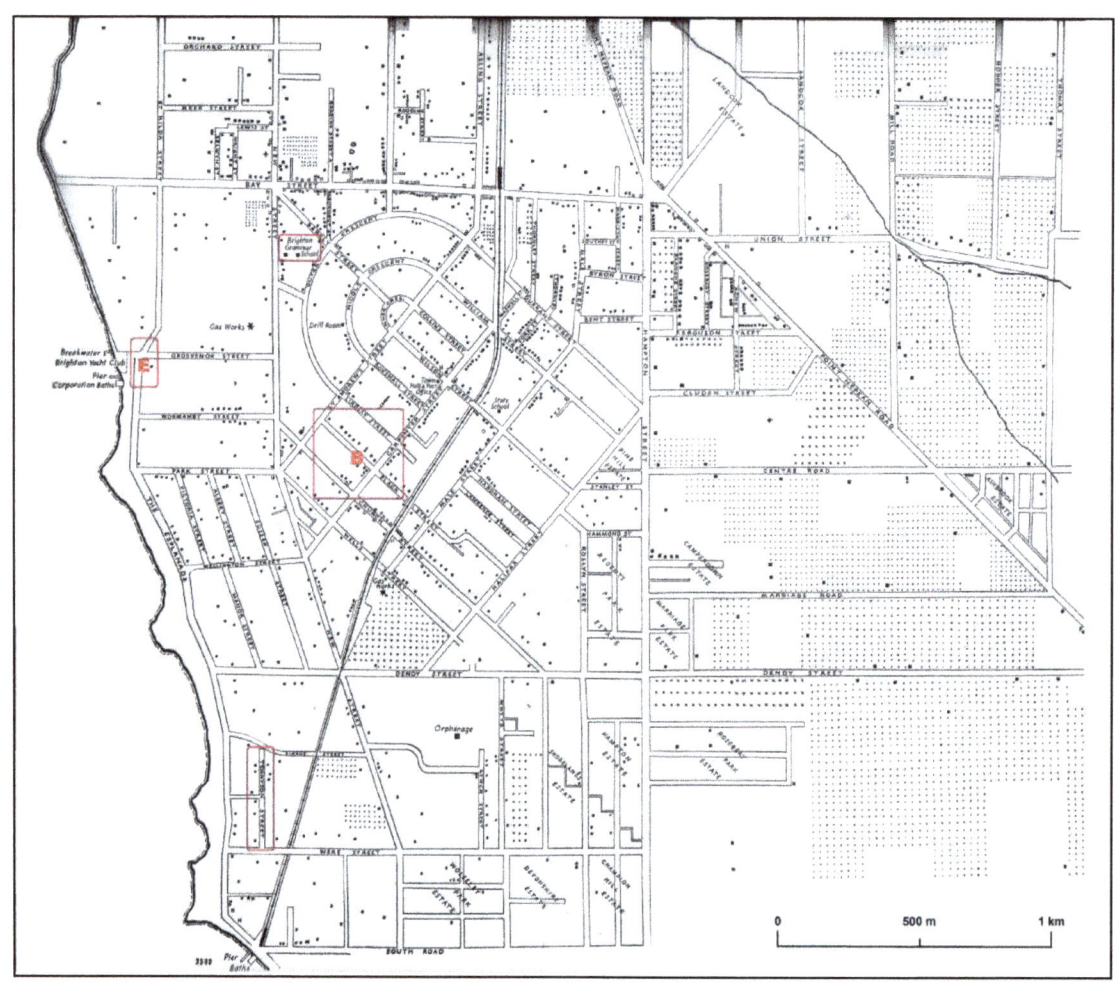

Brighton 1887
detail from the map of the Municipal District of Brighton in Bate, History of Brighton,
based on the Council Rate Book for that year
Marked with red are the area of the Esplanade [E] where Philip Crespigny had a house from 1889 to 1892
and where his father Philip Robert Crespigny died in 1889;
Tennyson Street, where Philip Crespigny rented a house named "Wyndcote" from 1892 to 1894;
Black Street [B], where Philip Crespigny had his house named "Vierville" from 1908;
and Brighton Grammar School, attended by Philip's sons Philip and Constantine Trent in the 1890s.

TABLE 3

THE BEGGS FAMILY IN AUSTRALIA DURING THE NINETEENTH CENTURY
A SUMMARY GENEALOGY

Note: The Beggs family genealogy is complex and confused, and there are differing reconstructions of the family tree. The table below, which is primarily concerned with the family in Australia, is based upon Henderson, *Early Pioneer Families*, 249-257, and Alexander/Persse, *Every Tree, Rock, and Gully*, viii-ix, supplemented by ancestry.com.au.
Not all the names in this table are indexed.

Irish origins

FRANCIS BEGGS (1770-1839)
married [1] *Jane* **Montgomery** (1778-1806)
    Thomas died in Ireland
    William Montgomery (1800-1874) died in Ireland
        m Martha **Gihon/Gihan** (1802-1890) died in Ireland
            Thomas Alexander (1839-1920) **moved to Australia**
                m Clamina Florinda **Faris** (1841-1895) [his cousin, as below]
            other issue
    Matilda died in Ireland
    Helen died in Ireland
married [2] 1805 *Clamina Lyons* **Montgomery** (1787-1821)
    Clamina Montgomery (1811-1890) died in Ireland
        m John **Faris** (1801-1861) died in Ireland
            Clamina Florinda (1841-1895) **moved to Australia**
            Francis Benjamin (1835-1860) **moved to Australia**
            John Lyon (1842-1882) **moved to Australia**
            William Irwin (1836-1882) **moved to Australia**
            other issue
    Francis (1812-1880) **moved to Australia**
    Sophia Montgomery (1813-1887) **moved to Australia**
    William Montgomery (1813-1887) died in Ireland
    Charlotte (b.1815) [twin of Hugh Lyons Montgomery below] died in Ireland
    Hugh Lyons Montgomery (1815-1885) [twin of *Charlotte*] **moved to Australia**
    George (1816-1879) **moved to Australia**
    Charles Montgomery (1819-1897) **moved to Australia**
    Catherine (b.1821) died in India

In Australia

THOMAS ALEXANDER **BEGGS** (1839-1920)
    married Clamina Florinda **Faris** (1841-1895)
        William John (1876-
        Grace Charlotte (1865-1920)
        Clamina Mary (1867-1867)
        Martha Sophia (b.1868)
        Clamina Elizabeth (b.1870)
            m Charles **King**
        Mary Montgomery (1872-1948)
            m Robert **Newton**
        Charlotte Faris (1874-1942)
            m John **Utberg**
        Frances Georgina (1880-1960)

CHAPTER FIVE

FRANCIS **BEGGS** (1812-1880)
    married 1849 Maria Lucinda **White** (1826-1914)
        Francis [Frank] (1850-1921)
            m Helen Rosalie "Rose" **Champion** [de] **Crespigny** (1858-1937)
        Elizabeth Persse "Lizzie" (1852-1908)
            m 1888 Francis **Beggs** (1857-1898) [her cousin, son of Charles
                  Montgomery (1819-1897) below]
        Gertrude (1854-1859)
        Charlotte (1854-1898)
            m 1888 Robert **McKissock** (1839-1899)
        Maria (1856-1902)
        Clamina ["Miney"/"Minie"] (1858-1904)
            m 1877 Walter Henry **Davidson** (1847-1916)
                Ethel (1878-1975)
                Walter Henry "Hal" (1879-1971)
                Alan (1881-1903)
                Beatrice (1883-1948)
                Francis (b.1885)
                Donald (b.1886)
                Norman (1889-1915)
                Samuel (b.1893)
                Hector (b.1895)
        Theodore (1859-1940)
            m 1918 *Agnes Jane* **Walpole** (1893-1918)
        Robert Gottlieb (1861-1939)
            m 1. 1882 *Maria Juana* **Balcombe** (d.1883)
                Robert Balcombe (1883-1954)
            m 2. 1905 *Amy Edith* **Ricardo** (1880-1940)
                Arthur Ricardo (1906-1978)
                Ralph (b.1907)
                Helen Elizabeth (1909-1984)
                George (b.1910)
                Barbara
        Hugh Norman (1863-1943)
            m 1897 *Mary Catherine Reeves* **Palmer**
                Norman Francis Henry (1898-1918)
                Beryl Charlotte (1900-1956)
                Hugh Carleton (1901-1904)
                Theodore George (1903-1936)
                Sandford Robert (1907-1984)
        Gertrude Dorothea (1866-1943)
            m 1894 Thomas Edward **White** (1864-1944)
                Robert Beggs (1902-1982)

SOPHIA MONTGOMERY nee **BEGGS** (1813-1887)
    married 1853 Humphrey **Grattan** (1823-1904)
        William (1855-1917)

Bushy Creek homestead of Hugh Lyons Montgomery Beggs and his son Francis

HUGH LYONS MONTGOMERY **BEGGS** (1815-1885)
    married [1] 1853 *Elizabeth* **Smith** (1828-1864)
        Catherine (1854-1939)
        Rose Annie (1858-1919) *m* 1876 William **Wood** (1850-1890)
            John Vivian Montgomery (1877-1945)
            Elizabeth Victoria Geraldine (1879-1879)
            William Bertram Montgomery (b.1880)
            Ruby Frances Emily (1883-1971)
        Francis (1858-1919) "Bushy" *m* 1905 Edith Mary **Turnbull** (1877-1956)
        Jane Frances (1860-1934) *m* 1887 Thomas **Dodds** (1847-1891)
        Kathleen Elizabeth (b.1888)
        Vair Montgomery (b.1891)
        Martha Florence (1864-1866)
    married [2] 1865 *Lavinia Mary Eugenia* **Heney** (1831-1925)
        Sophia (1866-1866)
        Lavinia (1868-1869)
        Sophia Montgomery Grattan (1870-1936) *m* Philip **Champion** [de] **Crespigny** (1850-1927) [formerly married to Annie Frances nee Chauncy]
            Francis George Travers (1892-1968)
            Hugh Vivian (1897-1969)
            Royalieu Dana (1905-1985)
            Claude Montgomery (1908-1991)
        Hugh Lyons Montgomery (1872-1949) *m* 1897 *Ethel Maud* **Murch** (1877-1966)
            Doris Montgomery (1899-1967)
            Mabel Goodwin (1903-1979)
        Mabel Georgina (1875-1951) *m* 1907 John Richard **Moodie** (1867-1932)
            John Claude Beggs (1908-1981)
            Annie Lavinia (Penny) (1910-1993)
            William Marcus (1911-1974)
            Dorothy Enid (1914-1968)
            Hugh David (1918-1994)
        Matilda Cairns (1876-1969)
        William Goodwin (1878-1957) *m* 1911 *Gwendoline Maud* **Fenton**
            Kenneth Montgomery (1912-1981)
            Stewart Goodwin (1916-1937)

CHAPTER FIVE

    GEORGE **BEGGS** (1816-1879)
        married 1855 *Charlotte Elizabeth* **White** (1836-1921)
           Frances Georgina (1856-1932)
           Catherine (1859-1938)
           Madeline (1860-1915)
           George Warren (1870-1873)

    CHARLES MONTGOMERY **BEGGS** (1819-1897)
        married 1851 *Charlotte Catherine Sophia* **Meehan** (1831-1917)
           Elizabeth Charlotte (1851-1927) *m* 1880 James Reginald **Paget** (1853-1896)
                Neville James (1881-1910)
                Charles Montgomery (1882-1918)
                William George Gordon (1885-1932)
                Marcella Sophia (1887-1973)
                Reginald Beggs (1889-1931)
                Elizabeth Florence (1891-1942)
           Clamina (1853-1918)
           Francis (1854-1898) *m* 1888 *Elizabeth Persse "Lizzie"* **Beggs** (1852-1908)
                [his cousin, daughter of Francis (1812-1880)]
           Sophia Irene (1855-1883)
           Adelaide Louisa (1859-1954)
                m 1885 Charles Thomas Stavely **Paget** (1859-1928)
                Leslie Beggs (1886-1917)
                Esmond Charles (1889-1917)
                Honora (1891-1953)
                Carlene Gertrude (1892-1897)
                Ernestine Montgomery (b.1896)
                Clifford Francis (b.1898)
           George William (1862-1865)
           Charles James (1865-1939)
           Mary Faris (1867-1896) *m* 1893 William **Chaffrey**
           Maude Gertrude (1867-1939)
           Ernest Grattan Neville Montgomery (1869-1954)
           Adamina ["*Minnie*"] *Matilda Margaret* (*c*.1870-1918)
                m 1890 Alexander Edward **Savage**

CHAPTER SIX

EURAMBEEN
1889-1904

The second marriage of Philip Champion Crespigny
The letters of Constantine Trent 1889-1896
Banks and the land: the crisis of the 1890s
The Eurambeen Letters 1898-1904

The second marriage of Philip Champion Crespigny
Annie Frances nee Chauncy, wife of Philip Robert and Charlotte Frances' son Philip and mother of his sons Philip and Constantine Trent, had died at Queenscliff in 1883.[1] Eight years later, on 2 November 1891, Philip married his second wife Sophia Montgomery Grattan Beggs (1870-1936) at Holy Trinity Church, Balaclava, close to Philip's residence at Brighton.

Sophia was the daughter of Hugh Lyons Montgomery Beggs, a brother of Francis and George Beggs. Francis' son Frank, husband of Philip's daughter Rose, was thus a first cousin to Sophia. Francis and George Beggs had been based on Eurambeen near Beaufort, and Frank had leased Eurambeen East in 1881. Hugh had purchased a separate property at Bushy Creek near Glenthompson, south of Ararat and he was succeeded there by his son Francis, Sophia's brother.[2] Though their holdings were a hundred kilometres apart the families were in regular contact and Philip Crespigny could have met Sophia at one of their gatherings.

The marriage of Crespigny-Beggs was reported at some length in the Melbourne journal *Table Talk* of Friday 6 November, with a detailed description of the dresses and the wedding presents.[3] As her father Hugh was dead, the bride was given away by Mr Humphrey Grattan, her uncle by marriage,[4] and the couple travelled to Lorne for their honeymoon.

Philip and Sophia would have four children, Francis George Travers (1892-1968), Hugh Vivian (1897-1969), Royalieu [Roy] Dana (1905-1985) and Claude Montgomery (1908-1991); they were half-brothers to the younger Philip and Constantine Trent.

The letters of Constantine Trent Champion Crespigny 1889-1896
Among the collection of letters that we believe were gathered by Ada Crespigny (1848-1927), which were then held by her nephew Constantine Trent CdeC (1882-1952), and which are now in the State Library of South Australia,[5] a few were written by or to Constantine Trent himself in 1889 and the early 1890s. Sent variously to and from Eurambeen and Melbourne, the letters themselves and items of internal evidence provide information on members of the family and their movements.

---

[1] Chapter Five at 198-199.
[2] On the acquisition of Bushy Creek by Hugh Beggs (1815-1885), see Chapter Five at 185.
Because of the number of men in the Beggs family with the same given name, this Francis Beggs (1858-1919) was often referred to as "Bushy:" *e.g.* 205 and 219 with note 33 below. An obituary was published in the *Portland Guardian* of 17 September 1919: Trove 63959688.
[3] Trove 147286033; Anne's Family History 2013/11/06. Entries also in the Queenscliff Sentinel, Drysdale, Portarlington and Sorrento Advertiser and the Euroa Advertiser: Trove 73592032 and 65531264.
[4] Humphrey Grattan, a family friend and sometime partner of Hugh, Francis and George Beggs, had married their sister Sophia Montgomery Beggs (1813-1887): Chapter Five at 184. This elder Sophia was the aunt of her younger namesake and probably her godmother.
[5] The provenance of the letters is discussed in Chapter Three at 113.

Chapter Six

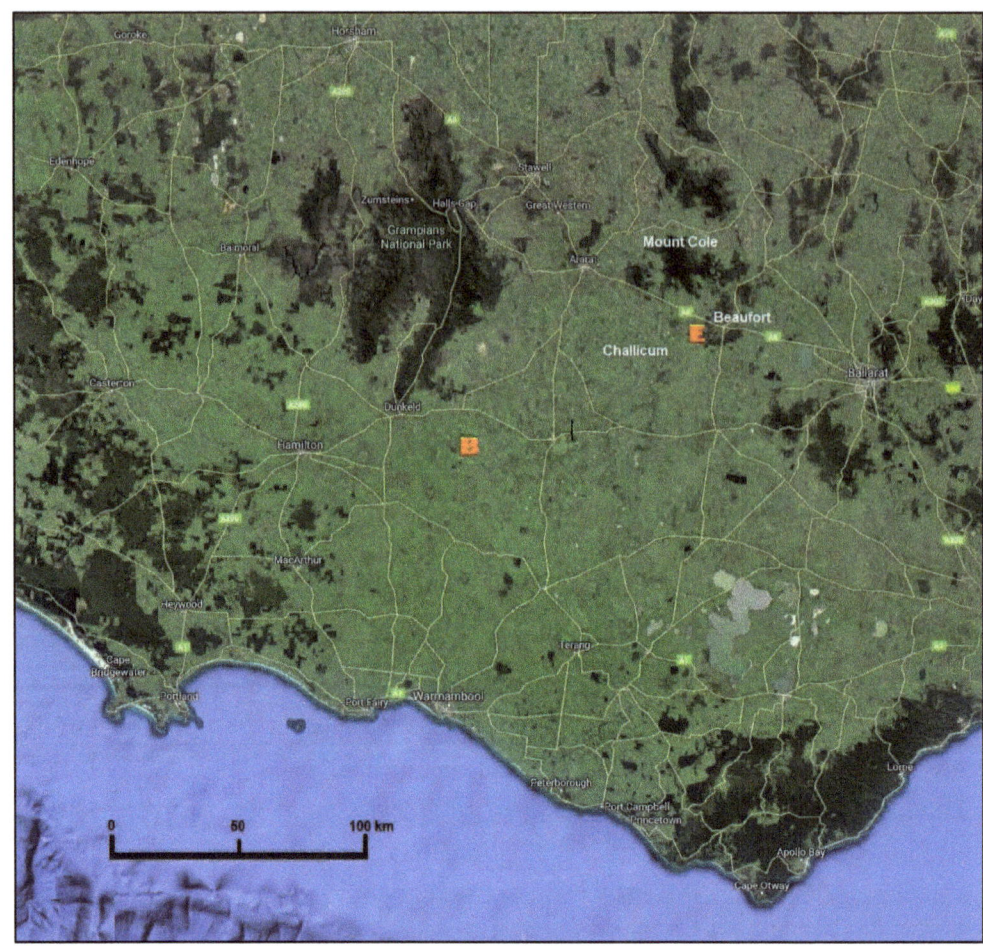

Part of the Western District of Victoria
E *indicates the area of the Eurambeen properties;* **B** *the site of Bushy Creek*
Mount Cole and Challicum are mentioned in Letter 23 written by Constantine Trent CdeC in December 1894

Eurambeen East homestead 2019
Photograph by Anne Young

The letters have been copy-typed more than once, so there may be errors in transcription, but in this series we may assume that mistakes of spelling and grammar reflect the original.

It must be noted, moreover, that the letters preserved were only a few among many which must have been written. They are valuable samples of experience, but there are many gaps between them, and they cannot be taken as a coherent account of events.

When their grandfather Philip Robert died in September 1889 Constantine Trent was seven and a half and his brother Philip (1879-1918) was ten. Three months later the two boys went to stay for the Christmas holidays with their aunt Rose and her husband Frank Beggs at Eurambeen East, close to Beaufort. The first letter in this series, number 18 of the whole collection, was written at this time by Constantine Trent to his aunt Ada.

Letter 18

Eurambeen East
BEAUFORT
Dec 24th 1889

My dear Ada,

We are going to the other House this afternoon.[6] I went down the fruit garden this morning and had some fruit.

Auntie Rose has a little dog called Mr Brown.

We have opened the cart and Phil took me for a raid.[7] Uncle Frank was so pleased with the little picture that I gave hem.

Now I must shut up.

Ever your
Con

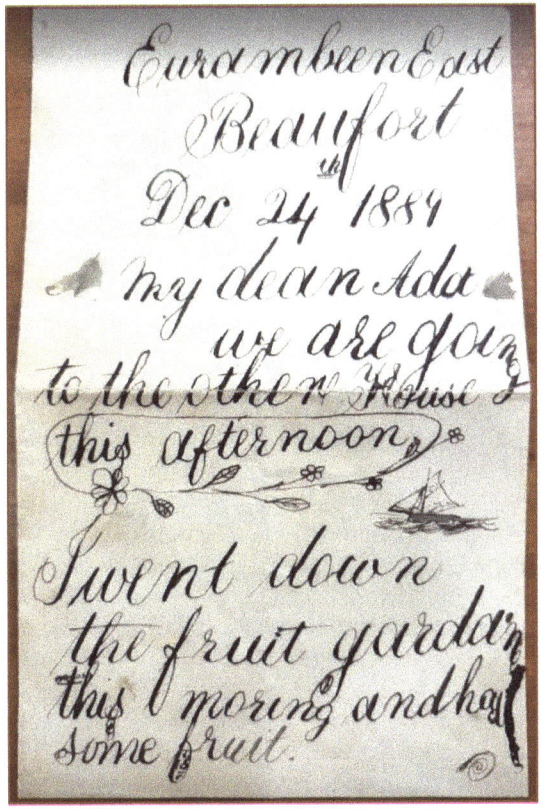 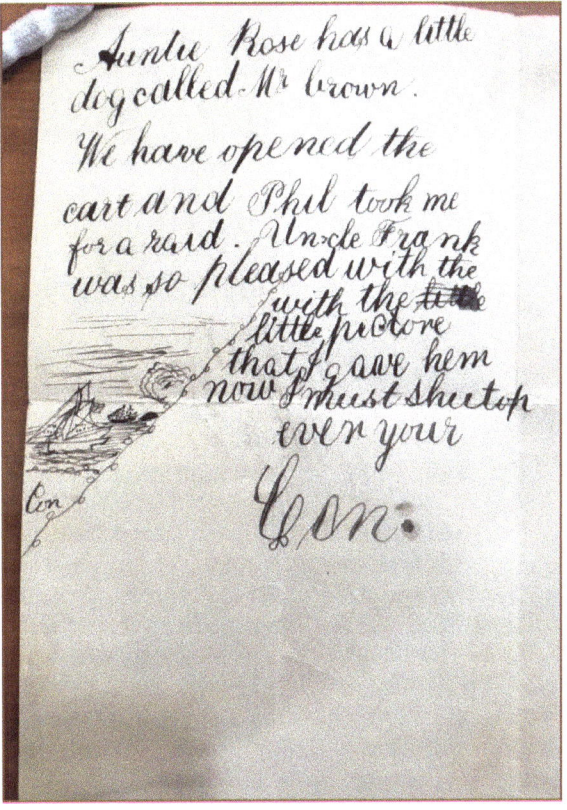

---

[6] The residents of Eurambeen East referred to Eurambeen [West] as "the other house" – and *vice versa*.
[7] One assumes it must have been a small, safe vehicle if a ten-year-old boy was allowed to pull or drive his younger brother in it.

CHAPTER SIX

From the references to Uncle Frank and Aunt Rose [Beggs], Letter 19 was also written from Eurambeen East, while the presents and the plum pudding indicate that it was Christmas time. From the composition style and the reference to Sophie as below, it would have been the end of 1890, one year after Letter 18; Constantine Trent was now eight years and ten months old.

Letter 19 [undated: Christmas 1890]
[Eurambeen East]

My dear Grannie, Papa, Auntie Ada and Auntie Vi,

Thank you so much for all the beautiful presents you sent me yesterday. I liked them all so much. I will tell you all I got:—

Uncle Frank	half a crown
Auntie Rose	scraps
Phil	two shillings
Sophie[8]	a pretty card
Minnie[9]	a knife
Tom[10]	a card
Pat	a knife and match box
Tim	a funny picture of Phil riding George[11]
Mr Gipton[12]	one shilling

For dinner we had parrot pie, curry and chicken and plum pudding. I ate a good lot but not quite tell my nose blead this time. Balkey came over here to dinner.[13]

We let off some of the fireworks and the rocket had the stick was put in wrong way, and Tom was holding it and all the sparks wend up his sleeve and he droped it and Uncle Frank wend to pick it up and it went off bung and he jumped a mile high in the ear.

Ever your loving
Con

---

[8] Sophie is probably Sophia Montgomery Grattan Beggs, who would become the second wife of Con's father Philip – the form is used in later letters written by Con when she is his stepmother. The time, however, is presumably before the marriage, or one would expect Philip to have been present; as it is, "Papa" is one of the people addressed in the letter – so he was not there.

[9] Minnie is Clamina Davidson nee Beggs, younger sister of Frank, note 123 to Chapter Five. She and her husband Walter had been in Queensland, but returned to Victoria about 1887 and now held Coliban Park near Elphinstone, southeast of Castlemaine and some 130 kilometres from Beaufort and Eurambeen.

[10] Tom appears several times below as a slightly older companion to Constantine Trent and his brother Philip. Pat and Tim cannot be identified.

[11] George is probably a horse.

[12] The surname Gipton is miswritten for Gibton.
Maria ["Mysie"] Gibton (1836-1926) came to Victoria from Ireland in 1853 at the age of seventeen. She was accompanying her father Robert Nassau Gibton – their mother had died a few years before – but he died soon after their arrival and Maria and her two brothers and two sisters had to fend for themselves. In Ireland, however, the Gibtons were known to the White family of Maria Lucinda the wife of Francis Beggs (Robert Nassau's brother William would marry Maria Lucinda's sister Adelaide Letitia in 1861), and Maria became nurserymaid and governess to the Beggs family in Victoria.
In 1860 Maria Gibton married Maria Lucinda's brother John Warren White. Their son Brudenell became Chief of the Australian General Staff. See Derham, *Silence Ruse*, 119-121, and note 143 below.
Mr Gibton would have been one of Maria's two brothers, working as senior assistants on the Eurambeen properties. The elder, named Robert Nassau like his father, had been born in 1827 and died at Warrnambool in 1891. The younger, William, was born in 1838 and died at Beaufort in 1928. At 225 below Letter 30 of February 1900 mentions "Old Gibbie," who must be William, but it is uncertain which of the brothers is referred to here.

[13] Balkey, also as Balkie or Balke and other variant spellings, was Robert Balcombe Beggs (1883-1954), son of Robert Gottlieb Beggs (1861-1939), younger brother of Frank the husband of Rose; Table 3 in Chapter Five at 204. His mother Maria Juana nee Balcombe had died at his birth in September 1883. A frequent visitor to Eurambeen East, he was a close friend of Constantine Trent, eighteen months the elder.

Letter 20, written when Con was ten years old, was addressed to his aunt Viola, now with her sister at Eurambeen East. His father Philip had lately rented a house named "Wyndcote" on Tennyson Street in Brighton,[14] and Con's grandmother Charlotte Frances was living there too.

Letter 20

"Wyndcote"
June 12/1892

My dear Auntie Vie,

    I hope you will not mind me not writing to you before but I have been busy with my lessons.

    Auntie Rose's hamper was so nice. I have eaten everything in it but the French mustard which Granny and I are just finishing now. I am getting on with my lessons very well.

    Charlie's poor brother's wife is dead after them only being marryed 6 mounths, is not it sad?[15]

    I was playing football yesterday and got a kick on the shin, and the other day strained my heel and do not know which leg to go laim on.

    I must shut up now as Ellen is going.[16] Give my best love to Uncle Frank and Auntie Rose and yourself.

Ever your loving
Con T. Ch - Crespigny

Letter 21 was written to Constantine Trent by his brother Philip, who was staying at Eurambeen East while Con was presumably at home in Melbourne. Philip was now fifteen years old, Con twelve.

Letter 21

Eurambeen East
BEAUFORT
11/11/94

My dear Con,

    I have been always going to write to you but never have so the news has been accumultaing [*sic*]. Buffer is looking very well and so is Sunbeam.[17]

    We all went for a drive today to Shirley to look for some wild ducks' eggs for Balkie who was with us.[18] Tedo was riding.[19] As soon as we got out of the buggy and started looking for the nest, I walked nearly over a tiger snake which I promptly killed and through into a water hole. When we went on a bit further Tedo saw another crawl into a drain. After a lot of trouble he and I ran him up a small drain (there was a lot of thorn interlaced with crape holes). Then we started hammering him, one each side of the drain, consequently splashing each other at every blow but we killed him and I fished him out of the water on the end of my stick.

    The other day Tom and I were racing little boats along the water race at the sheep-wash. We made a lot of boats and did not take them out and next day they stopped up the water pipes and we got into an awful row.

---

[14] A notice in the *Argus* of Tuesday 27 September records the birth of a son to the wife of Philip Champion Crespigny at Wyndcote, Tennyson-street, Brighton: Francis George Travers, first child of the marriage, had been born on 23 September.
[15] Charlie and his family cannot be identified.
[16] Ellen cannot be identified; she is probably not the Ellen O'[?] mentioned in Letter 29 at 222.
[17] From Letter 23 below at 214, Buffer is a dog and Sunbeam is a horse that Constantine Trent rides when he is at Eurambeen.
[18] Shirley is about fifteen kilometres south of Beaufort and some twenty kilometres from Eurambeen.
[19] Tedo is Theodore Beggs (1859-1940), owner-manager at Eurambeen [West]. Balkie and Balke below is Robert Balcombe Beggs (1883-1954): note 13 above.

Balke got some orchids sent him from Western Australia. We got some from the mountain too the other day so I suppose he will have some for you when you come up.

There was a pup lost here on Thursday week and I found him on Wednesday. He had not had a feed since and was alive but very thin.

With best love to all
Ever your loving
Phil

Philip CdeC (1850-1927) with members of his family in 1894
Constantine Trent, Sophia Montgomery Grattan nee Beggs, and Francis George Travers
From the collection of Philip's grandson John Chauncy CdeC (1908-1995)

The photograph is inscribed on the back – very faintly – as "Con, Sophie, Franky, Loo." The handwriting is probably that of Philip's sister Viola; the photograph may have been taken by her or possibly by Con's elder brother Philip, father of John Chauncy.

Dating is based upon the apparent age of "Franky" [Francis George Travers CdeC], who was born in September 1892 and appears at this time to be about eighteen months old. His half-brother Constantine Trent, born in March 1882, would then have been turning twelve.

Philip CdeC, now thirty-four, had been appointed Assistant Inspector at the Bank of Victoria four years earlier. He and his family were currently living at "Wyndcote" on Tennyson Street in Brighton, but they moved later that year to "Ottawa," a brick house on Gladstone Parade in Elsternwick.

Letter 22 was written by Constantine Trent to his father Philip one month after Letter 21, and Letter 23 was sent to his aunt Ada a few days later. He was now staying at Eurambeen with Frank Beggs and his aunt Rose, and it appears that his grandmother Charlotte Frances had joined the household.

In Letter 23 Con tells of an expedition to Mount Cole with Tom, but makes no mention of Philip. In his Letter 22 to Melbourne, however, he does not send him greetings. Philip was perhaps staying somewhere else over the holiday season.

The two shillings and sixpence [2/6] that Con mentions in Letter 22 was presumably a Christmas present which had arrived two days before.

Letter 22

Eurambeen East
BEAUFORT
27.12.94

A MERRY XMAS

My dear Papa,

I would have written and acknowledged your kind letter & 2/6 before this but I missed Monday's post and therefore could not write until today. Thank Sophie for the pretty card she sent me.

I am very glad you are pleased with my report and I think I will be moved into the LV [Lower Fifth] but I still rank 10th in form. I had hoped to move up a seat or two also but I don't suppose I could of, considering I was absent for 32½ days but still if I move into the LV it does not much matter.

I get a lot of birds' eggs about here, though it will soon be too late in the season. If that old guinea-pig doe has young ones try and tame them as much as you can and see that Maggie cleans out the boxes the way I told her.

Give Aunty Ada and Sophie my best love & thank Aunty Ada very much for the lovely card she sent me.

I must now wind up

Ever your loving
Con T C Crespigny

Give my best love to BB and a kiss. C T C C[20]
How is Rowly. C T C C[21]

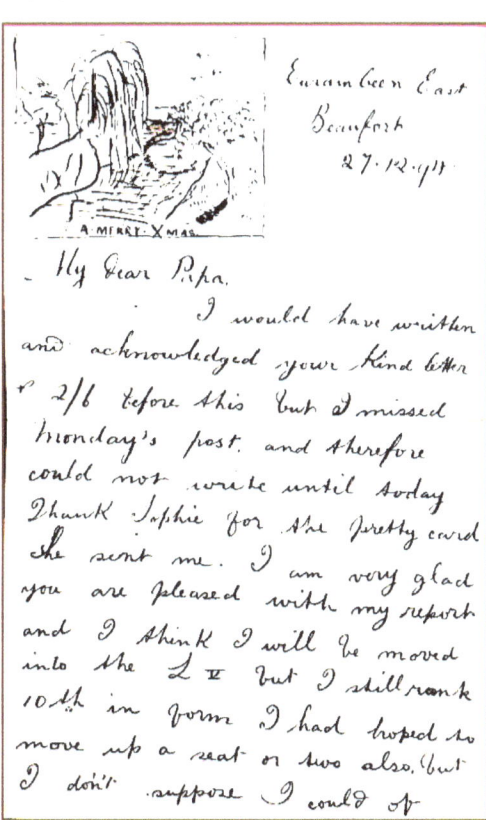

Con was a student at Brighton Grammar School. The Lower Fifth was the equivalent of present-day Year 10 but, unlike the present day, promotion from one level to another was not

---

[20] BB is probably "Baby Brother:" Francis George Travers, first child of Philip and Sophia nee Beggs and half-brother to Constantine Trent, was now just over two years old: note 14 above.
[21] Rowly cannot be identified; perhaps a dog?

Chapter Six

automatic; in principle, a student had to qualify for it. Since he would be thirteen in March of the year he entered that grade, he may have been a year ahead for his age.[22]

Letter 23
Eurambeen East
BEAUFORT
31st.12.94

A HAPPY NEW YEAR

My dear Aunty Ada,

    I got the fly-net all right last week. Thank you very much for it.

    Tom & I went up to the Cave on Mount Cole. I rode my own little mare, Sunbeam. When we got to the bottom of the mountain we had to leave our horses in another fellow's stable and start the stiffest climbing I have ever done, but when you get up to it the view is worth seeing, there is a great big rock about 1/2 a mile long and a 1/4 mile high out of which is cut a big lump just as if it was cut with a huge knife, and if you look away from it you see miles and miles away past Challicum nearly to the sea.[23]

    On going up to the cave we saw one snake but Tom could not get at it to kill it. It was fun rolling stones down, they went crash, crash, bang, bang, till they nearly came to the bottom.

    I have got 17 eggs since I have been up here, Golden Oriel's, fire-tail's, tom-tit's, swift's, wag-tail's, Australian thrushes and two other kinds but the nesting season will soon be over and then I won't get any more.

    Buffer is getting on well, he is as fat as a pig and still walks about with the same stately stride & still shakes hands with me.

    How is BB? I hope he is alright. Give him my love.
I must wind up now.

    Give my love to Pa, Sophie, and much for your self

Ever your loving
C T C Crespigny

A cave on Mount Cole

---

[22] As an example, Constantine Trent's son Richard Geoffrey, born in June 1907, was awarded the Second Form Prize in the Lower Fifth at Geelong Grammar School in 1921, the year that he turned fourteen.

[23] Mount Cole, 900 metres high, is thirty kilometres northwest of Eurambeen. Mount Challicum, 450 metres, is twenty kilometres to the south, almost due west of Eurambeen. The distance from Mount Cole to the sea coast at Warrnambool is some 150 kilometres, almost a hundred miles. See the map at the beginning of this chapter.

Mount Cole from Challicum 1852/53
Plate 39 of Cooper, Challicum Sketchbook

Last of this series, Letter 24 was written some eighteen months after Letter 23; Constantine Trent is now fourteen years old.

Letter 24　　　　　　　　　　　　　　　　　　　　　　　　　　Eurambeen East
　　　　　　　　　　　　　　　　　　　　　　　　　　　　　　　　　BEAUFORT
　　　　　　　　　　　　　　　　　　　　　　　　　　　　　　　　Aug 27th, 1896

My dear Auntie Ada,
　　You must not think me unkind for not writing before. I hope your cold is better. How is the parrot? You have not said anything about him in your letters or if the ferns are doing well. Have you planted out the seedlings yet? I hope you are not lonely down (there) without Grannie or me.
　　When Tom was staying here for the two or three days he shot a most beautiful lory parrot. I have had it stuffed in town and it looks so pretty.[24] Aunti Vi is much better today and says she feels quite different since she took the medicine.
　　Auntie Rose says that, as it is raining today, she will not send her bed-spread by this post for fear of its getting wet, but she will send it as soon as she can.
　　You need not be alarmed about me and the tiger as he has been stuffed twice and killed three times, at different places![25] Auntie Rose will have told you all the news. Give my love to all.

　　　　　　　　　　　　　　　　　　　　　　　　　　　　　　　　Ever your Loving
　　　　　　　　　　　　　　　　　　　　　　　　　　　　　　　　　　　Con

---

[24]　The unfortunate bird was presumably a lorikeet; they are very gaudy.
[25]　There is no other reference to a tiger[-snake?], alive or dead.

CHAPTER SIX

Banks and the land: the crisis of the 1890s

In 1889, soon after Philip Crespigny had been appointed Assistant Inspector of the Bank of Victoria, the bank and the colony as a whole entered a period of great financial difficulty. A land boom in the 1880s had seen enormous expansion of lending by banks, building societies and finance companies – "land banks" – and competition for clients meant that even the more cautious institutions weakened their requirements for granting credit. In 1889, however, a heavy fall in prices received for properties brought a vast number of bankruptcies, many of them at heavy cost to creditors,[26] and a failure in the money market as a whole, with building societies and then land banks driven to collapse, and increasing public concern. The results were spectacular: across all the colonies,

> Counting banks as any institution that called itself a bank and solicited public deposits, 54 of the 64 institutions operating in 1891 had closed by mid 1893; 34 of these closed permanently. Defining banks more narrowly, to exclude institutions more akin to building societies, only nine of 28 banks remained open continuously throughout the 1890s.[27]

The situation was particularly serious in Victoria, where speculation had been intense, and it was made worse by the fact that most of the funding for the boom had come from Britain – and British financiers were no longer willing to accept Australian assurances and maintain their former rate of investment. By April and May 1893 the banking institutions which had either closed or were suspending payment accounted for more than half of all deposits and notes in circulation, and the colonial governments did not have sufficient resources to cope with the potential shortfall.

The Bank of Victoria was one of those which closed its doors at the beginning of May, for it did not have sufficient specie to pay all those who sought to withdraw their money.[28] By an official sleight-of-hand, however, in 1891 the colonial government had passed a Voluntary Liquidation Act, amended in 1892, which allowed for the reconstruction of an "old" bank into a "new" one. In effect, provided that a majority of creditors approved, new shares were issued to depositors in exchange for the money owed them, while existing shareholders were called upon for additional capital. In announcing the meeting to discuss a Scheme of Compromise and Arrangement, the directors argued that

> The scheme of reconstruction will, it is believed, press as lightly as possible upon both shareholders and depositors.

Although it was an immediate strain and something of a risk, the re-arrangement was a great deal better than the alternative: absolute failure of the bank itself.

---

[26] Cannon, *Land Boomers*, 211-213, lists the insolvencies of 1892 and records their rates of "composition" – the amount each debtor paid in the pound: some were no more than a penny [240 pennies to the pound] and some even less. At 217 he notes that the stockbroker A F Dean had borrowed £18,700 from the Bank of Victoria; the "dividend" on his bankruptcy was one shilling in the pound – a twentieth of the amount he had owed.

[27] Fitzgibbon and Gizycki, "1890s Depression," 22; also Merrett, "Australian Bank Crashes of the 1890s Revisited."

[28] The report from the *Argus* of 10 May 1893 [Trove 8549228/301265], describing the new scheme of arrangement as below, stated that

> "A few weeks ago the bank had £1,200,00 worth of coins on hand, but the demand for payment of deposits was so heavy that now only £600,000 remained in its coffers,"

while

> "one depositor at a branch bank in Gippsland had recently called at the bank and demanded payment in gold of a deposit of £10,000."

The Land Boomers by Michael Cannon provides the major general account of the financial crisis, and records in particular the devastating effect of unemployment and destitution in a society with only the most minimal provision for social assistance. This, however, was not the only problem which faced the colonial economy, for the 1890s saw farmlands across Australia afflicted by rabbits and by drought.

Rabbits had been brought to Australia with the First Fleet in 1788, and Van Diemen's Land/Tasmania had experienced a plague of them in the 1820s, but the most serious development occurred after 1859, when a batch of wild and domestic rabbits, together with some hares, was introduced from England for hunting. When the new-comers interbred, however, the hybrid stock proved ideally suited for the local environment. Within a few years millions had spread across the country, and by the late 1880s colonial governments were offering rewards for new and successful methods of control.[29]

Rabbits damaged crops and grazing land, and in many areas they ate so much vegetation that the surface was reduced to dust. The effect was initially somewhat mitigated by the fact that much of the nineteenth century had been a wet period over much of Australia, while the late 1880s and early 1890s were years of particularly good rainfall. This encouraged the land boom, with all its financial implications, and also led to heavy stocking. In 1896, however, though there were floods in Gippsland, the winter rains failed over most of Victoria. That was the beginning of the so-called Federation Drought, a period of weak or intermittent rainfall which was not broken until 1903. Even after that, there was less rain than before, and the drought is now seen as a significant climate shift introducing a dry period in the first decades of the twentieth century.

For people on the land, the combination of difficult seasons and difficult banking had enormous effect. It is calculated that in 1892 Australia had more than a hundred million sheep but ten years later there were half the number, just over fifty million; cattle had similarly been reduced by forty percent, from almost twelve million to seven million.[30]

As flocks and herds were sold off to allow for the shortage of water and feed – compounded by the depredations of the ubiquitous rabbits – the beasts, their wool and their meat were placed on a falling market. With no effective government programs, moreover, loans or financial assistance were increasingly hard to obtain and increasingly expensive. Many small-scale farmers were driven from their land by the costs of buying feed, dealing with rabbits, damaging dust-storms and consequent repairs, while many large establishments, which had often been created by mortgaging one property to pay for the next, were either broken up or fell into the hands of financiers or rivals with ready cash.

The Beggs family were not small-holders, and they did have a degree of security and experience with their properties, but these were not easy times, and one thing that appears in the Eurambeen Letters which follow – sometimes stated explicitly, sometimes merely implied – is that money was short.

---

[29] The Wikipedia entry on "Rabbits in Australia" presents a good survey. See also *Australians 1888*, 65-67.
[30] See, for example, Australian Disaster Resilience Knowledge Hub [knowledge.aidr.org.au], National, 1895-1902, Environment – Federation Drought; and National Museum of Australia: www.nma.gov.au/defining-moments/resources/federation-drought.

Chapter Six

Eurambeen Station homestead
in the late nineteenth and early twentieth centuries

The Eurambeen Letters 1898-1904

The greater part of the last and longest series of letters in the family collection were written by Charlotte Frances to her eldest daughter Ada between 1898 and her death in November 1904. Now a widow in her late seventies, Charlotte Frances was living at Eurambeen East with her youngest daughter Rose and her son-in-law Frank Beggs, She was quite capable of travelling to Melbourne, however, and frequently did so.

At the time of the first of this series of letters, written in 1898, Charlotte Frances' son Philip was Assistant Inspector of the Bank of Victoria, based on Melbourne, and Ada was also living there in separate accommodation, possibly at Brighton where Constantine Trent was attending the Grammar School; his elder brother Philip, born in 1879, had already left school to begin a career in journalism. Charlotte Frances' second daughter Viola – like Ada, unmarried – was often at Eurambeen East but also travelled to Melbourne on occasion.

As in previous letters, not all the people mentioned can be well identified.

Charlotte Frances Champion Crespigny nee Dana c.1895
from Henderson, Early Pioneer Families of Victoria and the Riverina

Letter 25 is dated only by the day of the week and the day of the month. The year was probably 1898, however, and May was the only month in which the thirtieth day was a Monday. Constantine Trent was now sixteen; it appears that he had been unwell and had come to Eurambeen for convalescence during the school holidays.

Letter 25

Monday 30

Dearest Ada,

Con arrived safe on Saturday very jolly, Frank going to meet him, and I think except looking a little white that he is first rate. At present he has gone out to shoot a rabbit with Anna R who is staying here,[31] so he has great fun with Nan and she has been such a help to me and Rose who I'm sorry to say, has had a sharp turn at Influenza, <u>not</u> so bad as she was at Ottawa,[32] still a terrible headache and fever.

She is up today and is going to sit out on the veranda for a little. I hope she will soon be all right again. Her poor eye felt as if it was coming out. She sends her best love to you and says she is afraid, and so am I, that you will feel so lonely without Con and me. I wish you would go and stay somewhere to get a little change. I don't like to think of you being all alone.

Kate Beggs is staying with us and she is so nice and companionable, I like her so much, she is so kind to me. She is going down to Hawthorne. She has been staying with Bushy.[33] I'm glad Vi is going to stay on. I think it will do her so much good, and she seems to do so much better.

Con is in such splendid spirits. Well he may be dear boy. We have need to be proud of him. He is in a way about <u>you</u>. He thinks you will miss him so much and be dull.[34]

I'm sorry you made a mistake where to go for the steel beads, Numbers 12 and 10. You can get them at any fancy shop in town. They will cost about half a crown and the <u>finest</u> eyeglass cord at Craig's nine pence a doz yds. B[alcombe] would bring it up to me and I will send you a P[ostal] N[ote] for it.[35]

Mr Frazer has been so kind to Vi. <u>I don't like</u> him not making the [?illegible].

I have not unpacked all Con's things yet. I have such a lot to do with all the Poultry to look after now. Rose is not well but I think she will be all right by tomorrow. Phil is expected tonight.[36] I suppose the mail will bring us some news.

I have 4 beautiful young canaries and the other little hen sitting. Rose has 10 young ones I have to look after.[37] I have not a bit of news to tell you and will say goodbye as I'm

---

[31] Neither Anna R nor Nan immediately following can be identified.

[32] "Ottawa" was the name of the house that Philip was renting at Gladstone Parade, Elsternwick. He had previously been at "Wyndcote" in Tennyson Street, Brighton [above at 211], five kilometres to the south, but moved in 1894. Hugh Vivian, his second son with Sophia nee Beggs, was born at Elsternwick on 8 April 1897 and their third son, Royalieu Dana, was born there on 11 November 1905: *Argus* notices of 17 April 1897 and 18 November 1905: Trove 9185427 and 225182744.

[33] Hugh Lyons Montgomery Beggs, father of Sophia and second father-in-law of Philip CdeC, had established the property of Bushy Creek near Glenthompson, some hundred kilometres southwest of Beaufort. Following his death in 1885, the property was run by his son Francis, who was given the nickname "Bushy" to distinguish him from other men of the family named Francis: above at 205 and 207.

Catherine, born in 1854, was the eldest daughter of Hugh Beggs and sister to Francis.

[34] As in the introduction to this letter, it appears that Ada was in quite close contact with Constantine Trent when he was in Melbourne.

[35] "B" is Robert Balcombe Beggs, son of Robert Gottlieb the brother of Frank and husband of Rose: note 13 above.

[36] Philip CdeC (1879-1918), Con's elder brother, was now about nineteen.

[37] Charlotte Frances and her family were obviously keen on canaries and – from the postscript to Letter 30 at 226 below – were prepared to breed them for sale. She owned *The Canary Book* by Robert L Wallace, published by L Upcott Gill of London in 1884.

Chapter Six

tired from being up late. Con went with Anna & Katie to tea at the other house last night. Frank wld not leave Rose and we had been up till 3 with Rose the night before. Give my best love to Loo and Sophy and with very much for yourself

Ever dearest Ada,
Your loving Mother, C F C

Like Letter 25 above, Letter 26 is dated only to the day of Saturday. Assuming the order within this part of the series is correct, however, and given the reference to "blazing fires," it was written about September of 1898, at the end of winter when Constantine Trent was again on holiday from school. He had been suffering from a cold and was being treated with some care.

It appears that Charlotte Frances had travelled with him from Melbourne, probably by train as far as Beaufort, where they were met by Rose's husband Frank and Con's brother Philip to bring them by horse and carriage to Eurambeen.

Letter 26

Saturday

Dearest Ada,
    We arrived here all right and none the worse for the journey, and Con is as fit as a fiddle this morning. I cld not get him to have anything in Ballarat,[38] but Rose had a

---

Anne's Family History 9/1/2017 discusses the family breeding of canaries. In January 1917 Viola Julia CdeC donated a pair of canaries to the Beaufort Girls' Anzac Club in aid of the war effort. Another pair, given to the Beaufort, Waterloo and District 15th Infantry Brigade Comforts Depot were raffled and raised £1/7 [one pound and seven shillings], between a third and a half of the weekly basic wage for an unskilled labourer. Though bidding may have been generous for a good cause, this was a good deal of money for two canaries.

[38] Beaufort had had a railway station since 1874, so Charlotte Frances and her grandson had taken a through train from Melbourne, a journey of five hours. Many trains made a half-hour halt at Ballarat so that passengers could get off and buy a light meal.

delicious supper when we arrived, hot boiled chicken and mashed potatoes, coffee and hot scones Mary Jane insisted on making for us. Altogether it was delicious with the blazing fires. Both Con and I wished you were with us to have a little luxurious comfort and the loving welcome. Phil drove in and met us. Frank drove Con with the ponies and covered him up all over his head and mouth with a cloak. He did not cough once last night. I think he will soon pick up here. I feel still very tired and done up tho' I had a good night, lovely bed.

I hope you got home all right and went somewhere to tea. It will be so lonely for you, you will miss me so in my room. Mind and take care of yourself and take your tonic and get up your strength. Rose and Vi send you their best love and say they feel you will be so lonely. I have forgotten my Stropianthus and dropper.[39] Will you send it up by return? I must have been very bothered for I forgot my prayer book and bible. I must borrow.

Phil is just going so I must stop. Con sends his love and will write to his father next week.

Ever your Loving Mother

Kiss and hug my little [grandson?]. I think he wld have liked to come.[40]

In December of 1898 Melbourne and Victoria generally were affected by a heatwave, associated with the long Federation Drought; temperatures rose above 42 degrees Celsius.[41]

Letter 27

Sunday night, Dec 4/98

My dearest Ada,

I am sorry that you have been so poorly and do hope you have not bothered to do my commissions which can wait till you are well and the weather cool. Tell me what has been the matter with you, the old trouble I suppose. I feel very anxious about poor little Vivian, the heat has been so intense, and I hope Con takes care too coming home to lunch in it.[42]

I have had another bad day with poor Rose. I have just put her to bed with a terrible headache. She was better yesterday after two days in bed and this afternoon it came on again after dinner. She has never recovered [from] poor Vi's illness. She is completely run down. A complete change and rest is what she wants and what she can't get, no money. Poor Frank frets himself to death about her, always getting these crushing headaches.

It gave me a good deal to do to look after things for her and we are getting a new cook on Tuesday. Con will know, the old cook at the other house. When is he coming up? I'm so longing to see him. I feel so cut off from all somehow but dear Rose could not do without me and I could not be away from Con [?] any longer.[43]

---

[39] Stropanthus, extracted from a plant of that genus found chiefly in Africa, was used as a heart stimulant.
[40] This probably refers to Francis George Travers, eldest son of Philip and Sophia nee Beggs, who was now about six years old: above at 205 and 211.
[41] The *Canberra Times* of 21 December 1953 reported that Melbourne had lately recorded a maximum of 107.7 degrees Fahrenheit [42 degrees Celsius], the highest December reading since 1898: Trove 2907951.
[42] Hugh Vivian, second son of Philip and Sophia nee Beggs, born in April 1897, was eighteen months old.
  Constantine Trent was still attending Brighton Grammar School. Gladstone Parade in Elsternwick, where his family was living, was some three and a half kilometres from the school, a forty-minute walk. He would not have had time to walk there and back during a lunch hour, and it appears that Ada was living closer and that he went to her. It is hard to understand, however, why he did not take lunch at school; there may be some confusion.
[43] In this context, "Con" does not make sense. Charlotte Frances surely means that she feels obliged to be at Eurambeen East to help Rose, and she has just remarked on her concern about Constantine Trent, who is obviously at school in Brighton. We must assume there is a miswriting or a mis-copying.

Chapter Six

I have not a bit of news to tell you, everything is the same, one day like another. Will you enclose me the old Mutual Stores' bills which have been sent to Ottawa. They sent me a big bill to acct rendered and I want to know what it is for.[44]

Rose wrote to Vi today. We are so glad she is having such a time and <u>you</u> must get away with her somewhere for Xmas. The change will do you so much good and we would be so much happier if I knew you were enjoying yourselves. My hand is so swollen and painful I can hardly write. Give my dear love to Con and Loo and the little boys [her grandsons Francis and Vivian], not forgetting yourself.

Ever your loving Mother

Rose is better today and is just come into the dining room. The heat today is terrible – 103 in the Veranda. Tell my darling [Con] my hand is so swollen and painful I can't write to him and to take care of the <u>heat</u>. He wants a new Summer linen for hot days and when he comes a white coat or blazer, it saves his other clothes here.

Letter 28 is again essentially undated; identified only as Wednesday. A note by the transcriber Ms Walsh observes that, "By the writing this seems to be one of the later letters." Letter 29 is missing its first page and is likewise undated. Letter 30 was written in February of 1900, and the two which precede it in the series were presumably written in the summer of 1899-1900.

Letter 28

Vi's Room [at Eurambeen East]
Wednesday [c. 1900]

Dearest Ada and Con,

Just a line to say I am all right again and said good-bye to the doctor and poor dear Rose is up today but looks dreadful. She has had a very sharp turn and has suffered far more than I have. You know how I used to suffer with it at Elsternwick but I am all right now.

I hope to goodness you will succeed in getting me a decent attendant. Old Lucas has grown very disagreeable and cattish. Still she knows all my ways and is kind when I'm sick.[45]

Rose sends you both her dear love to you both and I shall be quite right in a day or two. I hope no one else will [be ill?]. God bless you both dears. I know you have been bothering yourselves about me.

Ever Your loving Mother, C F C

Transcriber Walsh notes that the first sheet of Letter 29 is missing, and there is no date.

Letter 29 [c. 1900]

... old friend Ellen O'[?], the Weres' old friends. She had been staying at the McPherson's, her Aunt's, the girl who milked the goat for me when you were crying for your milk.[46] I think she had been staying with Mr Shepperd and also at the Le Sneffs. The John Weres went to see her there.[47] She was so pleased to see me. When she left she threw her arms round me and kissed me. Her Mother is dead many years ago.

---

44 Ottawa is the name of the house of Philip CdeC in Elsternwick: note 32 above. "Account rendered" indicates that a detailed bill has been sent earlier but has not been paid and is now overdue. The original bills have evidently been sent to that address and Charlotte Frances has not seen them.

45 This does not seem to be the same Miss Lucas who is described on a number of occasions below as being gentle and helpful. The two [servants?], however, may have been related.

46 This was presumably soon after the family had arrived in Australia in 1852, when Ada, born in 1848, was a small child.

47 The 1903 Electoral Roll for Ballyrogan in the Division of the Grampians has the pastoralist John Charles Ware and his wife Annie Elizabeth living at Yalla-y-poora station [now Yalla-Y-Porra]. This is the family

Monday

We had a very pleasant evening, both afternoon tea and a <u>magnificent</u> iced cake with almonds all over it, and a lovely tea, 14 sat down to it. Con's ducks were most delicious, and a magnificent ham and meat pies, sweets of all sorts. I wished so much you could have had some of the good things and Loo would have enjoyed the ducks so much. Con and Rose were wishing he was there and you too. I was thinking all the time what a dull old Sunday you would all be having, without any servant.

After Tea, Frank drove me with Rose and Mr Minchin to the other house.[48] All the young people walked in the lovely moonlight. They stayed out playing games till nearly <u>10</u> when Frank came in and read prayers. After that, supper and home, Mr Hughes and all the whole crowd walking home Anna and Ethel, [illegible?] coming as well, having a little more refreshment.[49] They did not go till after the Hughes and Minchins drove home, near <u>12</u>, and then Con and Jack walked back with them enjoying the moonlight, no one wore any hats or bonnets, and all the white dresses looked so pretty. Trixey Hughes and Edith Minchin gave Rose pretty little presents.[50]

Vi is going to write in this but [?] has just driven up with Anna and Ethel to ask Con to drive Anna to Middle Creek to meet the train, as she goes home today.[51] She goes back to Geelong next week. She and Miss Pincott have got a <u>good business</u> there, decorating tables for teas and dinners, and also making blouses, hard work, poor things!

I don't think I have anything else to tell you, except all our very best love. Kiss dear little Vivie [grandson Vivian] for me. Don't delay about the <u>Clock</u> and tell Macbean to advise me of its coming. I can send for it. I expect a good long letter after this. Con sends his love and Rose says she will write on Wednesday, as it is washing day today, so much to be done. Vi does her room and the boys' room and the flowers.

I have written all this to make you feel less <u>lonely</u>, it must be so horrid without us all. We don't forget you.

Ever, dearest Ada,
Your loving Mother, C F C

Excuse mistakes.   Tell me in your next how Mrs Griffith is and give my love
I'm writing in such   to her when you see her.
a <u>Bedlam</u> of noise.   Miss Edith Minchin said she did not think Mr Ricketson left much.[52] Edith must have a good marriage settlement.[53]

Charlotte Frances refers to as Were. See also note 135 below.

[48] Corker Wright Minchin was Clerk of Petty Sessions at Beaufort. He and his wife Edith Christina Elizabeth [as below] are recorded in the Electoral Roll of 1903.

[49] Ethel Davidson (1878-1985) was the daughter of Walter Henry Davidson and Clamina nee Beggs, a sister of Rose's husband Frank: note 9 above.

Anna may be the same person as Anna R at 219 above, but she cannot be identified.

[50] Edward Walter Hughes (1854-1922) was the manager of the Bank of Victoria branch at Beaufort. When stationed at Dunolly in September 1883 he had married Jeannie nee Hawkins (1862-1941), and their first child, Victoria Beatrix, was born in April 1884; known as Trixey, she was now about fifteen years old. In 1906 Beatrix would marry Charlotte Frances' grandson Constantine Trent.

Anne's Family History 2018/04/02 has an account of Beatrix CdeC nee Hughes. Details of the wedding are given by Hudson, *Cherry Stones*, 84-87.

John Warren White (1863-1947), second child and first son of Maria ["Mysie"] nee Gibton and John Warren White (1828-1918), was commonly known as Jack: note 12 above and Alexander/Persse, *Tree, Rock, and Gully*, 167.

[51] Fifteen kilometres west of Eurambeen, Middle Creek was evidently a halting place on the local railway.

[52] As Edith Minchin was married to Corker Wright Minchin, the Clerk of Petty Sessions at Beaufort [note 48 above], it appears that "Miss" here is miswritten or miscopied for "Mrs." There is no mention of a daughter in the census of 1903.

[53] The birthplace of Edith Alice Mary Were in 1849 was registered as Cape St Mary [Cap Sainte Marie],

CHAPTER SIX

Letter 30

Friday Night, 9.2/00

My dearest Ada,

They are all gone to a moonlight picnic at the Reservoir in Beaufort,[54] except Vi, and she has gone to bed with indigestion but seems quite plucked up gossiping with Kate [McGregor] who came today to do the housework till Monday,[55] and she could not go as it is about her time and <u>too</u> much for her after her illness, poor girl.[56]

Lake Beaufort: the reservoir

We hope you are not very dull all alone. I hope to be home next week. I thought Flora would have been going back but she or Vi have written to Mr [?]for further leave.[57] She is a great help to Rose and can look after Vi when she wants it. Arthur goes back tomorrow but I could not go with him as he would be sure to go 2nd class.[58] I feel very anxious about poor Mr Fairclough's death if it will make any difference to Loo [Philip]. Let me know as soon as you hear anything.[59]

Madagascar. Her parents had come to Australia in 1839, so she was probably born on a voyage to England for a visit. There was no connection to the Ware family, miswritten Were, of note 47 above.

Henry Ricketson was born in Canada in 1825, and came to Australia in 1852. He and Edith married at St George's, Hanover Square, in London in 1884 and had two children.

Henry Ricketson died in December 1900. Despite Edith Minchin's doubts, the NSW Files of Deceased Estates record him as a Station Proprietor, with an estate valued at more than £100,000. His widow Edith was recorded in the Australian Electoral Roll of 1903 as living with her daughter Esther Edith at 39 Collins Street in Melbourne. She died in London in 1931 at the Grosvenor Hotel in Westminster, so she had surely been well provided for.

54 Beaufort reservoir, now known as Lake Beaufort, is just south of the town.
55 Kate McGregor is mentioned as a housemaid in Letter 43 below at 239.
56 "About her time," related to Viola, may be connected to menstruation.
57 Flora, here and immediately below, cannot be identified, nor her employer[?], whose name is illegible.
    References to Flora in Letter 30 at 225 and Letter 34 at 230 below, however, would indicate that she was a friend of the family.
58 Arthur, here and below, is Arthur Mitchell Hale (1880-1961). He was a first cousin of Constantine Trent, some two years the elder.
59 The death of Mr William Fairclough, manager of the London branch of the Bank of Victoria, had been reported by the Melbourne *Herald* on 8 February 1900: Trove 241253110. Among papers which carried the news, the *Bendigo Independent* remarked that Mr Fairclough had been a long-time manager of the branch in that city; he died of influenza at the age of sixty: Trove 179161672. Philip's first managerial appointment had been to the agency at Epsom, just north of Bendigo [Chapter Five at 191], so he probably

Sophy said in her letter to Frankie that he [Philip] was not returning till Tuesday and that he was coming up for Frankie.[60] If so I can return with him. I'm sure you will be glad to have me.

Rose, Flora and Frank spent the day at Stoneleigh yesterday and Rose looks all the better for her little trip and had a most delicious dinner.[61] She liked going to her picnic. I suppose they will adjourn to the Manse after for supper &c.[62] I don't expect they will be home much before one or 2.

Con looked so well and he is burnt as brown as a berry. Ethel [Davidson] went with Tedo to the Ararat Races.[63] She staid at [?]. Frank was going to take Con and Arthur and then at the last minute changed his mind. He is so afraid of a fire breaking out. After tea last night a great fire was seen near Tedo's paddocks and there was no end of commotion. The horses had to be hunted up and the men, old Gibbie and Frank, set out for it, Con on his bicycle, Tedo's men too, one of the farmers burning off a large paddock of stubble nearly a yrd high, with a heavy wind.[64] The brute never gave any notice. Poor Rose stood out by the tank for hours in fear of its coming on the run and the men had to remain until it was all safe. There is a fire on the Mountain now.[65]

Mrs Leithbridge called today, she has such a beautiful hooded buggie and pair of horses, by far the most stylish turnout here. Poor Mr Goodrich is still ill, Belkie drove him into Beaufort yesterday.[66] He was very poorly last night. I have missed him so much. He has been dreadfully hurt, his poor face and nose all battered, his knee, and internally, and he won't see a doctor. He is such a nice man, but not a ladies' man at all.

I'm sorry to see by Sophy's letters to Frankie, that she is still so unwell. I suppose it must be from the smell of the drainage got into her system. Frankie told me it used to make him sick. The dear little boy is looking much better and has never done one thing wrong since he has been here. I have been reading to him before I put him to bed, some of Hood's ridiculous poems and he squeaked with laughter.[67]

Con has grown ever so much and has a lovely time with the girls, and his gun. He will be well and strong.

I am enclosing you Gwen's letter. She sent me the photos of herself and little ones.[68] Be sure and write me about Loo. He will not have time to and I feel anxious.

With best love in which Vi joins
Ever, dearest Ada,
Your loving Mother, C F C

---

knew Fairclough well and may have been sponsored by him or had him as a referee.

[60] "Frankie" is Francis George Travers, son of Philip ChC and Sophia nee Beggs, who is now aged eight. The diminutive distinguishes him from Rose's husband Frank Beggs, his uncle by marriage.

[61] Stoneleigh, southwest of Beaufort, was owned by the Lewis family: below at 229 with note 87.

[62] The Manse is the home of the Reverend Joseph Johnstone and his wife May at Beaufort: note 79 below.

[63] "Tedo" is Theodore Beggs, elder brother of Frank, who managed Eurambeen.

[64] "Old Gibbie" is William Gibton, a brother of Maria ["Mysie] White: notes 12 above and 123 below.

[65] This is Mount Cole, just north of Eurambeen. There were reports of the fire – second of the season – in the Melbourne newspapers *Age*, *Argus* and *Leader*: Trove 196031834, 9048695 and 19852433. One house was lost, with several stacks of hay, quantities of fencing and five thousand acres of paddocks. The Beggs' property at Eurambeen lost 130 acres of grassland.

[66] Belkie is presumably a miswriting of Balkie, referring to Robert Balcombe Beggs: note 13 above.

Though Mr Goodrich is mentioned several times in these letters and was evidently a good friend of the family, he cannot be further identified

[67] The poet Thomas Hood (1799-1845) is probably best known now for "The Song of the Shirt," a fierce criticism of piece-work. He was also known, however, for comic verse, with much use of puns.

[68] Gwendolyn Blanche and her husband George Harrison CdeC are discussed immediately below.

Chapter Six

Would you very much mind putting my big canary cage under the tap and clean it for the poor little birds when I come. They will be so crowded I shall have to put them in a bigger cage till I sell them.

Letter 31

4.1.1901

Dearest Ada,

I send you poor Gwen's letter which show to Loo and please <u>return</u> to me. I am so sorry for them and it is very hard to lose so much money. Yr Uncle G[eorge Blicke] thinking Harry provided for by this wealthy man who adopted him and [then] Harry Trent, his godfather, left him nothing, Georgina getting George's money. Write and tell me what Loo thinks of it.[69]

I have not any news to tell you except that we got an inch of rain yesterday which I hope makes the grass grow. Poor Vi has been but so-so with one of her old attacks but seems all right today. The Frasers want her to spend the winter in Adelaide and go when all the gaiety will be when the Duke & Duchess of York will be there which if all goes on well she will do.[70] She and Rose send their best love to you.

Jenning's frame he made for me I got yesterday. It is most beautiful. I wish you could go and see them and tell them I think it so pretty. I was so glad to get your letter. I suppose you have seen Birdie.[71] Did you go to their party? Tell me about it. Phil was

---

[69] In a note to Letter 43 below Constantine Trent CdeC identifies Gwen as "the wife of Harry my father's first cousin" and adds that he corresponded with one of Harry's daughters.

George Harrison CdeC (1863-1945), known as Harry, was the son of George Blicke, second son of Charles Fox ChC and elder brother of Philip Robert. He married Gwendolyn Blanche nee Clarke-Thornhill (1864-1923) in 1890 and they had three children.

Harrison ["Harry"] Walke John Trent (1830-1899), godfather of Harry CdeC, was a cousin and fellow-officer of George Blicke. The Trent family had been wealthy but was less so now, so he had little to leave.

Harry CdeC, however, had been adopted by Oscar William Holden Hambrough (1825-1900), a very distant cousin, who owned Pipewell Hall in Northamptonshire and other properties. It had been expected that Harry would succeed to his estate, but his will left Harry no more than a life interest in some furniture and a pension from some of his land.

Before this, moreover, George Blicke had died in 1893, and all his property passed to Harry's sister Georgina Elizabeth (1856-1938).

The situation would have been clear from Gwendolyn's letter, but it has not survived, and Charlotte France's summary account is confusing without it. The affair is discussed in detail by *Anne's Family History* 2020/06/13: "Great expectations – disappointed." See also Letter 43 below with notes 126 and 128.

[70] The future King George V, then titled Duke of York and also Duke of Cornwall, was visiting Australia with his wife the duchess and future Queen Mary for the inauguration of the new Commonwealth.

The Fraser family of Adelaide is mentioned again at 228, but cannot be identified.

[71] Barbara Wilhelmina nee Walstab (1874-1949), known as "Birdie," had married Charlotte Frances' grandson

looking delicate from the exertion he went through saving the sheep from being burnt. The fire was so near Stoneleigh. Effie and Mary Whelan were hosing all the little outbuildings about the place. Roosts and Juggins' 400 sheep burnt but thanks to Phil none of Frank's.[72]

It is so cold today after the rain. I have not written to poor Edith yet. Write and tell me something about her.[73] I hope she is left decently off. I pity her with the first family. I will write tomorrow to Mrs Sheperd.

Con is in great form. SF has given him a song "The Queen's 15."[74] He and Jack sing whenever Rose has time to play for them. All the Davidsons were up last night dancing till 12 with Claude Campbell who I think goes to stay with George today.

Vi and Rose send their best love & so wld Con but he is out with his gun. SF is not living in town now. Since she came here, without telling her they all moved back to Euroa.

I'm so thankful dear little Vivie is so well and gaining in weight.[75] Give him a sweet kiss from poor old Grannie. B[alcombe] is looking so much better and is carpentering away in the veranda.[76] With my very best love to you all

Ever dearest Ada,
Yr lving Mother

Written in February 1901, Letter 32 includes references to Constantine Trent CdeC, who had now left school and was preparing to study medicine at the University of Melbourne.

Letter 32

Feby 18, 1901

Dearest Ada,

I intended to have written you a long letter yesterday but poor Rose had one of her severe headaches and we were without a housemaid, with a great deal to be done. Rose is better today I'm glad to say and will soon be all right again.

Con said he was going to write to his Father to say he will be home on Wednesday fortnight, with B[alcombe], the day after his 19th birthday.[77] You will be so glad to see him looking so strong and well. I shall miss him so much. He is such a good dear boy, and dear B also, he has never done <u>one naughty thing</u> since he has been here, and is one boy in a thousand. He is <u>implicitly</u> obedient & that is everything.

I'm afraid Loo will find the new work very heavy, and I'm sure will not agree with him half as well as the change & travelling.[78] Give him my best love.

I have no news to tell you, except that we drove into Beaufort on Friday and called on the Butler Johnstones and Michens [*sic*] and saw Mr Hughes and did all the usual shopping.[79]

Philip CdeC on 1 September 1900 at Holy Trinity Church in Kew, Melbourne.
The "Phil" immediately following, exhausted from saving sheep from a bushfire, was this Philip CdeC.

[72] There is a report of the fire in the *Camperdown Chronicle* of 1 January: Trove 28676565/4078730.

[73] Henry Ricketson, husband of Edith Alice Mary nee Were, had died in December just two months earlier. She was left very well off: note 53 above.

[74] SF cannot be identified. "The Queen's 15," referring by its title to Victoria's empire and dominions, was a patriotic Australian song composed by Alfred Wheeler (1865-1949), an Anglican minister, at the time of the South African War.

[75] Charlotte Frances' grandson Hugh Vivian, second son of Philip and Sophia nee Beggs, was now almost three years old: note 42 above.

[76] Robert Balcombe Beggs was a cousin and close friend of Constantine Trent: note 13 above.

[77] Constantine Trent's birthday was on 5 March, which this year fell on a Tuesday.

[78] Philip ChC was still Assistant Inspector of the Bank of Victoria, but it appears that he had been transferred from duties which required travel to different branches in the country, and was now more regularly at head office in Melbourne.

Chapter Six

Lizzie went to St Kilda to Sophy Hooker's on Saturday with Brien and was going to Colebin [Coliban] to stay with Mimie and Dora. She was coming back in a fortnight with Sophy so perhaps you could manage to see her.[80]

Mr Goodrich was here all yesterday afternoon and so enjoyed seeing all the <u>homes</u> in the old book, where he had been staying. It was quite an afternoon's amusement to him and me too.[81]

I hope you will go to see Mrs [?] now the [? are] gone, and write me a long letter of all your sayings and doings. It does not make you seem so far away. I often wonder what you are doing. You must miss me so much but you will soon have Don and it will not be so dull for you and lonely.

I hope Frank and Rose will be able to go to the opening of the Commonwealth and see the illuminations.[82] They very much wish to go as it will be a sight of a lifetime, and an Epoch in the History of England, and Mr and Mrs Fraser want Vi to see it all in Adelaide and stay all the winter. Ruth Minchen is such a nice lady-like girl, such a pleasant friend for Vi to have in Adelaide. I was a friend of her mother's, poor Ellen O'[?] in the early days.[83] She has sent me such kind messages since she went home. She said I was the most charming old lady she ever met. Mr Minchen showed me her letter. I ought to feel proud, but I'm afraid I am past all that sort of thing.[84]

Have you ever written to Montie since he left?[85] I hope I shall get my letter from you today. I told poor Loo <u>not</u> to bother to write to me when he has so much to do. Con says he will not write today as he had something to do for Frank who is getting a new servant today, and we have a new housemaid just come, who is already in her nice black dress and pretty white apron. The servants are all so good and kind to me, they can't do enough for me, and never let me put hand to do anything to help myself.

---

[79] Electoral Rolls list Joseph Butler Johnstone as a clergyman – presumably Anglican – at Beaufort; his wife was named May Dora Wickham.
　　On Corker Wright Minchin, Clerk of Petty Sessions at Beaufort, and his wife Edith Christina Elizabeth, see note 48 above, and further below with note 84.
　　Edward Walter Hughes, father of Beatrix/Trixey was manager of the Beaufort branch of the Bank of Victoria: note 50 above.

[80] Minnie [not Mimie] is Clamina Davidson nee Beggs, sister of Frank Beggs and sister-in-law to Rose. She and her husband Walter had at one time been in Queensland, but they had now returned and owned Coliban Park station. See note 9 above and note 123 to Chapter Five.
　　Lizzie is Elizabeth Persse Beggs (1852-1908), eldest sister of Rose's husband Frank Beggs: see note 122 with comment by CTCdeC.
　　Dora is probably Gertrude Dorothea White nee Beggs (1866-1943), youngest sister of Frank. In 1898 she had married her cousin Thomas Edward White (1864-1944), a nephew of Maria Lucinda the widow of Francis Beggs. At this time they had a property at Middle Creek, a short distance west of Eurambeen.
　　Sophy/Sophia Hooker cannot be well identified.

[81] This book may have been a collection of prints – probably not photographs – of houses in England.

[82] The first meeting of the Parliament of the new Commonwealth in Melbourne was opened by the Duke of York on 9 May 1901.

[83] Ellen O'[?] – the balance of the surname was evidently illegible – is mentioned also in Letter 29 as an old friend of Charlotte Frances, apparently from the time soon after the family arrived in Victoria in 1852.

[84] It appears from context that Ruth Minchen [*sic*] in Adelaide was related to the Minchins of Beaufort: note 80 above. The surname must have been miswritten or miscopied.

[85] Montgomery was a common given name in the Beggs family, but this man cannot be identified further.

Give all our best love to all and tell Loo the University fees are paid <u>not later</u> than the first.[86]

Ever dearest Ada,
Your loving Mother

The clock is the greatest comfort to R[ose] & F[rank] and B[alcombe] is so proud to get up with the alarm.

Ms Walsh the transcriber added a note to Letter 33: "This was in an envelope postmarked 5/3/01." It must have been misplaced, however, for the envelope surely relates to Letter 35, which was written on 4 March 1901, a Wednesday.

The reference to Constantine Trent's examinations and the university, to Christmas and to the heat, indicate that Letter 33 was written at the end of a year, probably 1901, in which case it should be placed in the series after Letter 38 below. It is also possible, however, that it refers to the previous Christmas of 1900, when Con was taking his matriculation examinations for entry to the university; in which case it should be placed near Letter 28. In either case, it is well out of order in the series.

Letter 33

Saturday [day, month and year not given]

Dearest Ada,

So glad to get your letter yesterday for I'm feeling so anxious about dear Con and his <u>exams</u> but I'm sure he will pass after all his hard work and if he does not it will not be his fault. Please give me the <u>earliest</u> news of him and give him my dearest love. I would have written to him but Rose has one of her very bad headaches and is sick and I have been with her since before ½6 this morning.

Frank went to the Shed at 5 and is not home till night & Vi calling me out of my sleep suddenly to go to her made me feel pretty bad myself but doctored up with whisky & tea.

We had a houseful of visitors yesterday. Effie & Henry Lewis came yesterday at 12 o'clock.[87] Poor Rose had such a bad headache she could not come in to dinner. They did not go till after 4 & Mr Hughes, Trixie & Edie Minchin came and did not leave till nearly six, then Mr Goodrich came so that altogether it was a hard day.

Tell Con to let us know when he is likely to come up. Henry Lewis told me that there will be no 2nd exams at Xmas. They have altered the rule, but I have my doubts about it tho' he is a University man. I shall want you to send me up some things by Con if you will let me know in time.

I am sending little Frank some of his sweet peas, let him have them, and the little biscuits are kisses to him and Vivi, the pansies are for Vivie. Birdie will tell you all about us.[88]

I must go to Rose as Vi has to see after things. Tell Con I think of him night & day. Ever dearest Ada,

Your loving Mother

---

[86] Constantine Trent, eighteen turning nineteen on 5 March 1901, was at Trinity College of the University of Melbourne, in his first year studying medicine.

[87] There does not appear to be a relevant Henry Lewis with wife nicknamed "Effie" in the electoral rolls of Victoria for 1903, but when Constantine Trent married Beatrix Hughes in 1910 their wedding presents included a number from the Lewis family of Stoneleigh: Hudson, *Cherry Stones*, 85. The family may have been registered elsewhere.

[88] Frank and Vivie [Vivian] are Charlotte Frances' two youngest grandchildren by her son Philip's second marriage to Sophia Beggs. Birdie is the wife of her eldest grandson Philip: note 71 above.

CHAPTER SIX

> The heat is terrific. I'm so glad you like your poor dress. You ought to have had a trained skirt but I know you would look just as well as any of them, also no <u>mistaking</u> a lady. Write soon. I miss you just as much as you miss me, tho' dear Rose's thoughtfulness & tenderness no words would express it. Frank also, one wld think I was a Queen.

Ms Walsh the transcriber also added a note to Letter 34: "This and the attached letter [33 above] were in an envelope postmarked 5.3.01. From the context they don't really seem to belong together." It appears that this letter too must have been misplaced. As above, however, the envelope surely relates to Letter 35 below, written on Wednesday 4 March 1901.

Given Viola's references to Rose's difficulties and her own, it seems probable that Letter 34 was written soon after Letter 33, possibly on the following Friday, six days later.

It may observed that while Charlotte Frances, now eighty years old, is physically able to travel to and from Melbourne, the family believes she needs an escort for the journey; they were no doubt correct.

Letter 34 [from Viola to Ada at Melbourne]

Friday [day, month and year not given]
Eurambeen E[ast]

> My dearest Ada,
>
> Will you be <u>too</u> lonely if Mother does not return next Tuesday? She is very anxious to go, thinking how lonely you will be if Sophie goes with Vivian but we find now as Mrs Soilleno has altered her arrangements, Flora can say here longer and she is such a help here to Rose & me too now I am not able to be of any use & of course Mother must not travel alone which is the difficulty, but I think she <u>really</u> wants to go & is rather vexed about it, but she is very well & lives on the fat of the land & has <u>every</u> that is good for her, but you know what she is like when she takes an idea into her head and of course we all feel uncomfortable about you.
>
> Write and say just what you would like and we will write often and tell you if there is any chance of sending Mother down with anyone else but really perhaps you will be glad of the rest after all your trouble with me, but be sure to write <u>by return</u> and say what you would like <u>best</u>.
>
> The old lady is quite cross about poor Flora going but now Rose has no house maid she is the greatest help though she is quite ready to give up her own pleasure and go with Mother but I don't see how we can possibly manage without her. I have been very seedy and am only recovering which is why I have not written to you. Arthur Richardson and his wife are staying here and Rose has so much to do.[89] Con is so brown and fat and you will love to see him so well but he will be very spoilt with all the good things.
>
> I had such a nice letter from Mr W thanking me for selling the maps. Have you called? I have never been outside the gate since I have been here as I have been too seedy and now have my friend but feel better.[90]
>
> Rose and Frank are driving Mother into Beaufort this afternoon to try and calm her down. Rose and they all enjoyed the concert in Beaufort on Wednesday. Of course I

---

[89] When Constantine Trent married Beatrix Hughes in 1910, their wedding presents included a silver jam dish and tumblers from Mr and Mrs A Richardson of Gorrin: Hudson, *Cherry Stones*, 86. Gorrin station at Dobie is on the Geelong Road ten kilometres southeast of Ararat. The woolshed is now registered by the Heritage Council of Victoria.

[90] The phrase "my friend' is presumably a reference to some recurrent discomfort, possibly menstruation.

could not go. Admiral Bridges, Mr Goodrich and everyone nice about were there.[91] I think it is I who could complain not poor old Mother.

Rose sends her best love and will write you a long letter on Sunday. She is worked to death and not over well. Do say if you have your spectacles and if your eyes are better.

Give my love to Loo. I am so sorry for his disappointment and he seems anxious about Sophie. Let us know all the arrangements. Perhaps you know of some one who could take Mother down. She is very bent on going.

This is a very stupid letter and hard to write as there is such a fuss going on. Write soon. I hate to think of you so lonely. With all our fond love,
Your loving Sister,

Vi

Letter 35, dated 4 March 1901, would have been sent in the envelope postmarked 5 March, mentioned in the introductions to Letters 33 and 34. Constantine Trent's birthday, the subject of discussion, was on 5 March, when he turned nineteen. He was currently at Eurambeen but would be travelling to Melbourne on Wednesday 6 March.

An appendix to this letter has a preliminary list of personal possessions that Charlotte Frances wished her grandson to receive when she died. This was a slight anticipation of her will; she would not die for another three years.

Letter 35

Monday, 4th March 1901

Dearest Ada,

The heat has been so terrible I could not write before this and I'm sorry to say Rose had another bad turn on Friday but is better now and working in the veranda with Con & Ethel. She is not well yet of a certain affair, now the 3rd week & it has made her so weak & white, but I hope she will soon recover her strength.[92] She sends many loving messages to you but is not strong enough to bother with pen and ink.

Our darling Con will be with you to lunch on Wednesday. He is going down in the A[delaide] express as he has a lot of things to see to in town before he goes out to you. He will tell you all about us. I'm afraid he will be very dull, poor darling, if he will have time to feel so. He did not go to the Hughes's last Friday. Rose was so poorly & the heat was so intense & he will have a quiet birthday. Poor Rose intended to have had such a nice birthday but it is out of the question now, she must not exert herself. It will be something for you to do and think of, making him comfortable. I will send some of his songs & do when he has time make him sing them. He depends greatly on his accompaniments being played well. I wish he could get some lessons.

Percy Smith was staying at the other house from Saturday till last night. He, Mr Goodrich & Tedo spent some hours here in the afternoon and we all sat with Rose in the veranda, the air was so cool after the night's rain. Vi, Con & Jack went back to tea & Prayers.

Will you ask Loo when he comes up to bring me some writing paper & envelopes. It is so dear here & I have only a few shillings left of my money. Con will tell you all about

---

[91] Rear-Admiral Walter Bogue Bridges (1843-1917) had been a captain in the Royal Navy on the Australia station in the 1870s and 1880s. He married Annie Caroline Wilson, daughter of an Australian landowner, and purchased Trawalla, a property just east of Beaufort, where he became a successful pastoralist, with a town house in Toorak; but *cf* note 100 below. Formally retired, he was eventually promoted Rear-Admiral by seniority. His obituary was published in the *Argus* of 29 December 1917: Trove 1671574; his will was proven with a value of almost half a million pounds: Trove 15765767.

[92] This may have been a miscarriage, but Letter 38 below mentions "bad turns," perhaps reflecting some form of epilepsy.

Chapter Six

us & Rose says his things will not all be ironed but she is sending them home <u>clean</u>. I hope Vi will have time to mend his socks.

I hope we shall have a line from you today. How do you like the stench of the Fox? He will eat all the Street's & Mr King's <u>fowls</u>.[93] With best love from all

Ever
Yr loving Mother

Appendix:

CONSTANTINE TRENT CHAMPION CRESPIGNY

For Con: March 4th, 1901
  Book Shelf & Chest of Drawers.
  All Books with his name written in them.
  Miniature by "Opie" of my Cousin Pulteney Sherbourne.[94]
  My jet locket with his Mother's Photograph in it.
  My gold Watch.
Any other thing belonging to me, he may <u>like</u> for my sake, let him have it, also black Cameo ring given to his Uncle Con, by the Officers of the Education Department.[95]

CHARLOTTE F CHAMPION CRESPIGNY

Ms Walsh the transcriber added a note: "Enclosed with this letter is a little pack of flowers, marked *Con. Picked from his dear Mother's grave*." Annie Frances ChC nee Chauncy had died on 21 February 1883 at Queenscliff, Victoria. Her gravestone in the cemetery there was engraved further with details of her sons Philip and Constantine Trent: Chapter Five at 197.

Letter 36

Friday, 22nd March 1901[96]

My dearest Ada and Con,

Thank you so much both of you for your dear kind letters yesterday, but darling Con I'm so <u>sorry</u> that you should have spent your poor slender income on me. The paper is lovely, and the pens beautiful. It was <u>just</u> what I wanted but still my <u>sweet</u> I know pretty well what it is, to be short of <u>cash</u>.

I had a very happy birthday, as far as it could be, away from you all. Frank drove Rose, B[alcombe] and myself into Beaufort and we had a most awful dust storm with a few drops of rain. I was nearly blown down and my parasol turned near the Bank. Rosie and I were going to Macfarlines but Rose made me go into the Bank where I staid all the afternoon. Mr Hughes gave me a pretty photo frame. Trixie was at home and they asked very kindly after you Con. They are always so hospitable.[97]

---

[93] This may be a reference to current politics, but it is not possible to trace it.

[94] Frances Johnstone Sherburne/Sherbourne nee Dana (1768-1832) was the sister of Charlotte Frances' father, William Pulteney Dana (1776-1861), and godmother of Charlotte Frances. Her son Pulteney Sherburne (1802-1831), Charlotte Frances's first cousin, is discussed in Chapter One at 18-20, with a reproduction of the miniature at 19. The picture is still with the family, by bequest from Constantine Trent to his son Richard Geoffrey CdeC, and since passed, under his instructions, to Richard Rafe CdeC as part of the collection of family pictures.

Though Charlotte Frances attributes it to "Opie," the miniature portrait cannot have been the work of the celebrated John Opie RA (1761-1807): born in 1802, Pulteney Sherburne was five years old when John Opie died.

One of the books as above was the large Bible which had been a godparent's gift to Charlotte Frances from Frances Johnstone Sherburne; it had already been specifically granted to Constantine Trent through his father Philip: Chapter Two at 44-45.

[95] Constantine Trent ChC (1851-1883) had been a Truant Officer in Brighton, and the ring was probably a farewell gift from his colleagues when he left for England in 1881: Chapter Five at 178 and 180.

[96] An annotation by CTCdeC identifies the date as "Her 81st birthday."

[97] William Duncan MacFarlane and his wife Jean were listed in the electoral rolls of Beaufort for 1903 and 1905; he is described as being of independent means.

Ethel [Davidson] and Vi had a great wetting driving from Stoneleigh. They could not hold up a parasol for the wind and dust. [?] gun came up yesterday. I have not an atom of news to tell you, except that we are all well.

Mr Hughes made Rose such a pretty blotting book and Mrs Beggs brought her from Ballarat some pretty flannel for a blouse and neck-tie of lace.[98] She had 3 presents in one day.

The Bank of Victoria building at Beaufort c.1900
Museums Victoria Collections

The new man seems to go on well, he is good with the horses and cows. 3 more new milkers in. Rose is going to try and get the prize for her butter next Wednesday and Alice for her bread. Frank is sending his two horses. I hope it will be a fine day for me to go.

I'm so glad the names are written down for the Hopetouns[99] and that you, Ada, are going to call on Mrs Turner, be sure and go on Mrs [Turner's "At Home"?] day, as they go out so much.[100]

The key of my cabinet was never sent back. If you can't find it let me know, as I have a duplicate but it is a pity to lose the key. I shall have to send you down another to get the duplicate out of my red box.

The Bank of Victoria building at 16 Havelock Street in Beaufort later became a Masonic Hall and has since been divided into three apartments. It would appear that the manager's residence was in the same building, and Charlotte Frances took refuge there rather than in the general office.

Beatrix/"Trixey" Hughes would marry Constantine Trent in 1906.

[98] Maria Lucinda nee White (1826-1914), widowed mother of Rose's husband Frank and the same generation as Charlotte Frances, lived at Eurambeen station with her son Theodore (Tedo) and his family: Derham, *Silence Ruse*, 205, Alexander/Persse, *Tree, Rock, and Gully*, 7 et saepe.

[99] Having arrived in Sydney at the end of 1900, Lord Hopetoun, first Governor-General of Australia, took the oath of office on 1 January 1901. Until the selection and initial construction of Canberra, however, Melbourne was the capital of the new Commonwealth, so his residence was established there.

[100] Mr and Mrs H M Turner of Trawalla gave presents when Charlotte Frances' grandson Constantine Trent married Beatrix Hughes in 1906: Hudson, *Cherry Stones*, 85. As in note 91 above, Rear-Admiral Bridges owned the station at Trawalla, but there is also a small settlement of that name, and it appears that the Turners also had a house in Melbourne.

CHAPTER SIX

> I have a letter to answer to Lizzie [Elizabeth Persse Beggs]. She is still at Macedon till after Easter with the Tricketts and I am a bit tired with nothing more to say, no news of any sort. With fondest and best love from us all
>
> Ever my dearest children
Your most loving old Mother and Grannie
C F Crespigny
>
> Dear Ada, I wish the next time you are in town you wld go to Stephen & Son and see if you could get me cheap a woollen shawl like the old one which Vi has to put on when I go out in the garden. You can often get them very <u>cheaply</u>, 3 or 4 shillings. If you saw old Stephen yourself and say it was for me he would send it up here and I could send a postal note for it. Don't give more than 4 shillings. Con cld bring it up. They are cheaper at Stephen's than anywhere else.

From the reference to Ottawa, which was the name of Philip's house at Gladstone Parade in Elsternwick, Ada was now living in that household. Given all the reassurances of affection, and expressions of concern about her loneliness, she may have shown signs of depression.

Letter 37

Eurambeen East
25th Nov 1901, Vi's birthday[101]

Dearest Ada,

You will be longing to hear that dear Con arrived all safe & sound & very hungry on Saturday night. Vi & Jack drove in for him & I was so happy to see his dear old sweet face once more. We all think he is looking splendid & in such good fat condition. He does your care more than cred[it] & has grown in breadth so, such good square shoulders and colour. He is so happy & delighted to be here again. He says everything tastes so nice. Rose had a lovely dish of sandwiches ready for him. He was so <u>terribly</u> hungry he ate all but the parsley garnish, and a lot of meringues Rose made for him filled with whipped cream. All the other house people were here to give him a welcome, Mr Goodrich says he is a very clever lad, he likes him so much. Mrs Beggs is giving him a party on Thursday.[102]

We are always thinking of you and hope dearest Ada you will take good care of yourself and <u>go out</u> as much as you can. We don't like to think of you being all by yourself, no one to utter a word in common with. You will have a good rest from anxiety and try to make a friend of Edith.[103]

The heat yesterday was terrible. You wld feel it upstairs at Ottawa. I wish you could see my flowers. I have never seen at any flower show pelargoniums and geraniums equal to mine in the immense bloom and size of flowers & I have struck all the cuttings myself. Frank and Rose say they have never had such a show of flowers before. The Petunias are magnificent, of every colour. They will all be over when you come. I send you some flowers to show the size and give Vivie after. All send their dearest love to you.

---

[101] Born in 1856, Viola Julia Constantia was now forty-five.

[102] Mrs Beggs is Maria Lucinda nee White, widow of Francis (1812-1880) and mother of Frank. She was living with her son Theodore at Eurambeen West.

Though Mr Goodrich is a friend of the family, he cannot be identified.

[103] This is probably Edith Alice Mary Ricketson nee Were, widowed twelve months earlier: note 73 above. Born in 1849, she was a year younger than Ada.

Con's clothes are all so beautiful and all came right in the old box, but remember the ivory box with fan in it is yours & also your bracelets with the ancestors. Kiss Vivi for me.

Ever dearest Ada,
Your most loving Mother

I feel so sick from the heat. I can't write more. Vi is on her bed & Rose & Con extended on the verandah chairs.

A postscript "Read this first" to Letter 38 has an update to problems mentioned in the main body of the letter.

Letter 38

December 12, 1901

Dearest Ada,

I have only time for a line this morning to thank you for the commissions which are beautiful, the comb such a comfort & the silk just what I wanted but I hope you did not give yourself too much trouble about it when you are not strong. The heat too was awful the last two days till a cool change yesterday. You must let me know how much I owe you for the comb & silk for no bill came & the parcel <u>open</u>.

I am so vexed that you shd have bought that lovely Snake Syringe for Con. You spend all your poor money on other people. Con was delighted with it & it is most useful to have by you but dear Ada we have never seen a snake this year, so few about, the <u>owls</u> and jackasses eat them all.[104]

Con sends you all sorts of loving messages & wld write but has a raging toothache the last few days in the tooth Fife stopped. He is going to have it out as soon as he can go up to Ararat. There is a splendid dentist Dr Palmer says. He is very well but we had a terrible day yesterday with poor Rose. She had one of her bad turns yesterday. Frank was at the dip but Con managed her splendidly. She was a long time in one of her old faints & sickness. Vi is perfectly useless with her foot which from the heat pains <u>her</u> but <u>forgets it</u> sometimes. Con is a <u>host</u> in himself.

I have a hundred things to do & must give Rose her mutton broth. She has had nothing for two days but is much better today. With dearest love & thanks for getting me the things, in haste

Your most loving Mother, C F C

READ THIS FIRST. I had no means of sending this to the Post which I'm glad of now. Rose is all right again now & Con's toothache all right. Rose made him drink porter, & it cured it & I think the pain comes from his cutting a wisdom tooth. He is looking so well & right & eats and enjoys everything. You would be pleased to see him which I hope you will soon & me <u>too</u>. The case you sent up he takes such an interest in, you wld laugh to see how he loves looking & examining it.[105] I do hope you are none the worse for going out in the heat. Ethel [Davidson] & Lizzie [Beggs] will be home this eve. I hope you have seen them. Write soon. Excuse scrawl. I had such a running about yesterday.

Friday 13 –

A last postscript:

---

[104] A "snake syringe" was a hypodermic syringe with a treatment for snake bites. Brinsmead's Pharmacy of Traralgon was advertising them at this time, including a compound with Chloride of Lime: *e.g.* Trove 59570046; the cost was £1 1shilling, about half the weekly wage of an unskilled worker.

Chloride of lime, Calcium hypochlorite [$Ca(ClO)_2$], is a bleaching agent, commonly used to purify water. Modern medicine does not regard it as effective against the venom of any snake.

By "jackasses," Charlotte Frances is referring to kookaburras.

[105] This may be a puzzle box with a trick opening.

Chapter Six

Letter cld not go yesterday. All well today and cooler. We have such a wretched servant for Cook & Laundress. Poor Rose who is far from strong so worried, the wash has come in & 15 shillings of collars & cuffs burnt to a cinder, put in the oven to <u>dry</u>, so <u>vexatious</u>.

In Letter 39 Charlotte Frances refers to her lack of money. It is uncertain whether it was a real problem or rather a sense of insecurity as she grew older. She did not receive a pension, and though she mentions shares and a dividend in Letters 41 and 44 her savings may have been affected by the financial crisis of the early 1890s and by the current drought.

Letter 39

March 13, 1902

Dearest Ada,

Thank you a thousand times for doing my commission so quickly. I have chosen a nice cashmere & am sending the dressmaker my skirt & a blouse that fits me well by this post, with directions how to make. I want the blouse made so that I can wear it in the evening and look <u>dressie</u> as a body <u>oppresses</u> me so.[106] I must have loose things, no train on the skirt. If you will have a look to it I shall be very glad.

I am very pleased to do the little bootees but can't do them very quick.[107] I have sent for the <u>wool</u> but perhaps you would order a <u>packet</u> of cream Andalusian wool not too fine & a pair of fine bone knitting needles with it. Put it down to me at Craig's & I will pay for it with my dress. Get the dressmaker to do it as cheaply as she can as I'm so hard up. She ought not to charge as much for a blouse as a body. I will trust it to you.

My old leg is much better & I'm able to get about a bit now. Thank my dearest boy for his nice dear letter & say I will write soon but am rather busy today. His poor birthday must have been an unmixed blessing with so many letters to write.[108] We all laughed tremendously at Edie's.[109] She gave it to us to read at the Hughes's & Trixie's.

Poor Ethel is a little happier. Her Mother is better. She has been awfully ill with double pneumonia. Mrs Stewart is with her & Dr Woolly has got a good <u>nurse</u>. Bob has gone to Swanwater. He is much better now.[110]

No news to tell you. Tell Con Arthur is awfully quiet & can't get a word out of him. I wanted to write to Loo but have not a moment today. Give him my love & say I have not forgotten him & love to the little boys.

Frank's twitching got all right here, poor little boy. Tell him I will write to him soon & dear little Vivie.[111]

Will you get an estimate from the dressmaker of what my dress will cost as I have so little cash & must cut my coat according to my cloth. Tell Con there is no jollity going on now he has gone. I wish Loo would write a kind letter to Rose. She & Frank said they have never had a line from him or Sophy since the boys went home. With much love to all,

Ever your loving old Mother, C F C

I have sent for wool so don't bother about it.

---

[106] "Body" probably describes a corset.

[107] Since Charlotte Frances's youngest grandson at this time was Hugh Vivian CdeC, born in 1897, while Royalieu Dana CdeC would not be born until 1905, the bootees were not intended for her immediate family; from Letter 41 written six months later, Charlotte Frances was knitting them for sale.

[108] Constantine Trent CdeC had turned twenty on 5 March, and was no doubt writing thank-you letters.

[109] Edie is Edith Minchin: note 48 above.

[110] Ethel Davidson's mother was Clamina nee Beggs, a sister of Frank. On the Stewart family, see note 125 below.

Swanwater, a pastoral property, gave its name to a district near Donald in Victoria, 130 kilometres north of Beaufort. Bob is Robert Gottlieb Beggs (1861-1939), brother of Theodore, Frank and Clamina.

[111] These are her grandchildren, Francis George Travers and Hugh Vivian CdeC, now ten and seven.

EURAMBEEN

At the end of her transcription of Letter 40, Ms Walsh notes that "This letter appears to be incomplete." Though it is dated to 22 March, Charlotte Frances remarks in the last line that she has received a large number of presents; her eighty-second birthday was on 22 February.

Letter 40

Saturday, 22.3.1902

My dearest Ada,

So good of you to write me such a nice letter, but I'm sorry, dear, you should spend your money on me, tho' I shall value the plants so much. The gloves fitted to perfection, & I'm sending the other pr back today. I must have my dress Monday. The Show is on Wednesday & I have not even my other dress to put on. I sent to Craig's for pattern. I don't care so much myself but it will disappoint Vi & Rose.[112]

Loo will show you his letter all about the fire. Is not Vi unfortunate, all her beautiful room burnt.[113]

Supposing Craig <u>can't send</u> my dress. If it is not in Beaufort Tuesday <u>morning I can't get it</u>, & they must send my old skirt. I have nothing to <u>wear</u>. Rose will be in to take her work for the Show on Tuesday. It is lovely.[114]

I will leave it to you to do your best for me I'm sending you PN [postal note] to get for me, & send by <u>Con</u>, two little pretty keepsakes for Edie [Edith Minchin] & Trixie [Hughes]. They have both given me such pretty little presents at Xmas & on my birthday, & I want you to choose for me some little dainty article in dress for Edie & some pretty little keepsake for Trixie. I will leave it to you, little Easter gifts. Deduct <u>your expenses</u> out for the 5 shillings <u>train fare.</u>

I'm perfectly addled with writing letters. I got so many presents yesterday.

Letter 41 was written after Charlotte Frances had been seriously ill and was still recovering. It is notable that she complains of the hot weather as early as mid-September.

Letter 41

23 Sept, 1902

Dearest Ada,

Your dear letter with the PN for 7s [postal note for seven shillings] found me sitting out in the veranda with Lucas and I walked there with her arm and my stick. I was there yesterday too, the weather has been so hot, so you will see I am getting much stronger. Thank my dear Con for his lovely long letter on Monday. Poor darling, I wish he would not bother about me.

Frank, Jack, Vi and Lizzie are all gone to the Ararat Show and F[rank] goes to be judge at the St Arnaud Show next Tuesday. Rose would not go to Ararat, she did not like to leave me so long but Miss Lucas is very good and takes too much care if possible, and has nothing objectionable about her. She is very gentle and kind and does all I want.

Mrs Hughes was here yesterday with Edie [Minchin]. Mrs Beggs sent me some beautiful spiced tongue. I wish you and Con were here to enjoy it. She is so kind and good to me.[115]

I have not a bit of news to tell you except we fear Mr Black will not get in for Beaufort.[116] I had two very kind letters from Loup today and hope to see him soon.

---

[112] This was the local Beaufort Show. Several major centres held shows at Easter, which fell in 1902 on 30 March. Beaufort, being smaller, had a shorter event a few days earlier.

[113] Letter 28 was written from "Vi's Room" at Eurambeen East, and this is presumably the room which was damaged. Charlotte Frances had evidently given more detail in a letter to her son Philip.

[114] The Show is presumably the local one at nearby Beaufort; it is now held in November.

[115] Mrs Hughes is Jeannie nee Hawkins: note 50 above.

[116] An election for the Victorian state parliament was held on Sunday 1 October 1902. The Ministerial

CHAPTER SIX

People all say they could not tell I had been ill by my face. My hands are getting a little better but my feet are very swollen still but the numbness in them is better.

Thank you so much dearest Ada for all the <u>trouble</u> you have had and <u>taken</u> about me. I so often think of it. I am always with you and my dearest Con in thought. When I was so dangerously ill at night, I often thought you and Rose gently laid your hands on me and Con putting my hair back, it all seemed so <u>real</u> but Nurse tells me sick people often had those fancies, but I'm sure there was no fancy, you <u>must</u> have been thinking of me. I could not mistake the feel of your hands.

Tell Con there is such a lovely book for him to read when he comes up, the one Rose bought in town – "The Hosts of the Lord" by F A Steel.[117] I'm going to try and knit my socks and bootees again. I'm quite proud of my seven shillings.[118] Make Loo give my M S Shares to the Manager.[119] Anyone cld give them, <u>you</u> or <u>Con</u> only to give them to the Manager and explain that I have been ill and tell him to send the whole caboodle to me here. The Shares are in my cabinet drawer, the lowest one. Rose won't let me write any more and with best love from us both

Ever and always

Your loving Mother

Dearest love to Con.

Three months after her letter of September, Charlotte Frances is still not fully recovered, and it appears that her companion Miss Lucas had to do some quite intensive nursing.

Letter 42

Tuesday, 23rd December, 1902

My dearest Ada,

I'm so grieved that you should have worried your poor self so much about my illness and I would have written to you but knew Rose would tell you everything about me and except a little cough I'm quite well and will soon be strong again, so <u>don't</u> dear have any fears for me.

I'm so glad Vi will stay over Christmas with you. It will be very dull here. We shall have a very quiet Xmas. Douglas has written again to Con to beg he will go down for his party and I think he will go on Monday, but whether he stays with Douglas or at home I don't know. Were you not glad he got his scholarship? I feel so proud of him and he is looking so much better.[120]

Edie is still here till tomorrow and helps Rose. Miss Lucas is a great comfort or what Rose calls a blessing and helps and makes the tea and tidies about. She is so good to me about all my dirty business and washes so kind, and it is such a comfort. I'm so glad you liked my little Xmas present and I'm sure you have advanced me half the money for my socks. It was so good of you going about them.

I had such a nice kind letter from Gwen yesterday which I will send you and Loo to read, also a picture of their new home. I think she is such a nice natural creature.[121] Rose

---

government was returned with an increased majority, but Mr A J Black, grazier, member of the Ministerial and Reform League for Ripon and Hampden, which included Beaufort, was defeated by Mr D S Owen, farmer, of the Opposition – the early Labour/Labor party – by 1164 votes to 1051.

[117] Flora Annie Steel (1847-1929), married to an officer in the Indian Civil Service, wrote many books based in India, and especially the Punjab. *The Hosts of the Lord*, published in 1900, told of missionary life.

[118] From context here and in the first paragraph, it appears that Charlotte Frances was knitting bootees and socks for sale in Melbourne by Ada: *cf.* note 107 to Letter 39 below.

[119] It is not possible to tell what investment this may relate to.

[120] Constantine Trent CdeC is now twenty years old. There are no details of the scholarship he had been awarded. His friend Douglas cannot be identified; he was probably a fellow-student of medicine.

[121] Gwendolyn Blanche nee Clarke-Thornhill, wife of George Harrison Crespigny, had corresponded earlier

and Con are both writing to you so I will stop. Write to me soon for it is such a comfort to me hearing from you for I'm always thinking of you. Give my love to Vi. I'm so glad she is enjoying herself.

Good-bye, dearest Ada, and may God bless and keep you well and send you some little happiness.

Ever Yr loving old Mother, C F C

Addressed jointly to Ada and Viola, who were presumably with Philip in Melbourne, Letter 43 is dated only as "Boxing Day – 26 December – and the year is not mentioned. Given the reference to the sale of a portrait of Mrs de Crespigny "last year," however, it is 1902.

Letter 43

Boxing Day [26 December]

Dearest Ada & Vi

Just a line, "not a morsel" as poor old Judge R used to say, to thank you for your pretty card, Ada, and Vi for her nice long letter.

We had a very quiet, delicious dinner yesterday, which we all did ample justice to. No one but ourselves and Con. I wonder he is alive to tell the tale. He had first goose, then chicken and ham, with the accompanying vegetables, plum pudding and cream, mince pies & raspberry jelly and custard, so you will know what our dinner was, and we hoped you were all enjoying yrs.

Ethel, Lizzie, Blakie [Balkie] and Hal came up after and Con went back to tea.[122] Rose and F[rank] went later. Miss Lucas and I and old Gibbie[123] tead and then went to bed. Edith is a splendid servant and we have Kate McGregor for house maid and Miss Lucas helps Rose so we are doing all right.[124] Lizzie gave me such a pretty green plush workbox and Mr Hughes a picture frame and Trixie a very pretty candlestick, Edie a handkerchief and almanac, and I had 7 letters with cards, one from Mr (Montrose) Stewart,[125] besides all the pretty ones Loo and Sophy & the little boys sent me. I'm too poor to buy so I made <u>10</u> little presents myself and Vi dear you will find your pincushion on your table when you come home.

Ask Loo to show you Gwen's letter and the pretty picture of the house.[126] I'm also sending the paper with a picture of Champion Lodge and Sir Claude with his distinguished shooting party.[127] Vi can bring them back to me, and in the "Graphic" there is a

---

with Charlotte Frances – as in Letters 30 and 31 at 225-226 above. They can never have met face-to-face, however, for she was born in 1864, well after Philip Robert and Charlotte Frances left for Australia.

[122] Annotations by CTCdeC identify these as Ethel Davidson, Lizzie [Elizabeth] Beggs, Balcombe Beggs and Hal Davidson. Walter Henry Davidson (1879-1971), known as Hal, was a younger brother of Ethel.

[123] An annotation by CTCdeC identifies "old Gibbie" as Mr Gibton: note 12 above.

[124] This servant cannot be Edith Minchin or Edith Were, as below; her surname is not known.

[125] An annotation by CTCdeC identifies "Montrose" as the name of the Stewart's house at Brighton Beach;. There is no Stewart family in the electoral roll for Brighton in 1903, but George and Nina Blanche Steward of Bay Street, Brighton, were listed in the roll for 1909; George Stewart is described as a bank manager, and a George Stewart was predecessor to Philip as General Manager of the bank of Victoria: below at 253.

[126] An annotation by CTCdeC: "Gwen the wife of Harry my father's first cousin. I correspond with Harry's daughter." It is discussed at 226 above, and see also note 121 above.

According to the British census of 1901, George H C de Crespigny and his wife Gwendolyn B C de Crespigny were living on private means in a house named Bryher on a street called Headlands in Kettering, Northamptonshire, with their three children, a cook and two female servants. Following the sale of the portrait of Dorothy ChC nee Scott, Harry's great-grandmother as below, however, the family leased the Hall, a large Elizabethan house with a fine garden at Burton Latimer, just east of Kettering. See *Anne's Family History* 2020/06/13.

[127] Sir Claude Champion de Crespigny (1847-1935), the fourth baronet, was a distant cousin of the Australian CdeC lineage: Sir Claude the first baronet (1734-1818), was the great-great-grandson of the fourth baronet; Charlotte Frances' son Philip was the great-grandson of the first baronet's younger brother Philip.

Chapter Six

much larger and better picture of Mrs de Crespigny. Harry sold the picture last year to the Liverpool Gallery and it was exhibited for the benefit of the Infirmary. It can't be Lady [de Crespigny] yr father's grandmother. Harry would not sell his great grandmother, but I don't know.[128]

Con goes down on Monday to Douglas, to stay for his party and will be back in two days but you will see him. He did not want to go as he had said goodbye and felt it so much he did not want to do it again. He is looking so much better and brighter.

I think all the young fellows are going to the Hughes to tea for a corobbery and Sports. Con sends you both his best love.

I have broken my specs and have only my eyeglasses which I can't see clearly with them. I am sending my specs to Gaunts but I shall not get them till next week and shall be in misery not being able to see. With all our best and fondest love.

Ever your loving Mother, C F C

Give Gwen's letter to Loo and be sure send it me back. I can't read my letter so excuse mistakes.

The portrait of Dorothy Champion Crespigny by George Romney 1790 and the Hall at Burton Latimer 1905

---

[128] The fourth baronet was well-known for his sporting activity, including the hunting and shooting of large numbers of wild animals in England and abroad. The hall at Champion Lodge, near Maldon in Essex, had a remarkable display of dead heads.

An annotation by CTCdeC reads: "She was the wife of Claude, afterwards the first baronet. I have a cutting of the picture. The original is in the public picture gallery at Chicago." This, however, is not quite correct: see RdeC, *Champions from Normandy*, 170.

Dorothy nee Scott was the fourth wife of Philip Champion Crespigny (1738-1803), younger brother of Sir Claude the first baronet. They were married in 1783. In 1790 a portrait of Mrs [Dorothy] Crespigny was commissioned from George Romney RA for the fee of £42, and she sat for him in March 1790.

Charles Fox ChC was the second son of Philip ChC and Dorothy nee Scott; George Blicke CdeC was the second son of Charles Fox and Eliza Julia nee Trent; and George Harrison ["Harry"] was the son of George Blicke and his wife Elizabeth Jane nee Buchanan.

Dorothy nee Scott was therefore Harry's great-grandmother. She was not, however, the wife of the baronet Sir Claude and did not have title as Lady de Crespigny.

On 27 April 1901 the painting was sold at Christies by George Harrison CdeC for £5,880; so Harry did sell [the portrait of] his great-grandmother. The amount realised by the sale would at that time have purchased a large house and land. The "Liverpool Gallery" would be the Walker Art Gallery of that city. The work was acquired by the Philadelphia Museum of Art in 1928.

It appears the portrait had come to George Blicke, and was then passed to Harry. It was not mentioned in his will – see above at 226, where we discuss the lost expectations suffered by Harry and his wife Gwen – but the sale enabled him to lease the handsome Hall at Burton Latimer: above at 239-240 and note 126.

In 1903 the first electoral roll was prepared for the new Commonwealth. Neither enrolment nor voting were yet compulsory, and women did not yet have the right to vote in Victorian state elections. They could, however, vote for the national parliament, so the Roll of Electors for the Division of Grampians voting at Beaufort Polling Place included all adult residents of Eurambeen, without distinction between Eurambeen proper and Eurambeen East.

Those of the surname Beggs who are listed, with their given names, sex and occupations, are:
- 63 Elizabeth Persse, F, home duties [sister of Francis/Frank Beggs, below];
- 64 Helen Rosalie, F, home duties [daughter of Charlotte Frances' and wife of Frank];
- 65 Francis, M, sheep farmer [Frank, son-in-law of Charlotte Frances];
- 66 Maria Lucinda, F, home duties [widowed mother of Frank];
- 67 Robert Gottlieb, M, farmer [brother of Frank];
- 68 Theodore, M, farmer [brother of Frank].

There were also two entries under the surname Champion:
- 173 Charlotte, F, home duties;
- 174 Viola Julia, F, home duties;

but two more under the Crespigny surname!
- 216 Constantia, F, home duties;
- 217 Frances, F, home duties.[129]

It appears that when Charlotte Frances and her daughter used the full surname of Champion Crespigny, their entries required two lines on the original written form. When the form was transcribed for printing, however, the lines were separated – so mother and daughter could theoretically have voted twice.

In practice, however, though Charlotte Frances was entitled to vote in the Federal election held on 16 December 1903, it is unlikely that she did so: voting was not yet compulsory; the context of Letter 50 below indicates that she did not readily travel as far as Beaufort; and though postal voting was formally available, the procedure was so awkward that it was effectively impracticable.[130]

Letter 44

Wednesday, 11.3.-03.

Dearest Ada,

Ethel [Davidson] will have told you all the little there is to say about us and also that I'm glad you gave the little sofa to Maggie V. I'm writing to ask you to send me by Vi, or Ethel, the china dessert dish and the two flat ones, to <u>match</u>, for poor Rose, who never got a single thing of your Aunt C's.[131] Pack them most carefully with plenty of newspaper round them and I think they would fit in one of those brown baskets, in my room, they are full of rubbish. When I left home or rather Ottawa one of them would be useful to me here. The big dish would go in <u>standing</u> and the flat ones standing up at each side.

Your straps I'm afraid Vi forgot. Did Con tell you of the beautiful present Sophy H[ooker] gave him. It was very kind of her. What beautiful things he got. Dear love, I'm

---

[129] *Australia, Electoral Rolls, 1903-1980*: 1903 pages 2 [Beggs], 3 [Champion] and 4 [Crespigny].

[130] *Anne's Family History* 2000/2/13 "Through her eyes: votes for women 1903," discusses Charlotte Frances' enfranchisement. *Cf.* Letter 51 at 249.

[131] Aunt C is Eliza Constantia Frances ChC. Youngest child of Charles James Fox ChC and sister of Philip Robert ChC. Born in 1825, she died unmarried in England on 23 May 1898. During the 1850s and 1860s she cared for her nephew, the elder Constantine Trent, when he was a child in his grandfather's household in England, and she attended him at his final years of sickness from 1881 to 1883. See, for example, Chapter Two at 76, Chapter Three at 114 and Chapter Five at 180-182.

Chapter Six

sure he would like to be 21 every day.[132] The silver mounted pipe his chum gave him and the silver cigarette case Loup and S[ophie] gave him were both the presents I had decided to give him. I'm glad I gave him money now.

You must miss him so much, but he seems so happy now. It is you I feel for. Give my love to Ethel. I hope you will go about with her and Vi. Rose took me out for a little drive yesterday and Mr Johnstone called on me but I was out. I will send down the little box in a day or two. The money is very acceptable. I want to pay Dr Jackson his 5 pounds and Harris but I must do some more work yet before I have enough. You did not say if the little bags would do. Are they <u>liked</u>? Shall I make some more?[133]

I got my little dividend from the Mutual yesterday, 4 shillings, but I owe a lot for whisky. I'm awfully sorry about poor little Frank's nose, and eyes and to wear specs, poor child. I hope the cauterising of his poor little nose won't hurt him much and that Vivie is quite well. Write to me soon and tell me everything.

Take Ethel to the Stewarts to call. Rose and Frank are going to Admiral B[ridge]'s to lunch on Saturday, by invitation, which will be very nice for them. Sophy H[ooker] will come and see me while they are away. I must write a line to Con. With best love to all

Ever my dearest Ada,

Your loving old Mother, C F C C

When you do my business take your expenses out of the cash.

Letter 45

Saturday, 11th April, 1903

Dearest Ada,

Only a moment to send you one line as they are sending in to Beaufort, just to say all are well and Con enjoying himself immensely of course. A bit of a turmoil with so many in the house, 15 to each meal.

I'm so disappointed that dear little Vivie did not get his little present on his birthday.[134] This horrid post is always going wrong and I'm afraid you wld be nervous. I miss you so among the home faces. I wish you were here. I hope you will not have any trouble with the children. Loo is enjoying himself so much but has a cold. He has been playing Golf all this morning and Yesterday with Alice W and the rest of them.

Sophy did not go out this morning. The young people went to the other house last night and were drenched coming home, except Vi who took her waterproof. I will write on Tuesday, if I am not <u>too</u> knocked up, but won't promise. Dear Con will have to go with the rest by the evening train. Rose up to her eyes in jellies and things, and a dance of about 30 tonight, to wax the floor.

Kiss the dear boys for me, in which their Father and Mother join. In haste with much love from us all, dearest Ada,

Yr loving Mother, C F C C

Letter 46 is dated to 5 May 1903, with a note that it was "Poor Con's 51 Birthday," and an annotation by CTCdeC identifies Con as "Uncle Con, my father's brother." On Constantine Pulteney Trent ChC (1851-1883), second son of Charlotte Frances and Philip Robert ChC, see Chapter Two at 74-76 and Chapter Five at 173-182. In fact he was born on 5 May 1851, so this would have been his fifty-second birthday.

Charlotte Frances is actively sewing and knitting small items for sale.

---

[132] Constantine Trent's twenty-first birthday was on 4 March 1903.
[133] As in Letter 41 and notes 107 and 118 above, Charlotte Frances was making small items for sale in Melbourne as a means to supplement her income.
[134] Hugh Vivian, second son of Philip and Sophia ChC, born on 8 April 1897, had just turned six.

Letter 46

5 May -03, Poor Con's 51 Birthday

My dearest Ada,

I was so glad to get your dear letter yesterday, but vexed to find you had been worrying yourself about me. My neuralgia is quite well and Rose took me out for a nice little drive and when we came home we found Philip Lewis had been here ever since we left, with Frank and Vi, all the people calling after the Ball. Rose will have told you all about their golf experiences at Yalla y-Porra and what a pleasant day they had.[135] We are always wishing you were with them to have a little enjoyment when there is anything going. We have had such a gay season.

Dear Con will be up tomorrow week and do not let him forget to bring me my papers he sealed up out of my drawers and I wish you would get me a box of foreign notepaper and envelopes from the Mutual and 2 qrt bottles of Whisky. If it is sent to the Cloakroom it has only to be put in the rack in the train and taken out at Beaufort. It will save me 2 shillings in carriage if you can manage it. Poor Con is always so hurried.

I had a nice letter from him with yours and am so glad he enjoyed the boat race. Why did not you go? I sent Mrs Macansh yesterday a beautiful pincushion and wrote her a little note. As Mrs Archer had the sofa. The pincushion was lace over orange silk, all tinselled with gold, and round instead of square. They all thought it lovely, but I'm not going to give any more of my work away, it is too expensive. I have just done 6 prs of little warm bootees for Mrs B[eggs?] when she is ready for them.[136] Did you ever give Birdie the little ones you could not sell?

I'm sending you her poor letter. She wrote me two days after Baby was born. Poor girl she is so happy with her little daughter.[137]

We all hate to think of your lonely evenings without a bit of fire and no one to speak to. I am always thinking of you. Miss Lucas would tell you how often we talk of you. Poor old thing took a great liking to you.

I am so glad poor Frank likes his school better. You could help him with his French, poor child.[138] Give him my best love and tell him I will write to him soon, but I do not expect him to write to me.

Is the book I sent Vivian nice? I thought it would be like our old Henny Penny book that was always such an amusement to the children.[139] Enclosed is a very interesting story

---

[135] Yalla-Y-Porra station, now registered by Heritage Council Victoria, is twenty-five kilometres southwest of Eurambeen. According to the Statement of Significance, during the second half of the nineteenth century the property was owned by the pastoralist John Ware. This is the family which Charlotte Frances identifies as Were in Letters 29 and 47: note 47 above.

[136] This is probably Maria Lucinda Beggs nee White at Eurambeen; she would have several grandchildren.

[137] Annie Frances, daughter of Charlotte Frances' eldest grandson Philip and his wife "Birdie" nee Walstab [note 71], was born on 25 April 1903. She was named for Philip's late mother Annie Frances nee Chauncy.

On 19 August 1901 Birdie had given birth to a stillborn son: Trove 10567379, quoting a Family Notice in the *Argus* of Tuesday 20 August. The reference to her happiness is likely a reflection of that earlier disappointment and sadness.

Annie Frances Champion de Crespigny was baptised at St Mary's Church of England in Caulfield, Melbourne, on 25 March of the following year, 1904. It is possible that her great-grandmother Charlotte Frances was able to attend.

It may be noted that the announcement of the stillbirth in the *Argus* in 1901 gave the surname as Crespigny, but the record of the baptism of Annie Frances in 1904 has it as Champion de Crespigny.

[138] Francis George Travers, known as Frank and now ten years old, was the eldest son of Philip CdeC and his second wife, Sophia nee Beggs. Ada had been born in France in 1848, shortly before her parents' marriage. Though the family left for Australia when she was just over three, she evidently had some knowledge of the language.

[139] Vivian, now six years old, was the second son of Philip and Sophia ChC.

Henny Penny, also known as Chicken Little, is the centre of a folk tale about a chicken which has an

CHAPTER SIX

of Byron Moor's I'm sending to Frank. His Mother can read it to him or you. He is so fond of flowers he will like it.[140]

Vi has two such lovely stud lambs she is rearing for Frank which is an amusement to her and they follow her about and jump about like dogs. Vivie would love them. Kiss and hug him for me and wish all our very best love.

Ever, dearest Ada,

Your loving Mother, C F CC

Write soon.

July 1903 saw a deal of social activity. Unfortunately, many of the names of friends and visitors are difficult to identify.

Letter 47

Monday, 5th July, 1903

Dearest Ada,

Con was going to write to you but has to go somewhere for Frank. He wants you to be sure and send him his shirts and collars not a day later than Thursday, as he wants them to wear on Friday at the Picnic.

I am very anxious about poor Vi and hope we shall welcome her home today. I'm sure she has been worse than you have let me know! I do read it between the lines of all your letters and cards, old as I am, you can't take me in.

Rose is so dreadfully busy, without any housemaid, and the crowd at the other house backwards and forwards here, teas and things, she has scarcely time to live, and with all the jam-making every day. She is in a state at not being able to write and was so hurt and vexed at not writing to poor Loo on his birthday.[141] Will you tell him so with her love.

The Whites are here every day.[142] We like Brudenell so much, he is engaged to Col[onel] Ricardo's daughter [Amy].[143] Trixie [Hughes] is coming to stay for the week today and [?] Henty comes today to the other house, so Con has plenty of fun.

I have missed Vi, but I hope she will be up today and we must nurse her up for Friday. The young Bridges, Lewis's, Percy S[taughton?],[144] Richardson's, Fores, Austins,

---

[140] acorn drop on its head and is convinced that the sky is falling and the world is coming to an end.
It is not possible to identify this author or the book. The *Australian Dictionary of Biography* has an entry for Henry Byron Moore (1839-1925), a public servant and businessman, but he is not a likely candidate.

[141] Philip CdeC ["Loo"] was born on 4 January 1850, so the anniversary had passed some time ago.

[142] The White family was closely linked to the Beggs: Alexander/Persse; *Tree, Rock and Gully*.

[143] Sir Cyril Brudenell Bingham White (1876-1940) became one of Australia's most distinguished soldiers. He has an entry in the *Australian Dictionary of Biography* and a biography by Derham, *Silence Ruse*.

Son of John Warren White and Maria ["Mysie"] nee Gibton, Brudenell White was related to the Beggs family by marriage. Having returned from the South African War in 1902, he was at this time attached to the Victorian artillery. At the beginning of 1904 he became aide-de-camp to Sir Edward Hutton, general officer commanding the Australian Military Forces. During the First World War, as Chief of Staff to General Sir William Bridges and then to Sir William Birdwood, Brudenell White was responsible for administration of the 1st Australian Division and later planned and supervised the successful evacuation of the ANZACs from Gallipoli in December 1915. He then held high command in France, became chief of the General Staff of the Australian Army, and was recalled from retirement in 1940 to take up that post again in 1940. He was killed in the air crash off Fairbairn airfield, Canberra, on 13 August of that year.

In November 1905 Brudenell White was married at Christ Church, South Yarra; his wife, however, was not Amy Ricardo but Ethel Davidson, who also appears in these letters. Amy Edith Ricardo (1880-1940), daughter of Colonel Percy Ralph Ricardo, had married Frank's brother Robert Gottlieb Beggs in September two months earlier: further details in Derham, *Silence Ruse*, 164-172. Robert Beggs' first wife, Maria Juana nee Balcombe, had died in child-birth in 1883.

Silence Ruse, 167, quotes scattered extracts from Eurambeen Letters of this period; the copies were provided by Royalieu Dana CdeC's widow Nancy nee Temple Smith.

[144] The Electoral Roll of 1903 lists Arthur John Staughton as a grazier living at Terang with his wife Esther Irving. Terang is 120 kilometres south of Eurambeen. Derham, *Silence Ruse*, 163, mentions the Staughton

Were's, &c &c all intend coming to the picnic. I shall be so very sorry if Vi is not strong enough to go. Miss Lucas and I will keep house.

I have had a long kind letter from Mrs S[taughton?]. She does not know Vi is in town. I have had such quantities of letters and cards, 6 on Saturday. B[alcombe Beggs?] says Vivian is the most beautiful child he has ever seen.

Poor Mrs Otter has been ill and is going to Sorrento for a change.[145] I had such an affectionate letter of good-bye from poor Douglas and as Jack [White] came from Sorrento, the day he came up he passed the *Medic* steaming down the Bay.[146] All join me in very best love to you all.

I forgot to tell you which please let Loo see that Con had a letter from poor old Phil begging him to go to Launceston next month to be with him while he had 13 teeth and stumps extracted under chloroform. He wants some one of his own to be with him and has offered, poor lad, to lend Con the £2.10.0 for the journey. He says the teeth are poisoning him, his mouth gets full of matter and he can't get into condition or good health till they are out.[147] Don't forget to show this to Loo. In haste

Ever Yr loving Mother, C F C

Letter 48

Wednesday, August 31, 1903

My dearest Ada,

Vi was so pleased to get your letter on Monday and please write to her again, a nice letter. She has been pretty bad since I am up with her scald, as she got a rash all over her which is most irritating; you know what it is like, but it will soon be better. She took the bandages off her legs too soon and they are very sore. She wants you to send her a packet of Vi-Cocoa. You will see it advertised everywhere. Dr Lethbridge will not let her have tea or coffee till her rash is well. Mind it is Vi-Cocoa.[148]

I have been attending to her and missed post time. Tell dearest Con his nice letter made me so jolly. Give him my dear love. I miss him terribly, so do Anna and Ethel.[149] I think they are going to write to Con. It was very good of you both to write me such long letters. There is no news. The other house men come back from Warreenbeen today with Hugh and his wife.[150]

I wish I had something to tell you but tell Con I have not even stalked a Turkey yet. Poor old Mack and Amy came and called in state upon me and they both cried so it was very sad. They took a lot of white flowers to Charlotte's grave.[151]

---

[145] family as neighbours and friends; it is possible that Percy S and Mrs S here and below are of that surname. Sorrento is on the Mornington peninsula, the eastern side of Port Phillip Bay. Lieutenant-Colonel and Mrs Otter had been guests at the wedding of Philip with Sophia Montgomery Grattan Beggs in 1891.

[146] Douglas, surname unknown, was a friend of Constantine Trent and probably a fellow-student of medicine above at 238. It appears that he had sailed for England on the ship *Medic*, which left Melbourne on 28 May: Trove 9804443. It was common for newly-qualified doctors to take passage as a ship's surgeon.

[147] Philip was at this time a sub-editor of the *Launceston Courier*.

[148] Vi-Cocoa was an enriched chocolate drink made with malt and hops.

[149] A friend of the family, Anna [Anna R?] appears several times with Ethel Davidson, but she cannot be identified.

[150] "The other house men" refers to the men from Eurambeen West, the "other house." There is a property named Warenbeen at Barwon Heads south of Geelong. Hugh Norman Beggs (1863-1943), youngest brother of Charlotte Frances' son-in-law Frank, had married Mary Catherine Reeves nee Palmer in 1897.

[151] Neither the visitors nor the deceased Charlotte can be identified.

Chapter Six

Dinner is ready and George is going for the mail so I must say goodbye. My dearest love to you and my darling Chubby,[152] ever

Your loving Mother, C F C

Vi will come down as soon as she is well.

Letter 49

24 November, 03

My dearest Ada,

I waited writing to you till Vi arrived last night, very comfortably. Jack went in for her and they brought Balcombe 2 to the other house.[153]

Vi tells me she has been poorly and also that you have not been feeling well. She looks rather delicate now but I hope that you dear Ada, will take care of yourself for I know how you look after every one else and yourself come last. We are longing to see our darling boy. I'm counting the hours till tomorrow night and only wish you were coming with him. I always miss and think about you when we are all together.

Thank you so much for your kind present of the clock which came yesterday. I am so sorry that you should spend your miserable little money on me when you have so many wants yourself and I am sure it cost you a lot. No one can tell how glad I am to hear poor Loo is better and nearly well Vi says. Give him my love and tell him how glad I am and hope the little boys are well and don't drink unboiled water. Dr Jackson told me how imperative it is to boil the water. He has it even in the bedrooms. Thank the dear little fellows for the flowers they sent me and kiss them for me.

It is so strange that Effie Lewis, should for 4 years have come here on the day we have heard of Con's passing, accidentally.[154] She sends him all sorts of kind messages. We are all hurry and bustle this morning, as Sophy Stretch, husband and son will be here to lunch to stay, I think, till Xmas.[155] Rose and Frank are driving in for them to meet the 12.16 train. The house will be pretty full.

Rose has done Con's room up so nicely, nice carpet and new rugs, curtains and red serge blind, and the bathroom will be such a comfort to him, what Frank calls his White Elephant for no one uses it except Loo and Con and visitors.

I have made such lovely Flags for the ship and it stands on a very pretty oval table in the hall. You have no idea how well it looks now it is cleaned, painted and revarnished.[156] I will write to you again soon and tell you everything. Give my love to Sophy and poor Loo. I can hardly believe I shall see my dear Con tomorrow. I'm so proud of him and it was with so much pride I read the three 135's in yesterday's *Argus*.[157] Frank will be down

---

[152] Though somewhat incongruous, for he was basically tall and thin, "Chubby" may be Charlotte Frances's nickname for her grandson Constantine Trent.

[153] "Balcombe 2" is very likely Balcombe Quick, who was a fourth-year student of medicine while Constantine Trent CdeC was in his fifth year: note 158 below. They were both at Trinity College.

Balcombe Quick became a distinguished surgeon, with an entry in *Australian Dictionary of Biography*.

[154] Constantine Trent ChC, second son of Charlotte Frances and Philip Robert ChC, born in 1851, died in England on 26 January 1883. The news of his death reached Australia about April of that year.

[155] When Constantine Trent married Beatrix Hughes in 1910, their wedding presents included two vases from Mrs Stretch of Colac: Hudson, *Cherry Stones*, 87. Colac is some 120 kilometres south of Beaufort at the edge of the Otway ranges.

[156] *Ariel*, the model of a two masted schooner, a type still common on the coast of Brittany, was probably built when Philip Robert and Charlotte Frances were at St Malo in the late 1840s: Chapter Two at 72.

Ariel remained at Eurambeen East until Frank and Rose Beggs moved to St Marnock station about 1907. After Frank's death in 1921 his widow Rose moved to Melbourne, and when she died in 1937 she left *Ariel* to her great-nephew Richard Geoffrey CdeC (1907-1966) who lived in Adelaide. For many years from 1950 to 1970 *Ariel* sailed off the beach at Grange: photograph in Chapter Two at 73. She has since been restored again and is at St Barbary in Lilli Pilli, New South Wales.

[157] 135 was Constantine Trent's student number. In its account of Annual Examinations, November 1903

for three days next Monday and you will have Con again on the 7th. I should love to see his degree conferred on him. Dear love from us all

Ever Yr loving Mother, C F C

Letter 50 is written by Charlotte Frances to her grandson Constantine Trent, who had just completed his Bachelor of Medicine [MB] degree at Melbourne.[158] As discussed below, it was written on the back of Letter 51.

Letter 50

Dec 3 '03

My dearest boy

Frank told me all about you and I quite agree with the month's holiday before you commence anything like work again. I shall expect you up as soon as you can after the 7.

The Bridges are going to town today. They devoted themselves to Rose. Vi and Sophy went to tea at the "Age." The two Basks were there. Frank was home before tea. They were all playing Bridge.

They all went to Beaufort yesterday for the opening of the Pavillion. Mr Stretch drove them with Jack in the waggonette. Mrs Hughes begged Rose to come and help her to entertain the Big people as the Councillors had asked her to give them tea so she went. There was no room for the others. Lady M'[cEacharn] and Sir Malcolm, the Bridges, Miss Budey and someone else.[159] Mrs Hughes took charge of the ladies for Tea while the men drank Champagne and "Speeched" in the Hall.

Lady M'C was Miss Watson of Bendigo. Her mother was old Dean Marcartney's Cook and turned the windlass for her husband on the goldfields. How your little apples swim, if you get a handle to your name and money!!![160]

Give my dear love to your poor Father. Frank says he is but so so. I'm longing to see him.

Ever Your Loving

Grannie

---

results, the *Argus* of 23 November records that student 135 had passed the three 5th year subjects of Forensic Medicine, Obstetrics and Disease of Women, and Surgery: Trove 10583675. The *Australasian* of 26 December reports that he had completed fifth year medicine: Trove 138696244.

[158] Con went on to complete his Bachelor of Surgery [BS] degree in 1904. He was then qualified to practice medicine and served as a resident in Melbourne hospitals, but he also gained the higher degree of Doctor of Medicine [MD] in 1906. Further details of his career are given by his entry in the *Australian Dictionary of Biography*: Chapter Seven at 258-259.

[159] The memorial to Queen Victoria at Beaufort is discussed by monumentaustralia.org.au/themes/people/imperial/display/93079-queen-victoria. An octagonal band rotunda, fifty feet [fifteen metres] tall, with a small clock-tower, the building was erected by subscription, but the clock was presented by Admiral Bridges: note 91 above.

The pavilion was opened Sir Malcolm McEacharn, Lord Mayor of Melbourne. Born in Scotland, he was a founding partner in the steamship company McIlwraith, McEacharn. He had been Mayor of Melbourne from 1897 to 1900 and was Lord Mayor (after the title was changed by King Edward VII) in 1903-1904. He was a member of the first Federal Parliament in 1901 and had been knighted in 1902.

[160] Lady M'C refers to Lady McEacharn. Born Mary Ann Watson, she was a daughter of John Boyd Watson and Mary Ann nee Covell. Her father began as a horse-groom but made his fortune on the goldfields of Bendigo and died a millionaire

The full proverb quoted by Charlotte Frances is "See how we apples swim, quoth the horse-turd:" *Oxford Book of Proverbs* [2nd edition, 1948], 13;. More detailed citations from the seventeenth century explain that pellets of horse-dung floating in a stream with some apples exclaimed, "How we apples swim!" The proverb relates to common people associating with and comparing themselves to their betters.

It is an interesting form of words for a grandmother to use to her grandson, though it is uncertain whether Charlotte Frances recognised the bawdier significance.

Chapter Six

The Queen Victoria Memorial Pavilion at Beaufort

Letter 51 was written to Charlotte Frances by Constance Kirkpatrick nee Chauncy. An annotation by CTCdeC remarks that the writer was "my aunt nee Chauncy."

Born in 1859, Constance was the sixth child of Philip Lamothe Snell Chauncy, and next younger sister of Annie Frances, first wife of Philip, so she was connected to Charlotte Frances by marriage. She had stayed with Philip and Annie Frances at Epsom in 1878-1879,[161] and married William Agar Arbuthnot Kirkpatrick in 1885. They lived in Bairnsdale, where she died in 1907.

Ms Walsh the transcriber notes that this letter was written on the back of the preceding one; in fact, however, it was the other way round. Constance wrote Letter 51 to Charlotte Frances on 1 December, and it arrived one or two days later. Charlotte Frances then wrote Letter 50 to her grandson Constantine Trent on 3 December, and – rather than using a separate sheet – she wrote on the back of Constance Kirkpatrick's so that he could see what his aunt had said.

Letter 51

1.12.3

My dearest Grannie

    I do indeed rejoice with you at Con's great success. Please give him my most hearty congratulations. He must have passed well to have a chance of the Melbne Hosp. I believe only the best 6 of the year have that chance. Get him to write when he can and tell me all about his prospects. I expect he is with you now.

---

[161] See Letter 14, written by Annie Frances on 25 January 1879 at 193-195.

We are up to our eyes in work preparing for Xmas exams &ct so I am tired as you may guess and still have other letters to write if my hand holds out. Agar has gone to a Political Meeting. I suppose I ought to have gone too but I have only one Politic – I am a freetrader & I don't want to bother about anything else.[162]

Goodnight, dearest Gran, and thanks so much for sending me the good news.

Ever Yrs lovingly
Connie Kirkpatrick

Love to the family

As in note 137 to Letter 46 at 243, Annie Frances, daughter of Philip and Birdie nee Walstab and first great-grandchild of Charlotte Frances, was baptised on 25 March 1904. The ceremony was held in St Mary's Church at Caulfield, Melbourne. It is not known whether Charlotte Frances was able to attend.

Four months later, on 14 July 1904, Philip and Birdie had another daughter, Lorna Blanche, but she was born in New South Wales at St Leonards in northern Sydney. There is no reason to believe that Charlotte Frances ever saw her.

Letter 52, last of the collection, was again sent by Charlotte Frances to her daughter Ada. Charlotte Francis's grandson Hugh Vivian, now five years old, was staying at Eurambeen. An annotation by CTCdeC says, "written 4 months before her death, Nov 9, 1904, aged 84."

Letter 52

Eurambeen East
July 23rd - 04

Received order & parcel quite safely, very much approved of and in good order. So glad to get yr letter. Nurse leaving Tuesday week.

Vivie sends you best love & is so much better, enjoying himself very much, looks more like himself, & is going out with Vi this eve for a little tea picnic with the Lambs.

L[oo/Loup: *i.e.* Philip ChC] home Monday, expecting him this eve. So good of you getting the work frames. Let me know how much they cost. Have my specs from Gaunt.

Will write soon again.

Yours always
C F C

Charlotte Frances Champion Crespigny nee Dana died at Eurambeen East on Wednesday 9 November, 1904. The death certificate gave the cause as "Phlebitis and Gangrene of the foot after two weeks." Phlebitis is a general term for inflammation of the veins, possibly associated with a blood clot, in which case it is now referred to as thrombophlebitis. It usually occurs in the leg and may block the flow of blood. In Charlotte Frances' case appears to have led to gangrene of the foot.

---

[162] The major debate in the early politics of Australia was between Free Traders and Protectionists, the latter seeking to exclude cheap foreign goods and labour from competition with Australian manufacturing. Victoria was strong for Protectionism, New South Wales for Free Trade; by the 1920s the battle had gone in favour of the latter and high tariffs were maintained until the latter part of the century

Pastoral families such as the Beggs and their associates were inclined to favour free trade: it assisted their sales overseas and tariffs meant that they had to pay higher prices for imported equipment. At the Federal election on 16 December 1903, the electorate of the Grampians returned a Protectionist candidate, Thomas Skene; the majority of the votes, however, went to his three opponents, all of whom supported Free Trade; Australia did not yet have preferential voting: see the *Age* of 23 December; Trove 189347883.

Hancock, *Australia*, 71-82, has a firm critique of Australian tariff polices in the mid-twentieth century; online at the-rathouse.com/ Revivalist4/RC_protect.

Chapter Six

A brief notice in the *Ballarat Star* of 11 November records the death of "two old and respected residents" of Beaufort. One of them was

> Mrs Charlotte Frances Champion Crespigny, a relative of the Messrs Beggs Bros, of Eurambeen, died at the Eurambeen Estate, from senile decay, at the ripe age of 85 years.[163]

The term "senile decay" was used quite loosely by doctors of the time. It is best interpreted simply as "old age." Letter 52 above certainly shows no sign of senile dementia.

Charlotte Frances' funeral was held at Melbourne on 11 November. Her death was announced in the *Argus* of that day, and a notice was published in the *Australasian* on 19 November.[164]

> **CRESPIGNY.—** On the 9th November, at Eurambeen East, Charlotte Frances, aged 85 years, widow of the late Philip Robert Champion Crespigny, police magistrate, and second daughter of the late Captain W P Dana, of HM 6th Foot (Royal Warwickshire Regiment).[165]

Charlotte Frances was buried at Brighton with her late husband Philip Robert Champion Crespigny.

---

[163] Trove 208876438. Born on 22 February 1820, Charlotte Frances was actually three months short of her eighty-fifth birthday.

[164] Trove 10349761 and 140775054.

[165] The regimental attribution is mistaken. William Pulteney Dana had been paymaster of the 6th Garrison Battalion stationed in Ireland from 1807 to 1814: Chapter One at 35-36. During that period the Sixth Regiment of Foot [identified as the Royal Warwickshire Regiment in 1836] was actively engaged against Napoleon, notably in the Peninsula War in Spain; William Pulteney Dana was not there.

*The gravestone of Philip Robert and Charlotte Frances Champion Crespigny
at Brighton General Cemetery; photograph by Anne Young*

His text is from the *Gospel of Saint Matthew*, Chapter XI, Verse 28:
　　Come unto me, all ye that labour and are heavy laden, and I will give you rest.

Her text is taken from the *Book of Revelations*, Chapter XIV, Verse 13:
　　Blessed are the dead which die in the Lord from henceforth. Yea, saith the Spirit;
　　that they may rest from their labours; and their works do follow them.

TABLE 4
THE CHILDREN AND GRANDCHILDREN OF CHARLOTTE FRANCES DANA

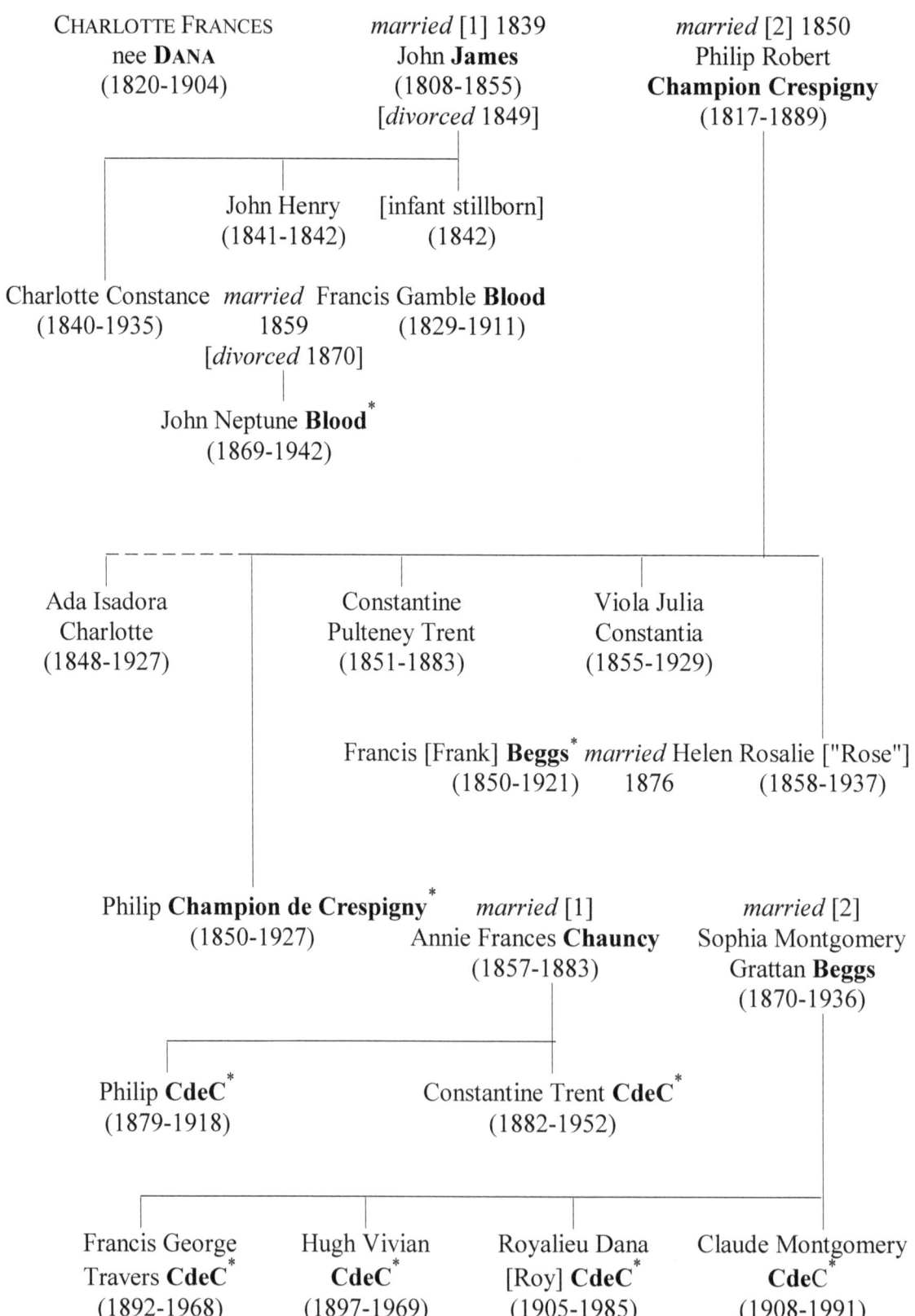

---

*   Individuals whose names are marked with an asterisk have an obituary or comparable entry in Chapter Seven following.

CHAPTER SEVEN

EPILOGUE: THE IMMEDIATE DESCENDANTS
OF CHARLOTTE FRANCES CHAMPION CRESPIGNY NEE DANA

Charlotte Frances Dana had seven children, all of whom except her son John Henry, born to her first husband John James, lived to maturity and, indeed, survived her. Only two, however – Charlotte Constance James and Philip Champion de Crespigny – had children of their own: Helen Rosalie "Rose" married Frank Beggs, but they had no children; the others never married.

It seems appropriate to provide brief accounts of these close descendants through a summary of entries in biographical dictionaries, obituaries or other sources of record. They are presented below for Philip and his six children, together with an account of John Neptune Blood, Charlotte Frances' only descendant through her daughter Charlotte Constance James. We also have entries for Rose and Frank Beggs, and a postscript on Charlotte Frances' daughters Ada Isadora Charlotte and Viola Julia Constantia.

This chapter does not have entries for Charlotte Frances' daughter Charlotte Constance James; nor for her son Constantine Pulteney Trent Champion Crespigny. Both are discussed in the body of the work.[1]

Philip Champion de Crespigny 1850-1927
[Eldest son by Philip Robert Champion Crespigny]

Portrait of Philip Champion de Crespigny from the Argus *of 12 March 1927*

---

[1] An account of Charlotte Constance James (1840-1935) is in Chapter Two at 66-67, and an account of Constantine Pulteney Trent Champion Crespigny (1851-1883) is in Chapter Five at 173-182.

CHAPTER SEVEN

Obituary from the *Argus* (Melbourne), 12 March 1927:[2]

MR P C DE CRESPIGNY
Death of Eminent Banker

It will be learned with regret that the death occurred yesterday at his residence in Brighton, at the age of 77 years, of Mr Philip Champion de Crespigny, long in the service of the Bank of Victoria.

Mr de Crespigny was born in France. His parents were British subjects. He came to Victoria with them, and joined the service of the Bank of Victoria in June, 1866, as a junior clerk. After spending a few years in country districts in service of the bank he was promoted to the position of manager at Epsom, and he filled a similar position at other country towns. Subsequently he was placed in charge of the South Melbourne branch of the bank. At the end of 1892 he was appointed assistant inspector, and he continued to act in that capacity until 1908, when he took the office of chief inspector. In 1916 he became general manager of the bank in succession to Mr George Stewart.

Under Mr de Crespigny's control the business of the bank made solid progress, and he had the complete confidence of his directors and shareholders. When negotiations were entered into some time ago for the amalgamation of the Bank of Victoria with the Commercial Banking Company of Sydney Mr de Crespigny took a leading part in carrying negotiations to a successful point. It was arranged that when the Bank of Victoria went into liquidation Mr de Crespigny was to be given a year's leave of absence on full pay, and at the end of that period he or his legal representative was to receive compensation for the loss of office as general manager of the bank.

The former Bank of Victoria building at 257 Collins Street, Melbourne, in 1918
National Library of Australia nla.pic-vn6388721
The building has since been demolished and replaced.

---

[2] Trove 3843151.

Mr de Crespigny was a son of Mr P Champion de Crespigny, who for some time was police magistrate and warden of the goldfields in the Maryborough and Ararat districts. He was a cousin of Sir Claude Champion de Crespigny, whose name is well known in British sporting circles.

Mr de Crespigny was twice married. His first wife was Miss Chauncy, and his second, who survives him, was Miss Beggs, of Bushy Creek. The family consists of six sons. The eldest was killed in action in Palestine during the war; the second, Dr de Crespigny, resides in Adelaide; and Dr Frank de Crespigny is at Ararat. Another son is squadron-leader Vivian Champion de Crespigny of the Royal Air Force.

During his long banking career Mr de Crespigny became known to a very large number of people in all walks of life who entertained for him feelings of the highest regard.

Extract from the entry in the *Australian Dictionary of Biography*
for his son Constantine Trent CdeC by Earle Hackett [see further below]:

Philip was a careful, conservative bank official who from 1866 aided the steady expansion of the Bank of Victoria. From 1916, as general manager, he played a diplomatic role in negotiations which led, at the time of his death, to the amalgamation of his bank with the Commercial Banking Co of Sydney. He had been a chairman of the Associated Banks of Victoria, president of the Bankers' Institute of Australasia, and a council-member of the Commonwealth Bureau of Commerce and Industry. Philip died at Brighton on 11 March 1927. He was survived by the two sons of his first marriage,[3] by his second wife Sophia Montgomery Grattan, née Beggs, whom he had married on 2 November 1891, and by their four children.

Philip Champion de Crespigny's house "Vierville" at 20 Black Street, Brighton
[*now renumbered as 18 Black Street*]
Philip and his wife Sophia nee Beggs lived here from 1908 until his death in 1927

---

[3] This, of course, is an error: as above and below, Philip's eldest son Philip, brother of Constantine Trent, had been killed in Palestine in 1918.

Chapter Seven

Philip Champion de Crespigny 1879-1918 [4]

[Eldest grandson by Philip Champion de Crespigny and Annie Frances nee Chauncy]

Notices from newspapers of 1918 and 1919 [collected by *Anne's Family History*]

The Argus, Melbourne, Monday 29 July 1918

DE CRESPIGNY. — On the 14th July, 1918, killed in action in Palestine, Trooper Philip (Phil) Champion de Crespigny, 2nd Light Horse, 1st Brigade, AIF, dearly beloved husband of Birdie and loving father of Frances, Lorna, Philip and Jack, eldest son of P C de Crespigny, Black Street, Middle Brighton.

(Inserted by his loving wife, Birdie.)

Worker, Brisbane, Queensland, Thursday 1 August 1918

MEN AND MATTERS

News has been received that Trooper Philip C de Crespigny was killed in action on July 14. Trooper de Crespigny was for some time a member of the literary staff of the "Worker" and the "Daily Mail." He was hon secretary of the Queensland branch of the Australian Journalists Association, of which he was one of the foundation members. Prior to coming to Brisbane he was attached to the staff of the Melbourne "Age," Hobart "Post," and other Southern papers.

De Crespigny was a very versatile and competent journalist, and his death is deeply regretted by a very wide circle. He enlisted in Brisbane early this year, and was attached to the Light Horse. He leaves a widow and four children.

---

[4] Philip CdeC is discussed by *Anne's Family History* 2013/04/25, with copies of the newspaper pieces transcribed below.

EPILOGUE

Brunswick and Coburg Leader, Victoria, Friday 2 August 1918
THE LATE P C DE CRESPIGNY
KILLED IN ACTION

Many Brunswick and Coburg residents will remember the name of Mr Philip C de Crespigny, who for some years was engaged in journalism here as its "Age" correspondent and also a editor and proprietor of a local paper. Mr de Crespigny stood as one of the selected Labor candidates for the Coburg Council, but was unsuccessful.

After leaving Brunswick Mr de Crespigny was engaged to a Hobart newspaper, afterwards going as chief of the staff to the "Daily Mail," Brisbane. He enlisted in the Light Horse for active service, and on 14th July was killed in action in Palestine.

The deceased married a daughter of the late Mr George Walstab, for many years sub-editor of the Melbourne "Herald," and leaves a widow and young family.

The Daily News, Perth, Western Australia, Saturday 10 August 1918
Melbourne "Punch" says that Philip Champion de Crespigny, reported killed in Palestine, was a dare-devil journalist when in Melbourne and elsewhere in Australia. He married a daughter of the late George Walstab, once a well-known figure in Australian literary circles, and an author as well as a dashing journalist.

Long, tall and thin, he was one of the "whitest" of men, with a heart like a horse where work was concerned. He joined up only a few months ago, and was attached to the 2nd Light Horse. His father is general manager of the Bank of Victoria.

The Australian Light Horse in Egypt
Trooper Philip Champion de Crespigny, identified by an inscription as the third from the left, was killed in action 14 July 1918
Photograph from the collection of his son John Chauncy CdeC

Chapter Seven

Worker, Brisbane, Queensland, Thursday 8 May 1919

"Socialism at Work"

Popularity of a Queensland Publication

The following cable message was published in the Brisbane "Courier" on Saturday last"

"In the House of Commons, Colonel Amery (Under Secretary for the Colonies), in reply to a question, promised to place in the library of the House of Commons a copy of the Queensland Government's publication, "Socialism at Work."

It is interesting to recall that the subject matter of the publication first appeared in the columns of the "Worker" (Queensland), for which paper the series of articles was specially written by the late Philip C de Crespigny. De Crespigny, who was one of the most widely known and one of the most capable journalists in Australia, was for a time attached to the Queensland Press, and during almost the whole his time spent in this state was a contributor to the "Worker."

The series of articles, "Socialism at Work," was written for the "Worker" to develop an idea which first presented itself in connection with the work of the Labor Government in Western Australia, but in the hands of de Crespigny they developed into a very valuable and very complete record of the work undertaken by the Queensland Government. After the articles appeared in the "Worker" they were to a slight extent remodelled by the author, and were subsequently issued by the Government as a record of its work and achievements.

There has been a good deal of speculation as to the authorship of "Socialism at Work," and both inside and outside Parliament a number of different people have been mentioned in that respect. Philip de Crespigny, who subsequently enlisted for active service in the Light Horse, was killed in action in Palestine just over twelve months ago.

Philip CdeC left Sydney on 2 March 1918 on the *SS Ormonde*, a troopship of the Orient Line. During the voyage to the Middle East he edited the journal *Billjim at Sea*; a souvenir volume was published as "A Memento of the ever-changing life on board a modern transport journeying from the Southern Cross with troops for the help of England."

During the First World War "Billjim" was a common term for Australian troops, particularly the Light Horse. It was more widely used than "Digger," while ANZAC related primarily to the Gallipoli campaign of 1915

The National Library of Australia has a copy of the souvenir volume of *Billjim*; it has been digitised at http://nla.gov.au/nla.obj-6388777.

Anne's Family History 2013/04/24 has an account of Philip's military experience.

Constantine Trent Champion de Crespigny 1882-1952
[Second grandson by Philip Champion Crespigny and Annie Frances nee Chauncy]

Entry in the *Australian Dictionary of Biography* by Earle Hackett[1]

Sir Constantine Trent Champion de Crespigny (1882-1952), medical practitioner, was born on 5 March 1882 at Queenscliffe, Victoria, second son of Philip Champion de Crespigny, bank-manager, and his first wife Annie Frances, née Chauncy (d.1883). Philip (1850-1927) was born on 4 January 1850 at St Malo, Brittany, France, son of Philip Robert Champion de Crespigny, police magistrate and goldfields warden, and his wife Charlotte Frances, née Dana. Family tradition claims descent from hereditary champions to the Dukes of Normandy in the eleventh century.[2] Huguenots, the family had moved to England after the revocation of the edict of Nantes in 1685.[3]

Constantine Trent was educated at Brighton Grammar School and Trinity College, University of Melbourne (MB 1903; BS 1904; MD 1906). From 1904 to 1907 he was a resident in Melbourne hospitals, and in 1907 he practised in the country at Glenthompson. Specializing in pathology, in 1909 he was appointed to the Adelaide Hospital. He continued his interest in laboratory medicine, being honorary director of the hospital's pathology services and lecturer in pathology in the medical school of the University of Adelaide from 1912 to 1919, but began private practice as a specialist physician in 1912.

Trent Champion de Crespigny was commissioned in the Australian Army Medical Corps in 1907. In May 1915 he joined the Australian Imperial Force as a lieutenant-colonel and was posted to the 3rd Australian General Hospital during the Gallipoli campaign. From February 1916 he commanded the 1st AGH at Rouen, France, returning to Australia in November 1917. He had been mentioned in dispatches and awarded the Distinguished Service Order in June. He then went back to England and in 1918 become consulting physician at AIF head-

---

[1] The text is slightly adapted and updated.
[2] The tradition is mistaken: see RdeC, *Champions from Normandy*, 5.
[3] The next paragraph has an account of Philip's career at the Bank of Victoria. It has been transferred to his own entry above at 255.

CHAPTER SEVEN

quarters in London. Next year he became a member of the Royal College of Physicians and returned to Adelaide.

His standing steadily grew as one of Adelaide's most reliable doctors. He was an honorary physician at the Adelaide and the Adelaide Children's hospitals. He became a fellow of the Royal College of Physicians (FRCP) in 1929 and was one of the senior Australian medical men involved in founding the Royal Australian College of Physicians, of which he was president in 1942-44. He published a number of medical papers, mainly in the *Medical Journal of Australia*, between 1914 and 1944.

Trent de Crespigny had a tall, spare figure, was well dressed and wore pince-nez. Proud of his ancestry, he spoke slowly, with a superior manner which isolated him from his associates and patients, especially women. Nevertheless his intellectual gifts as a diagnostician and his knowledge of scientific medicine were outstanding in South Australia in his time. A daughter-in-law said that he looked upon medicine as a detective looks upon crime—never ceasing to hunt for clues.

For nineteen years from 1929 he was dean and chief examiner in medicine at the medical school of the University of Adelaide. In 1908 he had started a research laboratory in pathology in a tin shed at the back of the Adelaide Hospital. He then solicited funds from private persons, charitable bequests and the State government so that an Institute of Medical and Veterinary Science could be built. In 1937 it was established by Act of parliament and he became the first chairman of its council. His portrait by Ivor Hele hangs there today.

Trent de Crespigny was president of the South Australian branch of the British Medical Association in 1925-26. In 1929 he presided over the medical section of the Australasian Medical Congress in Sydney. In 1941 he was knighted and became known as Sir Trent. Four years later he visited the United States of America where he inquired for the university into medical postgraduate education, especially as it affected medical officers returned from World War II.

His few intimates found 'Crep' a rationalist and a man of dry humour. Adelaide generally saw him as somewhat eccentric. He figured in apocryphal medical anecdotes: some of these concerned his deliberate manner and others his acerbic wit, or his inability to drive a motor car safely. In the 1930s he had been one of the first doctors to hire an aeroplane and pilot to visit distant cases. His advice to one of his children was: 'When in doubt, my dear, do the difficult thing'. He had a serious sense of private and national duty.

Sir Trent had married, on 11 September 1906 at Beaufort, Victoria, Beatrix Hughes (d.1943). On 13 December 1945 he married in St Peter's Cathedral Mary Birks Jolley, a teacher thirty years his junior. He died in Adelaide of hypertensive cardio-vascular disease on 27 October 1952, survived by two sons and two daughters of his first marriage and by his second wife and their daughter. His estate was sworn for probate at £8015. A colleague described his death as 'probably the greatest loss to the South Australian medical profession for the past thirty years'.

His eldest son Colonel Richard Geoffrey, OBE, (1907-1966) was a noted physician. His half-brothers, Air Vice Marshal Hugh Vivian, CB, DFC, MC, Croix de Guerre (1897-1969) and Group Captain Claude Montgomery, CBE (1908-1991) had distinguished careers in the Royal Air Force.

Francis George Travers Champion de Crespigny 1892-1968

[Third grandson by Philip Champion de Crespigny and Sophia Montgomery Grattan nee Beggs; their eldest son]

Francis George Travers CdeC
Captain in the Australian Army Medical Corps 1917

Extract from Henderson, *Early Pioneer Families of Victoria and the Riverina*, 239:[4]

> Born Brighton Beach, Melbourne, 23 September 1892. Educated Brighton Grammar School and Melbourne University; graduated MB BS 1916, FRACS 1928, House Surgeon Melbourne Hospital till 1917.
>
> Joined Australian Army Medical Corps during Great War and served in Egypt, Italy and France, rank Captain.
>
> Commenced practice Ararat 1919, Honorary Surgeon and Radiologist Ararat Hospital, Medical Officer Health for Borough and Shire Ararat.
>
> Married Beatrice Noel, daughter of James Spry Court, tea planter, Darjeeling, India, and later tea merchant, Melbourne.[5]

Francis George Travers CdeC   *Beatrice Noel CdeC nee Court*
(1892-1968)   *(1892-1958)*

---

[4] Slightly edited and adapted.
[5] Following the death of his first wife Noel, Frank married Adele Mabell Berthe nee Martel (*c.*1913-1990).

CHAPTER SEVEN

Hugh Vivian Champion de Crespigny 1897-1969[6]

[Fourth grandson by Philip Champion de Crespigny and Sophia Montgomery Grattan nee Beggs; their second son]

Air Vice Marshal Hugh Vivian Champion de Crespigny, CB, MC, DFC, Croix de Guerre,
Commander of the Royal Air Force in Iraq and Persia, at his desk.
Photograph by Cecil Beaton.

Entry in *Who's Who in Australia* 1965[7]

CHAMPION de CRESPIGNY, Air Vice-Marshal Hugh Vivian, CB [Companion of the Order of the Bath] 1943, DFC [Distinguished Flying Cross], MC [Military Cross], Croix de Guerre, FRGS [Fellow of the Royal Geographical Society], Regional Commander for Schleswig-Holstein, Germany, 1946 & 1947 (retired); Farming South Africa; former AOC [Air Officer Commanding], RAF [Royal Air Force] in Iraq and Persia.

Son of Philip Champion de Crespigny, Brighton, Victoria; *born* April 8, 1897, Elsternwick, Victoria; *educated* Brighton Grammar School.

2nd Lieutenant Royal Flying Corps 1915; World War I 1914-1919; transferred RAF 1918 (MC, DFC, French CdeG); Wing Commander 1930; operations North-West Frontier 1930, MID [Mentioned in Despatches]; command No 2 (Indian) Wing Station 1930-33; Air Staff HQ Inland Area 1934-36; Group Captain 1936-39; Air Vice-Marshal 1939, commanding No 25 Armament Group 1939; Labour Party candidate for Newark division of Nottinghamshire 1945 general election.

Married October 7, 1926, Sylvia E, daughter of Reverend R Usher, 3 sons and 1 adopted son; *recreation*, shooting; *clubs*, RAF (London), Victoria (Pietermaritzburg);
address, 31 Howick Road, Pietermaritzburg, Natal, South Africa.

---

[6] Hugh Vivian CdeC is discussed by *Anne's Family History* 2014/01/18.
[7] The text is paragraphed for clarity; abbreviations are explained or given full out.

Epilogue

Royalieu Dana ["Roy"] Champion de Crespigny 1905-1985

[Fifth grandson by Philip Champion de Crespigny and Sophia Montgomery Grattan nee Beggs; their third son]

From the late 1920s Roy was a farmer in the Avoca region of Victoria in partnership with his nephew Philip George CdeC. Though they were formally of different generations, they were close in age and close friends: born in 1906, Phil was the eldest son of Philip (1879-1918) [above]; Roy was the third son of his father's second marriage. The two young men worked together as share-croppers until 1934, when they jointly purchased Glenshee, a property near Elmhurst some thirty-five kilometres northeast of Ararat.

Three years later Roy married Nancy Temple Smith. Phil was best man, and Roy acted as his best man when he married Jane Elizabeth Beggs in 1940. Nan and Roy's son Royalieu Peter – also known as Roy – was born in 1943.

A childhood accident left Roy lame in one leg, so at the time of the Second World War he served only in the Home Guard. Phil, however, was in the army overseas, and qualified for Soldier Settlement on his return. The partnership was accordingly dissolved in 1946, and while Roy kept Glenshee Phil moved south to Wickliffe near Glenthompson.

Glenshee was sold in 1950, and Roy and Nan moved to Ecklin South, east of Warrnambool, where they lived for thirty years, with frequent family contacts. In 1964, however, their son Roy died suddenly while on a visit to New Zealand, he was not quite twenty-one.

On 16 February 1983 Roy and Nan's property was totally destroyed by the Ash Wednesday bushfires which devastated much of southwestern Victoria. They moved to Peterborough, where Roy died two years later, on 10 February 1985. Nan died on 24 August 2005.

The Wedding of Royalieu Dana with Nancy Temple Smith
at Saint Andrew's Church, Brighton on 9 November 1937;
Roy and Nan are on the right; best man Philip CdeC stands next to Roy
From Table Talk, Melbourne, 25 November; Trove 152536790

Chapter Seven

Claude Montgomery Champion de Crespigny 1908-1991

[Sixth grandson by Philip Champion de Crespigny and Sophia Montgomery Grattan nee Beggs; their fourth son]

Entry in Who's Who in Australia 1962[8]

CHAMPION de CRESPIGNY, Group Captain Claude Montgomery, CBE [Commander of the Order of the British Empire] 1954, jssc [graduated Joint Services Staff College] 1947; Staff, Defence Department Singapore Government 1958-61; attached HQ Far East Air Force 1955-58; Senior Personnel Staff Office HQ Flying Training Command 1954-55; AOC [Air Officer Commanding] RAF Station Tengah, Singapore, 1951-54; Deputy Director of Operations (Air Transport), Air Ministry, Whitehall, London 1949-51.

Son of late Philip Champion de Crespigny, Melbourne; *born* March 15, 1908, Brighton, Victoria; *educated* Haileybury College, Brighton, and Melbourne Church of England Grammar School.

Commissioned Royal Air Force 1928; Commanded No 61 Bomber Squadron 1939-40; Central Gunnery School 1941; RAF Station Tezpur, North Assam, 1942; 169 Wing (Burma) 1943-44; No 7 Air Navigation School 1945-46; Air Staff HQ Transport Command 1947-49.

Married February 1, 1933, Edith P [Patricia>"Pat"], daughter of Victor Cary-Barnard; *recreations*, yachting, shooting, fishing; *clubs*, RAF, Royal Lymington Yacht, Tanglin (Sing) *address*, Mulbrooks, Lower Buckland Road, Lymington, Hants, England.

Second Supplement of the London Gazette for Friday 30 April 1954

The Queen has been graciously pleased to give orders for the following appointments to the Most Excellent Order of the British Empire, in recognition of gallant and distinguished service in Malaya:

Group Captain Claude Montgomery CHAMPION DE CRESPIGNY, Royal Air Force

Pat [left] with Claude and a friend, England c. 1990
Photograph from Peter and Mariea ChdeC

---

[8] The text is paragraphed for clarity; abbreviations are explained or given full out.

Helen Rosalie "Rose" Beggs (1858-1937) and Francis "Frank" Beggs (1850-1921)
[Youngest daughter and her husband]

Punch, Melbourne, Victoria, Thursday 13 August 1908 "Fact and Rumour," page 24:[9]
Mr and Mrs Frank Beggs, who for many years have lived at Eurambeen East, are now settled in their new home at St Marnocks, Mr Beggs having purchased part of the Stoneleigh Estate in the Beaufort District.

Punch, Thursday 21 January 1909 "Fact and Rumour," page 25:[10]
Mrs C De Crespigny, of Brunswick-street, Fitzroy, and her little son, are visiting their relative, Mrs Frank Beggs, of St Marnock's, Beaufort.

> Note: Mrs C de Crespigny was Beatrix de Crespigny nee Hughes, wife of Constantine Trent CdeC; as was customary at that time the initial C was that of her husband. The 'little son was Richard Geoffrey "Geoff" CdeC (1907-1966).

Francis "Frank" Beggs (1850-1921) at St Marnock's, January 1908 with Richard Geoffrey CdeC (1907-1966), son of Constantine Trent CdeC and nephew of Rose[11]

The Pastoral Review, Victoria, Melbourne, Saturday 15 October 1921:[12]
Deep regret was felt at the death of Mr Francis Beggs, which occurred at St Marnock's, Beaufort, Vic, the end of August, at the age of 70 years. Mr Beggs had been ill for some time, and recently underwent a serious operation, from which he never fully recovered.

He was of a cheery, unassuming character, which made him a general favourite with all who knew him. With the exception of a trip to Ireland as a boy, and a couple of years in New South Wales, practically all his life was spent in the Western District of Victoria. Born at Geelong in 1850, he went inland with his parents at an early age, the family settling at

---

[9] Trove 176018320.
[10] Trove 176022294.
[11] Frank and Rose were very fond of their nephew, and he spent many holidays with them at St Marnock's. There was some idea that he might inherit the property, but he was only fourteen when Frank died, so that plan became impracticable and the station was sold to Franks' brother Theodore [below at 266]: personal communication from Geoff's cousin Philip George CdeC.
[12] Obituaries Australia, National Centre of Biography, Australian National University, http://oa.anu.edu.au/obituary/beggs-francis-95/text95.

CHAPTER SEVEN

Gnarkeet, near Pitfield. After about nine years they moved to Eurambeen, Beaufort, then known as Mt Cole Station.

He resided at Eurambeen East Estate for a considerable time, and some 14 years ago purchased St Marnock's. He was a prominent breeder of Merino sheep, the wool from St Marnock's always realising high prices on the market. His services were also much in request as a judge of Merinos.

In addition to sheep, Mr Beggs took a keen interest in horse breeding and racing in his younger days, his horses winning a number of events in the local Jockey Club's races at Ararat and Beaufort.

About 45 years ago he married Miss Helen R de Crespigny, a daughter of the late Mr P Ch de Crespigny, who survives him.

Argus (Melbourne), Tuesday 6 April 1937:[13]
The death occurred at North Brighton of Mrs Helen Rosalie Beggs, widow of the late Mr Francis Beggs, the original owner of St Marnock's Estate, Beaufort. She lived in the district many years and was closely associated with the local branch of the Australian Women's National League. The burial took place in the family burial ground at Eurambeen Estate.

Postscript: Ada, Viola and Rose
The Electoral Rolls of the newly-established Commonwealth of Australia for 1903 listed Charlotte Frances Crespigny and her daughter Viola, together with Frank and Rose and other members of the Beggs family all living at Eurambeen.[14]

In 1908, however, Francis and Rose Beggs moved to St Marnock's, and the rolls from 1909 to 1919 duly record them there, accompanied by Rose's sister Viola.[15]

When Frank Beggs died in 1921, St Marnock's station was purchased by his brother Theodore, and both Rose and Viola moved to Melbourne. The Electoral Rolls for 1922 and 1924 record them sharing a house at 250 Hampton Street in Brighton with their elder sister Ada.

Ada died on 29 November 1927 at the age of seventy-nine, and Viola two years later, on 12 October 1929, aged seventy-three. Soon afterwards Rose moved a little further north to 618 Hampton Street; she named the house St Marnock's after the property in the Western Districts. Her death in 1937 was recorded in the *Argus*:[16]

> **BEGGS** — On 28 March, at her residence, St Marnocks, Hampton Street, North Brighton, Helen Rosalie, widow of Francis Beggs, of St Marnocks, Beaufort.

Constantine Trent CdeC had been fond of his aunts Ada and Viola, and he was sad at what limited opportunities had been open to them as single gentlewomen and at their dependence upon others for financial support. He insisted that his own two daughters should have university educations:[17] Nancy graduated from Melbourne University and from Cambridge in England; Margaret had a degree from Melbourne.

---

[13] Trove 11054498.
[14] Chapter Six at 241.
[15] *E.g. Electoral Roll* for Division of Grampians, Sub-Division of Beaufort 1909 at 3 and 8; *Electoral Roll* for Division of Corangamite, Sub-Division of Beaufort 1919 at 3 and 9.
[16] Trove 11052467.
[17] Personal communication from Constantine Trent's son Richard Geoffrey CdeC.

Epilogue

John Neptune Blood (1869-1942)

[Grandson by daughter Charlotte Constance nee James, married to Francis Gamble Blood][18]

Obituary from the *Gloucester Citizen* (UK), Wednesday 30 September 1942

SUDDEN DEATH OF MAJOR J N BLOOD

THE DEATH OCCURRED SUDDENLY ON TUESDAY EVENING OF MAJOR JOHN NEPTUNE BLOOD, VD, MA, BCL, OF 1 MILLERS GREEN, GLOUCESTER, AT THE AGE OF 73. HIS WHOLE LIFE WAS DEVOTED TO PUBLIC WORKS, PARTICULARLY IN CONNECTION WITH DIOCESAN AFFAIRS.

On Tuesday evening, Major Blood was walking in Grey Friars, when he fell, and was taken to Sussex House. The City Ambulance was called, but he was found to be dead when he arrived at the Royal Infirmary.

Major Blood came of an old Irish family who lived in the Forest of Dean and at Huntley for many years. He moved to Gloucester some 10 years ago. He was a bachelor.

After leaving Cambridge University, where he gained the degree of Master of Arts, he studied law and was called to the bar in 1893. He practised on the Oxford Circuit, and for many years he was a familiar figure at Gloucestershire Assizes and Quarter Sessions.

Military Service

In his military career, Major Blood was an enthusiastic member of the old Volunteers, which later became part of the Territorial Army. He was captain of "A" Company, 2nd Volunteer Battalion, the Gloucestershire Regiment, for many years, and retired with the rank of major. During the last war [1914-1918], he returned to active duty, and commanded a defence detachment stationed at the Severn Bridge, Sharpness.

Towards the end of last century, Major Blood began his connection with Diocesan affairs which continued until his death. He first became secretary of the Diocesan Pensions Committee, and when this was merged in the Diocesan Board of Finance, he carried on his work as a member of that Board and of its Pensions Committee.

In this work, his legal knowledge was of great value in dealing with life insurance policies towards which the clergy received grants, and he did much technical work on their behalf. Another Committee of which he was a valued member was the Committee for assisting aged clergy and their widows.

Masonic Interests

He was also a member of the Diocesan Trust and of the Standing Committees of the Church Congress, the Diocesan Conference and the Three Choirs Festival. In addition he took a keen interest in other local bodies, especially those connected to St Mary de Lode.

A Mason for the greater part of his life, Major Blood was a member of the Royal Gloucestershire Lodge, of which he was Worshipful Master in 1903. He was Past Provincial Senior Grand Warden in the Royal Gloucestershire Chapter, he was Senior PX, and occupied the chair for five years between 1906 and 1952. He was also connected with other Lodges.

In business life, in addition to his practice as a barrister, Major Blood was a director of Westgate Motor House Co.

After a funeral service at St Mary de Lode, Major Blood will be buried at Huntley.

---

[18] Chapter Two at 67.

TABLE 5
THE GREAT-GRANDCHILDREN OF CHARLOTTE FRANCES DANA

son PHILIP CHAMPION DE CRESPIGNY (1850-1927)
    married [1] 1877 *Annie Frances* **Chauncy** (1857-1883)
        Philip (1879-1918)
            m Barbara Wilhelmina ["Birdie"] **Walstab** (1874-1939)
                Annie Frances (1903-1977)
                Lorna Blanche (1904-1962)
                Philip George (1906-2001)
                John Chauncy (1908-1995)
        Constantine Trent (1882-1952)
            m [1] 1906 *Beatrix* **Hughes** (1884-1943)
                Richard Geoffrey (1907-1966)
                Nancy (1910-2003)
                Margaret (1919-1989)
                Adrian Norman (1919-1993)
            m [2] 1945 *Mary Birks* **Jolley** (1915-1994)
                Charlotte (1948-)
    married [2] 1891 *Sophia Montgomery Grattan* **Beggs** (1870-1936)
        Francis George Travers (1892-1968)
            m [1] 1917 *Beatrice Noel* **Court** (1893-1958)
                Francis Philip ["Frank"] (1918-2010)
                James Vivian (1920-2006)
                Humphrey Moule (1922-2009)
                Peter (1926-)
                Rosemary (1932-)
            m [2] 1960 *Adele Mabel Berthe* **Martel** (1913-1990)
        Hugh Vivian (1897-1969)
            m 1918 *Sylvia Ethel* **Usher** (1901-1991) divorced
                Robert Vivian (1927-1989)
                Hugh Philip (1928-2004)
                Anthony Richard (1930-2008)
                Julian Augustus Claude (1934-1974)
        Royalieu Dana ["Roy"] (1905-1985)
            m 1937 *Nancy Temple* **Smith** (*c*.1914-2005)
                Royalieu Peter (1943-1964)
        Claude Montgomery (1908-1991)
            m 1933 *Edith Patricia ["Pat"]* **Carey-Barnard** (1911-2005)

BIBLIOGRAPHY

BOOKS AND ARTICLES

Alexander, Penelope, and Michael Collins Persse [editors], *Every Tree, Rock and Gully: a memoir of pioneering families: Beggs, Davidson, Persse, and White*, Grey Thrush Publishing [Oryx Publishing], St Kilda 2014

Alumni Cantabrigienses: a biographical list of all known students, graduates and holders of office at the University of Cambridge, from the Earliest Times to 1900 (ten volumes), compiled by John Venn and John Archibald Venn, Cambridge UP 1922-1953; internet edition 2011

Alumni Oxoniensis: the members of the University of Oxford, 1500-1714 (Series 1: 4 volumes), *1715-1886* (Series 2: 4 volumes)*, their parentage, birthplace and year of birth, with a record of their degrees, being the matriculation register of the university,* alphabetically arranged, revised and annotated by Joseph Foster, Klaus Reprint, Leichtenstein 1968

The Asiatic Annual Register or a view of the history of Hindustan and of the politics, commerce and literature of Asia for the year 1802, published at London in January 1803; The Wohl Library of the Institute of Historical Research, School of Advanced Study, University of London

The Asiatic Journal and Monthly Miscellany for British India and its Dependencies III (January to June 1817), Wm H Allen & Company for the East India Company, London 1817; Google Books

Australian Dictionary of Biography [*ADB Home*] at adb.anu.edu.au;
    Volume 1: 1788-1850 (1966), 278, has an entry for Henry Edmund Pulteney Dana by Marilynn L Norman

Australians: a historical library [created to mark the bicentenary of European settlement], general editors Frank Crowley, Alan D Gilbert, K S Inglis, Peter Spearitt, (10 volumes), Fairfax, Syme & Weldon Associates, Sydney 1987; the collection includes:
    Australians: a historical dictionary, edited by Graeme Aplin, S G Foster and Michael McKernan with Ian Howie-Willis;
    Australians 1838, edited by Alan Atkinson and Marian Aveling;
    Australians 1888, edited by Graeme Davidson, J W McCarty and Ailsa McLeary

Bailliere's Victorian Gazetteer and Road Guide: containing the most recent and accurate information as to every place in the colony, compiled by Robert Percy Whitworth, F F Bailliere, Melbourne 1865

Bate, Weston, *A History of Brighton*, Melbourne UP 1962

Beggs, Theodore, "The Beggs Family of Eurambeen," in Alexander and Persse [editors], *Every Tree, Rock and Gully*, 7-13; cited as "Memoir"

Blainey, Geoffrey, *The Rush that Never Ended: a history of Australian mining*, Melbourne UP 1964

——, *The Tyranny of Distance*, Sun Books, Melbourne 1966

——, *Black Kettle and Full Moon: daily life in a vanished Australia*, Penguin Books, Camberwell, Victoria 2003

Blake, Les, *Captain Dana and the Native Police*, Neptune Press, Newtown, Victoria 1982

A Book of South Australia: women in the first hundred years, collected and edited by Louise Brown, Beatrix Champion de Crespigny, Mary P Harris, Kathleen Kyffin Thomas and Phebe N Watson, published for the Women's Centenary Council by Rigby, Adelaide 1936

Brewster, Bea, *Amherst District Hospital 1859 to 1933: the outcome of compassion; the story of a gold rush hospital*, Talbot Arts and Historical Museum Inc, Talbot 2003

BIBLIOGRAPHY

Broome, Richard, *Arriving* [part of a 3 volume official anniversary history to commemorate 150 years of European settlement in Australia], Fairfax, Syme & Weldon Associates, Sydney 1984

Bryans, Dennis, "'A Tolerable Interpreter:' Robert Bell and the Chinese on the Ballarat goldfields," in *The La Trobe Journal* 92 (State Library of Victoria, December 2013), 126-143

The Cambridge History of Australia; volume 1, Indigenous and Colonial Australia, edited by Alison Bashford and Stuart Macintyre, Cambridge UP 2013

Campbell, F A, with supplements by others, *A Year in the New Hebrides, Loyalty Islands, and New Caledonia*, George Mercer, Geelong, and George Robertson, Melbourne 1873

Cannon, Michael, *The Land Boomers*, Melbourne UP 1966 & 1995

Cavanough, Maurice, and Meurig Davies, *Cup Day: the story of the Melbourne Cup 1861-1960*, Cheshire, Melbourne 1960

Chauncy, Philip Lamothe Snell, *Memoirs of Mrs Poole and Mrs Chauncy*, Lowden Publishing, Kilmore 1976

The Chronicle of Australia, Chronicle Australasia Pty Ltd, Ringwood, Victoria 1993

Chuk, Florence, *The Somerset Years: government-assisted emigrants from Somerset and Bristol who arrived in Port Phillip/Victoria 1839-1854*, Pennard Hill Publications, Ballarat 1987

Clayton, Ann, *Martin-Leake: double VC*, Pen and Sword, Barnsley, Yorks 1995

Connah, Graham, *'Of the Hut I Builded:' the archaeology of Australia's history*, Cambridge UP 1988

Cooper, Duncan Elphinstone, edited by Philip R Brown, *The Challicum Sketchbook 1842-53 and supplementary painting; introduced and edited*, National Library of Australia, Canberra 1987

Cross, F L [editor], *The Oxford Dictionary of the Christian Church*, Oxford UP 1958

Dana, Elizabeth Ellery (1846-1939) and Henry Wadsworth Longfellow Dana (1881-1950), with research by Benjamin Dana and Joseph Gardner Bartlett, *The Dana Family in America*, completed by the Dana Genealogical Committee and edited for publication by Thomas deValcourt: Cambridge Mass, 1956; Hathi Trust

Dana, Henry Wadsworth Longfellow (1881-1950), *The Dana saga: three centuries of the Dana family in Cambridge*, The Cambridge Historical Society: Cambridge, Mass, 1941; Hathi Trust

Dana, Rev John Jay, *Memoranda of some of the Descendants of Richard Dana*, Boston 1865; Google Books

Dana, Richard Henry Jr (1815-1882), *The Journal of Richard Henry Dana, Jr.* (3 volumes), edited by Robert F Lucid, Harvard UP [Belknap Press] 1968

de Crespigny, Rafe, *Champions from Normandy: an essay on the early history of the Champion de Crespigny family 1350-1800 AD*, Lilli Pilli, NSW 2017

de Serville, Paul, *Pounds and Pedigrees: the upper class in Victoria 1850-80*, Oxford UP 1991

Derham, Rosemary, *The Silence Ruse: escape from Gallipoli; a record andmemorkes of the life of General Sir Brudenel White KCB KCMG KCVO DSO*, Cliffe Books, Armadale, Victoria 1998

Double Time: women in Victoria – 150 years, edited by Marilyn Lake and Farley Kelly, Penguin Books, Melbourne 1895

Finnane, Mark, "Law and Regulation," in *The Cambridge History of Australia* 1, 391-413

Finn, Edmund [as "Garryowen"] *The Chronicles of Early Melbourne 1835 to 1852: historical, anecdotal and personal*, Fergusson and Mitchell, Melbourne 1888; arrow.latrobe.edu.au

Fitzgibbon, Bryan, and Marianne Gizycki, "The 1890s Depression," Chapter 6 in *A History of Last-Resort Lending and Other Support for Troubled Financial Institutions in Australia*, Research Discussion Paper 2001-07 of the Reserve Bank of Australia, Canberra 2001

Flett, James Edward, *Maryborough, Victoria: goldfields history*, Poppet Press, Glen Waverley 1975

Fordoński, Krzysztof, "Caroline de Crespigny translates Maciej Kazimierz Sarbiewski: forgotten Romantic poetess as translator of Neo-Latin verse;" researchgate.net/publication/271076379

Grayden, Bernard C [writing anonymously], *The Champion de Crespigny Chronicle*, ring-bound photocopies, Melbourne 1984; digitised at https://dcms.lds.org

Green, Walter Henry, *History, Reminiscences, Anecdotes and Legends of Great Sodus Bay, Sodus Point, Sloops Landing, Sodus Village, Pulteneyville, Maxwell and the environing regions, the Ridge Road and the 4-horse post coaches of pioneer days*, Sodus, NY 1947; Hathi Trust

Greenslade, Frank Nelder, *Mitchell Amen: a biography on the life of Reverend William Mitchell and his family*, Maylands WA, 1979 and 1983

Hamilton, John P, "Adjudication on the Gold Fields in New South Wales and Victoria in the 19th Century" [doctoral thesis, Macquarie University 2014], published by The Federation Press, Sydney 2015

Hancock, W K, *Australia*, Jacaranda Press, Brisbane 1961 [reprint of 1930 edition with a new preface by the author]

Hawes, Christopher J, *Poor Relations: the making of a Eurasian community in British India, 1773-1833*, Curzon Press, Richmond, Surrey 1996

Heckscher, Morrison H, *American Rococo, 1750-1775: Elegance in Ornament*, Metropolitan Museum of Art, New York 1992; Google Books

Henderson, Alexander, *Early Pioneer Families of Victoria and Riverina: a genealogical and biographical record* (2 volumes), McCarron, Bird & Co, Melbourne 1936

Hiscock, Peter McL, "La Trobe and his Horses: testing times," in *La Trobeana: Journal of the C J La Trobe Society* 17.3 (November 2018), 5-14

Holmes, Richard, *Redcoat: the British soldier in the age of horse and musket*, HarperCollins, London 2001

Hudson, Helen, *Cherry Stones; adventures in genealogy*, Pakenham 1985

Hunter, William Wilson, *The Annals of Rural Bengal* (Volume 1), New York: Leypoldt and Holt, 1868, 16-17; ebooksread.com

Jones, Helen, *In Her Own Name: women in South Australian history*, Wakefield Press, Adelaide 1986

Kingsley, Henry, *The Recollections of Geoffrey Hamlyn* [first published by Macmillan, London 1859], web edition by the University of Adelaide: ebooks.adelaide.edu.au

Kau, Marie, *From Back Creek to Talbot: what's in a name?*, Ballarat Heritage Services, Ballarat 2005

Kau, Marie [editor and compiler], *The Governor's Visit to Back Creek/Talbot, 17 October 1861*, Ballarat Heritage Services, Ballarat 2005

Letters from Victorian Pioneers: being a series of papers on the early occupation of the colony, the aborigines, etc, addressed by Victorian pioneers to His Excellency Charles Joseph La Trobe, Esq, Lieutenant-Governor of the Colony of Victoria, edited for the Trustees of the Public Library by Thomas Francis Bride, Government Printer, Melbourne 1898; text from archive.org; modern editions edited by CE Sayers were published in 1969, 1983 and 2004

The London Gazette at https://www.thegazette.co.uk

BIBLIOGRAPHY

Long, Charles R, *A History of State Education in Victoria*, Part II, Victorian Department of Education, Melbourne 1922

Lowndes, John, "The Australian Magistracy: from justices of the peace to judges and beyond," a paper presented to the Colloquium of the Judicial Conference of Australia 1999; at http://jca.asn.au/wp-content/uploads/2013/11/LowndesPaper.pdf

McNicoll, Ronald, *Number 36 Collins Street: Melbourne Club 1838-1988*, Allen & Unwin/ Hayes in conjunction with the Melbourne Club, 1988, second edition 2008

Merrett, David Tolmie, "The Australian Bank Crashes of the 1890s Revisited," in *Business History Review* 87 (2013), 407-429

The New Army List, Militia List, and Indian Civil Service List, exhibiting the rank, standing, and various services of every officer in the army serving on full pay, including the Royal Marines, and Indian Staff Corps etc, compiled by Colonel H G Hart, No CXXVII, John Murray, London 1870; archive.org

Pallot's Marriage Index, accessed through ancestry.com

Philippart, John, *The Royal Military Calendar, or Army Service and Commission Book: containing the services and progress of promotion of the generals, lieutenant-generals, major-generals, colonels, lieutenant-colonels, and majors of the army, according to seniority: with details of the principal military events of the last century*, third edition, London 1820; archive.org

Phipps, Pownoll William, *Life of Colonel Pownoll Phipps, with family records*, R Bentley, London 1894; archive.org

Picturesque Atlas of Australia, (3 volumes), edited by Andrew Garran, illustrated under the supervision of Frederic B Schell, assisted by leading colonial and Australian artists, Picturesque Atlas Publishing Company Limited, Sydney, Melbourne, London and Springfield, Mass, 1886-1888; online at the National Library of Australia

Poole, Daniel, *What Jane Austen Ate and Charles Dickens Knew: fascinating facts of daily life in the nineteenth century*, Robinson, London 1988

Randall, John, *Worfield and its Townships: being a history of the parish from Saxon and Norman times, and including notices of old families and documents contained in the parish chest*, Madeley, Shropshire 1887; openlibrary.org

Rothschild, Emma, *The Inner Life of Empires: an eighteenth-century history*, Princeton UP 2011

Russell, William [edited by Roger Hudson], *Special Correspondent of* The Times, London, Folio Society 1995

Searle, Geoffrey, *The Golden Age: a history of the colony of Victoria 1851-1861*, Melbourne UP 1977

Selby, Isaac, *The Old Pioneer's Memorial History of Melbourne; from the discovery of Port Phillip up to World War I*, Old Pioneers Memorial Fund, Melbourne 1924; "Revisited" edition published by Ian J Itter, Swan Hill 2015 at asrp.files.wordpress.com/2015/12/the-memorial-of-melbourne

Shorter, Edward, *The Making of the Modern Family*, Fontana/Collins, Glasgow 1977

——, *A History of Women's Bodies*, Allen Lane, London 1983

Stone, Lawrence, *Road to Divorce: England 1530-1987*, Oxford UP 1990

Strutt, William, *Victoria the Golden: scenes, sketches and jottings from nature 1851-1862*, with a narrative by Marjorie Tipping, Parliament of Victoria 1980

Sutherland, George, *The South Australian Company: a study in colonisation*, Longmans Green, London 1898

The Times Atlas: mid-century edition (5 volumes), London 1951-1959

Turner, Ian, "The Emergence of 'Aussie Rules,'" in *Sport I History: the making of modern sporting history*, edited by Richard Cashman and Michael McKernan, University of Queensland Press 1979, 205-226

The White Chrysanthemum; changing images of Australian motherhood, selected by Nancy Keesing, Angus and Robertson, Melbourne 1977

UK, Registers of Employees of the East India Company and the India Office, 1746-1939, The Wohl Library of the Institute of Historical Research, School of Advanced Study, University of London

Weber, Thomas A, "The Origins of the Victorian Magistracy," in *ANZ Journal of Criminology* 13 (1980), 142-150

Williams, David, *Beaufort Revisited; a sketchbook*, Beaufort Historical Society, 1990

Williamson, Charles, "The Pulteney Estates in the Genesee Lands," Chapter Four of *Saints, Sinners and Reformers: the Burned-Over District re-visited*, edited by John H. Martin and published in *The Crooked Lake Review* (Fall 2005): online at www.crookedlake-review.com/books/saints_sinners/martin4

Withers, William Bramwell, *The History of Ballarat, from the first pastoral settlement to the present time*, second edition, Niven & Co, Ballarat 1887; gutenberg.net.au

DIGITAL SOURCES

We refer to a number of sources found on the internet. We do not indicate the date of access, for many sites have been viewed on different occasions. All of them, however, have been checked during calendar year 2020.

ancestry.com.au *and* findmypast.com.au
> sources for records of births, baptisms, marriages, deaths and burials, probate and wills; also electoral rolls, census returns, military and civil appointments, *etc.*

Anne's Family History: an online research journal, compiled by Anne Young, at
> anneyoungau.wordpress.com
>> The footnotes refer to posts in Anne's online research journal by their date of publication. They can be retrieved using the internet address in the form https://anneyoungau.wordpress.com/yyyy/mm/yy.
>>> For example, https://anneyoungau.wordpress.com/2018/04/04 brings up the post on Daniel Dana published on 4 April 2018 referred to in footnote 4 on page 2.

Australian digitised newspapers retrieved from the Trove program of the National Library of Australia:
> References to "Trove nnnnn" can be retrieved using the internet address https://trove.nla.gov.au/newspaper/article/nnnnn.
>> For example, footnote 69 on page 74 has the reference "Trove 226324213" and the article can be retrieved through https://trove.nla.gov.au/newspaper/article/226324213.

British Library Newspapers, at Gale Primary Sources retrieved through nla.gov.au

British Newspaper Archive retrieved through findmypast.com.au

The Clergy of the Church of England Database [CCEd] at db.theclergydatabase.org.uk

History of Parliament online at www.historyofparliamentonline.org

Lockie, Mel, www.melocki.org.uk

Pattison, Andrew, *Shrewsbury Local History* at shrewsburylocalhistory.org.uk

U.S. Newspaper Extractions from the Northeast, 1704-1930 retrieved through ancestry.com

INDEX

aborigines [indigenous/native Australians], 70 *et passim*; Yarra Yarra tribe, 81
    Protector, 81, 84; Chief Protector, 90; Assistant Protector, 84, 90
    see also Native Police Corps
Aboyne, earldom, *see* Gordon family
Adams, John [US President], 2
    his wife Abigail, 3, 13
Addiscombe Military Seminary, 30-31
Adelaide, South Australia, 80, 184, 197, 226, 228, 246, 254, 259
    Adelaide Hospital, 259-260
    Adelaide Children's Hospital, 259
    Adelaide University, 259-260
Adelaide Lead at Amherst, gold riot, 111
Ah Sou [Chinese], 160-161,
Aiken, Andrew (*fl.*1813), 27; his wife, *see* Henrietta Laura Dana
—, Henrietta Laura (1813-*c*.1890), 27
—, John [father of Andrew], 27
Albert Park, Melbourne, 177-178
Albrighton, Shropshire [northwest of Wolverhampton], 15, 21, 31, 38, 41, 48
    Sutton House, 38, 50
Albrighton, Shropshire [north of Shrewsbury], 15
Albury, New South Wales, 186-188, 195
    Union Bridge over the Murray River, 195
Aldeburgh, Suffolk, 55; 57, parliamentary borough, 55; sale of the borough, 55, 173
Alice Downs station, Queensland, 194
Allaway, Steven/Stephen (*c*.1816-*c*.1875), 49
    his wife, *see* Helen Kinnaird Dana (1823-1882)
Allen, Thomas [greyhound trainer], 187
America, 1-3, 14, 40 *and see individual places*
    Declaration of Independence (1776), 32; Continental Congress, 2, 5
    Revolutionary War, 2, 5-6, 32
    see also United States
Amery, Leo (1873-1955) [British Colonial Secretary], 257
Amherst-Talbot, municipal borough, 111, 113, 115, 121, 127-128, 136, 145, 163
    Mayor, 128-129, 140; Council/Councillors, 128-129; Town Hall, 129; Roads Board, 129
    and see Amherst *and* Talbot
Amherst, William Pitt (1773-1857), first Earl Amherst, 111
Amherst municipal district and borough, Victoria, 100, 110, 128; Roads Board, 115
    Amherst [Mining] District, 128
    Adelaide Lead, 111
    Amherst parish [government district], 146 *and see* Amherst Anglican parish *above*
Amherst town [formerly Daisy Hill *q.v.*], Victoria, 101-102, 110-113, 115, 118, 124, 128, 133, 136-137, 150, 161, 163, 172; *see also* Talbot
    Crespigny's Hill, 113, 147; Pollocks Road, 147

Amherst town [continued]
    Clerk of Petty Sessions, 101, 111; Court of Petty Sessions, 111; Court House, 111, 125
    Magistrate, 111, 118, 121, 124-125, 128; police, 129
    Police and Commissioner's Camp *or* Warden's Camp, 111, 132; Gold House/repository, 125, 127; Warden, 128; Warden's office, 111, 127
    Mechanics Institute, 128, 134; Post Office, 127; Town Hall, 126-127; schools, 126-127, 134
    Anglican parish, 134-135; school, 127, 134
Amherst District Hospital, 132-133, 147; fete, 133-134
    Board of Management, 133; President, 133
Amiens, Treaty (1802-1803), 55, 57, 75
Anglo-Indian, 29-31
Anna, *see* Anna R
Anti-Transportation movement, 134
Antwerp, The Netherlands [later Belgium], 57
apoplexy, *see* stroke
Arab, ship, 79
Ararat, Victoria, 135, 161-165, 167, 169-173, 178, 183, 185-187, 189, 191, 193, 207, 220, 230, 238, 235, 237, 254, 261, 263, 266
    Coroner, 168, 170-172; District Surveyor, 168, 178, 191; Police Magistrate, 161, 168-169, 171, 183, 193, 200; Court House, 162; Gaol, 170; Hospital, 260; Land Board, 168, 178, 191; Lunatic Asylum, 168-169; Mining Board, 191; Shire Hall Hotel, 158; railway, 168; Warden of the Goldfields, 254
    Ararat Puppy Stakes, 187; Ararat Races, 225, 266; Ararat Show, 237
Ariel, model ship, 72-74, 246
Armagh, Ireland, The Royal School, 36
Armstrong, William (1755-1837), 27, 38
    his wife, *see* Matilda Dana
Arnot, Sandford, 30-31
Assam, India, 247
Aston Botterill, England, 8, 13; Rector, 8-9, 13
"Auld Lang Syne," song, 144
Australia, 49, 52, 54, 62, 65, 72, 74-76, 78, 101, *et saepe*
    Commonwealth of Australia [established 1901], 74, 226, 228, 233, 240
    Governor-General, 233; Parliament, 228; elections, 240-241, 248; Grampians Division, 222, 248
Australian Army/Australian Imperial Force [AIF], 259, 261
    ANZAC [Australian and New Zealand Army Corps], 244, 257
    Second Light Horse Brigade, 197, 255-257
    Australian Army Medical Corps, 259, 261
    First Australian General Hospital, 259
    Third Australian General Hospital, 259
    Volunteer Defence Corps [Home Guard], 263

INDEX

Australian Labor Party, 240-241
Australasian Medical Congress, 259
Australasian Steam Navigation Company, 179
Austria, 101
Avoca, Victoria, 111, 127, 130, 133, 142, 165, 263

Back Creek, Victoria, 102, 110-111, 116, 125, 132, 136; renamed as Talbot *q.v.*, 115
    Scandinavian Rush, 125
Bairnsdale, Victoria, 142-144, 157-161, 163, 248
    Coroner, 143; Police Magistrate, 142-143
Ballarat [Ballaarat], Victoria, 83, 87, 91, 97, 102-103, 105, 107, 111, 120, 122, 124, 131, 134, 142, 144, 158-159, 163, 170, 183, 193-195, 220, 232; District Surveyor, 193
    Nightingale Hotel, Ballarat West, 103
    Sturt Street, 97
    see also Eureka Stockade incident
Ballarat, Church of England diocese, 135
Bamford, Mrs [relative of the James family], 63, 65
Bank of Victoria, 94, 100, 140, 149-151, 153-154, 160, 167, 191, 195, 199, 215-216, 253; head office, 199, 227
    Local offices: Beaufort, 223, 227, 232-233; Elmore, 199; Epsom, 191, 193, 196, 224, 253; Gippsland, 216; Queenscliff, 196, 198; Sandhurst/Bendigo, 191; South Melbourne, 199, 253; London, 224
    Assistant Inspector of Branches, 199, 212, 216, 218, 227, 253; Chief Inspector, 253; General Manager, 253, 256
banking/financial crisis of the 1890s, 215
    Voluntary Liquidation Act [Victoria], 216
bankruptcy, *see* involvency
Barbados, West Indies, 210-211
    Ashton Hall Plantation, 210
Barkly, Sir Henry, Governor of Victoria, 116, 126
Barwon Heads, Victoria, 228
    Warenbeen station, 228
Bath, Somerset, 25, 55, 58
    Earl of Bath, *see* Daniel Pulteney
    Countess, *see* Henrietta Laura Pulteney
Bath, New York State, 33
Bath, order of knighthood, 54, 56, 154
Bathurst, New South Wales, 91, 97
Bathurst, Henry, Bishop of Norwich, 100, 103
    his daughter Caroline, *see* Caroline Champion de Crespigny
    his son Henry, 100
Batman, John (1801-1839), 74
Baxter, Stafford Squire, 55
Bayly family [*also as* Baily], 36, 39
—, Anna Penelope nee Grueber [wife of Henry], 36
—, Charlotte Elizabeth (1795-1846) [second wife of William Pulteney Dana and mother of Charlotte Frances Dana], 36-39, 49, 51, 53, 59, 67, 79; Table 1
—, Reverend Henry O'Neale (1756-1826), 36
—, John [father of Henry], 36

Beaufort, Victoria, 161, 164-170, 183-185, 189, 201, 207, 209-211, 213-215, 219-220, 223-225, 227-228, 230, 232-233, 236-237, 240-242, 246-247, 249, 259, 265-266; railway station, 220, 246; reservoir, 224
    County Court, 168; Court House, 168, 187; Court of Mines, 168; Court of Petty Sessions, 167-168, 187, Clerk of Petty Sessions, 167; Land Board, 191
    Beaufort Athletic Sports, 169; Beaufort Races, 265; Beaufort Show, 236-237; Queen Victoria Memorial Pavilion, 246-247
    Scharp's Hotel, 161; Golden Age Hotel, 169; Havelock Street, 169
    Beaufort Girls' Anzac Club, 220; Beaufort, Waterloo and District 15th Infantry Brigade Comforts Depot, 220
Beechworth, Victoria, 161
Beggs family, 127, 164, 176, 201, 207, 210, 228, 233, 244, 248 *and see* Table 3 *at* 203-206
[Table 3 has a full list of the members of the first generations of the Beggs family in Australia, but not all are included in this Index.]
—, Amy Edith nee Ricardo [second wife of Robert Gottlieb], *see* Amy Edith Ricardo
—, Catherine (1854-1939), 219-220; Table 3 *at* 205
—, Catherine (1859-1938), 186; Table 3 *at* 206
—, Catherine Sophia nee Meehan [wife of Charles Montgomery Beggs], 184; Table 3 *at* 206
—, Charles Montgomery (1819-1897), 183-184; Table 3 *at* 203 *and* 206
—, Charlotte Elizabeth nee White (1836-1921) [wife of George], 186; Table 3 *at* 206
—, Clamina Lyons nee Montgomery (1781-1821) [second wife of Francis (1770-1839)], 183, 185; Table 3 *at* 203
—, Clamina ["Miney/Minie"] (1858-1904), *see* Clamina Davidson
—, Clamina Florinda nee Faris (1841-1895) [wife of Thomas Alexander], 185; Table 3 *at* 203
—, Clamina Montgomery (1811-1890) [wife of John Faris], 185; Table 3 *at* 203
—, Elizabeth Persse"Lizzie" (1852-1908) 212, 219, 223-224, 239-240; Table 3 *at* 204 *and* 206
—, Frances Georgina (1856-1932), 186; Table 3 *at* 206
—, Francis (1770-1839), 183, 185; Table 3 *at* 203
    his wife, *see* Clamina Lyons nee Montgomery
—, Francis (1812-1880), 169, 183-186, 207; Table 3 *at* 203 *and* 204
    his wife, *see* Maria Lucinda White
    see also G and F Beggs partnership
—, Francis [Frank] (1850-1921), 164, 169-170, 176, 182-157, 163-164, 170, 172-178, 181-183, 185-191, 194-196, 201, 209-212, 218-221, 223, 225-226, 228-230, 232-237, 240-247, 251, 265-266; Table 3 *at* 204, Table 4; Table 5
    his wife, *see* Rose Champion de Crespigny

Beggs [continued]
—, Francis (1858-1919) ["Bushy"], 193, 207; Table 3 *at* 205
—, Gertrude Dorothea (1866-1943), 212; Table 3 *at* 204
—, George (1816-1879), 169, 183-184, 186, 188, 194, 207; Table 3 *at* 203 *and* 206
see also G and F Beggs partnership
—, George Warren (1870-1873), 186; Table 3 *at* 206
—, Hugh Lyons Montgomery (1815-1885), 183, 185-186, 193; Table 3 *at* 203 *and* 205
—, Hugh Norman (1863-1943), 183, 189, 245; Table 3 *at* 204
—, Jane nee Montgomery (1778-1806) [first wife of Francis (1770-1839)], 183; Table 3 *at* 203
—, Jane Elizabeth (1913-2005) [wife of Philip George CdeC], 263
—, Madeline (1860-1915), 186; Table 3 *at* 206
—, Maria Juana nee Balcombe (1860-1915) [first wife of Robert Gottlieb], 210, 244; Table 3 *at* 204
—, Maria Lucinda nee White (1826-1914) [wife/widow of Francis (1812-1880), referred to as "Mrs Beggs"], 183-184, 186, 194, 210, 228, 232, 234, 237, 240, 243; Table 3 *at* 204
—, Mary Catherine Reeves nee Palmer [wife of Hugh Norman Beggs], 254; Table 3 *at* 204
—, Robert Balcombe ["Balkie" and other spellings] (1883-1954), 210-211, 219, 225, 227, 239; Table 3 *at* 204
—, Robert Gottlieb ["Bob"] (1861-1939), 183, 189, 210, 219, 236, 240, 244; Table 3 *at* 204
—, Rose [Helen Rosalie] nee Champion de Crespigny (1858-1937) [wife of Frank Beggs], Table 3 *at* 204 *and see* Rose Champion de Crespigny
—, Sophia Montgomery (1813-1887), Table 3 *at* 204 *and see* Sophia Montgomery Grattan nee Beggs
—, Sophia Montgomery Grattan (1870-1936) [second wife of Philip CdeC (1850-1927)], 207, 210, 212, 219, 221, 243-244, 254; Table 3 *at* 205, Table 4; Table 5 *and see* Champion de Crespigny, Sophia Montgomery Grattan nee Beggs
—, Theodore ["Tedo"] (1859-1940), 183, 189, 211, 225, 232, 236-237, 240; Table 3 *at* 204
his "Memoir," 183-184, 186, 188-189
—, Theodore George (1903-1936), 189; Table 3 *at* 204
—, Thomas Alexander (1839-1920), 185; Table 3 *at* 203
—, William Montgomery (1800-1874), 185; Table 3 *at* 203
Mrs Beggs, *see* Maria Lucinda Beggs nee White
Beggs, G and F [partnership], 184
Bell, Henrie/Henry (1849-1891), 152-154

Bell [continued]
—, James Fraser (1847-1871) [planter in the New Hebrides], 152-155
—, Jessie Robina nee Kennedy (d.1880) [wife of Henrie], 154
—, Margaret Jessie Robina (1880-1957) [daughter of Henrie and Jessie; later Mrs Adams, then Mrs Reid], 154
Bellarine Peninsula, Victoria, 184
Belvoir, Victoria, *i.e.* Wodonga *q.v.*
Bendigo county, Victoria, 190
Bendigo, Victoria [town/city also known as Sandhurst until 1891], 96, 120, 124, 157, 160, 161, 163, 191, 193, 196, 199, 224, 247
Bengal, India, 6, 15-16, 55; Presidency, 16
Bengal Military Orphan Society, 29-30
Bengal Native Infantry, 28-29
see also India *and* East India Company
Bennett, Peter [sergeant in the Native Police Corps], 88-89, 93
Berbice [British Guiana], West Indies, 19-20
Canje Point, 19; New Amsterdam, 19-20
Bermuda, 174 *and see* West Indies
Besserot, Antoinette Camille nee Weber [wife of William Augustus Pulteney Dana], 98-99
Betsy [servant of the Chauncy family], 123, 125
Betton Strange, Shropshire, 223
Bible of Charlotte Frances nee Dana, 15, 21, 42-45, 65
Birbhum, Bengal, 15-16; Collector, 15-16
Birdwood, General Sir William, 227
Bissett, Mary Anne, *see* Mary Anne Walsh nee Bissett
Bitton, Gloucestershire, 47
Black Ball shipping line, 185
Black, A J [unsuccessful candidate for Victorian Parliament], 237
Blackall, Queensland, 194
"blackbirding," 155
Blackheath, Kent, 30
Blood, Charlotte Constance nee James, 67, 266 *and see* Charlotte Constance James
—, Francis Gamble (1829-1881), 67, 266; Table 4
—, John Neptune (1869-1942), 67, 266; Table 4
Blood *v* Blood [law case], 67 *and see* divorce
Bloomsbury, London, 30
Blowering, NSW, 186, 188
Blowering East station, 186
Blundell, Eliza, 55
—, George Snow, 47
Boglepore, Bengal [*also as* Boglipore, *now* Bhagalpur], 16-17
Bogong, NSW, 186, 188; [as Bayong], 186
Boston, Massachusetts, 2, 3, 13, 15-16
Bosworth, battle (1485), 11
Boulogne-sur-Mer, France, 54, 57, 68, 72
Bourke, Sir Richard, Governor of New South Wales, 72
Boyce, Margaret Mortimer [wife of Douglas Charles Kinnaird Dana], 49

INDEX

Boyle, sergeant of police at Talbot, 120
Boyne, Viscount, *see* Gustavus Hamilton
Brackenbury, Walter [Gold Commissioner at McIvor], 123
Bradford Estates, Shropshire, 14
Brady, Francis [complainant at the Gold Field's Commission of Enquiry 1855], 106-107
Branthwayte, Arthur (d.1808), 56
—, Elizabeth nee Phipps [wife of Arthur], *see* Elizabeth Phipps
Breconshire, Wales, 55, 58; High Sheriff, 55
Bridges, Rear Admiral Walter Bogue (1843-1917), 230, 233, 241
   his family, 244, 247
   his wife, Annie Caroline nee Wilson, 230
Bridges, General Sir William, 244
Bridgnorth/Bridgenorth, Shropshire, 39, 48
   Bridgnorth Grammar School, 39, 79
Bright, Victoria, 158-161, 163
Brighton, Victoria, 177, 189, 199-201, 203, 238, 244. 247, 253, 261; Bay Street, 239; Black Street, 177, 202, 254; Esplanade, 177, 199, 201-202; Hampton Street, 266; St Kilda Street, 177, 201; Tennyson Street, 202, 211-212, 219
   railway, 199
   Brighton Beach, 201-202, 261
   Brighton Grammar School, 177, 200, 202, 213, 218, 221, 259, 261-262
   Brighton General Cemetery, 233-234
   North Brighton, 266
Brigstock, Northamptonshire, 7, 9, 21, 26
   Vicar, 7, 21
Brisbane, Queensland, 255
Bristol, Gloucestershire, 23-26, 47, 119, 169
   Gaol, 25, 40, 48
Britain, 151 *and see* England *and* Scotland
British Army ranks *and appointments*: officer and commission, 81, 153, 162; Volunteer, 18
   Cornet, 54; Ensign, 18, 21, 27, 58, 173
   Lieutenant, 18-19, 21, 27, 35, 54, 58, [80-82], 175
   Captain, 35, 38, 48, 50-51, 56, 58, 67, 74, [80], 82, 82 [94, 98-99], 249
   Major, 22, 54, 210, 266
   Lieutenant-Colonel, 22-23, 36, 58, 173, 210
   Colonel, 18, 20-22, 27, 36
   Major-General, 23, 27, 39
   Lieutenant-General, 23-25, 27, 39, 54, 79, 69
   General, 6, 21
   Commander-in-Chief in Ireland, 27
   Barrack-Master, 19
   Paymaster, 22, 35-36, 48, 58, 249
   brevet rank, 22; half-pay, 18, 35, 38, 48, 50-51
British Army regiments *and other units*:
   First (Royal) Dragoon Guards, 55, 48
   First Regiment of Foot (Royal Scots), 18-19
   Sixth Regiment of Foot (Royal Warwickshire Regiment), 249
   Eleventh Regiment [in Victoria], 94

British Army regiments [continued]
   Thirteenth Regiment of Foot (1st Somersetshire) [formerly Pulteney's Regiment], 21
   Twentieth Regiment of Foot, 58
   Forty-First (Welch) Regiment of Foot, 175
   Fifty-Eighth Regiment of Foot, 19
   Sixty-Eighth Regiment of Foot (Durham Light Infantry), *218*
   Sixty-Ninth Regiment of Foot (South Lincolnshire), 173, 175
   Seventieth Regiment of Foot, 18-19
   6th Garrison Battalion, 22-23, 25, 35-36, 38, 48, 249
   Gloucestershire Regiment [Territorial Army], 266
   South Hampshire Regiment of Militia, 18
   School of Musketry, 58
British East India Company, *see* East India Company
British Guiana [formerly Guyana], 19 *and see* Berbice
British Labour Party, 245
British Navy, 100-101, 215; Captain, 20, 82, 103, 151, 230; Rear-Admiral, 230
Brittany, France, 67, 71-72, 246
Broadbent, Reverend Cornelius Farnworth, 39
Brooke, James, Rajah of Sarawak, 101
Brougham, Lord [Henry, first Baron Brougham and Vaux], 61
Brown, Margaretta Amyatt (c.1822-1855) [second wife of Charles John ChC], 67, 117
Brunel, Isambard [engineer], 114
Brunswick, Victoria, 240
Brussels, The Netherlands [later Belgium], 57
Buangor, Victoria, 170
Buffalo, New York State, USA, 32
Buffer [dog], 211, 214
Bullard, Anne (1629-1711)* [wife of Richard Dana (c.1617-1690), Table 1
Burdwan, Bengal, 6, 16
Burford [friend of Philip CdeC 1879], 182
Burma, 247; First Burma War (1824-1826), 19
Burrumbeet, Victoria, 163
Burton, Wiltshire, 19
Burton Lattimer, Northamptonshire, 239
   the Hall, 239-240
bushfires, 128, 144, 225-227
   Ash Wednesday 1983, 263
bushrangers, 82, 87, 94, 99, 111, 136-138, 140
Bushy Creek station, Victoria, 164, 185-187, 205, 207-208, 219, 254
Byron, George Gordon, Lord Byron, 100

---

* Until 1752 the official New Year in England and its colonies began on 25 March, so days before that were identified by two years: *e.g.* 1628/29, where 1628 was still the official year but 1629 was the year by present-day count. For practicality, we use the modern system.

Caen, France, 57
Calcutta, India, 15-17, 20, 28-29, 154
    Chouringhee district, 17
California, 1848 gold rush, 91
Calvinism, 29
Cambodia, ship, 76, 95-96, 115
Cambridge, Massachusetts, 1, 28, 35, 38-39
Cambridge University [England], 3, 33, 54, 58, 74, 266
    Christ's College, 7-8; Clare College, 26; Downing College, 58; Trinity College, 54; Trinity Hall, 58, 100, 103
    student categories; Nobleman, 58; Fellow-Commoner, 58; Commoner/Pensioner, 58; Sizar, 7
Cambridgeshire, England, 55
Campaspe River, Victoria, 184
Campbell, A [friend of Philip CdeC and Frank Beggs], 169-170
Campbell, Frederick Alexander, [traveller in the New Hebrides], 152, 154-155
    A Year in the New Hebrides, 154-155
Campbell, Lord [John, first Baron Campbell], 61
Camperdown, Victoria, 193
Canada, 18-20, 80, 93, 174, 224
canaries, 219-220, 225-226
Canberra, 233; Fairbairn air disaster (1940), 244
Cape Otway, Victoria, 88
Cape St Mary [Cap Sainte Marie], Madagascar, 208
Capetown/Cape Town, South Africa, 179
Captain Desborough [fictional character], 99
Cardiff, Wales, 175
Cardwell, Edward, British Secretary of State for War, 175
    his Regulation of the Forces Act, 175
Carroll, Michael Byrne MLA, 170-171
Cartwright, Harold, 210
Cartwright, Reverend Robert, 8
Cary-Barnard, Edith Patrica ["Pat"] (1911-2005) [wife of Claude Montgomery CdeC], 264
—, Victor, 264
Casterton, Victoria, 70
Castlemaine, Victoria, 101, 105-107, 109, 111, 115, 121, 123, 127, 138, 145, 161, 164, 194, 210
    Commissioner's Camp, 104
    Commission of Enquiry 1855, 106-107
    Goldfields Office, 106
    Survey Office, 106
Carlisle, England, 5
Cawnpore [Kanpur], India, 117-118, 107
censuses, British, 24-26, 28, 30, 38, 45-47, 49-50, 52, 55-56, 58, 74-76, 101, 113, 154, 173, 175, 239; Population Act 1840, 45
    Australian, 124, 128, 223
Ceylon, 19
Challicum, Victoria, 208, 214-215
Champion family [later Champion Crespigny and then Champion de Crespigny *qq.v.*],
    early history and background, 45-46
    variations of the surname, 77-78

Champion family [continued]
—, Marguerite nee Richard (1601-1682) [wife of Richard Champion], 68
—, Richard (c.1580-1669), 77
Champion Crespigny [surname; sometimes abbreviated as ChC], 45, 68-69 *and see* Champion de Crespigny
    family arms, 78
—, Charles [James] Fox (1785-1875), 54-59, 67, 72, 74-76, 78, 113-119, 173-175, 226, 239
—, Charles John (1814-1880), 57-58, 75-76, 113, 117, 173-174
    his wives, *see* Emma Margaret Smith, Margaretta Amyatt Brown *and* Frances Plunkett
—, Charles Stanley (1848-1907), 54, 75-76, 113-114, 116, 118 104-107, 173-175
—, Clarissa (1775-1836) [wife of Edward Toker], 47
—, Constantine Pulteney Trent ["Bar"?] (1851-1883), 70, 74-76, 113-114, 116-119, 136, 166, 173-182, 186, 192, 195-196, 201, 232, 241, 246; Table 4
—, Dorothy (1800-1800), 54
—, Dorothy nee Scott [wife of Philip ChC (1738-1803)], *see* Dorothy Scott
—, Eliza (1784-1831), 54, 223
—, Eliza Constantia Frances (1825-1898), 57, 75-76, 114-119, 166, 173, 176, 180-182, 186, 241
—, Eliza Julia nee Trent (1797-1855) [wife of Charles Fox ChC], 56, 74-76, 113-114, 173 *and see* Eliza Julia Trent
—, Eliza Julia (1819-1848), 57, 173
—, Emma Margaret nee Smith (1819-1848) [first wife of Charles John ChC], 75, 117
—, George (1783-1813), 54-55, 223
—, George Arthur Oscar (1894-1962), 210
—, George Blicke (1815-1895) [*also as* Champion de Crespigny], 57-58, 117, 173, 226, 239
    his wife, Elizabeth Jane nee Buchanan (1827-1897), 117, 239
—, Julia Constantia (1852-1876), 210
—, Margaretta Amyatt nee Brown (1822-1855) [second wife of Charles John ChC], 75, 117
—, Mildred Frances (1892-1946), 210
—, Philip I (1704-1765), 54
—, Philip II (1738-1803), 54-55, 58, 78, 173, 239
    his wives, 54, 239 *and see* Dorothy Scott
—, Philip (1765-1851), 55, 75-76, 173; Table 1
    his wife Emilia nee Wade (d.1832), 57, 75
—, Philip Robert (1817-1889), 53-54, 57-60, 64-72, 74, 76, 78, 95-100, 102-103, 105-121, 124-126, 128-149, 157-161, 163-174, 177-179, 182-183, 187, 191-192, 200-202, 207, 209, 226, 238, 241-242, 246, 249, 251, 253-254, 257; his grave, 249-250; Table 1, Table 4
—, Thomas (1763-1799), 55

INDEX

Champion de Crespigny [surname, sometimes abbreviated as CdeC], 45, 68-69 *and see* Champion *and* Champion Crespigny
  family arms, 78
—, Ada [Isadora Ada Charlotte] (1848-1927),* 52, 59, 64-65, 68, 70, 72, 76, 96, 113-114, 119, 121, 136-137, 140-141, 144, 157, 160, 166-167, 187, 189, 192-193, 195-196, 199-201, 207, 209-210, 212-213, 218-219, 221-222, 229, 232-234, 243, 251, 237-238, 253, 266; Table 4
—, Adele Mabelle Berthe nee Martel [second wife of Francis George Travers CdeC], *see* Adele Mabelle Berthe Martel
—, Adrian Norman (1919-1993), Table 5
—, Albert Henry (1824-1873), 101
—, Annie Frances nee Chauncy [first wife of Philip CdeC (1850-1927)], *see* Annie Frances Chauncy
—, Annie Frances (1903-1977) [daughter of Philip CdeC (1879-1918)], 226, 243, 248, 255; Table 5
—, Anthony Richard (1930-2008), Table 5
—, Augustus Charles (1837-1905), 101-103
—, Augustus James (1791-1825), 103
—, Barbara Wilhelmina ["Birdie"] nee Walstab (1874-1949) [wife of Philip CdeC (1879-1918)], 226, 229, 243, 248, 255; Table 5
—, Beatrice Noel nee Court [first wife of Francis George Travers CdeC], *see* Beatrice Noel Court
—, Caroline nee Bathurst (1797-1861) [wife of Heaton CdeC], 100-101
—, Charlotte (1948-), Table 5
—, Sir Claude (1734-1818), first baronet, 54, 58, 60, 78, 100, 239
—, Sir Claude (1847-1935), fourth baronet, 239, 254
—, Claude Augustus (1830-1884), 101
—, Claude Montgomery (1908-1991), 207, 243, 260, 264; Table 3 at 205; Table 4; Table 5
  his wife Patricia ["Pat"] [Edith Patricia Cary-Barnard] (1911-2005), 264; Table 5
—, Sir Claude William (1818-1868), third baronet, 103

---

* As discussed at page 78 above, the surname of the Australian family was changed in the latter part of the nineteenth century from Champion Crespigny to Champion de Crespigny. Philip CdeC (1850-1927): and his sisters Ada and Viola had the surname Champion Crespigny when they were born, but were generally known as Champion de Crespigny by the time of their death. We index them under the latter name.

Philip's brother Constantine Pulteney Trent, however, who died in 1883, always used the full surname Champion Crespigny. He is indexed in that style, distinguishing him from his nephew and namesake Constantine Trent CdeC (1882-1952).

Champion de Crespigny [continued]
—, Constantine Trent (1882-1952), 45, 70, 78, 113, 191, 196-197, 200, 201, 207-209, 211-231, 232-233, 236, 238, 241, 244-248, 251, 254, 259-260, 265-266; Table 4; Table 5
  annotations to family letters [*as* CTCdeC], 113, 116, 228, 232, 239, 242, 248
  his first wife, *see* Victoria Beatrix Hughes
  his second wife, Mary Birks nee Jolley (1915-1994), 113, 260; Table 5
—, Eyre Nicholas (1821-1895), 101
—, Francis George Travers [Frank] (1892-1968), 207, 212-213, 225, 236, 241, 243, 254, 261; Table 3 at 205; Table 4; Table 5
—, Francis Philip [Frank] (1918-2010), 68; Table 5
—, George Harrison ["Harry"] (1863-1945), 225-226, 238-239
—, Georgina Elizabeth (1856-1938), 226
—, Gwendolyn Blanche nee Clarke-Thornhill (1864-1923) [wife of George Harrison], 225-226, 238-240
—, Heaton (1796-1858), 100
—, Helen Rosalie ["Rose"], *see* Rose Champion de Crespigny/Beggs
—, Hugh Philip (1928-2004), Table 5
—, Hugh Vivian (1897-1969), 207, 219, 221-223, 227, 229-230, 234-236, 236, 241-244, 248-249, 254, 260, 262; Table 3 at 205; Table 4; Table 5
—, Humphrey Moule (1922-2009), Table 5
—, James Vivian (1920-2006), Table 5
—, John Chauncy ["Jack"] (1908-1995), 200, 212, 255; Table 5
—, Julian Augustus Claude (1934-1974), Table 5
—, Lorna Blanche (1904-1962), 248, 255; Table 5
—, Margaret (1919-1989) [daughter of Constantine Trent CdeC], 266; Table 5
—, Nancy (1910-2003) [daughter of Constantine Trent CdeC], 266; Table 5
—, Peter (1926-), Table 5
—, Philip (1850-1927) [nickname Loup-Loup, Loup or Loo], 45, 68, 62, 67, 70, 76, 78, 95, 112-113, 121, 136-138, 136-143, 150, 152-155, 160, 167-170, 177, 179, 183, 187, 191-202, 210-213, 216, 218-219, 221-222, 224-225, 227, 229, 232-233, 236-239, 242-244, 248-249, 251-254, 257-264; Table 3 at 205, Table 4; Table 5
—, Philip (1879-1918), 196-197, 200-201, 209-212, 218-220, 226-227, 229, 232, 243, 245, 248, 254-257; Table 4; Table 5
  Billjim at Sea, 257; *Socialism at Work*, 257
—, Philip George (1906-2001), 154, 255, 263, 265; Table 5
  his wife, Jane Elizabeth nee Beggs (1913-2005), 263
—, Richard Geoffrey (1907-1966), 74, 113, 214, 232, 246, 260, 265-266; Table 5
—, Robert Vivian (1927-1989), Table 5

Champion de Crespigny [continued]
—, Rose [<Helen Rosalie] (1858-1937) [wife of Frank Beggs], 72, 110, 112, 136-137, 141, 157, 160, 164, 166-167, 176, 180-183, 185-190, 193-196, 201, 207, 209-212, 215-242, 244, 246, 251, 265-266; Table 3 *at* 204; Table 4
—, Rosemary (1932-), Table 5
—, Royalieu [Roy] Dana (1905-1985), 207, 219, 236, 244, 263; Table 3 at 205; Table 4; Table 5
    his wife Nancy [Nan] Temple nee Smith (1914-2005), 263; Table 5
—, Royalieu Peter [Roy] (1943-1964), 263; Table 5
—, Sophia Montgomery Grattan nee Beggs (1870-1936) [second wife of Philip CdeC (1850-1927)], 207. 210, 212-214, 219-221, 225, 227, 229-230, 236, 239, 242-243, 246, 254, 261-264; Table 3 *at* 205; Table 4; Table 5 *and see* Beggs, Sophia Montgomery Grattan
—, Sylvia Ethel nee Usher [wife of Hugh Vivian CdeC], *see* Sylvia Ethel Usher
—, Viola Constantia Julia (1855-1929) [often known as "Vi"], 110, 112, 136-137, 157, 166, 196, 198, 201, 210-212, 215, 218-246, 249, 266; Table 4
—, Sir William (1765-1829), second baronet, 100, 103
    his wife Lady Sarah nee Windsor, 100, 103
Champion Lodge near Maldon, Essex, 239
charivari "rough music," [*à la Tipperary*] 132
Charles River, Massachusetts, 2, 3
Charlestown, Massachusetts, 3
Chauncy, Amy Blanche (1861-1925), 194-195
—, Annie Frances (1857-1883) [first wife of Philip CdeC (1850-1927)], 122, 168, 187, 191-198, 201, 207, 232, 243, 248, 254-255, 259; Table 3 at 205; Table 4; Table 5; photograph in a locket, 232; her grave, 197, 232
—, Clement Henry (1865-1902), 194-195
—, Constance "Connie" (1859-1907) [wife of William Kirkpatrick *q.v.*], 193, 195, 248-249
—, Frederick Philip Lamothe (1863-1903), 194-195
—, Philip Lamothe Snell (1816-1880), 122-125, 168, 191, 193, 230
    Memoirs of Mrs Poole and Mrs Chauncy, 122
    his first wife, Charlotte Humphreys nee Kemmis (1816-1847), 122
    his second wife, Susan Augusta nee Mitchell (1828-1867), 122-123, 191
—, Philip Lamothe (1851-1854), 123, 125
—, Theresa Snell ["Tise"], *see* Hale, Theresa Snell nee Chauncy
—, Theresa Susannah Snell (1807-1876), 122
    her first husband, John Walker (1796-1855), 122
    her second husband, George Herbert Poole (1806-1869), 122

Chauncy [continued]
—, William Snell (1820-1878), 195
—, William Snell (1853-1903), 195
Chelsea, London, 13, 20
    St Luke district, 20
Cheltenham, Gloucestershire, 26, 40, 58, 75, 113, 115, 119, 173-176, 182; Royal Parade, 173; Priory Street, 173, 176
    Cheltenham College, 116, 119
Cheshire, England, 1
Chester [horse], 191
childbirth, 125
    puerperal fever, 125
China, 111
Chinese miners, 111, 125, 160-161
    Chinese Proctor, 121; Chinese Protector, 121
Church of England churches in England:
    Chapel Royal at Whitehall, London, 6
    Chapel of Stanion in Northamptonshire, 7
    Saint Andrew's, Wroxeter, 11, 13
    Saint Anne's in Soho, London, 6, 15
    Saint Chad's, Shrewsbury, 23, 26
    Saint George's, Hanover Square, London, 24, 56, 224
    Saint Mary's, Shrewsbury, 26
    Saint Mary de Lode, Gloucester
    Saint Mary-le-Tower, Ipswich, 55
    Saint Mary the Virgin, Leyton, 20
    Saint Paul's Cathedral, London, 6, 60
    Saint Peter's, Leckingham, 173, 182
    Saint Peter's, Newnham, 45
    Saint Peter's, Worfield, 39-40
Church of England churches in Australia:
    Christ Church, Ararat, 183
    Christ Church, Geelong, 99
    Christ Church, South Yarra, 244
    Holy Trinity, Balaclava, 207
    Holy Trinity, Kew, 226
    Saint Andrew's, Brighton, 263
    Saint James', Melbourne, 93
    Saint Mary, Hotham [North Melbourne], 140
    Saint Michael, Talbot, 138
    Saint Michael and All Angels, Talbot, 135
    Saint Paul's, Ballarat, 193
    Saint Peter's Cathedral, Adelaide, 260
    Saint Stephen's, Richmond, 94
    St Mary's, Caulfield, 248
    Swan River parish in Western Australia, 191
Church of England churches elsewhere:
    British Chapel at Boulogne, France, 54, 57
    British Protestant Chapel at St Servan, France, 68, 70
    British Embassy at Paris, 67
    Saint Pauls' Cathedral, Calcutta, 29
Church of England offices:
    Archbishop of Canterbury, 51
    bishop, *see by diocese*
    archdeacon, 67
    rector, 7 *and see by parish*
    vicar, 7, 39 *and see by parish*

INDEX

Church of England offices [continued]
    curate, 9 *and see by parish*
    deacon, 6
    chaplain, 7
    clergyman/priest, 6-9, 15, 26, 39, 100-102, 134-135, 138-139, 227
    living and patron of a living [advowson], 7-8
Church of Ireland, 36; churches:
    Saint Mary's Cathedral, Limerick, 27
    Saint Munchin's, Limerick, 36
Church of Scotland [Presbyterian] church:
    Saint Cuthbert's, Edinburgh, 3
churches, other:
    Presbyterian church, Talbot, 135
    Scot's Church, Melbourne, 93
    Saint Patrick [Roman Catholic], Talbot, 123
    Wesleyan [Methodist] chapel, Launceston, 98
    Wesleyan [Methodist] church, Talbot, 116, 124
Clarke-Thornhill, Gwendolyn Blanche), *see* Gwendolyn Blanche Champion Crespigny
—, William Capel, 210
Clendinning, Martha, 124
Clevedon, Somerset, 182
Clifton, Gloucestershire, 47
Clive, Robert (1725-1774), 8
Clowe, Reverend A, 83
Clunes, Victoria, 97, 158-159, 167
Cobb and Co, coaching system, 187
Coburg, Victoria, 256
Cohn, Moritz, mayor of Amherst-Talbot, 133, 140, 143-144; his wife, 140
Colac, Victoria, 246
Coliban Park station near Castlemaine, Victoria, 194, 210, 227-228
Colles, James (1824-1893), 99, 140, 149
    his wife, *see* Cecile Sophia Dana
Commercial Banking Company of Sydney, amalgamation with the Bank of Victoria, 253
Commissioner of Crown Lands for the Goldfields [*also as* Goldfields Commissioner *and/or* Gold Commissioner], 97, 103, 105-106, 111-112, 123
    Assistant Commissioner, 97, 105-109, 112, 120, 129
    duties combined with/replaced by Wardens *q.v.*, 105, 110
    Police Magistrate and Commissioner, 111-112
    see also Warden *and* Magistrate
    Commissioner's Camp at Castlemaine (Mount Alexander), 104
        at McIvor/Heathcote, 123
        at Daisy Hill/Amherst, 111, 132
        see also Warden's Camp
    Commissioner's Tent at Ballarat, 87
Commissioner for Lands, Port Phillip District, 88
Commissioner for Public Works, Victoria, 114
Common Law [English], 51-52
Cook, Captain James, 151-152

Copley, John Singleton [American painter], 4, 15
Cornwall, England, 15, 43
Coroner, Victoria, 129, 143, 168, 170-172
Court, Beatrice Noel (1893-1958) [first wife of Francis George Travers CdeC], 261; Table 5
—, James Spry, 261
courts [England]:
    Court of Arches, 54-56, 59-61
    King's/Queen's Bench, 51
    See also divorce *and* House of Lords
courts [Victoria]:
    Supreme Court, 105-106, 131, 168, 170-171
    County Court, 105, 129, 168; judge, 105
    General/Petty Sessions, 117, 119, 129, 156, 158
    Clerk of Petty Sessions, 101-102, 111, 119, 129, 155, 207-208
    Police Court, 132 *and see by locality*
    Warden's Court, 132 *and see by locality*
    gold mining elective courts [1855-1857], 94
    Court of Mines, 105, 168
    court houses, 128 *and see by locality*
Cousen, James, defendant at Talbot, 130
Coventry and Lichfield, Church of England diocese, 8-9
Cox, Edward [landholder in Amherst-Talbot], 148
Crespigny/Crépigny, France, 77
Crespigny [surname], 45, 68-69 *and see* Champion Crespigny *and* Champion de Crespigny
    Crespigny's Hill, Amherst, Victoria, 113, 147
    Crespigny Street, Talbot, Victoria, 147
Creswick, Victoria, 142, 158, 166
"criminal conversation" [*crim con*], 60, 64, 66, 71 *and see* divorce
Cromartyshire, Scotland, 8
Croswell, Naomi (1670-1751) [wife of Daniel Dana (1663/4-1749)], Table 1
Crown Law Office, Victoria, 172 *and see* Law Department *and* Minister of Justice
Cumberland, England, 4
Cummins, Reverend R T, 193
Customs, Collector at Melbourne, Victoria, 79
Customs office at Launceston, Van Diemen's Land, 80

Daisy Hill Creek, 110, 124
Daisy Hill town [later Amherst *q.v.*], Victoria, 101-102, 110-111, 121
    Police and Commissioner's Camp, 111
Daisy Hill [present-day settlement], Victoria, 110-111
Daisy Hill Farm, Amherst, property of Philip Robert ChC, 113, 115, 119, 136, 140
    site and area, 145-149
    sales, 144-145, 147-148, 157, 160
    bushfire, 144; windstorm, 136
Dallimore, Miss [of Talbot], 141
Daly [magistrate at Ararat], 161, 167
Dan [tribe of Israel], 1

INDEX

Dana family: origin and variants of the surname 1; in America, 1-3; arms, 3-4, 44
—, Anna Penelope (1814-1890) [wife of William Henry Wood], 11, 36, 38-39, 49-52, 67, 79; Table 1
—, Anne Frisby (1803-1850), 33-35, 43, 52, 67; Table 1, Table 2
—, Antoinette Camille nee Weber [wife of William Augustus Pulteney Dana], 87-88
—, Augustus Pulteney (1851-1868), 100, 128, 149-150, 177
—, Barbara (1779-1779), 9, 27
—, Benjamin (1660-1738), 2; Table 1
—, Caleb (1697-1769), Table 1
—, Cecile Sophia (1845-1908) [wife of James Colles], 99-100, 137, 140, 149-150
—, Charles Edmund (1809-1836), 21, 28-31
—, Charles Patrick (1784-1816), 9, 14, 17, 28-30, 33, 39
—, Charlotte Elizabeth nee Bayly [wife of William Pulteney Dana], see Charlotte Elizabeth Bayly
—, Charlotte Elizabeth Kinnaird (1848-1848), 100
—, **Charlotte Frances** (1820-1904), 3, 15, 19, 21, 31, 38-40, 41-46, 48-49, 53, 58-59, 61, 64-68, 70-76, 78-79, 95-96, 98, 105, 110, 112-113, 115, 119, 121-122, 135-136, 139-140, 146-145, 149, 160-163, 166-167, 169-172, 174, 176-177, 182-183, 191-192, 198, 200-201, 207, 211-212, 218-251, 259, 266; Table 1, Table 4; Table 5; her Bible, 15, 21, 42-45, 65; her grave, 249-250
—, Daniel (1664-1749), 2; Table 1
—, Douglas Charles Kinnaird (1824-1878), 38, 49; Table 1
  his wife, see Margaret Mortimer Boyce
—, Douglas James Kinnaird (1815-1816), 38; Table 1
—, Douglas Kinnaird (1821-1821), 38; Table 1
—, Ebenezer (1711-1762), Table 1
—, Edmund, the Reverend (1739-1823), 2-11, 13-15, 21, 24, 26, 28, 31, 33, 35, 38-39, 45, 53; Table 1; his wife, see Helen Kinnaird
—, Edmund/William[?] (1802-1803), 33; Table 1, Table 2
—, Elizabeth Caroline (1767-1834) [wife of Thomas Oatley], 6, 9, 13-15, 24, 39; Table 1
—, Elizabeth Ellery, 1
—, Emma (1797-1797), 23
—, Frances Harriet/Harriett/Harriette Fitzpatrick (1807-1861), 28-30
—, Frances Johnstone (1766-1767), 6, 9, 11, 15; Table 1
—, Frances Johnstone (1768-1832) [wife of Joseph Sherburne (1751-1805) and godmother of Charlotte Frances Dana], 6, 9, 13-17, 19-21, 29-30, 42-43; Table 1
  her Bible, 21, 42-44 *and see* Charlotte Frances Dana

Dana [continued]
—, Francis (1743-1811), 2-5, 11, 13, 15; Table 1
—, Francis Richard Benjamin (1833-1833), 38; Table 1
—, Francis Richard Benjamin (1834-1854), 38, 49, 51; Table 1
—, George Jamieson Kinnaird (1849-1872), 99-100, 128, 137, 140, 149-155, 167
—, George Kinnaird (1770-1837), 9, 14, 18, 21-24, 27, 35-36, 39, 79; Table 1
  his first wife, see Arabella Belinda Forester
  his second wife, see Heloise Eliza Harris
—, Harriet (1774-1803) [daughter of the Reverend Edmund Dana and the Hon Helen nee Kinnaird], 9, 26
—, Harriet (1811-c.1875) [daughter of George Kinnaird Dana; wife of James Smith Junior], 25-26
—, Helen Gordon (1772-1855) [wife of John Gibbons], 9, 13-14, 26, 39; Table 1
—, Helen Kinnaird (1796-1854) [wife of George Edmund Oatley], 23-25
—, Helen Kinnaird (1823-1882) [wife of Stephen Allaway], 38, 49
—, Helen Matilda (1813-1813), 36, 67; Table 1
—, Henrietta Laura (1782-1814), 9, 27
—, Henrietta Matilda (c.1810-c.1818), 28-29
—, Henry (1741-1761), 2
—, Henry Bertie (1778-1798), 9, 27
—, Henry Edmund Pulteney (1817-1852), 38-39, 49, 65, 74, 79-82, 84, 86-90, 92-100, 140, 149, 155; Table 1
  his wife, see Sophia nee Walsh
—, Henry Edward Pulteney, *i.e.* Henry Edmund Pulteney (1817-1852) *q.v.*
—, Jacob (1655-1698), 2; Table 1
—, Joseph (1656-1670), 2; Table 1
—, Lydia (1755-1808), 2, 20
—, Maria (1787-1787), 9, 31
—, Matilda (1780-1837) [wife of William Armstrong], 9, 14, 27, 39
—, Obadiah (*fl.* 1678), 33
—, Richard (*c.*1617-1690), 1-2; Table 1
—, Richard (1700-1772) [father of Edmund], 2-4, 38; Table 1; his portrait, 4
  his wife, see Lydia Trow*bridge*
—, Richard Henry Junior (1815-1882), 2, 11, 13-14, 26, 30-31, 34-35, 38, 51, 53, 65, 71-72; Table 1
  Journal, 2, 26, 30-31, 34-35, 38, 51, 53, 72; *Two Years before the Mast*, 2
—, Richard Henry Senior (1787-1879), 2; Table 1
—, Thomas (1694-1752), Table 1
—, William Augustus Pulteney (1826-1866), 38-39, 46, 49, 74, 79, 88-90, 93-100, 140, 149-150; Table 1
  his first wife, see Sophia Cole Hamilton Walsh
  his second wife, see Besserot, Antoinette Camille Weber

283

INDEX

Dana [continued]
—, William Harry Pulteney (1844-1854), 93, 98, 100, 149
—, William Harry Pulteney (1858-1859), 98, 149
—, William Pulteney (1776-1861) [father of Charlotte Frances], 9, 14, 21-22, 27, 30-39, 48-53, 79, 232, 249; Table 1
    his first wife, *see* Anne Fitzhugh
    his second wife, *see* Charlotte Elizabeth Bayly
—, William Pulteney (1816-1817), 38; Table 1
Dana Street, Ballarat, 97
Dana Terrace/The Dana, *see* Shrewsbury
Danae [mythical princess], 1
Dane [*i.e.* Norseman], 1
Dane, William (16th century), arms, 4
Daniel [biblical prophet], 1
Darjeeling, India, 261
Davidson family, 211
—, Clamina ["Minnie"/"Miney"/"Minie"] nee Beggs (1858-1904) [wife of Walter Henry (1847-1916)], 194, 210, 223, 228, 236; Table 3 *at* 204
—, Ethel (1878-1985) [wife of Brudenell White], 194, 223, 225, 231-232, 235-236, 239, 241, 244-245; Table 3 *at* 204
—, Walter Henry ["Hal"] (1879-1971), 239; Table 3 *at* 204
Dayspring, ship, 152
Dean, A F [bankrupt stockbroker 1892], 216
debt, *see* insolvency
de Crespigny [surname], *see* Champion Crespigny *and* Champion de Crespigny
    miswritten as De Cressiguy, 53
Delhi, India, 118
dementia, *see* lunacy
Derry, Ireland, *see* Londonderry
D'Estair, Mr and Mrs, *i.e.* Philip Robert Champion Crespigny and Charlotte Frances James nee Dana *qq.v.*, 64, 67
D'Estrée, Mr and Mrs, *i.e.* Philip Robert Champion Crespigny and Charlotte Frances James nee Dana *qq.v.*, 67, 70
de Villiers, Christiaan [first commander of native police in Victoria], 83-84
Devon, England, 76, 171
Dickens, Charles, 53
Dighton, Arabella Veronica, *see* James, Arabella Veronica nee Dighton
Dinard, France, 70-71
Divinity, Bachelor of (BD) [University of Cambridge degree probably uncompleted by Edmund Dana], 7
Divinity, Doctor of (DD) [degree attributed to the Reverend Edmund Dana, probably wrongly], 15

divorce, procedures in England, 54, 59-61 *and see* marriage
    divorce of Charles Lord Kinnaird from Barbara nee Johnstone, 5
    divorce of John James Junior from Charlotte Frances nee Dana [James *v* James], 59-68, 70-72, 74, 174
    divorce of Charlotte Constance nee James from Francis Gamble Blood, 67
Doctors' Commons, London, 56, 60
Doughty, Mrs [widowed and remarried mother of James and Henrie Bell], 142
Douglas [surname unknown; friend of Constantine Trent CdeC], 238, 240, 244
Dover, Kent, 57, 64-65
Dow [surgeon and coroner at Amherst-Talbot], 133
Dowling, Charles Cholmeley [magistrate], 142-143, 158, 167
drought, 115; Federation Drought, 217, 221, 235
Dublin, Ireland, 22, 36, 38, 115, 183
    Trinity College, Dublin, 36, 184
Dunkeld, Victoria, 187; Athletic Sports Meeting, 187
Durban, Elizabeth Sarah, *see* Elizabeth Sarah Smith, 21
Durrell, Reverend Thomas, 101

Eaglehawk/Eagle Hawk, Victoria, 124, 161
East Anglia, England, 55, 57
East India Company, British, 5, 15-17, 30-31, 39, 56, 76, *see also* India *and* Bengal
    civil appointments: 6, 15-17; cadet, 39; Writer, 15; Factor, 15; Junior Merchant, 15; Senior Merchant, 15; Deputy Superintendent of Police, 15; Collector, 15
    military appointments: 47-48; Ensign, 28; Second-Lieutenant, 29; Lieutenant, 28; Captain, 28, 47, 56; Major, 56
    military units of the Bengal Native Infantry:
        Twenty-Third Regiment, 28
        Twenty-Fifth Regiment, 29
        Fifty-First Regiment, 56
    ships, 17, 20, 28, 29
Eaton Constantine, Shropshire, 9, 13; Rector, 9
Echuca, Victoria, 101, 186-187
Ecklin South, Victoria, 263
Edict of Nantes, Revocation (1684), 54, 259
Edinburgh, Scotland, 3-5, 154
Edith [surname unknown, servant at Eurambeen East], 239
Egypt, 22, 257, 261
Elba, 57
Ellenborough, Lord [Edward Law, first Earl of Ellenborough], 61
Elmhurst, Victoria, 263
Elmore, Victoria, 199
Elphinstone, Victoria, 210

Elsternwick, Victoria, 177, 186, 212, 219, 221-222, 233, 262
    Gladstone Parade, 177, 186, 212, 219, 221-222, 233
embezzlement, 130-131, 140, 167 *and see* forgery and fraud
England, 1-6, 11, 13, 15, 17-20, 22-25, 27-30, 33, 35, 38, 53, 55-57, 64, 70, 72, 74-77, 79, 93, 95-96, 98, 100-103, 111, 113-114, 116-117, 125, 132, 136, 140, 166, 173-174, 176, 180, 196, 217, 224, 228, 232, 239, 241, 244, 246, 256-257, 259 *and see individual places*
"England, Empress of the Sea," song, 144
epilepsy, 129
Epsom, Victoria, 191, 193, 195-196, 224, 227, 252
Estcourt [female servant], 63
Eurambeen station, Victoria [formerly Mount Cole station *q.v.* and then Eurambeen West], 164, 169, 176, 183-186, 201, 207-249, 266
Eurambeen East station, Victoria, 185-186, 188-189, 194, 201, 207-211, 213-215, 218, 221-222, 234, 236, 244, 246, 249, 266
Eurambeen West station, Victoria, 186, 211 *and see* Eurambeen station *above*
"Eurambeen Letters," 116, 194, 217-249
Eurasian, *see* Anglo-Indian
Eureka Stockade incident at Ballarat 1854, 105-106, 111, 121
Euroa, Victoria, 211

Falmouth, Cornwall, 15
Fairclough, William (*c.*1840-1900) [bank manager], 224
Faris, Clamina Florinda, *see* Clamina Florinda Beggs nee Faris
—, John (1801-1869), 185; Table 3 *at* 203; his wife, *see* Clamina Montgomery Beggs
—, Thomas (1844-1856), 185
Fawkner [member of the Gold Field's Commission of Enquiry 1855], 106
Feltrim, Ireland, 184; Feltrim Farm, 184 *and see* Violet Town, Victoria
Fenians, 174
Fiji, 152; Levuka, 152
Finn, Edmund [*alias* "Garryowen"], 89
    The Chronicles of Early Melbourne, 89, 93 *and see* Bibliography
Fitzball, Edward, librettist, 140
Fitzhugh family [USA], 33-34; Table 2
—, Anne (*c.*1784-1804) [first wife of William Augustus Pulteney Dana], 33-34, 43, 52-53, 67; Table 1, Table 2
—, Charles Carroll, 34, Table 2
—, Daniel Holker (1794-1881), 34-35; Table 1, Table 2
    his wife, *see* Anne Frisby Dana
—, Florence, 34, Table 2
—, Isabella, 35
—, Peregrine, 33

Fitzroy, Melbourne, Victoria, 265
    Brunswick Street, 265
Flemington, Victoria, 122-123
Flora [surname unknown; friend/companion at Eurambeen East], 224-225, 230
Florida, 6; British colony of West Florida, Governor, 6
forgery and fraud, 158-159 *and see* embezzlement
Folkestone, Kent, 58, 64-65, 173
football, Australian Rules, 150; Challenge Cup, 150
    Melbourne team, 150-151
    Royal Park team, 150
    South Yarra team, 150-151
Forest Creek, Victoria, 106-110, 120 *and see* Golden Gully *and* Golden Point fields
Forest of Dean, Gloucestershire, 49, 266
Forester, Arabella Belinda (1769-1836) [first wife of George Kinnaird Dana], 23-25; Table 1
—, Cecil (1721-1774), first Baron Forester, 23
—, Cecil Weld (1767-1828), second Baron Forester, 23-24
Fox, Charles James, British politician, 54, 106
forgery and fraud, 157-158 *and see* embezzlement
Frampton Cotterell, Gloucestershire, 24
Franc, Bridget [defendant at Ararat], 168
France, 22, 54-57, 67, 71, 75-76, 78, 95-96, 100, 151, 244, 253, 260 *and see individual places*
    French Revolution, 57
    1848 rebellion, 76
Francis, James Goodall, Commissioner for Public Works, Victoria, 114
Franklin, Sir John, Governor of Van Diemen's Land, 39, 79-80
Franklyn/Franklin Village, Tasmania, 98
Fraser family of Adelaide, South Australia, 226
Freemasonry, 266
Fyfe [potential magistrate at Amherst-Talbot], 129-130

Gallipoli campaign 1915, 244, 258-259
Ganges River, 16
Ganges, ship, 29
gangrene, 249
Gardner, Mary [servant], 46
"Garryowen," *see* Edmund Finn
Gauntlett, tea dealer of Bath, 100
Geelong, Victoria, 92, 95-96, 98-99, 137-138, 140, 149-150, 152, 158, 167, 183-184, 186, 189, 196, 223, 245, 265
    Geelong College, *see* Mr Morrison's College
    Geelong Grammar School, 214
George, Daniel [landlord at Brighton, Victoria], 199
Gem, ship, 152-154
Genesee Lands, New York State, USA, 32-33
Genesee River, USA, 32-33
Geneseo, New York State, USA, 33-34
Geneva, New York State, USA, 33
Geoffrey Hamlyn [novel] by Henry Kingsley, 99

INDEX

George III, King of Great Britain (1760-1820), 13, 21
George IV, King of Great Britain (1820-1830) *as* Prince Regent (1811-1820), 46
George V, King of Great Britain 1911-1936, *as* Duke of York and Cornwall, 226
  his wife, future Queen Mary, 226
Germany, 101, 262
Gibbons, Harriette Anne Matilda (1807-1885), 26
—, Helen Gordon nee Dana, *see* Helen Gordon Dana (1772-1855)
—, Helen Kinnaird (*c*.1805-1820), 26
—, Reverend John (1763-1858), 13, 26; Table 1
—, William Henry Kinnaird (1802-1873), 26
Gibraltar, 22
Gibton, Adelaide Letitia nee White (1841-1919) [wife of William (*fl.*1860)], 195
—, Maria ["Mysie"] (1836-1926), 210, 223, 225, 244
—, Robert Nassau (1799-1853), 210
—, Robert Nassau (1827-1891), 210
—, William (*fl.*1861) [lived in Ireland, 195
—, William Nassau ["Old Gibbie"] (1838-1928), 116, 210, 223, 225, 239
Gill, Samuel Thomas (1818–1880) [artist], 92, 94, 109
Gippsland, Victoria, 142, 217
  territory of the Port Phillip Bay District, 87-88
Glenshee station, Elmhust, Victoria, 263
Glenthompson, Victoria, 164, 185, 187, 207, 219, 259, 263
Gloucester, Church of England diocese, 266
Gloucester, Gloucestershire, 39, 180, 266
  Kingsholm Road, 180; Millers Green, 266
Gloucestershire, England, 23, 39, 41, 46-47, 49, 53, 59, 61, 75, 119, 180; Deputy Lieutenant, 49
Gnarkeet station, Victoria, 184, 265
gold, discoveries and rushes, 91-92, 97, 110-111, 129, 132, 145
  Scandinavian Rush at Back Creek, 125
goldfields, 92, 98, 102, 162
gold-mining: control, administration and licencing, 97-98, 115
  Act for the Better Management of the Goldfields (Act 18 Vict.37), 108
  Court of Mines, 105, 168
  gold mining elective courts [1855-1857], 94
  Gold Office/Goldfields Office, 95
  Gold Fields' Commission of Enquiry 1855, 106-107
  Gold Fields Royal Commission of Enquiry 1862-1863, 117
  Mining Board, 191
  see also miner's licences *and* miner's rights *and* Commissioner *and* Warden
Golden Gully field at Forest Creek, Victoria, 106
Golden Point field at Forest Creek, Victoria, 108-110
  Quartz Hill, 108-109

Goldsborough and Company, wool-brokers, 157-158
Goodrich, Mr [family friend at Beaufort], 225, 228-231, 234
Gordon family, Earls of Aboyne, 9
—, Helen (1689-1731) [mother of Charles, Lord Kinnaird], 9, 26
Gordon [doctor at Ararat], 171
Gorrin station at Dobie, Victoria, 230
Goulburn River, Victoria, 184
Gowangardie station, Victoria, 184
Grange, South Australia, 73, 246
Grant, Victoria, 157-158
Grattan, Humphrey, 184, 207; Table 3 *at* 204
  his wife Sophia Montgomery nee Beggs, 183-184, 207; Table 3 *at* 204
Gray's Inn, London, 64
Great Britain, ship, 114, 175
Greene, John, Bishop of Lincoln, 7
Greenwood, Mary Anne (1830-1901) [wife of Charles George Wood], 30
Gretna Green, Scotland, 5, 54, 132
Greyhound, ship, 185
greyhounds [dogs], 178, 187
Grosvenor, Countess, 20
Grosvenor Hotel, London, 224
Grueber family, 36
—, Reverend Arthur (1716-1788), 36
—, Daniel [father of Nicholas], 36
—, Nicholas [father of Arthur], 36
Gundagai, NSW, 188
Guyana/British Guiana, 19
Gwalior, India, 56

Haileybury, Hertfordshire, 31; East India College, 30-31
Hale, Amy Charlotte ["Tot" or "Totty"] (1870-1939), 194-195
—, Arthur Mitchell (1880-1961), 195, 224-225, 236
—, Philip Chauncy (1876-1962), 195
—, Samuel Aubrey (1847-1922), 195
—, Theresa ["Tise"] Snell nee Chauncy (1849-1886) [wife of Samuel Aubrey], 195 *and see* Chauncy, Theresa Snell
Ham, Thomas (1821-1870) [lithographer], 76
Hambrook [lawyer at the Gold Field's Commission of Enquiry 1855], 107
Hambrough, Oscar William Holden (1825-1900), *see* Holden Hambrough, Oscar William
Hamilton, Victoria, 98, 149, 187
Hamilton, Catherine [daughter of Gustavus Hamilton, Viscount Boyne, and mother of Clamina Lyons Beggs nee Montgomery], 183
—, Gustavus, fourth Viscount Boyne, 183
Hampshire, England, 20
Harefield House, Middlesex, 74-76, 102, 173-174
Harley, Shropshire, 9, 13, 24, 26; Rector, 9, 13-14, 26

INDEX

Harris, Heloise Eliza (c.1807-1874) [second wife of George Kinnaird Dana, later married to Russell Hipkins], 24-25, 48; Table 1
Hartford, Treaty 1786, 32
Harvard College/University, 2, 3, 7
Hastings, Edmund Trowbridge (1781-1861), 30
—, John (1754-1839), 2, 30
    his wife, *see* Lydia Dana
—, John Walter (1819-1883), 30-31, 35, 51, 53
[Le] Havre, France, 63, 67
Hawthorn, Melbourne, Victoria, 159-161, 177, 219
health and sanitation, 125 *and see individual diseases*
Heathcote [originally named McIvor], Victoria, 98, 105, 122-123, 191
heatwave, 221
Heidelberg, Germany, 101
Henderson, Reverend J D, 29
Henry VII, King of England (*reg.* 1485-1509), 11
Henry VIII, King of England (*reg.* 1509-1547), 29
Hereford, Church of England diocese, 9, 27
Herefordshire, 41
Hindes, Emily (1795-1870), 55, 57
—, Emily Crespigny (1813-1891) [wife of George Wymer], 55-57
Hipkins, Heloise, 25 *and see* Heloise Eliza Harris
—, Russell, 25
Hobson's Bay, *see* Port Melbourne
Hobart, Van Diemen's Land/Tasmania, 70, 139, 240, 255-256
Hoche, Lazare [French general], 27
Hodgson [member of the Gold Field's Commission of Enquiry 1855], 106
Holden Hambrough, Oscar William (1825-1900), 226
Homan, Reverend, Canon of Christ Church, Ararat, 183
Hood, Thomas (1799-1845) [poet], 209
Hooker, Sophy, 228, 241
Hopetoun, John Adrian Louis Hope, seventh Earl and first Marquess of Linlithgow, first Governor-General of Australia, 217
    Lady Hopetoun, 233
Horne [gentleman of Talbot], 130
horse accidents, 146, 148, 157, 159
Hoskins, H H [lawyer in Talbot], 130-131, 144; Mayor of Talbot, 131
Hotham, Sir Charles, Governor of Victoria, 110, 140
Hotham, suburb of Melbourne [now North Melbourne], 140
House of Commons, 257; elections, 8, 55
    Select Committee on Divorce Bills, 61
    see also Parliament, British
House of Lords, 3; Lord Chancellor, 60-61, 64
    in divorce cases, 59-64, 67
    see also Parliament, British
housing in the goldfields, 113
Houston, Texas, USA, 103

Hovenden, Mrs Everina, 29
—, Sophia, 29
—, Reverend Walter, 29
Howitt, Alfred William [magistrate], 142-143
Hudson River, USA, 32
Hughes family of Beaufort, 223, 231, 236, 240
—, Edward Walter (1854-1922), 223, 227, 229, 232, 239
—, Jeannie nee Hawkins (1862-1941) [wife of Edward Walter], 223, 237, 246-247
—, Victoria Beatrix ["Trixey/Trixie"] (1854-1943) [first wife of Constantine Trent CdeC], 223, 227, 229-230, 232-233, 236-237, 239, 244, 246, 260, 265; Table 5
Huguenots, 36, 54, 77, 259
Huntly, Victoria, 161
Hutton, General Sir Edward, 227

Ilminster, Somerset, 56; Dillington House, 56
immigration to Australia, 67-68, 70, 80-81, 84, 90
Inchture, Scotland, barony, *see* Kinnaird
India, 6, 8, 15-18, 20-21, 28-31, 40, 55-56, 154, 156, 180, 203, 237, 261-262
    Governor-General, 61, 99
    Indian Civil Service, 31, 237
    Indian Mutiny 1857-1858, 117
    see also East India Company *and* Bengal *and place-names*
Indians, American, 32
influenza, 219
Inglewood, Victoria, 157
insolvency, 25, 27, 48-53, 59, 79, 90
    procedures in England, 48
        Bankrupts (England) Act 1825, 48
        imprisonment for debt, 25, 48
        Insolvent Debtors [England] Act 1813, 48
        Court of Relief of Insolvent Debtors, 25, 48, 50
    see also banking/financial crisis in Victoria 1890s
Institute of Medical and Veterinary Science, Adelaide, 260
Ipswich, Suffolk, 55-56
Iran/Persia, 262
Iraq, 262
Ireland/Irish, 18, 21-23, 25, 27, 36-37, 39, 81, 135, 183-185, 188, 203, 210, 249, 265
    Famine 1845-1849, 183; *see also* Fenians
Ironmaster, 49
Iroquois tribes [America], 32-33
Isabella Watson [ship], 95
Isle of Wight, England, 56, 62, 64-66
Italy, 1, 57, 244, 261

James, Amelia Charlotte (1815-1893) [sister of John James Junior and wife of John Stanley], 47
—, Anne [nee Lloyd?] (1781-1863) [wife of John James Senior], 39, 47

INDEX

James [continued]
—, Arabella Veronica nee Dighton (1826-1923) [second wife of John James Junior], 66-67
—, Charles [brother of John James Junior] (1817-1851), 47, 64
—, Charlotte Constance (1840-1935), 45, 53, 63, 66-67, 76, 251-252; Table 4
—, Edward Lloyd [brother of John James Junior] (1811-1875), 47, 64
—, Frances (1819-1886), 47
—, John Junior (1808-1855), 39-40, 45, 53, 58-59, 61, 64-68, 71, 85, 113, 174, 251-252; Table 1, Table 4
—, John Senior (1781-1849), 39, 45, 47
—, John Henry (1841-1842), 45, 53, 251-252; Table 4
—, Mary Phoebe [sister of John James Junior and wife of Henry Sydney Wasbrough] (1813-1899), 47
—, Vera Maria (1853-1942), 66-67
James v James [law case], 59-67 *and see* divorce
John James and Son, Attorneys and Solicitors, 47
Johns, Reynall Everleigh [friend of the Crespigny family at Amherst], 129; *Diary*, 129
Johnstone family of Westerhall, Dumfries, Scotland, 3, 6, 9, 18, 39; arms, 3; baronetcy, 6, 13
—, Barbara [wife of Charles, Lord Kinnaird], *see* Kinnaird, Barbara nee Johnstone
—, Elizabeth, (1728-1813), 9
—, Sir James (1697-1772), third baronet, 3, 5
—, Sir James (1726-1794), fourth baronet, 3, 5, 14
—, John (1734-1795), 6-7
—, Sir William (1729-1805) fifth baronet, 6 *and see* William Johnstone Pulteney
Johnstone, Reverend Joseph Butler [at Beaufort, Victoria], 225, 227, 241
his wife, May Dora Wickham, 225, 227
Joint Stock Companies Act 1844, 53
Jones, C G [solicitor of London], 64-65, 67, 71
Jones, Mary [servant], 46
Jones, Reverend Richard, 21, 26
Justice of the Peace [in England], 55
Justice of the Peace [in Victoria], 129, 143, 167, 169-170, 178, 183, 187, 191

"Kathleen Mavourneen," song, 141
Keane, Sir John (1757-1829), 54
his wife, *see* Dorothy Scott
Keating, Archdeacon at the British Embassy in Paris, 67
Kemmis, Charlotte Humphreys, first wife of Philip Lamothe Snell Chauncy *q.v*, 122
Kendal, Westmorland, 1
Kensal Green, London, 24; All Souls Cemetery, 24
Kennedy, Jessie Robina (d.1880) [wife of Henrie Bell *q.v.*], 154
—, Margaret [mother of Jessie Robina], 154
Kent, England, 30
Kerang, Victoria, 101-102, 105

Kettering, Northamptonshire, 7, 21, 239
Kilmore, Victoria, 98, 123
King's Norton, Worcestershire, 49
King's Proctor, 223
Kingsley, Henry, *Geoffrey Hamlyn* [novel], 99
Kinnaird family, barons of Inchture, 3-6, 9, 39, 161, 183; arms, 3
—, Barbara nee Johnstone (1723-1865) [wife of Charles (1723-1865) below], 3-5, 9
—, Charles (1723-1767), sixth Baron Kinnaird of Inchture, 3-5, 7, 10, 22, 26
his mother, *see* Helen Gordon
his chaplain [Edmund Dana], 7
—, George (1691-1734), 21
—, George (1754–1805), seventh Baron Kinnaird of Inchture, 6
—, Helen (1749-1795) [wife of Edmund Dana], 3-5, 9-11, 14, 45; Table 1
Kipling, Rudyard, 17, 56
Kirby, Edmund Wilmer [solicitor of Bendigo], 196
—, Luisa Mary nee Turner, wife of Edmund Wilmer, 196
Kiribati [Pacific island], 152
Kirkpatrick, William Agar Arbuthnot, 231
his wife, *see* Constance nee Chauncy

La Trobe [*also as* Latrobe], Charles Joseph (1801-1875), [Superintendent of the Port Phillip District, then Lieutenant-Governor of Victoria], 74, 81, 84, 86-88, 90, 92-95, 97, 127
Labor Party, Australia, 237, 256-257
Lake District, Westmorland, 1
Lake Seneca, USA, 33
Lambe, Robert, Bishop of Peterborough, 6
Lamplough, Victoria, 133, 135
Lancashire, England, 1, 43
Langhorne, Reverend George, 83-84
Launceston, Van Diemen's Land/Tasmania, 79-80, 83, 98, 100, 149, 244
Customs Office, 80
Law Department, Victoria, 143 *and see* Minister of Justice *and* Crown Law Office
Learmonth, Victoria, 158, 167
Leckingham, Gloucestershire, 160, 169-170
Legislative Assembly *and* Legislative Council, *see* Parliament, Victorian
Lewin, Henry Ross [planter in the New Hebrides], 153
Lewis family, 229, 243
—, Effie [Euphemia?], 229, 244, 246
—, Henry, 229
—, Philip, 242
Leyton, Essex, 20
Lilli Pilli, New South Wales, 73, 246
Limerick, Ireland, 27, 36
Limited Liability Act 1855, 53
Lincoln, diocese, 7; Bishop, 7
Lincoln's Inn, London, 58
Lismore, Victoria, 184

INDEX

Little [sheep-owner in the Wimmera], 156
    Sterling v Little [law case], 167-168
Little Haywood, Staffordshire, 14-15; Bishton Hall, 14
Little Wenlock, Shropshire, 24; Curate, 24
Liverpool, Lancashire, 185
    Walker Art Gallery, 239
Livingstone County, New York State, USA, 27
Llangasty Talyllyn, Breconshire, 55
    Talyllyn House, 58
lockjaw [tetanus], 155
Lodden gold district, Victoria, 103
London, England, 4, 13, 17, 26, 54-60, 62, 64-67, 75, 95, 98, 106, 113, 118, 141, 154, 175, 179-180, 184, 260, 262, 264 *and see suburbs*
    Chandos Club, 103
    London Oriental Institute, 30-31
Londonderry/Derry, Ireland, 27
Lonsdale, William (1799-1864), Superintendent of the Port Phillip District, 74, 82-83
Lord Chancellor, 60-61, 64
Lorne, Victoria, 207
Loup/Loup Loup/Loo: nickname of Philip CdeC (1850-1827) *q.v.*, 113, 126
Louis Philippe, King of the French 1830-1848, 27, 68
Louis XIV, King of France 1643-1715, 78
Lovegrove, Jane (1822-1880), 101
—, William Augustus Decrespigny (1842-1918), 101
Lower Murray territory of the Port Phillip Bay District>Victoria, 87
Lucas, Miss [servant/companion at Eurambeen East; same as below?], 222
—, Miss [servant/companion at Eurambeen East; same as above?], 222, 237-239, 243-244
lunacy/dementia, 75-76, 101, 249
    Commission of Lunacy [England], 75
    lunatic asylums [Victoria]:
      at Yarra Bend, Melbourne, 138
      at Ararat, 168-169
Lurline opera, 140-141
Lymington, Hampshire, 264
Lyons family of Ireland, 183 *and see* Montgomery *and* Beggs families
—, Catherine nee Hamilton, *see* Catherine Hamilton
Lyons, Mathias [accused of assault at St Kilda], 178-179, 196, 201; his wife, 178-179

M'Alpine [tinsmith, deceased], 170
McCullough, James [officer in the Crown Law Office, Victoria], 159
McGregor, Kate [housemaid at Eurambeen East], 224, 239
McEacharn, Sir Malcolm Donald (1852-1910), 246
    Lady McEachern, *see* Mary Anne Watson
MacFarlane, Jean, 217
—, William Duncan, 217
McIvor/McIvoe[?], Helen Reid, 15, 43

McIvor [now Heathcote], Victoria, 98, 105, 122-123, 125; Surveyor, 122
    Gold Commissioner, 123; his Camp, 123
Macedon, Victoria, 217; Mount Macedon, 115
Madagascar, 224
Madden, Patrick [servant], 89
    Madden v Dana [law case], 88-89
magistrate in England, 10, 49
magistrate in Ireland, 93
magistrate in Massachusetts, USA, 2
magistrate in Victoria [*includes* Police Magistrate *and* Stipendiary Magistrate], 87, 90, 97, 102, 111, 115-116, 118, 121, 128-132, 138, 145-151, 155-160, 164, 167, 170, 174, 178, 180, 187, 200-201, 249, 254, 257; *see also by territory*
    licensing magistrate, 158
Majorca, Victoria, 119
Malahide, Ireland, 127, 183-184
    The Grange, 171
Malaya, 144
Maldon, Essex, 239
Maldon, Victoria, 105, 112
Malta, 22
Malvern Hills, Worcestershire, 119
Manchester, England, 1, 33
Manners [member of Ararat-Beaufort Land Board], 178
Manners-Sutton, Sir John Henry Thomas, Viscount Canterbury, Governor of Victoria, 166
Mansfield shire, Victoria, 167
Manton, Gildon [also miswritten as Gideon], 89
    his wife Julia Ann nee Walsh, 89
Maratha War, Third (1817-1818), 18
marriage legislation: in England, 4-5
    in Scotland, 4-5 *and see* divorce
Marnock [Irish saint], 189 *and see* St Marnock's
Martel, Adele Mabelle Berthe ["Dell"] (1913-1900) [second wife of Francis George Travers CdeC], 261; Table 5
Maryborough, Victoria, 99, 101-102, 110-112, 120, 126-127, 129, 131, 134, 139, 142, 159, 164
    Court of General Sessions, 131
    Warden of the Goldfields, 254
Maryland, USA, 33
Marylebone, London, 24
Massachusetts colony *later* Commonwealth/state in the United States, 1, 5-6, 13, 15, 32-33, 38-39, 50
    Supreme Court, 2; Chief Justice, 2
    Massachusetts Bay Colony, 32
    General Court, 2
Meadows, William [sheep drover], 187
Medic, ship, 244
Mediterranean Sea, 23, 57
Meehan, Catherine Sophia, 184 *and see* Beggs, Catherine Sophia nee Meehan
—, Jane, 184
Melbourne, ship, 175

INDEX

Melbourne, Victoria, 24, 74, 82-84, 88, 90, 92-94, 96, 98, 100, 106, 114, 121-124, 126-128, 136, 138, 149-150, 152, 154-155, 159-163, 167, 170, 172, 177, 179, 181, 184, 186, 189, 191-192, 194-195, 200-201, 207, 211-212, 218-221, 228, 230-231, 233, 237-238, 241, 244, 246, 248-249, 253, 255-256, 261, 264, 266
    Mayor/Lord Mayor, 247; Mayor's Ball, 167; Magistrate, 97, 149
    Collins Street, 94, 224, 253; Elizabeth Street, 94; Flagstaff Gardens, 93; Swanston Street, 94; William Street, 93-94
    see also churches *and* Port Melbourne *and* South Melbourne *and suburbs by name*
Melbourne Club, 94, 97
Melbourne Cup, 191
Melbourne Hospital, 230-231, 259, 261
Melbourne University, 227-229, 246, 259, 261, 266; Trinity College, 228, 245, 259
Melbourne and Hobson's Bay United Railway Company, 199; Brighton line, 199; South Yarra station, 199
Mercer [doctor at Ararat], 171
Metcalfe, ship, 17
Middle Creek, Victoria, 223, 228
Middlesex, 65-67, 102, 161
Minchin family of Beaufort, Victoria, and Adelaide, South Australia, 228
—, Corker Wright, 223, 227
    his wife Edith Christina Elizabeth ["Edie"], 223-224, 227, 229, 236-238
—, Ruth, 228
miners' licences, 92, 97, 103, 105, 110, 129
miners' rights, 94
Minister of Justice, Victoria, 142-143, 172 *and see* Law Department *and* Crown Law Office
Mitchell, Susan Augusta, second wife of Philip Lamothe Snell Chauncy *q.v*, 191
—, Reverend William (1803-1870), 191
Moglonemby station, Victoria, 185
Monckton, Frederick Odell [embezzler at Talbot], 130-131, 140
Montgomery family of Ireland, 170 *and see* Lyons *and* Beggs families
—, Clamina Lyons (1787-1821) [wife of Francis Beggs (1770-1839)], 183
"Montrose" house at Brighton, 239 *and see* Stewart family
Morgan *v* Holford [law case], 161
Mornington Peninsula, Victoria, 94, 244
Morrison, Reverend George (1830-1898), 100
    Mr Morrison's College [later Geelong College], 100, 149
Mount Alexander, 103-104, 105, 107, 121
Mount Cole, Victoria, 208, 212, 214-215, 225
Mount Cole station, Victoria [later renamed Eurambeen *q.v.*], 184, 266
Moyston, Victoria, 167

Muckleford, Victoria, land transactions by Philip Robert ChC, 112, 144, 147
Murray River, 101, 186-187, 195
"My Dear Old Wife and I," song, 144

"Nancy Lee," song, 194-195
Nangeela, sheep run, 80
Nantes, France: Edict and its Revocation, 54, 259
Napoleon Bonaparte, Emperor of the French, and wars, 18-19, 22-23, 36, 55-57, 75, 89, 100, 249
Narre Warren/Nerre Nerre Warren], Victoria, 84-85
National Anthem, 133, 144
Native Police Corps, Queensland, 88
Native Police Corps, Victoria, 74, 81-90, 91-95, 97, 99
    commander/Commandant, 74, 81-84, 89-90, 99
    officers, 74, 81. 86, 89-90, 92, 94
    non-commissioned officers, 86-87, 89-90, 92
    troopers, 82-90, 92, 94-95; uniforms, 86-87
    black trackers, 76-77
    see also police
Naylor [officer of the Castlemaine Gold Office 1855], 107
Neatishead, Norfolk, 100-101, 103
Neemuch, India, 56
Neilson [missionary in the New Hebrides], 155
Nelson, HMVS [*Her Majesty's Victorian Ship*], 149-150, 177
Nenagh, Tipperary, Ireland, 22, 25, 36; Vicar, 36
Netherlands, 54
    Netherlands/Dutch East India Company, 69
New Caledonia, 152; Nouméa, 152
New Hebrides [present-day Vanuatu], 151-155, 166, 191
    Vate/Éfaté island [*also as* Sandwich], 151
    Tanna/Tana island, 151-155
    Port Resolution, 151, 154-155
New South Wales, British colony and later Australian state, 74, 79, 90-91, 97, 105, 186-189, 194-195, 246, 248, 265
    Colonial government, 97
    Governors: Arthur Phillip, 82; Sir Richard Bourke, 72
    railway system, 186-188, 195
New York State, USA, 25, 32
New Zealand, 263 *and see* ANZAC
Newcastle-upon-Tyne, Northumberland, 95
Newnham on Severn, Gloucestershire, 39, 41, 45-47, 59, 61-62, 66-67; Back Lane, 38
Newport, John [nominal patron of a living], 9
Newry, Ireland, 27
Newark, Nottinghamshire, 245
newspapers, Australian:
    Advocate [Melbourne], 123, 149
    Age [Melbourne], 110, 125, 130-131, 138-139, 152-153, 159, 163, 179, 225, 248, 255-256
    Ararat Advertiser, 154

INDEX

newspapers, Australian [continued]
- *Ararat and Pleasant Creek Advertiser*, 161, 167, 169, 171
- *Argus* [Melbourne], 24, 92-95, 98, 109, 115, 125, 128, 131, 136, 138, 140, 151-153, 155, 161, 166, 168, 170-171, 173, 175, 178-179, 182, 188, 194, 196, 199, 211, 216, 219, 225, 230, 243, 246, 249, 251, 253, 255, 266
- *Australasian* [Melbourne], 95, 99, 173, 183, 246, 249
- *Avoca Mail*, 144
- *Ballarat Courier*, 158, 160, 167, 193
- *Ballarat Star*, 102, 131, 136, 138-139, 142, 145, 147, 152-153, 158, 161, 167-170, 187, 189, 191, 193, 249
- *Beaufort Chronicle*, 161, 167
- *Bell's Life in Victoria and Sporting Chronicle*, 150
- *Bendigo Advertiser*, 115, 161
- *Bendigo Independent*, 224
- *Brunswick and Coburg Leader*, 255
- *Camperdown Chronicle*, 193, 211
- *Cornwall Chronicle* [Launceston], 89, 95
- *Courier* [Brisbane], 241
- *Creswick and Clunes Advertiser*, 158
- *Daily Mail* [Brisbane], 255-256
- *Daily News* [Perth], 256
- *Dunolly Express*, 137
- *Euroa Advertiser*, 207
- *Evening News* [Sydney], 153, 186
- *Express* [Wagga Wagga, NSW], 194
- *Geelong Advertiser*, 99, 125, 152, 154, 167
- *Gippsland Times*, 142-143, 157
- *Hamilton Spectator*, 187
- *Herald* [Melbourne], 167, 224, 256
- *Hobart Courier*, 82
- *Illustrated Australian News for Home Readers*, 134
- *Launceston Advertiser*, 79
- *Launceston Courier*, 244
- *Leader* [Melbourne], 138, 153, 225
- *Maryborough and Dunolly Advertiser*, 115, 131, 138-139
- *Melbourne Daily News*, 74, 93, 95, 184
- *Mercury* [Hobart], 153
- *Mount Alexander Mail*, 107, 109-110, 138-139, 161
- *Mount Ararat Advertiser*, 167
- *New South Wales Government Gazette*, 186
- *North-Western Chronicle*, 127-128, 135
- *Ovens and Murray Advertiser*, 161
- *Ovens Spectator*, 161
- *Pastoral Review*, 176
- *Port Phillip Gazette*, 81, 93, 82
- *Port Phillip Gazette and Settler's Journal*, 90
- *Port Phillip Herald*, 89
- *Port Phillip Patriot and Melbourne Advertiser*, 89-90
- *Portland Guardian*, 207

newspapers, Australian [continued]
- *Portland Guardian and Normanby General Advertiser*, 115
- *Punch* [Melbourne], 138, 189, 194, 256, 265
- *Post* [Hobart], 255
- *Queenscliff Sentinel, Drysdale, Portarlington and Sorrento Advertiser*, 207
- *Sydney Morning Herald*, 179
- *Table Talk* [Melbourne], 186, 207, 263
- *Talbot Leader*, 99, 127, 129-131, 133-134, 136-137, 139-144, 146, 157-160, 163
- *Talbot Leader and North-Western Chronicle*, 127, 129-130, 135
- *Telegraph, St Kilda, Prahran and South Yarra Guardian*, 179
- *Tumut and Adelong Times* [New South Wales], 139
- *Victoria Government Gazette*, 101, 111, 134, 143, 168, 172
- *Victoria Police Gazette*, 161
- *Wagga Wagga Advertiser*, 194
- *Wagga Wagga Advertiser and Riverine Reporter*, 186, 194
- *Wallaroo Times and Mining Journal* [South Australia], 161
- *Weekly Times* [Melbourne], 152, 167, 201
- *Worker* [Brisbane], 255, 257

newspapers, British:
- *Bath Chronicle and Weekly Gazette*, 14, 25, 28
- *Belfast News-Letter*, 27
- *Berrow's Worcester Journal*, 67
- *Bristol Times and Mirror*, 67
- *Cheltenham Examiner*, 75
- *Dublin Evening Post*, 27
- *Folkestone Express, Sandgate, Shorncliffe & Hythe Advertiser*, 58
- *Gentleman's Magazine*, 28, 56
- *Gloucester Citizen*, 67, 266
- *Hampshire Telegraph and Sussex Chronicle*, 67
- *Hereford Times*, 59
- *Hull Packet and East Riding Times*, 59
- *Illustrated London News*, 52, 56
- *London Daily News*, 59
- *London Gazette*, 18-19, 21-23, 25, 27, 35, 48, 50, 53, 55, 58, 175, 264
- *London Standard*, 67
- *Morning Chronicle*, 26
- *Morning Post*, 20, 56, 53
- *Public Register and Daily Advertiser*, 31-32, 35
- *Punch*, 118
- *Reading Mercury*, 25
- *Silurian, Cardiff, Merthyr, and Brecon Mercury, and South Wales General Advertiser*, 161
- *The Era*, 62
- *The Times* [London], 61-64
- *Wolverhampton Chronicle and Staffordshire Advertiser*, 31

newspapers, Indian:
- *Calcutta Gazette*, 17
- *Madras Courier*, 17

INDEX

newspapers, United States:
    Columbian Centinel, 15
    Dansville Advertiser, 34
Nicholls, Emma [servant], 46-47
Nicholls, Mary [servant], 47
Nile, battle (1798), 22
Norfolk, England, 55-56, 89, 91
    Lord Lieutenant of the county, 18
Norfolk, ship, 98
Norman, William, 186-187
Normandy, France, 57, 68
    Champions to the Dukes, 257
Northamptonshire, England, 89, 91, 226
North-West Frontier, India, 262
Norwich, Norfolk, 101
Norwich, Church of England diocese, 100, 103
Notting Hill, London, 24

Oatley, Arabella Forester, 23-24; [as Isabella], 24
—, Reverend George Edmund (1796-1831), 24
    his wife, *see* Helen Kinnaird Dana
—, Mary (*fl*.1899), 24
—, Thomas (1767-1834), 13-15; Table 1
    his wife, *see* Elizabeth Caroline Dana
Odd Fellows, Independent Order [IOOF], 115
    Hall at Talbot, 129
Omeo, Victoria, 142, 157-158
O'[?]: full surname unreadable], Ellen, 196?, 207, 213
Opie, John RA (1761-1807), miniature of Pulteney Johnstone Poole Sherburne mis-attributed to, 232
Orr family of Ballarat, 194-195
O'Shanassy [member of the Gold Field's Commission of Enquiry 1855], 106
"Ottawa" house at Gladstone Parade, Elsternwick, Victoria, *q.v.*, 212, 219, 222, 233-234, 241
Otter, Lieutenant-Colonel, 244; his wife, 244
Otway Ranges, Victoria, 246; Cape Otway, Victoria, 88
Owen, D S [successful candidate for Victorian Parliament], 237
Oxford University, 24, 26, 33, 58, 67
    Christ Church, 9; Trinity College, 33
Oxfordshire, England, 101

Pacific Ocean, 152 *and see* South Pacific
Paimpol, France, 72
Pakington, Sir John, former Secretary of State for War and the Colonies, 84, 95
Palestine, 197, 254-257
paralysis [stroke?] of Philip Robert Champion Crespigny, 171-172, 200
Paris, France, 27, 53, 57, 63, 67, 100
    Prefecture of police, 69
    British Embassy, 67-68, 71
Parliament, British: Member, 8, 23, 54-55, 106, 117, 223
    see also House of Commons *and* House of Lords

Parliament, British [continued]
    private Act of Parliament, 60-61, 66-68 *and see* divorce
Parliament of Ireland, 54; Member, 54
Parliament of the Commonwealth of Australia, 228;
    elections, 240-241, 248
    Grampians Division, 222, 248
Parliament, Victorian, 98, 125, 128-129, 221;
    elections, 128, 237, 240
    members, 130, 170-171
    Legislative Council, 90, 128, 171
    Legislative Assembly, 128, 170-171
    Minister of Justice, 142-143, 172
    and see Law Department *and* Crown Law Office
Payne [servant], 107
pelvic cellulitis, 198
Peninsula War in Spain (1807-1814), 54, 249
Penlaye, Reverend John, 68, 70
Pentridge Gaol, Melbourne, 92
Pepys, Charles, Baron Cottenham, 61
Perseus [mythical hero], 1
Persia [Iran], 262
Perth, Western Australia, 256
Peterborough, Church of England diocese, 6-7
    Bishop, 6-7
Peterborough, Victoria, 263
Philadelphia, Pennsylvania, USA, 5
    Philadelphia Museum of Art, 239
Phipps family of the West Indies, 56-57
—, Constantine, 57
—, Elizabeth (1774-1836) [first married to John Trent, later to Arthur Branthwayte], 56-57
—, Penelope, 57
Phoenix, ship, 20
phlebitis/thrombophlebitis, 249
Pietermaritzburg, Natal, South Africa, 262
Pipewell Hall, Northamptonshire, 226
Pirton, Oxfordshire, 101, Vicar, 101
Pitfield, Victoria, 266
Pleasant Creek, Victoria, *see* Stawell
Pleurtuit, France, 70-71
Plunkett, Frances (1835-1908) [third wife of Charles John ChC], 75, 117, 174
    her second husband, *see* John Russell Reynolds
Plymouth, Devon, 76, 84, 184; Earl of Plymouth, *see* Windsor
Point Henry, Victoria, 96
Point Nepean, Victoria, 95
police in England, 49
police in Victoria, 82, 84, 86-87, 90, 129
    Superintendent, 97-99, 149
    Captain, 88
    Inspector, 98-99, 150
    Sergeant, 129
    senior constable, 129; constable, 129
    detective, 142
    police office, 95
    gold escorts/gold police, 94, 96-97

police in Victoria [continued]
    Mounted Police/Mounted Patrol, 90, 94, 129
        Commandant of the Mounted Patrol, 90, 94
    see also Native Police Corps
Police Magistrate, Victoria, *see* magistrate
Police Magistrate and Superintendent of the Port Philip District, 74
Poole, George Herbert (1806-1869), 111
—, Theresa Susannah Snell nee Chauncy [wife of George Herbert], *see also* Theresa Susannah Snell Chauncy
Port Adelaide, South Australia, 184
Port Fairy, Victoria, 82
Port Melbourne [Hobson's Bay], Victoria, 149, 152, 175, 179, 185
Port Phillip Bay, 95, 244
Port Phillip District, Australia, 74, 81-83, 86-87. *and see* Victoria
    Superintendent [Police Magistrate and Superintendent], 74, 81-82, 84, 86, 88, 90
Port Phillip Patriot Almanac and Directory, 90 *and see* newspapers
Port Resolution, New Hebrides, 151, 154-155
Port-St-Marnock, Ireland, 189
Port Wallaroo, South Australia, 161
Portland, Victoria, 82
Portland Bay, Victoria, 74, 80-81
    Territory of the Port Phillip Bay District, 87
    District of Victoria, 98, 149 *and see* Western District
Portsmouth, England, 17
Powlett, Frederick Armand (1811-1865), 88, 97
Prague, Bohemia [now the Czech Republic], 98
Prahran, Victoria, 178
Preemption Line, USA, 25
Presbyterianism, 29
Presland, Thomas Plowden, 26; his wife, *see* Harriette Anne Matilda Dana
Prime Minister of Great Britain, 61
Prince Regent, 54 *and see* George IV, King of Great Britain
Privy Council, 61
Protector of Aborigines, 81, 84, 90
Proctor/Protector of Chinese, 121
puerperal fever, 125
Pulteney family, 9, 183 *and see below*
—, Daniel, (*c.*1684-1731), 6
—, Frances (d.1782) [first wife of William Johnstone/Pulteney *as below*], 6, 9, 14
—, Harry (1686-1767), 6, 21
—, Henrietta Laura Johnstone (1766-1808), Countess of Bath, 14, 17, 27, 31. 35, 38
—, Margaret nee Stirling) [second wife of William Johnstone/Pulteney *as below*], 14
—, William (1684-1764), Earl of Bath, 6, 14, 21
—, William, (1731-1763), 6

Pulteney [continued]
—, William Johnstone [*later* Sir William Johnstone] (1729-1805), 6-11, 13-14, 16, 26-27, 31, 33, 35, 38-39, 51-52; portrait, 5
    his first wife, *see* Frances *above*
    his second wife, *see* Margaret Stirling *and above*
Pulteney Estates, New York, USA, 32-33
Punjab, India, 238
Purcell, Reverend John, 9
Quebec, Canada, 93
Queenscliff, Victoria, 196-198, 207, 232, 257
Queensland, British colony and later Australian state, 88, 155, 181, 194, 210, 228, 255, 257
Quick, Balcombe ["Balcombe 2", *cf.* Robert Balcombe Beggs], 245

R [full surname unknown], Anna, 219-220, 223, 245
rabbits, 217
Radcliffe [physician at Amherst], 133
Rae, Mr and Mrs, *alias* for Philip Robert Champion Crespigny and Charlotte Frances James nee Dana *qq.v.*, 64, 67
Raikes, Stanley Napier (1824-1891), 66
—, William Alves (1845-1920), 66
railway, in England, 10; railway clerk, 38, 51
—, New South Wales system, 186-188, 195
—, Victorian system, 186-187; Ararat region, 168, 170-171, 220, 223, 246; Melbourne-Adelaide, 220; Melbourne and Hobson's Bay United Railway Company [Brighton line], 199
Rance River in Brittany, 70
Ranelagh Gardens, Chelsea, England, 13
rape case, 130
Reading, Berkshire, 25
Receiver of the Droits of the Admiralty, 54, 60
Receiver and Paymaster, Victoria, 129, 142
Reward, ship, 88
Reynolds, Bertha Mitford, 51
Reynolds, John Russell (1828-1896), 75
Ricardo, Amy Edith (1880-1940) [wife of Robert Gottlieb Beggs], 244; Table 3 at 204
—, Percy Ralph (1855-1907), 244
Richard family of Normandy, 77
    Marguerite [wife of Richard Champion], 77
Richard III, King of England (*reg.* 1483-1485), 11
Richardson family, 244
—, Arthur, 230; his wife, 230
Richmond, Victoria, 90, 94
Ricketson, Edith Alice Mary nee Were (1849-1931) [wife of Henry], 208, 211, 218
—, Esther Edith (1885–1957), 208
—, Henry (1825-1900), 208, 211
Riverina district of southern New South Wales, 174
river-boats, 186

INDEX

Robertson, John G [squatter], 70
Robertson and Moffat, drapers of Melbourne, 179
Robinson, George, Protector of Aborigines, 81
Robinson, Peter, charged with theft, 121
Rochester, New York State, USA, 32
Rocky Waterholes [Kalkallo], Victoria, 123
Roman Catholicism, 29
Roman law, 51
Romney, George RA, portrait painter, 239
Ross, William Alister (d.1871) [planter in New Hebrides], 152-153, 155
Ross Hall, Shropshire, 23
Rouen, France, 65, 259
Roughton Hall at Worfield, Shropshire, 38, 40, 48-50, 53
Rowley, Dr Thomas, Headmaster of Bridgnorth Grammar School, 39
Royal Air Force, 238, 245, 247, 254, 262, 264
    Air Vice-Marshal, 262; Group Captain, 259, 262, 264; Wing Commander, 262; Squadron Leader, 254
    Royal Flying Corps, 262
    Second Lieutenant, 262
Royal Australasian College of Physicians, 259
Royal College of Physicians, 259
Royal Geographical Society, 103, 245
Russia, 2

S [surname abbreviated, possibly Staughton *q.v.*]
Saint Michael and Saint George, order of knighthood, 54
Saint Pancras, London, 25; workhouse, 25
"Saint Patrick's Day in the Morning," song, 144
Saint-Domingue [French colony, now Haiti], 22
Sadlier, John [policeman-historian], 94-95, 99
Sale, Victoria, 157
Salmon, FB, GC and EE [landholders in Amherst-Talbot], 148 *and see* Salmon Road, Amherst
Salop, *see* Shropshire
San Sebastian, Spain, 54
Sandgate, Kent, 101
Sandhurst, Royal Military College, 31, 39
Sandhurst, Victoria, *i.e.* Bendigo *q.v.*
Sarawak, 101; Rajah, Sir James Brooke, 101
Savage, Robert [sometime partner with Henry Edmund Dana], 80
Savoy/Piedmont, Italy, 1
scab disease of sheep, 167-168; Scab Act, 167
scarlatina/scarlet fever, 98, 100, 149-150
Schleswig-Holstein, Germany, 262
schools in Australia:
    Amherst Church of England school, 127, 134
    Amherst national school, 127
    Amherst Presbyterian school, 127
    Brighton Grammar School, 177, 200, 202, 213, 218, 221
    Geelong College, *see* Mr Morrison's College
    Geelong Grammar School, 214
    Haileybury College, Brighton, 263

schools in Australia [continued]
    Melbourne Church of England Grammar School, 263
    Mr Morrison's College [later Geelong College], 100, 150
    Victorian Education Act 1872, 164
schools in England, 49:
    Bridgnorth Grammar School, 39
    Cheltenham College, 116, 119
    Shrewsbury School, 28, 33
school in Ireland: The Royal School, Armagh, 36
sciatica, 129
Scot, Walter [servant of the Johnstone family], 5
Scotland, 3-5, 8, 152, 154, 167; Scots in Ireland, 36
Scott, Dorothy [fourth wife of Philip ChC (1738-1803), later married to Sir John Keane], 54-55, 239-240; her portrait, 239-240
Serjeant-at-Law, 62
Seven Years War (1756-1763), 5
Severn, River, 10, 49, 182
Shepparton, Victoria, 184-185
Sherburne family of Lancashire, arms, 43
Sherburne [*also as* Sherburn *and* Sherbourne] family of Cornwall, 15, 43
—, Frances Henrietta Laura (1803-1819), 17, Table 1
—, Joseph (c.1725-1763), 15; Table 1; *distinguish from* Joseph (1710-1799) *below*
    his wife Statira nee Fawkener, 15; Table 1
—, Joseph (1751-1805), 15-17, 20, 43; Table 1
    his wife, *see* Frances Johnstone Dana (1768-1832)
—, Pulteney Johnstone Poole (1802-1831), 17-21
    miniature, 19-20; wrongly attributed to John Opie RA, 232
Sherburne, Joseph of Boston (1710-1799), 15
    his son Joseph (1710-1799), 15
Shifnal, Shropshire, 26, 39, 48; Cosford Grange, 26
Shirley, Victoria, 211
Shrewsbury, Shropshire, 8-12, 15, 23-24, 26-28, 38-39, 41, 48-49, 53, 59
    Dogpole district, 31
    Holy Cross and St Giles district, 49-50
    Holywell Terrace district, 49-52
    Saint John's Hill district, 30, 48-49
    Saint Chad district, 29
    Abbey, 49
    Castle, 10-12, 49
    Castle Gate House, 10-11
    The Dana Terrace, 10-12, 48-49
    Gaol/Prison, 10, 12, 49
    Saint Chad's church, 23, 26
Shrewsbury School, 26, 33, 39
Shropshire, England [*also abbreviated as* Salop], 8, 10, 14-15, 21, 26-27, 30, 38-39, 41, 45, 48, 53
Sikhs, 180
Simla, India, 56
Singapore, 263
Sir Stephen Lushington, ship, 28

INDEX

Skene, Thomas, [successful Protectionist candidate for the Commonwealth parliament 1903], 248
Slut [sheepdog], 187
Smith, Elizabeth Sarah nee Durban [wife of James Kinnaird Smith], 26
—, Harriet Elizabeth [daughter of James Junior and Harriet nee Dana], 26
—, James (Junior) [husband of Harriet nee Dana (*fl.*1844)], 25-26
—, James (Senior), 25
—, James Kinnaird [son of James Junior and Harriet nee Dana], 26
Smith, Emma Margaret (1819-1848) [first wife of Charles John ChC], 67, 117
Smith, Isabella [wife of William Hamilton Walsh (1824-1853)], 93
Smith [lodging-house keeper at Shrewsbury], 48
Smith [mining surveyor at Talbot], 145
Smyth, C A [lawyer at Ararat], 170
Sobraon, ship, 179-180
Soldier Settlement program 1940s, 263
Solent strait, England, 65
Somerset, England, 21, 48, 170
Sonyea, New York State, USA, 34
Sorrento, Victoria, 244
songs:
    "Auld Lang Syne," 144
    "England, Empress of the Sea," 144
    "Kathleen Mavourneen", 141
    "My Dear Old Wife and I," 144
    "Nancy Lee," 194-195
    "Saint Patrick's Day in the Morning," 144
    "Sweet spirit, hear my prayer", 140
    "The Queens' 15", 211
South Africa, 28, 83, 262
    South African War (1899-1902), 227, 244
South Australia, British colony and later Australian state, 161, 196-197, 259 *and see by locality*
    South Australian Company, 80
South Melbourne, Victoria, 177, 199; Clarendon Street, 177, 199
South Pacific, 151-152 *and see* New Caledonia, New Hebrides, Fiji, Kiribati
South Yarra, Melbourne, 150-151, 185
Southampton, Hampshire, 63-65, 67, 84
Southsea, England, 17
Spain, 6, 46-47, 223
St Arnaud, Victoria, 237; Show, 237
Saint Pancras, London, 25
St Helena [island in the Atlantic], 180
St Kilda, Victoria, 161, 163, 167, 172-173, 178-179, 191, 196, 199-201, 228; Mayor, 178
    Lambeth Place, 163, 177; Grey Street, 172, 177; Robe Street, 172-173, 177-178, 199; Gurner Street, 177-178; South Beach [now St Kilda Beach], 178, 201
St Leonards, Sydney, NSW, 248
St Malo, France, 63-64, 67, 69-72, 103, 257; British Consulate, 69

St Marnock's [horse], 189
St Marnock's station, Victoria, 164, 184-185, 189-190, 265-266
"St Marnock's" [house at Brighton, Victoria], 189, 266
St Servan, France, 68, 70-71
Staffordshire, England, 14
    Stafford, 15
Stanion, Northamptonshire, 7; Vicar, 7
Stanley, Amelia Charlotte nee James [wife of John], 39
—, John [brother-in-law of John James Junior], 47
Stanley, [Edward George Geoffrey Smith-Stanley, Lord Stanley of Bickerstaffe, later fourteenth Earl of Derby], 61
Statesman, ship, 184
Staughton family, 244
—, Arthur John, 244
    his wife Esther Irving, 244
S[taughton?], Percy, 227
Stawell [formerly Pleasant Creek], Victoria, 164, 167, 171
Steel, Flora Annie (1847-1929), author, 238
    The Hosts of the Lord, 238
Stephenson, R, 29
Sterling *v* Little [law case], 167-168
Stewart, Prince Charles (1720-1788), the Young Pretender or "Bonnie Prince Charlie," 4-5
Stewart [Steward?] family at "Montrose" in Brighton, 236, 239
    George and Nina Blanche Steward [?], 239
Stewart, George [bank manager at Brighton; same as above?], 239
Stewart, George [General Manager of the Bank of Victoria; same as above?], 253
Stewart, James S [auctioneer at Talbot], 134
stillbirth, 45, 53, 59, 125, 243
Stipendiary Magistrate, Victoria, *see* magistrate
Stirling, Margaret [second wife of Sir William Johnstone Pulteney], 14
Stoke Doyle, Northamptonshire, 100-101, 103
Stoke-next-Guildford, Surrey, 30
Stoneleigh, Victoria, 225-226, 229, 232, 265
Stottesdon, Shropshire, 27; Vicar, 27
Strachan [member of the Gold Field's Commission of Enquiry 1855], 106
Stretch family of Colac, Victoria, 246
—, Sophia/Sophy, 246; husband and son, 246
stroke [apoplexy], 98, 102 *and see* paralysis
Strutt, William (1825–1915) [artist], 75
Sturt, Charles, 97
—, Evelyn Pitfield Shirley (1816-1885) [magistrate], 97, 100, 149-150
    Sturt Street, Ballarat, 97
Sudbury, Suffolk, 223
Suffolk, England, 55; Deputy Lieutenant, 173
Sunbeam [horse], 211, 214
Sunderland, County Durham, 95
Surveyor, Victorian government, 122 *and see by territory*

INDEX

Sutton House [The Old House] at Albrighton, Shropshire, 38, 50
Swan Hill, Victoria, 101
Swanwater station, near Donald, Victoria, 236
"Sweet spirit, hear my prayer," song, 140
Switzerland, 101
Sydney, New South Wales, 74, 81-82, 84, 90, 179, 186, 195, 233, 248, 257
    Commercial Banking Company of Sydney, 253-254
Symes [president of the Amherst Hospital Board], 133
Talbot county, Victoria, 127; shire, 127
Talbot District Lands Commission, 147
Talbot town [formerly Back Creek *q.v.*], Victoria, 99, 102, 110-113, 115-116, 121, 128-150, 149-150, 157-160, 163-164, 167, 171
    renamed from Back Creek, 126-127
    see also Amherst-Talbot *and* Amherst
    Avoca Road, 147; Crespigny Street, 147; Salmon Road, 147; Talbot Flat, 131
    Magistrate, 99, 121, 125, 142; police, 129
    Court House/ Police Court, 125, 129-130, 132, 135, 143, 158; Clerk of Petty Sessions, 130, 140
    Warden, 131; Warden's office, 116; Warden's Court, 143, 158
    Borough Hall, 142-143
    Independent Order of Odd Fellows; 127, Hall, 140-141; Theatre Royal, 127
    Talbot Brass Band, 143; Wrigley's Hotel, 145
    Anglican parish and church, 134-135
Talbot family of Ireland, 127
—, Richard, 127
—, Samuel, 127
—, William (1784-1845), 127
Tanna/Tana, New Hebrides, 151-155
    Port Resolution, 151, 154-155
    Mount Yasur, 155
Tarrangower, Mount, 105
    Tarrangower gold field, 105
tariff policies, Free Trade *v* Protectionism, 248
Tasman, Abel, 79
Tasmania [Van Diemen's Land to 1857],* 39, 79-80, 89, 95, 98, 127, 166, 217
Telford, Thomas [engineer], 10
Terang, Victoria, 244
Terrill [defendant at Talbot], 131-132
tetanus ["lockjaw"], 155
Texas, USA, 91
"The Queens' 15," song, 211
Thomas, William [Assistant Protector of Aborigines], 84
tinsmith, 157

---

* For the period before 1857 we commonly refer to the colony then known as Van Diemen's Land by its modern name Tasmania. Despite anachronism, it is more comprehensible to do so.

Tipperary, Ireland, 22, 36; High Sheriff, 36
    à la Tipperary, 132
Toker, Clarissa nee Champion Crespigny, (1775-1836) [wife of Edward], 56
—, Edward [lawyer], 56
—, Philip C [nephew of Charles Fox Crespigny], 56
Tolman, Susan/Susannah [servant], 174
Tonks, Reverend Nehemiah, 8
Toorak, Melbourne, 194, 230
toothache *etc*, 235, 244
Trawalla, Victoria, 233; Trawalla station, 230, 233
Trent family of the West Indies and Dillington House, Ilminster, Somerset, 56
—, Eliza Julia (1797-1855) [wife of Charles Fox ChC], 56 *and see* Eliza Julia Champion Crespigny
—, Francis Onslow (1797-1846), 56, 173
—, Harrison Walke John ["Harry"] (1830-1899), 226
—, John (1770-1796), 56-57
    his wife, *see* Elizabeth Phipps
—, John Constantine (1793-1846), 56
Trinity College, Dublin, 36, 184
Trinity College, Melbourne University, 228, 245
Trout River, Canada, battle 1870, 174
Trowbridge, Lydia (1711-1776) [wife of Richard Dana (1700-1772)], 2, Table 1
Truant Officer, Victoria, 178
tuberculosis [phthisis/consumption], 98, 149, 175, 196
Tumut, New South Wales, 186-188, 195
Turner, H M [of Trawalla], 233
    Mrs Turner, 233
Turner, Luisa Mary, wife of Edmund Wilmer Kirby, 196
Two Years Before the Mast, see Richard Henry Dana Junior
typhoid, 125
typhus ["ship fever"], 34

Udaipur, India, 56
United States of America [USA], 2, 18, 80, 117, 174, 184, 260 *and see individual places*
    President, 2, 13
    US Army: Captain, 2, 30; Colonel, 33
    War of 1812 against Britain, 18
    Civil War (1861-1864), 141
Uriconium [ancient Roman town], 10
Usher, Reverend Robert, 262
—, Sylvia Ethel (1901-1991) [wife of Hugh Vivian CdeC], 262; Table 5

Van Diemen, Anthony [Governor in the Netherland East Indies], 79
Van Diemen's Land [British colony; named Tasmania in 1857], 39, 79-80, 127, 217
    Colonial Secretary, 80; Colonial Treasurer, 39, 80
    see also Tasmania

Vane, William Harry, Earl of Darlington, 14
Vanuatu [present-day state], 151-152; Port Vila, 151-152
   see also New Hebrides
Ventnor, Isle of Wight, 62-63, 65-66
   Madeira Cottage, Whitwell, 62
Verdun, France, 56
Victoria, British colony and later Australian state, 74, 90 *et saepe*
   population 1851-1861, 91-92; census 1861, 128
   Governor, 110, 115-116, 126, 128, 140, 143, 166; Lieutenant-Governor, 74, 90, 93, 97, 127; Executive Council, 134, 172
   Chief Secretary, 130; Colonial Secretary, 92; Commissariat Department, 122
   Parliament, *see sub voce*
   see also Port Phillip Bay Settlement *and* Bank of Victoria
Victorian Alps, 142
Victorian Education Act 1872, 178
Victorian Native Police Corps, *see* Native Police Corps, Victoria
"Vierville" house at Black Street, Brighton, Victoria, *q.v.*, 202, 254
Violet Town, Victoria, 184-185
   Feltrim Road, 184-185
Vivian, Richard Hussey, first Baron Vivian, 54, 57, 223
von Guerard, Eugene/Eugen, 109, 162

Wade, Emilia (d.1832) [wife of Philip ChC], *see* Emilia Champion Crespigny
Wagga Wagga, New South Wales [commonly cited as Wagga], 186-188, 194
Wales, 41, 173
Walker, John (1796-1855), 122
Walker, Theresa Susannah Snell nee Chauncy, *see* Theresa Susannah Snell Chauncy
Wallace, William Vincent [composer], 141
Walsh [lawyer of Ballarat], 119
Walsh, Julia Ann [sister of William (1824-1853) and wife of Gildon Manton], 89
—, Sophia Cole Hamilton (*c.*1827-1860) [sister of William (1824-1853) and wife of Henry Edmund Pulteney Dana and then of his brother William Augustus Pulteney Dana], 89, 93, 97-98, 100, 149
—, William Hamilton (1784-1841), 93
   his wife, Mary Anne nee Bisset, 93
—, William Hamilton (1824-1853), 90, 93-94
   his wife, Isabella nee Smith, 93
Walsh, Ms W M [transcriber of family letters in the 1950s], 113, 118, 196, 222, 228-229, 232, 236, 248
Walstab, Barbara Wilhelmina, *see* Champion de Crespigny, Barbara Wilhelmina
—, George [father of Barbara], 256
Waltham, England, 20
Walton, defendant at Talbot, 120-121
Wando Vale station, Victoria, 80

Wangaratta, Victoria, 148
Warden of the Goldfields, 105-106, 108-112, 115-116, 120-121, 126, 128-129, 171-172, 254, 257 *and see* Commissioner *and* Magistrate; *see also by territory*
   Warden's Camp at Amherst, 132
   Warden's Court at Eaglehawk, 161
   Warden's Court at Talbot, 143, 158
   Warden's office at Amherst, 111, 125, 127
Ware,* Annie Elizabeth, 222-223
—, John Charles, 222-223
Warenbeen near Barwon Heads, Victoria, 245
Warfield, *see* Warfield
Warrnambool, Victoria, 176, 210, 214, 263; Woolaston/Wollaston station, 176
wars:
   American Revolutionary War, 2, 5-6, 32
   American Civil War (1861-1864), 141
   First Burma War (1824-1826), 19
   Napoleonic wars, 18-19, 22-23, 36, 55-57, 75, 89, 100
      Peninsula War in Spain (1807-1814), 54, 249
   Seven Years War (1756-1763), 5
   South African War (1899-1902), 227, 244
   Third Maratha War (1817-1818), 18
   War of 1812 [Britain against the United States], 18
   World War, First (1914-1918), 75, 244, 254, 257, 260-262, 267
   World War, Second (1939-1945), 260, 263
Wasbrough, Henry Sydney [brother-in-law of John James Junior], 47
Washington, George [US President], 33
Waterloo, campaign and battle (1815), 18, 23, 54, 57, 61
Watson [doctor in London], 117
Watson, John Boyd (1828-1889), 247
   his wife, Mary Ann nee Covell (1833-1915), 247
   his daughter, Mary Anne Dalton (1860-1934) [later Lady McEachern], 246-247
Watton [defendant at Talbot], 131-132
Weekley, Northamptonshire, 21, 26; Vicar, 21, 26
Wellington, Duke [Arthur Wellesley], 54, 61, 223
Wells [lawyer at Talbot], 132
Wenlock, parliamentary borough, 23
Were [surname miswritten for Ware *q.v.*], 222
Were, Edith Alice Mary, *see* Edith Alice Mary Ricketson nee Were
West Indies, 19, 22, 56
Westbury-on-Severn, Gloucestershire, 45
Westerhall, Dumfries, Scotland, *see* Johnstone family
Western Australia, British colony and later Australian state, 191, 212, 256-257
Wheeler, Rev Alfred (1865-1949), 227

---

*   In the Eurambeen Letters, this surname is often miswritten as Were.

INDEX

Western District/Portland Bay District, Victoria, 87, 98, 149, 164, 186, 208 *and see* Ararat, Ballarat, Hamilton, *etc*
Western Port, Victoria, 88
Westgarth [chairman of the Gold Field's Commission of Enquiry 1855], 106
Westminster, England, 24, 47, 224
Westmorland, England, 1
Weymouth, Dorset, 26
Whelan, Mary, 226
White family, 210, 244
—, Adelaide Letitia (1841-1919), *see* Gibton, Adelaide Letitia nee White
—, Charlotte Elizabeth, *see* Beggs, Charlotte Elizabeth nee White
—, Cyril Brudenell Bingham (1876-1940), 194, 210, 244
—, Ethel [wife of Brudenell White, later Lady White], *see* Ethel Davidson
—, John Warren (1828-1918), 210, 223, 244
—, John Warren ["Jack"] (1863-1947), 223, 227, 231, 234, 237, 244-246
—, Maria Lucinda (1826-1914) [wife/widow of Francis (1812-1880); often referred to as Mrs Beggs], 183-184, 186, 194, 210, 228, 232, 234, 237, 240, 243; Table 3 *at* 204
—, Thomas Edward (1864-1904), 212; Table 3 *at* 20
  his wife, *see* Gertrude Dorothea Beggs
Whitehall, London, 6-7, 264
Whittingham, George [brother-in-law of Walter Henry Davidson], 194
—, John [brother-in-law of Walter Henry Davidson], 194
Whittle [storekeeper at Talbot], 131
Wickliffe, Victoria, 164, 167, 171, 187, 263
Williamstown, Victoria, 150, 177; Cemetery, 150
Williamson, Charles [in Genesee Lands, USA], 33
Wiltshire, England, 19
Wimmera District, Victoria, 167
Windsor, Other Archer (1789-1833), sixth Earl of Plymouth, 100-101
—, Other Hickman (1751-1799), fifth Earl of Plymouth, 100
—, Other Lewis (1731-1771), fourth Earl of Plymouth, 100, 103
—, Lady Sarah (1763-1825) [sister of Other Hickman, wife of Sir William CdeC, and mother of Heaton CdeC], 100
Winter, Samuel Pratt [friend of the Dana family in Victoria], 98
—, Trevor [brother of Samuel], 98

Winterbourne, Gloucestershire, 23-25
Wintle [lawyer in Gloucestershire], 62
Wise, W M [auctioneer at Talbot], 144
Wodonga, Victoria [named Belvoir until 1869], 186-188, 195
Wolfendale, Mary [complainant of rape], 130
Wollaston station near Warrnambool, 164
Wolverhampton, Staffordshire, 15, 38
Wood, Charles George (1831-1892), 30
  his wife, *see* Mary Anne Greenwood
—, James Stead (1832-1855), 30
—, John Asprey (1806-1833), 29-30
  his wife, *see* Frances Harriette Fitzpatrick Dana (1807-1861)
Wood, Reverend John Mare (1780-1834), 26-27; Table 1
  his wife, *see* Harriet Dana (1774-1803)
Wood, William Henry (1810-1900), 11, 38, 50-52; Table 1
  his wife, *see* Anna Penelope Dana
Wood's Point, Victoria, 167
Worchestershire, England, 41
Worfield, Shropshire, 38-40, 45, 53, 61 [*as* Warfield]; Curate, 39
  Roughton Hall, 38, 40, 48-50, 53
Wotonga, ship, 179
Wrangham, Digby Caley, Serjeant-at-Law, 61-62
Wright [member of the Gold Field's Commission of Enquiry 1855], 106
Wroxeter, Shropshire, 8-11, 13-14, 20, 24, 26-28, 31, 38-39, 52, 59; Vicar, 8, 13; Rector, 14; Curate, 24
Wymer, Emily nee Hindes (1813-1891) [wife of George Petre], 55-56
—, George Crespigny (1836-1837), 56
  his grave, 56
—, George Petre (1788-1868), 56
"Wyndcote" house at Brighton, Victoria, 202, 211-212, 219

Yalla-y-Porra/Yalla-y-poora station, Victoria, 222, 242
Yarra River, 149
Yarra Bend Lunatic Asylum, 138
Yarra Yarra aboriginal tribe, 81
York and Cornwall, Duke and Duchess [future King George V and Queen Mary of Great Britain], 211
Yorkshire, England, 1, 51
Zeus [god], 1

www.ingramcontent.com/pod-product-compliance
Lightning Source LLC
Chambersburg PA
CBHW061537010526
44107CB00067B/2896